About the Cover

In this photograph, "The Sport Parade" (1932), the award-winning Soviet photographer Ivan Mikhaylovich Shagin (1904–1982) depicts a corps of female athletes marching through Moscow's Red Square. On the cover of this book, you see a version of Shagin's photo that has been colorized by the Russian artist Olga Shirnina (known as Klimbim), who specialized in imagining the full-color reality of historical black-and-white pictures.

Ivan Shagin, destined to become one of the Soviet Union's most successful photographers, grew up in an impoverished peasant family. His father died when he was eleven, and shortly afterwards his mother sent him to Moscow, where he worked to support the family in a small merchant's shop. He was too young to fight in the First

World War or to participate in the Russian Revolution of 1917; he became a sailor as a seventeen-year-old in 1919. After a three-year stint on a Volga River steamer, he returned to Moscow to take a job managing a cooperative store. He was successful and earned a respectable living but discovered photography during these years and became passionately devoted to it. Shagin's photographs were good enough to land him work as a professional photographer, and in 1928, he became a staff photojournalist for a local newspaper. Two years later he was named a special photo correspondent for the Soviet Union's most important youth newspaper, *Komsomolskaya Pravda*, where he worked until 1950.

In the 1930s, Shagin made photographs of famous Soviet figures and ordinary people. He depicted the Red Army as well as the Soviet navy and air force. During the Second World War, he would become one of his country's most prominent photo-chroniclers of the fighting, taking pictures of all the major battles.

Like other leading quasi-official Soviet photographers, Shagin became enamored in the 1930s of the public festivals organized by Joseph Stalin to portray Soviet society as young, vigorous, healthy, and strong. One of the most important of these festivals was the Sport Parade, also known as the Parade of the Athletes, which became an annual event in 1931. In these parades large numbers of physically fit young men and women performed gymnastic exercises, marched in formation, displayed weapons, and waved hundreds of red flags and banners, vividly displaying the colors of the communist state. Marchers also carried huge portraits of Stalin, who stood atop a high viewing stand and waved as the athletes paraded by.

In "The Sport Parade," Shagin focuses on the powerful women's bodies that fill the entire frame even as they seem poised to burst through it, so vigorous is their forward movement. Shagin's camera captures their vigor by highlighting the athletes' swinging arms, determined youthful faces, and well-nourished female forms.

There are important differences between the photograph's colorized version and the original black-and-white. The original highlights the women's white dresses while their flags nearly melt into the gray of the sky. The colorized photo makes the red flags so vivid against the blue sky that they compete with the dresses and draw the viewer's eye away from them. No longer are the female athletes the sole subject of the picture, as they were in the original. Now, the red symbolism of Soviet communism commands our attention as well.

Europe in the Modern World

A NEW NARRATIVE HISTORY

SINCE 1500

SECOND EDITION

Europe in the Modern World

A NEW NARRATIVE HISTORY

SINCE 1500

SECOND EDITION

Edward Berenson

New York   Oxford
OXFORD UNIVERSITY PRESS

Oxford University Press is a department of the University of Oxford.
It furthers the University's objective of excellence in research, scholarship,
and education by publishing worldwide. Oxford is a registered trademark of
Oxford University Press in the UK and certain other countries.

Published in the United States of America by Oxford University Press
198 Madison Avenue, New York, NY 10016, United States of America.

© 2021 by Oxford University Press

Library of Congress Cataloging-in-Publication Data

Names: Berenson, Edward, 1949- author.
Title: Europe in the modern world : a new narrative history since 1500 /
  Edward Berenson.
Description: Second edition. | New York : Oxford University Press, 2021. |
  Includes bibliographical references and index. | Summary: "Europe in the
  Modern World: A New Narrative History Since 1500 is an unusually
  engaging narrative history of Europe since 1500. Written by an
  award-winning teacher and scholar, the narrative highlights the major
  episodes of the European past and vividly connects those episodes to
  major international events"—Provided by publisher.
Identifiers: LCCN 2019059741 (print) | LCCN 2019059742 (ebook) | ISBN
  9780190078850 (paperback) | ISBN 9780190078874 (spiral bound) | ISBN
  9780190078942 (ebook) | ISBN 9780190078867 (epub)
Subjects: LCSH: Europe—History—1492- | History, Modern.
Classification: LCC D208 .B465 2020 (print) | LCC D208 (ebook) | DDC
  940.2—dc23
LC record available at https://lccn.loc.gov/2019059741
LC ebook record available at https://lccn.loc.gov/2019059742

Printing number: 9 8 7 6 5 4 3 2 1
Printed by LSC Communications, United States of America

To my mother, Claire Berenson, and the memory of my father, Norman Berenson (1919–2018), with gratitude and love.

Brief Contents

Contents

CHAPTER 8   From National Unification to Religious Revival, 1850–1880   *338*

List of Maps

Preface

Western Civ. was the first lecture course I taught as a new assistant professor at the University of California, Los Angeles. The student numbers were huge—more than five hundred, with a dozen TAs. Walking to my inaugural class, I felt none too confident. I had gotten lost on the sprawling campus, and a woman stopped me, intending to help. "Are you a freshman?" she asked.

Like many junior professors, I had just finished my dissertation, which focused on a single country and covered a span of just fifty years. Back in the 1980s, national histories were still in vogue. Now, as I contemplated teaching Western Civ., I suddenly had to think in terms of centuries, not decades, and dozens of countries, not one alone.

It turned out to be the hardest thing I'd ever done. I pulled near all-nighters several times a week. I was as sleep-deprived as a new teacher of Western Civ. as I would be ten years later as the new father of infant twins. Teaching Western Civ. was exhausting and exhilarating, humbling and illuminating; never had I learned so much so quickly. Midway through that first semester, a "mature student" who had returned to college in her fifties gave me a much-needed boost: "You're so young, and you know so much!" Little did she realize that eighteen hours earlier, I had known next to nothing of what I'd said in lecture that morning.

The teaching grew easier, though never easy, as the years went by. In that pre-electronics age, there were no laptops or cell phones to divert students' attention, though it still took some doing to keep five hundred students engaged, or at least awake. Many were innocent of European history, and nothing was more gratifying than when once-indifferent students came to talk with me after class. Still, I felt a little guilty when one especially curious freshman switched from pre-med to history. I didn't intend to affect anyone's career choice.

I taught Western Civ. every year for the first several years of my career and then, in the 1990s, branched out to world history. At New York University, what was long called Western Civ. is now "History of Modern Europe." Although several colleagues and I share responsibility for this course, I'm happy when my turn comes around—so much so that I decided to put my years of teaching and reading to the test by writing a textbook of my own.

I've long tried to give my teaching and writing a strong narrative thread, shaping my arguments and evidence into a set of true stories about the past. For this textbook, my goals haven't changed. I've done my best to narrate the major episodes and phenomena of European history vividly and engagingly and to connect the European story to a larger international history.

Four key features will, I believe, distinguish this book.

- **Biographies:** The Introduction, the Epilogue, and each of the book's fifteen chapters open with a biographical sketch. Illuminating, fascinating, and sometimes controversial individuals such as Martin Luther, Toussaint Louverture, George Sand, Leni Riefenstahl, and Ayaan Hirsi Ali give the events and ideas presented in the book a vibrant, human face.

- **Writing Exercises:** Each chapter connects to a series of writing exercises drawn from the historical content of the chapter and collected in the companion volume to this book. The exercises guide students, step by step, toward effective, polished expository writing in history and related fields. By completing the writing exercises, which are self-propelled and include an online component, students will vastly improve their written expression while—*without additional effort*—reviewing the material covered in each chapter. The writing program is unique to this book—no other history textbook has ever had anything like it.

- **Emphasis on an Updated Political History:** Some thirty years ago, when Western Civilization and European history textbooks began to feature social and cultural history, they helped bring our teaching up to date. But the new sociocultural history, novel as it was, often downplayed major developments in politics, ideas, warfare, and religion, the phenomena that distinguish—for better and worse—so much of modern European history. *Europe in the Modern World* reinvigorates those phenomena while doing justice to social and cultural life.

- **Detailed Attention to the Economy and Economic History:** The long-standing focus on social and cultural history has also obscured economics and economic history. In the wake of the Great Recession of 2008, *Europe in the Modern World* places economic phenomena—including monetary forces—front and center. Reading this book, students will understand the roots of our current economic dilemmas. And they will see the large role that economic developments—and the political, social, and cultural responses to them—play in shaping the political and social life of a given age.

Europe in the Modern World is, of course, no economics text. Here, economic history comes to life in vivid prose, as does the rest of my story, which tries to follow the example of narrative history at its best.

Changes to the Second Edition

- **A completely rewritten Chapter 2** opens with a new biography—of Roxelana, the wife of the Ottoman emperor Süleyman the Magnificent—and features a more extensive discussion of the Ottoman Empire. It also examines each of the states it covers as an empire, in one form or another; fully integrates material on Spain's American empire into the main discussion of Spain; and does the same for England, France, the Habsburgs, and Russia.
- **A completely new chapter, Chapter 3,** turns on the crises of the seventeenth century. Framed by the extraordinary global cooling of the time, it shows the connections linking the major events of the century: the Thirty Years' War, the two regicides and four deposed sultans in the Ottoman Empire, the "Great Trouble" in Russia, the Fronde in France, the civil war and two revolutions in England/Scotland/Ireland, and the Cossack massacres of Jews in the Ukrainian part of the Polish-Lithuanian Commonwealth.
- **The "Writing History" exercises,** formerly at the end of each chapter, are now located in *Sources and Writing Exercises for Europe in the Modern World* to allow more flexibility in how they are assigned.

Chapter-Specific Revisions

- **Chapter 4** includes a more in-depth discussion of Holy Roman Emperor Joseph II and "Enlightened Despotism."
- **Chapter 5** offers more coverage of the reverberations of the French Revolution in Germany and the Habsburg Empire.
- **Chapter 7** incorporates important new work on the Austrian Empire.
- **Chapter 9** has more, and substantially revised, material on Austria-Hungary, the Dual Monarchy, and nationalism.
- **Chapter 13** includes a new section on the Second World War in the Pacific.
- **Chapter 14** opens with a new biography of Ho Chi Minh.
- **An updated and expanded Epilogue** includes recent developments including Brexit, the Yellow Vest Movement, populism, and the COVID-19 pandemic.

Learning Resources for *Europe in the Modern World*

Europe in the Modern World offers both digital and print resources designed to increase student engagement and make teaching more efficient.

DIGITAL
ANCILLARY RESOURCE CENTER (ARC)

A convenient, instructor-focused destination for resources to accompany *Europe in the Modern World*, the ARC provides instructors and students with access to up-to-date learning resources at any time. In addition, it allows OUP to keep instructors informed when new content becomes available.

For instructors, the ARC for Europe in the Modern World includes:

- Oxford World History Image and Video Library: Includes PowerPoint slides and JPEG and PDF files for all the maps and photos in the text, an additional 400 map files from the Oxford *Atlas of World History*, and approximately 1,000 additional PowerPoint slides organized by themes and topics in world history. The Video Library includes ten videos, produced in collaboration with the BBC, on key topics in Western Civilization—from the Haitian Revolution to the atom bomb.
- Instructor's Resource Manual: Includes, for each chapter, a detailed chapter outline, suggested lecture topics, learning objectives, and suggested Web resources and digital media files. Also includes for each chapter approximately 50 multiple-choice, short-answer, and fill-in-the-blank questions. The test questions are available in a computerized test bank that can be customized by the instructor.
- PowerPoint slides and JPEG and PDF files for all the maps and photos in the text, lecture outline PowerPoint slides, and an additional four hundred map files, in PowerPoint format, from the Oxford *Atlas of World History*.
- E-version of *Sources and Guided Writing Exercises for Europe in the Modern World.*
- Oxford First Source, an online database of primary source documents. The continuously updated collection consists of approximately 450 documents for European and World History. These documents cover a broad range of political, social, and cultural topics and are indexed by region, period, and topic. Each document includes an introduction contextualizing the source. Review questions highlighting key themes additionally supplement select documents.
- Interoperable Course Cartridges. An interoperable course cartridge containing all of the instructor and student ARC resources can be seamlessly integrated with a variety of learning-management systems.

For students, the ARC for Europe in the Modern World includes:

- Enhanced eBook with embedded study aids, including interactive maps, interactive timelines, notetaking guides, primary sources, writing exercises, videos, and "Closer Look" image analyses.
- Student quizzes. Each chapter quiz includes approximately forty quiz questions with feedback. Note-taking guides, one per chapter, offer a systematic note-taking system designed to make students' note-taking more efficient.
- "Closer Look" visual analyses of selected artworks from *Europe in the Modern World*, accompanied by audio and quizzes.
- Flashcards of all the Glossary terms from the text.
- Weblinks that provide opportunities for further research.

PRINT

- ***Sources and Guided Writing Exercises for Europe in the Modern World***: Edited by Allison Scardino Belzer and Jonathan Perry, this companion sourcebook includes approximately 100 sources, arranged to match the organization of *Europe in the Modern World*. Each source is accompanied by a headnote and reading questions. Included in the volume are series of writing exercises, created by Catherine Johnson and Katherine Beals, that are drawn from the historical content of *Europe in the Modern World*.
- ***Mapping the Cultures of the West:*** Free when packaged with *Europe in the Modern World*, this map workbook includes approximately ninety color maps. The diverse set of maps examines both global and regional patterns of history. Each map section is accompanied by a headnote that provides historical context. Outline maps encourage students to see the connections between history and geography.

ENHANCED EBOOK

An enhanced eBook (9780190078867) is available online at RedShelf (www.redshelf.com), Chegg (www.chegg.com), or Vitalsource (www.vitalsource.com).

Acknowledgments

I wish to thank first the thousands of students at UCLA and NYU who have inspired my thinking and challenged me to make European history meaningful—and valuable—to them. Warm thanks go as well to Lisa Sussman, whose excellent work as my developmental editor added focus, precision, and clarity to every aspect of the project. Like Lisa, the outside reviewers commissioned by Oxford

University Press have made a vital contribution to this work. I'm deeply grateful to the following people for reviewing the second edition of *Europe in the Modern World:*

Alan Allport, Syracuse University

John Ashbrook, The University of Virginia's College at Wise

Stephen Auerbach, Georgia College

Allison Belzer, Georgia Southern University

Sarah K. Danielsson, Queensborough Community College of the City University of New York

Benjamin Frommer, Northwestern University

Andrew Keitt, University of Alabama at Birmingham

Matthew Lindaman, Winona State University

Paul D. Lockhart, Wright State University

Kenneth Pearl, Queensborough Community College of CUNY

Ron Rexilius, Houston Baptist University

Matthew Ruane, Florida Institute of Technology

Ruma Salhi, Northern Virginia Community College

Peter Sposato, Indiana University Kokomo

Lisa Tiersten, Barnard College

Steven Usitalo, Northern State University

Not only did they spot errors and omissions, but they also directed me to crucial secondary sources and gave me the benefit of their immense expertise, both as scholars and teachers.

I am also thankful for the exemplary work of the editorial and production team at OUP. Despite the tight schedule, Katie Tunkavige, Keith Faivre, and Michele Laseau pulled together the photos, maps, and other elements of the book into a harmonious whole. Warmest thanks, too, go to Francelle Carapetyan for her brilliant photo research. The result is, I think, an immensely pleasurable reading experience. Allison Scardino Belzer at Georgia Southern University, who edited the new edition of the sourcebook that accompanies *Europe in the Modern World*, also deserves my sincere gratitude for a job well done.

I am grateful as well to the many colleagues and friends whose deep knowledge of European history has boosted my own: Bob Brenner, Herrick Chapman, Ruth Harris, Tony Judt, Dominique Kalifa, Sam Lipsman, Arno Mayer, Jerry Seigel, and Debora Silverman, to name just a few. Sam's and Tony's lives were cut much too short, but I'll always have the memory of Sam's brilliant mind and the intellectual benefits of Tony's remarkable work. I want to give special recognition to Yanni

Kotsonis and Larry Wolff for the example of their work and for advising me about what to read in their respective fields.

My deepest gratitude goes to Charles Cavaliere, editor extraordinaire. Not long after arriving at Oxford University Press, Charles encouraged me to take on this project and, along the way, gave me exactly the right kind of support. When deadlines pressed, he subtly, but effectively, coaxed my collaborators and me to get our chapters done. Charles is the ultimate historians' editor, a talented professional with deep knowledge of the field and an unmatched understanding of the way it is taught in colleges and universities coast to coast.

Finally, a word to the students and professors using this book: I would love to hear from you, so please write (**edward.berenson@nyu.edu**) with any comments and questions that come to mind.

Edward Berenson
Tarrytown, New York
December 2019

About the Author

Edward Berenson is professor of history at New York University. He specializes in the history of modern France and its empire, with additional interests in the history of Britain, the British Empire, and the United States, as well as the history of memory and memorialization and the history of celebrity and charisma. He is an accomplished teacher, having received the American Historical Association's Eugene Asher Distinguished Teaching Award and UCLA's Distinguished Teaching Award. His contributions to French studies and to Franco-American understanding earned him a prestigious decoration from former French President Jacques Chirac: Knight in the Ordre national du Mérite (2006). Berenson has received fellowships from the National Endowment for the Humanities and the Social Science Research Council, and he is the author or editor of eight books, the most recent of which is *The Accusation: Blood Libel in an American Town* (2019). *The Accusation* tells the strange story of the lone case in US history of an anti-Jewish ritual murder accusation that engulfed an entire town.

Introduction

Europa

According to Greek mythology, a Phoenician princess named Europa woke up in fright early one morning from a disturbing dream. In the dream, two continents, one named Asia and the other nameless, took the form of women and fought over her. At daybreak, Europa and several other young noblewomen went to the seaside to gather flowers. The god Zeus saw them there, and he was immediately drawn to Europa, the most beautiful of the group. To attract her attention, Zeus transformed himself into a magnificent white bull, appearing powerful and gentle all at once. The bull smelled of flowers and lowed in a voice so melodious that it sounded like a song.

The young women began to pet and stroke him, and when he lay down in front of Europa, she climbed onto his back. Suddenly, the bull dashed toward the sea and plunged into the water with Europa clinging to his neck. Several supernatural figures joined them in the water, and Poseidon, the god of the sea and brother of Zeus, guided the way.

Europa realized that the bull must be a god and, terrified now, she begged him to take her back home. But the bull kept swimming ahead, telling Europa he loved her passionately. Before long, the Greek island of Crete appeared on the horizon, and landing there, Zeus returned to his human form. As a man-god, Zeus raped Europa—or in more polite versions of the story, seduced her—and she became pregnant with their son Minos, who would become king of Crete. Europa herself married a Cretan monarch, thus making herself a Greek and leaving her Asian identity behind (Phoenicia belonged to western Asia, Lebanon and Syria today). Eventually, so the story goes, she would give her name to the nameless continent of her dream.

Drawing on this myth, the ancient Greeks named their side of the Mediterranean Sea "Europe" to distinguish themselves from the supposedly inferior Asian side (the northeast corner of Africa was then considered part of Asia). The naming raises interesting questions, since Crete is closer to North Africa than to parts of ancient Greece, and by moving Europa from the Middle East to Crete, the myth appears to claim the huge Mediterranean Sea—and by extension, Greece as a whole—for what would later be called the "West."

Europa and the Bull. A relief in stone from the sixth century BCE representing Zeus, disguised as a bull, abducting the Phoenician princess Europa.

In any case, by "Europe," the Greeks meant what are now Greece, the westernmost parts of Turkey, and the Balkans (Albania, Serbia, Croatia, and neighboring countries). Only later, probably after Charlemagne (742–814) became Holy Roman Emperor and ruler of Christendom, did "Europe" come to stand for something close to its meaning for us today. ≡

What and Where Is Europe?

Although we think we know what we mean by "Europe," in reality its boundaries, both geographical and conceptual, are unclear. Is Great Britain part of Europe, even though it does not belong geographically to the continent? What about Ireland and Iceland, both even further detached from the European landmass than Great Britain? Although Iceland is only a candidate for membership in the European Union, the multinational organization of European states, Ireland belongs, as did the United Kingdom until the end of January 2020. To add to the ambiguity, Switzerland, a country that sits close to the center of what used to be known as Western Europe, does not belong to the European Union, whereas two countries on the periphery of the continent, Portugal and Greece, have been members since the 1980s (see Map I.1).

And speaking of Western Europe, there were considerable periods when people in the western part of the continent did not consider those in the East—Poles, Hungarians, Romanians, and so on—true Europeans. Now all three countries belong to the European Union, and age-old distinctions between Western and Eastern Europe are gradually fading away.

Finally, take the region's two largest countries, Russia and Turkey, both of which have at times played key historical roles in Europe and at other times have seemed to stand outside it. Russia extends from the Baltic Sea, considered part of European geography, all the way across the Asian landmass to the Pacific Ocean, where it borders on China and North Korea and nearly touches Japan. Is Russia part of Europe or Asia or both? As for Turkey, a small section of the country sits on the European continent, and the rest is separated from it by only a narrow strait. But its dominant Muslim religion has long made it seem distinct from the largely Christian countries to its west. Still, Turkey's ancestor, the Ottoman Empire, extended into the heart of Europe for centuries, and like the Russians, the Ottomans were key players on the European stage. Both the Russian Empire and the Ottoman Empire will figure prominently in this book.

≡ **Europa on the Twenty-Euro Note**. The latest issue of the European common currency, the euro, features an image of Europa on its 20-euro note.

≡ **Europa.** Detail from the Twenty-Euro note.

So, of course, will the British Empire, which took its relationship to Europe seriously but for centuries was at least as concerned with India, Africa, and the Middle East as with Germany, Russia, and France. Like Britain, several other European powers—France, Spain, the Netherlands, and Portugal—possessed large overseas empires, and throughout this book we will view them not merely in their European guise but in their imperial, international one as well.

The other countries conventionally considered part of Europe—the Austrian empire, the various German and Italian states, Scandinavia, and Poland—had largely continental concerns, with different measures of importance at different times. These states and regions, plus the countries created after the First World War and following the collapse of the Soviet Union in 1991, will receive due attention here.

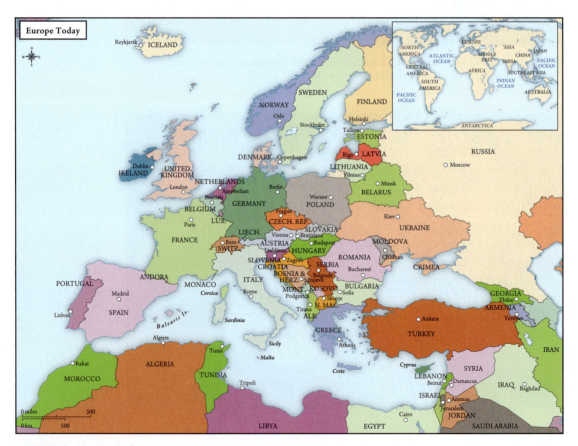

≡ **MAP I.1** Europe Today

Why Europe?

In 1500, when the main narrative of this book begins, it was far from obvious that Europe, however we define it, would come to dominate the globe economically and militarily by the early twentieth century (only to cede that dominance after 1945 to the Soviet Union and the United States, and then to the United States alone). In the seventeenth and eighteenth centuries, Europe experienced powerful competition from Manchu China, also known as Qing (formerly Ch'ing) China, which during its heyday, from 1644 to 1800, expanded the country's borders to roughly their current dimensions and encompassed more than 300 million people. Qing China was an economic powerhouse that used its vast resources to develop a strong domestic economy and play a major role in international trade.

What ultimately gave Europe, or at least northwest Europe (Britain, France, the Netherlands, Germany), its edge? This now-classic question was raised by Karl Marx in the nineteenth century and by legions of historians and social scientists after him. Throughout most of the nineteenth and twentieth centuries, the answer seemed obvious: Europe had jumped ahead for cultural, or economic, or political reasons already by the sixteenth century. But recent research comparing China and Europe has cast doubt on this answer by showing the dynamism of Qing China.

The best current answer to the question of why northwest Europe, in particular, took a great leap forward in the nineteenth century turns on two main points: 1) the European slave trade and Europe's exploitation of land and labor in the Americas; 2) Europe's relative abundance of coal.

By 1800, Northwestern Europe, the Yangzi Delta in China, and other advanced regions of Asia were running out of land, as their manufacturing economies expanded and population grew. While China and Japan possessed only a limited ability to address this problem, the British, in particular, solved it through the power of its state and its willingness—and ability—to use coercion and military force. British merchants, backed by a powerful navy, seized human beings in Africa and worked them as slaves in the Caribbean and the American South, where extensive lands were available for cultivation. By colonizing or controlling these lands, the British were able to compensate for their deficit of land at home. The terrain they controlled overseas gave them the cotton and foodstuffs they needed to supply their textile manufacturers and feed their workers, most of whom were no longer needed for agricultural pursuits.

With Britain's land shortage alleviated, the British, and eventually other peoples of Western Europe, now benefited all the more from a key accident of nature: Europe's large, accessible deposits of coal—far larger than existed in East Asia, which had to rely for energy on dwindling stocks of timber. Thanks to their coal,

Europeans could develop energy-intensive industries whose products—cotton textiles, metals, and a variety of consumer items—proved highly valuable on the world market and gave Europeans the ability to import food and cotton at relatively low prices. On the whole, Europeans were now better fed and clothed than people elsewhere, and these advantages allowed European populations to soar and thus to provide cheap labor for their burgeoning industrial concerns and manpower for their armies. East Asia, meanwhile, stagnated with its labor-intensive, unmechanized industry and agriculture. Chinese and Japanese trade leveled off or even declined, and East Asia, like most other parts of the world, became vulnerable to European domination.

Europe in 1450–1500

None of this was foreseeable in 1500. At that point, no European country was as yet an empire, and most were barely even states. Take, for example, England and France, both of which had been divided internally by the endless Hundred Years' War (1337–1453). The century of fighting had angered peasants, who were heavily taxed to pay for the war, and alienated leading noble families from their kings, whom they deemed too weak to prevail. In England, two of the greatest of those families, the houses of Lancaster and York, fought in the War of the Roses (1455–1487) for control of the throne. The country began to unify only after Henry Tudor (1457–1509), an independent Welsh nobleman, subdued both sides and made himself king. His family or offshoots from it would rule England for the next two centuries and in doing so create the basis for a centralized state, brutally colonizing Ireland in the process.

In France, too, the Hundred Years' War had strengthened the great nobles at the expense of the kings, but when Charles VII assumed the throne in 1422, he asserted royal power by creating Western Europe's first standing army and imposing taxes that did not require the consent of France's representative assembly, the Estates General. In exchange, however, he had to give tax exemptions to the nobles and clergy who led those assemblies, thus creating revenue problems that would haunt French monarchs for centuries.

Charles and his son Louis XI (ruled 1461–1483) used his army not only to fend off the English and subdue rebellious nobles, but also to expand the kingdom of France. Strategic marriage alliances with neighboring royal families enlarged France still further, making it the leading continental power by 1500.

In the late fifteenth century, France's greatest continental rivals were in the Iberian Peninsula (today's Spain and Portugal) to its south. There, the two largest kingdoms, Castile and Aragon, came together after King Ferdinand of Aragon (1452–1516) married Queen Isabella of Castile (1451–1504) in 1469. Ferdinand's territories included a large swath of southern Italy and several Mediterranean islands. Ferdinand and Isabella expanded their potential holdings by marrying their children into Portugal's royal family and especially through a marriage alliance with the powerful Habsburgs, who ruled much of South and Central Europe and what are now parts of eastern France, Belgium, and the Netherlands.

While making these far-flung European marriage alliances, Ferdinand and Isabella also launched their army against Granada, the lone remaining Muslim territory in Iberia—the other Muslim lands had been conquered earlier—and defeated it in 1492. In that same year, the two monarchs forced Spain's Jews and Muslims either to convert to Christianity or face expulsion from their homes, and they sent Christopher Columbus on his famous voyage of discovery, which gave them a foothold in the New World. After Ferdinand died in 1516, his grandson Charles presided over Europe's largest empire, as he inherited not only his grandparents' Spanish, Italian, and French territories but also the vast Habsburg domains passed down from his mother. In Italy, only the republics of Florence and Venice and the pope's temporal domain, the Papal States, lay outside his realm (see Map I.2).

The other large empire of the 1400s, that of the Ottomans, came from outside Europe but spread gradually and inexorably into European lands. In 1453, they captured Constantinople, the capital of the Byzantine Empire (now reduced to a couple of enclaves that were absorbed a few years later), and moved into the Balkans, eventually taking Bosnia, Romania, the northern Black Sea coast, and most of Hungary. They battled the prosperous Italian city-states of Venice and Genoa for control of trade in the Adriatic and eastern Mediterranean Seas, and in the early sixteenth century conquered Syria and Iraq before expanding into North Africa. For the next 350 years, the Ottomans would rule about a third of Europe and half of the Mediterranean rim.

To the Ottomans' north stood the joint kingdom of Poland and Lithuania (later known as the Polish-Lithuanian Commonwealth), which like Aragon and Castile had come together as a result of a marriage alliance. By the early 1500s, Poland-Lithuania had extended its reach into a large part of Central and Eastern Europe, including what are now the Baltic States. Prussia, later to become a great European power, was at this point a minor **duchy** whose overlord was the king of Poland.

To the east of this huge state sat Muscovy, later Russia, which expanded by beating back the Mongol empire and strengthening the authority of its monarch, who became known as tsar (the Russian word is ultimately derived from the Roman title Caesar). In northern Europe, a group of commercially successful city-states along the North and Baltic Seas had come together in the Hanseatic League. To oppose the league, Norway, Denmark, and Sweden (which included Finland) joined in an alliance that lasted until the 1520s, when Sweden broke free to establish an empire of its own.

In Central Europe, the main political entity was the Holy Roman Empire, a loose confederation of more than three hundred principalities, city-states, duchies, and religious jurisdictions known as **bishoprics** that extended over a huge area. Despite the empire's size, its power was constrained by the weakness of its ruler, the Holy Roman Emperor, who was elected to his throne rather than inheriting it. Beginning in the mid-1400s, the head of Austria's powerful Habsburg family

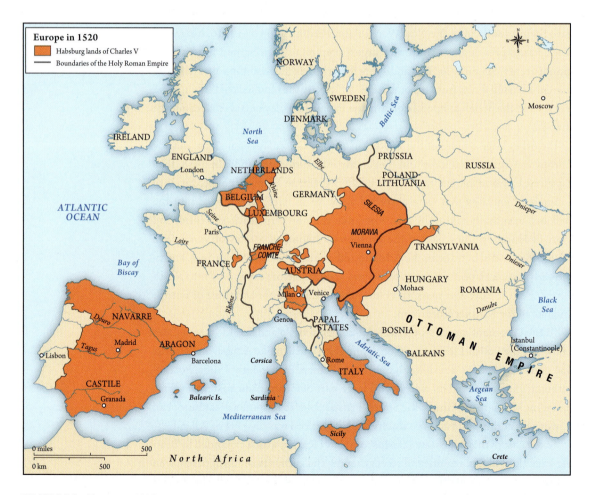

≡ **MAP I.2** Europe in 1520

was always elected emperor (except for one brief period), but even so, he had to recognize the autonomy of the empire's seven electors in order to retain the crown. The electors' power thus prevented the empire from consolidating into a unified state. So did the Protestant Reformation, which divided the empire's inhabitants into Protestants and Catholics and kept many of them at each other's throats.

Agriculture, Industry, and Trade in 1450–1500

The Reformation (see Chapter 1) would trigger a bloody Peasants' War (1524–1525). At the beginning of our period, most peasants—the overwhelming majority of Europeans—were poor and oppressed. Rapid population growth in the fifteenth century had increased competition for an essentially fixed amount of land. This competition allowed landlords to raise rents, which peasants mostly paid in kind, that is, by giving up much of their produce and performing unpaid labor every week.

Peasants tried to escape these increasingly difficult conditions by fleeing to cities, where they would be free of the landlords' control. To keep peasants on the land, large proprietors, especially those in Eastern Europe and Russia, used their political clout to turn peasants into **serfs**—unfree laborers tied by law to the land-lords' domains. In doing so, landowners prevented peasants from moving to cities, which declined as a result. Throughout much of the period covered in this book, cities in Eastern Europe were fewer and more sparsely populated than in Western Europe, where serfdom no longer existed.

Not that peasants in the West were completely free. Most continued to owe uncompensated labor services to their lords, while paying high rents and taxes. And given the sparseness of industry and commerce in 1500, they had few alternatives to agricultural pursuits. To make ends meet, every member of a peasant household had to work. Both men and women labored in the fields, while women also cared for young children, prepared meals, and looked after the home. Children tended any livestock a family owned and helped with myriad other tasks.

The peasant diet consisted mostly of bread, since grains—wheat, rye, barley, and oats—were the main crops Europeans grew. Often there was too little to go around, and families tried to supplement their meager diets with whatever fruits, nuts, vegetables, and herbs they could find or cultivate. If they kept animals, there would be small amounts of meat, butter, cheese, and milk. Peasants were thus poorly nourished, especially considering the hard labor they put in. On average, Europeans were more than a foot shorter than they are today. A great many children did not survive their first year, and women commonly died in childbirth. Few peasants lived to a ripe old age.

The peasants who became most prosperous were those who accumulated enough land to cultivate a surplus that they could market for cash. Some profited from climates that enabled them to produce items much in demand—olives, wine, and fruits—while others gained from harvesting the raw materials for fine woven cloth: silk, wool, and flax (linen). Peasants, for the most part, did not make cloth themselves. That would come later, when agricultural families also produced textiles at home.

In 1500, skilled craftsmen, mostly in the cities of northern Italy, the Netherlands, England, and parts of France, spun wool, silk, and flax into yarn and then wove the strands into cloth. These workers, who toiled punishing hours but remained poor, were not protected by the **guilds** to which the elite of working people belonged, especially in industries such as printing, tailoring, shoemaking, carpentry, and the like. Guilds established standards of quality, regulated working conditions, and set prices as best they could. They limited the number that could work in any field by requiring lengthy apprenticeships and allowing only those who had demonstrated the ability to produce high-quality goods to establish businesses of their own.

Guild members ranked among the most privileged workers in Europe and represented only a small percentage of those who labored for a living in 1500. The rest lived precarious lives and did what they could to make ends meet: carrying goods from place to place, working as servants, running errands, and loading and unloading ships, among other things. Many of these workers were too poor to marry and have families and often floated from town to town looking for jobs.

Their activities were nonetheless important, and not infrequently they contributed to a growing international commerce. Europeans had long traded with countries around the Mediterranean basin, easily accessible by boat, and in the North and Baltic Seas. An increasingly brisk trade also existed on both sides of the English Channel and in the Black and Aegean Seas, where European merchants met caravans bringing goods overland from India, China, and Central Asia.

As this Euro-Asian trade expanded throughout the fifteenth century, the Portuguese had a different idea: they sent ships south toward West Africa in search of gold and eventually slaves. In the 1450s, they landed on the shores of the Mali empire, one of Africa's largest and most powerful, where they bought captive men. The Portuguese deposited them on the African islands they had discovered and forced them to produce sugar, for which Europeans had developed an insatiable demand. The use of enslaved Africans to cultivate sugar under a merciless tropical sun marked the beginning of a terrible, if lucrative, slave economy that would last for centuries (see Map I.3).

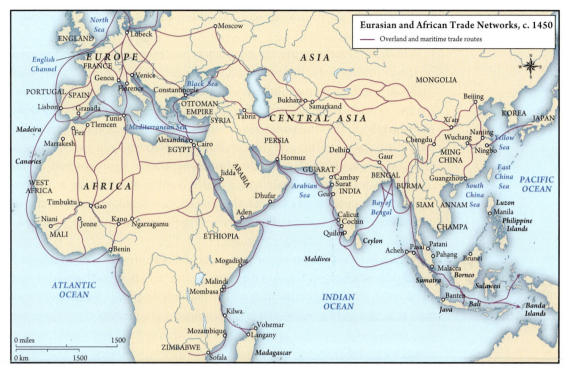

≡ **MAP I.3** Eurasian and African Trade Networks, c. 1450

Religion, Culture, and Intellectual Life in 1450–1500

Although the Portuguese and a great many others who traveled in 1450–1500 did so in search of economic gain, some went to distant lands as expressions of religious faith—either as pilgrims or missionaries. The latter were especially drawn to the New World, where millions of indigenous people seemed ripe for salvation through conversion to Christianity. Europeans did not blame the Native Americans for their "pagan" beliefs, and missionaries not infrequently attempted to convert thousands at a time.

Europeans showed far less tolerance for those closer to home, where "heretics," Jews, and Muslims faced persecution, banishment, and death. In the thirteenth century, England expelled its entire Jewish community, and France temporarily excluded Jews a century later. They migrated south and east, where they settled in the major cities of Italy, Spain, and Central and Eastern Europe. Jews chose cities rather than the countryside, because they were commonly prohibited from owning land. Eventually, the Jewish quarters of cities turned into **ghettos**, to which most Jews were confined.

In the late fifteenth century, the expulsion of Jews resumed, as Bavaria banished its Jewish population in the 1480s and Spain a decade later. A great many Jews took refuge in the Ottoman Empire, which allowed its Jewish and Christian minorities to practice their religions freely, although they had to pay special taxes for the privilege. The Ottomans were far more tolerant of religious difference than most Christian countries, and the Ottomans accepted not only Jewish refugees and Christian dissidents but also the Muslims expelled in the 1490s from Spain. The Ottoman Empire also tolerated a sizable number of Orthodox or Eastern Christians who populated the Byzantine Empire, conquered by the Ottomans in 1453. (There had been a formal split between the Eastern and Western, or Roman Catholic, branches of Christianity in 1054.)

In the mid-1400s, the Ottomans' looser attitudes toward religion were replicated in Italy, where educators began to depart from what until then had been an almost exclusive focus on religion. As trade and manufacturing grew in Italian city-states such as Venice and Florence, civic leaders decided that education should have not only a religious purpose but a practical, worldly one as well. Schools should prepare young men—women were largely excluded from formal schooling—for careers in business and for public engagement by giving them broad "humanistic" training focused on literature, history, mathematics, and the arts. This training would teach budding merchants and bankers to manage businesses, and even more important, it would help them understand human nature and past experience and how to use that understanding to shape the affairs of their cities. Crucial to these new capacities was the ability to write and speak logically, persuasively, and eloquently.

The sources of this humanistic education lay not primarily in religious texts, although these remained important, but in the literature, speeches, and historical narratives produced by the great writers and statesmen of Ancient Greece and Rome. This "**Renaissance** humanism," so named by nineteenth-century historians for the fifteenth century's "re-naissance" (rebirth) of classical learning, spread quickly from Italy to the Netherlands, the two great commercial centers of the time. It later influenced the Catholic world's most successful teaching order, the Jesuits, who would educate many of Europe's greatest minds and most important leaders. Even so, **humanism** hardly touched ordinary people, most remaining illiterate and immersed in an oral culture whose main features were religious, spiritual, and supernatural.

Among Europe's literate minority, however, the spread of humanism—and soon of Protestantism—was accelerated by the invention of the mechanical printing press in the mid-fifteenth century. Although forms of printing had developed centuries earlier in China, and several European inventors worked on it as well, the individual most closely associated with the printing revolution was the German goldsmith Johannes Gutenberg (c. 1400–1468). After more than a decade of experimentation, Gutenberg developed a process for turning chunks of metal into reusable, moveable letters that could be arranged into words and sentences to create a large plate of type. Each plate was covered with ink and then pressed onto sheets of paper, which, in turn, were cut into pages and bound into books.

Gutenberg and his partners developed the first printing presses in the 1450s, and the new, relatively inexpensive technology spread extraordinarily fast. By 1500, perhaps twenty million printed books had been published, a number that far surpassed the sum of all handwritten books disseminated from ancient times until then. The ability to mass-produce books created a genuine cultural revolution, an intellectual upheaval that allowed for the transformation of religious belief and practice and an unprecedented advancement of knowledge. Thanks to the invention of print, the radical theologian Martin Luther (1483–1546) could broadcast his revolutionary views far and wide (see Chapter 1), as could the great astronomer Galileo Galilei (1564–1642) a century later (see Chapter 4).

The Structure of This Book

We will encounter Luther, Galileo, and fourteen other exemplary men and women in the biographies that open the chapters of this book. The point of the biographies is to introduce you to the main themes of each chapter by considering them through the prism of an individual life. You will see how certain key figures embodied or exemplified the events and phenomena of each historical period covered.

After the opening biography, each chapter proceeds chronologically and thematically, emphasizing the most important political and economic phenomena in Europe as a whole and in the countries most prominent during a given period. The nature of states and empires directly affected their inhabitants' lives, the more so as new technologies enabled them to extend their reach, and we will consider politics in some detail. We will also pay considerable attention to economic phenomena and economic history, reminded as we are of the weight of economic forces after struggling to overcome the lasting effects of the "Great Recession" of 2008–2009 and then the devastation caused by COVID-19.

Beyond politics and economics, the chapters of this book also devote considerable attention to society and culture and, where appropriate, to religion and intellectual life. Since Europe extended its influence into the rest of the world, dominating Africa, Asia, and the Americas for much of the period since 1500, we examine Europe's role in the world at large and connect European events to their broader international context. Still, this is a history of Europe rather than a history of the world, and the focus here is on Europe, as we have (rather broadly) defined it.

By studying this history, you will be able to understand more fully the events of our contemporary world. At its best, history is a set of true stories and reasoned interpretations written to draw readers in. That is the kind of history we have attempted to present here—history in a compelling narrative mode.

KEY TERMS

bishoprics *xlii*

duchy *xli*

ghettos *xlvi*

guilds *xliv*

humanism *lxvi*

Renaissance *xlvi*

serfs *xliii*

 For digital learning resources, please go **https://www.oup.com/he/berenson2e**. Turn to the back of the book to see the list of primary sources and writing exercises provided in the accompanying *Sources and Guided Writing Exercises for Europe in the Modern World*

Europe in the Modern World

A NEW NARRATIVE HISTORY

SINCE 1500

SECOND EDITION

The Age of Religious Reform, 1490–1648

Martin Luther

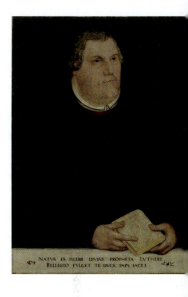

According to legend, Europe's explosive religious reformation began on a dark and stormy night. In July 1505, a young law student named Martin Luther (1483–1546) journeyed on foot back to his university in Erfurt, a small city in central Germany, after a short visit home. Suddenly, a violent thunderstorm burst over him and a bolt of lightning knocked him to the ground. In awe and terror, Luther called out to the Virgin Mary's mother: "Help me, St. Anne! I will become a monk." If Anne allowed him to live, he would renounce his legal studies—and a potentially lucrative career—and devote himself to God.

Martin's father, Hans, a former peasant who had married up and achieved a modest success in business, was unhappy about his son's change of heart. Hans had great ambitions for Martin, a brilliant student who he hoped would become a prosperous professional man, maybe even a counselor to the local prince. A well-off Martin would mean that Hans and his wife could expect to live to a ripe old age comfortably supported by their son. It would be a waste of Martin's great talents for him to become a monk, which required a vow of poverty and the surrender of all worldly possessions.

Martin recounted the thunderstorm story to his father, and that story has become part of Luther lore. But it is likely that the epiphany in the thunderstorm never happened. Even before making the long, mid-semester trip home, Luther probably had already decided to radically change his path in life, and he wanted to ask for his parents' consent. His father doubtless objected, and perhaps to convince him, Martin invented the thunderstorm experience as God's confirmation that he should become a monk. Hans Luther responded that, instead, the lightning bolt was a sign from the devil and that Martin should beware. In the end, Hans reluctantly accepted his son's altered path. Like essentially everyone in sixteenth-century Europe, Hans Luther believed in God and Jesus and could not help but admire those who devoted their lives to serving the Lord.

Back in Erfurt, Luther entered perhaps the city's most rigorous Catholic monastery, the so-called Black Cloister of the Observant Augustinians. There, Luther shaved his head, donned jet-black robes, and moved into a cell barely large enough for a bed. The new monk's day began at 2 a.m., when he was awakened for the first of seven worship services. When not in the chapel,

Luther devoted himself to private prayer and contemplation. The Augustinians' self-denial went beyond the rejection of worldly goods; they endured the torments of hunger, thirst, cold, and sleeplessness to demonstrate how little their own bodies mattered and how deep was their love of God.

No one loved God more than Martin, and Martin demonstrated that love through daily confessions. Since cloistered monks had little inclination, and even less opportunity, to commit sins, they rummaged through their thoughts and emotions in search of anything impure. Luther was nothing if not assiduous in this effort, and he became obsessed by the fear that he could never rid himself of sinful feelings like jealousy, envy, and lust. He despaired of ever meriting God's grace. The harder he tried, the more he came to believe that all efforts to contribute to his own salvation were futile.

Fortunately, Luther was not left to simmer endlessly in his increasingly dark views of himself. His intellect earned him entry into the fine university at Erfurt, where he moved after five years in the Black Cloister. At the university, he learned about how the great theologians of the past had answered the questions about sin and salvation that tormented him. Luther's teachers told him that God was righteous and good by definition and that human beings were God's opposite—sinful and weak. But biblical passages suggested that because humans were capable of guilt, the feeling of having done wrong, they had a spark of goodness within them and thus were capable of taking steps to redeem themselves.

These ideas failed to satisfy Luther's steadfast belief in his own sinfulness; to divert him from his constant worry, his superiors convinced him to earn a doctorate and begin teaching at the University of Wittenberg in eastern Germany. Like young university professors today, he had to prepare several brand new lectures every week. In doing so, Luther systematically thought through the spiritual and theological problems that had long tormented him. The end result was a religious revolution, perhaps even a revolution in the fullest sense of the word.

Luther began with the idea of righteousness, the state of moral perfection and complete absence of sin. As he delved deep into the Bible, especially the book of Romans, the new theology professor determined that there were two kinds of righteousness. The first was the one Christian theologians had long identified, the righteousness of God. But the second stemmed from a new insight on Luther's part. It was the righteousness that God freely gave to those who believed in Him. This idea, simple

Timeline

1480	1500	1520	1540	1560	1580	1600	1620	1640	1660	1680

1478–1834 Spanish Inquisition

1483–1546 Martin Luther

1492 Muslim Grenada falls to Spanish forces of Aragon and Castile;
Spanish Jews forced to convert or be expelled

1517 Luther posts his 95 Theses

1519 Zwingli extends Luther's reforms

1520 Luther is excommunicated

1521 Diet of Worms, Edict of Worms, Luther condemned to death

1523 Thomas Müntzer popularizes Anabaptism

1524–1526 Peasants' War

1529 Holy Roman Emperor defeats the Ottomans at Vienna

1534 Henry VIII declares himself Supreme Head of the Church in his kingdom

1536 Calvin publishes the *Institutes*

1540 Jesuits established as official religious order

1545–1563 Meetings of the Council of Trent

1547 Charles V defeats Schmalkaldic League

1555 Peace of Augsburg

1558 Elizabeth I becomes queen of England

1559–1560 Scottish rebellion against Catholic rule

1562–1598 French wars of religion

1572 St. Bartholomew's Day Massacre of Huguenots

1589 Henry IV converts to Protestantism
and is crowned King of France

1598 Edict of Nantes establishes religious
toleration in France

1609 Declaration of the Dutch Republic

1618 Defenestration of Prague

1618–1648 Thirty Years' War

1648 Treaty of Westphalia

as it sounds, turned traditional theology upside down. No longer did people have to strive, however imperfectly, to be righteous toward God. Instead, God, in his mercy, conferred his righteousness on them. To open the possibility of salvation, individuals needed only to have faith, to believe in God's goodness and mercy, while recognizing their own inherent sinfulness.

This notion, which Luther later termed "**justification [acceptance] by faith alone**," had revolutionary implications because it did not require that individuals do anything to merit salvation. In fact, Luther told his students, there was nothing human beings could do. As he had discovered about himself, no matter how hard he tried, he could never rid himself of impure thoughts and emotions. Worse, his efforts to attain a state of grace amounted to a kind of blasphemy, an unholy, prideful belief that he could be as pure as God. The same thing, Luther said, happened to those who tried to earn God's favor by doing good works. They egotistically became convinced of their own righteousness without in any way impressing God—or Christ, who asked only that people believe in His willingness to extend mercy to them even though they did not deserve it.

Luther developed these views gradually after he assumed his university teaching position in 1512. Five years later, he stepped outside the classroom to place his increasingly unorthodox ideas before the public at large, presenting them in the form of **95 Theses**, which, according to legend, he nailed to a church's wooden door. Among other things, his theses challenged the heightened effort by Catholic leaders to strengthen Church finances through the sale of **indulgences**. The Church "indulged" people's sins before they died if they did something to merit a pardon, which in theory might consist of a spontaneous act of charity but in practice usually meant payments to the Church.

In Luther's era, Catholics believed that virtually no deceased person went straight to heaven. Some descended to Hell but most found themselves in a kind of halfway house known as Purgatory, where they had to work off the sins they had accumulated while alive. The more sins committed, the longer they had to stay. Earning indulgences before death shortened the sentence in Purgatory, either for the individual who earned them or for someone already there. Family members helped deceased relatives by buying indulgences on their behalf.

Luther was far from the first theologian to criticize indulgences, but thanks to the relatively new medium of print, he reached an unprecedented number of people with his vehement, skillful response to a particularly egregious example of their abuse. In 1515, the pope arranged for a huge sale of indulgences in Germany to finance a lavish new structure, the Basilica of St. Peter in Rome. In effect, the pope decided to pay for his construction project by selling people shares of stock whose "dividend" was a partial reprieve from Purgatory. The effective salesmanship of Johann Tetzel, the Dominican friar charged with hawking indulgences, made them highly popular. In his sales campaign, Tetzel pioneered what we now call the advertising jingle: "As soon as the coin in the coffer rings, a soul from purgatory to heaven springs."

Such naked commercialization infuriated Luther, a theologian for whom nothing was more serious than salvation. As if Tetzel was not crass enough, in 1515 a young German prince named Albert of Hohenzollern went even further: he agreed to make a large cash payment to Pope Leo X in exchange for Leo's agreement—against all precedent—to permit Albert to hold two positions as archbishop at once. The pope knew that Albert lacked the funds to make this payment, so he authorized the prince to raise the agreed-upon sum by selling a huge number of indulgences to people living under his rule. The process was complicated, and to oversee it, Albert enlisted Europe's largest financial institution, the Fugger Bank, which also advanced money to the pope.

These transactions proved beneficial all around: Fugger made a sizable commission, Albert got his new archbishop's cloak, and the pope brought in some much-needed cash—in this case, to help finance the construction of St. Peter's Basilica. The problem was that the entire arrangement rested on what was supposed to be a grave spiritual matter, the pardoning of sin. For Luther, the sale of Church-minted certificates of forgiveness turned divine justice upside down, as one of his 95 Theses declared: "All those who consider themselves secure in their salvation through letters of indulgence will be eternally damned, and so will their teachers."

With this uncompromising statement, first written in Latin and then popularized in a fluid German translation, Luther became notorious overnight. And almost immediately, Church officials—including Albert, now a cardinal—moved to silence him. In a 1519 debate, a papal emissary tried to get Luther to retract his thesis about indulgences. Instead, the German professor opted for outright heresy by maintaining that he understood scripture better than popes and councils of cardinals. Such an assertion was unpardonable, and in 1520, Luther found himself excommunicated from the Catholic Church.

Fortunately for the now-notorious German professor, Luther had a powerful protector in Frederick the Wise, the ruler of his home province of Saxony. Frederick gave Luther the chance to redeem himself by inviting him in 1521 to the **Diet of Worms**, a meeting of the principal German rulers under the leadership of Charles of Habsburg, the elected emperor of the Holy Roman Empire (HRE). Luther's invitation to speak there was to be a show trial of sorts, an occasion for the theologian to take back everything publicly. Instead, he doubled down, saying (as legend has it), "Here I stand; I can do no other." This legend has the ring of anachronism, making Luther sound like a nineteenth-century individualist. What he actually said, "my conscience is captive to the Word of God," conforms to his writings and to the thought structures of the time. Religious radicals like Luther did not see themselves as rugged individualists, but rather as channels through which the Holy Scriptures could speak their divine truths.

Having failed his test at Worms, Luther escaped with his life only because Frederick the Wise agreed to hide him from the Holy Roman Emperor, who in the **Edict of Worms** (1521) sentenced him to death as a heretic and banned his writings. Unable to teach, Luther occupied himself by translating the Bible into a beautiful form of German that was at once colloquial and literary, accessible and sophisticated, while remaining faithful to the ancient Greek and Latin texts. In many ways, Luther's vernacular bible created the modern German language. He then refined the language with his almost superhuman output of books, pamphlets, letters, and transcribed lectures and conversations.

During his thirty most productive years, Luther averaged a book every other week—the modern edition of his collected works encompasses one hundred large tomes. Luther alone provided work for dozens of printers, whose Gutenberg-inspired presses, invented around 1450, made the spread of religious reform possible in the sixteenth century. During the six years following the publication of Luther's 95 Theses, the

≡ **Luther Bible.** In 1521, Luther translated the Bible, until then available only in Greek and Latin, into a beautiful German prose. The Bible was now accessible to far more people than ever before.

production of printed material in Germany grew by a factor of six, thanks in part to the three hundred thousand copies of Luther's work.

This extraordinary output made Luther the Catholic world's best-known and most hated "heretic." Church leaders burned his books in massive bonfires and claimed that Luther's mother was a prostitute who conceived him in casual sex with the Devil. Luther responded by calling the pope a "man of sin and son of perdition" whose dominions were "more corrupt than any Babylon or Sodom ever was." Luther added that true prayer required Christians to curse the papacy: "If I say, 'Holy be Thy name,' then I must add, 'Cursed, damned, and disgraced must be the papists' name.'"

After his excommunication in 1520, Luther burned all his bridges with the Catholic Church, never to turn back. He and his disciples created what amounted to an alternative religion known as the Evangelical faith or **evangelicalism**, because it was centered on Christ and grounded in the Word of God. Only later would the new faith be called Lutheranism. But whatever its name, Luther's theological innovations and harsh criticism of "Roman" Catholicism, now separate from "German" evangelicalism, transformed Christianity and, with it, the Western world—forever. ≡

The Beginnings of Religious Change

Once Luther had begun the process of religious reform, it quickly escaped his control and rival forms of Protestantism came into being. As we will see, the most important was Calvinism, the new denomination created by the French theologian, John Calvin (1509–1564), in the 1540s. Still other forms of the new religion followed, some so radical that Luther would not have recognized them.

Because human beings take their deepest beliefs very seriously, disputes between Protestants and Catholics regularly led to war during the sixteenth and seventeenth centuries. The era of religious reform turned out to be one of the most violent in European history, perhaps the most violent until the world wars of the twentieth century. Not only did Protestants and Catholics do battle with each other, but different Protestant sects fought among themselves. In combating what Catholics considered a terrible new heresy, leaders of the Roman Church worked to both stamp out the new version of Christianity and reform their own. As we will see, a Catholic reformation accompanied the Protestant one, creating a revolution in religious belief.

Innovative as he was, Luther did not produce the first efforts to reform the Catholic Church or the first splits within it. Long before him, critics had called for the purification of the Church—for a renewed spirituality to counter the "worldliness" of religious officials and their political and financial patrons. Scholars regularly interpreted and reinterpreted the meaning of what God revealed to humankind, and there was always a variety of opinion within the admittedly tiny theological world.

In the late fourteenth century, differences within the Church became so sharp that clerical and political leaders could not agree on who should be pope. From 1378 to 1417, two popes reigned simultaneously, one in the southern French city Avignon, the other in Rome. (For six of those years, a third pope entered the fray.) A single legitimate pope eventually emerged, but the episode lowered the papacy's esteem and created the precedent of a divided Church, a precedent to which Protestants would later refer.

Protestants would likewise remember the various "heretical" movements within the supposedly universal Church. In the mid-fourteenth century, the Oxford theologian John Wyclif (1330–1384) anticipated what would later become key Protestant themes by arguing that believers should follow the dictates of scripture rather than those of the pope. For that reason, the Word of God should be accessible in the people's own language, English, and not just Latin. Long before Luther, Wyclif denounced the materialism and worldliness of the priesthood and advocated a purer spirituality. His followers, ridiculed as "Lollards" (speakers of nonsense), suffered persecution and harassment until they gave up their beliefs or went underground.

Wyclif's ideas did not disappear, however, for they influenced the prominent Bohemian (Czech) theologian Jan Hus (1369–1415), who developed the Englishman's ideas into a popular movement for Church reform. Hus conducted religious services in the local Czech language, rather than Latin, earning him the support of Czech nobles and peasants, eager to promote their tongue against the German-speakers who dominated them politically. The Czech nobility could not, however, prevent Hus from being convicted of heresy and burned at the stake in 1415. Infuriated, his many supporters rose in rebellion and took Hussite ideas in new and even more radical directions, although they had to practice their faith discreetly at best.

Related to these developments were efforts by secular rulers—the French and Spanish kings, the Holy Roman Emperor, city leaders, and landed noblemen—to assert their independence from the pope and take control of certain religious institutions and practices within their domains. The upshot of these struggles for authority and financial resources between secular rulers and the pope was that the relatively powerful kings of France and Spain and the Holy Roman Emperor could assert independence from the Church and did not therefore need to break with it. The small German principalities and city-states, by contrast, had minimal military and financial might and could get out from under the pope's domination only by rejecting Catholicism altogether—not that every German political entity would. As a result, there were political, and not just theological, motivations behind the religious choices of the sixteenth and seventeenth centuries, that is, of the Protestant and Catholic Reformations, to which we will now return.

The Protestant Reformation

The Reformation began with Luther in Germany and soon expanded to Denmark, Switzerland, Eastern Europe, England, Scotland, and France. As the new religious ideas spread, they underwent a variety of changes and ultimately produced several different versions of what would soon be called Protestantism.

Luther and Religious Reform in Germany

Martin Luther stood out as a great theologian, but he was also a political activist. In 1520, Luther's *Open Letter to the Christian Nobility of the German Nation* called on German leaders to help him reform the Church. The nobles who adopted Luther's evangelical faith created new religious institutions and decreed that all their subjects would become evangelicals as well.

Although Luther himself never produced a systematic statement of evangelical beliefs—a younger colleague, Philipp Melanchthon (1497–1560) did so instead— Luther nonetheless decided what his most essential religious reforms would be. Clerical marriage ranked high on his list, and in 1525, Luther wedded a former nun, Katharina von Bora (1477–1552). Gone was the key Catholic notion that even within marriage, sex had the whiff of sin. Justification by faith alone, of course, became a fixed element of Luther's embryonic religion, which abandoned for good the Catholic notion that individuals could nudge themselves (or their relatives in Purgatory) into heaven by confessing sins, performing selfless acts, or buying indulgences. Christians, Luther said, should do good things for others not to gain salvation but because that was the right way to live.

In spearheading these changes, Luther developed a novel form of religious culture. He dismissed the Catholic idea of humankind as God's triumphant creation in his image, what he called "a theology of glory." Instead, Luther made the individual Christian into a humble, passive sinner, a "man without qualities" who

 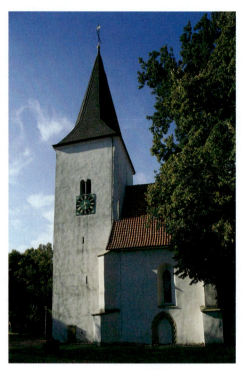

≡ **Contrasting Church Exteriors.** This pair of German churches highlights the difference between the Reformation era's elaborate Catholic cathedral and the simple, unadorned early Lutheran church. In Luther's view, Catholic churches heretically exalted man's creations over God's.

could do no more than quietly have faith that Christ would bestow his grace on him. This Protestant modesty would reveal itself in the form of plain, whitewashed churches designed as centers of unadorned humility and direct contact with the Word of God. They stood in stark contrast to Catholicism's great gothic cathedrals. In Luther's view, these luxurious temples, festooned with statues, bloody crucifixes, and elaborate stained glass windows, heretically exalted man's creations over God's.

Luther enjoyed the support of several German princes, but Europe's most important monarchs largely shunned him. In 1521, England's King Henry VIII (1491–1547), later to create his own form of Protestantism, published a tightly argued defense of traditional Catholicism that earned him the title "defender of the faith." The Holy Roman Emperor, as we have seen, sentenced Luther to death, and the French king Francis I (1494–1547) remained an orthodox Catholic. Before 1550, King Gustav I of Sweden (ruled 1523–1560) and King Christian III of Denmark (ruled 1534–1559) were the only monarchs to make Lutheranism the official religion of a major European power.

Zwingli and the Radicalization of Religious Reform

Because Luther changed some aspects of Christian ritual and belief while leaving many intact, it was inevitable that other, more radical, reformers would emerge. Luther's earliest prominent competitor was a learned ex-priest from Zurich, Switzerland named Huldrych Zwingli (1484–1531). Although Luther claimed Zwingli had been possessed by the Devil, he was in fact a sober religious scholar influenced by the brilliant humanist scholarship of Erasmus of Rotterdam (1466–1536), the great Renaissance writer. Zwingli mastered Erasmus's Greek and Latin versions of the New Testament, believed to reproduce the Word of God more faithfully than the Catholic Church's official, thousand-year-old Latin translation known as the "Vulgate." For those who knew Greek, Erasmus's New Testament seemed, as he put it, to "bring you . . . the speaking, healing, dying, rising Christ himself." Erasmus's texts opened Zwingli's eyes, and together with a near-death experience in 1519, gave him a new structure of belief. Like Luther, Zwingli now maintained that the Word of God as revealed in scripture trumped everything else, whether the rules and traditions of the Church or the decrees of a pope. When several of his associates deliberately ate sausages during Lent, Zwingli (who didn't partake) preached a sermon justifying the transgression because the holy scriptures do not mention any such prohibition.

From here, Zwingli went on a rampage of reform. Since the Gospels did not forbid clergy to marry, Zwingli not only took a wife but denounced the Catholic clergy for hypocritically keeping concubines. In Zwingli's Zurich, only two sacraments remained—baptism and Communion—and even Communion changed. In the latter, also known as the Eucharist, the priest consecrates bread and wine in a process called transubstantiation that turns these two "elements" into the body and blood of Christ. The consecrated bread and wine retain their outward physical properties, but their reality has changed in accordance with Jesus's words at the Last Supper: "This is my body . . . this is my blood." Zwingli considered this Catholic belief pure superstition. How could the two "elements" be Jesus' body and blood? Christ, after all, had left the Earth for good when he ascended into heaven. Zwingli insisted that Jesus's words at the Last Supper should be understood metaphorically rather than literally, that the bread and wine represent Christ in spirit only. Here, Luther strongly disagreed, maintaining that Christians must believe in the real presence of Christ during the Eucharist because scripture commanded it.

These differences appeared meaningless to the Holy Roman Emperor, who in 1529 extended the Edict of Worms from Luther to the entire band of religious dissidents, all now branded as heretics and condemned to death. Fortunately for the dissidents, they had influential allies, as six princes of the HRE and fourteen chiefs of its Free Cities (city-states with special status) had adopted the new evangelical faith and signed a joint "protestation"—hence the term "Protestant"—against the renewed Edict of Worms.

But despite this unifying political stance, Luther and Zwingli could not overcome their theological disagreements. Zwingli rejected the statement of Lutheran beliefs known as the Augsburg Confession (1530) and declined to join the Schmalkaldic League, the defensive alliance formed (in the German town of Schmalkalde) to protect Lutheran cities from the Holy Roman Emperor's army. When several Catholic cantons of Switzerland attacked the Protestant city of Zurich, killing Zwingli, the Lutherans refused to intervene.

Even without Zwingli, Zurich remained in the Protestant camp, and other Swiss and south German cities gradually abandoned Catholicism in favor of religious reform. A key center of innovation was the Imperial Free City of Strasbourg, then in western Germany, and moderate reformers there tried to bridge the differences separating key Protestant and secular leaders. They also did what Luther never could: build a carefully structured church with a clear set of rules and ways to discipline its members.

Thomas Müntzer's Radical Anabaptism

In their moderation and desire to cooperate with other religious and secular leaders, the Strasbourg reformers could not have differed more from the religious radical Thomas Müntzer (1480–1525), whose name is closely associated with **Anabaptism** (rebaptism). Müntzer and his followers wanted to return Christianity to its origins as a small sect whose purity put it at odds with political authority. According to Müntzer, when the Roman Emperor Constantine converted to Christianity in the fourth century and made it the official religion of a powerful state, it became corrupted as a result. Church and state reinforced each other by ensuring that everyone automatically became a Christian through infant baptism. Strength lay in numbers, but by failing to make Christianity a conscious, adult choice, as it had been for the earliest adherents of the faith, religious and political officials allowed insincere and faithless people to call themselves Christians. This, according to Müntzer, was the source of most of Catholicism's ills. The answer was to forego infant baptism and limit Christian belonging to those who chose, as adults, to be baptized. This idea was much too radical for reformers like Luther and Zwingli, who viewed infant baptism as the way to discipline the political and religious community by having people live their entire lives within the confines of the faith.

Anabaptism and the Peasants' War

In 1523, Müntzer took up residence in a tiny Saxon town, where he married a former nun, created the first church service entirely in German, and evoked spirited participation by having congregants sing hymns (prayers set to music). These innovations were popular, but Müntzer got himself into trouble when he insisted on giving local residents tests of faith to distinguish "real" Christians from supposedly faithless ones. The princes of Saxony summoned him to explain himself, which he did by denouncing them to their faces as "eels [who] immorally in one great heap" had sex with snakes, "priests and all the evil clerics." Müntzer added that the kingdom of God would soon do away with all earthly kingdoms like their own. After this performance, Müntzer had to flee Saxony for his life. He ended up in Mühlhausen, an Imperial Free City in Thuringia (central Germany), where he and an associate tried to replace the existing town council with an "eternal council" that would rule according to divine justice and the Word of God. Town leaders initially resisted Müntzer but soon became engulfed in a rebellion linked to the **Peasants' War** (1524–1526) raging at the time (see Map 1.1).

Historians disagree over the nature of the relationship between the Reformation and this peasant uprising, but there was a clear connection between the two. Although Luther wanted freedom from what he considered false Catholic belief, he had no interest in social upheaval and preached against it. Peasants, however, chafing under the burden of high taxes, serfdom, and other forms of unpaid labor, probably heard Luther's message of freedom but not of obedience to secular authority.

In 1524, when farmers in the Black Forest region of southern Germany faced new limits on their ability to fish and hunt and thus to feed their families, they rose up in rebellion. Over the next two years, the insurrection spread into surrounding German lands and eventually to Switzerland and Austria. Not until the French Revolution in 1789 would there be a larger rural uprising in Europe.

In the name of Christ and the Gospel, armed peasant bands seized castles, nobles' houses, monasteries, and even a few cities. In 1525, their leaders drew up a document called the **Twelve Articles of Memmingen** that justified their rebellion on the grounds that "Christ has delivered and redeemed us all . . . by the shedding of His precious blood." The Twelve Articles demanded the abolition of serfdom, the restoration of hunting and fishing rights, tax reductions, and an end to obligatory unpaid labor. These economic planks were couched in religious terms, as peasant rebels maintained that the Gospel forbade the kinds of burdens imposed on them. In doing so, they linked in radical ways the Word of God with the requirements of economic and social righteousness.

Although most of the Peasants' War took place in rural regions, it spilled over into cities as well. Under Müntzer's leadership, Mühlhausen became a center of rebellion as Anabaptists pillaged monasteries and drove the mayor and councilors out of town. Müntzer made himself a theocratic ruler, and from his new

The Peasants' War, 1524–1525

▨ General area of conflict	✳ Urban violence
▨ Areas of severe conflict	— Boundary of the Holy Roman Empire

☰ **MAP 1.1**   The Peasants' War, 1524–1525

pulpit he urged local artisans and farmers to join the wider Peasants' War. He did so with violent, apocalyptic rhetoric, convincing some three hundred people that the "end time" heralding Jesus's Second Coming had arrived. "Let not mercy seize your soul," Müntzer declared. "Let your swords be ever warm with blood!" He convinced his tiny troop that they were invulnerable and led them into the battle of Frankenhausen, where forces of the Holy Roman Empire wiped them out. Some six to eight thousand peasants were slaughtered as well, and Müntzer was captured, tortured, and beheaded. In the twentieth century, East German communist mythology glorified Müntzer as a precursor of Marx and Lenin; in reality, he was a Reformation radical overcome with apocalyptic zeal.

The Politics of Religious Strife

After Müntzer's execution, Imperial troops finished off the peasant rebellion with great brutality. Although these same troops would soon threaten the Reformation itself, Luther applauded their acts of retribution against the peasants. In a polemic unsubtly titled *Against the Robbing and Murdering Hordes of Peasants* (1525), the theologian urged Germany's secular leaders to serve "as God's sword on earth to knock down, strangle, and stab the insurgents as one would a mad dog." Zwingli followed suit with a pamphlet of his own, and both men identified Anabaptists as particularly at fault. Zurich turned against the sect, executing hundreds, often by drowning. Magisterial reformers may have rebelled against the Catholic Church, but they showed no mercy to those who rebelled against them.

With the Peasants' War, Luther's religious revolution turned violent. It would remain so for the next century and a half, as Protestants fought among themselves and especially as Protestants and Catholics squared off. The first armed conflict between forces of the old and new religion took place in the Kingdom of Denmark, where victory in a civil war of 1536 allowed King Christian III to overcome Lutheranism's foes. A decade later, Emperor Charles V decided it was time to stamp out the Protestant heresy in his German domains. He went to war against the religious reformers banded together in the Schmalkaldic League, defeating them decisively in the spring of 1547. With the Protestant princes once again under his control, Charles imposed something close to Catholic orthodoxy on most of their cities and towns.

Charles V's overwhelming victory altered the balance of power between the Holy Roman Emperor and local rulers in Germany to such an extent that several Catholic princes feared that their own traditional autonomy might be compromised. They withdrew their troops from Charles's army, allowing the Schmalkaldic League to restart the fight. The emperor might have won again, except that France's Catholic king, Henry II (1519–1559), intervened on the Protestant side. In this case, as in others to come, power politics overcame religious conviction. Henry, worried that Charles had become too great a continental rival, encouraged division within the Holy Roman Empire by helping the Protestant princes within it regain their autonomy. The French efforts succeeded, and Charles and his brother Ferdinand, soon to be the new Holy Roman Emperor, were forced to roll back the Catholic victories of 1547.

In the ensuing **Peace of Augsburg** (1555), the princes of the Empire gained the right to determine the official religion of the territories they ruled. This outcome enhanced the autonomy of the princes vis-à-vis the Emperor and divided the HRE in two, exactly as the French king had wanted. Its eastern and southern lands remained Catholic, while its central and northern lands became Protestant. Although the Augsburg treaty theoretically offered protection to the minority religion in each region, the German population largely reshuffled itself along religious lines; either people converted to their prince's religion or they moved to a different state (see Map 1.2). What the Peace of Augsburg failed to do was to allow for any form of Protestantism other than the Lutheran faith. Under Lutheran princes, Anabaptists and Zwinglians were regularly persecuted and even killed. So were Calvinists, who set out from Geneva, which had recently joined the Swiss Confederacy, to reform the reformers. Although their version of Protestantism was largely barred from German lands, it would quickly spread to France, the Netherlands, England, Scotland, and ultimately the United States.

Calvinism

John Calvin (1509–1564), a French lawyer and theologian who fled to Switzerland for religious reasons, was in many ways Luther's opposite. Calvin's great personal restraint contrasted with Luther's dramatic, even flamboyant, personality. The Frenchman wrote relatively little but spoke a great deal (260 sermons a year), unlike the German, who seldom sermonized but wrote at the preposterous rate of two books a month. Calvin composed his sermons in bed and delivered them

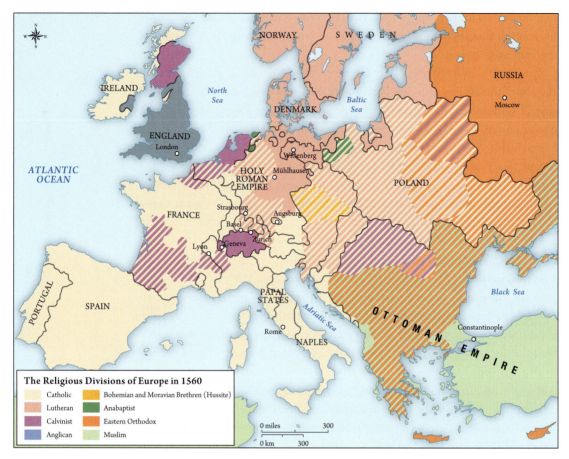

≡ **MAP 1.2**   The Religious Divisions of Europe in 1560

without notes; Luther depended on ink and paper. Highly disciplined himself, the Frenchman imposed tight discipline on his followers and created an orderly, doctrinaire, and hierarchic church. Luther did little to censor his often impulsive words and left to others the creation of a useable religious doctrine and well-functioning set of church institutions.

Calvin's personal restraint kept him largely silent about his early life and the reasons for his disillusionment with Catholicism. He told no stories of thunderstorm conversions or of dramatic confrontations with the Emperor or representatives of the pope. We know that Calvin's father was a lawyer and notary attached to an ecclesiastical court and that he intended his son to be a priest. Young Calvin did, in fact, study theology at a Parisian *collège* (secondary school), but after graduating, switched to the law. He then studied Greek, Hebrew, and classical philosophy—subjects that gave him the tools to immerse himself in the New Testament and eventually to write and speak about it in a clear and pleasing French. In Paris, he became attached to scholars whose humanistic inquiry moved them to question certain fundamental tenets and practices of Catholicism. When several of his mentors were declared heretics and burned at the stake in November 1534, Calvin decided to pack his bags. He landed in Basel, Switzerland, where he began work on what was to become the founding document of a new Calvinist religion, *Institutio Christianae Religionis* (An Instruction in Christian Faith), known in English as the *Institutes*.

Calvin first published his work anonymously and in Latin in 1536; he expanded and revised it continuously throughout his life. It began as a short six-chapter catechism or outline of the main religious principles he wanted to advance. The final version, published in Latin in 1559 and in French a year later, reached eighty chapters, divided into four sequential books. His first French translation of the work in 1541 proved to be one of the earliest modern masterpieces in that language and made Calvin, like Luther, a linguistic pioneer.

In the first sentence of the *Institutes*, Calvin outlined the argument that shapes the entire work: "Nearly all wisdom we possess, that is to say, true and sound wisdom, consists of two parts: the knowledge of God and of ourselves." Calvin went on to say that the more we learn about God and ourselves, the more we come to understand how fully inadequate we are. God is righteous and perfect, humans are sinful and indelibly flawed. Like Luther (and St. Augustine before him), Calvin wrote that even the best among us do not possess the talents and abilities to pull ourselves up from our sinful, fallen state. A merciful God can choose to save us, but not because of anything we do to deserve it.

John Calvin. A French lawyer and theologian who disputed Catholic doctrine, Calvin fled in 1535 to Switzerland, where he established a new form of Protestantism known as Calvinism.

Predestination and the Creation of a Calvinist Church

Although Calvin is widely known for the idea of **predestination**, the notion that God decided in advance who would be saved and who would not, it was mostly his successors who championed the idea. Still, Calvin maintained in the *Institutes'* later chapters that salvation was an extraordinary gift from God, and as such, it had to be reserved for a small "elect" (pre-)destined to be saved. It is likely that Calvin played down predestination because it seemed to suggest that human beings had no free will, that they were subject to a divine determinism over which they had no control. Melanchthon argued instead that God "called" those who were to be saved

a militant force whose members wanted to emerge from the shadows and assert their right to practice their faith and eventually to reform the country as a whole. They now boldly held services in public spaces and sang their metrical (rhythmic) psalms with growing verve. The words were simple and easy to memorize, which meant that even illiterate people could learn them. And once learned, psalms allowed large numbers of people, rich and poor, male and female, urban and rural, to participate in Protestant devotion—and not only in church.

In the summer of 1558, some four thousand Calvinists camped out in a Parisian park, singing psalms at the top of their lungs. On this and other occasions, mass singing became a tool of Protestant conversion, turning individuals into a crowd capable of drawing others into the fold. Particular psalms could evoke particular emotions or ideals. Psalm 115, for example, which denounced idols of "silver and gold, made by human hand," could move a crowd to smash up church interiors.

Catholics despised Protestant psalm singing precisely because it was so effective. When Catholic leaders burned Protestant "heretics" at the stake, they were known to first cut out their tongues. The persecution of Calvinists thus continued—despite Catherine's attempts at religious moderation—and French Protestants and Catholics soon came to blows, with gruesome acts of violence on both sides. On March 1, 1562, the leading Catholic nobleman, Prince Francis de Guise (1519–1563), organized an assault against a group of Protestants worshipping legally, if discreetly, in a barn. Guise's henchmen killed fifty congregants in cold blood. The following month, France's top Protestant nobleman, Louis, Prince de Condé (1530–1569), called for retaliation against Guise and the Catholics who supported him. That declaration led to a religious civil war in France that lasted forty years.

One of the first acts of war was Guise's assassination by a militant **Huguenot**, as French Calvinists were now called. Guise was attacked while his Catholic army fought to retake the city of Orléans, which the Huguenot army had captured along with dozens of other French cities and towns in the early 1560s. In taking them back, Catholic soldiers massacred hundreds of Huguenots, their bodies mutilated and burned as part of a ritual intended to purify France. Huguenots retaliated in kind. In 1567, their leaders, the Prince de Condé and Admiral Gaspard de Coligny, attempted to kidnap the child-king Charles IX and seize the French capital. Catholic forces foiled the effort, and when an assassin nearly killed Coligny in the summer of 1572, Huguenots became even more incensed.

Their leaders had congregated in Paris for a wedding intended to bridge the kingdom's religious divide. Margaret de Valois, the daughter of Catherine de' Medici and sister of Charles IX, was set to marry the son of the Protestant King of Navarre, a small province between France and Spain. The marriage took place, but it unwittingly set the stage for the worst atrocity of France's religious war. On Sunday, August 24, 1572, Saint Bartholomew's Day, King Charles ordered royal troops to kill the Huguenot elite encamped in Paris. The king and his still-powerful mother, Catherine de' Medici, feared Huguenot violence in response to Coligny's near-assassination and decided on a preemptive strike. The royal family's murderous example inspired Catholic extremists in the capital to embark on a murderous rampage of their own. Over the next three days, they seized every Protestant they could find and strung them from lampposts before savagely mutilating their bodies. These Paris killings evoked copycat atrocities in the provinces; when the killing was done, some five thousand Huguenots lay dead.

By the end of the sixteenth century, religious battles had cost thousands of additional lives, including that of another duke of Guise and of a reigning French king, Henry III (ruled 1574–1589), who was crowned after his brother, Charles IX, died at age 23. Having ordered the assassination of Guise in 1588, Henry was murdered in retaliation a year later. Several leading Huguenots and members of Guise's Catholic League followed them to their graves. Meanwhile, the king of Spain, Philip II (ruled 1556–1598), stirred the pot, hoping to gain power at France's expense both by inflaming the country's political divisions and by placing an ultra-Catholic on the throne. Philip's machinations backfired, however, as they motivated French noblemen and other influential people to put an end to France's civil war.

A compromise solution presented itself in the form of King Henry of Navarre, who by a quirk of fate became the murdered Henry III's legitimate successor (neither Henry III nor his brothers produced a male heir, and French law forbade women to rule). Despite Navarre's well-known Protestant beliefs, moderate Catholics and Protestants alike threw him their support. But when Catholic extremists opposed him, he had to lay siege to their main stronghold, Paris, before he could claim the throne. In the process, several thousand—perhaps as many as thirty thousand—Parisians died of starvation. To unify

≡ **St. Bartholomew's Day Massacre.** Beginning on Saint Bartholomew's Day, August 24, 1572, France's royal troops and Catholic extremists undertook a massacre of Protestants that left some 5,000 dead.

the country, Navarre converted to Catholicism, saying, according to legend, "Paris is worth a mass." (He probably did not actually make this statement, but it conveys the meaning of his religious compromise.)

After being crowned Henry IV in a solemn mass at Notre Dame Cathedral, the new king (ruled 1589–1610) concluded a peace treaty with Philip II of Spain and signed the famous **Edict of Nantes** (1598), which established religious toleration in France. Protestants were now free to practice their faith under the protection of special law courts and military forces. This edict made France one of the rare European countries to allow both Protestants and Catholics to worship legally—the only others were Poland-Lithuania and Transylvania. For his pains, Henry IV suffered two assassination attempts in the 1590s before succumbing to the knife-thrust of the Catholic militant François Ravaillac in 1610.

Other Calvinist Gains

Also known as the "Reformed" religion, Calvinism maintained its strongholds in Geneva and southern France while it spread to the Polish-Lithuanian Commonwealth, England, Scotland, the Netherlands, and Transylvania (a region formerly in Hungary, now part of Romania). The Polish-Lithuanian Commonwealth stood out as the largest and one of the most populous countries of sixteenth- and seventeenth-century Europe. It lasted until the late eighteenth century, when the wars and political realignments of the time erased it from the map. During its Reformation-era heyday, the Commonwealth boasted a multiethnic population and an unprecedented degree of religious diversity. Here, Calvinist noblemen, Lutheran city-dwellers, Lithuanian Orthodox Christians, a sizable Jewish community, and a Catholic monarchy and peasantry lived in relative peace.

Peacefulness did not characterize the religious reform movement in the Netherlands, a territory that, in the sixteenth century, belonged to Spain. The Reformed religion took hold in the Dutch provinces after 1560 in part because Spanish Catholicism, with its inquisitions and quest for religious purity, discussed later in this chapter, felt particularly oppressive, especially with Spain's army there to enforce them. Protestants rebelled against Spanish rule and after decades of bloody fighting succeeded in 1609 in establishing a Protestant Dutch Republic—but only in the north. The southern Netherlands (Belgium today) remained Catholic and part of the Spanish Empire until the French revolutionary era. The new Dutch Republic featured a rigid Calvinist church, but because Calvinism never gained the status of an official state religion, Dutch people could be, in effect, partial members of the church, free of its tightest rules. As a result, the Dutch Republic became a land of relative religious freedom, open to dissenting scholarship and, increasingly, to the presence of a large and prosperous Jewish community.

Elsewhere on the European continent, Calvinism took shape, if only briefly (1570s–1620s), in one key German state, the Rhenish Palatinate, which then returned to Lutheranism. In Transylvania and the non-Ottoman part of Hungary, Calvinism emerged as a quasi-state religion. The failure of Hungary and Transylvania's Habsburg rulers to stave off the Ottoman armies in the 1520s discredited the Habsburgs and their Catholic religion, whose supposed corruption was blamed for the defeat. As in the Netherlands, the Reformed religion brought opponents of the Habsburgs together and gave them an organized way to express their contempt for the dynasty. Calvinism also served as a bulwark against Ottoman Islam, which threatened to overrun the entire region. The turmoil in France and the Netherlands—and later in the Holy Roman Empire—sent waves of Calvinist refugees to Transylvania, where they helped combat the Catholic enemy.

In the Netherlands and Transylvania, Calvinism provided a set of organizing principles for rebellions against foreign rule. The same was true of Scotland in the 1550s and 1560s, which was essentially governed from France. Scotland's official monarch was Mary Queen of Scots (1542–1587), crowned at nine months of age in 1542 shortly after the death of her father, King James V. Her mother, Mary of Guise, belonged to the ultra-Catholic French family whose patriarchs inflamed the religious conflicts in France. A small group of Scottish evangelicals conspired against the two Marys in the mid-1540s, but they failed to displace them. One of the conspirators, John Knox (1514–1572), escaped to England and then to Geneva, where he studied at the feet of John Calvin. He returned to Scotland in 1559 to participate in a political/religious rebellion against Mary of Guise's French, Catholic rule. Protestant crowds pillaged monasteries and churches, stripping them of the "graven images" (statues, graphic crucifixes, and the like) forbidden by the new Calvinist theology. Knox found himself pleasantly surprised by this popular "iconoclasm" (opposition to idols), which marked the beginning of the end of Scottish Catholicism and French rule.

Knox and his colleagues created a new Scottish church, a "Kirk," as it was called in Scots, modeled along Genevan lines. The Kirk itself would be "presbyterian" (from the Greek word for "elders"), that is, directed not by bishops, as in Catholicism, but by committees of pastors, elders, and other laymen. This structure gave the Scottish church considerable independence from the now-adult Mary Queen of Scots, who returned home to rule in 1560 after the death of her husband, the French King Francis II. Mary brought with her an extraordinary royal melodrama in which she acquiesced to the murder of her second husband, a cousin and Catholic member of her own Stuart family, and then agreed to marry his accused killer, a Protestant and leading Scottish earl. This sequence of betrayals produced a mini–civil war that pitted Protestants against Catholics. The Protestants won, and

Mary fled to England, leaving her infant son, James VI, as the titular Scottish king. James was raised a Protestant, and Mary lived under house arrest in Elizabethan England for the next twenty years. She was beheaded in 1587 after being convicted of conspiring to kill Queen Elizabeth and restore Catholicism in her realm.

The Protestant Transformation in England

This Scottish melodrama paled in comparison with the one that had taken place in England under King Henry VIII (1491–1547). Between 1509 and 1547, the King married in rapid succession six women, two of whom he had executed. The libidinous king also took another half-dozen mistresses, two eventually promoted to wife. The marriage saga began in the late 1520s, when Henry asked the pope to annul his marriage to Catherine of Aragon (1485–1536) after she had failed to provide him with a male heir. Henry claimed that God must be punishing him for having wedded Catherine, who happened to be his dead brother's widow. The pope, however, refused to endorse the King's effort to elude the sacrament of marriage. There were solid religious grounds for the pope's decision, since Catholic marriages were indissoluble, but political motives counted as well. God may not have been angry with Henry VIII, but Rome was furious over his refusal to contribute troops to the (losing) fight against the Turks in Southeastern Europe. Henry responded by declaring independence from the pope and making himself Supreme Head of the Church within his kingdom, a declaration ratified by Parliament in 1534. No other European monarch had repudiated the pope's spiritual authority so unambiguously; he found himself excommunicated as a result.

Having been ejected from the Catholic Church, Henry needed an alternative. Protestantism was the obvious answer, especially since certain prominent English theologians and landed aristocrats had become attracted to the new evangelical faith. So had members of England's urban elites, whose commercial links with Protestant parts of Germany and Scandinavia had exposed them to the new religion. The existence of an English-language Bible, translated by William Tyndale in 1526, helped as well. To solidify the new religious orientation, Henry VIII selected as his Archbishop of Canterbury—England's chief religious authority—a reformer named Thomas Cranmer. The new archbishop quickly annulled Henry's marriage to Catherine of Aragon and blessed his union with his former mistress, Anne Boleyn (1501–1536), who had become a knowledgeable advocate of religious reform. Another of the king's lieutenants, Thomas Cromwell, then dissolved the country's monasteries and began to sweep away the remaining vestiges of Catholicism. But Henry VIII was nothing if not fickle and soon decided that

Cromwell had gone too far, executing him for treason and heresy. In an effort to steer a more "moderate" course, Henry burned three evangelicals while "balancing" these actions by executing three loyalists of the pope. One evangelical who managed to escape the fires later commented bitingly that Henry celebrated each of his marriages by having someone burned at the stake.

Despite these religious and personal zigzags, Henry VIII managed to transform the religious orientation of his kingdom in the space of a decade and a half. He succeeded in doing so because of the existing interest in Protestantism and because England was far more unified politically than any continental kingdom or empire. That unity made it difficult for centers of religious and political opposition to emerge, at least up until the mid-seventeenth century, when Parliament itself would become a source of religious opposition to the crown (see Chapter 3).

The succession in 1547 of Henry's young Protestant heir, Edward VI, allowed Cranmer to pursue the religious reform effort that had been interrupted a few years earlier. The archbishop created a Book of Common Prayer that laid out a Protestant service to replace the Catholic Mass, and he had composers write non-Catholic music—with words in English rather than Latin—to accompany the new rituals. To Cranmer's dismay, and soon demise, Edward died at age fifteen, making his Catholic half-sister, Mary, the first woman to rule England. "Bloody Mary," as her opponents called her, moved quickly to restore Catholicism by purging the country of its leading Protestants. She had Cranmer and three hundred others burned at the stake, while forcing a great many other visible reformers into exile abroad. Had Mary lived to a ripe old age, England might have returned for good to the Catholic fold. But she died in 1558 at age forty-two, turning the throne over once again, this time to her Protestant half-sister Elizabeth.

During her long reign (1558–1603), Queen Elizabeth established England's identity as a Protestant country once and for all. Catholics would not disappear, but Protestantism, soon in many varieties, would be the overwhelmingly dominant religion. Elizabeth retained the Book of Common Prayer and the new Protestant service but kept many of Catholicism's outward forms. Church leaders were still called bishops, and they wore traditional clerical robes. Many of England's old cathedrals, with their vivid imagery and awe-inspiring architecture, escaped the iconoclastic violence so common in other Protestant countries. This religious moderation convinced a growing number of theologians and lay people that the queen was not Protestant enough. These "Puritans," as their opponents called them (they labeled themselves "Godly"), wanted a purer, more disciplined church, one that resembled Calvin's Geneva with its allergy to pomp and circumstance.

☰ **Queen Elizabeth I.** During Elizabeth's nearly fifty-year reign, England developed a distinctive form of Protestantism, known as Anglicanism, that would shape the country's religious and political culture for centuries to come.

That discipline would extend to popular culture, which Puritans considered overly bawdy and profane.

On the national level, Puritans played a key role in preventing Elizabeth from marrying a European Catholic monarch, as she wanted to do, but their success in this effort backfired against them politically. Unable to conclude a suitable marriage, Elizabeth styled herself the "Virgin Queen," which gave her an air of sanctity and shamed those who said she was not pure enough. Given Elizabeth's considerable popularity and her victorious wars against Spain in the 1580s, it became difficult for the Puritans to oppose her too strenuously. As a result, Puritans remained a minority force within English Protestantism.

The Catholic Reformation

The Protestant Reformation changed the religious and political face of Europe and, for a time, put Catholicism on the defensive. But the old Church never accepted its diminished stature. Almost as soon as the Protestant Reformation began, Catholics fought back on multiple fronts—theological, military, educational, and political. This response was long known as the "Counter-Reformation," but that is too negative a way of framing it. Much of the Catholic reaction to the Protestant challenge was positive, in the sense that it attempted to revitalize Catholic education and make Catholic practice and belief more effective, more appealing, and in certain ways, more like Protestant ones. A Catholic reformation paralleled the Protestant Reformation. Still, part of the Catholic response involved the repression of unorthodox beliefs and military efforts to roll back Protestantism's territorial gains. Church leaders and Catholic rulers launched inquisitions against perceived heretics, created an "Index" of forbidden books, assassinated key Protestant figures, and sent troops into "reformed" regions. For that reason, the term "Counter-Reformation" captures certain elements of what occurred.

Taken together, the Catholic reformation and Counter-Reformation achieved considerable success, both in strengthening Catholicism and in reversing Protestant gains. A once-threatened Catholic Church had gone on the offensive and largely prevailed.

Reformation and Counter-Reformation	
1415	Jan Hus burned at the stake as a heretic
1515	Pope arranges for huge sale of indulgences in Germany
1517	Martin Luther makes public his 95 Theses
1519	Near-death experience sets Zwingli on path of radical reform
1520	Luther excommunicated from the Catholic Church
1521	Edict of Worms sentences Luther to death
1524–1526	Peasants' War in Germany
1525	Thomas Müntzer, leader of Anabaptists, is executed
1530	Augsburg Confession summarizes Lutheran belief
1534	Ignatius of Loyola founds Society of Jesus; Henry VIII declares himself Supreme Head of the Church in England
1536	John Calvin publishes his *Instruction in Christian Faith*
1547	Schmalkaldic League (Protestant) decisively defeats Catholic forces
1545–1563	Council of Trent meets to reform the Catholic Church
1555	Emperor Charles V accepts the Peace of Augsburg
1558	Philip II becomes King of Spain
1572	St. Bartholomew's Day Massacre, Paris
1587	Mary Queen of Scots beheaded
1598	Edict of Nantes establishes religious toleration in France

The Catholic Recovery

The Catholic recovery of the late sixteenth and early seventeenth centuries was not the first one the old Church had achieved. We have seen how it overcame the heretical movements and schisms of the Middle Ages. In the second half of the fifteenth century, it faced a much graver, even unprecedented, threat in the form of a powerful Ottoman advance into Southeastern Europe. But Catholic forces halted that advance outside Vienna in 1529 and then, beginning at mid-century, gradually pushed it back.

If Catholic Europe found itself on the defensive against the Islamic Turks, the Catholic rulers of Spain, King Ferdinand of Aragon (1452–1516) and Queen Isabella of Castile (1459–1504), took the offensive against the two non-Christian societies entrenched in the Iberian Peninsula, the Jews and the Islamic "Moors." In the 1480s, agents of Isabella's new Catholic Inquisition burned more than seven hundred "Judaizers" alive and ordered Spanish Jews in general either to convert to Christianity or leave the peninsula. About one hundred thousand chose to flee, creating a large Sephardic (after *Sefarad*, the Hebrew word for Spain) diaspora. The Jews who stayed converted to Catholicism, but Spanish officials and much of the population believed that most conversions were insincere and proceeded to harass and persecute former Jews (*conversos*) for centuries to come. As for the Muslims of Spain, they found themselves subject to similar treatment after their kingdom of Grenada fell to Spanish forces in 1492. Most Iberian Muslims fled to North Africa.

The success of Spain's Inquisition led to a tighter, more disciplined Spanish Church that purged itself of the kinds of abuses that would soon galvanize reformers in Germany; there was no controversy over indulgences in Spain. When Ferdinand and Isabella's grandson, Charles V, became king of Spain and Holy Roman Emperor, the Spanish monarchy dominated Italy, and with it, the pope. This domination constrained the pope's powers but also ensured that both Italy and Spain would remain free of any Protestant taint.

The Council of Trent

Germany, as we have seen, enjoyed no such immunity. By the time Charles V and his brother Ferdinand of Austria defeated the Ottomans at Vienna in 1529, Protestantism in Germany was already entrenched. And once it became clear that Lutheranism could not be defeated militarily, Charles sought to convene a general council of the Church to resolve Europe's religious disputes. By bringing reformers and traditionalists together, he hoped to enact compromises that would return all Christians to a common fold. But power politics entered into the equation when France's Catholic king, Francis II, acted to block any religious resolution in Germany that could reunify the HRE and thus tip Europe's balance of power toward Charles and away from France.

When the General Council finally met in 1545 in the small alpine town of Trent, the French boycotted the event, and no Protestants showed up. Worse, only two Spanish bishops and a lone German bishop bothered to come. That the other representatives all hailed from Italy hardly made it a *general* council of the Church. With no official Protestant representation and the papal delegates in control, the Council of Trent hardened the Catholic-Protestant divide rather than healing it through compromise, as Charles V had hoped. The Council's first significant decree held that God's truths "are contained in written books and in unwritten traditions." This statement explicitly contradicted Protestantism's belief in the truth of scripture alone. The Council's second key decree went right to the core of the Catholic-Protestant split by rejecting the Protestant maxim of justification (salvation) by faith alone. The Council maintained that human beings have free will and can merit God's grace through the good works they perform, especially by participating in the Church's seven traditional sacraments—baptism, eucharist, confirmation, reconciliation (confession), anointing of the sick, marriage, and holy orders (joining the priesthood). A third decree affirmed the Catholic doctrine of transubstantiation, once again contradicting Protestant beliefs.

The Council of Trent met off and on until 1563, but not until its final session (1562–1563) could it genuinely be considered a *general council* of the Church. Only then did it include significant numbers of bishops from Spain and France. Its most tricky discussions turned on whether the pope, then Pius IV (1499–1565), or the council of bishops enjoyed supreme religious authority. But while the Council dithered, the pope took action. He made the Church into a top-down hierarchy under his command.

Beyond these administrative questions, the Council issued a series of decrees destined to remain in force for the next four centuries. Most important was the creation of a standard church service, or **mass**, in Latin rather than the different vernacular (e.g., French or German) languages. Another decree called for a well-trained clergy and seminaries in every diocese of the Catholic world. Seminarians would prepare to teach their flock the basic elements of Catholicism using a standard catechism (summary of religious doctrine), itself the product of Trent. It went without saying that priests would instruct parishioners never to look at materials placed on the papal Index of forbidden books, established at the time of Trent; if they did, the Holy Office, or papal inquisition established in 1542, would haul them in.

The Jesuits

The conclusion of the Council of Trent in 1563 marked the beginning of a period in which the Catholic reformation and Counter-Reformation worked together and reinforced each other. Central to this process was a new religious organization, the Society of Jesus, commonly known as the **Jesuits**. The order grew out of the intense personal and religious experiences of a Basque nobleman, Ignatius Loyola (1491–1556), whose earliest ambition was to serve the Castilian king in battle and at his court. Loyola fought valiantly against the French and in 1521 suffered serious injuries to his legs. During his long convalescence at home, he read the Catholic devotional works his parents had collected and experienced a religious awakening that transformed his goals in life. Instead of attending to his king as a

≡ **Ignatius Loyola.** A Basque nobleman, Loyola founded the Jesuit order and styled himself a religious knight in the service of the Church and the pope.

knight and courtier, he decided to serve God and the pope as a religious warrior. In one sense, he remained what he had always been, a chivalric Spanish nobleman possessed of the crusading spirit, but rather than combating the French enemy or the Muslim infidel, he would now fight for the strength and glory of the Church.

After relearning to walk, Loyola took a pilgrimage to the shrine of the Black Madonna at Montserrat, where a vision of the Virgin Mary moved him to trade his nobleman's cloak for the rags of a religious hermit. As he stalked the countryside, he attracted a devoted group of followers with whom he shared his religious visions and mystical experiences. He began to record these experiences in a series of writings that he would later publish as the *Spiritual Exercises* (1548), a book destined to become one of the classics of Catholic thought. Loyola's charismatic personality and impromptu congregation worried local Catholic leaders, who brought him before an Inquisition court. He escaped conviction for heresy but judged it advisable to leave Spain. His destination was Paris and the Sorbonne, where he intended to undergo rigorous theological training and be ordained as a priest. In Paris, as in Spain, he attracted a loyal following, whose members included another Basque nobleman, Francis Xavier (1506–1552), and an international cohort of dedicated young men. After being ordained as priests, Loyola and his fellows traveled to Rome, where the pope declared their new ten-member Society of Jesus an official religious order in 1540.

From the start, the Jesuits raised eyebrows. Their dedication to self-reflection and a kind of mystical spirituality earned them the ongoing hostility of the Spanish Inquisition, which feared their unorthodox religiosity and independence of mind. And to the discomfort of other religious orders, the Jesuits refused to be cloistered inside a monastery. "The world is our house," declared a new member in the 1550s, when the Society expanded rapidly. Their goal was to take the Catholic message to the streets, to prisons and hospitals, and soon to the peoples of colonial North and South America, India, and China, where Society members ranked among Europe's first missionaries abroad. The Jesuits achieved remarkable successes in converting colonized people, but they often suffered cruelly for their efforts, becoming martyrs to the cause of Catholic renewal. Those willing to be martyrs often made the best recruits, and from the original ten Jesuits of 1540, the Society mushroomed to thirteen thousand members in dozens of countries by century's end.

In addition to missionary work, the Jesuits took on two main tasks. The first was to provide a high-quality Catholic education, and the second—often related to the first—was to combat Protestantism and annul its political and spiritual gains. Loyola interacted easily with political and economic elites, and his fundraising efforts enabled him to create the Society's first secondary schools ("colleges," as they were called at the time) and make them free of charge. The early colleges proved enormously successful, earning Jesuits the reputation of being Europe's best educators, at least in Catholic countries. Because Jesuits valued scholarship and placed teaching at the core of their religious mission, their schools became centers not just of religious instruction but of humanistic learning as well. They trained secular leaders—lawyers, scholars, government officials, and even ruling princes—as well as future bishops and cardinals. Famous graduates included Holy Roman Emperor Ferdinand II, Cardinal Richelieu of France, and the great philosopher René Descartes. Nobles and other elites clamored to have their sons (girls were not eligible) educated by Jesuit fathers, and they eagerly committed themselves to funding a growing number of Jesuit academies. From two in the 1540s, the number of Jesuit colleges expanded to 35 in 1556, 144 in 1579, and 550 in 1626. By 1773, when the Vatican briefly suppressed the Jesuit order, they had established 800 colleges throughout the Catholic world, including several in Asia and the Americas.

The Jesuits devoted many of their best people to the educational mission, but the Society was above all a militant organization structured hierarchically along military lines and fitted out for battle. Its generals deliberately sent their top soldiers into the middle of religious civil wars and to places like Ireland, where Jesuits worked to shore up the Catholic population in the face of English efforts to subvert it. In England, Jesuits risked their lives giving spiritual aid and comfort to a persecuted Catholic minority. Once a formerly Protestant state or city returned to the Catholic fold, often by the force of arms, Jesuits quickly established schools designed to create an entrenched, well-educated Catholic elite.

If Jesuits shunned the monastery, the leaders of Tridentine (post–Council of Trent) Catholicism tried to ensure that members of female orders would remain inside the cloister. In the past, convents had often been open to the outside world, places where women could come and go according to the needs of their families, which were often considerable. Convents provided one of the few respectable alternatives to marriage in a society in which custom prevented a substantial percentage of elite women from finding husbands.

In most parts of Europe, nobles and other elites provided dowries—substantial sums of money or valuable possessions or both—to their daughters upon marriage. Dowries were meant to help found a new household and add to its status and financial security. The larger the dowry, the more desirable the woman and the higher the wealth and standing of the husband she could attract. If a family had several daughters, it made sense to devote its dowry resources to just one or two of them to ensure the best possible matches. But this strategy left many young women without dowries and unable to marry, which presented problems for them and their families. Unmarried adult women were considered a threat to the social order, since they might draw the attentions of married men, potentially creating scandalous relationships and illegitimate children. Europeans doubtless exaggerated this threat, but they commonly believed that the sexuality of unmarried women had to be contained. Convents appeared to solve this problem. Women who entered them took a vow of chastity, and in any event, their behavior could be closely monitored while in the cloister. It was fine for them to go back and forth between the convent and their parents' home, since there too, they could be closely supervised.

Even so, the bishops meeting at Trent disliked this situation. They worried that women who left the convent, however briefly, or received visitors there, however tight the surveillance, opened themselves—to say nothing of inherently lustful, sinful men—to sexual temptation. Clerics were fully aware of such temptations, since despite the priestly requirement of celibacy, churchmen—including bishops, cardinals, and the popes themselves—had often kept mistresses and sired children by them. The Council of Trent succeeded to some extent in imposing sexual discipline on the clergy; it remained to impose that discipline on unmarried women.

To do so, church elders decreed that women who entered convents must be confined there, forbidden to leave or to receive visitors. Even family members could speak to them only through a heavy screen that obscured them from view. Elite families resented these new restrictions, and certain prominent nuns resisted them. But officially, at least, the cloistering of women members of religious orders won out. To ensure the nuns' obedience, male clergymen replaced female leaders as supervisors of convents. Even under these new conditions, however, many of the elite women sent to convents used their social standing and familial protection to quietly subvert the new rules. One new female religious order, the Ursulines, even managed to retain the right to participate in their communities. They provided charity, visited hospitals, and taught the catechism under the cover of a male religious order whose leaders vouched for them. In the mid-seventeenth century, the Ursulines freed themselves altogether by establishing a convent, a girls' school, and a hospital in New France (now Quebec).

The Counter-Reformation

By reaffirming the basic tenets of Catholicism and denying any legitimacy to Protestants, the Council of Trent stabilized the old faith and gave its leaders the confidence to take the offensive against their religious opponents. As we have seen, the Jesuits were key to both the confidence and the offensive. So were a variety of Catholic political leaders determined to use their power, including military power, to retake provinces and peoples lost to the Protestant foe.

When Philip II became King of Spain in 1558, he gave his full backing to Catholic orthodoxy, aiming the religious fervor still directed against Jews and Muslims against Protestants as well. He and his successors acted through the offices of the Spanish Inquisition, whose regular tribunals investigated tens of thousands of cases and sentenced some fifty thousand people in Europe and the

≡ **The Council of Trent.** Holy Roman Emperor Charles V convened the Council of Trent (1545–1563) in an effort to reunify a splintered Christian church. Instead, the Council hardened the Catholic-Protestant divide. It succeeded, however, in reforming Catholic doctrine and practice.

colonial dominions of Mexico and Lima between 1540 and 1700. Prosecutions reached their height in the late sixteenth century, when Moriscos (converted Muslims) and suspected Lutherans faced interrogation, torture, and burning at the stake.

Many of the victims were, in reality, neither Muslims nor Lutherans, but by making an example of them, the Inquisition fostered obedience in the rest of the population. Still, repression constituted only one part of the Spanish story. More important to the maintenance of a solidly Catholic population was the work of missionaries, at home as well as in the colonies, who brought the catechism to the masses. By the late seventeenth century, the overwhelming majority of Spaniards had internalized proper religious conduct and belief.

For all these reasons, Spain never became a battleground in the struggle between Catholicism and Protestantism, except in its distant Dutch provinces. The heart of the intra-Christian conflict resided in France, Germany, and Eastern Europe. Poland-Lithuania became one of the first regions in which Catholics turned back the Protestant tide. Beginning in the 1570s, the Jesuits invested heavily there, and leading Catholic families sent their sons to the growing number of Jesuit schools. By the late seventeenth century, most Polish noblemen had renounced Protestantism, and their country became a reliably Catholic state.

The Jesuits scored similar successes in the southern provinces of the Netherlands, which unlike their northern counterparts remained solidly within the Catholic fold. Meanwhile, Jesuits and other religious orders helped restore an almost completely vanquished Catholicism in Hungary, although the Habsburg army had to finish the job. Early in France's wars of religion, Jesuits joined the battle against Protestantism there, and French seminaries trained hundreds of Irish priests determined to return home to lead the fight against their English Protestant colonizers. Together with a group of influential writers, these newly minted priests linked Ireland's Gaelic language and culture to the Catholic religion and helped make Irish identity synonymous with Catholicism (see Map 1.3).

In the Holy Roman Empire, Catholic rulers, reduced to a minority in the early to mid-sixteenth century, regained confidence after Trent and asserted their authority. In the mid-1560s, the Duke of Bavaria suppressed the religious freedom of his Protestant noblemen and invited Jesuits to train a new Catholic elite. Three decades later, Ferdinand II (1578–1637), the new ruler of Austria, put his own Jesuit education to work by undertaking a vigorous campaign to roll back the substantial gains Protestants had made in his territories. His campaign proved successful, and it encouraged him to seek election as king of Bohemia, where he planned to suppress "heresy" in this supremely heretical place. There, Jan Hus had rebelled against the Catholic Church already in the early 1400s, and Lutheranism and Calvinism had firmly taken hold a century later.

Named king of Bohemia in 1616, Ferdinand immediately began to harass Protestant congregations, censor their publications, and dismiss Protestants and Hussites from their government offices. These provocative actions in a country where Protestantism had seemed secure evoked a powerful reaction against the new king. During a meeting of leading Protestant noblemen in Prague, the Bohemian capital, participants tried to execute three of Ferdinand's royal representatives by ejecting them from a third-story window. A pile of rotting garbage broke their fall, and they survived, albeit in humiliation and covered with filth. Protestants throughout Europe applauded what came to be known as the "defenestration of Prague" (May 23, 1618), while Ferdinand, buoyed by the "miraculous" survival of his men, became all the more determined to make the Bohemian nobles pay.

Both sides had already organized military alliances, the Protestant Union and the Catholic League, and by the 1610s, both seemed ready for war. The Catholics represented the stronger force, for despite the newfound alliance of Lutherans and

NORWAY

SWEDEN

COURLAND

SCOTLAND

DENMARK

*North
Sea*

Baltic Sea

PRUSSIA

IRELAND

POMERANIA

POLAND-
LITHUANIA

Dublin

MECKLENBURG
BRANDENBURG

ENGLAND

UNITED
PROVINCES

Berlin

Warsaw

London

Amsterdam

Wittenberg

SILESIA

Antwerp

Münster

SPANISH
NETHERLANDS

Schmalkalden

Prague

BOHEMIA

MORAVIA

HUNGARY

Worms

Paris

Strasbourg

Vienna

Vassy

BAVARIA

AUSTRIA

*ATLANTIC
OCEAN*

FRANCE

Zurich

ALSACE
SWITZ.

Geneva

Trent

Milan

Brescia

SAVOY

Bordeaux

Ravenna

Avignon

Florence

OTTOMAN
EMPIRE

*Adriatic
Sea*

NAVARRE

SPAIN

ITALY

Rome

Madrid

Naples

PORTUGAL

0 miles   200

0 km   200

The Religious Divisions of Europe, c. 1600

▮ Protestant majorities	▮ Areas regained by Catholic efforts
▮ Significant Protestant minorities	▮ Predominantly Catholic

MAP 1.3   The Religious Divisions of Europe, c. 1600

Calvinists, the two groups disliked and distrusted each other almost as much as they disliked and distrusted the Catholics. This division did not prevent Bohemia's Protestant nobility from rescinding the election of Ferdinand as their king and replacing him with Friedrich V (1596–1632), the devoutly Calvinist ruler of the Palatinate in northwestern Germany. Ferdinand did not take kindly to this affront, and the brewing conflict between Friedrich and him, one representing a militant Catholic Counter-Reformation and the other a re-energized Protestantism, soon unleashed a generation of war. Called the **Thirty Years' War** (1618–1648), this religious struggle took proportionally more European lives than any other conflict until the World Wars of the twentieth century. In German lands, as much as 30 to 40 percent of the population died early as a result of the fighting and the famine and disease it caused (see Chapter 3).

The Thirty Years' War

Although skirmishes began in 1618, the real fighting came in November 1620, when Ferdinand II, having been elected Holy Roman Emperor the previous year, sent a seasoned Habsburg army against Friedrich and his Calvinist fighters. This conflict, known as the Battle of White Mountain, ended badly for the Calvinists, who had alienated their Lutheran and Hussite brethren and lost four thousand men. The defeated Protestant noblemen had to convert to Catholicism or flee the country. Leaving nothing to chance, Jesuits appeared on the scene to oversee the conversions and ensure at least an outward allegiance to the Catholic faith.

The outcome of White Mountain encouraged the Catholic League to take the offensive against Calvinists, Lutherans, and Hussites alike. In 1622, they overran the Upper Palatinate and sacked the city of Heidelberg. They then destroyed what remained of the Hussite church and expelled from Ferdinand's core territories in Austria all Protestant landowners who refused to renounce their faith. The victors of these battles imposed on the vanquished Protestants a harsh Edict of Restitution (1629), which returned to the Catholic Church all lands seized by secular authorities since 1552 and banned Calvinism throughout most of the HRE.

This Edict proved so extreme that it finally produced an alliance of German Lutheran and Calvinist princes, which had been elusive until then. Most significantly, the Catholic offensive made Gustavus Adolphus (1594–1632), the king of Lutheran Sweden, fear that the Catholic League would attack his kingdom, and he sent a large army to stop it. Gustavus styled himself a Protestant savior, and by 1631 he had reversed the course of the war. A year later, the savior became a martyr, as the Swedish king fell in battle.

At about the same time, an entire German city was martyred as well. After a long siege by Catholic forces, the overwhelmingly Protestant city of Magdeburg, long a proudly independent Imperial Free City, was brutally sacked by the imperial troops. Most of Magdeburg's twenty thousand residents died at the hands of invading soldiers or in the fires deliberately set to "purify" the town. This massacre stands as one of the most violent episodes of the entire Reformation period.

≡ **Siege of Magdeburg.** In one of the bloodiest episodes of the Thirty Years' War, Catholic forces sacked the Protestant city of Magdeburg (eastern Germany) in 1631 and killed some 20,000 people.

In a terrible irony, the atrocity of Magdeburg occurred when the religious motivations of the Thirty Years' War were already on the wane; it was rapidly becoming a contest for power in Central Europe largely independent of religious affiliations. German Catholic princes now worried that Emperor Ferdinand II had amassed power at their expense, and the desire to remain independent trumped their religious commitments. They withdrew military support from the Catholic League.

Meanwhile, the French began to worry as well, concerned as always over any signs of growing HRE strength. In this case, politics clearly outweighed religion, since a cardinal of the Catholic Church, the Duke of Richelieu (1585–1642), King Louis XIII's prime minister, set his country's foreign policy. Richelieu intervened on the Swedish side, battling Habsburg and Spanish armies and enabling German Protestants to elude defeat. Even the pope, fearing excessive Habsburg and Spanish power, remained neutral in the final decades of the war, as did the Protestant king of England, who faced rebellion and civil war at home.

The Thirty Years' War finally ended in 1648, when the **Treaty of Westphalia** froze Europe's religious divisions for centuries to come. The signers, Catholic and Protestant alike, affirmed the independence of the Calvinist Netherlands and permanently split German territories into a predominantly Protestant North and a mainly Catholic South. Hungary, Austria, Bohemia, and most other Habsburg provinces of Central and Eastern Europe returned to the Catholic fold. These

The Thirty Years' War	
1618	Bohemian revolt against Habsburg rule
	Defenestration of Prague
1619	Ferdinand II is elected Holy Roman Emperor
	Frederick, elector of the Palatinate, is elected king of Bohemia
1620	Catholic victory at Battle of White Mountain
1621	Truce between Spain and the Netherlands expires; war between Spain and the Netherlands begins
1626	Imperial forces defeat armies of Christian IV of Denmark
1629	Edict of Restitution bans Calvinism from most of the Holy Roman Empire
1631	Swedes under Gustavus Adolphus defeat imperial forces at Breitenfeld
	Catholic forces sack Magdeburg
1632	Death of Gustavus Adolphus
1635	Peace of Prague
1643	French defeat Spanish in the Netherlands
1648	Peace of Westphalia

developments contained the power and reach of the militantly Catholic Habsburgs, while granting Sweden significant new territories and enshrining it as a Protestant Great Power on the continent. Perhaps most significant, the Treaty of Westphalia introduced the idea that the object of statecraft in Europe should be the creation of a **balance of power** in which no single country, kingdom, or empire should be allowed to dominate the continent—or for that matter, the New World, to which the European rivalries had spread (see Map 1.4).

Perhaps the key unintended consequence of the Thirty Years' War was to establish an unprecedented measure of official religious tolerance in German lands. For the first time, it became legal to practice the Calvinist faith within the Empire, while Lutheran subjects in Catholic states and Catholic residents in Lutheran lands gained the right to worship privately "without investigation or disturbance." In Europe as a whole, the terrible toll of the Thirty Years' War convinced both Catholic and Protestant rulers of the folly of religious crusades and opened them to the peaceful compromise solutions of diplomacy. Wars, of course, often ensued, but rarely now for religious reasons. Continental Europe's religious passions seemed finally to have burned themselves out.

Europe in 1648

▨	Spanish dominions
▨	Austrian dominions
▨	Brandenburg-Prussia
▨	Swedish dominions
Lützen	Major battle of the Thirty Years' War
——	Boundary of Holy Roman Empire

≡ **MAP 1.4**   Europe in 1648, with Locations of Major Battles of the Thirty Years' War

Reformation Society and Culture

Much of our story of the age of religious reform has necessarily centered on popes and kings, clergymen and theologians, nobles, and other social elites. These were the major actors in this extraordinary, and often tragic, religious, social, and political drama. For that reason, historians know the most about them. But there were millions of other actors as well, actors whom we have occasionally glimpsed in the German Peasants' War, in urban uprisings, and as soldiers in many of the era's religious battles. We have a good idea of what religious reformers said with the great masses of peasants and artisans in mind. But we need to ask to what extent, and in what ways, ordinary people understood the words directed at them.

From the Peasants' War, we know that certain Protestant ideas sank in because the rural rebellions of the 1520s differed from the many similar rebellions of the past. Never before had peasant rebels explained their desire for lower taxes and fairer treatment in terms of "Godly law" or the authority of scripture. Nor had they explained their hostility to the landlords who exploited them by deciding "henceforth to have no lord but God alone." Further evidence that new religious ideas had entered the consciousness of ordinary people came in the waves of iconoclasm that washed over Scotland, Switzerland, and the Netherlands, often to the horror of their social superiors. People learned through sermons, pamphlets, or printed pictures that the creation of "graven images" violated God's Ten Commandments and took it upon themselves to strip churches of these now forbidden idols.

Witchcraft

The "witch craze" of the Reformation period tells us even more about the popular resonance of the era's new religious ideas. Although witch-hunting had occurred in the Middle Ages, it soared to an unprecedented peak after Martin Luther appeared on the scene. He did not cause it, of course, but the intense religious contestation of the time, when heresy threatened and the Apocalypse loomed, made the Devil and his harem of witches seem an ever-present danger. Amid the religious fervor, preachers and politicians, fearful of the opposing side, demanded uniformity and purity and singled out individuals or groups that appeared to subvert them. This preaching stirred up general social fears and convinced ordinary people that the calamities they all too often faced—epidemics, crop-destroying storms, droughts, and fires—represented the work of the very witches of whom their leaders spoke. Between the early sixteenth century and the early eighteenth century, some one hundred thousand people, mostly women, found themselves accused of witchcraft, often by their neighbors. About forty thousand were put to death, far more than the number of supposed heretics burned at the stake.

Why were most alleged sorcerers female? People of the early modern era commonly believed that women possessed voracious sexual appetites, and the large number of unmarried women, especially widows, threatened to unleash those appetites on hapless men. Having tasted the pleasures of the flesh, widows supposedly constituted a particular sexual danger, which may explain why those accused of witchcraft tended to be older women living alone.

These considerations raise the general question of the role and status of women during the era of Protestant and Catholic reformation. Did women suffer or profit from these religious transformations—or both? Protestantism exalted the status and importance of marriage and family life, and pastors were encouraged to marry and make their families a model for everyone else. But this was not necessarily a good thing for women.

For Calvin, the family served as a miniature church in which fathers assumed the role of a minister charged with educating and disciplining their wives and children. Luther, for his part, declared that husbands could subject their wives to "reasonable" physical punishment and that "women should bear children to death—that is what they are for." Still, Luther did not feel that way about his own wife, so it may be that, in practice, Protestant wives established a fair amount of informal authority within the outward form of the patriarchal family.

One problem for Protestant women was that they no longer enjoyed the alternative to marriage that existed in the Catholic world, namely becoming a nun and entering into a marriage with Christ. The cloister isolated and confined the women who entered it, but it also freed nuns from the close supervision of male

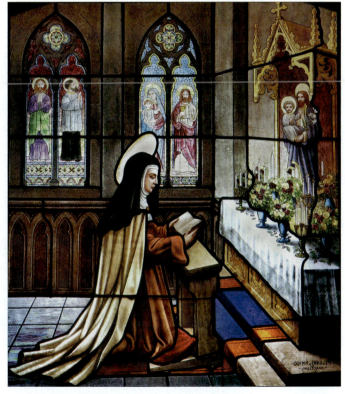

≡ **Teresa of Avila.** A Carmelite nun and ultimately a saint, Teresa wrote an autobiographical work, the *Vida*, which stands as one of the great Catholic writings of her time.

family members and gave them the ability to develop deep and reflective spiritual lives.

The Carmelite nun Teresa of Avila (1515–1582), who ultimately became a saint, composed a spiritual autobiography, the *Vida*, which stands as one of the great Catholic writings of the time. Teresa founded several convents, and the success of her religious order earned her the admiration of leading Jesuits and even of King Philip II, whom she met in person. Although subject to the oversight of men, Teresa developed the ability to live the life she sought. She possessed, as one admirer later wrote, "the gift of making men give her the orders she wanted to obey."

The Visual Arts

As Teresa of Avila's story shows, written texts took on importance for Catholics as well as Protestants during this period. Such was not the case with the visual arts. Catholic painting and sculpture had long been resplendent with sensuality—vivid, colorful, and rich. Jesus, the Virgin Mary, and a great many saints loomed over parishioners in every medieval church, while statues, busts, and frescoes filled every nook and cranny, with religious murals plastered onto the walls. Post-Tridentine churches maintained this intense visual tradition and often added to it.

Protestantism, by contrast, especially its Calvinist variety, found such visual exuberance blasphemous and wasteful, a violation of the Second Commandment's prohibition of "graven images." (Catholics believed that this prohibition belonged to the First Commandment's injunction to "have no other gods before me" and thus that it applied to idols and not to God or Jesus.) As Calvin wrote, "all

≡ **Rembrandt van Rijn, Ahasuerus and Haman at the Feast of Esther (1662).** This painting depicts a key episode from the Bible's Book of Esther. Queen Esther, a Jew, convinces her husband, the Persian King Ahasuerus, that her cousin Mordechai had been wrongly accused of disrespect by Persia's religious leader, Haman. When told of Haman's treachery, Ahasuerus decided to hang the religious leader on the gallows erected for Mordechai, thus sparing him and the rest of Persia's captive Jews.

attempts to depict [God] are an impudent affront . . . to his majesty and glory." Images were idols by definition, which meant that good Christians not only had to remove them from existing churches but also refrain from making new ones.

Because Protestantism frowned on religious art, painters and sculptors turned to secular subject matter. In the Calvinist Netherlands, which became a great center of seventeenth-century art, the "Dutch masters" painted landscapes, still lifes, portraits of prosperous people, and realistic scenes of the everyday world. Religious subjects were not prohibited altogether; painters just had to represent them in the form of history, as scenes from the Bible brought to life.

Rembrandt van Rijn (1606–1669) stood out as the period's exemplar of this kind of biblical art. Despite these concessions to religious history, the strictures against art for devotional purposes moved painting in Protestant countries from the sacred to the profane. Art detached itself from religion, and in this sense, if not in many others, the Reformation served the purposes of secularization, the creation of spheres of life separate from religion and the church.

Conclusion: The Reformation's Outcomes and Results

Once upon a time, historians viewed the Reformation as a crucial step on the road to liberty, modernity, and secularism. As we have seen, it was much more complicated than that. First, there was nothing inexorable about the process. Although about half of Europe lived under Protestant governments or culture at the end of the sixteenth century, a hundred years later the Protestant share had declined to one-fifth. Because people took their religious beliefs, practices, and commitments seriously, efforts to change them resulted in violence and war.

Between 1517, when Luther posted his 95 Theses, and 1660, Europe enjoyed only about ten years of total peace. Tens of thousands of people died, and a great many more found themselves displaced. The Reformation produced Europe's greatest population movements, both voluntary and involuntary, between the "barbarian" invasions of the Roman Empire (400–800) and the First World War (1914–1918). The era's warfare was expensive and logistically complex; to finance and organize it required expanded bureaucracies and centralized governments.

The religious wars thus favored the strongest and best-organized kingdoms and made them even stronger, in some cases by transferring power away from nobles and parliaments and in others by creating closer ties between privileged elites and the crown. For this reason, one key outcome of the Reformation was the emergence not of liberty but of powerful "absolutist" states (see Chapter 2)—especially in France, Prussia, and the Habsburg Empire—none of which showed tolerance toward minority religions. Even English monarchs, their prerogatives intermittently constrained by Parliament, sometimes ruled arbitrarily and more than in any other Protestant country had their religious and political opponents killed.

If Catholicism and Protestantism constituted the minority religion in different parts of Europe, Jews were almost everywhere a tiny persecuted group. They were barred from Spain, Portugal, and England; confined to ghettos in Italy; and accused throughout the continent of using the blood of murdered Christian children in various religious rites. The great humanist scholar, Erasmus, a relative voice of tolerance in the early sixteenth century, wrote vicious anti-Semitic polemics, while Luther argued that synagogues should be burned and Jewish literature forbidden in retribution for the killing of Christ.

During the Reformation, the Jews' outcast status made them adept at finding places where they could live in relative peace. The Ottoman Empire ranked high on their list, as did Poland-Lithuania. The Jews' most important haven was doubtless the city of Amsterdam, the bustling commercial capital of the Calvinist Netherlands, which distinguished itself as seventeenth-century Europe's most open, tolerant place.

In the sixteenth century, Hungary, Transylvania, Bohemia, and Poland showed glimmers of religious toleration, but the Counter-Reformation mostly snuffed them out. Toleration reemerged in the seventeenth century, but the price for it was high. The Dutch had to endure sixty years of brutal warfare with Spain, while in Germany, Protestants and Catholics alike paid for the toleration legislated in 1648 in rivers of blood. The Reformation did produce a measure of religious freedom, as the old story about it maintained, but it usually did so against the wishes of most of its leaders, whether Catholic or Protestant.

As for secularization, if anything, the Reformation made European society more religious rather than less. Great theologians like Luther and Calvin thought deeply about scripture and communicated their ideas widely, while Catholics renewed their faith and catechized the population after the Council of Trent. Not until the Enlightenment of the eighteenth century would it become possible to imagine a world distanced from God.

KEY TERMS

95 Theses *6*

Anabaptism *14*

balance of power *40*

Diet of Worms *8*

Edict of Nantes *24*

Edict of Worms *8*

evangelicalism *9*

Huguenot *22*

indulgences *6*

Jesuits *31*

"justification [acceptance] by faith alone" *6*

mass *31*

Peace of Augsburg *17*

Peasants' War *15*

predestination *19*

Thirty Years' War *38*

Treaty of Westphalia *39*

Twelve Articles of Memmingen *15*

For digital learning resources, please go to **https://www.oup.com/he/berenson2e**. Turn to the back of the book to see the list of primary sources and writing exercises provided in the accompanying *Sources and Guided Writing Exercises for Europe in the Modern World*

States and Empires, 1450–1700

Roxelana, the Ottoman Queen

In 1516, a troop of Tatar slave-raiders swept into Ruthenia (present-day Ukraine) and seized a young Christian girl—along with perhaps 30,000–40,000 others. We don't know the child's name, but she would later be called Roxelana, which means "the maiden from Ruthenia." The thirteen-year-old, chained to other captives, must have been terrified and bewildered, cringing in fear of the alien men who had taken her. She could not have known that a glorious future awaited her.

The raiders had come from the Crimean Khanate, a protectorate of the Ottoman Empire. Their job was to seize thousands of non-Muslim children every year and sell them to well-to-do Turkish families and often to agents of the Ottoman sultan, who would press them into the service of his court. Slaves came not only from Ruthenia but also from the Balkans (present-day Serbia, Bulgaria, Greece, and the other countries of Southeastern Europe), lands the Ottomans had annexed in the fifteenth century. The slave trade was big business: the tax revenues it generated gave the Ottomans their greatest source of income.

The slave trade also gave the Ottoman Empire its elite soldiers, high civil servants, and the future mothers of its sultans—in addition to many of its household laborers. Unlike the Western Europeans, who confined virtually all of their slaves to the lowliest positions in society and treated them barbarously, the Ottomans sorted their captives by talent, intelligence, adaptability, and strength. Female slaves were also judged by beauty, charm, and grace. The top male slaves were drilled as elite warriors or educated to serve the state. The top female slaves were trained to please sultans and princes and encouraged to appeal to them sexually.

Beginning in the early fifteenth century, sultans officially slept only with the enslaved women chosen for their harems. Ottoman rulers ceased to marry because they did not want to elevate another family to a status similar to their own. In Western Europe, kings married women from other royal families, which added to the power and standing of the other families and made their members—and especially their offspring—potential rivals of the king. Sultans avoided these dangers by procreating only with slaves seized from poor Christian parents, who lost their daughters forever.

We lack exact information about the enslaved Roxelana's early fate. Whoever purchased her would have shipped her from the slave market at Caffa (now Theodosia) on the Crimean Peninsula across the Black Sea to Istanbul, the Ottoman capital. She must have distinguished herself as a potential concubine for the sultan or sultan-to-be, for she next appears in the historical record as a member of the sultan's harem living in what was known as the Old Palace. There, she and other young enslaved women shared quarters with various officials tasked with preparing them for the sultan's bed. Enslaved girls selected for this role did not have much of a choice: either they submitted sexually or they lived out their lives, at best, in lowly menial jobs.

As she prepared to be a royal concubine, Roxelana learned the Turkish language and converted to Islam. She also learned that physical allure, the ability to illuminate her master's desire, was not enough. Women of the royal harem also had to demonstrate the ability to nurture princes and princesses and prepare them for their royal lives. Although concubines were slaves, their children became fully legitimate members of the sultan's family, the boys potential heirs to the throne. As guardians of princes and princesses, royal concubines received sophisticated educations in history, literature, music, and the arts—educations far more advanced than those of most free-born Ottomans. That instruction was especially important for a concubine who gave birth to a boy. According to Ottoman custom, the new mother would never again be invited into the sultan's bed; now her sole, all-encompassing duty was to serve as advisor and guide to her son as he prepared to succeed his father one day.

Roxelana, just seventeen years old, must have caught the eye of Süleyman I shortly after he became sultan in September 1520. Their first child, Mehmed, was born just a year later. As a boy, Mehmed was Süleyman's potential heir, and his princely standing transformed the status of his mother Roxelana, now elevated to the palace elite. But she faced competition from Süleyman's former concubine Mahidevran, with whom he had also conceived a son, Mustafa, a few years before Mehmed was born. Both boys were eligible to succeed their father, because the Ottomans did not observe the tradition of primogeniture, or inheritance by the firstborn child, common in the kingdoms and empires of the West. Roxelana's role, like Mahidevran's, was to ensure that her son won the contest for the succession.

Timeline

1450	1520	1540	1560	1580	1600	1620	1640	1660	1680	1700

1453 Ottomans capture Constantinople

1492 Columbus lands in the Caribbean; beginning of Columbian Exchange

1494 Treaty of Tordesillas divides the New World between Spain and Portugal

1500–1550 Half of all revenues accruing to the Portuguese crown come from overseas trade

1516 Roxelana captured by slave-raiders in Eastern Europe

1519 Charles V becomes Holy Roman Emperor

1519 Hernando Cortés lands in Mexico

1520–1566 Reign of Ottoman sultan Süleyman I

1523 Sweden breaks free of Danish rule

1527 Gustav I convenes Swedish Riksdag (parliament)

1531–1533 Francisco Pizarro defeats the Incan Empire

1534 Süleyman makes Roxelana queen

1540s England begins colonization of Ireland

1569 Poland unites with neighboring Lithuania to create Polish-Lithuanian Commonwealth

1571 Spain occupies the Philippines

1572 Polish parliament wins right to elect king

1580 Spain annexes Portugal

1581 The northern part of the Spanish Netherlands declares independence from the Spanish crown

1600 Queen Elizabeth charters English East India Company

1602 Dutch East India Company founded

1603 James I succeeds to English throne

1607 Jamestown settlement founded by the Virginia Company

1613 Michael Romanov establishes Romanov dynasty in Russia

1614 Beginning of tobacco cultivation in Virginia

1618–1648 Thirty Years' War

1619 Dutch establish commercial base of Batavia in today's Indonesia

1624 Virginia becomes a royal colony

1643–1715 Reign of Louis XIV

1660s Slave-based production of sugar expands in the Caribbean

1682–1725 Reign of Russian tsar Peter the Great

1685 French government issues the *Code noir* designed in part to make treatment of black slaves less inhumane

c. 1700 More than three-quarters of all those who cross the Atlantic are African slaves bound for the New World

It is at this point that Süleyman broke with Ottoman custom by continuing to sleep with Roxelana, despite her having given him a son. Süleyman and Roxelana seem to have developed strong feelings for each other, and he refused to give her up. Over the next few years, Roxelana and Süleyman conceived a daughter and three more sons. He had no children with any other woman during the whole of his unusually long reign (1520–1566) and appears to have been monogamous, something nearly unprecedented for an Ottoman sultan.

As the mother of four Ottoman princes, Roxelana ascended to the upper reaches of the Ottoman Empire's female elite, ranking second to Süleyman's mother Hafsa and above Mahidevran, the mother of the sultan's oldest son. After Hafsa's death in 1534, Süleyman took yet another unprecedented step: he married Roxelana and made her his queen. The slave girl became the reigning partner of one of the most powerful monarchs on earth, and with Hafsa gone, the most important woman of the realm.

Having become the first Ottoman queen in nearly a century, Roxelana was free to invent her role. Almost immediately, she moved from the Old Palace, the province of women, to the New Palace, the sultan's home and the province of men. The New Palace was the seat of government, and Roxelana, with Süleyman's apparent approval, began to participate in political affairs. So important did she become that the rumor mill claimed she had bewitched her sultan and kept him under a spell. How else, critics whispered, to explain his monogamy, the marriage, and Roxelana's residence in the heart of the New Palace? The reality was that Roxelana had become an astute advisor, and Süleyman depended on her, as he had long depended on his mother. This was especially true during his long military campaigns, when he remained away from Istanbul for as much as two years at a time.

During these periods, Roxelana became the sultan's chief lieutenant in Istanbul, reporting to him about the situation there and seeing to many essential tasks of government. She also assumed key diplomatic duties, writing to European kings and queens and gathering intelligence whenever she could. Another of her crucial tasks was the mentorship of her oldest son Mehmed, age thirteen at the time of the Iranian wars of the mid-1530s. And she used the immense wealth that Süleyman had bestowed on her to build mosques, hospitals, and charitable institutions, which added immensely to her prestige. She did all this while remaining largely unseen, for elite Muslim women were required to avoid the gaze of men outside their family.

Roxelana's huge authority earned her the growing enmity of Ottoman officials unaccustomed to powerful women. Leaders of the Janissaries, the empire's elite fighting force, "hate her and her children," a knowledgeable foreigner wrote, and they decided to back Mustafa as heir to the throne rather than one of Roxelana's sons. Süleyman, however, stood firmly behind his queen and produced a quiet uproar when he had Mustafa executed in 1552 to remove him from the succession. The killing of potential heirs was common in the Ottoman Empire, as this was deemed the only way to prevent the usurpations and civil wars that occurred so regularly in European kingdoms. But Mustafa's supporters were horrified by this turn of events and blamed Roxelana for his death.

The queen was doubtless pleased that one of her sons would be the next sultan, but which one? She had three eligible boys. Fortunately for the queen's peace of mind, she died before her son Selim had his brothers and their male children killed to make himself the sole heir to the throne. Powerful as she was, Roxelana could not change this feature of Ottoman political culture. But she nevertheless showed that a woman could participate in the affairs of state and enabled elite woman after her to do the same.

The Ottoman Empire

Süleyman and Roxelana's Ottoman Empire was Europe's most powerful state. Its rivals were all empires as well. Süleyman's closest competitor was the Spanish Empire, which briefly incorporated the Holy Roman Empire (1519–56) and later the Portuguese Empire (1580–1640). The Netherlands broke off from Spain at century's end, and the new Dutch Republic formed an empire of its own. England began its own imperial venture at about the same time, and so did France. While the Ottomans, like the Holy Roman Empire, Sweden, Poland-Lithuania, and later the Russian Empire, largely conquered contiguous territories, the other European states expanded overseas. In every case, the conquests were designed to enhance the power and prestige of the monarch, emperor, or sultan and also to seize valuable resources, build wealth through trade, convert people to the dominant religion, and protect the empire's flanks from encroachment by rival empires. In the case of overseas empires, monarchs could generally rule more absolutely abroad than at home, because the far-off colonies tended to have fewer representative assemblies, free cities, and privileged regions than the European homelands. Of course, distance limited the reach of European monarchs, as did the wealth of settlers abroad, who sometimes developed the ability to trade directly with other colonies or empires without sending their goods through the mother country's European ports. All of these empires contained a variety of different peoples, although no other empire matched the diversity of the Ottomans, who ruled over a vast array of peoples and included Catholics, Orthodox Christians, and Jews as well as the Muslim majority. The Ottomans, like the other empires, had to manage these differences, and some managed them more successfully than others. The Ottomans ranked among the most successful, as they tolerated the religious diversity of their subjects. The other empires, except for Poland-Lithuania, were loath to accept minority religions and often excluded or oppressed them.

The Rise of the Ottoman Empire

The Ottoman Empire originated in the early 1300s, when a Turkic leader named Osman Gazi (1256–1326) seized territory from the faltering Byzantine Empire (395–1453). Osman gained a foothold in what is now northwestern Turkey and expanded from there into western Anatolia and around the Sea of Marmara, ultimately landing on its European side. Ottoman troops marched into Bulgaria, northern Greece, and parts of Serbia before crossing back into Asia, where they moved eastward into the heart of Anatolia. After failing to capture the Byzantine capital Constantinople at the dawn of the fifteenth century, Osman's heirs built a powerful navy to prepare for a second attack, which they launched in early 1453. The Byzantine capital, built at the end of a peninsula, was protected by steep walls on its eastern, western, and southern flanks. On the north side of the peninsula, a taut metal chain stretched across the waterway leading into the city and prevented enemy ships from coming in. After failing to cut the chain in late April, the Ottoman Sultan Mehmed II circumvented it by hoisting his ships onto greased logs and rolling his fleet along the rim of the waterway before depositing his boats inside the chain. This brilliant logistical and tactical move enabled Mehmed to tighten his siege of the city, which he captured in May 1453.

Constantinople, renamed Istanbul, became the capital of a rapidly expanding Ottoman Empire (see Map 2.1). The Ottomans succeeded, in part, by learning from those they conquered. This once-nomadic people imbibed the vibrant urban culture of Greek and

≡ **MAP 2.1**   Ottoman Expansion c. 1200–1453

formerly Roman cities, learned seafaring and commerce from the great Italian city-states, and enriched their culture with elements of all three monotheistic religions (Judaism, Christianity, and Islam). The Ottoman elite remained true to Islam, the principal religion of the places they seized early on.

Once the Ottomans had forged their huge Mediterranean empire, they needed to find effective ways to hold it together. The first step was to create an absolutist central government, which at first meant managing the succession from one sultan to his heir. As we have seen, the leading contender had his brothers and half-brothers and their male children, even babies, killed.

These brutal methods prevented the sultan's family members from forging rival centers of power, but the Ottoman rulers were not content to stop there in the effort to secure their monopoly of power. They also prevented the emergence of a European-style nobility by giving the highest positions in the realm—governorships, army commands, treasury directors—to slaves. Even the grand vizier, the empire's highest-ranked official, and members of the sultan's royal council were slaves. The great advantage for the sultan of having slaves as his top military and governmental figures was that virtually his entire elite literally belonged to him. He could dismiss them from their positions at will and even execute them if he chose. When powerful non-slave elites emerged in local areas, as they did from time to time, the sultan moved them to distant corners of the empire, where they lacked the influence to turn themselves into European-style magnates capable of vying for the throne.

The Ottoman regime thus concentrated unprecedented power in the hands of the sultan, far more than any European monarch enjoyed. He used that power to build a superior military organization. Thanks to the enslaved but privileged Janissaries and the ability of regional leaders loyal to the sultan to muster large numbers of soldiers, the Ottomans possessed, already in the early 1500s, a standing army of nearly one hundred thousand troops. Their European rivals had to undergo great financial strain just to bring together ten to twenty thousand

The Devshirme. To avoid concentrating substantial power in the hands of the Ottoman nobility, the empire's sultans imposed the Devshirme, a tax in human beings, on their Christian subjects. Under this taxation system, the Ottomans harvested an annual crop of young Christian boys, who were enslaved, converted to Islam, and trained to serve in the sultan's special fighting force, the Janissaries. The ablest among them rose to top positions in the imperial government.

men. The Ottomans' military advantages, together with Europe's ferocious internal conflicts, enabled the Ottoman Empire to expand continuously at Europe's expense until the late seventeenth century, when Ottoman finances began to suffer.

The Expansion of the Ottoman Empire

But for nearly two centuries following the Ottoman seizure of Constantinople, the empire expanded relentlessly, as shown on Map 2.2. These conquests gave them a large measure of control over the lucrative seagoing trade in the Aegean, Ionian, and Eastern Mediterranean Seas. They also enabled the Ottomans to profit from overland trade routes across Asia and into the Indian Ocean via the Persian Gulf and Red Sea, which the empire secured in the early 1500s. By defeating the Shi'ites of Iran in 1514, the Ottomans became the world's dominant Islamic power, and their victory over the Mamluks, the rulers of Egypt and much of the present-day Middle East, placed the holy cities of Jerusalem, Medina, and Mecca within their domains. Control over these cities arguably made the Ottoman Empire the guardian of the

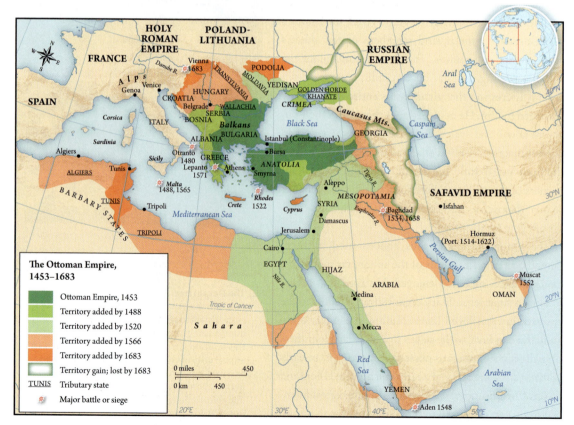

≡ **MAP 2.2** The Ottoman Empire, 1453–1683

Western world's three monotheistic religions. Jerusalem formed the sacred center of Judaism, Christianity, and Islam, while Mecca and Medina represented respectively the birthplace of the prophet Muhammad and the capital of his Islamic empire. These three cities, along with Constantinople, long the capital of Eastern Christendom, gave the Ottoman Empire enormous prestige as both a religious and secular power.

During the reign of Süleyman I and his sixteenth- and seventeenth-century successors, the empire grew still further, making it a huge Eurasian expanse. The Ottomans maintained their control over these far-flung and incredibly diverse regions by sending trusted people, often the sultan's adult sons, to govern them while refusing to empower local elites. But while ruling from the center, the sultans also granted their provinces a fair amount of cultural and religious autonomy—as long as the inhabitants and their religious leaders swore allegiance to them and their lieutenants. This approach allowed the empire to absorb a wide variety of peoples—Greeks, Serbs, Hungarians, Arabs, Tatars, Kurds—while offering protection and tolerance to the empire's religious minorities, Orthodox Christians, Catholics, Protestants, and Jews. This tolerance largely prevented the kinds of murderous conflicts that occurred in Europe during the Reformation, when rulers tried to impose a single dominant religion on all of their subjects. The Ottomans' relative religious tolerance also meant that a great many Jews and non-Catholic Christians preferred the Ottoman Empire to the Habsburg Empire, also known as the Holy Roman Empire, where non-Catholics often faced severe religious repression.

Having extended their domains from east-central Europe to Arabia and North Africa, the Ottoman empire occupied a strategic position that gave them access to vast riches and cultural accomplishments. By the time of Süleyman's death in 1566, his empire had become a major force in Europe and the dominant power in western Asia and North Africa. It would remain so until the eighteenth century.

Spain and the Spanish Empire

The Ottoman push into Eastern and Central Europe placed the growing empire into direct competition with the Spanish Habsburgs, Europe's other expansionist power of the sixteenth century. As we saw in Chapter 1, Charles V, the grandson of Ferdinand and Isabella, became king of Castile and Aragon and Holy Roman Emperor between 1516 and 1519. His parents' and grandparents' marriage alliances made him ruler of a vast European territory that, in addition to Spain, included parts of eastern and northern France, the Netherlands, the southern half of Italy, Austria, and other regions of Central Europe. Charles would soon add an enormous empire in the New World. Later, the Habsburg lands of Central and Eastern Europe would be separated from the Spanish Empire, but Spain added to its overseas domains by occupying the Philippines in 1571 and took more European territory when it annexed Portugal in 1580. Even without the Habsburg territories, Spain constituted an enormous, if unwieldy, empire.

The prelude to Spain's overseas conquests began in August 1492, when Christopher Columbus (1451–1506), having convinced Ferdinand and Isabella to help finance him, set out on a small voyage west across the Atlantic Ocean to China, a shortcut, he thought, to the riches of the East. Admiral Columbus did not seek to prove that the earth was round instead of flat—this was common knowledge among the well-informed—but rather that China was closer than most Europeans believed and that Spanish ships could get there relatively quickly by sailing due west. Columbus vastly underestimated the size of the globe and calculated that China was just three thousand miles from Spain, one-quarter of the actual distance.

Taking off from southern Castile, Columbus sailed southwest to the Canary Islands, which Castilians had recently seized. The Canaries proved to be a crucial starting point, because only from there, and not from any Spanish port, could the explorer pick up the trade winds that would propel him directly across the Atlantic. After nearly a month at sea, his crew sighted a small Caribbean island and then traveled to Cuba and Hispaniola (present-day Dominican Republic and Haiti). Columbus thought the first island was Japan and the second China. After leaving part of his crew on Hispaniola, he returned to Spain, where the king and queen greeted him as a hero. A few months later, Ferdinand and Isabella sent Columbus back to "China," this time with a huge fleet of seventeen ships, fifteen hundred crewmen, and a bevy of priests, doctors, artisans, and many others. Although he never, of course, found China, he did explore the Caribbean, Central America, and parts of northeastern South America.

The Columbian Exchange

Columbus's "discoveries," as the Europeans termed them, were notable, but far more important was the **Columbian Exchange**—the transfer of plants and animals, insects and diseases, between two parts of the planet that had never before experienced any sustained contact. Beginning with Columbus, European ships served as transatlantic Noah's Arks that transported plants and animals unknown in the Americas until then: sugar cane, wheat, bananas, and coffee; livestock such as cattle, sheep, and horses (corn and potatoes, among many other things, would flow in the opposite direction). In addition to the plants and animals that the Europeans had loaded onto their ships, they unwittingly carried a great many stowaways hidden in their hulls: earthworms, mosquitoes, cockroaches, honeybees, dandelions, African grasses, and an immense number of rats (see Map 2.3).

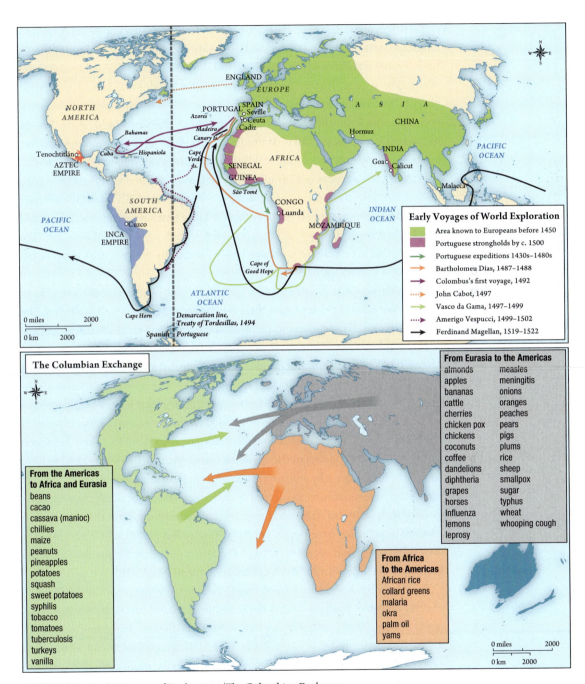

From Eurasia to the Americas

almonds	measles
apples	meningitis
bananas	onions
cattle	oranges
cherries	peaches
chicken pox	pears
chickens	pigs
coconuts	plums
coffee	rice
dandelions	sheep
diphtheria	smallpox
grapes	sugar
horses	typhus
Influenza	wheat
lemons	whooping cough
leprosy	

The Columbian Exchange

From the Americas to Africa and Eurasia

beans
cacao
cassava (manioc)
chillies
maize
peanuts
pineapples
potatoes
squash
sweet potatoes
syphilis
tobacco
tomatoes
tuberculosis
turkeys
vanilla

From Africa to the Americas

African rice
collard greens
malaria
okra
palm oil
yams

Early Voyages of World Exploration

- Area known to Europeans before 1450
- Portuguese strongholds by c. 1500
- → Portuguese expeditions 1430s–1480s
- → Bartholomeu Días, 1487–1488
- → Columbus's first voyage, 1492
- ⋯→ John Cabot, 1497
- → Vasco da Gama, 1497–1499
- ⋯→ Amerigo Vespucci, 1499–1502
- → Ferdinand Magellan, 1519–1522

≡ **MAP 2.3** Early Voyages of Exploration/The Columbian Exchange

These species transformed the ecology of the New World, changing the American landscape for the better and the worse. But one kind of newcomer was catastrophic—the microbes that cause epidemic disease. Before the arrival of Columbus and those who followed him, the viruses that cause smallpox, influenza, hepatitis, measles, encephalitis, and pneumonia and the bacteria that produce diphtheria, cholera, typhus, scarlet fever, and meningitis did not exist in the New World. Their absence meant that native people had no immunities against them, the immunities that had formed in Europeans and Africans as they adapted over the eons to these ailments.

Within a few decades of Columbus's arrival, over 75 percent of the native population was dead. In some areas almost everyone perished. To take one example: before Columbus landed on Hispaniola, it is likely that several hundred thousand people lived there. Thirty-four years later, fewer than five hundred were left. The export of Old World diseases inadvertently caused the greatest demographic catastrophe in human history.

This unfathomable disaster made it easier for Columbus's Spanish successors to conquer vast areas of the Americas; there were fewer and fewer people in the way. The first to stake out territory there was a former notary named Hernando Cortés (1485–1547), who landed in Mexico in April 1519. There, he met the great Aztec emperor, Montezuma (1466–1520), who welcomed the Spaniard to his capital Tenochtitlán (present-day Mexico City). Cortés reciprocated by killing Montezuma and conquering his empire—with the help of the Aztec ruler's local enemies. Mexico now became Castile's first major colonial possession on the American mainland. Spanish control over the immense Inca Empire followed in 1531–1533, when Francisco Pizarro (1471–1541) defeated the Peruvian forces. Pizarro, like Cortés before him, completed his conquest by enlisting the enemies of the ruling empire on his side. His own forces were too meager to succeed on their own. The two Spanish conquistadors justified their seizure of Aztec and Inca lands and the destruction of the existing civilizations by pointing to the pope's **Treaty of Tordesillas** (1494), which purported to divide the New World between Portugal and Spain, giving the former Brazil and the latter the rest of America and the Caribbean (see again Map 2.3).

These new Spanish lands proved highly valuable, for they contained rich veins of silver and gold. Spanish settlers harvested the precious metals by forcing indigenous people—and eventually African slaves—to labor in dangerous, unhealthy mines. The Spanish did so with the help of local intermediaries on whom they depended to recruit and organize a labor force largely uninterested in working for the colonists. In exchange, the intermediaries took a share of the profits. They also moderated the colonists' efforts to exploit the indigenous laborers, often in the face of rebellions—or the threat of rebellion—against their Spanish overseers. Indigenous people benefited not only from these intermediaries, but also from the work of certain missionaries, who early on convinced Queen Isabella to forbid the enslavement of Native peoples. The most famous of these early missionaries, the Dominican friar **Bartolomé de las Casas**, argued that the Natives had developed an advanced culture and that, as Catholics, the Spanish had no right to oppress them. But de las Casas, however influential, represented just one voice among many. He was often ignored, and the harsh conditions of work took a serious toll in Native people's lives, as did the European diseases that continued to decimate the Native population.

Fortunately, many survived, including members of

≡ **La Malinche.** A young woman from Mexico's Gulf Coast, La Malinche was enslaved and given as a gift to the region's Spanish conquerors. She impressed Cortés with her beauty and intelligence and became his interpreter, advisor, and lover. She served as an intermediary between the Spanish and the indigenous people of eastern Mexico

the Aztec and Inca elite. Spanish colonists, mostly male, married or at least fathered children with women of these elites, creating a group of mestizo, or mixed, people who would populate much of Spanish America. Spanish colonists never married the African women conscripted into slavery for the sugar plantations of Cuba and Santo Domingo, but these white men not infrequently mated with them, forcibly or otherwise, producing yet another kind of mixing in Spanish America. The Church offered no protection to people of African origins, whether mixed or not, and slavery blighted the Spanish colonies as it later would the British ones.

As time went on, certain plantation owners and mining magnates became fabulously wealthy. They paid the taxes they owed by sending some of their silver and gold back to Spain, where the sixteenth-century monarchs, Charles V and Philip II, were heavily in debt and desperately needed the cash.

The Troubled Government of Spain

Why were Spain's rulers saddled with a huge amount of debt? A key reason was their efforts to concentrate political power in their hands. To do that, they had to curtail the authority of the **Cortes**, Castile's representative assembly that, in

≡ **The Rich Mountain of Potosí.** This c. 1603 image of Potosí's famous Cerro Rico shows not only the legendary red mountain with its silver veins but also workers, most of them native Andeans, refining silver by mercury amalgamation, and antlike llamas carrying ore down the mountain. The ore-crushing mill in the foreground is powered by a stream of water supplied by canals coming down from artificial reservoirs built high in a neighboring mountain range.

theory, possessed a fair amount of sway over the king by virtue of its ability to approve taxes. But the Cortes contained only thirty-six members, which made it easy for the Spanish monarchs to buy their agreement to taxation by showering them with lucrative offices and exempting them from any taxes they approved. Since Spain's clergy and nobility were largely exempt as well, the tax burden fell mainly on those of modest means. Tax receipts were therefore low relative to the size of Castile's population, and they dropped all the more because the king had delegated revenue collection to private financiers known as **tax farmers** and to individuals who had purchased offices in the government bureaucracy. These financiers and **venal officeholders** kept a significant portion of the proceeds for themselves.

Castile's narrow tax base and low receipts made it impossible for revenues to keep up with outlays, given the cost of colonial expansion and near-constant wars.

The Spanish Habsburg kings fought France throughout the first half of the sixteenth century, and as we saw in Chapter 1, faced religious separatism in German-speaking Europe. Beginning in 1568, Spain conducted an eighty-year-long battle against the northern provinces of the Netherlands, which had converted to Protestantism and grown rich through overseas trade (see below). The Spanish also confronted the Ottoman Empire in Hungary, the Mediterranean, and even in the outskirts of their own Habsburg capital, Vienna.

To close their budget deficits, Spain resorted to massive borrowing and the sale of most governmental offices. In 1598, principal and interest payments on outstanding *juros* (loans secured by future tax receipts) amounted to 100 percent of the king's annual revenues. That is, after servicing just one kind of outstanding loan, the Castilian government had no money for anything else. This reality meant skyrocketing budget deficits and further borrowing at interest rates of 20 to 30 percent due to the perceived riskiness of these loans. Castile's inability to pay its debts forced royal officials not just to sell offices—one office for every 166 inhabitants—but entire villages and towns. In the late sixteenth century, Castilian kings began to auction off their own people, turning their municipalities over to private landlords, who now exercised near-absolute legal authority over their residents.

The sale of offices and towns was designed to raise funds to improve Spain's military effectiveness, but other financial expedients compromised it instead. Perpetually

≡ **Seville, ca. 1580.** This painting by the Spanish painter Alonso Sánchez Coello shows the city humming with activity. Atlantic shipping works its way up the Guadalquivir River, much of it carrying silver mined from Spain's colonies in the Americas.

short of funds, the kings sold military commissions to the highest bidders, many of whom turned out to be ineffective battlefield commanders. To make matters worse, Castilian kings delegated the responsibility to create, and finance, military companies to powerful noblemen, who sometimes used soldiers for their own purposes—to control rebellious peasants, for example—before sending them into battle against Spain's enemies. Spain's cash-strapped kings thus sacrificed a good measure of control over their fighting forces and, with it, their chances of battlefield success.

Beginning in the 1530s, the gold and silver mined in Spain's New World colonies promised to help with the kingdom's budgetary problems, but only a modest percentage of these precious metals flowed into Spain. The lion's share ended up in China—in exchange for the colonists' purchases of spices, porcelain, and silk—and in Italy, the Netherlands, Germany, and Eastern Europe, where Spain's wars were fought. Even worse, the influx of silver produced a Europe-wide price inflation that impoverished a Spanish population already suffering from highly regressive taxation (see Map 2.4).

Spain tried to maintain control over the influx of silver and its overseas trade by requiring that all ships to and from the New World pass through a Spanish port, first Cádiz and then Seville, where they would be subject to taxes destined for the royal coffers. To ensure that this actually happened and, in general, to rule effectively over their American possessions, Spanish monarchs organized their New World territories into two powerful administrative units: the **Viceroyalty of New Spain**, which governed all of Central America, the Gulf Coast, Florida, Cuba, Santo Domingo, and Venezuela, and the **Viceroyalty of Peru**, which governed the entire west coast of South America, from Columbia to Chile. These two viceroyalties, each divided into **audiencias**, ruled the Americans more absolutely than the monarchy ruled its lands in Europe. In the New World, no representative assemblies, venal officeholders, aristocratic landowners, religious authorities, or town councils constrained Spain's authority, as they did in Europe. Still, the immense size of Spain's American possessions made it impossible to oversee them completely or to check the power of individuals grown wealthy from America's increasingly lucrative overseas trade with China and Europe.

New World riches did little to solve Spain's Old World problems of warfare and soaring debt. Overwhelmed with both, Charles V decided in 1556 to give up his throne and divide his realm. He conferred the title of Holy Roman Emperor on his brother Ferdinand, who now controlled the Habsburg lands of Central Europe, a region consumed as we have seen by the fierce religious conflicts of the Reformation. Charles gave the rest of his domains to his son Philip II (1527–1598), who now ruled over Castile and Aragon in Spain; Milan, Naples, and Sicily in Italy; the Netherlands; and the two viceroyalties of America.

MAP 2.4   European Claims in the Americas, c.1600/World Silver Flows, c. 1650

Philip allied himself to England by marrying Mary Tudor, the daughter of Henry VIII, who became the reigning English queen in 1553. She lived only another five years, and her early death ended the brief pact between Spain and England. When Elizabeth I acceded to the English throne and confirmed its Protestant character, Philip tried to restore England to Catholicism by pitting the Spanish Armada (flotilla) against the English fleet. England's victory in 1588 ended for the time being the threat of a Catholic restoration in Elizabeth's realm.

Having lost ground against Protestantism in England and in the face of the Netherlands' powerful Calvinist revolt, Philip turned his attention in the late sixteenth century to his American colonies. In the viceroyalties of New Spain and Peru, which contained a quarter of a million European settlers and a huge indigenous population, he encouraged the work of Catholic missionaries and tightened his administrative control. But Philip's deep indebtedness stripped him of the resources needed to keep his colonies firmly in line. Increasingly, American merchants ignored the requirement to send their goods and silver shipments to Seville, trading with one another and evading Spanish taxes.

While trying to maintain his hold over Spanish America and dealing with wars and crises in Europe, Philip II inherited the Portuguese throne, which had become vacant after its king died childless in 1578. This inheritance gave Philip a second empire, this one older than his own.

Portugal and the Portuguese Empire

A small kingdom on the western edge of Europe, Portugal had long been a seafaring country. To compete with its larger and more powerful European neighbors, Portugal took to the sea in search of trading opportunities and the wealth it hoped would follow. Beginning in the early fifteenth century, the Portuguese explorer known as **Prince Henry the Navigator** and several of his successors sailed south to Africa, where they first surveyed the coast of Morocco and continued on to Senegal and the Congo, which they reached in the 1440s. Their voyages succeeded in part because they astutely combined knowledge and technology gleaned from a variety of cultures: ship design from northern European and Mediterranean mariners, the magnetic compass from Chinese sailors, the **astrolabe** from Arab astronomers, and geographic understanding from experienced Italian navigators.

Portuguese sailors began to buy and sell enslaved Africans in the 1440s, but mainly they purchased gold mined in what is Ghana today. Until then, Arab traders had monopolized the commerce in gold, traveling back and forth across the Sahara Desert between the Mediterranean and the "gold coast" of West Africa. The Portuguese found a cheaper, faster way to transport gold from Africa to Europe—by ship instead of over land—and this new source of wealth enriched their state. They also bought spices and ivory from local peoples as well as other tropical commodities hotly in demand. In the process, Portuguese agents claimed several Atlantic islands—Madeira, the Canaries (later ceded to Spain), and the Azores—where they began to cultivate sugar in a dress rehearsal for the massive sugar plantations they would soon establish in northern Brazil.

The growing and processing of sugar is difficult, backbreaking work that requires a huge amount of manual labor in hot climates. That Europeans often refused to do this work encouraged sugar cultivators to purchase slaves in Africa, where states victorious in war captured defeated people and enslaved them. There had long been a slave trade from Africa to the Middle East, and now a new European demand for slave labor encouraged Africans to capture more people and sell them in exchange for guns and other European commodities.

In African societies enslaved people often found themselves living relatively close to home in familiar circumstances and sharing dwellings and working conditions with the families that owned them. When Africans were sold to European slave traders, they were completely uprooted from their lives. Slavers force-marched their captives under grueling conditions from the African interior to the coast and then stuffed them into the filthy, stifling holds of ships waiting to take them across the Atlantic. Food and water were scarce and disease was rampant. In the early decades of the transatlantic slave trade, only about half of the captives made it to their destinations alive.

As they exported human beings from Africa to the Americas, Portuguese and other European slave traders imported Christianity to Africa. In the early 1500s, Catholic missionaries converted Nzinga Nkuwu, ruler of the huge central African kingdom of Kongo, who in turn allowed the conversion of a great many of his people (on his baptism he became King João I of Kongo). The missionaries succeeded in this effort in part because many of Catholicism's key ideas—heaven, a priesthood with special powers, saints and supernatural beings, rituals involving water—resembled the religious notions and practices native to the region. Africans could adopt the new religion without having to alter their beliefs and practices very much. Still, the people of Kongo were recognized as Christians, and their kings complained that by enslaving them, Europeans not only depopulated their

≡ **Queen Nzinga's Baptism.** This seventeenth-century watercolor depicts the baptism of the central African Queen Nzinga (not to be confused with her namesake, Nzinga Nkuwu). Queen Nzinga's Catholic baptism did not prevent her from making alliances with non-Catholics, both African and European, in long and violent struggles with neighbors and the Portuguese.

country and disrupted its social structure but also violated fundamental Christian beliefs. Europeans largely ignored these appeals.

After landing in Kongo, Portuguese explorers continued further down the African coast. In 1497, Vasco da Gama sailed around the southern tip of the continent and into the Indian Ocean, where he discovered an extraordinarily active trade. For centuries, Chinese, Arab, Malay, and other merchants had been transporting African products such as ivory to Europe and China and Asian products, especially spices, to Europe. The Portuguese joined this ongoing trade by forcibly inserting themselves into key locations and establishing fortified trading posts known as **factories** there. They built factories on the west and east coasts of Africa as well as in the Persian Gulf, western India, Malaya, and Macao in China. Strings of these posts formed mini-colonies that housed storage facilities, merchants, and the soldiers sent to protect them. Local people were willing to trade with the Portuguese because their factories served as secure way stations and their armed ships inspired the confidence that their products and purchases would reach their destinations intact (see Map 2.5).

At first, the Portuguese government exerted firm control over this Afro-Eurasian trade and reaped substantial profits and tax revenues from it. Between 1500 and 1550, half of all revenues accruing to the Portuguese crown came from this overseas trade. But eventually, other empires began to outcompete the Portuguese, and local merchants used the factories for their own purposes, trading with one another directly rather than relying on Portuguese intermediaries and routing their products exclusively through Portuguese ports.

A key reason for the defiance of these intermediaries was that the Portuguese were thin on the ground. Unlike the Spanish monarchy, which sent hundreds of thousands of settlers to the New World, Portugal was sparsely populated and could not spare many people to settle abroad. In Africa and Asia, the Portuguese mostly confined themselves to their fortified posts, sending a total of just ten thousand soldiers and administrators abroad. The great exception was Brazil, where Portuguese planters built extensive sugar plantations and imported more than a million Africans to work as slaves. From the sixteenth to the nineteenth centuries, Brazil would be the world's number one destination for enslaved human beings. The colony would become far more prosperous than Portugal, so prosperous that in the early nineteenth century, the Portuguese king moved his entire government there, leaving Portugal behind.

The Netherlands and the Dutch Private Enterprise Empire

When the Portuguese crown fell in 1580 to the Spanish monarch Philip II, the Portuguese empire found itself in competition with a new Dutch empire, which like Portugal belonged to the Spanish king—at least on paper. In 1581, after a

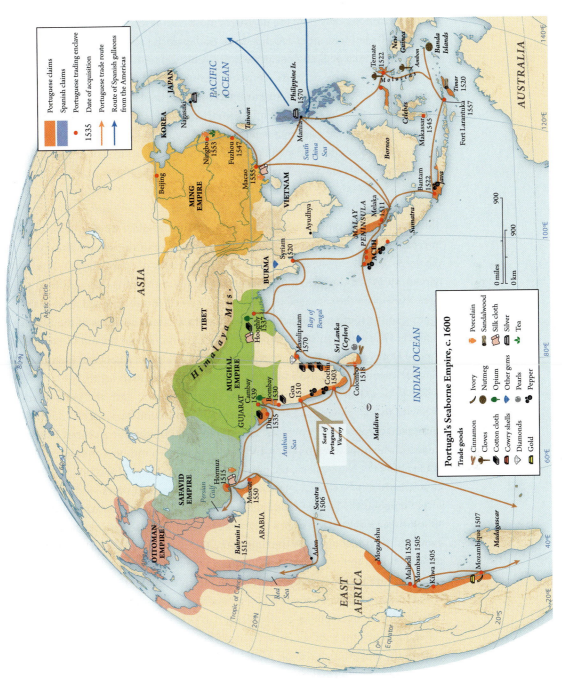

MAP 2.5   Portugal's Seaborne Empire, c. 1600.

Portuguese claims
Spanish claims
Portuguese trading enclave
1535   Date of acquisition
Portuguese trade route
Route of Spanish galleons from the Americas

Portugal's Seaborne Empire, c. 1600

Trade goods

Cinnamon
Cloves
Cotton cloth
Cowry shells
Diamonds
Gold
Ivory
Nutmeg
Opium
Other gems
Pearls
Pepper
Porcelain
Sandalwood
Silk cloth
Silver
Tea

thirteen-year-long rebellion, the northern, mostly Protestant, part of the Spanish Netherlands declared independence from the Spanish crown. Dutch grievances against Spain included religious persecution, political repression, and the menacing presence of a large Spanish army on Dutch soil. Philip II believed it was his duty to restore Catholic orthodoxy to a part of his realm that, in his view, had succumbed to the Calvinist heresy. Philip also tried to establish centralized rule over a Dutch territory that had long been governed by local aristocrats and wealthy urban elites. These elites did not take kindly to Philip's efforts to subordinate them to his own officials sent from Spain.

Dutch Independence

This Spanish intervention had begun in 1568 and would continue, with brief interruptions, for eighty years. These wars drained a Spanish treasury already on the verge of bankruptcy and reduced the effectiveness of Spain's largely mercenary army. When the government failed to pay the mercenaries, they refused to fight. Even when they engaged in combat, the Spanish forces confined most of the fighting to the southern Netherlands, leaving the United Provinces of the North at peace. (The southern Netherlands, mostly Catholic, would remain in Spanish hands.) Dutch elites used the respite to establish a new government and eventually a Dutch Republic. They also added to their already substantial wealth.

The government of what became the Dutch Republic gave the lion's share of power to the provincial Estates (representative assemblies) of the country's seven semi-autonomous provinces. Each estate sent delegates to a central Estates General, which set foreign policy and made decisions about war and peace. But even on these vital questions, the power of the Estates General was limited, since its policies had to be ratified by each of the seven provincial estates.

As a republic, the Netherlands did not have a king, although the leaders of most of its provinces agreed to assign a measure of executive power to a chief executive known as the **stadtholder**. At the time of the Dutch rebellion, the stadtholder position belonged to the nobleman William of Orange, but he was assassinated by a Spanish loyalist just a few years after the Dutch declared their independence. William's son Maurice succeeded him as stadtholder, and the office, now hereditary, developed the trappings of monarchy.

But, in reality, the rural and urban elites who dominated the Estates continued to make the most vital decisions, especially in the realm of trade. These elites had derived their wealth from banking, the slave trade, and international commerce. In the late sixteenth century, they found themselves in conflict not only with Spain but, as already noted, with Portugal as well. For the Dutch, Spain constituted a political problem and Portugal an economic one. The latter's capital, Lisbon, was the European center of the all-important spice trade with Asia, and that center was now closed to Dutch merchants. To procure the coveted spices, especially nutmeg and cloves, for which Dutch consumers seemed to have a bottomless demand, Dutch traders had no choice but to deal directly with producers and merchants of the spice islands, now part of Indonesia.

The Dutch Empire

To manage this vital commerce, several leading members of the Dutch merchant elite devised a new kind of empire, one based on private enterprise rather than the state. The vehicle for this new empire was the **Dutch East India Company** (VOC, after its initials in Dutch), a privately owned monopoly that projected the Netherlands' economic might into Asia and the Indian Ocean.

The VOC was a **joint-stock company**—the ancestor of the modern corporation—owned by a group of shareholders and managed by a board of directors. The great virtue of this business arrangement was that it could mobilize large amounts of capital from many different investors. The joint-stock company also minimized risk by dividing any losses among all the shareholders. Any costs an individual incurred were limited to the portion of the company, often relatively small, he owned. The joint-stock company thus allowed for the financing of risky enterprises such as overseas trade, since the hazards were widely shared.

In the early seventeenth century, the VOC quickly amassed a large treasury, which it used to build a fleet of ships designed both to transport valuable cargoes and to engage in war. Although a business enterprise, the VOC acted like an aggressive, imperial state. The Dutch used force to outcompete their Spanish and Portuguese rivals and to compel local growers and traders to deal exclusively with them. By 1669, the company owned nearly 200 ships, fielded an army of 10,000 soldiers, and employed 50,000 civilians. Its armed vessels were prepared to fight off pirates,

≡ **Batavia.** In the early seventeenth century, the Dutch East India Company built an extensive commercial network in South Asia, and Batavia (now Jakarta) became its principal port and the hub of the Netherlands' informal empire in the region.

attack competitors, and establish militarized trading bases in parts of Asia close to sources of desirable goods. To oversee its operations, the VOC created a central hub called Batavia (now Jakarta, Indonesia) on the island of Java. It then fanned out into Malaya, Bengal (in India), Ceylon, Thailand, China, and Taiwan (then called Formosa), where VOC leaders established secondary commercial bases. They also built a way station in the Cape of Good Hope, which marked the beginning of a stormy Dutch settlement there.

From Batavia and their other commercial bases, the VOC seized routes controlled by the Portuguese and required local elites not to trade with any other European power. If they did, the VOC punished them with great brutality, destroying crops and massacring entire villages. At home, the Dutch government may have been unusually tolerant; in Asia, the VOC brooked no opposition. By the 1650s, the company had ejected the Spanish and Portuguese from the Indonesian spice market and established a near-monopoly there. To increase supply and outcompete local growers, the VOC built its own plantations staffed by slaves and turned the city of Batavia into a large commercial marketplace. A fair number of Dutch settlers established themselves in Batavia, marrying indigenous women and creating mixed-race offspring whose linguistic and cultural connections to local people helped the VOC manage its private empire.

By the early eighteenth century, the VOC's profits had made Amsterdam one of the wealthiest cities in the world. But the company's greatest asset, its private financing through stock purchases, would also prove to be its greatest weakness. Faced with intense British competition after the mid-eighteenth century, the VOC, as a private firm, could not draw on the vastly superior resources of the Dutch state to maintain its monopoly. When the British began to seize the VOC's markets, investors took fright and pulled their money out of the company. Having been the world's richest corporation in the 1670s, it sank into bankruptcy in 1798.

England and the British Empire

Although Britain's East India Company, founded in 1600, would eventually drive its Dutch counterpart out of business, the British government and economic elites only gradually and hesitantly embraced imperial expansion. In the sixteenth century, English merchants did fairly well in international trade without government involvement or the creation of monopolies and other institutions dedicated to overseas trade. England was still a small island-nation overshadowed by a much wealthier and more populous France and locked in competition with Spain, which came close to defeating it at sea in 1588. Domestically, England had traversed many decades of religious turmoil beginning with Henry VIII's rupture with the

Catholic Church. When Henry's daughter Elizabeth became queen in 1558, her country was still smarting from its religious wounds. Catholics were disappointed that Elizabeth's short-lived predecessor, Mary Tudor, had not restored their faith, and Protestants were divided between moderates and radicals, between those who wanted to maintain some of the trappings of Catholicism and those who wanted to rid their land of all vestiges of "popery."

England's Political Institutions

England's greatest strengths—but also some potential weaknesses, as we will see in Chapter 3—lay in its political institutions. Unlike France and Spain, England emerged from the Middle Ages with a healthy tradition of participatory politics at the local level and a robust representation of those localities at the center of the realm. England's kingdom-wide **Parliament** differed from its counterparts on the continent by containing two chambers, Lords and Commons, instead of three (nobles, clergy, and commoners). The House of Lords resembled Europe's noble estates by including just one social category, noblemen, but the House of Commons represented the country as a whole (although people of low and middling social status only indirectly). As such, the Commons could stand as an effective counterweight to the king—unlike the "estates" of the continent, which kings could manipulate by pitting one estate against the others. This tactic worked because no single estate could plausibly claim to represent the entire country.

In England, Parliament became indispensable during the endless wars of the fourteenth and fifteenth centuries, when the kings regularly needed it to approve new taxes, and the Commons, in particular, developed substantial power. But so did financiers and tax farmers, since the royal treasury needed to float short-term loans while it waited for tax receipts to trickle in. Venal office holding became a temptation as well, because it seemed a sure way to raise additional funds. Parliament vigorously opposed the sale of offices, but after the wars ended in the 1450s and the kings' revenue needs declined, they only rarely called Parliament into session. Fewer Parliaments meant fewer checks on the explosion of venal office holding and the awarding of honors and sinecures (paid positions requiring very little work) in exchange for cash. By the dawn of the seventeenth century, a once-powerful Parliament took a backseat to venal officeholders, tax farmers, and financiers, who served the monarch as the monarch served them.

Things began to change after James I (1566–1625) acceded to the throne in 1603, and Parliament reclaimed some of its earlier powers. Unlike his predecessor, Queen Elizabeth, James spent money freely, and when he asked Parliament to help cover his huge personal debts, the MPs (Members of Parliament) balked. In doing so, they set a precedent for parliamentary oversight of the king's finances—and a new degree of parliamentary independence—that would grow more stringent as his reign progressed.

Facing a revival of Parliamentary power, James tried to extend his authority by creating a "Great Britain" that united England and Scotland, the independent kingdom on England's northern border. Thanks to complicated dynastic arrangements, James had inherited both the English and Scottish thrones, but the Scots successfully resisted the union of the two. They feared the imposition of England's religious arrangements onto Scotland and being overshadowed by their more prosperous southern neighbor. For the time being, the two kingdoms remained separate and distinct, even though they shared the same king.

The Beginnings of the British Empire

James enjoyed more success in Ireland, whose king he also became in 1603. Henry VIII had begun the English colonization of Ireland in the 1540s, and it continued through the whole of Elizabeth's reign. The Irish resisted fiercely, and the English used brutal tactics against them. In an attempt to pacify and "civilize" Ireland, Elizabeth sent Protestant settlers there—Ireland was overwhelmingly Catholic—and gave them "plantations" (colonial settlements) throughout the island. Irish men and women were to work for these English—and some Scottish—landlords, who would also dominate the Irish government. King James, for his part, stepped up the "civilization" of Ireland by creating large plantations in the most rebellious, anti-English section of the country, Ulster in the north. He did so through the wholesale confiscation of Ulster's lands, which he awarded to English and Scottish colonists, who were required to be Protestant and English-speaking and forbidden to hire Irish laborers. They would import English and Scottish ones instead. Through these settlers, James hoped to supplant both Irish Catholicism and the Gaelic language native to the country. What actually happened was that most of Ulster's Gaelic peasants remained in the province—and true to their Catholic faith—but were forcibly relocated to the least productive lands of the region. This displacement all but guaranteed the persistent poverty of the Irish peasantry and their undying hatred for the English.

Beyond the Irish plantations, two other forms of colonization took place during James's reign: the effort to displace the Dutch VOC from its dominance in Asia and the establishment of settlements along the Atlantic seaboard of North America. In 1600, Queen Elizabeth chartered the **East India Company** (EIC), granting it a monopoly (within the British Isles) over trade in the Indian Ocean. The new company immediately found itself in competition with Portuguese traders and the Dutch East India Company and decided to concentrate on India, where neither competitor had established a strong presence. From India, which was then controlled by the Mughal Empire (a successor of the Mongols), the British bought silk, indigo, saltpeter (nitrates used in fertilizers and gunpowder), tea, and cotton textiles, and sold these goods for a huge profit at home.

During the first century of its existence, the EIC did nothing to challenge the Mughal Empire politically; the two sides derived mutual benefit from their relations. The Mughals profited from the access the EIC gave them to the huge European market, and the EIC from the huge returns they earned as middlemen between Indian producers and European buyers. The EIC did, however, offer financial support to local rulers who sought greater independence from their Mughal overlords, and the company employed, in considerable numbers, the subjects of those local leaders. These Indian employees traveled throughout Asia and coastal Africa on EIC business, and some settled in the EIC's commercial hubs, extending an existing Hindu diaspora.

Much of the trade between India and Europe was one-way: Europeans wanted to buy a great many Indian products, but most Indians found little to purchase in Europe that they didn't already make themselves. The EIC thus transported goods to Europe and silver, as payment, to India. This was yet another reason why silver mined in Spanish America ended up in Asia rather than Spain. The precious metal enriched entrepreneurs and governments in India and China and helped those countries keep pace with Europe—even exceed Europe—in economic development.

The Asian trade also made the EIC's shareholders wealthy men. Their wealth enabled them to extend their operations deeper and further into Asia and to build what amounted to a private army and navy, which they used to drive the Portuguese and most other competitors out of business. The shareholders' riches also gave them a growing influence in England and Scotland as well. The company hired a great many Scots, who had fewer economic opportunities at home than their English counterparts, and as key figures in the EIC, these Scotsmen identified with England and the English and helped pave the way for the union of Scotland and England in 1707.

After unification, leaders of the new Great Britain recognized the financial power—and imperial potential, for good and ill—of the EIC and began, in the late eighteenth century, to bring it under the auspices of the state. The government, in turn, supported the company by using the royal navy to protect its sea routes and by passing Navigation Acts that required goods produced in Asia and America to be transported in British ships. These navigation acts would later be a major bone of contention in the British Empire's North American colonies.

The British Empire in North America

The Virginia Company, chartered in 1606 as a private enterprise like the EIC, quickly departed from its model. The Virginia Company's original investors were motivated by political and religious ideals as well as economic gain. These investors saw North America as a virgin territory in which they could build a community from scratch and, in the process, convert the "heathen" American Indians to Protestantism.

In April 1607, Captain Christopher Newport (1561–1617) landed on a finger of land near the southern end of the Chesapeake Bay, with 105 prospective Virginia settlers on board. The spot had the virtue of being without Native inhabitants, but in most other ways, it was a disaster: poor soil, undrinkable salty water, and endless swamps perfect for breeding mosquitoes. Still, the area seemed defensible against attack, so Newport's group decided to stay. They named their new home Jamestown after their king.

The English had no right to claim this land. Their government told them, correctly, that the pope had, without justification, awarded this territory to Spain in his decree of the 1490s. But the English government, like the pope, overlooked the people who already occupied what would become Virginia. This part of North America was called Tsenacommacah and belonged to a coalition of Algonquian tribes dominated by the paramount chief Wahunsenacawh, known to the English as Powhatan (c. 1548–c. 1618), a ruler who had gained control over a large part of the Chesapeake region. Unlike the Aztecs, with their huge pre-Cortés population of between five million and twenty-five million, Powhatan's people numbered only about fifteen thousand. But Powhatan was well protected and kept himself out of the Europeans' clutches, as Montezuma had failed to do. Still, relations between the two groups deteriorated quickly, and the emperor stopped supplying food to the newcomers, who soon began to starve. Within eight months of their arrival, nearly two-thirds were dead. Efforts to reinforce the settlement with new recruits had the same result. Between 1607 and 1624, 80 percent of the seven thousand settlers shipped to Virginia died young. What saved the precarious settlement were regular shipments of food from England, and, beginning in 1614, the cultivation of tobacco.

King James I hated smoking, calling it "lothsome to the eye, hatefull to the Nose, harmefull to the braine, [and] daungerous to the Lungs." But he soon discovered that it could be taxed, and always short of funds, he made Virginia a royal colony in 1624 and encouraged its growth. Tobacco production soared from 50,000 pounds in 1620 to 25 million pounds annually a century later. Jamestown not only survived, it became rich.

With tobacco hotly in demand, Virginia landowners needed a large influx of labor. To keep costs down, they used **indentured servants**, individuals who agreed to work for a set number of years without pay in exchange for their passage to the New World. Between 1607 and 1700, nearly half of all Europeans who went to British North America arrived in this way. They came not only to Virginia, but also to several of the other British colonies established in North America during the seventeenth century—especially Maryland, Delaware, and New Jersey—as British colonialism crept up and down the Eastern Seaboard.

Early on, Virginia needed more laborers than any other

☰ **Tobacco.** Although King James I considered tobacco "harmfull to the braine," the addictive plant became immensely popular in Europe and turned Virginia into one of England's most prosperous colonies.

colony, and tobacco growers there tried to enlist Native peoples ("Indians" to the Europeans), and even to enslave them, but their numbers remained relatively small. So, at first, did the number of enslaved Africans. Slaves cost more than indentured servants and therefore were rare in North America during the first century of British colonization. Why, then, did African slaves come to vastly outnumber Europeans and Native peoples as laborers on North American plantations?

The answer turns, in part, on different susceptibility to disease. Europeans and Native peoples were highly prone to malaria and yellow fever, both transmitted by mosquitoes. The malaria-carrying mosquitoes had been inadvertently exported to the New World from the swamplands of southeastern England, while the yellow fever carriers had come from Africa. Malaria, in particular, thrived in the swampy environs of the Chesapeake Bay and in marshy lowlands to the south and west where tobacco and later cotton were grown. Yellow fever plagued Caribbean islands like British-controlled Jamaica, where sugar became the dominant crop. The Europeans and Native peoples working in these regions contracted these diseases and died in horrendous numbers. Half of all the Chickasaw of the Carolinas died between 1685 and 1715, while the Quapaw people of Arkansas nearly became extinct.

Meanwhile, the relatively small number of African slaves working in the American South enjoyed much greater longevity, despite their harsh working and living conditions. Planters did not know what modern medicine has learned, namely that Africans possess both genetic and acquired immunities to malaria and yellow fever, while Europeans and Native Americans, for the most part, have neither. But tobacco growers in Virginia and sugar magnates in the Caribbean, where the British, Spanish, and French established huge slave-based plantations, could observe that Africans survived relatively well and the other peoples did not. Planters thus decided to purchase mounting numbers of African slaves, despite their relatively high cost (see Map 2.6).

The enslaved population grew to such an extent that by the eighteenth century, more than three-quarters of all those who crossed the Atlantic were African slaves bound for the New World. These developments do not mean that malaria and

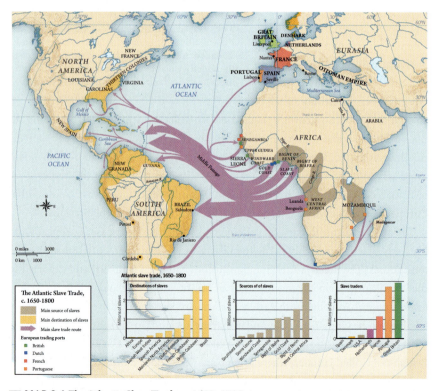

≡ **MAP 2.6** The Atlantic Slave Trade, c. 1650–1800

yellow fever *caused* slavery; earlier precedent, prejudice, and religion—the notion that Europeans were God's people and Africans were not—did much to spur black slavery as well. But tragically, the Africans' ability to resist disease helped make them the victims of one of the worst forms of oppression the world has known. And with the overwhelming majority of Africans in the New World living as slaves, blackness became associated with slavery and inferiority and whiteness with freedom and superiority. To Europeans, these conditions increasingly seemed natural, even God-given, and not the result of conquest and greed.

France and the French Empire

British settlers in the New World were not the only ones to rely on slave labor. So did the Portuguese in Brazil, the Spanish in Cuba and Santo Domingo, and the French in the sugar-based colony they built in Saint-Domingue (present-day Haiti). The French came relatively late and somewhat hesitantly to empire. Their early efforts to settle in North America either succumbed to weather and disease or to Spanish efforts to wipe them out. In any case, French kings concerned themselves far more with establishing and expanding their position in Europe than in gaining footholds or major trading positions overseas.

French Political Institutions: The Nobility and the King

Throughout the Middle Ages, French kings extended the lands they ruled far beyond their private domains in and around Paris. In the process, they found themselves overwhelmed with the legal business of managing conflicting claims to land and other resources. In England such claims were resolved by local landlords with legal authority in their own decentralized jurisdictions. French kings, by contrast, were centralizers who kept legal and administrative matters in their own hands by creating eleven monarchical courts of law, one in Paris and ten dispersed around the country, known as *parlements*. Despite the name, these were judicial institutions, not legislative bodies like England's Parliament. The French parlements, established between the fourteenth and sixteenth centuries, dispensed justice in the name of the king; they formed part of a centralized administration rather than a counterweight to it, although their mostly aristocratic members retained some ability to question decisions and rulings made by the king.

In addition to these monarchical courts of law, French kings established a financial administration to oversee the collection of the tax on land, known as the *taille*, and certain sales and excise taxes. Like the courts of law, the financial administration was hierarchical and centralized and designed to serve the king. Until the early sixteenth century, the king or his agents appointed people to these offices, but in 1525, King Francis I decided to put these positions up for sale. He was desperate for revenue to fight his increasingly costly wars against his continental rival, the Holy Roman Emperor, Charles V.

The French monarch lacked revenue because tax receipts were grossly inadequate. Francis, like several kings before him, refused to call into session the representative body known as the **Estates General**, which in medieval times had approved new taxes. By declining to convene the Estates, French kings prevented the nobility, who dominated this assembly, from having a collective say in the affairs of the realm, as their counterparts did to some extent in England and elsewhere in Europe. French kings thus ruled their country largely on their own, allowing them to claim "absolute" authority. The problem was that this arrangement gave French rulers no sure mechanism for approving—and legitimizing—new taxes. When they tried to raise them on their own, it seemed like an arbitrary act imposed on the kingdom without anyone's consent. For that reason, tax increases often produced resistance and thus failed to boost revenue very much, especially since, by custom, nobles were largely exempt. Instead of raising taxes to meet expenditures, Francis I—and his successors—stepped up the sale of offices and borrowed ever larger sums.

The offices sold included judgeships, financial administrators, tax assessors, military positions, the kings' household managers, and a large number of clerks, among many other posts. These positions were desirable, and a great many people wanted them—so much so that the kings invented a host of new offices and sold the same offices to two or three people. In 1515, there were 4,081 royal officers; a century and a half later, the number had skyrocketed to more than 46,000. The most prestigious of these positions gave their owners titles of nobility, which for a fee could be passed on to their heirs. These **venal** offices both limited and enhanced royal power. They limited it by making offices a form of private property independent of the king, who except in unusual situations could not fire the occupant. But venal office holding enhanced the monarch's power by tying officials to his regime. Their fortunes depended on the king's fortunes, which gave them plenty of incentive to support what he did.

Beyond the sale of offices, French kings raised money by borrowing constantly. And no monarch borrowed more than Louis XIV, whose long reign lasted from 1643 to 1715. Louis sold government bonds to French and international financiers, tapped officeholders for short- and long-term loans, and even had military commanders advance money to pay the costs of war. France's supposedly absolute ruler thus found himself beholden to bankers and moneylenders of various sorts. Even worse, France's tax collection system compromised royal power all the more.

There was nothing even remotely like the Internal Revenue Service Americans know today. Instead, monarchs had to rely on **tax farmers** to collect taxes for them. Farmers advanced the government a lump sum and, in exchange, kept all the tax money they collected—often 20 percent more than what they gave the king. This represented a huge loss for the king from an already inadequate tax base, built as it was on impoverished peasants and exempted nobles. Tax farming thus made kings, like their counterparts in Spain, dependent on financiers, who in turn were beholden to the king for their business. It was an exchange in which the king received cash and loyalty, but at a high financial price.

A New Nobility

The possibility of using great wealth to purchase high office with noble status created a new kind of nobleman, what the French called **nobles of the robe**, after the elaborate robes that judges and other magistrates wore. These new nobles contrasted with the old landowning military nobility, the **nobles of the sword**. But as time went on, the contrast faded. Robe nobles began to purchase large landholdings and to live for at least part of the year as traditional nobles on the land. Meanwhile, sword nobles became less likely than in the past to lead armies into war. Fearing armed competition from them, kings discouraged their military activity, and increasingly, military commanders were those who purchased their commissions rather than being called, as in the past, by God and king to fight.

In addition, by the seventeenth century, traditional nobles increasingly found themselves attracted to Paris and to the royal court, where they mixed with robe nobles, blending the two noble cultures together. By then, the essential division within the nobility was no longer between sword and robe, but between poor and rich. Poor nobles were consigned to the land, whose productivity grew slowly at best during this period, while wealthy nobles combined their (sometimes substantial) landed resources with the far superior sums they could gain from service to the state. When Louis XIV built the great chateau of Versailles (1660s–1680s) and encouraged nobles to live there, he did not, as historians once believed, emasculate them by confining them to a gilded cage. If anything, they became wealthier and more powerful than ever before. But now their power increasingly lay in their connection to the state, their proximity to the king. Nobles depended on Louis XIV more than they had on his predecessors, but he depended on them as well, especially on their commitment to his regime.

The corollary to the buildup of Louis XIV's authority at home was his effort to achieve great feats of glory abroad. He did so by conducting a series of European wars (discussed in Chapter 3) and developing a colonial empire. He tried to dominate that empire economically through the policy of **mercantilism**—the requirement that the colonies trade exclusively with France. Unfortunately, for Louis, mercantilism did not bring significant revenues to the crown.

The French Empire

A key reason for the disappointing returns hinged on France's relatively late entry into the competition for colonies. By the time the French created their own East India Company (1664) and tried to develop overseas trading posts and markets, the Portuguese, Dutch, and English had an insurmountable head start. Still, French merchants succeeded in colonizing some bits and pieces of land: coastal areas of present-day Senegal and the islands of Réunion and Mauritius in Africa, Pondicherry on the southeast coast of India, the riverbanks of the St. Lawrence and Mississippi in North America, and three islands in the Caribbean. These footholds could not compete with the far more robust hubs and circuits created by their Dutch and British counterparts.

The French government under Cardinal Richelieu (1585–1642), chief minister to King Louis XIII, planned to send some 4,000 settlers to Quebec, but by the time of Richelieu's death, only 300 had arrived. While sparsely settled farmers scratched out a living along the banks of the St. Lawrence, fur traders did considerably better, supplying Europeans with warm coats and hats. But the largely nomadic fur traders remained few in number and did little to develop the colony. The fishing industry in the waters of Newfoundland and Nova Scotia proved lucrative for a time, but the French forfeited these territories in treaties of 1713 and 1763 after losing wars against Britain.

The fur trade and fisheries, important as they briefly were, paled in comparison with the sugar production established on the Caribbean islands of Martinique, Guadeloupe, and Saint-Domingue. On these islands, the treatment of black slaves was so harsh that the French government developed a set of regulations known as the *Code noir* (1685) designed in part to make it less inhumane. The code forbade plantation owners to torture, mutilate, or execute their slaves and required them to provide enslaved people with adequate food and shelter. But French planters mostly ignored these rules, convinced, as one colonial governor put it, that "blacks must be led like cattle" (see Map 2.7).

Slavery and Race

This was the dominant but not the exclusive view. Since European women largely shunned the Caribbean, considered dangerous and inhospitable, French men regularly made black women their mistresses, frequently subjecting them to coercion and violence. These unions produced mixed-race children and eventually a new racial category, "people of color," intermediate between whites and blacks. Their

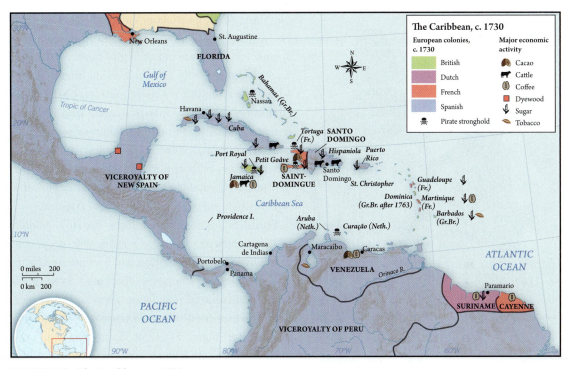

The Caribbean, c. 1730

European colonies, c. 1730
- British (green)
- Dutch (pink)
- French (orange/red)
- Spanish (blue)
- Pirate stronghold

Major economic activity
- Cacao
- Cattle
- Coffee
- Dyewood
- Sugar
- Tobacco

≡ **MAP 2.7**   The Caribbean, c. 1730

numbers grew steadily over the eighteenth century, as many were granted freedom and became property owners, even slaveholders. People of color gained a measure of recognition from the white elite and ultimately became a potent political force.

The existence of mixed-race "people of color" highlighted a new status hierarchy based on the color of one's skin. Until the conquest and settlement of Asia, Africa, and the Americas, with the inevitable mixing of populations that resulted, Europeans identified the different categories of people by referring to "blood." Nobles had "blue blood," whose supposed purity they sought to protect by prohibiting marriages to commoners. Europeans also used the word "blood" to refer to what we nowadays term "nationality," "ethnicity," or religious affiliation. Thus, there was "French blood" or "English blood" and Catholic, Protestant, Jewish, and Muslim blood, which a great many people believed should never be mixed.

Sometimes, Europeans substituted the term "race" for "blood," as in the "German race," but in the New World, "race" increasingly became associated with skin color. In the colonies of North and South America, the new understanding of race determined an individual's standing in society. At the top were "pure" European whites, then white-Native mixtures, white-black, Native-black, and so

≡ **Black Women and Women of Mixed Race.**
Although European leaders condemned the racial
mixing that resulted from their enslavement of
Africans and conquests in the New World, the
number of people of mixed race grew rapidly. To try
to stem that growth, Europeans outlawed marriages
between whites and people of other races. These
laws did little, however, to prevent the birth of
mixed-race children.

on. These new categories of race and status bounced
back to Europe and around the world. They led to laws
against intermarriage out of fear of diluting the white
race with supposedly inferior colored blood. Thus, a
Virginia law of 1691 outlawed marriages between an
"English or other white man or woman," and a "negroe,
mulatto [mixed race], or Indian man or woman." Of
course, white male plantation owners continued to
have children with enslaved black women, but they
almost never married those women or recognized as
legitimate the mixed-race children they fathered.

Saint-Domingue differed from Britain's colonies
in North America in that a considerable proportion
of the mixed-race population had become free by the
mid-eighteenth century (see Chapter 5). Even so, the
size of the enslaved population grew rapidly as plantation owners tried to meet the insatiable European
demand for sugar. By 1750, Saint-Domingue produced more of it than all the British sugar islands
combined. This was fortunate for France: after the various European wars of the eighteenth century, most of
which spilled over onto the Americas, Saint-Domingue
and a few other dots of territory would be all that was
left of the French empire in the New World.

Russia and the Russian Empire

While Spain, the Dutch Republic, Britain, and France
expanded overseas and sent European settlers abroad,
Russia made its imperial conquests within a huge continent peopled by a dizzying array of ethnicities, languages, and religions. Russia, like the Ottoman Empire,
became a multinational empire par excellence (see Map 2.8).

Russia took its name from a group of Scandinavian warriors known as Rus', who
beginning in the eighth century had established themselves on the river routes between the Baltic and Black Seas, controlling trade with the Byzantine Empire and
the Islamic East, and soon merged with the local Slavic population. In the fifteenth
century, local rulers in the east-central portion of that region seized territory

European Overseas Empires, 1492–1715	
1492	Christopher Columbus makes landfall in the Caribbean; beginning of the Columbian Exchange
1492–1600	275,000 enslaved Africans transported to the Americas
1498	Vasco da Gama (Portugal) rounds Cape of Good Hope and reaches India
1500–1600	Indigenous population of the Americas declines by 90 percent
1521	Tenochtitlán (Mexico City) surrenders to Hernando Cortés
1533	Spanish conquistadors execute Inca ruler Atahualpa
1600	English East India Company (EEIC) founded
1602	Dutch East India Company (VOC) established
1619	Dutch trading hub of Batavia founded by Dutch on island of Java
1607	Jamestown colony founded by English
1614	Tobacco cultivation begins in Virginia
1650–1750	Nearly three million enslaved Africans transported to the Americas
1685	France issues the *Code noir* regulating treatment of black slaves
1691	Virginia outlaws marriages between whites and blacks
1715	Tobacco production in Virginia approaches 25 million pounds annually
1750	French colony of Saint-Domingue produces more sugar than all British sugar islands combined

from the declining Mongol Empire and established a state based in Moscow. The Muscovites then fanned out in all directions, bringing fellow Slavs as well as Baltic peoples to the west and north under their control and moving into Siberia and across Central Asia. Rulers ensconced in Moscow maintained control over these diverse peoples by using four strategies. First, the Muscovites declared that all lands belonged to them and then "magnanimously" granted those lands back to local elites in exchange for loyalty and support. Second, Moscow's rulers (called grand dukes until Ivan IV assumed the title of tsar in 1547) married their sons and daughters into the families of local elites, thus creating long-lasting familial bonds. Third, they gave key representatives of these elites top positions in the government, a strategy that rewarded loyalty with influence. Fourth, they allowed subject peoples a great deal of cultural and religious autonomy—like the Ottoman Empire

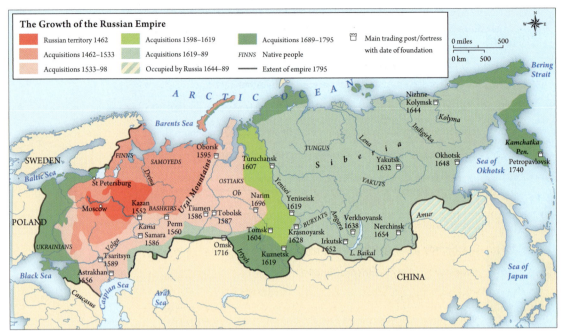

The Growth of the Russian Empire

Russian territory 1462	Acquisitions 1598–1619	Acquisitions 1689–1795	Main trading post/fortress with date of foundation
Acquisitions 1462–1533	Acquisitions 1619–89	FINNS Native people	
Acquisitions 1533–98	Occupied by Russia 1644–89	Extent of empire 1795	

☰ **MAP 2.8**   The Growth of the Russian Empire

again. Muslims were not forced to adopt Orthodox Christianity, Russia's dominant religion, nor were they required to speak Russian or to abandon longstanding cultural practices and traditions. These efforts did not always work as planned, but in general they proved remarkably successful in discouraging rebellion and in holding Russia's far-flung empire together.

This situation held true until the Time Of Troubles (see Chapter 3), a tumultuous period that began with the death of the feeble Tsar Feodor in 1598. It persisted in violence and warfare until the contending forces compromised on a new tsar, Michael Romanov (1596–1645) in 1613. Michael established a dynasty destined to rule, increasingly absolutely, until the Russian Revolution of 1917. Michael maintained the tradition of giving local elites almost total control over the peasantry. Landowning nobles feared that peasants would leave their domains to work under better conditions elsewhere, and already in 1597 the regent Boris Godunov had forbidden peasants to leave the landed estate where they worked. Over the course of the seventeenth century, Russian peasants became **serfs**, unfree laborers whose incomes and resources were kept artificially low by their inability to bargain with any landowner. The tsar also suppressed representative assemblies (the last were held in the 1680s) and, thus, most independent power in relation to the central government. Members of the nobility would periodically rebel against these conditions and did so emphatically under Michael's son and successor Alexei, as we will see in Chapter 3. But their successes were rare and short-lived.

When Peter I (Peter the Great, ruled 1682–1725) became tsar, he was determined to make Russia a major European power by going to war against neighboring kingdoms, especially Sweden. To fight these wars, he made the Russian government even more autocratic, tripling taxes, conscripting peasants into the army, and requiring nobles to serve in the army or government bureaucracy for life. Peter also forced peasants to produce weapons and other war materiel by conscripting them to work in mines and manufacturing plants, which belonged to the state. After initially losing battles to the Swedes, Peter ultimately defeated them in 1709, conquering large swaths of land along the Baltic Sea.

Peter, like Louis XIV, wanted to express his glory through large construction projects in his name. Only, unlike Louis, who limited himself mainly to a grand new home, the Chateau of Versailles, Peter built himself an entirely new city, which he immodestly dubbed Saint Petersburg. He created his new capital city on near-virgin territory captured from Sweden in 1703. To complete this vast construction project quickly, Peter forced hundreds of thousands of peasants to work around the clock to build the city's streets, houses, palaces, and churches. The laborers lived in abject misery as they fashioned what would be one of the world's most sumptuous, magnificent cities.

≡ **St. Petersburg.** Peter the Great's glittering new capital city, built on the western edge of his empire, faced Europe rather than Asia (on which Peter had turned his back).

Sweden and the Swedish Empire

Until 1703, Sweden competed against Russia with considerable success, despite its small population and meager resources. Sweden owed its achievements to the ability of its sixteenth- and seventeenth-century kings to mobilize the society, from top to bottom, for war.

The Emergence of a Strong Swedish State

In the early 1500s, Sweden was a northern European backwater loosely ruled by Denmark, then the strongest state in the Baltic region. Although Sweden included most of present-day Finland, its population amounted to less than a million people at a time when its largest neighboring states, Russia and Poland-Lithuania, contained ten million and six million respectively. Even geographically tiny Denmark housed about a million souls. Sweden's capital, Stockholm, with its 6,000 inhabitants, seemed little more than a large village. By comparison, the population of Moscow exceeded 100,000 and Paris 200,000. With just a single port on the North Sea, Sweden was largely isolated from Western and Central Europe, and its lone port on the Baltic Sea was its tiny capital, Stockholm. In any event, Sweden did not have much to trade. Its normally cold climate became even colder between the late sixteenth and late seventeenth centuries (on global cooling, see Chapter 3), and the low average temperatures gave Sweden a short growing season and meager agricultural output. As for its three important natural resources, wood, copper, and iron, none would be properly exploited until the seventeenth century.

These disadvantages had made Sweden vulnerable to Danish domination beginning in the late fourteenth century. But a Danish effort to impose harsher rule in the early sixteenth provoked a Swedish rebellion led by a young nobleman named Gustav Vasa, who became King Gustav I (1496–1560) of Sweden in 1523. As a Lutheran, Vasa led his country into the Protestant Reformation and, in the process, seized the Catholic Church's extensive landholdings in his realm. The king gained the loyalty of the nobility by giving them a large portion of this land, but he also kept quite a bit of it for himself, boosting the royal domain from 3 percent to 21 percent of Sweden's farmland.

This farmland, extensive as it was, did not make Vasa especially rich, and to gain the resources he needed, he shared power with a representative assembly known as the **Riksdag**. This body gave representation not only to nobles, clergy, and city-dwellers, as many German diets did, but to the peasantry as well. The peasant representation was unique in Europe. It gave the peasantry a measure of protection from a landed nobility intent on exploiting them economically and moved peasants to reciprocate by throwing their support to the king. In the Riksdag, the king created a coalition of peasants, city-dwellers, and minor nobles, which he could use to stymie the demands of the noble elite.

During the reign of Gustav I, Sweden became a stable, fully independent kingdom. Under his three sons, who ruled one after the other, the country began to expand into an empire, intending to bolster Sweden's security in the face of threats from Denmark, Poland-Lithuania, and Russia. In a series of sixteenth-century wars against these neighbors, Sweden prevented any encroachment on its territory and captured pieces of present-day Estonia and Russia. To fight these wars, the Swedish kings taxed their impoverished peasantry heavily and took a toll in blood by conscripting thousands of them into the army. The peasants, accustomed to hardship, mostly accepted these burdens because their representation in the Riksdag and large degree of landownership made them feel as though they were fighting for a country that belonged to them.

After its initial territorial gains of the late sixteenth century, Sweden mostly marked time until one of Gustav I's grandsons, Gustav II Adolf, known as Gustavus Adolphus, took the throne in 1611. The new king improved the administration of the country by creating schools and universities to train bureaucrats, and he convinced members of the noble elite to serve as high administrators in his realm. By doing so, he attached the upper nobility to himself and his government, thus preventing them from becoming a powerful opposition force, as this group was in other European states.

Sweden Becomes a Regional Power

Gustavus faced the same enemies as his ancestors, but with his strengthened administration and larger peasant army, he was better equipped to confront them. In 1617, he crossed the Baltic Sea, taking Ingria and Karelia, which today belong to the Russian Federation. Then, in the 1620s, Gustavus seized the city of Riga and much of what is now Latvia. Together, these conquests rounded out Sweden's Finish possessions and claimed a large slice of territory on the eastern Baltic coast.

Gustavus's kingdom was now an imperial power, albeit a minor one. What made him and his country a major European player was his intervention in the Thirty Years' War (1618–1648). As we have seen, this destructive conflict pitted large Protestant and Catholic armies against each other throughout German-speaking Central Europe. By the end of the 1620s, the Catholic forces had beaten back their Protestant enemies and restored the old religion in many places that had embraced the Reformation in the previous century. Gustavus worried that the triumphant Catholic army would join with one of Sweden's traditional opponents, Catholic Poland, and threaten his homeland. To forestall that danger, he launched his army across the Baltic in ships laden with 14,000 men. Once in northern Germany, he

≡ **The Lion of the North.** In this idealized depiction, Gustavus Adolphus leads a cavalry charge at the Battle of Lützen, in Saxony, in November 1632. He wears a simple leather coat that afforded him little protection, and he was killed later that day.

gained extensive financial support from France, which, although a Catholic country, favored the Protestants for geopolitical reasons in the Thirty Years' War. France wanted to weaken its main rival on the continent, the Holy Roman Emperor and leader of the Catholic forces. Gustavus seemed the perfect vehicle for achieving France's objectives, and French money enabled him to hire mercenary soldiers and expand his army to an impressive 100,000 men. With this army, Gustavus turned the tide of the war and came to be known as the "Lion of the North." He did not live to savor his victory, falling on the battlefield in November 1632.

Gustavus's military successors rampaged through Germany and came close to laying siege to Vienna, the Habsburg capital. But even Germany's Protestants, ostensibly saved by the Swedish army, denounced it, because the multitude of Swedish-affiliated soldiers fed themselves by seizing local crops and livestock. German Protestants, as well as Catholics, demanded to be rid of these northerners when the long war finally ended. At the peace settlement in 1648, Swedish acquisitions were limited to some small pieces of territory on the north German coast and a couple of islands in the Baltic Sea. Still, Sweden had gained considerable prestige as a European power and the military might to extend its imperial holdings in the decades to come.

Germany and the Holy Roman Empire

During the long Thirty Years' War, Germany, which constituted the largest portion of the Holy Roman Empire, remained a patchwork of about two dozen essentially independent states and hundreds of tiny jurisdictions only loosely joined together by the HRE's weak political structures. In the governing systems of these quasi-sovereign states and independent jurisdictions, a ruling prince—or sometimes bishop or archbishop—exercised sole authority over lawmaking, internal order, defense, and foreign affairs. During the Reformation, as we have seen, German princes added the power to determine the religion of their subjects. The main German states had representative assemblies known as **diets**, which usually enjoyed the right to approve new taxes, although during the Protestant-Catholic wars of the sixteenth and seventeenth centuries they rarely denied their princes' requests. The religious uniformity of each state meant that diet members shared religious beliefs and goals with the prince and thus sided with him, even though by doing so they reduced their leverage. A strong tradition of princely prerogative embedded in Germany's system of Roman law gave the princes still more sway over the diets, whose members were in any case divided into three distinct estates. Those divisions made it difficult for them to act in unison against the wishes of the prince, who used their differences to his advantage.

When German princes began to face regular military conflict in the early sixteenth century, they created strong administrative apparatuses to organize people and resources for combat. Since the states were relatively small, they had to manage themselves as efficiently as possible. To do so, they created bureaucracies composed not of venal officeholders, as in France and Spain, but of salaried administrators. German princes did not need to sell government offices, because their avoidance of warfare before 1500 enabled them to confront the new world of religious conflict without the massive debts common elsewhere in Europe. So did the willingness of diets to vote new taxes when the prince requested them. Equally important was the excess of young men with humanistic educations and legal training readily available to staff the new bureaucracies.

The years from 1500 to 1648 saw the opening of eighteen new German universities—far more than elsewhere in Europe—where young scholars could prepare to serve their princes, as Martin Luther's father wished his son had done (Chapter 1). After the end of the Thirty Years' War in 1648, most German princes felt free to do away with their diets or dramatically reduce their influence. They now ruled unconstrained by representative assemblies or venal officeholders, using salaried bureaucrats to govern with near-absolute authority.

Austria, Bohemia, and Hungary: The Limits of Habsburg Authority

Although the Habsburg monarchs, in their guise as Holy Roman Emperor, ruled German-speaking Central Europe indirectly at best, they presided more completely, at least in theory, over two other realms: Austria and Bohemia (see Map 2.9). Still, in Austria, which included the Habsburg capital, Vienna, two phenomena limited the Habsburgs' authority: a long tradition of local autonomy in the country's various regions (e.g., Lower and Upper Austria) and relatively powerful representative assemblies. These assemblies employed well-paid administrators who collected taxes; recruited soldiers; oversaw judges, teachers, doctors, and other professionals; and

≡ **Map 2.9** The Habsburgs in Central Europe, 1618–1700

governed the peasantry, who owed their primary allegiance to local landlords rather than to the Habsburg ruler in Vienna.

What gave Austria a semblance of unity was, first, a powerful Counter-Reformation church (see Chapter 1) that imposed religious obedience and orthodoxy, and second, a group of powerful landed magnates whose domains covered much of the country and who served as pillars of the Church. The magnates usually saw eye to eye with the Habsburg kings and endorsed their authority, with troops when necessary.

As we saw in Chapter 1, Bohemia (part of today's Czech Republic) had enthusiastically joined the Reformation in the sixteenth and early seventeenth centuries before being forcibly returned to Catholicism early in the Thirty Years' War. Because Catholic Habsburg armies had defeated the Protestant Bohemian ones, Bohemia found itself subjected to the Habsburgs, who became its hereditary rulers and all but disbanded the country's representative assembly. Catholicism became the only legal form of Christianity, while the courts and administration now answered directly to Vienna and no longer to Bohemian officials in Prague.

Despite these developments, Bohemia retained considerable autonomy from the Habsburg court. The latter's bureaucracy did not possess the manpower to govern Bohemia directly and thus had to rely on powerful Czech magnates to manage the country for them. In exchange, the magnates were rewarded with titles, offices, property, and nearly complete control over the peasants who worked on their extensive lands. Since the Habsburg court could not do without these magnates, they became the de facto rulers of Bohemia despite the country's official subservience to Vienna. Average Bohemian peasants—and small noblemen as well—possessed less independence than before the Counter-Reformation, but their country remained a politically distinct entity within a sprawling Habsburg monarchy that had to be content with keeping its various regions on a long political leash.

The same was true of Hungary, which fell partly under Habsburg control after the Ottoman Sultan Süleyman I attacked the long-independent country in 1526 and seized two-thirds of its territory. The Habsburgs took the rest. In Hungary, not unlike Bohemia, landed elites exercised the lion's share of authority by controlling local leadership positions, judicial institutions, and other key offices in the government. With many levers of power in their hands, the Hungarian elites granted themselves large tax exemptions and placed substantial burdens on the peasantry, whose lives they largely controlled. Even under Habsburg rule, Hungarian elites maintained substantial autonomy from the government in Vienna, and in the late 1600s, they succeeded in driving out the Ottomans.

Poland-Lithuania

In Poland, like Hungary, the landed nobility dominated the government at the expense of their kings, whose powers were sharply constrained by a representative assembly called the **Sejm**. When Poland united with neighboring Lithuania in 1569, making the Polish-Lithuanian Commonwealth one of the largest and most populous European states, the pattern of noble domination characterized the country as a whole. In 1572, the Sejm ruled that its members would select the Polish-Lithuanian kings, and it restricted the power of the monarchs they chose. Polish kings could not raise taxes, summon the army, or alter the rights and privileges of the nobility without the Sejm's explicit consent. In addition, the Sejm stripped the kings of their judicial power and gave itself full control over the government's finances. So suspicious of political authority did the Sejm become that it enacted the *liberum veto,* a rule granting any single Sejm member the ability to block legislation he disliked and eventually to end a session altogether.

The resulting vacuum of central authority nearly paralyzed the Polish-Lithuanian state and made it a choice target for surrounding countries eager to expand their territory at the Commonwealth's expense. Russians invaded in 1654, and Sweden, Brandenburg-Prussia, and Ottoman-ruled Transylvania followed suit. Predictably, Poland-Lithuania suffered a series of stinging military defeats, losing Baltic territories to Sweden and the Ukraine to the Cossacks, independent bands of varied origins but including many escaped Russian serfs. The **Cossacks**, named from a Turkish word for a nomad or adventurer, were fierce horsemen who roamed freely in the lands north of the Black Sea. They increasingly saw themselves as fierce defenders of the Orthodox Church and harbored a particular hatred for the Catholic Poles and for Jews, murdering tens of thousands in the seventeenth century (see Chapter 3).

The Polish nobility, meanwhile, tightened their hold over the country's social and economic life. To

☰ **The Polish Rider.** This mysterious painting, from about 1655 and ascribed to Rembrandt, captures the romance many in the West have felt toward Poland throughout its history. The young man on horseback has been described variously as a mounted Polish knight, a Cossack, or even a figure from the Bible.

keep agricultural domains in their hands, they forbade city-dwellers to buy landed estates. To grant themselves commercial advantages, they exempted nobles, but not other social groups, from all tariffs on imported goods. As for the agricultural economy, the Sejm passed laws requiring peasants to work one day each week without pay and kept their wages down by restricting their right to leave one noble's property for another.

Unlike Sweden, where political institutions enabled the king to limit the power of the wealthiest noble magnates, in Poland-Lithuania the structure of the Sejm allowed the magnates to dominate not just the king, but all the other social groups as well. By the early 1600s, the magnates had used their power to buy up the properties of the lesser nobility and reduce many of them to penury. The largest noble estates became so extensive that they resembled small countries with their own cities and towns, private armies, courts of law, and a host of officials, all employed by the magnate who owned the estate. To maintain their vast riches and power, the magnates kept the central government of Poland-Lithuania as weak as possible. In the long run, this selfishness proved counterproductive. In 1795, after nearly 150 years of incursions by neighboring powers seeking to overwhelm the feeble Polish state, the country disappeared from the map.

Prussia

One of the countries that took handsome advantage of the Polish weakness was Brandenburg-Prussia (after 1715, simply Prussia). This German state freed itself from the Habsburgs and became the most successful example of "bureaucratic absolutism," rule by a powerful monarch backed by a service nobility tied to him. In the sixteenth and seventeenth centuries, Brandenburg was a medium-size northeastern German state of little consequence. Sweden's powerful army occupied the country during the Thirty Years' War and in doing so inadvertently taught its rulers, all members of the Hohenzollern family, how to organize a successful military conquest.

Combining armed force and strategic marriages, the Elector of Brandenburg, Frederick William (ruled 1640–1688), expanded his territory as shown on Map 2.10. To maintain his grip on these lands in the face of potential Swedish and Polish designs on them, Frederick William needed as strong an army as possible. This required tax revenue, which he successfully extracted from his Estates by the tried and true practice of exempting their members in exchange for making everyone else pay. He also promised to support their efforts to force peasants to work on their lands for minimal compensation.

The leaders of the different Estates found themselves so satisfied with these arrangements that they allowed Frederick William to impose new taxes without their

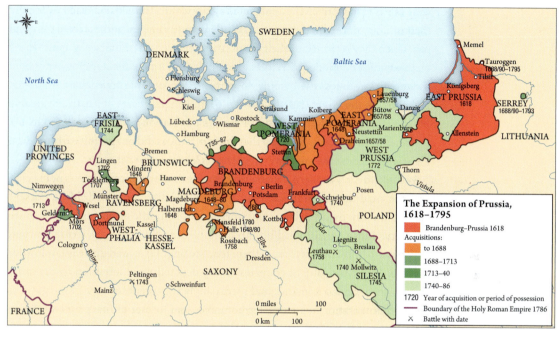

≡ **MAP 2.10** The Expansion of Prussia, 1618–1714

consent. His ability to do so marked the beginning of the end of the Estates' political leverage and the start of Hohenzollern efforts to rule Brandenburg-Prussia on their own. Frederick William and his successors, Frederick I (ruled 1688–1713, assuming the title of king) and Frederick William I (ruled 1713–1740), ignored or disbanded what remained of their Estates. They then enlisted educated noblemen and other academically trained individuals into a new administrative apparatus whose main functions were to collect taxes and organize a powerful standing army. As in other German states, Prussia's administrators were salaried professionals who served at the pleasure of the ruler; Frederick William and his successors refused to have their powers limited either by representative assemblies or venal officeholders. Still, the absence of a regular parliament meant that there was no entity within the Prussian government with the independence and credibility to endorse and legitimize the king's request for more revenues. As a result, Prussia routinely found itself short of funds, especially in wartime.

To remedy the problem, the kings tried to avoid war by building a standing army large enough to discourage military intervention from other states. Frederick William I financed the standing army by dramatically cutting non-military costs and by having landed noblemen conscript (draft) their peasants into reserve army units they commanded. During planting and harvest time, the peasant-soldiers were released to work on the land, but they stood fully trained and ready to resume their military duties on short notice. While in uniform, peasants received minimal pay; when they returned to their farms, they received no military pay at all. These methods allowed Frederick William I to double the size of his standing army even though his revenues rose by only 44 percent. The larger army enabled Frederick II, known as the Great (ruled 1740–1786), to conquer parts of Austria's valuable province of Silesia in 1745, raising Prussia's population by 60 percent and its tax revenues by 40 percent. But even these new resources did not permit early modern Prussia to become the great military state its leader wanted it to be.

What held early modern Prussia back was its limited ability to tax its noble elite and the rigid agricultural economy that the nobility controlled. Most peasant farmers did not own the land they worked and had little opportunity to acquire property. They therefore had no incentive to improve their agricultural output, which was barely enough to keep them fed, pay their taxes, and give the landowner his due. As for the lords themselves, many devoted more attention to the army than to their landed domains, and increasingly they went to work in the government administration, which preferred nobles and former military officers. Some Prussian nobles worked to improve their agricultural output and to turn it into products for sale, and the most successful among them marketed their grain far and wide. Still, until the late eighteenth century most noble landowners obeyed Frederick the Great's strictures against what he termed "inappropriate" commercial and industrial activities. Overall, the combination of a constrained peasantry and a non-entrepreneurial landowning elite produced a relatively, if not wholly, stagnant economy that limited the resources that Frederick's powerful administrative state could extract. Prussia's "bureaucratic absolutism" did not yet contain the elements necessary to create a great continental power.

Conclusion: The Rise and Decline of European Empires

Between 1500 and 1700, Europe featured a shifting balance of states that were all empires as well. Throughout most of this period, the Ottomans enjoyed the strongest, most expansive empire, which grew from its early conquests in the Black Sea region to encompass the entire Anatolian Peninsula, much of today's Middle East and North Africa, and a large piece of Southeastern Europe. This vast Eurasian empire fell behind its Western rivals only after they grew wealthy from their expansion into Asia and North America. Spain and Portugal were the first European empires to profit from their ventures overseas, but by the seventeenth century, they found themselves eclipsed by the Dutch and British empires. Sweden, too, expanded overseas, but in its case, the sea was the narrow Baltic, so its colonial possessions were close to home. This proximity did not, however, help Sweden hold on to their Baltic lands, because they sat close to other empires as well.

Russia was one of them, and the Russian Empire grew entirely over land, which did not make it any less of an empire. In Central and Eastern Europe, the Habsburg Empire pushed into Hungary in the early sixteenth century but found itself buffeted by religious warfare a century later. Poland combined with Lithuania to swell into a large Eastern European state, one that encompassed the present-day Baltic states, Ukraine, Belarus, and parts of Germany. Farther to the west, France captured neighboring territories in the seventeenth century and seized some colonial possessions abroad. England, meanwhile, incorporated Scotland, while colonizing Ireland and North America and making economic and political claims in India.

None of these developments was smooth. Every empire faced competition and confrontation with the others, and in the seventeenth century, as we will see in Chapter 3, several of them endured crises so severe that their Eurasian homelands almost fell apart.

KEY TERMS

astrolabe 66

audiencias 64

Bartolomé de las Casas 61

Batavia 71

Columbian Exchange 58

Cortes 61

Cossacks 93

diets 90

Dutch East India Company 71

East India Company 74

Estates General 80

factories 68

indentured servants 77

joint-stock company 71

mercantilism 81

nobles of the robe 81

nobles of the sword 81

Parliament 73

Prince Henry the Navigator 66

Riksdag 88

Sejm 93

serfs 86

stadtholder 70

tax farmers 62

Treaty of Tordesillas 60

venal 80

venal officeholders 62

Viceroyalty of New Spain 64

Viceroyalty of Peru 64

 For digital learning resources, please go to **https://www.oup.com/he/berenson2e**. Turn to the back of the book to see the list of primary sources and writing exercises provided in the accompanying *Sources and Guided Writing Exercises for Europe in the Modern World*

3

Crises of the Seventeenth Century

Louis XIV

Louis XIV (1638–1715) became king of France in 1643, when he was just five years old. His feeble father, Louis XIII, had died at age forty-one. Because the new child-king was too young to rule, his mother, Anne of Austria (1601–1666), together with his godfather, Cardinal Jules Mazarin (1602–1661), governed the country in his name. Mazarin was the protégé of Armand Jean du Plessis, better known as Richelieu (1585–1642), Louis XIII's chief minister and a cardinal of the Catholic Church. Richelieu had restrained the powers of France's great noblemen and made the kingdom a powerful, centralized state. He did so by recruiting writers to extol the king and defend his policies and by sending royal representatives called **intendants** into the French provinces to attempt to root the monarch's power into the fabric of local life.

When Mazarin succeeded Richelieu as chief minister in 1642, he followed his mentor's policies in guiding France through the final years of the Thirty Years' War and then in a mildly successful military campaign against Spain (1657–1659). These wars proved so costly, however, that they alienated rich and poor alike: the rich because Mazarin used them to extort "loans" and an increasing array of other payments; and the poor, because as a group they shouldered the lion's share of France's highly regressive taxes.

Wars and taxes proved so burdensome that between 1635 and 1660, France witnessed 282 rural and urban uprisings, many of which turned into pitched battles between the authorities and the people. Beginning in 1648, top noblemen also turned against the child-king in a rebellion known as the **Fronde**. This elite defiance sparked a popular upheaval in Paris so powerful that it forced Anne, Mazarin, and the young Louis XIV to flee the city for their lives. Louis's near-abdication encouraged several of France's wealthiest regional leaders, or **magnates**, to form personal armies in an effort to restore the power and independence they had lost under Richelieu.

The Fronde lasted five years and subsided only when certain magnates shrank back from an effort by some nobles to side with Spain against France, which would have threatened the integrity of the realm. The rebellion ended for good when Louis XIV, now age sixteen, was officially crowned King of France in 1654.

The experience of the Fronde convinced Louis XIV of the need not just to reign, as his father had done, but to rule as well—in large part by commanding the loyalty and deference of France's leading nobles, the only group with the potential to dilute his power. To achieve this goal, Louis built a sumptuous palace in Versailles, about twelve miles south of Paris, and made it essential for the greatest nobles of the land to reside there for much of the year. It quickly became a sign of great prestige to live in Versailles, and virtually every member of the nobility wanted to be invited there. Now, nobles gained power and standing not by asserting independence from the king, but by proximity to him. This situation enhanced the king's power while giving the nobility new sources of wealth, namely the ability to profit from the resources that Louis XIV could confer on them.

To gain access to these resources, whether richly paid sinecures or immensely profitable offices, nobles had to win the king's favor. They understood that Louis XIV preferred those who had impressed him with their loyalty and their ability to add to his grandeur. At Versailles, he created a hierarchy of those closest to him, and he displayed and reinforced that hierarchy through the rituals of his highly choreographed days.

Louis arose every morning at 7:30 a.m. He never awoke alone or with his queen or one of his mistresses but always with a select group of France's top dignitaries—all wealthy, powerful noblemen—who had been admitted to his chamber and ringed his bed. They watched as the king donned his robe and moved across the room to his dressing table, where they hoped to gain his attention. Everyone living at Louis's vast palace of Versailles, all five thousand of them, not including the five thousand soldiers encamped outside, rose at dawn to prepare for the king's *lever* or awakening.

Only the most honored of these **courtiers** actually got to witness this first official event of the king's daily routine, but the other, mostly noble, residents jostled one another in an effort to get as close to the "Sun King" as they could. As Louis's valets began combing his hair, officers of the bedchamber (as they were called) cracked open his door. Immediately, the second level of dignitaries came rushing in. Their objective was for the king to notice them so that they might ask for a favor, pension, government position, or one of the many other rewards Louis had the power to grant. He spoke to the lucky few and ignored the rest.

His grooming complete, the bedroom door swung fully open and the scores of other privileged people who held *entrées de la chambre* or admission tickets pushed

Timeline

1580	1600	1620	1640	1660	1680	1700	1720	1740	1760	1780

c. 1590–1720 Little Ice Age

1598–1613 "Great Trouble" in Russia

1603 James I succeeds to the English throne

1603–1703 Ottoman Empire sees ten sultans come and go, with two murdered

1618–1648 Thirty Years' War

1643–1715 Reign of Louis XIV

1642–1645 English Civil War

1645–1669 War between Ottoman Empire and Venice over control of Crete

1648 Cossack attacks in Ukraine reduce Jewish population by 50 percent; tsarist regime nearly collapses due to internal unrest

1648–1653 Fronde rebellion in France

1649 King Charles I of England executed

1658 Sweden defeats Denmark in Dano-Swedish War; Swedish Empire attains its greatest extent

1685 Louis XIV revokes the Edict of Nantes

1688–1689 Glorious Revolution in England

1688–1697 Nine Years' War

1699 Ottomans ejected from Hungary and lose parts of Greece to Venice

1700–1721 Great Northern War ends Sweden's dominance of the Baltic

1702–1714 War of the Spanish Succession

toward the king. They too hoped to get close enough to exchange a word or simply to gain a sign of recognition from him. Meanwhile, Louis's attendants finished dressing him, and once satisfied with his regal appearance, Louis headed toward the chapel with the three groups of courtiers in tow. The walk from the king's apartment to the chapel produced another round of discreet (and not so discreet) jostling of exquisitely dressed ladies and gentlemen eager to elbow into proximity to the king. Sometimes, all they wanted was a greeting, preferably by name.

After the church service, Louis left his courtiers behind to meet with his top ministers and counselors. He was a hands-on king who made all major governmental decisions himself. During these meetings and the king's lunch, which he took alone, courtiers gathered in the palace's gardens, where they discussed who had received favors and who had been rebuffed. Everyone watched for the king to reappear, hoping to position themselves to accompany him on his daily walk around the manicured grounds or, better yet, on his hunt. The king ate his dinner in public, but courtiers were forbidden to address him. They then joined him for the operas, plays, and other spectacles that he staged at Versailles. Louis's bedtime ritual or *coucher* mirrored the morning *lever* in reverse. By the time the king had closed his eyes, the courtiers found themselves exhausted from a long day of gossiping, partying, and waiting—anxiously or confidently—for signs of recognition or favor from him.

The king's *lever* and *coucher,* together with the other carefully staged events of his day, served as both real and symbolic manifestations of his power—or at least of what Louis intended to project. He created a public aura of grandeur and glory, a set of images crafted by artists and wordsmiths hired to inspire awe and reverence and the obedience these emotions produced. In symbolic terms, the *lever* and *coucher,* also the French words for the rising and setting of the sun, likened Louis XIV to the great celestial body for which the Sun King had been named.

Still, there were limits to his power. His Achilles heel was the immense cost of the long series of wars he conducted throughout his reign. To finance these wars, Louis imposed high taxes on his people, especially on those least able to pay, and he landed the kingdom massively in debt. Louis XIV may have gained the nobles' support, but he lost the backing of many of his subjects. Peasants and workers constantly rebelled against the costs of his wars, and their rebellions, along with the wars that sparked them, mirrored the situation elsewhere in Europe and the rest of the world. ≡

Upheavals of the Seventeenth Century

During the entire seventeenth century, Europe enjoyed just three years of peace. Throughout the other ninety-seven, at least two countries, and usually several, were always at war. The worst conflict was doubtless the Thirty Years' War (1618–1648), which, as we have seen, devastated much of German-speaking Central Europe. That war took proportionally more lives than any other from the beginning of European settlement until the murderous First World War (1914–1918). Virtually every European country participated in one way or the other in the Thirty Years' War, and the Treaty of Westphalia that ended it marked a lull in the fighting rather than a definitive peace.

In 1640, England erupted in a terrible civil war that engulfed Scotland and Ireland and ultimately led to revolution and the execution of the English king, Charles I. This English conflagration coincided with the Fronde in France and upheavals in Sicily, Naples, Spain, Portugal, Russia, Ukraine, the Netherlands, and the Ottoman Empire. On the other side of the world, China exploded into a civil war that ended in 1644 with the fall of the Ming Dynasty, which had ruled the country for nearly three centuries. After England calmed down temporarily in 1660, Denmark experienced a revolutionary change of regime and rioting broke out in Moscow. In 1688, England would undergo yet another revolution, this one beginning with a Dutch invasion of sorts—key English elites had invited them in—and the fall of another king. Each of these developments can be traced to conflicts over religion, politics, taxation, and social change, among other things. But they took place against the backdrop of changes in climate so severe that parts of Europe saw three of the coldest years in eight centuries and endured average temperatures well below what anyone could remember. This global cooling caused massive hardship, and it is not unlikely that it had something to do with the unprecedented political eruptions of the time.

The Little Ice Age

As its name suggests, the **Little Ice Age,** which lasted from the late sixteenth century to the early eighteenth, represented an era of extraordinary cold. During the bitter winter of 1620–1621, rivers normally frozen only part of the time became so thick with ice that merchants and farmers could drive heavy carts across them from December to March. It was so cold that people could traverse the Bosporus, the strait separating Europe from Asia, on foot. A few years later, the still below-normal temperatures produced some of the rainiest summers and snowiest winters on record. Driving rain and melting snow produced rushing waters, and rivers everywhere surged over their banks, washing away crops, livestock, houses, and people as well.

These conditions persisted for decades. In 1641 Scandinavia endured the coldest average temperatures in history. The thermometer stayed so low in northern Europe that during the winter of 1657–1658 the Swedish king staged an unprecedented assault on the Danish capital Copenhagen by launching his army on foot across the deep-frozen Baltic Sea. In 1654 people in the Balkans went without wine and olive oil for the entire winter because both of these staples froze solid in their bottles. Fish froze within blocks of ice, and human beings were found with their hands fused to the oars of their boats. In the Alps, the permanent mountaintop glacier moved a full mile downhill, and entire villages succumbed to the advancing ice. In London the deep freeze was more productive: merchants created an entire shopping district known as the "frost fair" atop the petrified waters of the Thames River, which obliged the vendors by freezing repeatedly as the century wore on.

When spring finally arrived, melting mounds of snow inundated low-lying regions. In the Dutch Republic, floodwaters burst through dikes and ruined lands long reclaimed from the sea. Meanwhile, in Paris, the Seine River, which has flooded sixty-two times in all of recorded history, registered eighteen floods in the seventeenth century alone. The flip side of floods was drought, also caused by the strange weather conditions of the century. In 1651 southern France saw not a single drop of rain for the entire year, and in England drought conditions persisted for several years beyond the mid-century mark. In 1666 the tenacious drought helped spark the Great Fire of London, which gutted much of the old central city. This disaster came on the heels of London's Great Plague of 1665—the last outbreak of the bubonic plague in England—which may have killed 100,000 people. In Romania the drought lasted throughout much of the 1680s. And in the lands between the Aegean and Black Seas, the drought of 1659 was the worst in a thousand years.

☰ **Ice City.** The citizens of Antwerp in the Spanish Netherlands (now in Belgium) enjoy winter pastimes on one of the city's many frozen waterways during the winter of 1622–1623.

The extreme cold, along with frequent floods and droughts, had devastating effects. It was so cold in 1628, the "year without a summer," that a great many crops failed to grow, resulting in a general shortage of food. In Central Europe of the 1630s and early 1640s, summertime frosts wiped out a multitude of crops. In England, according to historian Joan Thirsk, "bad weather ruined the harvests of corn and hay for five years from the autumn of 1646 onward." Over the following sixteen years, there would be ten harvest failures, each causing malnutrition and, for the poorest people, starvation. In Scotland at about the same time, "The long great rains for many weeks did prognosticate famine," wrote Robert Baillie, a Presbyterian minister active in Scottish politics. In France, meanwhile, average temperatures dropped so low from 1648 to 1650 that harvests came late and produced wine so inferior that vintners had to sell it for a loss, thus ruining their livelihoods. While wine prices sank, poor grain yields dramatically increased the price of food and led to widespread misery, especially among the poor. Crop failures meant not only that people went hungry but also that livestock starved to death. The loss of animals produced a dearth of meat, which added all the more to the malnutrition of the time.

Even those capable of feeding their families in the face of soaring grain prices found themselves with no money for anything else. This situation reduced demand for manufactured goods and thus threw many artisans and craftsmen out of work. With no job, laborers could not begin to afford the high price of food. Malnutrition weakened people's immune systems and left them vulnerable to disease and stunted growth. Rates of death and disability soared during these frozen years. So did people's anger over their plight—anger that often erupted into rebellion, especially given the high taxation imposed on ordinary people to finance the seventeenth century's incessant wars.

When farmers and other rural laborers found themselves with too little to eat, they abandoned their plots and their homes and fled to nearby cities, where they hoped to find work. As rural areas emptied out, cities became overcrowded, in part because most were surrounded by natural

≡ **Feeding the Poor.** In this painting from about 1646 by the Spanish painter Bartolomé Esteban Murillo, solemn-looking children and the elderly give thanks to the kneeling St. Diego of Alcalá for a ration of food. Seville, where Murillo spent most of his life, suffered several crop failures, disastrous floods, and repeated outbreaks of famine and the plague between 1626 and 1679.

barriers or walls designed to keep enemy armies out. These barriers left cities with no room to grow, which meant that the burgeoning number of immigrants had to squeeze into less and less per capita space. Living in such close quarters made people susceptible to highly infectious diseases such as smallpox and the bubonic plague, whose germs rampaged with particular force through the poorest sections of cities and towns and killed tens of thousands in a matter of days. Fires also spread rapidly through neighborhoods packed with hastily built dwellings subdivided into multiple apartments and crammed tightly together.

Cities were especially vulnerable to grain shortages, because their large populations—Istanbul housed 800,000 in 1650, and London, Naples, and Paris over 300,000 each—required massive amounts of food brought in from agricultural regions often hundreds of miles away. When harvests failed, the urban poor went hungry and not infrequently starved to death. Poor nutrition left pregnant women, always vulnerable in the premodern period, especially defenseless against disease. Huge numbers died in childbirth, and many of those who survived lost their babies in the first year of life. Still others killed their own babies to avoid having extra mouths to feed. These tragic developments revealed themselves in the statistics of the time: seventeenth-century London recorded twice as many burials as baptisms.

Harvest failures and grain shortages were hardly unique to the seventeenth century, but during this period of global cooling, Europe, like the rest of the world, saw far more such shortages than in centuries past. Part of the problem turned on the contrast with the sixteenth century, when global temperatures averaged somewhat higher than normal; this encouraged peasants to plant crops on higher-altitude lands which had, until then, been left uncultivated. The additional crops fed more people, and population grew. But when temperatures dropped in the seventeenth century, these higher-altitude lands became vulnerable to summer frosts and short growing seasons, which regularly made them unproductive. Without good harvests from these newly cultivated lands, the relatively high population levels reached in the sixteenth century could not be maintained. In some places, the number of inhabitants declined by as much as 30 to 40 percent between 1590 and 1650.

It seems clear from these developments that the global cooling of the seventeenth century contributed to the difficult living conditions of the time. But what caused this dramatic climate change? Clergymen said the strange weather represented God's punishment for the sinfulness of humankind. "Why hath the Earth sometimes too much raine?" asked one pamphlet. "Because the Lord is pleased in judgement to send it." Others blamed witches for brewing the awful weather, and the height of the era's witch craze coincided with the coldest, wettest years.

In May 1626, authorities in southern Germany tortured and then executed 900 supposed witches, men as well as women, for having caused a hailstorm that brought winter temperatures and destroyed acres of crops. Beyond witchcraft, it was the putative sinfulness of the theater, with its sexual innuendo and bawdy dialogue, that made God angry and moved him to unleash plagues of biblical proportions.

Not everyone agreed with this religious diagnosis. Those more scientifically inclined noted, thanks to the telescopes invented early in the seventeenth century (see Chapter 4), that sunspots had virtually disappeared. From 1612 to 1614, stargazers recorded about 100 sunspots a year, but the number dropped almost to zero in 1617 and stayed low for decades. By 1645, astronomers were looking at the heavens thousands of times a year, and only rarely did they record any solar flares—on average just one sunspot a year. In modern times, the annual number of sunspots tends to exceed 100 (see Figure 3.1).

Scientists of the seventeenth century did not understand this solar activity very well, but they were right about the connection between sunspots and climate. Today's climatologists generally find that a decrease in sunspots correlates with lower temperatures and more extreme weather patterns on earth. With fewer sunspots, less solar energy reaches our planet. Another explanation of the global cooling advanced at the time and confirmed by scientists today is the seventeenth century's unusual number of volcanic eruptions. These events spat dust clouds into the air, and those clouds blocked some of the sun's warming rays. Another climate culprit was the equatorial weather pattern known as **El Niño.** In normal years, El Niño winds blow into Asia monsoon rains essential for irrigating Chinese and Japanese crops. But every so often, these winds weaken significantly, and instead of sending precipitation to China

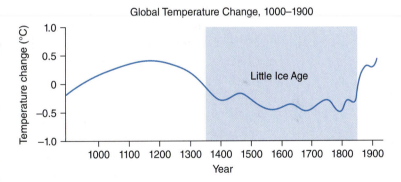

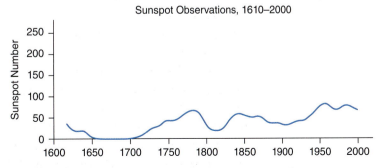

≡ **FIGURE 3.1** Global Temperature Change, 1000–1900, and Sunspot Observations, 1610–2000

and Japan, they blow rainclouds only as far as North America, which experiences excessive rainfall and flooding. Deprived of rain, Asia becomes parched with drought. Europe, in turn, suffers unusual cold. Normally, a weak El Niño occurs just once every five years, but in the seventeenth century, it happened almost every other year. The effects were serious, for they exacerbated the extreme weather already resulting from infrequent sunspots and frequent volcanic clouds. These climate conditions contributed in their own right to the misery of the seventeenth century, but combined with the near-constant warfare of the era, they took a devastating toll on human life.

Wars of the Seventeenth Century

"In the present century," wrote Christina, the former queen of Sweden, "the whole world is at arms." She made this comment in 1683, at the beginning of a war between the Ottoman Empire and a coalition of four other states: Russia, the Habsburg Empire, Poland-Lithuania, and Venice. This conflict would last sixteen years and cost nearly 400,000 lives. During Christina's century, wars occurred more often and lasted about three times longer than in any century since 1400. And the years from 1640 to 1660 saw more civil wars than any other equivalent period in human history. This was true not just of Europe but of Asia—and especially China—as well. There wars, including civil wars, engulfed virtually the entire seventeenth century.

Millions of soldiers and untold numbers of civilians were drawn into the conflicts. At the height of the Thirty Years' War, more than 300,000 troops battled one another in Germany, and during the civil wars of the 1640s in England, Scotland, and Ireland, about 100,000 joined the near-constant fighting. In the 1670s and 1690s, Louis XIV boasted a standing army of a quarter of a million men. Most of these soldiers were mercenaries who had to be paid to fight, and their wages added a large amount to the already huge costs of feeding and clothing them, manufacturing weapons and munitions, and fortifying and provisioning cities likely to be under assault. Much of the era's warfare involved laying siege to major cities and other strategic places. Building city walls and other fortifications was phenomenally expensive, as was the weaponry needed to breach them.

To finance these wars, kings and emperors had to mobilize vast sums of money. Between 1618 and 1670, the Dutch Republic's richest province, Holland, increased its debt by nearly 3,000 percent. Taxes skyrocketed as well, adding 33 percent to the price of bread and more than doubling the price of beer. Taxes had similar effects throughout Europe, and peasants and other working people found themselves, at best, barely making ends meet, and, at worst, falling into destitution. To make matters even worse, the various armies tended to live off the land, seizing food, water, shelter, and other resources from farmers already struggling to feed themselves. Even "friendly" armies, such as the Catholic forces fighting in the Catholic parts of Germany, inevitably harmed the people they were intended to support. And no war proved deadlier than the Thirty Years' War of 1618–1648.

Germany and the Thirty Years' War

In Chapter 1, we sketched the milestones of this war: the formation of opposing religious armies, the Protestant Union and the Catholic League; the Defenestration of Prague (1618), when Protestant dissidents ejected three Catholic officials from a third-story window; the Battle of White Mountain (1620), when the Catholic army dealt its Protestant counterpart a devastating defeat; the Edict of Restitution (1629), which returned to the Catholic Church all the lands that Protestants had stripped from it since 1555; the Sack of Magdeburg (1631) in which Catholic forces wiped out 90 percent of the city's 25,000 inhabitants; the Swedish King Gustav II's convincing victory of 1632 over the Catholic forces; and the relentless fighting of the next sixteen years. This fighting pulled in the Dutch Republic, Denmark, Poland-Lithuania, France, and Spain, making it more than just a German war or a Catholic-Protestant conflict. Catholic France contributed to the Protestant side, because Richelieu considered the Holy Roman Emperor, the titular head of the Catholic cause in Germany, France's greatest European threat (see Map 3.1).

≡ **A World at Arms.** These two paintings by the Flemish painter Pieter Snayers capture the immensity and terrible suffering of the constant fighting that ravaged Europe for most of the seventeenth century. *Left:* The Battle of White Mountain, a pivotal battle in the early phase of the Thirty Years' War, in which 50,000 soldiers fought. *Right:* The siege of Aire-sur-la-Lys, in northern France, 1641. Starving Spanish soldiers freeze in the snow. Visible behind them are the fortifications of the town.

Because this three-decade-long war coincided with some of the worst years of the Little Ice Age, its effects were particularly devastating. During the immediate run-up to the war in 1617 and 1618, frigid weather and excessive rain destroyed crops throughout Germany and left large numbers of people desperately short of food. Hunger and the anxiety it caused put both Protestants and Catholics on edge and convinced many on both sides that their religious enemies bore responsibility for the hardships they faced. The weather remained unusually harsh throughout much of the first decade of the Thirty Years' War, and in 1628, the "year without a summer," the people's suffering became unbearable. Cold weather lasted so long into the normal growing season that grains and grapes were stillborn on their stalks and vines, leaving too little food and drink. This was especially problematic because the Catholic army alone numbered 130,000 troops. Soldiers seized what they needed, and ordinary people starved, often to death.

In some years, average temperatures reached normal levels, but even then, people had to contend with severe weather. In 1642 an unending series of storms raged through the winter, spring, and summer. They produced the worst floods in memory, along with hailstones the size of baseballs and frosts lasting until the middle of June. In many places, there would be nothing to harvest in the fall. The terrible cold did have one positive effect: the frigid temperatures of August 1647 and of the following winter convinced Sweden's victorious generals to stop fighting and send their exhausted, frostbitten army home. Sweden even accepted a compromise peace that gave it a fraction of the money its leaders had originally demanded of their enemies. On October 24, 1648, Sweden and the other belligerent powers signed the Treaty of Westphalia, which restored land and the right to worship to Protestants, diluted the Holy Roman Emperor's power, allowed exiles to return to their homes, and, perhaps most important, left Europe less polarized by religion, if only because sectarian passions had burned themselves out. What is more, the intervention of Catholic France to offset the Catholic Holy Roman Empire set the stage at Westphalia for a general "balance of power" designed to prevent future wars by keeping any individual state from growing too strong. The balance, as we will see, failed to hold for very long, but the concept endured until the First World War.

Overall, the costs of the Thirty Years' War itself were horrific. Some two million soldiers, mostly German, perished and another three million noncombatants lost their lives. Since the fighting took place unevenly throughout Germany, the losses were uneven as well. In the Rhine Palatinate and Württemberg, both in southern Germany, about half of the population perished during the war. The same was true of the north German states of Mecklenburg and Pomerania. Bavaria, Franconia, and Hessen in the south lost between one-third and one-half, as did Saxony and Brandenburg in the north. Many people died from the fighting itself, but severe weather, malnutrition, disease, and lack of shelter also took a dreadful toll. In the once-prosperous surroundings of Magdeburg where some of the worst fighting took place, two-thirds of the structures were leveled.

Not only did the long war destroy people and material goods, it also wrecked Germany's impressive cultural advances. Its long-active printing presses went silent, music compositions declined, and intellectuals endured religious persecution, often preventing them from doing their work. The great astronomer Johannes Kepler (1571–1630), a Protestant, had to flee one home after the other as Catholic forces moved in. He found himself menaced not just by Catholics, but

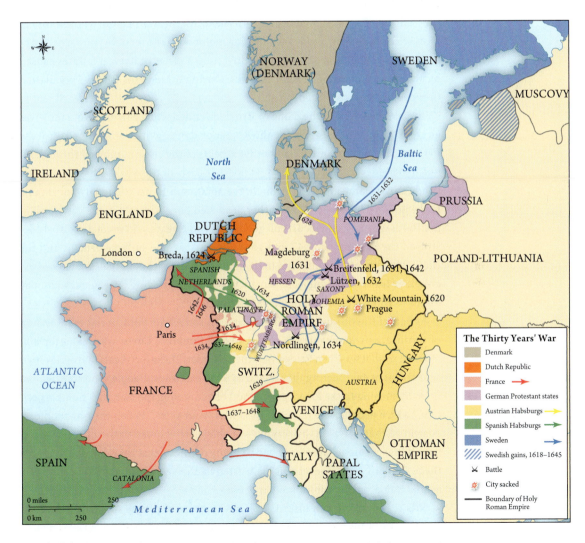

≡ **MAP 3.1** The Thirty Years' War

also by Lutherans who considered his views too Calvinist. Meanwhile, his mother, Katharina, faced accusations of witchcraft for which she was jailed and threatened with torture. Kepler had to put his astronomy aside as he devoted himself to saving his mother.

Russia in the Seventeenth Century

Russia stayed out of the Thirty Years' War, but since the late sixteenth century, it had been engulfed in losing wars with Sweden and the Polish-Lithuanian Commonwealth. These wars coincided with a two-decade-long crisis known as the "Time of Troubles" that began with the death of Tsar Feodor, who expired in 1598 without an heir, and reached its low point with the terrible famine of 1601–1603. This long period of hunger resulted from a series of harvest failures caused by below-freezing summer temperatures. During these years, Russia's population dropped by as much as 25 percent.

The political void of the Time of Troubles ended when Michael Romanov was elected tsar in 1613, establishing the Romanov dynasty that ruled Russia until the February Revolution of 1917. But other aspects of the crisis continued throughout much of the seventeenth century. As in other parts of the world, Russia's climatic conditions became miserable again in the 1620s and 1630s and nearly unbearable in the 1640s. Unusually cold weather produced poor harvests in the early part of the 1640s, drought and locusts plagued the middle years, and premature frosts destroyed the harvests of 1647 and 1648. Russia's people suffered cruelly, and the country's population continued to decline. Tsar Michael nonetheless imposed ever-heftier taxes on his subjects, largely to finance a growing bureaucracy and pay for his ongoing wars against Poland and Sweden.

As part of Russia's defense, Michael and his son Alexei built an elaborate system of fortifications known as the Belgorod and Simbirsk Lines, which ran for 800 miles near what was then Russia's southern border. These fortifications represented a great feat of engineering, but the costs were excessive. People protested against them by turning to the lone legal method of addressing the tsar, the "humble petition," which people were required to sign as "your slave." When the tsar's subjects demeaned themselves in this way, he was obliged to respond to their concerns. But he and his successor Alexei received so many petitions that they decided to ignore them. In April 1648, Alexei sent his trusted lieutenants to intercept a particularly adamant one, and he left Moscow without seeing it.

This breach of custom infuriated large numbers of people suffering from food shortages and high taxes. In June, scores of petitioners came together to present their grievances to Alexei in person. Again, the tsar's guards intercepted the petition and, adding injury to insult, opened fire on the crowd. In response, several people burst into Alexei's private quarters in the Kremlin and tried to deliver their petition to the tsarina, the tsar's wife. A day later, a huge crowd surrounded the tsar on his way out of church, and once again, he refused to accept their petition. His chief advisor, the enormously wealthy magnate Boris Morozov, then ordered the palace guard to disperse the crowd by force. Guard members, however, had not been paid for months, and they sided with the petitioners, refusing to fire on them. With no one to stop them, crowd members, joined by palace guardsmen, stormed into Morozov's residence and destroyed everything in sight. They then killed four of the tsar's top officials and demanded that Morozov and two other ministers blamed for the high taxes be turned over to them. Knowing that the ministers would be killed, the tsar stalled. Meanwhile, protesters set fires throughout the Russian capital; with trees and shrubs parched by the drought of that year, the city went up in flames. Some 50,000 buildings were reduced to smoking ruins, and 2,000 people died.

Again, protesters demanded the heads of Morozov and other officials while threatening the tsar himself. The very existence of the regime was now in doubt. As one petitioner declared, "The whole world is shaking." To shield himself, Alexei sacrificed his treasury minister, Peter Trakhaniotov, and promised to exile Morozov to a monastery far from Moscow. But even this did not end the unrest. To calm the situation, Alexei responded favorably to more than seventy petitions demanding concessions and reforms. He then agreed in mid-1648 to convene a representative assembly, the *Zemskii Sobor*, which had not met regularly for several decades.

The assembly brought together representatives of Russia's various social groups, but the nobility dominated the body. Alexei convinced the assembly to include measures designed to severely punish the forms of mass protest that had nearly overturned the regime in June 1648. In exchange, the tsar gave the nobility full control over their serfs (peasants), who were not only forbidden to leave their lord's domains but also stripped of their personal property, which would now belong to the lord. Any serf who had fled to a city or town or to regions like Siberia outside of any noble's control could be forcibly returned to his master. Serfs essentially became slaves, as nobles were granted the right to buy and sell them at will. The tsar had not wanted to grant the nobility such comprehensive control over the peasantry, because he intended to use peasants as homesteaders who would expand Russian territory to the north and south. But the protests of 1648 convinced him that the stability, even the existence, of his regime required the allegiance of the nobility; to assure it, he had no choice but to sacrifice both the peasantry and his expansionist aims.

≡ **Tsar Alexei of Russia.** The long reign of Alexei (1645–1676) was filled with crises, and the tsar relied on advisers who often failed him. In this painting, Alexei wears the royal regalia that symbolize his sovereignty and legitimate his rule.

Alexei's arrangement with the nobility resolved Russia's severe mid-century crisis, but it did not fully stabilize his government. If anything, the effects of the Little Ice Age in Russia grew worse in the second half of the century. The years from 1650 to 1680 registered the coldest falls, winters, and springs in a half-millennium. Crop failures and food shortages occurred with depressing regularity and coincided with severe unrest, both religious and political. A series of ecclesiastical reforms enacted in the 1650s by Russia's most important religious leader, Nikon, the Patriarch of Moscow, split the Russian Orthodox Church and led to the violent suppression of traditionalists known as Old Believers. This conflict would divide Russian society until the revolution of 1917. In 1670 the Cossacks, led by the charismatic Stepan Razin, staged a major rebellion that mobilized tens of thousands of people beyond the Cossacks themselves. The uprising lasted for more than a year before finally succumbing to a tsarist counterattack—but making Razin a folk hero for centuries.

Not long after the regime subdued this latest rebellion, Russia went to war against the Ottoman Empire, and in 1700, it would begin a twenty-one-year-long fight against Sweden. More normal climatic conditions greeted the new century, and Russia's victory in 1721 proved a major turning point for the Russian Empire, which now joined the ranks of Europe's great powers.

The Decline of the Polish-Lithuanian Commonwealth

The same was not true of the Polish-Lithuanian Commonwealth, despite its military and political successes of the first half of the seventeenth century. At its height, the Commonwealth had become very large, encompassing much of present-day Poland, Lithuania, Belarus, and Ukraine, along with pieces of Russia, Latvia, and Estonia. Its Ukrainian regions were particularly desirable, because they featured some of Europe's most fertile soil. People from all over Central and Eastern Europe migrated there, but the Commonwealth's noble-dominated government granted much of the Ukraine's land to a handful of powerful noble magnates. Those magnates hired estate managers who often treated the peasant population harshly, squeezing them for ever-higher rents and taxes. Some of these managers, although only a small minority, came from the region's growing Jewish population, and they evoked resentment from the mostly Catholic peasantry.

Resentful as well were the Cossacks, a militaristic people accustomed to their independence and determined to defend their rights. Some Jewish managers doubtless treated Cossacks badly, but the Cossacks owed their troubles mainly to the loss of lands they had traditionally controlled to Poland's noble magnates. The Cossacks also suffered from the consequences of climate change. Extremely cold weather in the spring and summer of 1641 to 1643, as well as the massive snows and rains of spring 1646, the exceptionally long winter of 1646–1647, and the floods of spring 1648, turned the Ukraine's normally fertile land into a fount of famine. The Cossacks blamed the Jews for their problems and went on the war-path against them. In June 1648, they slaughtered some 6,000 Jews in the town of Nemyriv, now in central Ukraine. A month later, Cossacks killed another 12,000 Jews in Polonne (western Ukraine) and forced another 8,000–10,000 to flee for their lives. Some 3,000 Jews were sold to Tatars as slaves. Overall, the Jewish population of the Ukraine dropped by 50 percent during the summer of 1648.

The Ukraine's peasants did not fare much better during these years, and they erupted in rebellion against their noble lords. The Cossack leader, Zynoviy Bohdan Khmelnytsky, took advantage of the chaos to launch an attack against the Polish government, whose representative assembly, the Sejm, was deadlocked in the summer of 1648 over the effort to elect a new king. In September, Khmelnytsky defeated the Polish army, and in a truce negotiated with the new Polish king, John Casimir, the Cossack leader won a measure of financial aid for his people. Backed by Ukraine's Orthodox clergy, Khmelnytsky also won a series of religious concessions, especially the expulsion of all Jesuits and remaining Jews from the Ukraine and the right of Orthodox Christians to worship freely.

The truce between Khmelnytsky and Casimir was short-lived: in 1651, the Polish army returned to the region and defeated the Cossacks, whose powers and independence were once again reduced. To regain them, Khmelnytsky asked Tsar Alexei for help. With the Sejm paralyzed once again, Alexei declared war on the Polish-Lithuanian Commonwealth with the intention of regaining lands lost to Poland in earlier conflicts and to defend the Cossacks of Ukraine. In May 1654, Russian troops captured the city of Smolensk as well as Vilnius, the capital of Lithuania (the city was then known as Wilno or Vilna; the population was largely Polish and Jewish).

The entire Commonwealth seemed on the verge of collapse, and this situation moved the Swedish king, Karl X Gustav, to grab some of the spoils. In July 1655, he invaded Poland, capturing its two most important cities, Warsaw and

Krakow, three months later. King John Casimir fled the country, and the entire Commonwealth fell into Swedish hands, albeit briefly. Almost immediately, Russia declared war on Sweden, whose forces were stretched too thin to hold onto Poland and fight off Russia at home. Karl X Gustav abandoned the Commonwealth, the better to defend the core areas of his kingdom. As Sweden and Russia fought, Poland suffered from more frigid winters and harvest failures and contended with two epidemics of bubonic plague. Finally, in 1661, Sweden and Russia signed a peace agreement that left each country with exactly the same amount of territory as before this latest round of fighting began. The Commonwealth and Sweden also signed a treaty in which no significant territory changed hands.

All this warfare—between Poland-Lithuania and Russia, Poland-Lithuania and Sweden, Sweden and Russia, not to mention the rebellion of the Cossacks and the slaughter of Ukraine's Jews—came at a massive cost to ordinary people in all these countries. Not only did they pay for these wars in taxes, and as soldiers in blood, they footed these bills amid the worst climatic conditions in centuries.

The Rise and Fall of the Swedish Empire

While Sweden fought against Russia and the Polish-Lithuanian Commonwealth, Denmark tried to take advantage of the situation by launching an attack against Sweden in 1657. But the Swedish king, Karl X Gustav, mounted a counterattack so powerful that his forces succeeded in taking the strategic Danish lands ringing the North Sea and Baltic coasts of the Swedish peninsula. These conquests gave Sweden key ports facing northern and Western Europe and substantial control over access to the Baltic Sea.

The gains completed a Swedish expansion begun a half-century earlier (see Map 3.2). It was now an empire and had to behave like one—that is, its leaders had to manage diversity. In addition to its long-standing population of Swedes and Finns, Sweden now contained significant numbers of Danes, Germans, Poles, Estonians, and Latvians. That most of these peoples adhered to the Lutheran faith helped keep the empire together, but the Danes and Germans, in particular, resented their new rulers. These groups looked for support to Denmark and the HRE, both of which, together with neighboring Russia, feared as well as resented the new Swedish empire in their midst.

The problem for Sweden was that, even with its territorial gains, it remained relatively weak. Sweden's late-seventeenth-century population of 2.5 million paled in comparison with the population of the other European powers, and as a largely agricultural economy with mediocre crop yields, it did not stand to gain very much from trade. Its peasantry was poor, especially after so many decades of constant

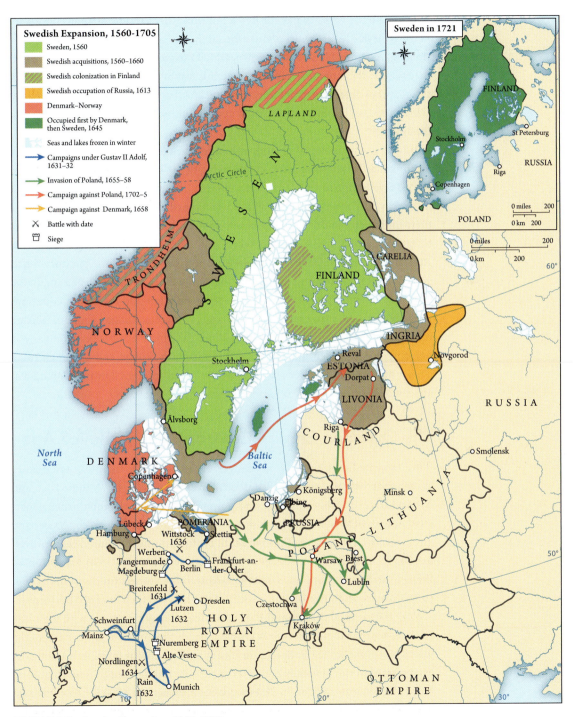

≡ MAP 3.2   Sweden Expansion, 1560–1705

warfare and the taxes to pay for it. To improve the peasants' fortunes, Sweden's kings of the late seventeenth century forced their wealthiest nobles to transfer substantial amounts of land to the crown, which the government then sold or rented to peasants. The monarchs accomplished this feat by maneuvering in the Riksdag, the country's representative body, to create an alliance of peasants, city-dwellers, clergy, and lesser nobility against the upper nobility, which was then outvoted in the assembly.

Having lost a great deal of land, a considerable number of nobles went to work for the state. This development, combined with the kings' control of the Riksdag, turned Sweden into a quasi-absolutist empire. Its kings were strong internally but limited in their ability to project that power abroad. Sweden's neighbors perceived these limitations, and at the dawn of the eighteenth century, they banded together to exploit them. In the Great Northern War (1700–1721), a shifting coalition of Russians, Prussians, Danes, and Poles stripped Sweden of all the territory it had gained in the seventeenth century save for the lands along its North Sea and Baltic rims. In the end, Sweden, with its meager population and resources, could not measure up to the vastly more populous and prosperous Russian Empire. Sweden managed, however, to outlast Poland-Lithuania, which faced repeated invasions not only from Sweden but also from Brandenburg-Prussia and Ottoman-ruled Transylvania. In 1795, after nearly 150 years of intermittent fighting, Poland disappeared from the map.

The Ottoman Empire Confronts the Little Ice Age

The Ottoman Empire was in no danger of falling apart. In 1600, its territory stretched across huge swaths of southern Europe, Anatolia, the Middle East, and North Africa. Its army was large and powerful, its capital, Istanbul (then generally known as Constantinople), a showcase of wealth. But despite the power and glory it enjoyed at the end of the sixteenth century, the next hundred years proved extremely difficult for the Islamic regime. Between 1620 and 1690, the Ottoman Empire saw the murder of two of its sultans and three others overthrown. Its centuries-long territorial expansion screeched to a halt and then began to decline.

Why this reversal of fortunes? Part of the reason may have to do with the Little Ice Age, which was more severe in Ottoman lands than in many other parts of the world. Not every corner of the empire felt equal effects, as the farmlands among the Mediterranean rim generally enjoyed the sun and rain needed to raise basic food crops plus tobacco and cotton. But on coastal plateaus and hillsides, too little rain fell in many years to grow grains and vegetables without irrigation, which mostly did not exist. Inland regions fared even worse, as even in good years temperatures remained low and drought was common. Unfortunately, good years all too often gave way to bad ones, when spring and summer frosts combined with a lack of rain decimated the harvest and left farmers with little or no food to sell—or even to feed themselves.

The dearth of food dramatically raised mortality rates; in several parts of the Ottoman Empire, population declined by 40 to 50 percent between the late 1500s and 1650. The situation became especially dire in Egypt between 1640 and the early 1650s, when El Niño left the Nile Valley with so little rainfall that the river barely overflowed its banks. Since Egypt "is a desert with a river running through it," farmers can raise crops only because, in normal years, the Nile floods the adjacent strips of land, producing the irrigation needed to grow food. Egyptian crops fed Istanbul, a huge city of 700,000 in 1650, and when the Nile suffered from drought, the Ottoman capital went hungry. Popular unrest often ensued, and that unrest commonly sparked, or dovetailed with, political crises to produce dramatic, regime-changing effects.

Such political turmoil was largely new to the seventeenth century. During the previous hundred years, the Ottoman Empire remained highly stable. Between 1512 and 1595, there were just four sultans, with one of them, Süleyman I, serving a record forty-four years. The contrast is stark with the period from 1603 to 1703, when the empire saw ten sultans come and go, the shortest tenure lasting just three months. In the sixteenth century, every sultan reigned until he died a natural death; in the following century, two were deposed and then murdered and three found themselves simply deposed—one of them twice.

The instability began in 1595, when Sultan Mehmed III had all nineteen of his brothers killed. His agents also murdered several pregnant members of his harem, just in case they were carrying boys. When Mehmed III died eight years later, only two potential heirs were left: his sons Ahmed, age thirteen, and Mustafa, four. Ahmed became sultan and allowed Mustafa to live; he needed a potential heir and was too young to father any sons. Surprisingly, Ahmed kept his younger brother alive even after he had a son. When Ahmed died in 1617, he left two young men, his son Osman, age fourteen, and Mustafa, now eighteen years old, as rivals for the throne.

Mustafa's supporters won out, and he succeeded his brother. But he proved mentally unbalanced, and Osman's backers deposed him. Unfortunately, Osman seemed unbalanced as well, and he imposed a series of harsh religious restrictions, which alienated the empire's top Islamic leaders. This unpopular sultan then had to confront several weather-related challenges. During the severe winter of 1620–1621, the Bosporus froze solid and no food shipments arrived in Istanbul for over a month. Starvation set in. To make matters worse, Osman declared war on Poland, and to feed his army, he monopolized a large portion of an already scarce food supply. The unusual cold persisted into the spring and summer of 1621, leaving both his capital city and his troops wanting for food. His underfed army fought poorly, and Osman had to withdraw from the Polish campaign in defeat. More bad weather in the spring of 1622 exacerbated the food shortage and turned the elite Janissaries against him. Several of them seized the sultan, humiliated him in public, and then strangled him to death. This was the first murder of a sultan in Ottoman history; it would not be the last.

With Osman gone, Mustafa returned to the throne, but his mental condition was no better than before, and, if anything, the climatic conditions were even worse. In 1622 Istanbul registered the highest food prices of the entire seventeenth century, creating widespread misery. And in the winter of 1622–1623, bubonic plague gripped the city. At first, Janissaries punished Mustafa's grand viziers for this situation, killing several. Finally, in September 1623, the elite soldiers turned on the sultan himself, and Mustafa found himself deposed for the second time. Unlike his predecessor, he was allowed to live, albeit confined to a cave-like room deep in the bowels of the palace.

The new sultan, the fourth in six years, was an eleven-year-old boy named Murad. Like Mustafa and Osman, his reign was plagued by usually severe weather, which returned with a vengeance in 1630. A dearth of rain produced widespread famine, and in Istanbul, the drought left numerous city-dwellers dying of thirst. In response, rebellions broke out in the capital and elsewhere around the country, and Murad's top officials took the blame. Insurgents forced the sultan to give them his grand vizier and several other top officials. They were all killed on the spot.

When Murad finally got the insurrection under control, he ordered a brutal repression of suspected rebels and the execution of officials blamed for the misery that had sparked the rebellion. The sultan also

≡ **Imperial Hall, Topkapi Palace.** Shortly after they conquered Constantinople, the Ottomans began the construction of a new palace for their sultans: Topkapi Saray. The Topkapi is a veritable mini-city, with schools, barracks, a hospital, an armory, and most important, the living quarters, or harem, for the ruling family. Located at the very center of the palace complex were the private apartments of the sultan, which included the Imperial Hall where the sultan would receive members of his family and closest advisors.

took under his wing a radical religious movement called the Kadizadelis (the followers of a preacher named Kadizade), endorsing their views about the immorality of coffee, alcohol, and tobacco and decreeing the death penalty for people who consumed them in public. Murad's reign lasted a respectable sixteen years, and after he died in 1640, he was succeeded by Ibrahim, dubbed the "mad sultan" for his myriad health and emotional problems. During the eight years of his reign, Ibrahim named and then deposed more than a dozen grand viziers; dismissed ten chief muftis, Islam's top legal expert; and fired dozens of provincial governors. The beginning of the end came for him when he attacked the Venetian island of Crete. The Venetian navy replied by blockading the Dardanelles, the narrow strait that leads to Istanbul. The blockade prevented food and supplies from reaching the Ottoman capital, and characteristically for the seventeenth century, it coincided with several bouts of bad weather and other natural disasters: floods in 1646, drought in 1647, and a powerful earthquake in 1648 that destroyed Istanbul's main aqueduct. The drought had already compromised the city's water supply; the tremor left much of the capital high and dry.

The war against Venice, meanwhile, cost 100,000 lives and squeezed higher and higher taxes from an Ottoman population already suffering cruelly. With the people at a boiling point and rebellions breaking out around the empire, key Muslim figures blamed the situation on the supposed irreligion of the empire's top officials. Under these circumstances, a group of Janissaries murdered Ibrahim's grand vizier and threatened the sultan himself. Fearing that he would be deposed, Ibrahim tried to kill his son to prevent him from taking his place, but the chief mufti stepped in on August 8, 1648, and had Ibrahim deposed. Ten days later, the mufti issued a fatwa, or legal ruling, that led to the second regicide in twenty-six years. Ibrahim, already locked in a cage, was strangled to death.

Ibrahim's son Mehmed IV took over as sultan, and the situation stabilized for a time, especially after the Ottomans defeated the Venetians in 1656 and lifted the long blockade of Istanbul. But shortly afterwards, a rebellion broke out in Anatolia, and this time a climate disaster helped save the day for the regime. A brutal winter in 1657–1658 deprived the rebels of food, and the movement petered out. But Mehmed's reprieve would be short-lived. In 1659–1660, much of the empire suffered the most severe drought in a thousand years, causing crops everywhere to fail. In Istanbul, bone dry from the drought, the city's multitude of wooden buildings went up in flames. The damage was vast, especially in the Christian and Jewish quarters of the city.

This disaster did not deter Mehmed from embarking on a new round of warfare. In a series of campaigns in Hungary in the 1660s, Ottoman forces rounded out the empire's possessions there, and shortly afterwards, ejected all remaining Venetian troops from Crete. Despite these victories, the Ottoman Empire's many decades of political turmoil, with its regicides and depositions, to say nothing of the effects of climate change, left Mehmed's realm in a weakened state. In 1683 the Habsburgs took advantage of this weakness by assaulting Ottoman positions in Hungary and along the Adriatic coast. Mehmed had trouble feeding his troops, and they overthrew him in September 1687, marking yet another removal of a sultan. By 1699, the Ottomans found themselves ejected from Hungary, which became a Habsburg possession, and they lost parts of Greece to Venice. These were the first territorial losses for the Ottoman Empire since the early 1400s. The empire would regain its footing in the eighteenth century, but never again would it be the equal of the great central and western European powers.

France and the Crisis of the Seventeenth Century

France was one of those powers, although it suffered mightily between 1620 and 1660. The seventeenth century began well enough for Louis XIII, who became king in 1610. His realm's 20 million inhabitants made France the most populous country in Europe, and its fertile agricultural lands gave it an adequate supply of food. But his kingdom was plagued by two problems: its deep religious divisions between the majority Catholic population and the minority Protestants, or Huguenots, and its seemingly perpetual war against Spain.

Although Louis XIII's predecessor, Henry IV, had signed a truce with the Huguenots known as the Edict of Nantes (1598, see Chapter 1), Louis, less tolerant, resolved to deprive them of the territories and cities they controlled. Between 1620 and 1624, Louis integrated the kingdom of Navarre, at the west end of the Pyrenees, into France, in part to reduce the large Protestant presence there. Three years later, Louis and Richelieu laid siege to France's port city La Rochelle, which was, in effect, the Huguenot capital. English forces intervened several times to break the siege but did not succeed. La Rochelle finally surrendered in October 1628. Richelieu's victory left all French Protestants highly vulnerable and strengthened the French state by extending Louis XIII's authority deep into what had been a largely autonomous region of the country.

After defeating the Huguenots, Louis and Richelieu revived France's longstanding conflict with Spain by sending an army into Spanish-controlled northern Italy. But the French found themselves stymied by a weather-induced famine in 1629–1630 and then by an epidemic of bubonic plague. Undeterred, Richelieu continued the war. He also sent large subsidies to the Dutch republic and Sweden, the former allied with France against Spain and the latter leading the thirty-year-long fight against the Holy Roman Empire. These subsidies, to say nothing of France's own warfare, cost a fortune and required Richelieu to raise taxes dramatically. This move evoked a great deal of domestic unrest, especially in 1631, when another famine gripped the country. Taxes continued to rise after France stepped up its war against Spain in the mid-1630s, and with each increase, more rebellions flared—fourteen urban insurrections in 1635 as opposed to six a few years earlier. In 1637, the combination of bad weather, higher taxation, and the increasingly aggressive recruitment of French soldiers produced one of the largest rural rebellions in French history: the **Croquants** of the southwest.

"Croquant" can be loosely translated as "hayseed" or "bumpkin," derogatory terms that the peasant rebels never used. They referred to themselves as "the people" or "the communes," meaning all the villagers of a particular region. In general, French peasants willingly paid what they considered "just and reasonable" taxes, but they became incensed when imposts suddenly rose high above reasonable levels. Peasants especially hated the people who came into their communities to forcibly collect taxes, which the cash-poor peasants paid by giving up cattle and pigs or the seeds destined for the following year's crop. Livestock and seeds were precious; transferring them to the state threatened their livelihood and sometimes their lives.

Beginning in 1636, peasants responded to these tax collections by banding together in an ad hoc army. These armies were led by local priests, judges, and lower-ranking nobles from the region. The peasant fighters were hostile not to the king, who had been duped, they falsely believed, by his advisors, but to the government officials charged with collecting their money. The Croquant army seized as many of these officials as they could and often treated them brutally, hanging them and dismembering their bodies. To discourage future tax collectors, Croquants pinned severed body parts to doorways and other visible places.

The Croquant rebellion reached its height in 1637, when the government raised the *taille*, the main land tax, by 33 percent. By early May, the rebels had coalesced into an ad hoc militia of 30,000 armed with pikes, pitchforks, and muskets. Their objective was to take Bordeaux, the largest city in southwestern France, after occupying smaller cities like Bergerac along the way. From Bergerac, the Croquants demanded that all tax collectors be punished and that the region's defunct representative assembly, the Estates of Périgord, be revived. The insurgent army constituted a serious threat to the king's effort to centralize power, and he launched a royal army against them. Louis XIII's battle-hardened troops easily overwhelmed the poorly armed Croquants, who suffered 1,500 deaths before scattering into the countryside.

Their rebellion had raised hopes of relieving the peasants' tax burden and of ending military recruitment, but beyond those hopes, the Croquants possessed no coherent ideology or program for political change. They thus did not threaten the existing political order, which, if anything, was reinforced once the Croquant movement unraveled. This did not mean, however, that Louis XIII and Richelieu had vanquished their opposition. In July 1639, less than two years after the Croquants' defeat, a new rebel peasant army emerged. This time, it came from Lower Normandy, which for historical reasons bore a disproportionate share of the kingdom's tax burden and had faced a 500 percent tax increase since 1630. Suddenly, French tax collectors found themselves besieged by a group of workers called the *Nu-pieds* ("barefoot ones"), who, for their living, trudged barefoot on Normandy's beaches collecting salt from the sea.

Poorly paid though they were, the Nu-pieds were required, like everyone in France, to pay a huge tax on salt, even the salt they themselves had harvested. To protest the salt tax, the Nu-pieds killed more than 100 people thought to be tax collectors and formed a new ad hoc army to confront France's regular army sent in to punish them. The Nu-pieds fought valiantly but ultimately lost, although not until the government diverted troops away from its endless war against Spain.

The Fronde

Fortunately for France, Spain had been weakened by its own endless war against the Netherlands and by a rebellion in Portugal. In 1643, Mazarin, Richelieu's successor as chief minister, pushed Spanish forces out of southern France and successfully resisted an invasion from the Spanish Netherlands. But these battles, successful as they were, mired France deeply in debt. The many peasant revolts had reduced tax revenues and forced Mazarin to borrow massively to finance his wars. To repay these loans, the chief minister ordered huge tax increases and sold a plethora of new offices in government.

The Parlement of Paris had the power to question these taxes, but not to block them. This relative impotence made members of the Parlement, along with other elites, extremely unhappy about these imposts, especially after Mazarin eliminated many of their cherished exemptions. Elite Frenchmen became even unhappier in 1648 when the chief minister sent tens of thousands of people to prison for failing to pay their assessments. And they became enraged when he created a host of duplicate offices that diluted the value of those for which these wealthy Frenchmen had paid huge sums of money.

Two key members of the Paris Parlement made strong speeches opposing the new taxes and venal offices, and their words quickly saw print. Circulating throughout the French capital, these speeches convinced many people to stop paying their taxes. At this point, Mazarin had a chance to sign a peace treaty with Spain, but his refusal to do so depleted the French treasury all the more. It did not help that bad weather ruined much of the harvest in 1648 and stirred unrest throughout rural and urban France. When the Parlement alleged that several of Mazarin's creditors had committed fraud, the rest of his lenders refused to offer any more funds for fear of being investigated as well. By mid-1648, the government teetered on the brink of bankruptcy.

Rather than negotiate with the Parlement, Mazarin doubled down by arresting one of his chief critics in the body, a magistrate named Pierre Broussel. His arrest triggered a huge uprising in Paris in which protesters erected more than 1,000 barricades and smashed doors and windows by launching rocks from slingshots called *frondes.* To quiet the rebels, Mazarin released Broussel from prison, only to have him and others print up a large number of anti-Mazarin pamphlets dubbed *Mazarinades.* Several authors of these tracts and other members of the Parisian elite now effectively took over the city in a movement soon known as the *Fronde.*

The *frondeurs* sought relief from high taxation and an end to the absolutist rule established by Louis XIII, Richelieu, and Mazarin, an absolutism that had cost the French elite large sums of money and many of its traditional privileges, especially exemption from key taxes. They also wanted to end the war with Spain, which was a main source of France's dire financial straits. Such was the hostility to Mazarin and Louis XIV's mother Anne that they spirited the boy-king out of Paris before he could be deposed.

Meanwhile, the frondeurs published a blizzard of pamphlets criticizing the crown and demanding major reforms. This material circulated in a country suffering in 1648–1649 from an unusually cruel winter followed by a huge snow melt and torrential rains. Paris flooded, as did the grain belt south of the city. The harvest was partially ruined, and the shortage of gain doubled the price of bread. A single loaf cost more than the average unskilled worked earned in a day. Starvation set in, and angry crowds demanded the ouster of Mazarin. What may have prevented the Fronde from overthrowing him and potentially Louis XIV was the trial and execution of England's King Charles I (see below). This regicide so terrified the

≡ **The Fronde.** A Fronde leader urges Parisians to revolt against Cardinal Mazarin. The Seine, visible in the background, flooded its banks numerous times in the seventeenth century.

elite French people leading the rebellion against Mazarin that the Parlement of Paris decided to drop its opposition to him.

Other nobles, however, kept the rebellion alive, and the Prince of Condé, the head of one of France's greatest noble families, nearly succeeded in replacing Mazarin. In the political chaos that ensued, France experienced another bout of Little Ice Age weather. In February 1651, the Seine overflowed its banks once again, causing widespread misery. The following spring, food prices in southern France reached their highest levels of the century and provoked dozens of rural and urban revolts. Elsewhere, there was flooding, famine, and disease. A group of nobles sympathetic to Condé formed an ad hoc legislature called the Assembly of Nobles, which demanded that Anne convene the Estates General, the kingdom-wide representative assembly that had not met since 1614. Anne promised to take this step but never intended to follow through. Condé had hoped to lead the Estates, and when it became clear that it would not be called, he forged an alliance with King Philip IV of Spain, who promised to help the French prince restore order in his country. In 1652, Condé tried unsuccessfully to take control of Paris, after which his supporters seized the government of Bordeaux and called for the establishment of a republic, as in England.

The radical developments in Bordeaux raised new fears of regicide in France, and those fears allowed Anne and Mazarin to regain control of the situation there. The chief minister attracted enough loans to buy the support of key members of the Parlement and other top noble families. Louis XIV, now age fourteen, returned to Paris and restricted the Parlement's ability to meddle in the affairs of state. Still, Louis faced a powerful new rebellion in Bordeaux, a fronde by Catholic reformers known as Jansenists who were incensed over Mazarin's efforts to have the pope condemn them. Meanwhile, Condé threatened to march on Paris, this time at the head of Spanish troops. Luckily for the young king, the Bordeaux rebellion petered out, as a key Jansenist leader sustained a debilitating injury, and a truce between France and Spain ended Condé's threat. France had come close to revolution, but in the end not close enough. The different frondeurs—magistrates, clergy, nobles, princes, city leaders, and ordinary people—possessed no common or compatible set of ideas and objectives that could hold them together well enough to overthrow the regime. The Fronde subsided, and Louis XIV was poised to rule in his own right.

To avoid any future Frondes, Louis stripped parlements and other institutions of much of their power and resolved not to appoint leading nobles or top religious figures—Richelieu and Mazarin were both noblemen and cardinals of the Catholic Church—to the key positions of state. These posts would go to men of middle-class birth who, unlike top nobles and prelates, would have no ready-made power bases of their own. They would owe their positions and authority entirely to the king. Louis XIV had made his power absolute—or so he thought.

Absolutism and Its Limits

How accurate was Louis XIV's belief in the absolutism of his rule? The French theologian and political philosopher, Jacques-Bénigne Bossuet (1627–1704), made the most celebrated case for the **divine right of kings**, the notion that monarchs ruled absolutely in God's name. But Bossuet added that precisely because kings represented God on earth, they could not do anything they pleased. Their actions were limited by the responsibility to obey God's laws, which prohibited them from treating their subjects arbitrarily—although those subjects had no right to judge or challenge the actions of their king. Louis took his responsibility to God seriously but interpreted that responsibility as he wished. He thus often behaved arbitrarily and intransigently, producing opposition that he could have avoided. The behavior of other European monarchs had the same result, and with their constant wars, they made a great many people suffer cruelly.

Although only minimally constrained by God's laws, Louis faced several earthly checks on his authority. The most important of those checks had to do with money. Constantly short of cash, as we have seen, Louis had to turn the offices of his government into the private property of his wealthiest subjects. Doing so cost him a measure of authority and power. So did his indebtedness to financiers: Louis XIV borrowed more than any French king before or since.

Had Louis XIV avoided some of the five wars he fought from the mid-1660s to 1714, he might have ruled more absolutely than he did.

The Wars of Louis XIV, 1660s to 1714

In 1665, Louis picked a fight with Spain by issuing a false claim to the Spanish Netherlands. Louis sent his army into this territory and met so little Spanish resistance that the neighboring Dutch Republic became alarmed.

≡ **The Chateau of Versailles—Hall of Mirrors.** In this ornate palace, completed in 1682, King Louis XIV presided over some 5,000 of his country's leading nobles and shaped an ambitious, adventurous foreign policy.

Now France and the Netherlands went to war, drawing several nearby states into the conflict. After six years of furious fighting, which spilled over into Italy and the Caribbean, France gained nothing but a few morsels of land on its northeastern border. The costs, however, were staggering, as evidenced by the size of Louis XIV's army. In 1525, the French military numbered about 40,000 men. During the Thirty Years' War, it stood at 125,000, and now in the war against the Dutch, it swelled to 280,000 (peaking at 420,000 in 1697). To pay the costs of men and munitions, Louis's ministers tried to raise taxes, but as usual, they had to exempt members of the elite and divert resources from the foreign wars to domestic efforts to quell revolts by peasants unwilling to pay ever-higher sums. The only way to bring in the needed money was to borrow it by floating new loans, creating new venal offices, and selling titles of nobility outright.

A comparison with Britain highlights just how dysfunctional French government finances were. Although the British economy was about half the size of the French, the British government raised as much money for warfare as its enemy across the English Channel. While France resorted to a series of complex and ultimately self-defeating expedients, the British Parliament came to a consensus over the need to raise funds to finance the wars against France. British elites, for the most part, were not exempt from taxes, and their willingness to shoulder a higher fiscal burden encouraged the rest of the country to do so as well. When the English king needed to borrow money, he issued government bonds called "treasury orders," whose interest and repayment were guaranteed by Parliament. That guarantee gave ordinary people the assurance that loans to their government were a good, safe investment (much as US treasury bills are today), and this public confidence filled the treasury with ample short-term loans at interest rates far lower than those in France.

Rather than acknowledge France's grave fiscal problems and the opposition they produced, Louis XIV blamed the mounting dissidence on two religious groups: Jansenists and especially the Huguenots, whom he decided to tolerate no more. In 1685, he revoked the **Edict of Nantes,** which had allowed French Protestants to worship freely, and ordered the destruction of all Protestant churches. About a hundred and fifty thousand Huguenots fled the country, while several times that many took their religious practices underground. Many of those who left France went to the Netherlands and England, where political and religious leaders proved only too happy to publicize Huguenot condemnations of the cruelty and bigotry of Louis XIV. This anti-French propaganda proved highly useful in steeling the Dutch and English people for the series of wars yet to come.

In the first, the Nine Years' War (1688–1697), the French fought a coalition of German states, the Dutch Republic, and England, the latter two countries now ruled by the same man, the Dutchman William III (1650–1702). The effort to combat several countries on multiple fronts required a massive, unprecedented mobilization of men and resources. It strained the French economy to the breaking point but resulted in few territorial gains. Amid staggering losses on the battlefield, famine haunted the civilian population at home. For a great many of Louis's subjects, the Sun King was now shrouded in clouds.

A measure of light peeked through during five short years of peace (1697–1702). But war loomed once again when the Spanish king died in 1700 and two opposing candidates claimed the right to succeed him. One candidate was the Archduke Charles of Austria, a member of the Habsburg family, and the other was Philip of Anjou, a member of the Bourbon family and grandson of Louis XIV. Each claimed so much from the Spanish succession as to put Europe's fragile balance of power at risk. European leaders tried to hammer out a compromise that would limit Habsburg and Bourbon gains and preserve the European balance, but intransigence in several quarters kept a general agreement out of reach. The answer, once again, was war.

This new conflict, the **War of the Spanish Succession**, lasted twelve years (1702–1714) and nearly shattered Louis XIV's reputation for good. It cost tens of thousands of lives on all sides and engulfed not only Europe but the Caribbean Islands and parts of India and North America as well. It contributed to widespread famine in Europe and turned people everywhere against their governments. Finally, in 1713–1714, the exhausted European powers came to the kind of agreement they should have reached a dozen years earlier. In the treaties of Utrecht and Rastatt, named after the Dutch and German towns where negotiations took place, Philip of Anjou, now dubbed Philip V of Spain, received the Spanish throne and its New World possessions but gave up his claim to succeed Louis XIV as king of France. Meanwhile, Archduke Charles of Austria, newly elected Holy Roman Emperor, renounced his claim to the Spanish throne and received in compensation most Spanish territories in Italy and the Netherlands (see Map 3.3).

Although Louis XIV did not succeed in making his grandson heir to his throne, he nonetheless clawed his way back from a series of humiliating defeats in the 1700s, recapturing small territories on France's eastern and northern borders. But Louis XIV's efforts to dominate the European continent had failed, and his half-century of wars had inflicted terrible suffering on his people and mountains of debt and administrative dysfunction on his state. Ironically, the "absolutist" power that had enabled Louis XIV to pull his country into war after war left the French monarchy in a severely weakened state.

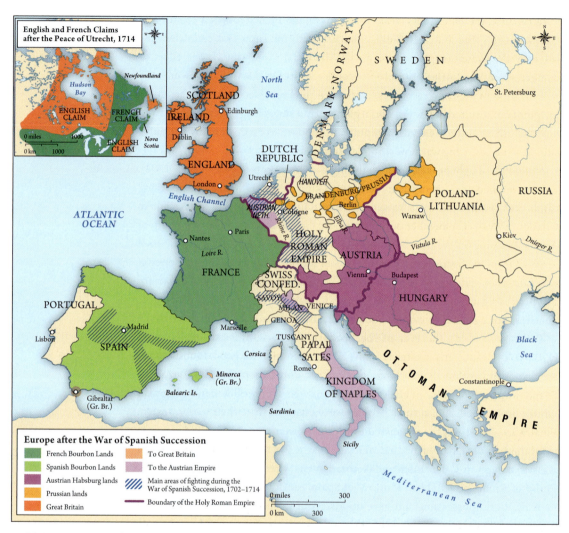

≡ **MAP 3.3**   Europe after the War of the Spanish Succession

England's Road to Revolution and Civil War

When James I became king in 1603, he too claimed to be an absolute ruler. But overspending forced him to go to Parliament for additional funds, and this financial vulnerability allowed the legislative body to wrest a measure of power from the monarchy. Over the next two decades, the balance of power continued to shift, albeit subtly, in Parliament's direction. In 1621 King James called the body into session to approve taxes to finance England's participation in the Thirty Years' War. The MPs, gripped by anti-Spanish and anti-Catholic fervor, not only granted the taxes but drew up a petition requesting war with Spain and proposing that the king's son Charles (1600–1649) be married to a Protestant. Until now, it had been generally understood that Parliament did not participate directly in the framing of foreign policy and especially not in creating royal marriage alliances. But Parliament was becoming increasingly assertive and independent, and both James and Charles felt their kingly prerogatives under attack. James sharply denounced the petition, and Parliament shot back by accusing him of violating their free speech, "the ancient and undoubted birthright … of the subjects of England." In response, the king angrily dissolved Parliament, forfeiting the funds for war. This unexpected peace turned out to be a blessing in disguise: the El Niño weather of 1621 dumped torrential rains on much of England, ruining the harvest and producing severe shortages of food.

Unable to fight Spain, James decided to make peace by offering to marry Charles to the daughter of the Spanish king, Philip IV. When negotiations with Philip IV broke down, James quickly substituted a similar arrangement with France, and Charles now wedded Louis XIII's sister, Henrietta Maria (1609–1669). The Catholic marriage already aroused opposition among Parliament's leaders, Protestants all; they were outraged when Charles agreed to allow Henrietta Maria to practice her Catholic religion and raise her children, Charles' heirs, in the faith. To key MPs, the danger was clear: Catholicism could be restored as England's dominant religion. When Charles became king in 1625 and attempted to conduct foreign policy without convening Parliament, the rift between him and leading MPs widened into a chasm of mutual hostility.

In 1628, Parliament drew up a Petition of Right, whose purpose was to wrest power away from the king. The Petition declared that the monarch could not impose taxes without Parliament's consent or imprison English subjects arbitrarily, both of which Charles believed to be well within his royal rights. In response, the king dissolved Parliament, which he had done regularly since assuming the throne. Charles also launched wars against Spain and France, whose costs made the kingdom's debts soar to four times its revenues. Charles's efforts to derive funds from sources beyond Parliament—excise taxes, loans, import and export duties—angered MPs and the public at large, widening the cleavage between king and Parliament and causing unrest around the country. Bad weather associated with the Little Ice Age exacerbated the turmoil, as floods devastated crops in 1629 and extreme cold ruined the harvest in 1630, 1632, 1633, and 1635. The 1630s turned out to be the coldest decade in 800 years. Adding to the misery, a series of droughts took a bitter toll in 1634, 1636, and 1637. Charles got through the decade by refusing to call Parliament into session, and most important, by generally staying out of the Thirty Years' War.

English Protestantism Divides in Two

Still, this long, terrible war had revived the English Protestants' longstanding antagonisms against their Catholic countrymen, as had Charles's marriage to a Catholic princess. But even more than the disputes between Protestants and Catholics, it was the religious battles within Protestantism that set the country on edge. Beginning in the early seventeenth century, clergymen trained at Oxford and Cambridge universities rejected the Calvinist ideas about predestination dominant until then in **Anglicanism**, England's official version of Protestantism. These clergymen feared that if people believed God had chosen only a small "elect" for salvation, the majority of people, considering themselves damned in advance, would see no point in attending church, performing the sacraments, and obeying their priests. To counter this danger, opponents of predestination, known as Arminians after the Dutch Reformed theologian Jacobus Arminius (1560–1609), urged clergymen to attract people to church with beautiful, elaborate rituals and awe-inspiring cathedrals, their religious services highlighted by sermons couched in soaring, emotional language.

These ideas horrified English **Puritans**, for whom elaborate ritual and sumptuous cathedrals were sacrilegious and smacked of Catholicism. Puritans already worried about King Charles I's "papist" tendencies and loathed the Arminian theologian William Laud (1573–1645), whom Charles had named Archbishop of Canterbury, England's highest religious post. As England's religious leader, Laud purged the ministry of Puritan preachers and took control over book licensing, which enabled him to censor the press. Clergymen who defied him found themselves subject to heavy fines and even hauled before the Star Chamber, a secret court that imposed gruesome punishments such as cutting off people's ears and branding them with hot irons. A number of Puritan leaders and ordinary believers fled to America to escape Laud's religious oppression and harsh justice.

≡ **Puritans.** These Protestant purists disliked elaborate religious ritual and thought England's sumptuous Anglican cathedrals smacked of Catholicism. Puritans considered William Laud, King Charles I's Archbishop of Canterbury, a papist.

The combination of repression and emigration enabled Laud to maintain his power in England, although his religious authoritarianism, along with Charles's apparent desire to rule without Parliament, produced a great deal of disaffection. Opposition broke into the open when the king and his archbishop tried to impose Arminian reforms in Scotland, where Charles also ruled, but where a strict Calvinism had long held sway. Thousands rioted in the streets, and their leaders adopted a National Covenant that rejected the king's religious reforms and declared the independence of the Scottish Church (the Kirk) and, implicitly, of the Scottish people, from English rule.

In response, Charles led an invasion force into Scotland, which an ad hoc Scottish army promptly defeated, thanks to the king's inexperience as a military leader and clever strategy by the Scots. In addition, many English soldiers proved reluctant to fight against fellow Protestants from Scotland, who shared many of their own grievances against a now unpopular king. Facing what appeared to be a national emergency, Charles convened a new Parliament and asked it to approve funds to turn back the Scottish advance. Parliament, however, imposed strict conditions on the appropriation, and rather than agree to them, Charles dissolved this "Short Parliament," as it came to be known, after three weeks.

Charles then convened a "Long Parliament," destined to remain in session from November 1640 to April 1653, an unprecedented period of time. But it, too, made clear that there would be no funds until the king stopped imposing taxes without Parliament's consent, dropped the persecution of Puritans, and dismissed the royal favorites—hand-picked assistants on whom he had showered wealth and influence. With Scottish forces encamped in northern England and a great many English in sympathy with them, Parliament held the upper hand. Charles was powerless to prevent the impeachment of Archbishop Laud and the execution of his favorite and principal advisor, the Earl of Strafford (1593–1641). Like the Russian tsar and Ottoman sultan, Charles was forced by his opponents to sacrifice his chief lieutenants.

Strafford's execution, along with a so-called Army Plot in which Charles threatened to use military force against Parliament, created a climate of fear and anxiety in which people on both sides detected assassination plots and political conspiracies everywhere. This highly fraught emotional climate was exacerbated by the climate rigors of the Little Ice Age: the late 1630s and early 1640s were plagued by frigid weather, crop failures, and the resulting shortages of food.

The miserable weather had also contributed to Charles's defeat at the hands of Scotland, and now he faced a rebellion in Ireland. In the fall of 1641, Catholic insurgents seized key parts of the country and demanded political and religious freedom from their Protestant overlords. The fighting was murderous in itself, and the especially rigorous winter made things immeasurably worse. Catholic forces punished the Protestants seen as exploiting them by stripping them of their clothes and forcing them, naked, into the snow and bitter cold. The number of deaths from exposure to the elements exceeded that of the actual fighting, even though the combat involved gruesome atrocities on both sides.

Protestant leaders in England accused the king of supporting the Catholic side in the Irish struggle, and a group of MPs tried to raise an army to put the Irish rebellion down. But John Pym, who had emerged as Parliament's leader, vetoed the idea, fearing that Charles would turn the army against him and his supporters. The king then decided to raise a fighting force without the MPs' consent, and Parliament responded by creating an army of its own. By mid-1642, what were now two armed camps, **royalist** and **parliamentary**, faced off against each other, and the country braced for civil war.

The English Civil War

Over the next several years, the two sides battled each other to stalemate—at great cost in blood and treasure. About one in eight English men fought in one army or the other, and about 250,000 people—4 percent of the population of England, Scotland, and Wales—lost their lives. The number of casualties as a proportion of the overall population was probably higher than in any other British conflict until the First World War. Exacerbating the human toll were poor harvests in Scotland and Ireland that led to "so cruel a famine," as one contemporary put it, "which hath already killed thousands of the poorer sort."

On the surface, the main cause of the fratricidal conflict was the struggle for political supremacy between the king and Parliament. But perhaps more important were the deep religious divisions that shook England to its core and set that country on a collision course with Scotland and Ireland. In England, the royalist side came to identify itself with Anglicanism, the form of Protestantism established by Queen Elizabeth and reshaped by Archbishop Laud. The parliamentary side, hostile as a whole to Laud's authoritarian "papist" church, was nonetheless divided into two opposing tendencies, Presbyterians and Independents. The former advocated a centralized church and the latter a decentralized religious institution under local control. As the civil war continued, Presbyterians came to dominate Parliament, and Independents reigned in the army.

These religious and political conflicts produced a blizzard of pamphlets and other printed materials, as each side sought to make its case. Under these circumstances, royal censorship disappeared, and English men and women enjoyed an unprecedented freedom of expression. In 1639, England saw the publication of just one newspaper; three years later, there were more than sixty. The active public debate gave England a degree of popular democracy that it would not experience again until the twentieth century.

Amid this public contestation, the military conflict continued unabated. The war finally ended when **Oliver Cromwell** (1599–1658), a brilliant young general, routed Charles's army in June 1645. Presbyterian leaders in Parliament now tried to reduce the army's influence by sending part of it to Ireland and disbanding the rest. But most members of the **New Model Army**, as the parliamentary force now called itself, wanted to remain in England and in uniform, at least until they received their back pay. Soldiers marched to London, where they fraternized with radical groups such as the **Levellers**, whose demands for civil rights and religious toleration accorded with those of the radicalized New Model Army.

To battle these radical soldiers, Charles raised a new army of his own, allied this time with Scottish forces that also opposed the New Model Army. In this new conflict, known as the Second Civil War (1648), Cromwell soundly defeated the Scottish troops, while another parliamentary army trounced Charles's royalist force. But Cromwell's victory, instead of gaining the support of Parliament and the people, aroused widespread sympathy for Charles. The New Model Army was increasingly seen as brutal and arrogant, while English men and women professed to remember the gentleness of the king. Feeling betrayed, leaders of the New Model Army purged Parliament of its Presbyterian majority. The result was a "Rump Parliament" whose leaders, all Independents, charged the king with treason for conducting a war against his own people. Some members tried to head off a guilty verdict by negotiating secretly with Charles, but he refused all compromise. Treason carried the death penalty, and the magistrates who took up the case ruled that the king be taken "to the place of execution, where his head should be severed from his body." In a public ceremony on January 30, 1649, an executioner chopped off his head.

The English Revolution

We have seen that Ottoman sultans regularly killed aspirants to the throne and that contenders killed potential competitors. In two cases, reigning sultans were murdered. In France, kings were assassinated in the sixteenth and seventeenth centuries, while the young Louis XIV had to flee Paris for his life. But the execution of the

≡ **The Execution of Charles I.** In January 1649, England's revolutionary "Rump Parliament" indicted Charles for treason, and a newly created High Court sentenced him to death. The execution shocked a great many English people and polarized a deeply divided country all the more.

English king was unprecedented in European history. The act was revolutionary in the modern sense of the term, since Charles was stripped of his royal sanctity and charged with treason, as if he were an ordinary man. His supporters considered this charge absurd, since, in their view, Charles incarnated England and could not commit treason against himself. But Charles's opponents not only dethroned him before taking his life, but effectively abolished the monarchy itself, albeit temporarily.

Charles's conviction and execution thus represented a complete break from the past, a break that some believed would turn England into a "new Jerusalem," a nation governed by saints dedicated to building a perfect heaven on earth. Some of those who held such beliefs thought the way to achieve this earthly Kingdom of God was to give everyone the right to vote. Others wanted to do away with churches, ministers, and services and accepted no earthly authority—only God's. Still others wanted to create a Christian commonwealth by abolishing commerce and private property and distributing land to the poor. Elizabeth Lilburne (died 1660), wife of a Leveller leader, led a fight for women's rights.

These radical, utopian projects alienated most English men and women, including the majority of the purged Parliament. They wanted not a New Jerusalem but rather to live in an orderly society that allowed individuals to enjoy basic liberties without turning society upside down or encouraging what they considered religious zealotry. Having made himself England's leader, Cromwell somehow had to reconcile his country's opposing religious and political tempers; he mostly did so by having his large standing army impose order, sometimes arbitrarily and with force. Eventually, Cromwell seized dictatorial powers in an effort to keep his fragmented country intact. In Ireland, his military dictatorship turned into conquest pure and simple, as the English army subdued and then colonized the country, plundering its people and evicting tens of thousands of Irish from their lands.

The Restoration

Cromwell's death in 1658 doomed his shaky regime, and it fell less than two years later. Charles II (1630–1685), the son of the executed king, assumed the throne. To mark the end of the English Revolution, royalists unearthed Cromwell's body, chopped it to pieces, and stuck his head on a pole outside Parliament's meeting place, where it stood for twenty-five years. The new regime was called a "restoration," but it did not turn back the clock to the 1630s; too much had changed during the two decades of civil war and revolution. Parliament had emerged stronger than ever before, as had the Anglican Church, although it no longer held a monopoly over English religious life. Religious Dissenters—Baptists, Quakers, Presbyterians—were here to stay.

The English government changed dramatically as well, becoming sounder financially and more efficient than ever before. The new Treasury Order, as we have seen, gave the state a relatively inexpensive way to obtain credit, and revenues soared after reformers placed tax collection in the hands of salaried officials rather than tax farmers. These developments did not mean, however, that relations between Charles II and Parliament were harmonious or that religious passions had been stilled.

When the king's brother and heir, the future James II (1633–1701), publicly converted to Catholicism in 1673, Charles faced a powerful resurgence of anti-Catholic feeling, fueled all the more by the king's efforts to forge a military alliance with Catholic France. Leading MPs claimed that a vast "Popish Plot" threatened to destroy the country and introduced a bill designed to exclude James from the royal succession. Their bill created an "exclusion crisis" and reordered English politics by creating the two opposing political parties, Whigs and Tories, destined to confront each other for the next 150 years. The Whigs came together to prevent James from inheriting the throne, while the Tories remained loyal to the Stuart monarchy, James as well as Charles.

Despite the Whigs' resistance, James II succeeded his brother as king in 1685. When his Catholic wife, Queen Mary Beatrice, gave birth to a son in June 1688, opposition to him reached a fever pitch. Now, James had a Catholic heir and the potential to restore Catholicism in England. What is more, he was planning to ally with Louis XIV in a new war against the Dutch. To block a powerful Anglo-French alliance against his country, the Dutch stadtholder William of Orange prepared an invasion

Glorious Revolution. This dramatic event deposed England's quasi-Catholic King James II and imported a Dutch Protestant nobleman to take his place. The revolution forbade Catholics to occupy the English throne and increased the powers of Parliament at the monarchy's expense.

of England. He did so in collaboration with key English Whigs, who at William's request had "invited" the Dutchman to "investigate the state of English liberties." William did not come alone. Accompanying him were some twenty thousand troops and a fleet of five hundred ships. In effect, the Whigs, together with a large share of England's military and naval commanders, encouraged a foreign invasion of their homeland to block a potential Catholic restoration and a Catholic alliance with France against the Protestant Dutch.

After two of James's top generals switched sides, the already feeble opposition to William collapsed, and England was under his control. But what legitimacy did he enjoy? James was still king, and his baby son (James III) was his heir. Neither William nor his wife, Mary Stuart (1662–1694), the daughter of James II, had a rightful claim to the throne, even though much of the English elite, as well as ordinary people, wanted to put them on it. To do so, parliamentary leaders declared that James II had broken his contract with his people (even though no contract had ever existed) and that he had "abdicated the government; and [left] the throne … vacant," neither of which was true.

By deposing James and anointing William and Mary as the joint rulers of the Kingdoms of England, Scotland, and Ireland, Parliament's Whig leaders had carried out a revolution, a revolution by—and largely for—English Protestant elites. It would be known as the **Glorious Revolution of 1688–1689**, a political transformation that barred Catholics from the throne, strengthened the powers of Parliament, and limited, though far from eliminated, those of the king.

In accepting the throne, William and Mary agreed to a new Bill of Rights that enshrined the people's ability, through Parliament, to petition their government, consent to taxation, bear arms, enjoy protection from cruel and unusual punishment, and vote freely (although not democratically). These rights turned William and Mary and their heirs into constitutional monarchs who governed jointly with Parliament.

William and Mary, like the four kings who had preceded them, ruled England and Scotland as two separate kingdoms. But under strong pressure from English leaders, the Scottish Parliament agreed in 1707 to merge with its English counterpart and meet from then on in London. In effect, Scotland had united with England and Wales in a new political entity known as Great Britain. (Ireland would not be invited to join until nearly a century later.) The new enlarged kingdom was set to play a dominant role on the world stage, thanks to its modernized bureaucracy, revolutionary system of public finance, constitutional government, and the colonies in Asia, North America, and the Caribbean that would add handsomely to its wealth.

Conclusion: Global Cooling and Its Turbulent Effects

People living in the seventeenth century experienced a dizzying array of crises: near-constant warfare—including devastating religious and civil wars—along with revolutions, insurrections, regicides, and the regular murder or execution of grand viziers, chief ministers, royal favorites, and religious leaders. These deadly, chaotic events took place against the backdrop of a dramatic global cooling whose extreme weather patterns ranged from freak summer frosts to hard winter freezes. The thick, encrusted ice enabled entire armies to thunder over bodies of water that, in normal times, would not have withstood a family of four (see Map 3.4 and the table following it). Rivers that normally flooded once or twice a century now overflowed their banks

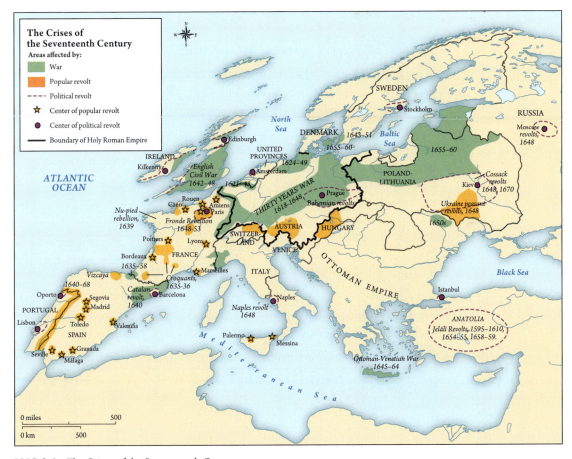

MAP 3.4   The Crises of the Seventeenth Century

The Little Ice Age in Europe, 1590–1684	
1590–1650	Climate-induced food shortages lead to 40 to 50 percent decline in population in many parts of the Ottoman Empire
1600–1700	The Seine River floods eighteen times; London records twice as many burials as births
1601–1613	Famines in Russia reduce population by as much as 25 percent
1608	Thames River freezes over; would do so ten times in the eighteenth century
1620–1621	Bosporus Sea separating Europe from Asia freezes over; heavy rains destroy harvest in England
1622–1623	Bubonic plague strikes Istanbul
1628	Temperatures throughout Europe are so persistently cold that it was "the year without a summer"
1629–1631	France ravaged by famine and bubonic plague
1630	Istanbul reels from drought and famine
1630s–1640s	Repeated droughts and crop failures throughout Europe; England suffers coldest decade in 800 years
1640–1650	Egypt suffers from extreme drought
1641	Scandinavia endures the coldest average temperatures in history
1641–1648	Famine grips Ukraine due to cold weather, excessive snow, and flooding
c. 1645	Stargazers record, on average, just one sunspot a year
1644–1648	Locusts and premature frosts destroy the harvests in Russia
1651	Southern France does not see a single drop of rain for the entire year
1655–1660	Poland suffers from bitter cold and bouts of bubonic plague
1657–1658	Swedish army assaults the Danish capital Copenhagen by marching across the frozen Baltic Sea
1659–1660	Ottoman Empire suffers most severe drought in a thousand years
1683–1684	"Great Frost" in England; Thames River completely frozen for two months

every five to ten years, while the Nile, whose expected floods irrigated the desert, all too often barely lapped over its rim. The result was severe food shortages, and even famine, not to mention epidemic diseases fueled by the weakened immune systems of malnourished people. Many of the worst consequences of the Little Ice Age clustered around the mid-seventeenth century, which witnessed a series of earth-shaking events: the murder of the Ottoman sultan (1648), the existential threats against the French monarchy (1648), the near collapse of Russia's tsarist regime (1648), and the execution of the English king (1649).

It would be wrong to say that the global cooling of this time *caused* the political upheavals experienced in almost every region of the globe. But it is likely that the effects of the Little Ice Age set people on edge and exacerbated the political, religious, and social conflicts of this turbulent time. Had weather patterns been normal, it seems reasonable to suppose that some of the conflicts would have been avoided and that others would have been less severe. The environment matters, even if it is global cooling, rather than the global warming more familiar today.

We know a great deal about the environmental conditions of the seventeenth century in large part because of the intense effort of those years to understand the workings of the earth and the planetary system to which our world belongs. This quest for understanding led to great advances in science, many of which occurred amid the turmoil of the seventeenth century, and eventually to the explosion of knowledge and thought known as the Enlightenment. We will turn to science and Enlightenment in Chapter 4.

KEY TERMS

Anglicanism   *132*

courtiers   *100*

Croquants   *123*

divine right of kings   *127*

Edict of Nantes   *128*

El Niño   *107*

Fronde   *99*

Glorious Revolution of
1688–1689   *138*

Great Trouble   *101*

Intendants   *99*

Levellers   *135*

Little Ice Age   *103*

magnates   *99*

New Model Army   *135*

Oliver Cromwell   *135*

parliamentary   *134*

Puritans   *132*

royalist   *134*

War of the Spanish
Succession   *129*

For digital learning resources, please go to **https://www.oup.com/he/berenson2e**. Turn to the back of the book to see the list of primary sources and writing exercises provided in the accompanying *Sources and Guided Writing Exercises for Europe in the Modern World*

Science and Enlightenment, 1600–1789

Galileo

Galileo Galilei (1564–1642) epitomized the new scientific methods of the seventeenth century, especially empiricism and experimentation. These methods involved the effort to understand the natural world through direct human observation rather than the dogmas established by philosophers and the Catholic Church. Galileo came from an accomplished—if impoverished—family, and like many gifted boys in this situation, he entered a monastery and prepared to become a monk. After completing his secondary schooling at the monastery, Galileo decided the religious vocation was not for him and entered the University of Pisa in 1581, where he studied medicine and mathematics. These were important fields but less esteemed than theology and "natural philosophy," the study of the natural world or what we now call "science."

Natural philosophy had been dominated since the thirteenth century by a Christianized version of the writings of the ancient Greek philosopher Aristotle (384–322 BCE), whose views had congealed into a rigid orthodoxy during the Middle Ages. When Galileo arrived at the University of Pisa, he necessarily entered into a world of Aristotelian belief grounded in a set of maxims and understandings that philosophers dogmatically embraced.

Aristotelians believed that everything that existed in the world and the heavens was already known. The task of philosophers was to explain why those known things appeared to us the way they do and why they exhibit the behavior and actions we observe. Their explanations came not from experimentation, but from a set of already established principles. For example, heavy objects fall because they seek their "natural" place on the earth, while light objects such as air and fire rise.

In distinguishing between things that fall and things that rise, Aristotle identified four elements: earth, water, air, and fire. The first two possess "gravity," which explains why they fall when displaced above their natural location, and the latter two possess "levity," which explains why they ascend when unnaturally situated on the ground.

Aristotle based the existence and properties of these elements on the idea that the earth occupies the center of the universe. Heavy objects fall toward that center and light ones rise away from it. Aristotelians knew that the earth occupied the center because contemplation of the heavens had shown that the sun,

moon, planets, and stars—all perfect spheres—moved at regular, predictable speeds around it and always in a perfect circular motion. These heavenly objects, Aristotle reasoned, had to differ, in their essence, from earthly phenomena, which were often irregular, unpredictable, and ephemeral. What loomed above the earth could not, therefore, be composed of any of the four terrestrial elements. Instead, heavenly bodies were all made of a single element, which Aristotle called "aether," a substance that produced neither gravity nor levity but rather perpetual circular motion. Because the motion of the heavens seemed so perfectly regular, Aristotle believed that nothing about them ever changed. That is, there could be no planets, moons, or stars beyond those that already existed, which meant those that appeared to the naked eye.

These Aristotelian ideas dominated the European universities of Galileo's time to such an extent that it was difficult to think outside of them. But even as a student, the young Galileo realized that certain of these ancient ideas did not pass muster. He noticed, for example, that hailstones of very different sizes hit the ground at the same time, and thus disputed Aristotle's widely accepted notion that the bigger and heavier an object, the faster it fell.

The observation of hailstones constituted a rudimentary empirical test, an effort to see what happened in the natural world. The next step was to make precise measurements of natural phenomena. Philosophers had known since the fourteenth century that bodies accelerate as they fall, and Galileo hoped to find a mathematical formula that would express this acceleration by using empirical techniques. His method was ingenious: he figured out how to slow movement enough to make it measurable. He placed

How Galileo Measured Acceleration. Galileo observed that all unimpeded falling bodies accelerated at the same rate, but to measure that acceleration he had to slow the falling objects down. He did so by placing a ball on a gently sloping plane and timing its movement with a pendulum. He demonstrated that the speed of an accelerating body increases in direct relation to time and that the distance it travels increases in relation to time squared.

Timeline

| 1600 | 1620 | 1640 | 1660 | 1680 | 1700 | 1720 | 1740 | 1760 | 1780 | 1800 |

1610 Galileo's *Starry Messenger*

1632 Galileo's *Dialogue Concerning the Two Chief Systems of the World—Ptolemaic and Copernican*

1637 René Descartes' *Discourse on Method*

1651 Thomas Hobbes' *The Leviathan*

1660 Royal Society of London founded

1687 Isaac Newton's *Mathematical Principles of Natural Philosophy*

1689 John Locke's *Second Treatise on Government*

1739 Sophia's *Woman Not Inferior to Man*

1740–1786 Reign of Frederick the Great of Prussia

1748 Montesquieu's *The Spirit of the Laws*

1751–1772 Publication of *Encyclopedia*

1757 David Hume's *Natural History of Religion*

1759 Adam Smith's *The Theory of Moral Sentiments* and Voltaire's *Candide*

1762 Rousseau's *Emile: or On Education* and *The Social Contract*

1762–1796 Reign of Catherine the Great of Russia

1763–1783 Publication of Macaulay's *History of England*

1776 Adam Smith's *The Wealth of Nations*

1779 David Hume's *Dialogues Concerning Natural Religion*

1780–1790 Reign of Joseph II of Austria

1787 Mary Wollstonecraft's *Thoughts on the Education of Daughters*

1791 Olympe de Gouges' "The Declaration of the Rights of Woman and the Female Citizen"

1792 Wollstonecraft's *A Vindication of the Rights of Woman*

a ball on a gently sloping plane and marked its positions at intervals of about a half-second, timed by a pendulum. This experiment demonstrated that speed increases in direct relation to time and that distance increases in relation to time squared. That is, in ten seconds, the ball's speed will have increased by a factor of 10 and it will have moved 100 units of distance (Galileo used millimeters). When he tried planes with different angles of incline, he obtained the same result, thus confirming the original test.

From this experiment, Galileo extrapolated, correctly, to all falling bodies: the distance fallen would always be the square of the time elapsed and speed would increase in direct relation to time. Galileo had derived a mathematical rule from an experimental procedure, a process at odds with traditional Greek views that divorced mathematics, supposedly a realm of abstract perfection, from the operations of the material world.

In experimenting with descending objects, Galileo broke with Aristotelian orthodoxy not only by using an empirical method but also by asking a non-Aristotelian question. He wanted to know not *why* things fall, the question Aristotelians had asked and answered—falsely in Galileo's view—but rather *how fast*. Galileo's question was mathematical, rather than philosophical; its answer provided useful information about the world.

Galileo proved to be a brilliant mathematician, and even without earning an academic degree, he was appointed professor of mathematics at the prestigious University of Pisa in 1589. While teaching there, Galileo became interested in tides, and that interest pointed him to the heavens and the study of astronomy, a field in which Aristotelian philosophers had established a set of clear-cut, unalterable truths.

Two letters of 1597 suggest that, by that date, Galileo had come to believe that the apparent movement of the moon, planets, sun, and stars made sense only when understood from the startlingly new perspective of Nicolaus Copernicus (1473–1543). A Polish cleric and astronomer, Copernicus believed that the sun, not the earth, occupied the center of our planetary system and that the earth, like the other planets, revolved around the sun. Copernicus's views were radical, even blasphemous, and although the Danish astronomer Tycho Brahe (1546–1601) advanced a compromise between the Aristotelian and Copernican understandings of the planetary system, Galileo—like his contemporary, Johannes Kepler (1571–1630)—believed Copernicus was right.

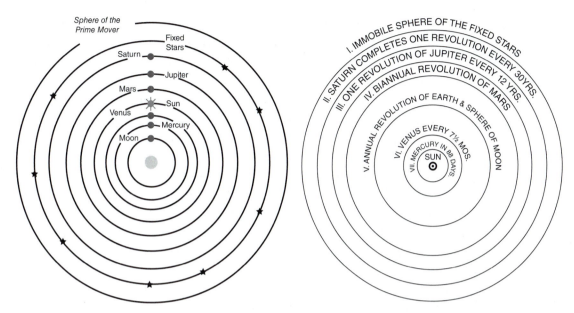

≡ **Aristotle versus Copernicus.** Aristotle posited a universe with a stationary earth at its center surrounded by a moon and planets that circled it in fixed orbits (left). The stars were plastered, immobile, onto the heavens. Copernicus, by contrast, placed the sun at the center of a solar system whose planets, including the earth, revolved around it in circular orbits (right).

Copernicus did not possess the scientific instruments needed to prove that the planets revolved around the sun; he simply advanced a hypothesis to this effect based on the observations of planetary movements that he and other astronomers had made. But Tycho imagined a more complicated version of the traditional geocentric (earth-centered) heavenly map in which every planet but the earth revolved around the sun, which then dragged all five planets with it in orbit around an immobile earth. Tycho backed his view with a series of measurements made with instruments he had created, but his model seemed needlessly cumbersome. In addition, as Kepler demonstrated, Tycho's model could not account for the fact that Mars, in particular, appeared to move at varying speeds.

For Kepler, the data showed that not only did all the planets, including earth, have to revolve around the sun, but the very planetary speeds and trajectories Tycho had documented meant that the shape of each planet's orbit had to be an **ellipse** (oval). In correctly substituting an elliptical orbit for the circular ones taken for granted for more than two thousand years—including in Copernicus's heliocentric

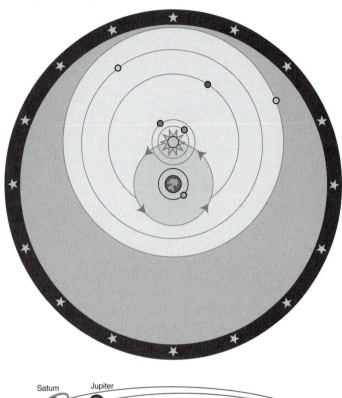

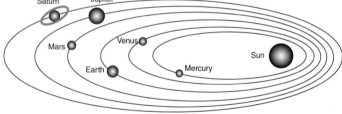

≡ **Tycho Brahe versus Kepler.** Tycho Brahe proposed a complex planetary system in which every planet but the earth revolved around the sun, which then dragged the five known planets with it around the earth (top). Kepler showed that Tycho's schema could not account for the movement of Mars and that all planets, including the earth, revolved around the sun in elliptical, rather than circular, orbits (bottom).

(sun-centered) model—Kepler made almost as much a break with the past as had his Polish predecessor. Even more important, Kepler anticipated Isaac Newton in suggesting that planets moved not of their own volition, as Aristotle had thought, but because they were pulled by a magnetic force emanating from the sun.

The elliptical orbit was for Galileo yet another nail in the coffin of the Aristotelian approach. In adopting the Copernican system, as modified by Kepler, Galileo disputed the very structure of the Aristotelian universe—and with it, most of Aristotle's fundamental tenets. If, for example, the earth was just one planet among many, it could not be true that it consisted of "elements" entirely different from the lone element—aether—that comprised the sun, moon, planets and stars. Logically, all these bodies must be made of at least some of the materials found on earth. Similarly, the mathematical principles of motion that Galileo discovered must apply everywhere, not solely to our own planet.

When Galileo made these arguments at the beginning of the seventeenth century, he possessed no empirical proof that Copernicus and Kepler were right. In fact, to most people their ideas seemed patently absurd. Everyone knew from daily experience that the earth stood still; otherwise, you would be able to *feel* its motion, just as sailors could feel the motion of a moving ship. Besides, everyone could see by looking at the sky that the heavens moved. In 1600, there were perhaps a dozen people in all of Europe who believed in a heliocentric planetary system. One of them, the Italian philosopher Giordano Bruno (1548–1600), was burned at the stake.

Under these circumstances, Galileo understood that he would be able to convince others of the truth of the Copernican system only when he could demonstrate that truth empirically. To this end, Galileo began to experiment with an instrument of Dutch origins that made distant objects appear closer. In 1605 he built a spyglass capable of spotting ships hours before they came into port, and by 1609 he had created what he dubbed a "telescope," a device whose curved lenses magnified distant objects by a factor of twenty. This instrument allowed Galileo to see the heavens as no one had seen them before, and what he observed allowed him to confirm Copernicus's key ideas about the nature and structure of the solar system. The telescope—and the phenomena it revealed—so impressed Grand Duke Cosimo II de' Medici, the ruler of Florence, that he made Galileo his official court mathematician.

Galileo's observations, along with Cosimo's patronage, gave the astronomer the confidence to publish his work, and the book that resulted, the *Starry Messenger* (1610), created a sensation. The literate public found the book fascinating, but Aristotelian philosophers were determined to destroy it. They dismissed the objects that appeared in the lens as optical illusions and Galileo as a fraud. It is notable that the *Starry Messenger* evoked far more hostility from academic philosophers than from officers of the Church. But as Galileo's fame spread and Europe's educated elite became familiar with his critique of the Aristotelian worldview, certain clergymen became concerned. In December 1614, a Dominican monk named Thomas Caccini gave a sermon that denounced Galileo for contradicting Holy Scripture. By claiming that the sun stood still and the earth moved, Galileo supposedly denied the miracle of Joshua in which God stopped the sun and moon to give the Israelites more daylight to complete their victory over the Amorites (Joshua 10). If the sun never moved, Caccini asked, how could God have stopped it?

Galileo found this attack disturbing, because it took religion into scientific territory. If the Church were to take sides on a purely scientific matter, and scientists were to prove it wrong, Galileo feared that the Church's authority would suffer, which as a faithful Catholic, he wanted to avoid at all costs. Christians, Galileo said, were free to believe in the miracle of Joshua, but as a matter of faith, not as a scientific phenomenon. To remain good Catholics, believers need not take biblical texts literally.

The mathematician-astronomer enjoyed considerable support within the Church for such views, but by the mid-1610s, with the long conflict between Protestants and Catholics about to explode into the Thirty Years' War (Chapters 1–3), the critique of Galileo for contradicting the Bible began to take a toll. Catholic leaders became increasingly sensitive to charges that Galileo's liberal interpretations of scripture were aiding and abetting Protestants.

In 1616, the Inquisition took up Galileo's case. After considerable debate, it forbade him to argue "that the sun is in the center of the world and totally immovable" or "that the earth is . . . in daily motion." Despite Galileo's efforts to prevent the Church from taking a position on scientific matters, it did just that, saying that the Copernican system "contradicts the express opinion of Holy Scriptures in many places."

Galileo's supporters within the Church interpreted the Inquisition's ruling as barring him only from defending the Copernican propositions in question, not from describing them in his teaching and writing. Galileo proceeded with this "description" in his *Dialogue Concerning the Two Chief Systems of the World—Ptolemaic and Copernican* (1632), an argument in favor of the Copernican system thinly veiled as a debate between an Aristotelian and a Copernican.

Religious authorities in Rome cleared the *Dialogue* for publication, but in August 1632, the Inquisition overturned their ruling and ordered all sales to stop. The Inquisitors then summoned Galileo, now almost seventy years old, to stand trial in Rome. Apparently, one of Galileo's Aristotelian enemies had convinced Pope Urban VIII that the Inquisition had forbidden Galileo not only to defend Copernicanism, but also to discuss it in any way. Galileo agreed to admit some errors and to make changes to his *Dialogue,* with the expectation of lenient treatment in exchange. He was shocked when a harsh sentence came down: imprisonment for life.

Galileo's patron in Florence had his sentence commuted to house arrest for life, which allowed the astronomer to continue to write and even to see his *Dialogue* translated into Latin and circulated widely in Europe. Galileo's final and perhaps best work, *Two New Sciences* (1638), would also be widely circulated. It laid out his findings about the structure of matter and the laws of motion, shaping the work of the greatest scientific thinkers of his era and the next. ≡

A Scientific Revolution?

Although Galileo found himself subject to the disciplinary authority of the Catholic Church, he lived at a time when a variety of people and events raised questions about authority of all kinds. As we saw in Chapter 1, the Protestant Reformation dislodged the authority of what had been Europe's overwhelmingly dominant religion. Meanwhile, the European encounter with the Americas showed that Aristotle was wrong in believing that everything about the world was already known.

If the voyages of Columbus and the explorers who followed him showed that the earth was larger, richer, and more complex than Europeans had thought, Galileo did much the same thing for the heavens. His telescope revealed moons, planets, and stars that earthlings had never seen and showed that the stars must be immensely far away. Not only was the earth much larger than previously suspected, so was the universe.

Meanwhile, the explosion of print in the sixteenth century made the new discoveries about the earth and the heavens accessible to unprecedented numbers of people, who could now read books in their own vernacular languages. The availability of printed materials also helped create other centers of learning besides monasteries and universities, which remained under the sway of Aristotelians and therefore largely closed to new approaches to the natural world. In the seventeenth century, natural philosophers in England, France, and Italy established scientific societies dedicated to the creation and dissemination of new forms of knowledge. England's Royal Society of London, founded in 1660 and still in existence today, played a particularly important role in fostering scientific innovation and the spread of new knowledge (see Map 4.1).

Despite such developments, most educated, knowledgeable people resisted Copernicanism until the eighteenth century, and in general, the findings of Galileo and his great, innovative contemporaries—Francis Bacon (1561–1626) in England and René Descartes (1596–1650) in France—were slow to take hold. For this reason, recent historians have been much more reluctant than their predecessors to call the advances of the sixteenth and seventeenth centuries a "scientific revolution." Knowledge of the natural world, and the means of developing that knowledge, changed significantly during this period, but the changes were more gradual and evolutionary than abrupt and revolutionary.

The World as Machine

One of the most important changes involved the effort to compare natural phenomena to machines. For Aristotle, natural phenomena were **animistic**;

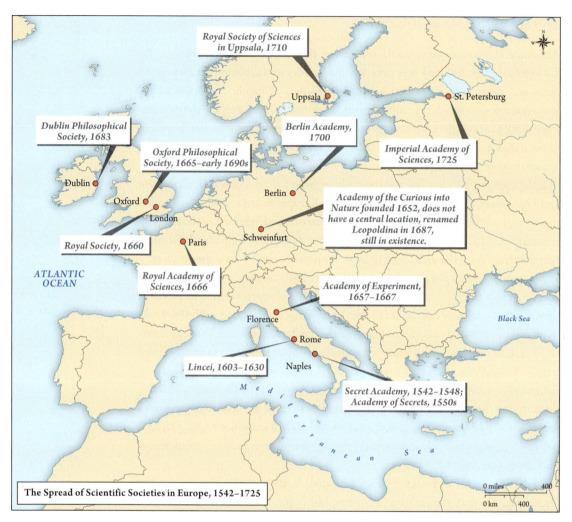

≡ **MAP 4.1** The Spread of Scientific Societies in Europe, 1542–1725

they resembled living things in having goals and aspirations—in being motivated to reach a particular state. Heavy substances fall because they "seek" their natural place at the center of the universe. Flames rise because they "aspire" to their natural place in the air.

In the seventeenth century, natural philosophers replaced animistic explanations with **mechanistic** ones by denying that inanimate objects possessed will, intention, and desire and comparing a purely human creation—a machine—to nature. As the Frenchman Pierre Gassendi (1592–1655) put it, "concerning natural things, we investigate in the same way as we investigate things of which we ourselves are the authors." It did not matter, in other words, whether objects were man-made or God-made; they have comparable characteristics and can be understood using the same procedures and approaches. Such an idea would have sent Aristotle, who considered nature and human artifice utterly different, spinning in his tomb.

The central metaphor for the new "mechanical philosophers" was the clock. By the sixteenth century, most European cities and good-sized towns possessed elaborate public clocks designed to dramatize

☰ **Clock on a Medieval Church.** The clock became the central metaphor for the "mechanical philosophers" of the scientific revolution. Like the elements of the natural world, the clock, once set in motion, operates entirely on its own. It needs neither divine intervention nor human qualities such as desire or will.

the passing of time. Although created by human beings, a clock was a mechanical device; once set in motion, it operated on its own, its pendulum moved by gravity, its gears by the force of a pendulum and a spring. Its hands needed no human intervention or human qualities like desire or will. "The several pieces making up [a clock]," said Descartes, move "without anything of knowledge or design; yet each part performs . . . as regularly and uniformly as if it knew and were concerned to do its duty."

The natural world was similar, the new philosophers said. Once God had created the world, it operated on its own. Like a clock, natural phenomena such as falling objects or rotating planets worked by purely mechanical processes that scientists could discover and understand. Because the mechanisms of the natural world were knowable, scientists could create new mechanical devices based on the principles of nature they observed.

In 1644, Galileo's secretary, Evangelista Torricelli (1608–1647), resolved to show that air possessed weight and to disprove Aristotle's long-accepted animistic notion that "nature abhors a **vacuum** [space with no matter, not even air]." In his experiment, Torricelli filled a glass tube closed at one end and open at the other with liquid mercury. The mercury, a relatively heavy substance, pushed all the air from the tube. Torricelli then inverted the tube, open end down, into a dish of mercury. The substance began to drain from the tube and then stopped.

≡ **Evangelista Torricelli's Barometer.** To show that air possessed weight, Torricelli filled a glass tube with liquid mercury and inverted it into a dish of mercury. He observed that only a small amount of the mercury from the tube drained into the dish. This was because the pressure of the atmospheric air weighing down on the mercury in the dish kept the column of mercury up. In performing this experiment, Torricelli inadvertently invented the barometer, a device that measures the pressure of air.

If water and other liquids truly abhorred a vacuum, none of the mercury should have drained out. It drained to some extent and then stopped, Torricelli argued, not because it only *partially* abhorred the vacuum inside the tube—the Aristotelian fallback position—but because the pressure of the atmospheric air pushing on the surface of mercury in the dish kept most of the mercury inside the tube. When the air pressure, or weight of the air, equaled the weight of the mercury in the tube, the two substances came into balance, and the mercury ceased to fall. The height of the mercury thus served as a measure of the pressure of the air; without intending to, Torricelli had invented the **barometer** (from Greek *baros* 'weight' and *metron* 'measure'). "We live," Torricelli declared, "at the bottom of an ocean of . . . air, which by unquestioned experience is known to have weight."

To test this conclusion, the French philosopher Blaise Pascal (1623–1662) decided to see what would happen when the same experiment was done at different altitudes. In 1648 Pascal's brother-in-law placed one of Torricelli's barometers at the bottom of a mountain in central France and then carried another to the summit 3,000 feet above. Sure enough, with less atmosphere weighing down on the mercury in the mountaintop barometer, it stood three inches lower than the mercury in the one at the mountain's foot. The experiment appeared to confirm that air pressure declined as altitude increased. Air was not everywhere the same, as Aristotelians believed, and it clearly had weight. The experiment converted Pascal to the mechanical view of the world.

The Experimental Method

Conversions such as Pascal's led a great many natural philosophers of the mid-seventeenth century to declare the old Aristotelian philosophy dead and to enthrone a new mechanical, empirical one in its place. The leading natural philosophers now maintained that knowledge of the natural world came not from the wisdom of classical texts but from the direct experience of observation and experimentation, from work scientists did for themselves.

Perhaps the philosopher most identified with this new point of view was Francis Bacon (1561–1626). As a high English government official, Bacon was especially interested in what we today call **technology**—that is, applied knowledge. Above all, Bacon wanted science to discover new knowledge and better ways of accomplishing necessary tasks rather than endlessly discussing things already known, which, in his view, was one of the Aristotelians' greatest sins. For that reason, he emphasized the value of recent inventions such as gunpowder, the magnetic compass, and printing with moveable, reusable type. The authors of these inventions tended to be artisans working with their hands rather than university-trained philosophers spinning arguments in their heads. What science could and should do, Bacon said, was to make such inventions less haphazard and more the result of formal scientific inquiry and experimentation with a practical goal in mind.

Bacon's influence was such that British natural philosophers, as a group, became particularly wedded to empirical investigation through experimentation. Their Royal Society of London dedicated itself to the experimental method and to publicizing the results of their members' work. The Society's most influential founding fellow, Robert Boyle (1627–1691), became famous for his series of public experiments with the air pump, an invention created by his assistant, Robert Hooke (1635–1703).

To conduct his experiments, Boyle used a pump to suck the air out of a globe made of glass. Before extracting the air, Boyle placed Torricelli's barometer inside the glass globe. As he pumped out the air, the mercury fell lower in the tube until it dropped almost to the level of the dish. In performing this experiment, Boyle reproduced in his laboratory the same phenomenon Pascal had observed on the mountaintop in central France. Just as the mercury level dropped in tandem with air pressure at higher altitudes, so too did it fall when Boyle removed air from the glass globe, thus reducing the air pressure inside.

The point of this experiment was to demonstrate that natural scientists could build machines or other artificial devices that replicated important aspects of nature—in this case, air pressure and vacuums—and then use this man-made device to investigate the truths of the natural world. To establish the authenticity of his experiments, Boyle asked other scientists to observe them and then published elaborate descriptions of what he had done.

But not everyone was convinced. The English political philosopher Thomas Hobbes (1588–1679), who we will revisit later in the chapter, maintained that Boyle had no way of *proving* he had created a vacuum—or something close to it—inside the glass globe. Boyle answered that rather than provide absolute proofs, his experiments enabled him to formulate a probable explanation of air pressure and its effects, an explanation on which a great many knowledgeable men of science could agree. This, Boyle said, was the best science could do. Even today, most science operates this way. Science provides explanations that produce consensus—until a better explanation comes along.

Descartes and the Quest for Certainty

Boyle's **probabilistic** form of knowledge satisfied the members of England's Royal Society as well as others in the British Isles, but on the European continent the leading natural philosopher, Descartes, insisted on certainty. To achieve it, he sought to provide a set of understandings grounded in the absolute truths of mathematics.

Certainty was crucial, Descartes wrote, because the undermining of Aristotelianism in the late sixteenth and early seventeenth centuries had given rise to a widespread skepticism, a broad sense of doubt about all efforts to explain natural phenomena. Hobbes's doubts about Boyle's experiments are an example of such skepticism, as was the growing belief that, all too often, people's senses could not be trusted. After all, they regularly fell for optical illusions and failed to detect the movement of the earth through space. Nor could we be confident, skeptics added, in the viability of human reason. Because even the most intelligent people make errors, we cannot necessarily trust the conclusions they draw.

How, Descartes asked, could such skepticism be overcome? In his most famous work, the *Discourse on Method* (1637), the French philosopher argued that there was at least one phenomenon about which he could have absolute certainty, namely his own existence. "I think, therefore I am," wrote Descartes, maintaining that an individual's consciousness of himself proves that he exists. The fact that I can think thoughts, and know that I have those thoughts, demonstrates beyond a shadow of doubt, the philosopher said, that I am real.

Having established the certainty of his own existence, Descartes then argued that the philosophical implications of this certainty were that God must necessarily exist as well. We know this, he said, because of the problem of doubt. To be human is to be full of doubt. This makes

≡ **Cartesian Thought.** In his famous *Discourse on Method,* Descartes devised what became an influential proof of the existence of God and a critique of philosophical skepticism (the notion that essentially nothing could be convincingly explained).

us imperfect, because a perfect being would not be consumed with doubt. Now, imperfection has meaning only in relation to perfection. But since we humans are imperfect, we must have developed the idea of perfection from a being that, unlike us, is perfect—God, who therefore must exist.

The next step in Descartes' argument was to establish that God's perfection meant that he would not want to mislead us about the phenomena we perceive "very clearly and distinctly." A perfect God, Descartes said, would not have created human beings incapable of apprehending the world he had made. For this reason, the skeptics must be wrong.

From here, Descartes went on to say that it must be possible to develop a complete understanding of how and why the world works as it does. The understanding Descartes developed, which amounted to a general theory of everything, was built on the premise that there were just two kinds of phenomena: matter and mind. In Descartes's view, the human body belonged to the category of matter—wholly defined by its ability to take up space. All of matter's other apparent properties—color, texture, odor, light, etc.—actually reside in the human mind. We perceive or experience these properties because the motion of a particular piece of matter triggers our senses, which in turn leaves imprints in our mind.

Descartes' natural world is completely filled by matter of different sizes and shapes; there is no empty space—no vacuum. In the beginning of time, this matter was inert; it began to move when God gave it its initial jolt. Very quickly, everything began to move, as each piece of matter, which Descartes called **corpuscles,** jostled against the others it touched. Because the universe is finite, the moving matter could not extend outward forever but rather bumped up against the edges of existence and eventually began to spin around in a great circle, causing every other piece of matter to spin as well. The universe for Descartes was thus an enormous vortex, a huge whirlpool of spinning matter.

For Descartes, this whirlpool was what explained the movement of the planets in their orbits and also caused humans to see the sun as a great ball of light. While his explanation may seem fanciful today, Descartes's attempt to understand matter completely and systematically, along with his apparent proof of the existence of God, made him enormously influential. In addition, his crucial contributions to algebra and geometry deepened mathematics and set the stage for Isaac Newton's development of calculus.

Isaac Newton: The Way Gravity Works

If Descartes and Cartesian philosophy remained popular in France and elsewhere on the continent, in England members of the increasingly influential Royal Society championed the work of Isaac Newton (1642–1727). While living at his family's country estate in the late 1660s, Newton began to work on a question raised by Galileo in 1632: If the earth spins on its axis, why is it that people and objects do not fly off its surface? This question prompted Newton to consider the relationship between **centrifugal force**, which thrusts objects away from a central point, and gravity, which pushes them back down toward the center. Gravity, he reasoned, must counteract the effects of centrifugal force, but precisely how it did so and how the relationship between the two could be expressed mathematically would take Newton nearly two decades to work out.

Newton took a crucial step forward during a visit by Edmund Halley (1656–1742), after whom Halley's comet is named. Halley asked Newton what would be the path of any object orbiting a stationary body. After giving Halley's question a great deal of thought, Newton's answer was that the moving body would trace out an ellipse.

Why an ellipse? Newton based his reasoning on Kepler's ideas about planetary motion and a 1644 work by Descartes, who had demonstrated that any object, once set in forward or backward motion, will forever move in a straight line at constant speed as long as nothing interferes with its motion—e.g., gravity, friction, wind, and the like. In the vacuum of space, Newton added, an object like the Moon would perpetually move straight ahead but for the gravitational force exerted by the earth. At each point on the Moon's path, the earth's gravitational pull attempts to reel it in, but the Moon's inertia counteracts that pull just enough for it to fall into an elliptical-shaped orbit.

It was one thing for Newton to make this claim about a moving object like the Moon and quite another to provide a mathematical proof of the principles of gravitational attraction. His effort to do just that produced the Englishman's

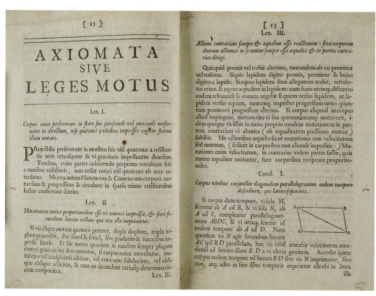

≡ **Newton's *Principia*.** In his most influential work, Isaac Newton demonstrated the laws of gravitational attraction and developed a comprehensive understanding of the physical world. That understanding would underlie the field of physics until the early twentieth century, when Albert Einstein revealed the limits of Newton's thought.

most famous and influential work, the *Philosophiae Naturalis Principia Mathematica* (*Mathematical Principles of Natural Philosophy*), commonly known as the *Principia* (1687). This work would underlie the field of physics until Albert Einstein's contributions superseded it in the early twentieth century.

In the *Principia*, Newton established the three key features of gravity: it was a predictable force that acts on all matter in the universe; objects of greater mass exert more gravitational force on each other than do those of lesser mass; and the further two objects are apart, the less the gravitational pull between them. It is important to note that although Newton elaborately explained gravity's effects and how to calculate gravitational force, he admitted that its cause remained "unknown to me." At one point, Newton suggested that God produced gravitational attraction by intervening directly in the universe all the time. Although the mutual attraction of the planets in the solar system should disrupt their orbits and cause the system to collapse into itself, God's regular, timely interventions kept the system in proper working order and prevented any catastrophic crash. As a committed Christian, Newton liked this explanation, because it demonstrated not only the existence of God but the need for his perpetual engagement with his creation.

Milestones of the Scientific Revolution	
1543	Copernicus, *On the Revolution of Heavenly Bodies*
1576	Construction of Brahe's observatory begins
1591	Galileo's law of falling bodies
1609	Kepler's third law of motion
1610	Galileo, the *Starry Messenger*
1620	Bacon, Novum Organum
1632	Galileo, *Dialogue Concerning the Two Chief Systems of the World*
1637	Descartes, *Discourse on Method*
1660	Boyle, *New Experiments Physico-Mechanical*
1687	Newton, *Principia*

Newton's critics, especially the German Gottfried Leibniz (1646–1716) and the Dutchman Christiaan Huygens (1629–1695), lambasted him for failing to provide a physical, material explanation of the causes of gravitational attraction. Instead, Leibniz said, Newton advanced the unphilosophical notion of gravitation as a "perpetual miracle." And not only was Newton unphilosophical, he was irreligious as well. The Englishman had implicitly denied God's perfection, Leibniz maintained, by imagining that he had created a solar system so rickety that it required his constant intervention just to keep it from falling apart.

Newton brushed off these criticisms; as the long-standing president of the Royal Society, he occupied a position of great power and prestige in his home country and enjoyed the support of England's clerical leaders. His many disciples took up his defense, and his ideas enjoyed such widespread support that they became a new orthodoxy, a set of positions far truer and more useful than those of the Aristotelians, but an orthodoxy nonetheless.

"Enlightenment": From the Natural World to the Study of Humankind

While Newton outlined the operation of the natural world, others began to examine the workings of a distinctly human realm, a realm that belonged to the natural world but that held a special place within it. Humans obeyed the laws of gravity and motion, but they also possessed reason and emotion, unlike, say, a falling stone, and those qualities gave them a unique relationship to everything else.

If the greatest philosophers of the seventeenth century thought and wrote about what we today call "science," the most prominent ones of the eighteenth century mainly thought and wrote about religion and government, taking into account questions of equality and inequality, reason and emotion, and what it meant to be a human being. Key thinkers still performed scientific experiments and made significant advancements in mathematics, but in the eighteenth century, philosophers focused more on people and society than on motion, gravity, and the heavens.

As a group, these philosophers made a major departure from existing forms of explanation and understanding by denying that God had established, once and for all, the parameters of social, political, and religious life. Human beings, the philosophers said, were fully capable of shaping society, government, and religion for themselves. Just as seventeenth-century scientists had understood the natural world as operating on its own, free of God's—or an Aristotelian—will or design, so their eighteenth-century successors depicted society and government as human creations rather than ones shaped largely by God.

Before delving into these eighteenth-century philosophers—**philosophes**, the French called them—it is important to note that they represented a minority of the era's authors. As the costs of printing declined, more writers than ever before had their works published. And the relative prosperity of the years between the peace agreements of 1714 and the outbreak of the French Revolution in 1789 enabled more people than ever before to purchase books and newspapers and gave them the leisure time to read. They read a great many religious booklets; travelers' accounts of distant, "exotic" places; and a pile of almanacs filled with popular sayings, facts, and predictions about the weather, harvests, and the price of food. History books and advice manuals for young adults, not to mention pornographic works, were enormously popular as well.

≡ **Madame Geoffrin's Salon.** In eighteenth-century France, intelligent, wealthy women such as Madame Geoffrin played host to the greatest minds of their day. Geoffrin, in particular, helped familiarize influential people with the best of Enlightenment thought.

A complete history of eighteenth-century literary life would consider all of these writings. But given the intellectual power and influence of a handful of writers who exemplify what is commonly known as the **Enlightenment**, we will focus on them. The Enlightenment is what historians in the nineteenth and twentieth centuries tended to call the body of philosophical writings of the eighteenth century, whose authors referred to "enlightenment" as a process rather than a distinct historical phenomenon.

Enlightened ideas were developed and disseminated in a set of institutions, both formal and informal, which historians have called the **public sphere.** This public realm of ideas originated in France in the late seventeenth century, when prominent women attached to the court of Louis XIV invited people to their homes for the reading and discussion of plays, poems, and other writings. The hostesses of these gatherings, known as **salons**, decided whom to invite, which works and authors to present, and, in many cases, how the discussion would proceed.

In the eighteenth century, salons extended far beyond court society to encompass a much broader intellectual and social elite. Hostesses still held high social standing and considerable wealth; under their leadership, intellectual life now filtered into the society at large. In the salon, women and men interacted much more equally than ever before, and male writers acknowledged the power and authority of the women in charge. The Swiss philosopher Jean-Jacques Rousseau

(1712–1778) intensely disliked that authority, and he accused salon leaders of side-stepping their "natural" maternal roles and of emasculating the men invited into their lairs.

Why, in a society in which men held a near-monopoly of power, did women emerge as leaders of the salon? The answer has to do with the widespread seventeenth- and eighteenth-century belief that women were the bearers of culture and "civilization." As mothers, they transmitted these attributes to their children—in addition to the manners and proper behavior taught at the dinner table and around the house. As organizers of salons, women served as social and intellectual mothers to a new generation of people eager to be endowed with the new culture, ideas, and values of their day.

The salon accustomed people to meeting together to discuss books and ideas, and by the mid-eighteenth century, those discussions had extended beyond the private home and into a more genuinely public sphere, a realm of ideas that already existed in Britain and came to exist throughout the European continent. The public sphere was composed of members-only organizations such as Masonic lodges in France and the Habsburg Empire, as well as more open institutions such as "patriotic" associations in Germany, scientific and agrarian societies in Habsburg lands, and learned academies in several countries. The public sphere also featured informal gathering places such as cafés, clubhouses, and literary societies. The members-only organizations brought together people of high social standing. Many of the informal organizations were open to essentially any literate man, thus enabling people from different walks of life to rub shoulders as they discussed literature, philosophy, and current events. Newspapers and other forms of periodical literature, most of them new to this period, became the intellectual arteries of the public sphere, the channels through which information and ideas circulated from organization to organization, city to city, and country to country. From the political authorities' point of view, this intellectual ferment could be worrisome, because it threatened to nurture religious and political dissent.

Also worrisome, at least to a considerable number of men, was the new prominence of women. Western society had long considered women inferior to men, but that inferiority was taken for granted and seldom discussed. This silence ended in the eighteenth century, when essentially everything seemed open

≡ **Immanuel Kant.** In "What Is Enlightenment?" Kant argued that, all too often, people fail to think for themselves, preferring to blindly follow those in authority. To be enlightened was to develop one's own reason and apply it to the surrounding world.

to debate, even long-taboo subjects such as the existence of God. In this context, the influence of salon leaders and other intellectually inclined women suddenly brought front and center the question of **gender**. Writers now asked about the meaning of masculinity and femininity, the proper role of women and men in society and the family, and the particular attributes of men and women, whether biological, emotional, or intellectual. As we will see, an impressive array of women writers maintained that society's hierarchy of men over women was artificial rather than natural and could be undone as the process of enlightenment progressed.

"What Is Enlightenment?"

The most celebrated definition of the process of enlightenment came from the German philosopher, Immanuel Kant (1724–1804), who called it "man's release from his self-incurred immaturity." In Kant's view, people became stuck in a childlike state by failing to think for themselves. Humans could release themselves by following their own reason rather than the dictates of someone else.

"Man's self-incurred immaturity," Kant said, applied to religion as well as politics. People blindly followed church dogmas rather than judging whether those dogmas made sense. In politics, people obeyed authority even when it had them do irrational, unreasonable things—as when instructed to kill in the name of religion. Radical as Kant's views appear, they did not move him to take a public stance against organized religion and existing political authority. He maintained that people needed to outwardly obey religious and political leaders, while keeping their evaluations of those leaders to themselves. Only genuine philosophers—Kant did not say precisely who belonged to this category—should discuss the reasonableness of established religion and politics, and they must do so privately, among themselves, and not in front of ordinary people.

As much as Kant believed, in theory, in the necessity of enlightenment, in reality he thought it should occur gradually and with the least disruption possible. Kant's ideas may have had radical implications in the long run, but like most other "enlightened" people of the eighteenth century, he was no revolutionary.

Natural Law and the Nature of Human Beings

Kant's belief that enlightened people must judge religion and politics for themselves summed up the most important intellectual developments of the eighteenth century, and his views sharply contradicted the ideas almost universally held before then. Prior to the seventeenth century, a great many ideas about human life turned on Thomas Aquinas's (1225–1274) Christianized version of Aristotle's extensive writings about **natural law**, the idea that human beings lived according to a set of rules inscribed by God. Since God had embedded the same rules in everyone, all people were alike in fundamental ways, which meant that they had a natural tendency to live together in communities and to cooperate with one another. People lived, Aquinas maintained, according to two "primary precepts," which were also biblical commandments: "love thy neighbor as thyself" and "do unto others as you would have others do unto you." In addition, all human beings possessed "innate ideas" or "innate senses" that enabled them to perceive the world exactly as God had created it and to distinguish between good and evil while sharing a common belief in God.

The English philosopher John Locke (1632–1704) contradicted Aquinas's views by maintaining that at birth the human mind was a blank slate without any innate ideas. People's understanding of the world came entirely from their engagement with it, from the perceptions of their senses and their experiences of the environment around them. Even the knowledge of God, Locke said, came from individuals' experiences of the world. This view met with a great deal of criticism, especially from theologians, who said that nothing in the material world could resemble God. But certain of Locke's contemporaries, deeply influenced by the encounter with Africans and Native Americans, decided that Locke's views about innate ideas and sensory experience were right. That the newly discovered peoples appeared so different from Europeans seemed to undermine Aquinas's idea that all humans shared the same nature and perceived the world in essentially the same ways.

Beyond the encounter with distant people, developments in Europe itself convinced some writers, most famously Thomas Hobbes, that human beings were not, as Aquinas had claimed, naturally cooperative and sociable. Observing the terrible brutality of the Thirty Years' War and the English Revolution (Chapters 1–3), Hobbes decided that "man is a wolf to man." Each individual wanted to gain advantages over all the others, and to do so would readily harm other human beings rather than try to live sociably and peacefully with them. For this reason, people lived in fear of one another and were governed by a single overarching principle: self-preservation, the desire to protect and preserve one's life—at the expense of others, if necessary. Each individual's ultimate goal was to live as long as possible while trying to satisfy limitless desires.

But if people, by nature, were disinclined to live together in peace, how could the existence of functioning societies be explained, and how, in the future, could a lasting peace come about? To answer these questions, Hobbes asked readers of his book *The Leviathan* (1651) to imagine human beings in their natural state, or as he put it, in "the state of nature." Because people naturally tried to defend themselves and gain advantage over others, the state of nature would be nothing other than a "war of every one against every one" in which all human beings faced constant danger and life was "solitary, poor, nasty, brutish, and short."

These conditions existed because "natural" man was free to do as he pleased, and what pleased him was to fulfill his own desires whatever the cost to others. But in this situation, no one was truly free, because any individual who gained a measure of wealth and power would inevitably face successful attacks from those who wanted to seize what he had gained. Human beings, in Hobbes's view, highly radical for the time, were relatively equal to one another in strength, stamina, and intelligence, which meant that no one would be able to maintain a superior position for very long. By positing a natural equality, Hobbes shocked aristocrats and intellectuals for whom hierarchy and inequality seemed natural.

Not only were people essentially equal, in Hobbes's view, but they also possessed a common rationality that enabled them to emerge from the state of nature. At some point, Hobbes wrote, people would recognize the futility and irrationality of their situation and decide, collectively, to give up their freedom to do as they pleased. In effect, they would gather together all their individual freedoms and bestow them on what Hobbes called a "leviathan," an absolute ruler or ruling group that alone would possess the power to crush any individual's effort to gain power and wealth at other people's expense. It did not matter for Hobbes whether the leviathan was a monarch or a committee of leaders as long it held a monopoly of power and authority and every member of society agreed to submit to it.

This collective agreement would create what Hobbes called a "commonwealth," a community of people who voluntarily traded their freedom for security and in doing so embraced absolutist rule. This was a highly pessimistic view of humankind, as it portrayed people as incapable of freedom and unable to live in peace except when under the thumb of a coercive state.

Pessimistic as he was, Hobbes stood out nonetheless as an extraordinarily innovative and radical thinker. He posited a natural law independent of God's designs and denied the existence of sharp natural inequalities

≡ **Leviathan.** In this work, Thomas Hobbes argued that human beings in their natural state were condemned to a perpetual "war of every one against every one." The only way to leave this "state of nature" was for all human beings to give up their freedoms and agree to obey a "leviathan," an all-powerful ruler who would suppress each person's natural aggression, covetousness, and greed.

within the human race. Perhaps most important, he claimed that societies were the purposeful creations of human beings rather than fixed structures established by God and ruled by divinely chosen individuals. In Hobbes' commonwealth, groups of people decided for themselves who should exercise authority over them. In so arguing, Hobbes opened the way to modern political thought.

Locke, Mandeville, and the Scottish Enlightenment

Many influential political thinkers after Hobbes agreed that people could—and should—form their own governments, but they disagreed that every member of a society had to submit to an all-powerful sovereign as the price of membership in the commonwealth they had created. Locke argued in his *Second Treatise on Government* (1689) that human beings possessed the potential to regulate their own political and social affairs. Property owners, he said, would come together, as they had during the Glorious Revolution of 1688 (Chapter 3), to establish a set of laws designed to protect their holdings and guarantee their security. In doing so, propertied men would create a functioning "civil society," which they would govern in collaboration with a hereditary monarch whose powers were limited by representative institutions, especially Parliament, led by those same propertied men.

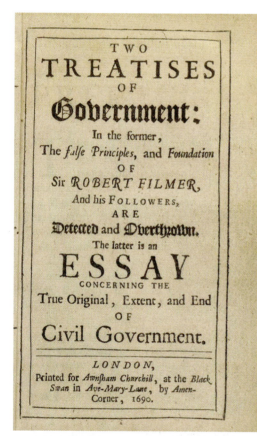

A Just Government. John Locke's solution to the ills of man's natural state was not an absolute ruler but rather a "just government" created by the property-owning members of a society and grounded in their consent. These property owners would devise a set of laws designed for their mutual protection and security.

Property, according to Locke, did not exist at the first stages of the state of nature, since God gave the earth to everyone in common. But early on, individuals took bits of these common resources and applied their labor to them, making them vastly more productive and valuable. This increased value justified the claim that a cultivated piece of land, or a stone fashioned into a tool, should belong, as private property, to the individual responsible for creating it. In this way, labor created property, and individuals benefited humankind as a whole by exercising their private desires for gain.

Because other people benefited from each individual's labor, people in Locke's state of nature were linked to one another by the labor they unwittingly contributed to the common good. Locke's natural man was thus more sociable and more benign than Hobbes's natural man, and no less rational. Even so, human reason was too unreliable for society to automatically regulate itself. Locke believed that private property had to be secured by a body of law and a government to enforce it.

These considerations moved late-seventeenth-century philosophy away from the bleak views of Hobbes. But not until the eighteenth century would European writers provide a fuller sense of how and why people could live successfully in societies without excessive government constraint. For these European thinkers, it was people's "passions" or "sentiments," what we would call emotions today, which drew them together and gave them the potential to live in peace.

The Anglo-Dutch philosopher Bernard Mandeville (1670–1733) was closest to Hobbes in positing that human beings naturally wanted to dominate others and to gain advantages for themselves. But Mandeville maintained that humans gradually learned the futility of trying to dominate others physically and decided instead that they could gain superiority by behaving in ways that would earn other people's esteem. The more an individual was esteemed and admired, the more he would loom over his fellows, thus inflating his self-love, or pride, a feeling natural to human beings. Excessive self-love could produce egotism, but the desire to be esteemed had crucial positive effects. It moderated an individual's behavior by discouraging him from doing things to others that would forfeit their esteem and cause him shame, the opposite of pride. In other words, people behaved decently toward others not because they were inherently sociable, as Aristotelians maintained, but out of fear of being shamed and therefore of suffering damage to their self-love.

The Scottish philosopher David Hume (1711–1776) followed Mandeville in believing that people behaved decently toward others because they wanted their esteem and respect and were moved by the "passions" of ambition, vanity, and self-love. But unlike Mandeville, Hume believed humans to be governed by more positive passions as well, especially by "friendship, generosity [and] public spirit."

For Hume, passions were central to all human beings and more important than reason, which "is, and ought only to be, the slave of the passions." His focus on the passions was designed to show the extent to which human beings naturally and automatically connected with one another and why Hobbes's "war of every one against every one" did not accurately describe the human condition.

If for Hume self-love and the desire for esteem moderated people's behavior and made them more sociable, the passion of sympathy, built into the fiber of human beings, better explained why people took naturally to living in society. Sympathy makes us care what happens to other people and to identify with them. When they laugh, we laugh; when they cry, we cry as well. Sympathy overcomes self-love and moves us to admire and emulate those who may be better and more virtuous than we are.

The idea of sympathy also animated the thought of Adam Smith (1723–1790), Hume's fellow Scotsman and close friend. As the author of *The Wealth of Nations* (1776), Smith is best known today as one of the world's seminal economists, but he was also a premier moral philosopher, having published in 1759 the *Theory of Moral Sentiments*. For Smith, sympathy comes from our imaginations, from our ability to envision ourselves in the place of someone else. If we watch someone suffering, we "form some idea of his sensations [and] enter, as it were, into his body, and become in some measure the same person with him."

Sympathy is not limited to pity or compassion; it also leads to happiness and delight, as when we witness someone's good fortune. But we do not identify with everyone. We try to sympathize only with actions and emotions we consider appropriate. The passion of sympathy thus allows us to judge what others do. We identify with these people, but since we are separate from them, we have the ability to judge them impartially.

The experience of judging others enables us to judge ourselves. We can do so with some accuracy because our sympathy allows us to imagine how others are likely to judge us. This imagination overcomes the distortions produced by our own self-love, and combined with the knowledge we have of ourselves, permits us to evaluate our motives and actions reasonably well.

In judging ourselves by standing imaginatively in other people's shoes, we create what Smith called an "impartial spectator." This creature of our imagination may not be perfect, but the more we turn to it, the better our capacity to judge—and therefore control—ourselves becomes. This self-control combined with our ability to identify with others makes cohesive societies possible and renders intrusive, oppressive government unnecessary.

Hume's and Smith's optimistic views about people's ability to live peacefully together in cohesive societies stemmed in part from their relatively happy social, political, and religious circumstances. Scotland's incorporation into Great Britain in 1707 endowed them with a constitutional government that limited the king's powers and gave political voice to propertied, educated men like themselves. The new political order allowed greater freedom of political and religious expression than anywhere in Europe except perhaps for the Dutch Republic. In a sense, Scotland felt freer than England did, since the British government resided in London, far away from the Scottish cities of Glasgow and Edinburgh, which were highly autonomous and lightly ruled.

Smith's views about sympathy highlight aspects of his economic theory often overlooked. He is well known for his argument in the *Wealth of Nations* (1776) that the **division of labor**—breaking down tasks into a series of small operations handled by different workers—vastly enhances the productivity of industry; what often remains unacknowledged is the extent to which his ideas about sympathy made him sensitive to the negative aspects of this phenomenon.

The division of labor makes manufacturing vastly more efficient than when a single worker performs every task himself. Smith's famous example of this phenomenon involves the making of a pin, which can be broken down into eighteen subtasks. If a team of ten people shares these tasks, with each individual doing the same one or two of them repeatedly, its members can produce 48,000 pins in a day. But if each individual works separately and does all eighteen different tasks, he or she is lucky to produce one pin a day, or ten pins for the team.

Smith did not merely applaud this enhanced productivity. He also sympathized with working men over the division of labor's mind-numbing, dehumanizing effects. The division of labor, he wrote, yokes workers to tasks "so simple and uniform as to give little exercise to the understanding; while [making] their labor . . . so constant and so severe, that it leaves them little leisure and less inclination to apply to, or even think of any thing else." If left uncorrected, Smith argued, workers' minds would be so dulled as to make them unable to imagine an impartial spectator and for that reason incapable of judging themselves and others. They might, as a result, fail to recognize threats to civil liberties, or they might behave in ways that would invite government oppression.

Smith's solution to the harmful effects of the division of labor was for the government to provide a free public education to all working people. Such a public service would supply the mental exercise and stimulation that repetitive labor took away. Educated workers would be able to accurately judge their leaders, and having been re-energized by schooling, would work more diligently for the common good.

Smith's fellow Scotsman Adam Ferguson (1723–1816) was somewhat less optimistic about the ability to undo the negative effects of the division of labor, but Ferguson shared Smith's belief in the importance of sympathy in forging human relationships and in making societies work. In fact, Ferguson did not believe that genuine human life existed outside of society; there was no such thing, in his view, as a pre-social state of nature. If we were to send an individual to the desert alone, Ferguson wrote, he would become "a plant torn from its roots." His human form "may remain, but every faculty droops and withers; the human personage and the human character cease to exist."

Because Ferguson rejected the idea of a pre-social state of nature, he did not believe, as Hobbes did, that humans developed from the state of nature to the state of society. Instead, human advancement went from the less to the more civilized. "Primitive" people like those encountered in the Americas were no less social than modern people; the difference between them turned on the moderns' greater knowledge, technology, and experience of the world.

In a sense, Ferguson maintained, primitive people are more social than modern ones, since modern trade and commerce can create ruthless forms of competition that move each individual to deal with others "as he does with his cattle and his soil, [merely] for the sake of the profits they bring." On this point, Smith and Hume disagreed with Ferguson. For Smith, commerce brought people together far more than it drove them apart, and for Hume, modern urban societies were far more social than primitive village-oriented ones.

Despite these differences, the Scottish thinkers agreed with one another far more than they disagreed. The upshot of their anti-Hobbesian ideas about the naturalness of sympathy and sociability was the optimistic notion that human beings, no matter how superficially diverse, were programmed to understand and get along with one another and thus could—and should—govern themselves.

Rousseau and Natural Man

Jean-Jacques Rousseau (1712–1778), who also criticized Hobbes, resembled the Scots in other ways as well. Rousseau hailed from a Calvinist country, Switzerland, which, like Scotland, had developed a large measure of religious toleration. In Rousseau's home city of Geneva, an important group of religious leaders deemed human beings inherently good rather than depraved and sinful, as orthodox Calvinists thought. Rousseau drew on this moderate Protestantism as a source of his belief in equality and simplicity as essential human virtues. But unlike his Scottish counterparts, Rousseau was pessimistic about the ability of human beings to live peacefully in society.

Although Geneva, like the Scottish capital Edinburgh, featured a vibrant publishing industry and allowed for significant political participation, Rousseau did not benefit from the same tolerance that Scottish intellectuals enjoyed. Geneva's political elite, relatively open-minded on religious matters, remained intolerant when it came to political dissent. Once Rousseau began to publish philosophical works critical of existing social and political arrangements, city leaders moved to silence him. For this and other reasons, the adult Rousseau took up residence across the border in France.

Rousseau quickly found France inhospitable as well, and Hume, who admired his work, offered him refuge in England. But the two men did not get along, and Rousseau parted company with him and the rest of the Scottish Enlightenment. The Genevan differed, in particular, from Ferguson, who considered humans inherently social beings. Rousseau, by contrast, posited a pre-social state of nature in which the first humans lived in isolation from one another and depended on no one but themselves. They built nothing permanent and lived only in the present, having no conception that a past or future could exist. Pre-social humans had little need for rational thought, since their behavior was largely governed by their senses: hunger, danger, warmth, cold, and the like. Because they had no sustained interactions with other people, they felt no need to dominate others or even to distinguish themselves from other human beings.

Rousseau outlined these ideas in his famous *Discourse on the Origins of Inequality Among Men* (1754), which argued that human beings were better off in the state of nature than in the societies that evolved from it. Unlike the Scottish writers, who believed that humans progressed from savagery to civilization, Rousseau portrayed "civilization," the complex societies of eighteenth-century Europe, in largely negative terms.

Rousseau's natural man enjoyed freedom and independence, but once societies formed, people "everywhere [lived] in chains." If for Mandeville and the Scots society is natural and desirable, for Rousseau it is unnatural and undesirable—unless it can be carefully reconstructed in ways he outlined in two utopian books of 1762, *Emile: or On Education* and the *Social Contract*. Rousseau admitted, however, that the social reconstruction he had in mind would be difficult to achieve. It would have to be built in part by educating people in isolation from society and in part by having them take guidance from a benign "legislator," who would, in effect, teach them how to rule themselves. Rousseau suggested that without such careful reconstruction, society inevitably creates hierarchy, which leads to constant warfare and ultimately to authoritarian government, the only force that can end the chaos. Rousseau's state of society resembled Hobbes's state of nature, and like Hobbes, Rousseau foresaw the emergence of a leviathan. But whereas Hobbes saw the leviathan as just and necessary, Rousseau considered it oppressive.

Civilization and "Primitive" Man

These ideas about the state of nature and "natural man" developed in the context of a world vastly enlarged in the minds of European observers by the encounter with the peoples of Africa and North America. Although most eighteenth-century thinkers rarely left their own cities and towns let alone traveled to the Americas,

≡ **Rousseau's Noble Savage.** Rousseau thought human beings were better off in the state of nature than in the civilized world. He thus idealized the "noble savage," a simple, unspoiled individual uncorrupted by the greed and vanity of Europe's hierarchical, uncaring civilization.

a growing number of "traveler-philosophers," eager to see and experience the world for themselves, set sail for Africa, the Americas, China, and the Pacific islands. The more Europeans confronted the vast array of peoples from the different parts of the globe, the more pressing the questions about the nature of these "others" became. To what extent were they human beings like the ones Europeans knew?

The most common European view was that African or American tribesmen were primitive versions of themselves. As the French traveler-philosopher Joseph-Marie Degérando (1772–1842) put it, the explorer "who sails to the farthest corners of the globe, travels, in fact . . . in[to] the past." By getting to know the "savages" encountered there, the traveler glimpses his distant European ancestors.

Implicit in this view was the notion that human beings and human societies evolved from primitive to modern, from the state of nature to the state of civilization—or as Ferguson thought, from the less civilized to the more civilized. Different peoples evolved at different rates, and Europeans pronounced themselves the most highly evolved of all. But why, asked the traveler-philosophers and their more sedentary counterparts, was this so? A common answer, articulated most forcefully by the French political philosopher Charles-Louis de Montesquieu (1689–1755), turned on climate. Hot climates made people lethargic, which supposedly explained the backwardness of Africans and American Indians. Cold climates like those of the Mongols made them overactive and aggressive in an effort to stay warm. Their inability to keep still stunted them intellectually. Europeans alone possessed a temperate climate, allowing them to avoid the extremes of lethargy and hyperactivity, and thus to evolve at a deliberate, even pace.

This view of climate seemed commonsensical to many, but Hume objected to it, as did the French philosopher, essayist, and playwright François-Marie Arouet (1694–1778), universally known by his pen name, Voltaire. Why is it, Voltaire asked, that ancient Greeks and Egyptians were highly advanced for their time, but eighteenth-century Greeks and Egyptians mostly backward? Their climates, after all, could not have changed all that much. What differed was their government. They had good governments in ancient times and poor, oppressive ones today. Even Montesquieu admitted that oppressive living conditions could undo the positive effects of climate. "Slavery," he wrote, "debases, weakens and destroys the spirit, while liberty shapes, elevates and fortifies it."

If climate did not explain human differences, what did? Poverty, lack of education, absence of contact with other people—all these man-made phenomena, wrote Hume, not natural ones like climate and geography, prevented some people from advancing as rapidly as others. Alleviate poverty and ignorance, and any people would advance rapidly. This was so, wrote Kant toward the end of his career and Hume throughout, because all human beings were fundamentally the same. They all possessed sympathy, the ability to feel for and identify with other people. That quality gave everyone the potential to live peacefully together and overcome through commerce, education, and human generosity what the two philosophers thought to be superficial differences: skin color, language, clothing, customs, and knowledge.

Despite this general view, Hume nonetheless echoed the common European prejudice against Africans. "Negroes," he said, "[are] naturally inferior to the whites." Hume's Scottish colleague, the legal scholar Lord Kames (1696–1782), refuted this view, arguing that Hume mistook the Africans' natural condition for the enslaved state in which most eighteenth-century Europeans observed them. Slavery, Kames said, deprived Africans of the ability to act human, although not of the idea of what it meant to be human. The gap between the two sank them into despair and deprived them of motivation to improve their lives. They became uncivilized not because of any natural inferiority, but because of their terrible, inhuman living conditions had made them that way.

Rationality and the Critique of Religion

For Rousseau, all human beings living in society had to endure terrible, oppressive conditions, which is why he imagined a state of nature in which people, largely isolated from one another, enjoyed safety and security. In many ways, Rousseau's state of nature resembled Judeo-Christianity's Garden of Eden, and as we have seen, he drew on other religious ideas in promoting the virtues of equality. Rousseau showed little hostility to religion in the body of his work, and Kant disliked religion only when it was dogmatic. Such was equally true of Mandeville and some of the Scottish thinkers we have discussed.

But despite their generally benign views of religion, Mandeville and the Scots nonetheless sketched out a world independent of God's will and designs, as did

Kant in positing a realm of pure "phenomena" wholly governed by the mechanical laws of cause and effect. Rousseau, meanwhile, imagined a political realm grounded in a social contract that owed nothing to God.

If God did not play a direct role in human life, various European philosophers asked, why did we need him, and for what purposes? And did we need established churches and organized religion, and if so, how much of what they taught should we believe? In Scotland, some theologians maintained that humans were by nature benevolent and thus could behave morally and understand the difference between good and evil without already having knowledge of God or going to church. These views at first disturbed Scotland's religious establishment, known as the Kirk, but as the eighteenth century progressed, reformers came to define a new position within the Kirk that helped make Scottish Presbyterianism tolerant of religious dissent.

Hume agreed that people could lead virtuous, moral lives without believing in God but took the questioning of traditional religious belief even further. Hume wanted to know how humans develop religious belief and how we know whether that belief is true. The Scotsman pursued these questions in two crucial works, the *Natural History of Religion* (1757) and *Dialogues Concerning Natural Religion*, published posthumously in 1779. In the first book, Hume maintained that humans develop religion out of fear of the unknown. When something bad happens, they invent a god that must have caused it and then proceed to appease him so that the bad phenomenon will not happen again. The efforts to appease typically involve rituals of sacrifice or repentance, and with these rituals, religious practice begins.

Thus for Hume, religion originates in human ignorance, and his idea that humans create God, rather than the other way around, horrified leaders of the Kirk, who labeled Hume an atheist. But Hume did not say that because people created God, it followed that God did not exist. Rather, Hume granted the *possibility* of God's existence but wanted proof. Many of Hume's contemporaries argued that proof lay in the complex reality of the natural world, which could not have come to exist on its own. It must instead have been created by some extraordinary force, a divine Designer, or God, with the incomprehensible power to create all natural things. (This argument exists today as "intelligent design," often proposed as an alternative to Darwinian evolution.)

This "argument from design" was built on an analogy with human inventiveness. Just as people designed houses and machines, so the entire natural world must have been the result of some kind of design, although one vastly more intelligent than any human could produce. Hume rejected this argument, maintaining that it is wrong to make the jump from human design to God's design. To assume that God created the universe because God is like man, only immeasurably more powerful, is both to make a false analogy and to demean God. If God exists, Hume wrote, surely he cannot be compared with us.

Again, Hume did not flatly deny God's existence but rather said we could not demonstrate it by the kinds of arguments advanced in his day. Traditional theologians readily agreed that human reason was too weak to apprehend the fullness of God. But in their view, the answer to this dilemma was not Hume's skepticism but rather religious faith. We must *believe* in God precisely because we are too weak and sinful to reach upward to him in any other way.

National Differences in Enlightenment Thought

It is notable that no one prevented Hume from publishing his radical, even "blasphemous," religious views, although the *Dialogues Concerning Natural Religion* did not see print until after his death. By the late eighteenth century, freedom of expression in Scotland had trumped the power of traditionalists in the Kirk. Moderates within the Kirk sympathized with, and participated in, the new developments in Scottish philosophy. As a result, there was no split in Scotland between philosophy and religion, which meant that even when writers such as Ferguson, Smith, and Hume raised questions about certain religious beliefs, they mostly did so without attacking Christianity itself.

This relatively tolerant Scottish situation resembled in certain ways that of other Protestant countries, especially the Netherlands and Prussia under Frederick the Great, who banned prosecutions for heresy, gave rights to Jews, and declared, "everyone must be allowed to choose his own road to salvation." Beyond Protestant Europe, religious toleration grew as well in the largely Catholic Habsburg Empire. The reform-oriented Emperor Joseph II (1741–1790, ruled 1765–1790) gave extensive rights to non-Catholic Christians—Protestants and Eastern Orthodox adherents—and eventually to its growing number of Jews. Such toleration stood in stark contrast to the religious and political environment in eighteenth-century France, which turned a great many French philosophers into enemies of Christianity and the Church.

In France, kings still claimed to rule by divine right, and Catholicism remained the official state religion. The Catholic Church, which had emerged from the Reformation more powerful than before, worked hard to impose orthodoxy on religious practice and expression. The royal government actively censored religious and political writing, and in the first half of the century, far fewer newspapers, pamphlets, and books saw print in France than in Great Britain.

In this context, French writers and philosophers often found themselves silenced and oppressed; denied the ability to speak freely about religious issues, they turned against the "irrationality" of Catholicism and the Church. Many also disliked monarchy, at least as practiced in France, and found few redeeming qualities in the political institutions that surrounded it. For these reasons, French religious and political writing tended to be sharper and more extreme than its Scottish, German, and Austrian counterparts.

Voltaire and the Critique of Religion in France

The most famous French critic of Christianity was Voltaire, a philosopher who authored more than two hundred books and pamphlets and twenty thousand letters, many of which criticized what he considered the falsehoods of Christianity.

Voltaire lived in a huge chateau with his lover, a noblewoman, Emilie du Châtelet. Together, they acquired one of the largest private libraries of the time and studied Newtonian physics, French and English history, and especially the Bible and biblical commentary. Châtelet was as brilliant as Voltaire, and she developed an intellectual reputation unusual for women of her day. Her French translation of Newton's *Principia Mathematica*, a work that few people could understand, demonstrated her scientific prowess and deep understanding of mathematics. She corrected errors Newton had made and added her own algebraic postscript to the work. Voltaire, who popularized Newton's work in France, learned a great deal from her but was ambivalent about her intellectual powers, calling her "a great man whose only fault was being a woman."

Voltaire and Châtelet poured over the Old and New Testaments and found themselves horrified by what they read. The Old Testament, Voltaire said, reeked of "historical monstrosities which are repellent to nature and good sense." How could we possibly believe, Voltaire asked, the stories of snakes that talked, of women turned into columns of salt, of men who slept with their sisters? Even more ridiculous, he added, was Noah's ark, which somehow carried two hundred species of animals, including fourteen

≡ **Francois-Marie Arouet (Voltaire).** The author of more than 200 books and pamphlets, Voltaire mercilessly criticized Christianity and mocked many of its fundamental beliefs. Even so, he thought religion necessary, if only to discipline the supposedly unruly, unintelligent common man.

elephants, and the food to nourish them for nearly a year on a boat smaller than the gardens of his chateau.

Turning to the New Testament, Voltaire claimed that Jesus was just one of many equally insignificant itinerant preachers in Judea (today's Israel and Palestinian territories) and dismissed as absurd the idea that he was born of a virgin mother impregnated by God. Even more laughable, he said, was the notion that Jesus was at once God and the son of God. Voltaire added that no Roman historians or other writers of Jesus's time, beyond his loyal disciples, recorded the historical events so prominent in the Gospels: the virgin birth, the three philosophers guided by a newly created star, or the "darkness at noon" with which God punished the earth for the crucifixion of his son. These events, Voltaire concluded, were pure fiction concocted to take advantage of ignorant people.

Voltaire enjoyed making fun of what for him were ridiculous stories that defied common sense. But he did not consider them harmless. The New Testament, he declared, created a religious sect that wished "to annihilate all the others." Its quest for exclusivity and purity turned Christians against one another, and against Muslims and Jews. The result, he claimed, was centuries of religious warfare and nine million people dead.

Voltaire's most sustained critique of Christianity came in his *Philosophical Dictionary* (1762), a book studded with his trademark irony and satire. In his entry entitled "Faith," Voltaire has a fictionalized pope admitting that faith makes no sense. "Tell me," says the pope, "what merit one can have in telling God that one is persuaded of things of which in fact one cannot be persuaded?"

Such views did not make Voltaire an atheist. He believed that a great Creator existed, although one who did not intervene in the everyday world. What troubled Voltaire was the Judeo-Christian understanding of God, who was supposedly loving and benevolent but, in fact, allowed a great deal of evil and suffering to exist. If the Judeo-Christian God was good, why, Voltaire asked, had he so severely punished Adam and every human after him just "for having swallowed an apple?"

The traditional Catholic answer had to do with original sin and free will. Beginning with Adam, humans showed themselves to be sinful creatures, but their free will gave them the ability to overcome their depravity. Evil existed because humans chose to behave badly. For Voltaire, this answer was no answer at all. Why, he asked, did God create humans as creatures prone to sin and suffering?

A highly influential non-clerical response to the "problem of evil" and human suffering came from the German philosopher Leibniz, who argued that a benevolent God created a universe beneficial in the long run to everyone. The problem was that human beings' understanding of God was too limited to see that this was the case. A terrible thing that happens to us now, Leibniz maintained, ultimately serves a good purpose. It is just that this good purpose exists in a divine plan inaccessible to us. Evil, Leibniz said, is like a dissonant chord in music. By itself, it sounds terrible, but placed within a long symphony, it sets off the other chords and adds to the beauty of the composition. Leibniz called "**theodicy**" the idea that God created the universe as a perfect symphony imperceptible to human beings.

Voltaire found theodicy not only unconvincing but dangerous, for it encouraged people to accept the world as it was rather than to improve it. Along with many other European writers, Voltaire saw the terrible Lisbon (Portugal) earthquake of 1755 as proof that the benevolent God of Christian theology—and Leibniz's philosophy—did not exist. How, Voltaire asked, could such a God have allowed Europe's third largest port city to be thoroughly decimated, first by the quake, then by a huge tidal wave, and finally by fires that set what was left of the city ablaze?

For Voltaire, a disaster of such proportions could not possibly belong to a divine plan that would render it good in some distant future. "At the frightful sight of their smoking ashes," Voltaire wrote, "will you say, in seeing this mass of victims: 'This is the result of eternal laws directing the acts of a free and good God!'" Voltaire's story *Candide* (1759), perhaps his most famous work, mocks Leibniz by concluding, with bitter irony, that the series of disasters Candide faces—earthquakes, tsunamis, war, torture, starvation—will be "for the best" in the long run and that he lives in the "best of all possible worlds."

Despite his relentless condemnation of traditional Christian belief and practice, Voltaire, like many other French philosophers, thought religion necessary for the common man (although not for members of the enlightened elite like him). A religion's moral strictures could control people's boisterous behavior by convincing them that eternal damnation awaited them if they failed to obey their betters. "If God did not exist," Voltaire allegedly said, "it would be necessary to invent him."

Religion had its necessary, benign features, even for Voltaire. But when it came to politics, religion was dangerous, for it could lead to despotism when a leader claimed to rule by divine right. As Voltaire's comrade, Denis Diderot (1713–1784), wrote, despotism occurs when "one man—proud, evildoing, self-interested, and vicious—rules men with impunity in the name of God" and when "it is a crime to examine his commands, and an impiety to oppose him." In making this comment, Diderot had the French kings in mind.

As if to confirm Diderot's description of them, French royal officials worked hard to prevent the sale and circulation of his and Jean Le Rond d'Alembert's (1717–1783) *Encyclopedia* (1751–1772), the great compendium of seventeenth- and eighteenth-century knowledge and the flagship publication of the Enlightenment.

The *Encyclopedia* stretched over twenty-eight volumes and included nearly 72,000 articles and more than 3,000 illustrations. Its goal was "to change the way people think" by bringing together in a single set of books everything that was known—practical, philosophical, mathematical, historical, literary, and much else besides. The *Encyclopedia* was at once a manifesto of the new science and philosophy discussed in this chapter and a detailed "how-to" book that explained everything from how to build and operate a printing press to how to identify and classify the different forms of life—plants, animals, and human beings.

In an introductory essay, d'Alembert divided the *Encyclopedia's* content into three forms of knowledge: memory/history, reason/philosophy, and imagination/poetry. The successive volumes banished theology, long the "queen of the sciences," to the margins and subjected the Catholic Church to mockery and satire, although the various authors generally did so subtly and indirectly in an effort to escape the heavy hand of government censors. Diderot and d'Alembert's audience quickly learned to read between the lines, to crack the code of subterfuge and insinuation to perceive the fullness of their critiques. But so too did the censors. As soon as the first volume appeared, Diderot and d'Alembert found themselves roundly condemned.

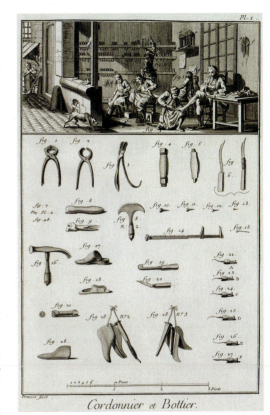

The *Encyclopedia.* This monument of the French Enlightenment was at once a manifesto of the era's new science and philosophy and a "how-to" manual that explained everything from how to make shoes and boots to how to identify the various forms of life.

To defend their work, the two editors enlisted the support and participation of the most illustrious writers of the day—Voltaire, Rousseau, Montesquieu, and many others. However, government leaders, top clergymen, Jesuits, and conservative aristocrats mercilessly attacked the enterprise. Pope Clement XII declared that any Catholic who failed to burn all copies he owned would face excommunication from the Church.

Few printed works had been more thoroughly condemned, but the *Encyclopedia* had become so popular among educated readers and so profitable for publishers that Diderot and d'Alembert had no trouble finding people to print and distribute their books (see Map 4.2). The very government official, Guillaume-Chrétien de Lamoignon de Malesherbes (1721–1794), in charge of suppressing the *Encyclopedia* surreptitiously allowed it to be published under a different title.

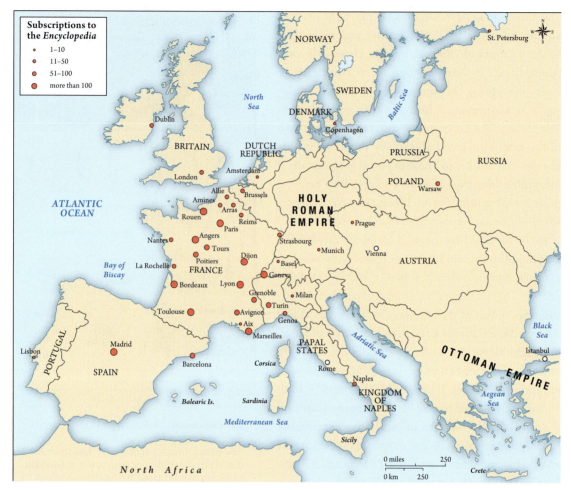

Subscriptions to the *Encyclopedia*

- 1–10
- 11–50
- 51–100
- more than 100

≡ **MAP 4.2** Subscriptions to the *Encyclopedia*

And when this ruse proved too cumbersome, booksellers simply arranged for the volumes to be printed in neighboring countries and then smuggled past sympathetic border guards into France. The country's official censorship, offset by lax enforcement of the censors' work, proved a great boon to dissident writers like Diderot. Their books appeared all the more important precisely because the government tried, albeit unsuccessfully, to ban them.

The original editions of the *Encyclopedia* were expensive and therefore accessible only to a narrow, wealthy elite. Most readers of the *Encyclopedia* and other key Enlightenment works came from the upper ranks of society—lawyers, high office-holders, the upper clergy, educated aristocrats, and other dignitaries. Businessmen, no matter how wealthy, rarely had the time or inclination to read philosophical works, and most working people possessed neither the means nor the literacy to enjoy them. Still, Enlightenment ideas gradually filtered into a growing periodical press, pamphlet literature, and the burgeoning category of pornographic works, many of which mocked kings and queens, clergymen, aristocrats, and the like. It was through these more popular works that elements of the Enlightenment critique of political authority and the Church reached ordinary people and influenced their actions and beliefs.

The Theory and Practice of Government

If philosophers like Diderot convinced growing numbers of people that France's monarchy was "self-interested and vicious," leading Enlightenment figures did not agree on what kind of government would be better. To help them decide, Montesquieu, a French nobleman, undertook to analyze them all in what became his most famous work, *The Spirit of the Laws* (1748), a book banned by French censors and the pope.

Montesquieu identified three possible forms of government: republics, monarchies, and despotism. **Republics** could be either "democratic" or "aristocratic," that is, ruled either by all the people or by a small elite. In **monarchies**, one person held all the power but governed according to "fixed and established laws" and could not therefore rule arbitrarily, which is precisely what despots could do. Under **despotism**, a single individual rules "without law and . . . drags everything along by his will and his caprice."

Each form of government possessed an underlying principle. For republics the principle was "virtue," for monarchies "honor," and for despotism "fear." In Montesquieu's view, virtue and honor were acceptable founding principles, but fear was not. For that reason, only republics and monarchies were legitimate forms of government. Montesquieu's ideas, diametrically opposed to those of Hobbes, moved him to distinguish between European governments and "Eastern" ones (Turkey, Persia, and China). The former were mostly legitimate republics or monarchies and the latter despotisms, where custom and climate supposedly yoked their people to rulers who prevented them from enjoying the benefits of "civilization" (liberty, science, progress, and sophisticated arts) increasingly common in Western Europe.

Montesquieu's preferred government was a republic-monarchy hybrid, a "moderated monarchy" similar to the one he observed in Britain. There, a monarchy coexisted with an aristocratic republic, and the king shared power and authority with a propertied elite, itself divided into two categories: a small, hereditary House of Lords and a considerably larger, elected House of Commons. The three categories—monarch, Lords, and Commons—checked and balanced one another and prevented any individual or group from gaining too much power—at least in theory. This idea deeply influenced the American Founders, especially James Madison, the key author and defender of the Constitution and Bill of Rights, who inscribed checks and balances into the very fabric of US law.

Voltaire and other French writers shared Montesquieu's admiration of Britain's form of government, but they did not believe France could reproduce it. French writers thus looked elsewhere in Europe for a kind of monarchy that might be preferable to a French monarchy they considered increasingly despotic. They discovered what came to be called "enlightened despotism," governments of strong monarchs who sought to use their power to improve society in ways championed by leading philosophers of the eighteenth century.

Voltaire found himself drawn to Prussia's Frederick the Great, who saw himself as a "first servant of the state." Frederick worked tirelessly to modernize the Prussian bureaucracy, to advance the arts and other highlights of European "civilization," develop the Prussian Academy of Sciences, and to promote religious tolerance. Frederick made French, the language of "enlightenment," the official tongue of his court and engaged in a fifty-year-long correspondence with Voltaire, whom he invited to live in his French-named palace, Sanssouci ("without worries"). Frederick, like Europe's other "enlightened despots," Russia's Catherine the Great (ruled 1762–1796) and Austria's Joseph II, also took steps to make his economy more modern and productive, to promote education, to modernize his army, and generally to reform society from above. Under Joseph's mother, Maria Theresa (1717–1780, ruled 1740–1780), the Habsburg empire became the first European state to make public education mandatory for both sexes, although, in practice, too few schools existed to educate everyone.

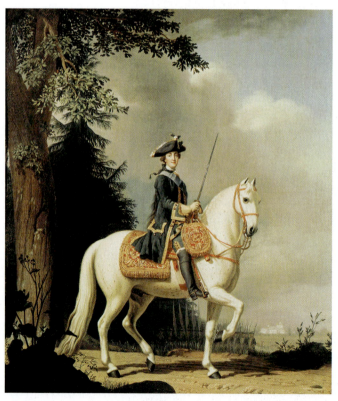

≡ **Catherine the Great.** Devoted to high culture and Enlightenment thought, Catherine not only ruled her vast Russian Empire but wrote stories and plays, corresponded regularly with Voltaire and Diderot, and developed a modern school for girls. She made a valiant, but ultimately unsuccessful, effort to reform her country's rigid political and social structures.

Along with Frederick, Voltaire corresponded regularly and over many years with Catherine the Great, who also developed close intellectual relationships with Diderot and Jacques Necker (1732–1804), the economist and future prime minister under France's Louis XVI. Catherine offered refuge to Diderot after the French government threatened to imprison him. A devotee of high culture, Catherine wrote stories and plays, created an impressive art collection, and tried to develop modern, Westernized schools. She created her country's first state-run school for girls, something that did not exist elsewhere in Europe, and tried (without success) to reform her government in ways Montesquieu would have approved. In advancing these reforms, Catherine paid homage to her predecessor as tsar, Peter the Great (ruled 1682–1725), who strengthened and expanded his country while trying to remodel his government and society along Western European lines.

Voltaire and Diderot admired Catherine, in part because she was originally from Germany, an area of Europe that the French philosophers considered "civilized." When she became Russia's tsarina after helping stage a coup d'état against her husband, Tsar Peter III, Voltaire applauded her attempts to bestow the supposed benefits of European civilization on a country he deemed backward, even barbaric. In endorsing Catherine's work, Voltaire distinguished between an advanced, cultivated Western Europe, anchored by France and Britain, and an Eastern Europe said to resemble the "barbarism" of Asia more than the "civilization" of the West.

Even so, Voltaire, along with a variety of other Enlightenment writers, believed Eastern Europe had the potential to be civilized, thanks in large part to Catherine's vast, despotic powers. She had used them, Voltaire said, first to lift her long-backward country out of barbarism and then to shine the light of civilization onto the lands between Russia and Germany by conquering them militarily. In the process, Voltaire urged the tsarina to push the "savage" Turks out of Europe and claim the vacated lands for "civilization." "These barbarians," the philosophe wrote, referring to the Ottomans, "deserve to be punished," even "exterminated," because they "neglect all the fine arts" and "shut up women." Voltaire would also have approved of the Habsburg rulers Maria Theresa and especially Joseph II. By lightening the burdens on peasants and reining in the aristocracy and the Church, both extended the benefits of "civilization" to the easternmost reaches of their domains, territories that included parts of today's Poland, Slovakia, Ukraine, and Romania.

Voltaire extolled Catherine the Great without ever visiting her country, but Diderot actually traveled there in 1773. Once in Russia, he met regularly with the tsarina and continued to admire her. Diderot was, however, less optimistic than Voltaire about Catherine's ability to raise Russia to the level of the West. "To civilize all at once such an enormous country," Diderot declared, "seems to me a project beyond human forces." With such judgments about Russia—and similar ones about Ottoman Europe and Eastern Europe—Diderot, Voltaire, and many of their Enlightenment colleagues established a template for understanding the eastern parts of the continent that would continue to shape Western discourse about them into the twenty-first century.

That Voltaire and Diderot corresponded with two "absolutist" monarchs, Frederick and Catherine the Great, and apparently admired them both makes it difficult to consider either philosopher an advocate of political participation for the masses. Certainly, neither was a democrat, and neither opposed monarchy on principle. The one French philosopher who called for an equal political voice for all male citizens was Rousseau, although he too did not reject monarchy on principle.

Women and the New Philosophy

Rousseau was adamant that men alone should participate in politics and the public sphere; women's place, he claimed, was in the home. Although, like most eighteenth-century writers, Rousseau sought to erase women from political life, he did not erase them from the public debates of his time. In fact, the writings of Enlightenment philosophers, including women philosophers, devoted a huge amount of attention to the nature of women and their role in society and the family. Mandeville became one of the first to take up what later would be called the "woman question." As we have seen, he believed that feelings of shame had the positive effect (for men) of improving people's behavior. But for women, Mandeville believed shame had the negative consequence of placing unjust constraints on them and forcing them to suppress their passions. Women, Mandeville said, were just as naturally sexual as men, but the man-made rules of society required women to remain chaste until marriage and display modesty in their sexual demeanor throughout their lives. Those tempted to behave otherwise knew they would be shamed and ridiculed and banished from polite society. They thus either consciously kept their sexuality in check or internalized the codes of society and acted as if they were, by nature, modest and chaste.

Hume agreed with Mandeville that female chastity was "artificial" rather than natural, the product of social rules, education, and the requirements of husbands and fathers. But if they considered women no less sexual than men, neither Hume nor Mandeville went so far as to argue that women were the equals of men in other respects. Hume asserted that "nature has given man the superiority above woman, by endowing him with greater strength both of mind and body." He added, however, that only in barbarous or despotic societies did men lord their superiority over women by treating them brutally, selling them, enslaving them, or confining them, by force and custom, to the home. In civilized societies, men tempered their superiority, even denied or disguised it, through "gallantry," through the respectful, kind, and generous treatment of women. One of the main measures of progress and civilization, wrote Hume and other members of the Scottish Enlightenment, was the level of consideration shown toward women. Their own society, they thought, had developed such consideration, while less advanced ones had not.

Although some women writers of the eighteenth century accepted such ideas, many prominent ones rejected the premise of male superiority on which they were based. In *Woman Not Inferior to Man* (1739), a writer who used the name Sophia maintained that women were the intellectual equals of men and that the differences between the two sexes were minimal. This equality meant that there were no legitimate reasons for excluding women from positions in the church, government, and army and that they were denied these opportunities only because of men's prejudice and desire to keep these jobs for themselves.

While Sophia focused on equality, the distinguished English historian Catharine Macaulay (1731–1791) took up the notion of gallantry, which she condemned for allowing men to feel good about their treatment of women while subjecting them to "a total and absolute exclusion of every political right." That women were treated with kindness and a condescending indulgence did nothing to allow them the independence and political equality they deserved.

Macaulay was a prolific writer whose eight-volume *History of England* (1763–1783) attracted a great deal of attention, as did her pamphlets on electoral reform, constitutional theory, and the American Revolution. Like Hume, who also wrote a multivolume *History of England*, Macaulay maintained that English liberty emerged not through some special wisdom or aptitude of her compatriots but through the chance occurrences of historical events. English philosophers, she said, began to theorize about liberty only after English people had stumbled on the practice of liberty in their reactions to the despotism of James I and Charles I in the first half of the seventeenth century. In making this argument, Macaulay showed a modern sensibility by maintaining that human beings, not God, were in charge of their own destiny, although not necessarily in ways they consciously understood. And because people controlled their destiny, they had the right to devise their own governments and to change them "according to the dictates of experience and [their] better judgment." These beliefs made her highly sympathetic to the American Revolution and evoked criticism from advocates of hereditary, monarchical rule.

Although Macaulay did not write specifically about women in her works of history, she took up the issue of female equality in her final work, the *Letters on Education* (1790), in which she argued that boys and girls should have an identical education. Schooling was crucial, she wrote, because human beings are highly changeable, and a comprehensive system of tax-funded national education would enable governments to turn all young people, girls as well as boys, into moral, politically engaged citizens. In making this argument, Macaulay directly challenged the views of Rousseau, who claimed that since women were by nature intellectually inferior to men, it would be pointless to give boys and girls the same kind of education.

Rousseau was perhaps the most prominent advocate of the notion that women's bodies determined the kinds of lives they had to lead. As he put it, "the male is male only at certain moments; the female is female her whole life . . . everything constantly recalls her sex to her." No woman should be active in society, because each needs a "soft sedentary life to suckle her babies and to give [constant] care and tenderness to hold her family together." Men, like children, needed women to care for them, and it was this feminine nurturing, Rousseau said, that fortified men morally and spiritually to employ their superior rational abilities in an all-male political sphere.

Macaulay rejected Rousseau's ideas as degrading to both men and women, for they portrayed men as morally incomplete and women as intellectually incompetent. But Macaulay admitted that even though Rousseau was wrong to say that men, by nature, were intellectually superior to women, most women behaved as though he were right. Society, she wrote, rewarded women for being modest and retiring and for devoting themselves to the care and pleasure of men. It punished them for cultivating their minds and bodies and, in any case, made it difficult for them to develop intellectually by barring them from schools.

The English philosopher Mary Wollstonecraft (1759–1797) made this point even more forcefully in what was to become her most famous book, *A Vindication of the Rights of Woman* (1792). If women appeared to be less rational and less accomplished than men, Wollstonecraft wrote, it was because society had forced them into narrowly prescribed "feminine" roles and denied them education, excluded them from the professions, and relegated them to the home.

Women, Wollstonecraft added, had adapted all too well to these conditions, gratefully accepting male gallantry and doing their best to please and entice men in return. They had become preoccupied with outward appearances and sought to relate to men mainly as sexual beings. A sound moral education, Wollstonecraft maintained in *Thoughts on the Education of Daughters* (1787), would help undo the damage the rules and conventions of society had done and develop the rational intellect that women, no less than men, possessed. To put her ideas into practice, she helped establish an intellectually rigorous school for girls.

As important as education was, it alone did not suffice. Women, Wollstonecraft said, needed civil and political rights, for if they lacked the ability to contribute directly to the public realm, men would not take them seriously. Women would fall back on their traditional roles as nurturers and seducers, which had long been their only way of influencing men, and through them, society at large. If women gained political rights, the moral regeneration achieved in schools like the one she created would spread into society and transform public life.

Wollstonecraft believed that such a transformation was taking place in the new United States, and, like Macaulay, she became an ardent supporter of the American Revolution, which inaugurated, in her view, "a new epoch in the history of mankind." What she particularly admired about the new American political culture was the "innocent frankness that characterizes the American women, and the consequent friendly intercourse that subsists between the sexes when gallantry and coquetry are equally out of the question." Wollstonecraft was less enamored of the French Revolution, whose violence she deplored, but she would have supported the writings of her French contemporary, Olympe de Gouges (1748–1793).

Gouges (born Marie Gouze) rose from obscure small-town origins to make a name for herself in pre-revolutionary France and then to play a significant role in the French Revolution itself. Already a widow at seventeen, Gouges took off for Paris in 1770 with her infant son, Pierre. In the mid-1780s, she began to write, and in less than a decade produced more than forty works—literary essays, political pamphlets and manifestos, and plays with a political point of view. Her best-known theatrical work took a strong stance against slavery and earned her the hatred of planters and sugar merchants, who owed their wealth to human bondage.

Ridiculed for her radical views, Gouges turned in response to the condition of women. She argued that just because women were physically different from men did

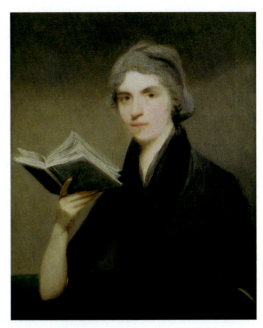

≡ **Mary Wollstonecraft.** In a series of influential, radical works, Wollstonecraft argued that women were the equals of men, despite appearances to the contrary. Women seemed inferior only because they had long been denied education, excluded from the professions, and relegated to the home.

not mean they lacked the brainpower and commitment to their country to help solve its problems. Women should, therefore, possess the same political rights as men. In the wake of the French Revolution of 1789 (Chapter 5), Gouges issued a blizzard of newspaper articles and pamphlets and insisted on the right to speak at political meetings from which women had been barred. Her most significant intervention came in 1791, when the parliament was debating France's new revolutionary constitution. Fearing that women would be completely left out, she published a bill of rights for women, which she called "The Declaration of the Rights of Woman and the Female Citizen." It paralleled "The Declaration of the Rights of Man and Citizen," adopted during the opening phase of the Revolution, but unlike the original, explicitly gave rights to women. Where the Declaration of the Rights of Man declared, "Men are born and remain free and equal in rights," Gouges' version countered, "Woman is born free and remains equal to man in her rights." For advancing such ideas and denouncing French revolutionaries for failing to extend liberty and equality to women, she was sent to the guillotine in 1793.

Major Works of the Enlightenment		
1689	*Two Treatises of Government*	John Locke
	An Essay Concerning Human Understanding	
1707	*Theodicy*	Gottfried Wilhelm Leibniz
1733	*Philosophical Letters of the English*	Voltaire
1748	*The Spirit of the Laws*	Montesquieu
1751–1772	*Encyclopedia*	Denis Diderot
1755	*Discourse on the Origin and Basis of Inequality among Men*	Rousseau
1757	*Natural History of Religion*	David Hume
1759	*Candide*	Voltaire
	Theory of Moral Sentiments	Adam Smith
1762	*The Social Contract*	Rousseau
1763	*Treatise on Toleration*	Voltaire
1763–1783	*History of England*	Catherine Macaulay
1764	*Philosophical Dictionary*	Voltaire
1776	*The Wealth of Nations*	Adam Smith
1784	*"What Is Enlightenment?"*	Immanuel Kant
1789	*"Slavery of the Negroes"*	Olympe de Gouges
1792	*A Vindication of the Rights of Woman*	Mary Wollstonecraft

Conclusion: The Accomplishments of the Enlightenment

Gouges' writings about slavery joined those of Montesquieu and Kames and made her a key contributor to one of the central debates of the second half of the eighteenth century. Human bondage, after all, violated essentially everything enlightened writers stood for, especially sympathy for others in distress. The existence and persistence of slavery led some writers of the period to question the widely accepted idea that Europeans were more civilized than everyone else.

Still, most eighteenth-century observers accepted the notion that Europe had progressed enormously since the early seventeenth century, when Galileo first challenged Aristotelian certainties, and in many ways they were right. Galileo had played a major role in creating a new understanding of the natural world based on empirical observation rather than the accepted, though untested, ideas of antiquity and the Middle Ages. His successors—Descartes, Torricelli, Pascal, Bacon, Boyle, and Newton—extended and deepened his pioneering work.

Although the study of "man" made somewhat less progress than the study of the natural world, eighteenth-century philosophers nonetheless established the responsibility of human beings for their own condition and raised questions about the received truths of all major religions. Enlightenment writers, especially women writers, undermined the notion that women were inherently inferior to men and claimed political and civil rights for the female half of the human race. As philosophers debated the question of who should enjoy political rights, they turned to the study of government and examined the nature of republics, monarchies, democracies, and despotic forms of rule. If writers such as Montesquieu and Voltaire rejected "oriental" despotism in Western Europe, they embraced "enlightened" despotism as a solution for the supposed backwardness of Russia and Eastern Europe, as the only way to bestow "civilization" on the region's "primitive" peoples.

The New World was also said to contain primitive peoples and unsophisticated European emigrants, but the American Revolution forced European writers to take notice of the upstart United States. The establishment of a republic there in 1776 created what amounted to a natural experiment that tested people's ability to govern themselves. Macaulay, Wollstonecraft, and a great many other Enlightenment philosophers decided that the Americans had passed the test. In 1789, as we will see in Chapter 5, the French undertook an even more radical experiment in human governance whose results are still being debated today.

KEY TERMS

animistic *151*	Enlightenment *161*	public sphere *161*
barometer *154*	gender *163*	republics *181*
centrifugal force *158*	mechanistic *152*	salons *161*
corpuscles *157*	monarchies *181*	technology *155*
despotism *181*	natural law *163*	theodicy *178*
division of labor *169*	philosophes *160*	vacuum *153*
ellipse *147*	probabilistic *156*	

For digital learning resources, please go to **https://www.oup.com/he/berenson2e**. Turn to the back of the book to see the list of primary sources and writing exercises provided in the accompanying *Sources and Guided Writing Exercises for Europe in the Modern World*

5

The Era of the French Revolution, 1750–1815

Toussaint Louverture

"I was born a slave, but nature gave me the soul of a free man ... I want Liberty and Equality to reign in Saint-Domingue [Haiti]." So declared Toussaint Louverture, one of the most remarkable figures of the French revolutionary era.

The French Revolution broke out in the spring of 1789, and by the time it was over in 1815, it had transformed France and left a deep imprint on Europe and the world. The revolution swept away a centuries-old monarchy and nobility, confiscated the extensive landholdings of the Catholic Church, transformed understandings of politics and society, disrupted empires, and gave French people and other Europeans a taste of democracy and civil rights. The French Revolution also led to the modern world's only successful slave rebellion, a cataclysmic event in which enslaved people in Saint-Domingue not only won their freedom but made themselves full-fledged citizens of France.

François-Dominique Toussaint Louverture (c.1743–1803), a black man born in slavery, played a commanding role in Saint-Domingue's slave revolt of 1791–1793. By 1798, he had made himself the military governor and de facto ruler of what had been France's most lucrative colonial possession. He then led the effort to throw off what remained of colonial rule and to create a new country called *(h)ayti* (Haïti in French) or "land of high mountains," the name used by the island's original inhabitants.

Toussaint Louverture came from a West African family of warriors and princely leaders. Although his father had been captured in Africa and sold into slavery in the New World, his grandfather probably—we do not know for sure—was a provincial governor or royal official in the West African kingdom of Dahomey (present-day Benin), an important precolonial state. Toussaint grew up hearing stories of his ancestors' military bravery, or perhaps invented those stories later in life, and concluded that black people had been warriors and kings and that slavery was far from their natural state.

In the mid-1770s, Toussaint's master freed him and gave him a modest plot to farm. Unlike Saint-Domingue's *gens de couleur*, individuals of mixed race, Toussaint had no white relatives. Thus, even though he was no longer a slave at the time of the French Revolution, he remained on the lowest rung of the

Général Toussaint Louverture (1743-1803)
Précurseur de l'Indépendance d'Haïti

colony's strict racial hierarchy, with whites at the top, mixed-race people in the middle, and individuals of pure African descent at the bottom.

Although there are few reliable details about Toussaint Louverture's early life, we know that he learned to read and write, which was unusual for enslaved Africans, and that he possessed a strong intellect. Toussaint seems to have read certain key Enlightenment writings and found himself attracted to the work of the prominent French abolitionist Abbé Guillaume Thomas Raynal (1713–1796), who predicted that a black hero would lead a successful slave revolt in Saint-Domingue.

Although Toussaint's ability to write in French remained rudimentary, he understood the importance of written expression and recruited dozens of educated white secretaries to put his thoughts to paper. In the letters that have survived, we can see that Toussaint thought deeply about military strategy, understood the nuances of diplomacy, and developed a clear sense of how Saint-Domingue should make the difficult transition from slavery to freedom. In some ways, he resembled Napoleon Bonaparte—some called him "the black Napoleon"—since, like Napoleon (1769–1821), his military genius allowed him to ride the wave of revolution from a modest position in society to the heights of political power.

In 1793, with revolutionary France at war against the other European countries, Saint-Domingue's slave revolt became implicated in the conflict when Britain and Spain invaded the French colony in an effort to seize it for themselves. Spain was the weakest of the three countries contending for control in Saint-Domingue, and to bolster its military fortunes, Spanish officials offered to free all leaders and soldiers of the slave revolt who agreed to fight for them against the French. This offer prompted Toussaint Louverture and several other black commanders to defect to Spain.

Toussaint was already a free man, but he feared that if the French prevailed they would re-enslave him, and he was ambivalent at best about the French Revolution. Although the revolution was devoted to "Liberty, Equality, and Fraternity," its leaders refused to grant freedom to enslaved people in France's colonies.

Not until the spring of 1794 did Toussaint Louverture join the French side. He did so shortly after the French revolutionary parliament decreed the emancipation of Saint-Domingue's slaves and made all adult black men full-fledged citizens of France. This dramatic, unprecedented French decree was based in part on the

Timeline

| 1750 | 1755 | 1760 | 1765 | 1770 | 1775 | 1780 | 1785 | 1790 | 1795 | 1800 | 1805 | 1810 | 1815 | 1820 |

1756–1763 Seven Years' War

1771 Maupeou disbands Parlement of Paris

1774–1793 Reign of Louis XVI

1777 Necker appointed minister of finance of France

1785 Parlement of Paris refuses to approve loans

1788 French treasury suspends payments to creditors

1789 May 5 Convening of Estates General

June 20 Tennis Court Oath

July 12–14 Necker removed from office; attack on the Bastille

August 4 Nobles renounce their privileges; *Declaration on the Rights of Man and Citizen*

October 6 Parisian women march on Versailles

November Parlement nationalizes Church property

June 20, 1791 Royal family attempts to flee Paris

1791–1803 Rebellion in French colonies

April 1792 France declares war on Austria

August 1792 Sans-culottes attack Tuileries; royal family flees to Assembly

September 1792 "September Massacres," Convention meets; new parliament strips king of titles and declares France a republic

January 1793 Louis XVI executed

March 1793 Vendée Rebellion

1793–1794 The Terror

1794 Robespierre is executed

1794–1799 The Directory

November 1799 Coup establishes Napoleon as First Consul

1801 Napoleon signs Concordat with pope

1801 Toussaint becomes governor of Saint-Domingue

1802 Napoleon becomes First Consul for life

1804 Napoleon crowned Emperor of the French, issues Napoleonic Code

1812 Napoleon advances to and retreats from Moscow

April 1814 Allied forces defeat Napoleon, who is exiled to Elba

1815 Returning Napoleon defeated at Waterloo, exiled for life

revolutionary ideology of freedom and equality and in part on the pragmatic realization that the badly outnumbered French forces in Saint-Domingue could hold the colony only if the island's talented black commanders and rebel soldiers agreed to fight with them. Both commanders and soldiers had shown that they would ally with Europeans in exchange for their freedom, and the French decree likely convinced them that France was a more reliable liberator than either Britain or Spain.

Toussaint's defection from Spain to France delighted French officials in Saint-Domingue, who expressed the hope that "all the Africans [would] imitate his generous repentance and defend their freedom by fighting for France." Toussaint, for his part, now publicly embraced the French Revolution and the language of the Enlightenment. "We are republicans," he declared, "and consequently free according to natural right." He denounced the kings "who dare to claim the right to reduce men to slavery when nature has made them free." Toussaint's dedication to freedom and equality did not prevent him from behaving ruthlessly in pursuit of his goals. He methodically stripped his rivals of power and regularly reminded the freed slaves of their debts to him and the French of the crucial military forces he controlled.

In late 1794, Toussaint, along with the mixed-race commander André Rigaud (1761–1811) and other indigenous leaders and troops, contained the British advance in Saint-Domingue and helped retake Guadeloupe. After 1795 they no longer had to face troops from Spain, which had withdrawn from the war against France. The British, however, clung to parts of the island, and when they launched a new offensive in 1796, Toussaint repelled it. After this new military success, French authorities named Toussaint commander in chief of the entire French army in Saint-Domingue, not just its black auxiliaries. In this role, the former slave became the de facto ruler of the island.

After seven years of bloody fighting, Saint-Domingue's economy was devastated, many of its once-opulent mansions and sugar fields burned to the ground. As the colony's leader, Toussaint decided to restore plantation sugar production. He forced all ex-slaves not serving in the army to work on plantations—often for their former masters—which he considered the only efficient way to produce the sugar and other tropical products so highly valued in Europe. To many ex-slaves and French revolutionaries, Toussaint's effort looked like a betrayal of the revolution and a return to the Old Regime.

While Toussaint enshrined the abolition of slavery and racial hierarchy in the constitution he framed in 1801, in other ways, Toussaint set his nascent country back. By making landed property "sacred and inviolable," his new constitution permitted former slave owners to reclaim their plantations and unfairly rewarded the black and mixed-race generals who had seized abandoned domains during the long years of fighting. Perhaps most important—and most ominous—Toussaint made himself a virtual dictator, who as "ruler for life," according to the constitution, presided over a parliament devoid of power and a population with no meaningful political and civil rights.

For fear of another French intervention, Toussaint did not formally declare Saint-Domingue independent from France, but his new constitution advertised his true, independence-minded intentions. So did his foreign policy. At a time when France and the United States were at odds, Toussaint established friendly relations with the new American republic and encouraged direct trade between Saint-Domingue and other countries in violation of French colonial rules.

Napoleon Bonaparte, who had emerged as the undisputed French leader in 1800, did not accept this state of affairs. In 1802 he sent an enormous, 25,000-man army to restore colonialism, slavery, and the slave trade in France's former Caribbean possessions. In the end, Napoleon succeeded in reestablishing colonial rule in Martinique and Guadeloupe, but Toussaint and his lieutenants blocked him in Saint-Domingue. Sadly for Toussaint, he fell into a French ambush and was spirited off to France, where he died in a dank prison cell.

≡ **Fighting in Saint-Domingue.** Bloody, murderous fighting on the Caribbean island began with the revolt of enslaved people in 1791 and continued until the final defeat of Napoleon's forces some thirteen years later. This painting of 1802 by the Polish artist January Suchodolski shows Poles fighting with the French army against the black Haitian troops.

Napoleon later admitted "it was a great mistake to have wanted to subdue [Saint-Domingue] by force; I should have contented myself to govern it through the intermediary of Toussaint." But Toussaint would not have been anyone's intermediary, not even Napoleon's. Under Toussaint's leadership, the people of Saint-Domingue had transformed a slave revolt into a revolution, and like the French Revolution that had triggered it, the Haitian Revolution would not be overthrown. Both would serve as precedents and models for revolutionaries to come. ≡

Origins of the French Revolution

To understand how and why the French Revolution and its Haitian offshoot became precedent-setting "world historical events," as the German philosopher Friedrich Hegel called them, we must look back to the last decades of the eighteenth century and to the origins of the upheaval of 1789. In the mid-1780s, the French royal government of Louis XVI faced a political and economic crisis so severe that it paralyzed the state and sapped much of the public's confidence in the king and his ministers. No single factor—or collection of factors—made revolution inevitable, but in the 1780s several relatively recent developments in France's economy and society, politicized by the newfound power of public opinion, brought a variety of deep structural problems to a head. Those problems mostly turned on the royal government's inability to finance its operations, which was itself the product of the kings' inability or unwillingness to reform France's dysfunctional political system and status hierarchy. As a result, France confronted one crisis after the other between 1750 and 1789—a financial crisis, a political crisis, a public opinion crisis, and a crisis of frustrated expectations—which together launched the country deep into the political unknown.

The Financial Crisis

As we saw in Chapter 2, France's financial crisis had been brewing for a long time. Beginning in the sixteenth century, the country's ceaseless wars regularly emptied the royal treasury and sank the monarchy deeper and deeper into debt. Because the nobility remained largely exempt from the chief forms of taxation, monarchs could attract money from wealthy noblemen only by borrowing from them and by selling them offices. But venal office holding made government highly inefficient and officeholders difficult to control. Nothing was more emblematic of this irrational system than **tax farming**, which allowed elite individuals to purchase the right to collect taxes on behalf of the king, while keeping a healthy portion of the proceeds for themselves.

Despite the weakness of the French treasury and the advice of his finance minister, Jean-Baptiste Colbert, Louis XIV fought a series of wars of unprecedented length and cost, overwhelming the state's financial system to an unparalleled degree. His successors tried to repair this situation by undertaking or encouraging the seizure of colonies and commercial bases in the Caribbean, North America, Africa, China, and India and then retaining a portion of the income generated there. But the need to defend those colonies from rival European powers, especially the British, forced France to fight a series of wars for control of shipping lanes, ports, sugar islands, and the lucrative slave trade. Colonies cost far more to manage and defend than they brought in and added to France's enormous pile of debt.

Since France was a continental power in addition to a maritime one, it increasingly had to battle both on land and at sea. This was the case during the Seven Years' War (1756–1763), when France fought Prussia in Europe and Britain in North America, the Caribbean, India, and elsewhere around the world (see Map 5.1). These conflicts ended disastrously for the French, who lost Canada and India to the British and went even further into debt. Interest payments to the crown's creditors

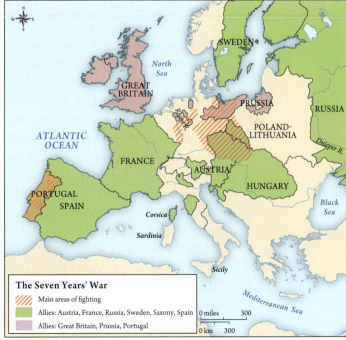

≡ **MAP 5.1** The Seven Years' War

now absorbed 60 percent of all tax revenues, leaving far too little for everything else. Even so, the French government dug itself further into the red by financing the American colonists' effort to throw off British rule (1776–1783). The effort proved a rousing success, but once again, the French crown could fund this latest war only by increasing its debt load—now at exorbitant interest rates, since creditors considered loans to France risky in the extreme.

While the French state found it increasingly difficult and costly to borrow money, its British rival could borrow easily and at far lower rates. Britain could do so thanks to a pair of key institutions that France did not possess: a national bank with the authority to issue government bonds (that is, to solicit loans from the public) and a political institution, Parliament, which constitutionally guaranteed that the bonds would be repaid. Without such institutions, French leaders found themselves unable to repair their ruined system of state finance and to prevent the royal government from heading toward collapse.

The Political Crisis

Although France lacked a national representative assembly like Britain's Parliament, it possessed thirteen regional judicial institutions called ***parlements***. These institutions were appeals courts with the power to review all royal legislation and reject any law they considered flawed, although the king could override them. Parlements had existed in France since the Middle Ages but exercised only modest authority until after the death of Louis XIV, who had held them at bay. When his great-grandson, the five-year-old Louis XV, succeeded him to the throne in 1715, the absence of an adult king vastly reduced royal power and enabled the parlements, especially the Parlement of Paris, to fill the relative political void. Parlements now pressured the king (or his regent while Louis XV remained a minor) by publishing their dissents, called "remonstrances," and sparking debate around them in France's fledgling "public sphere."

From the 1720s until 1789, one of the main issues addressed by parlements and the public sphere was the problem of taxation. To raise desperately needed revenues, Louis XV (1710–1774, ruled 1715–1774) and his successor, Louis XVI (1754–1793, ruled 1774–1792), broke with precedent and tried to reduce or abolish tax exemptions for the rich and privileged. In this effort, both kings enjoyed only limited success, since, to their surprise, the non-exempt made common cause with the exempt. Ordinary people, like many parlementaires, believed the royal court to be extravagant and corrupt, wasteful of the revenue it took in. When the king tried to limit or abolish tax exemptions in the wake of the costly Seven Years' War, the parlements said no, and the weight of public opinion supported them.

In response, France's chief minister, René-Nicolas-Augustin de Maupeou (1714–1772), disbanded the Parlement of Paris along with four of its key provincial counterparts, while emasculating the rest. These actions of 1771 raised a powerful hue and cry from parlementaires and their growing number of supporters, who saw Maupeou's acts as a despotic coup d'état, which is exactly how Diderot and other Enlightenment philosophers characterized them. When Louis XVI assumed the throne in 1774, he decided he had no choice but to restore all the deposed parlements. This move gave him immense popularity—at least for a time. But it foreclosed the possibility of new taxes and made the crown's financial situation even worse.

To address it, Louis XVI called in a skillful Swiss banker named Jacques Necker (1732–1804) to direct the crown's budget. To cut government costs, Necker eliminated hundreds of venal offices without reimbursing their owners and began the process of transforming France's mighty tax farmers into mere salaried bureaucrats. In doing so, he tugged at the roots of France's entire social and political system, which had long rewarded certain people with wealth, status, and privilege and, in exchange, endowed the king with their loyalty and financial support. But Necker was no match for the hordes of noble officeholders, tax farmers, parlementaires, and financiers, whose entrenched interests and comfortable lives he had threatened. They forced Louis XVI, already uneasy about upending France's sociopolitical status quo, to fire him and reverse his reforms. Yet again, the French government found itself back at square one: it had to borrow at high interest rates to stay alive.

The constant borrowing alarmed the Parlement of Paris, which after 1785 refused to approve any more loans. Now the French government had no way to service its debts, let alone administer a country of 25 million people. Bankruptcy loomed. After several futile attempts to prevent financial collapse, a potential solution finally emerged: the Parlement of Paris agreed to approve a new short-term loan, but only if the king revived the **Estates General**, France's dormant, kingdom-wide representative body, which had not met for almost two centuries and existed only as a vague historical memory.

By tradition, the Estates General consisted of three chambers—one each for the clergy (First Estate), the nobility (Second Estate), and the commoners (Third Estate). In calling for a new Estates General, the Parlement of Paris said, in effect, that no existing institution had the credibility to reform France's political and economic system and thus to restore confidence in the finances of the realm. In 1788, Louis XVI had no choice but to call the Estates General into being.

A FAUT ESPERER Q'EU SE JEU LA FINIRA BENTOT

☰ **The Three Estates.** Before the French Revolution, the clergy and nobility (First and Second Estates) were accustomed to being supported by the commoners (Third Estate), who encompassed more than 80 percent of the French population and performed most of the country's useful work. In the lead-up to the meeting of the Estates General in May 1789, leaders of the Third Estate wanted to move their group from the bottom to the top.

The Public Opinion Crisis

The king had no choice in part because parlementaires and a growing number of pamphleteers had mobilized public opinion against him. In 1771, at the time of the Maupeou coup, about 300 pamphlets were published in France. Sixteen years later, during the controversies surrounding the king and the Parlement of Paris, more than 1,000 pamphlets came out. Most chastised the king for wasteful spending, excessive luxury, unfair and burdensome taxation, and especially for "despotism," whether in his effort to silence the parlement or to impose higher taxes.

Also deemed "despotic" was the king's decision to remove traditional price controls on grain, which had long kept down the cost of bread, the nutritional mainstay of most French families. A group of economists called **physiocrats** had convinced Louis's advisors that allowing grain prices to rise naturally with demand would encourage French farmers to produce more of it and that the larger supply would ultimately bring prices back down. In the end, they believed, France would produce more food at about the same prices as under the system of controls.

Unfortunately for Louis XVI, things did not work out that way. France's archaic agricultural system, with its old-fashioned technology and multitude of tiny, inefficient farms, did not allow for a substantially higher output of food. Prices went up and stayed up, because demand still outstripped supply. Worse, the king also relaxed restrictions on the export of grain, which meant that the supply of grain in France dropped rather than increased. The inevitable result was skyrocketing prices, made even worse by successive years of poor weather and thus smaller harvests than usual.

As high grain prices caused widespread misery, pamphleteers encouraged ordinary people to contrast their hunger with the splendor and profligacy of Versailles. In 1785 Queen Marie-Antoinette (1755–1793) was falsely said to have purchased a diamond necklace for the huge sum of two million French pounds, but a great many people believed the story. In the 1770s and 1780s, it seemed all too plausible, especially to working people, that the king and queen would spend millions on baubles instead of fulfilling their traditional obligation to protect them from want.

The Church appeared equally guilty of indifference to ordinary people, and although few read the works of Voltaire and Diderot, Enlightenment criticisms of the Church and Catholicism circulated by word of mouth and influenced people indirectly. The majority of French men and women did not become irreligious, but they lost a measure of faith in the institution and personnel of the Church. This was especially true in regions of the country with significant numbers of **Jansenists**, reform-minded Catholics who criticized the luxury and worldliness of official Catholicism. The Church, in turn, ruled Jansenist beliefs heretical, forbade parish priests to administer the sacraments to them, and censored their writings. The royal court, as we saw in Chapter 4, resorted to censorship as well. But by the second half of the eighteenth century, the flood of pamphlets, newspapers, and books could not be contained. Eventually, the king's advisors and supporters concluded that since dissenting ideas could not be blocked, they would now have to argue against them.

By joining the debate rather than trying to squelch it, the king hoped to gain a measure of good will; instead, he compromised his authority by engaging with his critics on an equal plane and then lost many of the debates. When, for example, members of the court argued that France was, by nature, a hierarchical society with the king, representing God, at the top, they seemed to support entrenched privilege against the legitimate aspirations of the majority of the country.

The Crisis of Frustrated Expectations

Those aspirations had been fueled by a significant economic expansion in the eighteenth century. On the eve of the French Revolution, France's gross domestic product, having grown 130 percent (36 percent allowing for inflation) between 1715 and 1789, was more than three times that of Great Britain. French agricultural output doubled in value between 1700 and 1789, while trade and commerce tripled during the same period. Especially lucrative were colonial products such as sugar, coffee, and tobacco, whose profits stimulated the development of manufacturing and trade within France itself.

Unfortunately, these positive developments had uneven effects. Industry and commerce, which benefited at most one-fourth of the people, expanded much more rapidly than agriculture, whose growth barely kept up with the country's population increase. And since agricultural output was itself uneven, people in some parts of the country—particularly the region surrounding Paris—ate better than people in the south and west.

Even those whose economic situation had improved often did not feel better off; they could see that a select portion of the population had prospered considerably more or that their expectations of improvement had not been met. One of Alexis de Tocqueville's great insights about the origins of the revolution was that people measure their well-being in relative terms. Even if they are doing better than in the past, which most French people of the late eighteenth century were not, they feel aggrieved if others are doing better than they.

Paradoxically, then, France's economic growth and prosperity, relatively healthy as they were, created more dissatisfaction than satisfaction and added to the widespread discontent of the late 1780s. This was especially true in that France's economic growth was overwhelmed by its increase in government spending, which in real terms grew twice as fast as the economy as a whole. Faced with the difficulty of raising taxes on those best able to pay, French monarchs tried to fill some of the gap between expenditures and revenues at the expense of the poor.

Given high food prices and high taxation, large numbers of people found it increasingly difficult to make ends meet. And just at the moment when they most needed the government's help, it completely ran out of cash. On August 16, 1788, the royal treasury suspended all payments to creditors; France was officially bankrupt, its government in disarray. Everything now hinged on the Estates General, which Necker, who had returned to Paris as finance minister, declared would meet in the spring of 1789.

Because the Estates General was an institution that harked back to the past, calling it into session seemed like a conservative solution; privileged parlementaires, high clergymen, and other elites quickly championed the idea. But conditions had changed so much since it last met (1614) that the new Estates General would bring not conservative reform but revolutionary change.

France's New Social Structure

In 1614, France was a hierarchically ordered society with a huge distinction between the nobility (about 1 percent of the population) and everyone else. By 1789, France's social structure had become far more complex, in part because of the growth of its economy. Alongside the wealthy, powerful nobles who belonged to—or helped finance—the royal court stood a considerable number of non-nobles whose riches from trade and commerce in some cases rivaled those of the most prosperous noblemen. Some of the new rich lived like noblemen in the Caribbean colonies of Saint-Domingue and Martinique, while others bought huge noble domains called *seigneuries* in France. These merchants, bankers, and industrialists still belonged to the Third Estate, even though almost everything else about them appeared noble.

One key result of these developments was that France's once sharply defined social structure now became blurred. Officially, the country remained a hierarchy of orders with the clergy and nobility at the top. But in terms of wealth, a growing number of commoners now outranked a large part of the nobility. In terms of behavior and lifestyle, wealthy commoners often looked like nobles, especially now that prosperous noblemen had begun to act like merchants and bankers by investing in colonial plantations, trade corporations, and, of course, government bonds. But just because prosperous commoners and nobles looked and acted more and more alike did not mean that all distinctions between them had dissolved. In fact, the more commoners outwardly resembled nobles, the more noblemen emphasized what still set them apart: their titles, heritage, and special privileges, especially tax exemption.

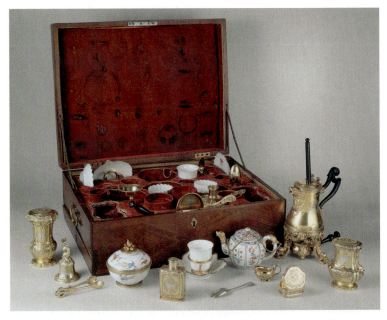

The Queen's Travel Kit. In the eighteenth century, prosperous middle-class people acquired the means to enjoy luxury items reserved until then for the aristocracy. These items included the coffee and sugar produced on Caribbean plantations by enslaved Africans. Queen Marie Leczinska could not travel without them, or so her husband, King Louis XV, apparently believed. He gave her this kit as a gift after the birth of their son, the future King Louis XVI.

The effort to maintain these distinctions helps explain the difficulty of reforming France's fiscal system and thus of reducing its perennial budget deficits. Noblemen wanted not only to protect their wealth from royal taxation but also to retain their special status as members of a titled, tax-exempt elite. Commoners who lived nobly, along with many who did not, resented these distinctions, which to them seemed irrational and unjust.

The Revolution

It was in this fraught social context that elections to the Estates General took place. Necker announced that each estate would hold elections separately and that each would have equal representation in the Estates General when it met in May 1789. Nobles, who constituted no more than 1 percent of the population, would have the same political weight as members of the Third Estate, who encompassed perhaps 98 percent. Enlightenment writers had argued against what they considered the artificial distinctions of title and birth, and those arguments had helped convince a great many commoners that each of them should have the same political voice as each member of the nobility. Reinforcing this view was the commoners' experience as the equals of nobles in the public sphere—in salons, Masonic lodges, scientific societies, local academies, and the like.

Under these circumstances, leaders of the Third Estate began to push for two changes with respect to the precedent of 1614: the "doubling of the Third," so that the Third Estate would have as many representatives in the Estates General as the First and the Second combined, and "voting by head" (individual representative) rather than by estate. If voting went by estate, the clergy, dominated as it was by noblemen, would side with the nobles, and the Third would always lose two to one. If voting went by head, and the Third was doubled in size, it would likely prevail. To ensure their domination of the Estates General, most nobles opposed voting by head, while candidates for the Third Estate made this question a potent campaign issue, arguing that any other arrangement would be unfair. The campaigns lasted for months and evoked a political debate and an explosion of political writing unprecedented in French history.

This explosive political activity took place against the backdrop of the worst economic conditions in recent memory. Soaring bread prices and high unemployment left a great many people hungry and miserable, and in 1789 an exceptionally cold winter made their conditions even worse. These dire economic circumstances heightened an already tense, agitated political situation. French people became mobilized all the more when villagers, townsmen, and city-dwellers met to draft "lists of grievances" (*cahiers de doléances*), as the king, following the procedures of 1614, had told them to do. When asked to discuss and then record what troubled them, French voters let loose with detailed lists of problems: taxes, unfair privileges, the requirement to perform unpaid labor, dues or fees assessed by noblemen on peasant-owned land, and the **tithe**, or 10 percent tax levied by the Church.

The process of drafting the cahiers reinforced the already widespread idea that things had gone terribly wrong and that the country desperately needed reform. A host of political writers eagerly addressed that need, none more influentially than a young liberal-minded clergyman, Emmanuel Joseph Sieyès, usually called the Abbé Sieyès (1748–1836). His celebrated pamphlet "What Is the Third Estate?" became a bestseller in part by arguing "The Third Estate is everything" and the First and Second Estates nothing. Sieyès identified the commoners with "the nation," a term increasingly prominent in 1789, and suggested that as long as the First and Second Estates tried to maintain a separate, privileged identity, they placed themselves outside the nation, a political entity composed of people of equal political standing. Echoing Enlightenment writers, Sieyès maintained that

Frenchmen were no longer subjects of a king but members of an independent political community capable of deciding how it wanted to be governed.

Sieyès's ideas proved immensely influential, and they dovetailed with the notion of voting by head. This, along with the dissolution of the three estates into one, is what many delegates of the Third Estate wanted when the Estates General convened in Versailles. When the clergy and nobles, backed by the king, refused to grant these demands, the Third Estate declined to participate in any deliberations. A six-week-long stalemate ensued.

The Tennis Court Oath. In June 1789, members of the Third Estate withdrew from the Estates General and, meeting in an unused tennis court, vowed to remain in session until the king recognized them as France's official parliament. Noblemen did not join representatives of the Third Estate until later, but the revolutionary artist Jacques-Louis David portrayed all three estates as bonded together in the foreground of this painting of 1791.

Meanwhile, popular unrest grew day by day, as nothing was being done to address France's deepening crisis. Finally, on Sieyès' suggestion, the Third Estate's representatives walked out of the Estates General, never to return. They cast about for a place to meet and finally came upon an indoor tennis court, the Jeu de Paume, where they declared themselves the true representatives of the French nation, or the National Assembly. A small number of clergymen joined them, and the National Assembly vowed to remain in session until the king recognized them, and not the Estates General, as France's official parliament. This act of defiance, known as the **Tennis Court Oath**, marked the beginning of the French Revolution.

The Revolution Takes Off

King Louis XVI, upset by the commoners' defiance of order and tradition, initially refused to acknowledge the National Assembly. Its members held firm, however, and at the end of June 1789, the king appeared to give in. But behind the scenes, key members of his court had quietly ordered the French army to amass in Versailles and at strategic points on the outskirts of Paris. By the second week in July, royal troops seemed ready to forcibly disband the National Assembly and subdue the restive city of Paris. Necker opposed these plans, and on July 12 the king removed him from office.

When news of Necker's dismissal reached Paris, the city exploded in rebellion. A crowd of Parisian workers and shopkeepers broke into government armories and seized a huge cache of weapons. On July 14, crowd leaders decided to attack the **Bastille**, a notorious prison that dominated the eastern half of Paris, where large numbers of working people lived. Because political prisoners had once been confined there, the Bastille symbolized despotism and arbitrary rule, even though in 1789 only a handful of inmates were left. The ad hoc rebel force, strengthened by deserters from the royal army, stormed its ramparts and killed the Bastille's commanding officer. Insurgents cut off the dead man's head and mounted it on the tip of a pike. Other insurgents followed suit with four more severed heads, which they soon paraded around the city as trophies of the day's events. This was the Revolution's first public display of gratuitous violence; it would not be the last.

The Bastille's remaining defenders surrendered the fortress to the rebels, who also seized control of other strategic parts of the city. Almost immediately, political writers began to characterize the storming of the Bastille as the founding act of the French Revolution, and it is still seen that way today. But the events at the Bastille constituted just one episode, albeit an important one, of a powerful urban insurrection that left the French capital in rebel hands. Under these circumstances, the king had no choice but to accept the National Assembly as the official new parliament. This institution alone possessed the authority and the legitimacy to calm the Paris population and send the people home.

As part of the calming process, the National Assembly established a citizens' militia, the National Guard, charged

≡ **The Storming of the Bastille.** On July 14, 1789, a large crowd of Parisian working people stormed the Bastille, a nearly empty prison that nonetheless stood as a stark symbol of royal despotism. After hours of fighting, the crowd smashed through the ramparts of the old fortress, capturing and killing the captain of the prison guard. The insurgents severed the dead man's head and displayed it on the tip of a pike.

with maintaining order. But the revolutionaries knew that, in the long run, order would have to be grounded in a new and more equitable political system. To create it, they immediately set out to frame a written constitution, just as the American revolutionaries had done two years earlier.

The first step was to draft a statement outlining the basic rights, freedoms, and duties of the French people. The document that resulted, the **Declaration of the Rights of Man and Citizen**, became the law of the land on August 26, 1789. As we saw in Chapter 4, Olympe de Gouges found this document wanting, given its focus on "man" and not men and women. But in 1789, most French people, although not the majority of nobles or the king, considered the document a great step forward. With statements such as "Men are born and remain free and equal in rights" and "The free communication of ideas and opinions is one of the most precious of the rights of man," the Declaration established political liberties unprecedented in France.

The Great Fear

After the fall of the Bastille on July 14, ominous rumors began to circulate in the countryside, especially the rumor that vengeful aristocrats planned to starve the peasantry to death by having an army of "brigands" destroy their crops. Rumors quickly turned into reality in people's minds, and a "Great Fear" gripped the peasantry, thousands of whom preemptively attacked noble chateaus to prevent aristocrats from unleashing the brigands. Peasants also sought to lighten their financial obligations by burning the documents that showed the centuries-old payments and taxes ("seigneurial dues") they owed local noblemen. In some cases, peasants torched the entire chateau.

To stem this revolutionary tide—and create a more equitable regime—a group of liberal noblemen in the Assembly renounced their age-old privileges. On the night of August 4, 1789, one nobleman after the other rose to

≡ **Declaration of the Rights of Man and Citizen.** This *Declaration*, framed in late August 1789, became one of the founding documents of the French Revolution. It outlined the basic freedoms, rights, and duties of the French people. Because the *Declaration* spoke of "man" but not "woman," Olympe de Gouges challenged the document by publishing her own, unofficial *Declaration of the Rights of Woman and the Female Citizen.*

demand the elimination of seigneurial dues, venal office holding, unpaid labor services, tax exemptions, and tithes to the church. Although these radical concessions were not enacted into law until a few weeks later, August 4 stands as one of the most revolutionary moments in world history. On that single night, a regime of privilege and hierarchy, in place for a millennium, collapsed into dust.

In a sense, the nobles simply ratified what had already occurred, since by burning tax rolls, peasants had made clear that they would no longer pay seigneurial dues. But it was crucial to transform this fait accompli into law: it reassured an agitated, paranoid peasantry, calming the countryside and allowing the fall harvest to take place.

If a measure of calm settled over rural France, such was not true of Paris, where unemployment and food prices remained high. On October 6, a large group of Parisian women, traditionally responsible for feeding their families, marched out to Versailles to confront the king, whom they blamed for their economic hardship and suspected of conspiring against the revolution. Members of the National Guard, commanded by the Marquis de Lafayette (1757–1834), scrambled to follow the women's lead. In Versailles, marchers invaded the palace, threatened the life of the queen, and were mollified only when Louis XVI agreed to move his court to Paris, where the people hoped they could keep him under control.

When the royal family abandoned the Chateau of Versailles, long the glittering symbol of France's absolutist monarchy, the Revolution took yet another radical step. Not only had the king's power been sharply limited, but he now lived under the watchful eyes of the people of Paris. They wanted to love him in his new constitutional guise but did not quite trust him to merit their affection.

The Women's March. In October 1789, a large group of working women, traditionally responsible for feeding their families, marched from Paris to Versailles to confront King Louis XVI. They blamed him for their economic hardships and wanted to force him to improve their plight. Fearing for his life and that of his queen, Louis XVI agreed to return to Paris, where the people could hold him hostage to their needs.

The Revolution Settles In

The leaders of the former Third Estate understood that the people of Paris and the countryside had been crucial to their political fortunes and that without their intervention, the revolution would have stalled. Even so, middle-class revolutionaries feared popular violence and declined to give the poor full citizenship rights. But even as they excluded "passive" citizens—one-third of adult French men—from the right to vote, revolutionaries expanded citizenship in other ways. In December 1789, Protestants gained the right to vote and hold office (if they owned enough property), and two years later, Jews gained citizenship rights as well. For the first time in French history, Protestants and Jews possessed the same political standing as Catholics.

Even those denied the right to vote and hold office could participate in politics in other ways. Anyone with the relatively modest funds to buy a uniform could join the National Guard, and when political clubs—fledgling political parties—began to spring up in 1790, anyone could attend meetings, even women, depending on the club. The first and most important club was the **Jacobins**, named after the former monastery where its members met in Paris. Early on, the Jacobins attracted more than two hundred members of the National Assembly and featured well-known figures like Lafayette, famous for fighting alongside George Washington in the American Revolution, and up-and-coming politicians like Maximilien Robespierre (1758–1794).

Beyond political clubs, large numbers of people participated in politics by demonstrating in the streets, often to denounce high food prices or express displeasure over the doings of the Assembly and the king. As in October 1789, women regularly took the lead in protesting the cost of food and in agitating for changes in the nature and structure of the family. Thanks in part to women's political activity, the Assembly legalized divorce in September 1792 and gave women equal inheritance rights a year later. When the Revolution turned against traditional Catholicism and the Church, women played a prominent role in advocating for the freedom to worship as they pleased.

Religion and Revolution

By late 1789, the controversies over Jansenism as well as Enlightenment critiques of traditional Catholicism had reduced the Church's authority and tied it in people's minds to the discredited monarchy. When members of the Assembly looked for new sources of revenue, they felt secure in seizing them from the Church, which owned vast expanses of land.

In November 1789, the Assembly nationalized all Church property and used it as backing for new paper money called *assignats* created to pay off France's gigantic public debt. Initially, the assignats had a positive effect, as they allowed France to retire some of its obligations and to stimulate its moribund economy by increasing the money supply. But there were too few assignats to solve France's financial problems, so to raise additional cash, the revolutionary government began to sell off the former Church property. It mostly did so without redeeming the assignats, as it had promised. The government, that is, kept the proceeds instead of using them to pay off holders of the paper, which remained in circulation.

The land sales brought in substantial sums and satisfied, to some extent, the peasants' hunger for property. But once the former Church properties were sold, there was nothing to support the assignats, since they could no longer be redeemed, and nothing to limit the number of assignats that could be printed. As the government turned out more and more, their value plummeted, and they became essentially worthless by 1796.

Meanwhile, clergymen and devout French men and women denounced the confiscation of Church lands as an unconscionable attack against Catholicism. Many deeply religious people turned against the Revolution for good. Polarizing the situation all the more, the government decided in early 1790 that the Church as a whole, and not just its lands, would be governed by the state. Under what was called the **Civil Constitution of the Clergy**, priests and bishops, now deprived of tithes and the income from confiscated lands, became salaried employees of the government. No longer would the pope name bishops and the bishops appoint parish priests; both would be elected by their parishioners. The pope's role in French religious affairs would be honorific at best.

The Civil Constitution evoked a howl of protest, and in 1791 the pope denounced it. In response, the Assembly required all clergymen to sign an oath of obedience to the new set of rules. About half of French priests refused to sign, and as punishment, these "refractories," as they were called, received no salary from the state.

This situation opened a major, hugely consequential, rift in the French Revolution. Ardent revolutionaries condemned the refractory priests and urged people to boycott them. Sincere Catholics, meanwhile, faced what was for many an impossible choice. If they accepted the sacraments from a "constitutional" priest—one who had signed the loyalty oath—they risked being ostracized by the Church and thus the danger of eternal damnation. But if they took the sacraments only from refractory clergy, they risked being labeled "counterrevolutionaries" and traitors to the new French nation.

The rift between Catholicism and the Revolution would become a chasm a few years later when revolutionary leaders replaced the traditional Christian calendar with a revolutionary one and embarked on a campaign of "dechristianization." The traditional calendar marked time in relation to the birth of Christ—the year 1 AD (Anno Domini or Year of Our Lord) was the year of his birth—and it organized the year around the major Christian holidays. Seeking to dethrone Christianity symbolically, the revolutionaries decided to mark time in terms of the political events in France. September 22, 1792, the day the French Republic was declared, would now be Day 1 of the Year I. Events that occurred before that inaugural day, including the birth of Christ, would be symbolically consigned to a barbaric prehistory largely to be forgotten, except of course for the French Revolution itself and the lives of key Enlightenment figures like Voltaire and Rousseau. In the new revolutionary calendar, all references to Christian holidays and saints' days were removed and the weeks and months measured in "rational"—that is, decimal—terms, ten days to a week and three ten-day weeks to a month.

This symbolic assault against Christianity was followed by more concrete forms of attack. Refractory clergy faced the danger of execution and had to leave the country or go into hiding. Most churches were closed and religious practice forced underground. Traditional worship gave way to a Cult of the Supreme Being that found few supporters beyond its main proponent, Robespierre.

The End of the Monarchy

King Louis XVI deeply resented these efforts to revolutionize Catholicism and the Church and refused to accept sacraments from constitutional priests. When politically active Parisians learned of his stance, they gathered outside his residence, the Tuileries Palace, to protest this apparent disrespect for the Revolution. The protesters refused to disperse, and the royal family began to feel unsafe. Louis XVI's two brothers had already fled the country, along with a growing number of noble **émigrés**, and the king decided to join them in exile.

On June 20, 1791, the king, queen, and their two children disguised themselves as middle-class people and furtively left Paris in a horse-drawn coach. They made it all the way to the town of Varennes, just thirty miles from the Belgian border, before being recognized by a local postmaster. Louis XVI and his family were taken as prisoners and brought back to Paris in disgrace—not only for having fled

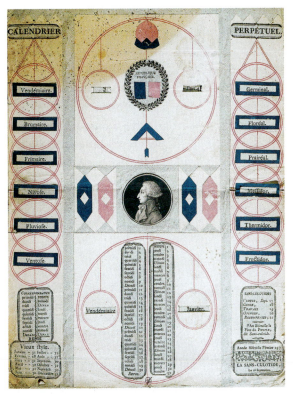

The Revolutionary Calendar. In a symbolic act of "de-Christianization," the French revolutionaries jettisoned the traditional Christian calendar, which measured time in relation to the birth of Christ. They replaced it with a calendar whose Year I began on September 22, 1792, the day Louis XVI lost his throne. The new revolutionary calendar divided time along "rational" decimal lines by carving each thirty-day month into three ten-day weeks.

Paris but for writing a letter denouncing the Revolution and hinting at plans to overthrow it. Shortly after the king's return, radicals organized a huge demonstration against him, which the National Guard put down with force, killing more than fifty people.

This repression quieted the crowd, and revolutionary France might have settled into a constitutional monarchy, albeit with a reluctant monarch, had it not been for the wars that broke out in 1792. Even before the flight to Varennes, thousands of French émigrés, including about two-thirds of the French army's officer corps, had taken up residence in Prussia and Austria and urged the emperors of those countries to invade France and overturn the revolution. It now appeared that Louis XVI saw an invasion by neighboring countries as his best hope for regaining his old authority. Meanwhile, the **Girondins**, a faction of the Jacobin Club soon to be expelled, wanted war as well. The Girondin leader, Jacques Pierre Brissot (1754–1793), believed that war would discredit the king once and for all and sweep away the moderates in the Assembly who supported him.

Robespierre and other Jacobins showed more caution. They believed that with most French officers in exile and the army in disarray, their country was ill prepared to fight a European war. But Brissot won the argument, and in April 1792, France declared war on Austria, which together with Prussia attacked France from the north and west.

The early fighting proved disastrous for the French, whose forces had to cede France's borderlands to the enemy. Revolutionary leaders declared that the Austrians and Prussians wanted not just to overthrow the revolution but to conquer France, and that defense of the fatherland and the revolution were one and the same. To support the revolution was to be a French patriot; to oppose it a traitor—just like the émigrés and the king.

≡ **Sans-Culotte Woman.** The radical working people of Paris, known as sans-culottes, successfully pushed the revolution to the left between 1792 and 1794. Male sans-culottes, without the knee breeches (*culottes*) characteristic of aristocratic men, wore long pants instead. Female sans-culottes dressed in simple, unadorned frocks and engaged in political combat alongside the men.

These notions radicalized Parisian working people, who now proudly took the name ***sans-culottes*** (without knee breeches) to distinguish themselves from traitorous aristocrats, who wore stockings and knee-length trousers (culottes) rather than the long pants of working men. On June 20, 1792, armed sans-culottes invaded the newly elected Legislative Assembly and accused the king of conspiring with the enemy. They blamed France's military losses not on its unprepared and poorly equipped army, but on aristocratic plots and conspiracies that supposedly had compromised the French troops' ability to fight. Six weeks later, the sans-culottes attacked the Tuileries Palace, forcing the royal family to take refuge inside the Assembly chamber. Radicals massacred some 600 members of the king's personal bodyguard, and the sans-culottes, encouraged by certain Jacobin leaders, threatened violence against the Legislative Assembly itself.

In response, the representative body voted to dissolve itself, even though it had existed for less than a year. In the fall, there would be elections for yet another national parliament, the **Convention**, which, it was said, would truly represent the nation. For the first time, all adult men would have the right to vote. But women would still be excluded—despite demands by Olympe de Gouges and leaders of the women's clubs for political standing equal to men. The revolutionaries had, after all, promised liberty and equality, and activist women demanded that those promises be kept.

In early September, even before the Convention could meet, violence broke out yet again, when crowds of people stormed into prisons and slaughtered more than 1,000 inmates. The Prussian army was heading toward Paris, and many of the city's residents were convinced that convicts languishing in Parisian jails had somehow conspired with the enemy to permit them to break through the French defenses. These "September Massacres" represented the most gruesome episode of revolutionary violence to date.

In 1789, that violence had been relatively restrained and broke out mainly in response to the king's efforts to undo the political liberties the Third Estate had won. But by 1792, with the country facing occupation by surrounding powers and in extreme economic distress, popular violence took on a sharp, hysterical edge. Radical journalists like Jean-Paul Marat (1743–1793) whipped up people's fears and convinced them that particular individuals or groups bore responsibility for their plight. These supposed conspirators needed to be stopped before they did more damage to the Revolution.

It was true, of course, that by 1792 the Revolution had made plenty of enemies, but most had nothing to do with the Austrian and Prussian military successes, nor had they, as Marat claimed, conspired to starve the sans-culottes. Still, it could be emotionally satisfying to find a person or people to blame, since it seemed to follow that by eliminating them, the problems would disappear. By the fall of 1792, no one seemed more blameworthy than the king. He had, after all, tried to flee the country into the arms of the enemy.

When the Convention met in late September 1792, Jacobin leaders, backed by the sans-culottes, made it clear that the monarchy had to go. On September 22, the new parliament stripped the king of his titles and declared France a republic. Louis XVI, now known by his un-royal name, Louis Capet, was accused of treasonous relations with the enemy and forced to stand trial for his crimes.

These developments polarized France all the more, dividing the country between those who accepted the new republic and those who refused it. Even the republicans were divided, as the Jacobins mostly wanted to execute the king, while the Girondins did not. Rather than search for common ground, political opponents saw each other as enemies with whom no compromise was possible. Since France lacked strong parliamentary traditions, representatives possessed little experience in the art of negotiation and compromise, which influential journalists and politicians presented as forms of betrayal and deceit. And when the possibility of conciliation arose, the sans-culottes were perpetually ready to block it—with violence, if necessary—in the name of revolutionary purity.

What is striking about the growing divide of 1792–1793 between Girondins and Jacobins was just how similar in socioeconomic terms the two groups were. But their beliefs drove them further and further apart—especially concerning the fate of the king.

After a short trial and guilty verdict in December 1792, Jacobins and Girondins began a long and contentious argument over his sentence. Voices from all over the country weighed in. When the Convention's ballots were counted in late January 1793, the Jacobins had won by a single vote. Louis XVI went to the guillotine on January 21, 1793.

Once again, a revolutionary people had killed their king. In Britain, where Charles I had died on the scaffold 144 years earlier, Prime Minister William Pitt nonetheless called Louis XVI's execution "the foulest and most atrocious act

☰ **The Execution of Louis XVI.** In January 1793, the revolutionary Convention (parliament) voted by a narrow margin to condemn the king to death. He was executed in a public ceremony, his severed head held high for all the world to see.

the world has ever seen." Pitt decided to enter the war against France in alliance with the Dutch Republic, Spain, Portugal, Austria, Prussia, and several Italian states. In early 1793, France stood alone against virtually the entire European world.

Civil War and Terror

To face this vast array of foreign armies, the Convention decided to conscript 300,000 new French soldiers. While most recruits submitted to the draft and agreed, reluctantly or eagerly, to defend the fatherland, conscription met with widespread resistance in some areas of western France, where a pro-Church and pro-king population was already up in arms over the persecution of refractory priests. In March 1793, a violent antirevolutionary civil war, known as the **Vendée rebellion**, broke out in this part of the country.

Jacobins and Girondins differed over how best to quell this conflict, violently or leniently, and once again the sans-culottes sided with the Jacobins. On June 2, 1793, sans-culottes invaded the Convention and forced the expulsion of the Girondins and the arrest of their leaders. The French Revolution was now entirely in the radical Jacobins' hands, although always under the watchful eyes of the sans-culottes.

The workaholic, single-minded Robespierre, a former provincial lawyer, emerged as the Jacobins' undisputed leader, and he solidified his power by seizing control of the twelve-man ruling junta called the **Committee of Public Safety** (CPS). The purpose of this committee was to streamline the government, which had lacked executive authority since the early days of the revolution, and to mobilize the country both to put down the Vendée rebellion and to defeat the military coalition of enemy states.

In September 1793, Robespierre decided that the revolution could defeat its internal and external enemies only by adopting a policy of "terror." By terror he meant the ruthless suppression of all enemies, actual and potential, and the use of extreme measures, backed by the threat of the death penalty, to preserve the revolution. Robespierre's supporters believed that the end justified the means—that authoritarian methods could and should be used to prevent France's democratic revolution from being overturned.

≡ **Robespierre.** As leader of the Jacobins and mastermind of the Terror, Robespierre presided over the most radical phase of the French Revolution. Under his reign, a great many French men and women, including several prominent revolutionary leaders, were sent to die in the guillotine. In provincial cities and the French countryside, thousands more lost their lives as revolutionary forces put down the Vendée and Federalist rebellions of 1793.

Robespierre's uncompromising attitudes earned him a great many enemies, especially in provincial France, where in the summer of 1793, Marseille, Lyon, and Bordeaux joined the rebellion against the Paris-centered revolution. These "federalist" insurgents did not support the Church and king as did their counterparts in the Vendée, but Robespierre saw the two revolts as equally counterrevolutionary and resolved to crush them both. In the fall of 1793, the CPS sent troops into the rebellious provinces, where leaders of the various insurgencies were rounded up and put to death. In the Vendée, priests and rank-and-file rebels were executed en masse, many by being hog-tied and drowned in the Loire River. In this, the opening phase of the Terror, 15,000 to 20,000 people lost their lives—not including the thousands more who died in the fighting.

For the sans-culottes and some Jacobins, even these measures seemed too mild. To reassure them, the CPS sent Marie Antoinette and the Girondin leaders to the guillotine in October 1793. The Committee then decreed that anyone suspected of a political crime could be arrested, with no evidence of wrongdoing required. It expanded the revolutionary tribunals charged with trying suspects and (mostly) condemning them to death. The Committee also established price controls (the "maximum") on all basic commodities, dispatched revolutionary commissars to provincial cities to rule them with an iron hand, and sent "revolutionary armies" of sans-culottes into the countryside to force peasants to sell their grain at the low prices set in Paris.

The government, Robespierre declared, would be "revolutionary until the peace"—centralized, authoritarian, and ruthless—and limited by no constitutional constraints or even by the rule of law. Rather than the moderate constitutional monarchy advocated by most revolutionaries in 1789–1791, France's political system had come to resemble the quasi-despotic governments of earlier in the century.

In certain ways, the Terror worked very well. It stamped out most internal enemies, real and imagined, and its highly centralized government successfully mobilized the country for war. By requisitioning grain and other supplies from peasants, revolutionary leaders kept the cities and the armies supplied. The lives of working people improved, and a fair number supported the Terror—at least until being sent off to war.

To pursue an all-out military effort, the regime decreed the **_levée en masse_** or universal conscription, which created a fighting force of unprecedented size. A new cohort of four hundred thousand soldiers joined the three hundred thousand already in the field, forming a vast citizen army that confronted the smaller, largely mercenary armies of the other European powers. With battle-hardened commanders at the French army's helm, the revolutionary forces, motivated by patriotic zeal or fear of the state, or both, rolled over enemy troops, ejecting them from France in the spring of 1794 (see Map 5.2).

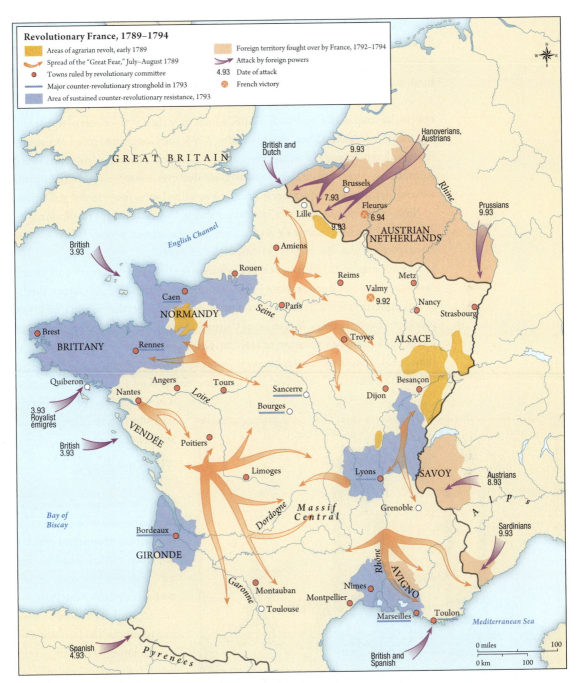

Revolutionary France, 1789–1794

- Areas of agrarian revolt, early 1789
- Spread of the "Great Fear," July–August 1789
- Towns ruled by revolutionary committee
- Major counter-revolutionary stronghold in 1793
- Area of sustained counter-revolutionary resistance, 1793
- Foreign territory fought over by France, 1792–1794
- Attack by foreign powers
- 4.93 Date of attack
- French victory

≡ **MAP 5.2** Revolutionary France, 1789–1794

The End of the Terror

With the war now going well for France, Georges Danton (1759–1794), a highly popular member of the Jacobin Club, Convention, and CPS, began to argue for a moderation of the Terror and efforts to wind down the war. These "indulgent" positions prompted a harsh reaction from extremists known as Hébertists, who attempted a coup d'état against the CPS, which they thought—falsely—to contain too many Indulgents. Thus, in early spring 1794, the Committee faced challenges from both the left and the right—political designations invented during the French Revolution—that is, from Hébertists who wanted even more terror and Indulgents who wanted less. Robespierre responded by sending both groups to the guillotine.

Now, essentially no one was safe, as several of the most ardent revolutionaries succumbed to the guillotine's blade. So began the "Great Terror," when anyone Robespierre and a few colleagues suspected of a political crime, or the potential to commit one, could be rounded up, summarily tried, and executed—all on the same day. Between April and late July 1794, some two thousand people perished.

Robespierre saw the Terror as a vast ritual of purification that would ultimately produce what he called a "Republic of Virtue." His was a strange understanding of virtue, and after the execution of Danton, Robespierre's colleagues realized that they could, and likely would, be next. To prevent that outcome, certain influential members of the Convention had him arrested, and on July 28 (9 Thermidor, Year II on the revolutionary calendar), the guillotine sliced off Robespierre's head.

The Directory, 1794–1799

The "Thermidorians" who took over after Robespierre's execution found themselves with a favorable military situation but a difficult domestic one. To prevent a recurrence of the Terror—and to keep their heads—they had to subdue the Jacobins and sans-culottes, the main forces behind the state violence of 1793–1794. Fortunately for the Thermidorians, the country was weary of conflict, and they succeeded in closing Jacobin

EGTE AFBEELDING VAN DE GUILLOTINE TE PARYS.

≡ **The Guillotine.** Designed as a "humanitarian" instrument to prevent botched executions, the guillotine came to symbolize the Terror and a revolution that had gone too far.

clubs and in breaking up the sans-culottes' main organizations. They then wrote a new, less democratic, constitution that sought to rule out dictatorship by giving executive authority not to a single person but to a "Directory" of five members. The Directors often failed to see eye to eye, but they agreed that politics should not tack too far to the left or the right. They steered a middle course by ruthlessly suppressing demonstrations and annulling elections deemed too favorable to royalists or Jacobins. In doing so, the Directory showed little inclination to establish a regular, smoothly functioning constitutional regime.

Major Events of the French Revolution	
May 5, 1789	Estates General convenes at Versailles
June 20, 1789	Tennis Court Oath
July 14, 1789	Storming of the Bastille
July–August 1789	The Great Fear
August 4, 1789	National Assembly abolishes feudal privileges
August 26, 1789	National Assembly issues "Declaration of the Rights of Man and Citizen"
October 5–6, 1789	Women march on Versailles and force royal family to return to Paris
November 1789	National Assembly confiscates church lands
July 1790	Civil Constitution of the Clergy establishes a national church; Louis XVI reluctantly agrees to accept a constitutional monarchy
June 1791	Royal family is arrested while attempting to flee France
April 1792	France declares war on Austria
September 22, 1792	National Convention abolishes monarchy and declares France a republic
January 21, 1793	Louis XVI is executed
February 1793	France declares war on Britain, the Dutch Republic, and Spain
April–June 1793	Robespierre and allies organize the Committee of Public Safety
1793–1794	The Terror
October 16, 1793	Marie-Antoinette is executed
February 4, 1794	National Convention abolishes slavery in all French territories
July 28, 1794	Robespierre is executed; Thermidorian reaction begins
1795–1799	Directory rules
1797	Napoleon defeats Austrian armies in Italy and returns in triumph to Paris
November 9, 1799	Napoleon overthrows the Directory and seizes power

Still, the frequent elections of 1795–1799 gave French men the experience— even if not the full reality—of democratic politics. They enjoyed considerable freedom of the press, speech, and assembly, and many developed the habit of thinking seriously about politics. Even without the right to vote, women, too, participated in politics as never before, going to meetings, joining demonstrations, and following the political process along with their men.

Although these political experiences were short-lived, French people would not forget them. They constituted an apprenticeship in democracy on which later generations would build. But in the late 1790s, the Directory was too shaky and institutionally weak to take its own democratic arrangements seriously. It counted on military victories to maintain its hold on power and a semblance of legitimacy. Under the command of Napoleon and other top generals, the French army won battle after battle, knocking the Dutch, Prussians, Spanish, and Austrians out of the war.

Britain, Russia, and the French Revolution

The British, alone, refused to give in, protected as they were by the world's most powerful navy, by a burgeoning economy, and by an empire that, despite its loss of the Thirteen Colonies in 1781, was a great source of economic and political strength. In 1800, Britain traded on highly favorable terms with virtually the entire world and enjoyed especially lucrative economic relationships with the new United States, colonial Jamaica and other Caribbean islands, and increasingly the resource-rich Indian subcontinent, which the East India Company (EIC) and the British state were making into the "jewel" in its colonial crown (see Chapter 2).

In the 1780s, British writers led by Adam Smith and Edmund Burke (1729–1797), the philosopher and Member of Parliament, harshly criticized the EIC's treatment of the Indian people and demanded that the government rein the company in. Once the French Revolution broke out, its ideas about liberty and equality crossed the English Channel, encouraging British dissidents to demand greater freedom both at home and in India, better conditions for working people, and a more representative Parliament. Burke did not, however, join this group. Although he had supported the American Revolution, he stood apart from Thomas Paine (1737–1809) and other British reformers by condemning the French Revolution. For Burke, the French upheaval had gravely and dangerously erred by trying to transform politics and society overnight.

By the mid-1790s, the British government had subdued its internal Jacobin sympathizers and joined the war against France. Britain used its powerful navy to challenge France in the Caribbean and to deter any French effort to invade the British

Isles, including Ireland, which was forcibly integrated into the British Empire in 1801. Napoleon was all too aware of this naval strength, and rather than confront British warships in their home waters, he led his army across the Mediterranean to Egypt, where he hoped to disrupt Britain's lucrative trade with India. But once the French fleet had deposited Napoleon and his troops on Egyptian soil in July 1798, the British navy stranded them there by destroying the French vessels anchored in Aboukir Bay.

Napoleon expected the Egyptians, whom he saw as oppressed by cruel Ottoman overlords, to greet him as a liberator; they strenuously resisted him instead. But even as the French invasion went from bad to worse, Napoleon proved himself to be a master of propaganda, sending back to France images of military triumph and cultural discovery and boasting of a successful effort to "civilize" the Egyptian people. The French thought him a great hero. To preserve his reputation in the face of an imminent military disaster, Napoleon slipped out of Egypt and returned to France before the collapse of the French forces, which could now be blamed on someone else.

In the meantime, the Belgians and Italians staged a successful rebellion against the French occupation of their territories, and for the first time, an increasingly powerful Russia entered the war against revolutionary France. Under Catherine the Great, who ruled from 1762 to 1796, Russia expanded into what are now Belarus, Ukraine, Lithuania, the Crimea, and the eastern shore of the Black Sea, having put down a serious rebellion by Emelian Pugachev (1742–1775). This Cossack fighter was hostile to Catherine for stripping his people of their traditional independence and claimed to be the real Peter III, the tsar whom Catherine had married and then overthrown. Peter III was seen as more favorable than she to the Cossacks and serfs who made up the bulk of Pugachev's army.

After overcoming the Pugachev threat in 1774, Catherine rationalized and strengthened the administration of her country, affirming her status as an absolute ruler, although supposedly an "enlightened" one. This status did not prevent her from maintaining the institution of serfdom, which critics had begun to oppose but which the nobility considered its most important privilege, one that even an absolute ruler could not undermine.

When the French Revolution broke out, Catherine distanced herself from the Enlightenment writers she had corresponded with and exiled any Russian intellectuals who expressed even cautious support for the principles of 1789. Her officials censored books and newspapers and seized printing presses deemed to have published offensive works. There would be no revolutionary contagion in Russia, which would fight off and on against the French Revolution and Napoleon until 1815.

Revolution in the French Empire

France's reverses in Egypt and Europe in 1798 coincided with a new rebellion in the Vendée and a nearly successful royalist effort to capture France's crucial Mediterranean port of Toulon. Suddenly, the French republic seemed to be falling apart, and the Abbé Sieyès, now a Director, enlisted Napoleon in a plot to replace the increasingly ineffectual Directory with a new, authoritarian regime. On November 9, 1799, they led a coup d'état that established a three-man executive authority called the Consulate. Napoleon was named First Consul, a title borrowed from Ancient Rome, and he quickly pushed Sieyès and the third Consul aside. By early 1800, Napoleon, born in obscurity, had made himself the effective ruler of France.

Napoleon would soon play a major role in France's Caribbean colonies—Martinique, Guadeloupe, and Saint-Domingue—which had been in revolt since 1791. On the eve of the French Revolution, Saint-Domingue reigned as the most productive colony in the world, outperforming all of Spain's New World colonies combined. Its enslaved workers harvested huge quantities of sugar cane, coffee, indigo (a vegetable dye), cacao, cotton, and tobacco. Some of these products, especially sugar, were also grown on the smaller islands of Martinique and Guadeloupe (see Map 5.3).

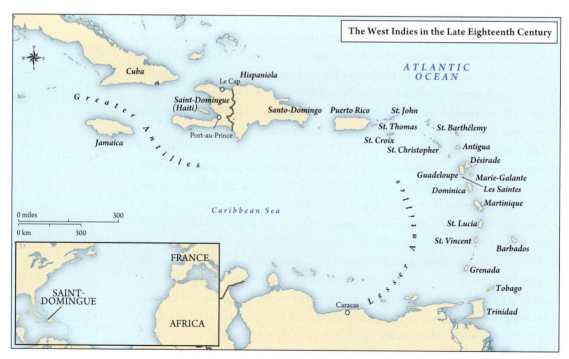

≡ **MAP 5.3**   The West Indies in the Late Eighteenth Century

As we have seen, certain Enlightenment philosophers deemed slavery immoral and inhumane, and the royal government regularly worried that plantation owners abused their slaves, though it did little to stop that abuse. Slavery and the slave trade were just too profitable, and besides, the Caribbean islands were too far away for the French government to exercise much oversight. By 1789, the slave population of Saint-Domingue had reached 465,000 (89 percent of the inhabitants), many of them recent arrivals from Africa. There were just 31,000 whites (6 percent) and 28,000 free people of color (5 percent), mostly individuals of mixed race (mulattoes). Although the United States in the late eighteenth century was 100 times the size of Saint-Domingue, it contained less than half as many slaves.

The treatment of slaves was even harsher in Saint-Domingue than in the southern United States, in part because the French colony had so many more blacks than whites. The vastly outnumbered Europeans lived in constant fear of slave rebellions and counted on extraordinarily cruel punishment to keep blacks in line. Slaves who hit white people were tortured and killed, as were those who tried to run away.

When word of such treatment reached France, anti-slavery sentiment increased. In 1788, the philosopher Nicolas de Condorcet (1743–1794) joined with other like-minded people to create the **Society of the Friends of Blacks**, which advocated the abolition of the slave trade and eventually of slavery itself. In condemning this institution, members of the society publicized the new idea of **human rights**, the notion that a set of fundamental rights—and especially the freedom from servitude—applied to all human beings without exception.

These ideas filtered back to Saint-Domingue, Martinique, and Guadeloupe, where white plantation owners denounced them vehemently and free people of color listened with interest, even though about a quarter of them owned slaves. Having escaped human bondage, the mixed-race population still lived as second-class citizens, and they were receptive to Enlightenment ideas about freedom and equality.

When revolution broke out in France, the Caribbean colonies sent competing delegations

≡ **Jean-Baptiste Belley.** Born in Africa, Belley became the first black person and former slave to serve in the French legislature. He is posed next to a bust of the eighteenth-century abolitionist Guillaume-Thomas (Abbé) Raynal.

to Paris, one composed of white planters, the other of free people of color. The white delegates emphasized the importance of the plantation economy and the need to keep its slave system intact. For them, this meant maintaining the strict racial hierarchy by refusing any concessions to those of mixed race, to whom many whites were related by blood. Led by the lawyer and slave-owner Vincent Ogé (1755–1791), free people of color maintained that the National Assembly had to extend full political rights to the mixed-race population. Otherwise, its members might ally with the slaves and foment a revolt that would "see blood flowing, our lands invaded, the objects of our industry ravaged, our homes burnt." For the time being, the white planters won the argument, but Ogé had made inroads among an influential minority of Assembly members that included Lafayette.

Caribbean slaves gained no representation in Paris, but they learned about the revolutionary developments occurring there from former slaves who worked on ships sailing between France and the Caribbean. The royal governor of Saint-Domingue reported that slaves were told that the poor people of France had killed their masters and now ruled themselves. "We must expect strange revolutions," wrote his counterpart in Guadeloupe.

The first revolt came not from the slaves but from the free people of color. Having failed to gain equal rights for those of mixed race, Ogé returned to Saint-Domingue in October 1790 and led 350 mixed-race people in a rebellion against the local regime. Planters and French soldiers stationed there put it down, executing Ogé in February 1791. This rebellion foreshadowed the massive slave revolt that broke out in late August 1791. Insurgents burned dozens of plantations near the city of Cap Français, pillaged their masters' houses, and exacted revenge for years of brutal treatment by mutilating, raping, torturing, and murdering the whites in their paths. More than 100,000 slaves were involved, and by mid-September much of northern Saint-Domingue lay in smoking ruins.

For the time being, the rebellion did not spread to Martinique and Guadeloupe, but the whites there prepared for trouble. To prevent any alliance between slaves and free people of color, white planters in Martinique granted mixed-race people the right to vote. But the whites of Saint-Domingue refused to follow suit, staging a rebellion against the French assembly's efforts, later retracted, to grant full political rights to people of color whose parents had also been free.

This white intransigence angered the free colored population and sparked a new uprising of slaves. Together, white and mixed-race fighters, backed by a small contingent of troops from France, slowed the spread of the slave revolt, but they could not crush it. The blacks retained control over the ruined plantations of Saint-Domingue's Northern Plain, where they created a new, black-run society marked not by sugar production and large-scale plantations but by small peasant farms. The former slaves had no desire to return to grueling plantation labor, even though their leaders wanted them to do just that. A plantation economy would have enriched the emerging black elite and produced the sugar needed to buy weapons and ammunition for the war against the French.

Although short of arms and other supplies, the slave rebels benefited from the persistent inability of whites and free people of color to create a durable alliance. Rather than accept the equality of their mixed-race neighbors, many of Saint-Domingue's whites, backed by French troops stationed on the island, rebelled against the "civil commissioners" sent from France to govern the colony. In response, the commissioners allowed mixed-race soldiers to form their own militias independent of the regular French army and urged them to put down the white rebellion. The representatives of France's revolutionary government were now closely allied—and dependent on—Saint-Domingue's *gens de couleur*.

Meanwhile, the whites of Saint-Domingue, now facing a triple threat from the civil commissioners, the free people of color, and the slave revolt, shifted their allegiance from France to Britain. The British had joined the European war against France in early 1793 and promised to maintain slavery throughout the Caribbean. Since Spain was also at war with France, its leaders decided to send troops from Santo Domingo into Saint-Domingue to seize parts of the French colony. As we have seen, the Spanish promised freedom to Saint-Domingue slaves who agreed to help put down the revolt. Some slaves, in other words, could earn their freedom by fighting to keep other slaves in chains.

Under these circumstances, it was the civil commissioners—that is, the official representatives of the French revolutionary government—who faced a triple threat: from Saint-Domingue's white planters, the British, and the Spanish, the latter now allied with Toussaint and other leaders of the slave revolt. To complicate matters all the more, the civil commissioners suddenly found themselves subject to the authority of General François Galbaud, the newly appointed governor of Saint-Domingue. In theory, Galbaud represented the same revolutionary government as did the civil commissioners, but as the owner of slave plantations on Saint-Domingue, he sympathized with the rebellious whites and looked down on the colony's free people of color.

On June 20, 1793, Galbaud launched several shiploads of soldiers against the commissioners holed up in Cap Français and inadequately protected by a band of mixed-race soldiers. In desperate need of reinforcements, the commissioners made an earth-shattering decision: they promised freedom from bondage and citizenship in the French republic to any enslaved person who agreed to take up arms in their defense. The black slaves of Cap Français and the surrounding region responded to this offer en masse, forcing Galbaud and his terrified white troops to flee to the relative safety of the French ships moored off the coast. The general himself plunged into the water rather than wait for a rowboat to arrive.

To force the rest of the whites out of the city, the most elegant in the colony, the black rebels set its buildings aflame. Some 3,000 people of all races died in the fighting and the fires, making it the worst case of urban violence in the history of the New World to date. The violence was terrible, but the rebel slaves had saved the republican government in Saint-Domingue—at least for the time being. The blacks, however, saw no reason to continue fighting for the French Revolution unless its leaders abolished slavery altogether, and not just for those who agreed to join the French army.

With British and Spanish forces threatening the very existence of the French colony, the commissioners decided to take this momentous step. On August 29, 1793, they issued an emancipation proclamation, seventy years before Abraham Lincoln would do the same in the United States. Five months later, France's revolutionary parliament, the National Convention, officially confirmed the commissioners' proclamation, decreeing, "slavery of the blacks is abolished [and] all men living in the colonies, without distinction of color, are French citizens and enjoy all the rights guaranteed by the constitution"—that is, the same rights as white men (which white women did not share).

The emancipation decree moved significant numbers of black fighters to defect from the Spanish side and return to Saint-Domingue, where they joined the battle against the British. The most prominent of these defectors was Toussaint Louverture, who, as we have seen, became Saint-Domingue's military leader and de facto ruler of the island. Napoleon did not accept Toussaint's independent stance and took advantage of an 1802 truce with Britain to reclaim Saint-Domingue. In that effort, more than fifty thousand French soldiers died, many from diseases to which the black soldiers were immune. Although the French had vowed a "war of extermination" against civilians and soldiers alike, Saint-Domingue's black army dealt Napoleon an unprecedented defeat—even with Toussaint languishing in a French prison (see Map 5.4).

In 1803, under the leadership of Jean-Jacques Dessalines (1758–1806), the Haitians transformed the world's first successful slave rebellion into a victorious anti-colonial war of independence. The costs in human and material terms were staggering, as perhaps a third of the country's black population died in the struggle. The bitter feelings left by more than a decade of insurrection and war were such that when Dessalines emerged victorious, he ordered the extermination of

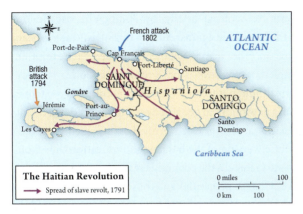

MAP 5.4   The Haitian Revolution

MAP 5.5   France's Retreat from America

all whites who had not managed to flee. Dessalines himself survived less than two more years, falling to assassins in 1806. Haiti then descended into political instability and economic misery, exacerbated in 1825 by steep, French-imposed reparations payments to compensate deposed slave owners, and in 1915 by a two-decade-long military occupation by the United States.

France's loss of Haiti ruined Napoleon's plans for a revived French empire in the Americas and contributed to the westward expansion of the United States (see Map 5.5). After Spain ceded the vast Louisiana Territory to France in 1800, Napoleon intended to make those North American lands the source of food and supplies for an expanded plantation economy in Saint-Domingue, Martinique, and Guadeloupe. But Haiti's independence deprived France of the world's most profitable sugar-producing island and thus of the need for lands to support it economically in North America. Napoleon also decided that rather than defend a large swath of the American continent containing few European inhabitants, he should husband his resources for a renewed war with Britain and the conquest of Europe. In 1803, Napoleon sold the Louisiana Territory to the United States for 15 million dollars, or 4 cents an acre. Had France succeeded in maintaining its American empire, the historical trajectory of the United States might have been altered beyond recognition.

Napoleon's European Empire

Napoleon, however, pivoted back to Europe, where he would leave a deep imprint on the continent as a whole. He justified his seizure of power in late 1799 by promising to rid France of the chaos of the revolution while maintaining its gains.

He fulfilled part of that promise, at least briefly, by ending the decade-long anti-revolutionary war—on the battlefield against Austria in 1801 and at the peace table with Britain a year later. In other areas, Napoleon fulfilled the revolution-aries' desire to create a complete set of laws—the **Napoleonic Code**—that ap-plied equally to all adult men, although it treated women as second-class citizens. He maintained the revolution's new political geography of eighty-six departments or states. And he devised a national system of government-supported secondary schools that constituted an elitist version of the basic public education the revolu-tion had sought—but failed—to create. In the economic realm, Napoleon affirmed the revolution's confiscation of Church properties and those of noble émigrés. This redistribution of land from the Church and nobility to the people constituted the revolution's most important economic reform, and Napoleon gained a great deal of goodwill by affirming it.

If Napoleon completed the revolution's work in the realms of law, geographical organization, education, and land redistribution, he overturned it in most other ways. Almost immediately after assuming power, Napoleon replaced "liberty, equality, and fraternity" with order, hierarchy, and property. He established order in Martinique and Guadeloupe by restoring slavery and the plantation economy, and in mainland France by creating an illiberal state complete with censorship, arbitrary arrest, and tight surveillance of all potential opponents.

Equality succumbed to hierarchy when Napoleon deprived the ballot box of meaning and instead vested the lion's share of political authority in himself and his administrative state. "The government," he declared, "is the center of society like the sun; all the various institutions must orbit it without ever deviating." The bottom-up configuration of elected officials that the revolution had intended to create gave way under Napoleon to an apparatus of absolutism that made Louis XIV's state seem weak by comparison.

With his new government in place, Napoleon sought to achieve reconciliation with the Catholic Church, many of whose priests had been harassed and killed under the Terror. Napoleon was himself indifferent to religion, but he saw it as an essential ingredient of social order. In late 1801, after eight months of arduous nego-tiation, Napoleon signed a **Concordat** with the pope. This agreement ended all re-strictions on Catholic worship imposed during the revolution, reopened shuttered churches, and erased the distinction between constitutional and nonconstitutional clergy. Catholicism was declared "the religion of the great majority of French citi-zens," although not, as under the Old Regime, the single official religion of France.

In exchange for this Catholic restoration, the pope officially accepted the con-fiscation and sale of Church lands and agreed to the revolutionary precedent of making priests and bishops salaried officials of the state. The Catholic Church, long the spiritual partner of French monarchs, was now the servant of Napoleon's post-revolutionary regime.

After concluding the Concordat, Napoleon moved to solidify his personal power. In 1802 he became First Consul for life, and in 1804 he crowned himself Emperor of the French. The pope blessed the new title, which Napoleon meant to be hereditary. To win the endorsement of the elite, or at least to keep its members quiet, Napoleon re-created the nobility, although a nobility of service to the state. To receive the people's blessing, he organized a referendum in which all adult men were asked to vote yes or no to his new hereditary monarchy. With public opposition forbidden and the results "enhanced," Napoleon appeared to receive the public's overwhelming support.

To women, Napoleon offered few benefits. The Code obliged wives to obey their husbands, who were supposed to give them financial support in exchange. Women would need that support, since the Code awarded husbands control over all wages earned by their wives and over all property held in common with them. Only with

≡ **Napoleon the Great.** This pair of iconic paintings from the Napoleonic period presents the emperor in heroic guise. On the left, Jacques-Louis David's *Napoleon Crossing the Alps* (1805) idealizes Napoleon as a valiant soldier, while J. A. D. Ingrès's *Napoleon on the Imperial Throne* (1806) portrays him as if he were the Sun King, Louis XIV, himself.

their husbands' consent could women bring civil suits to court, sell property, and take out loans. It was much easier for men to divorce their wives than vice versa, especially when it came to adultery, which the Code made nearly impossible for a woman to prove against her husband.

Workers, like women, were treated as children. They needed a certificate of good conduct signed by a former employer to obtain a new job—a requirement that discouraged workers from demanding higher pay or better working conditions. In any case, workers' organizations were illegal and strikes forbidden. In disputes between workers and employers, government officials almost always sided with the employer.

Like Louis XIV before him, only more so, Napoleon did everything he could to enhance his public image. Coins bore his likeness, as did public art and monuments built in his honor. Engravers created thousands of lithographs (inexpensively reproduced drawings) that circulated throughout the country and portrayed him as a great hero and savior of France. Napoleon had the country's top artists paint him in mythical, almost religious, hues, and he commissioned a series of monumental buildings designed, in part, as shrines to his regime.

In many ways, Napoleon lived up to the exalted image he created of himself, especially on the battlefield. He personally led armies in more than sixty battles and became legendary not only for his bravery but also for an apparent invulnerability. He survived unscathed after horses were shot out from under him nineteen times. So much did Napoleon bolster his soldiers' morale that his presence, it was said, equaled fifty thousand men.

Beyond this battlefield charisma, the French Emperor achieved his stunning military successes by building on the French Revolution's main military innovation, the creation of a citizen army staffed by unprecedented numbers of men. No traditional European army could match France's new fighting force. In addition to their numbers and the quality of their battle-tested officers, French soldiers had since 1792 developed a culture of patriotism forged in the effort to protect their country from foreign invasion. The feelings of national pride spilled over onto Napoleon's regime—at least as long as he continued to achieve great victories.

During Napoleon's first eight years in power, he and his forces lost only two major battles, one in Saint-Domingue and the other at Trafalgar, Spain, in 1805 against the legendary British naval commander Horatio Nelson. On the European continent, Napoleon appeared invincible. In late 1805, he crushed Austrian forces in Bavaria and again at the Battle of Austerlitz (December 2, 1805) in Bohemia, this time defeating the Russians as well. As soon as Prussia re-entered the war the following year, Napoleon promptly routed its forces at Jena and Auerstadt. In 1807 he forced Russia out of the war (see Map 5.6).

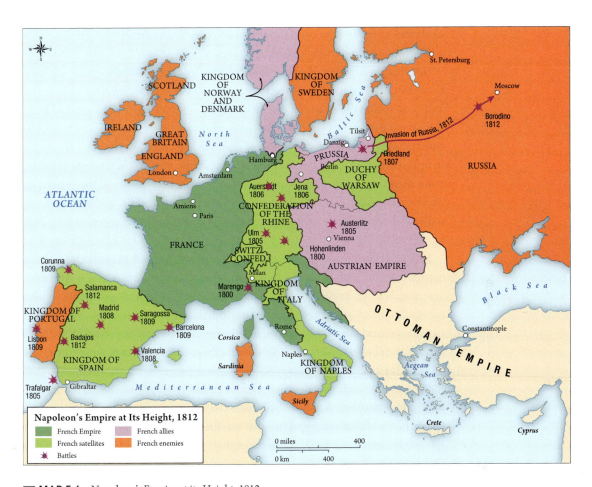

≡ **MAP 5.6**   Napoleon's Empire at its Height, 1812

When the smoke cleared, much of Central and Southern Europe found itself under Napoleon's control. Prussia was dismembered, with key western and eastern provinces becoming French satellite states known respectively as the Kingdom of Westphalia and the Duchy of Warsaw. Napoleon made northern Italy, western-most Prussia, and the Austrian Netherlands parts of France and turned the rest of Italy and the former Dutch Republic into French colonies. In 1806, he abolished the thousand-year-old Holy Roman Empire, reorganizing its over three hundred ministates into just thirty-three.

In creating his de facto colonies, Napoleon extended to them what he considered the major gains of the French Revolution: the abolition of monasteries, serfdom, and seigneurial dues; the subordination of church to state; and full civil rights to Jews and other religious minorities. He replaced existing laws with the Napoleonic

Code and opened positions in the army and government service, long reserved for noblemen, to members of the middle classes.

Napoleon's engineers built roads, bridges, and canals throughout his new European empire, partly to speed the movement of troops, but also to improve local and regional economies, which needed a boost. Parts of Europe had been devastated by years of warfare, and their economies were damaged by the "**continental system**," Napoleon's embargo on trade with Britain. Although Napoleon designed his continental system to isolate Britain economically, it harmed Europe more than the British Isles, which could still trade with Asia and the Americas, thanks to Britain's control of the seas. Europeans, meanwhile, suffered from the reduced ability to buy relatively inexpensive British products and export their own goods to British ports.

Still, some European manufacturers profited from the lack of competition from more efficient British firms and thus found aspects of the continental system congenial to them. Overall, Napoleon's efforts to reshape Europe pleased some people, especially liberal, commercially oriented individuals, and displeased others, particularly conservative landed elites. But almost no one in the dependent territories appreciated the taxes Napoleon imposed on them or the quotas of army conscripts he made them fulfill.

In Prussia, which was defeated and dismembered but not conquered in full, political leaders responded to Napoleon's challenge by undertaking a series of reforms, many of them inspired by what the French emperor had done. Reformers abolished serfdom in 1807, although in reality, most peasants remained unfree. Only a handful could afford the compensation payments required of them in exchange for their release from bondage. Officials also limited the ability of guilds (organizations of craftsmen and other workers) to fix prices and wages and generally to restrict the market in goods and services. These reforms laid part of the groundwork for Prussia's economic expansion of the mid-nineteenth century, but they were partially and unevenly applied. So was the abolition of tax exemption for nobles, which was discussed more than enacted.

A more significant reform involved the abolition of restrictions on what members of the different estates (status groups) could do. Nobles were now free to take up middle-class occupations in business, law, banking, and other realms, and middle-class people as well as peasants could buy noble properties, although in practice such purchases were rare. By making land and labor more mobile, these new possibilities, like the abolition of fixed status groups, prepared the way for the economic development to come. The extension of primary education to middle- and even lower-class children, already begun before the French Revolution, also boosted the economy, as did the creation of secondary schools and a new (Humboldt) university in Berlin. The growth of literacy during this period enabled the Prussian government to spread anti-French propaganda and to develop a measure of popular patriotism to steel the population for future conflict with France.

In the political sphere, reformers made the Prussian government somewhat more efficient than before the Napoleonic eruption, but the king and traditional elites resisted the writing of a constitution and the creation of a Prussia-wide parliament. Both would have limited their powers and given representation to members of the middle classes. The army, like the government, experienced changes designed to meet the challenges represented by Napoleon's conscript forces, but here, too, the reforms proceeded slowly and unevenly.

The Habsburg Empire, renamed the Austrian Empire in 1804, its ruler Francis I (1768-1835) now the emperor of Austria, also suffered military and territorial losses to Napoleon and undertook reforms in response. Austria's changes were less ambitious than those of Prussia, but in the military realm they were significant. Incompetent generals lost their commissions, while the treatment of common soldiers became less inhumane. New reserve battalions enabled the army to mobilize larger numbers of men when war broke out, and Francis's brother, the Archduke Johann, developed a "home militia" designed to protect Austria's myriad localities from the incursion of foreign troops. Service in the militias was compulsory for all men between eighteen and forty-five not already serving in the army. This new organization did much to connect Austria's various peoples to their emperor and empire and helped develop in them dual identities as at once members of a distinct group—Bohemians, Slovenes, Croatians—and as citizens of a multinational empire that transcended those groups.

In Prussia and Austria, as in the lands conquered by

≡ **The Departure of the Militiaman.** Johann Peter Krafft's, *The Departure of the Militiaman* (1813) represented a popular Austrian patriotism triggered by the Napoleonic wars and depicted a stoic, if idealized, commitment of its people to the defense of the realm.

Napoleon or his allies, people came together in common opposition to the French and in an emerging national feeling, or in Austria a greater commitment to the empire. Just as the French Revolution had created the sense of belonging to a French nation, so the revolution in its Napoleonic form produced a sense of national belonging in the Germans and Italians, among others, who strained under its yoke.

The national awakenings in Germany and Italy were largely political and cultural phenomena rather than military ones, although in Italy organized bandits attacked French officials and secret societies known as *carbonari* operated underground. Only in Portugal did the resistance to Napoleonic rule involve large-scale fighting. Although the Portuguese king, Dom Pedro IV (1798–1834), fled to Brazil in the wake of the French invasion of 1807, local fighters, aided by British soldiers, held Napoleon's forces at bay. But in the process, Portugal lost its hold over Brazil, which had achieved considerable autonomy even before Napoleon's invasion helped free the South American colony for good.

In Spain, the clergy and nobility rebelled against the installation of Napoleon's brother Joseph as their king by organizing groups of peasants called guerrillas (marking the origin of modern "guerrilla" warfare) to attack the French. These military efforts, however, forced the Spanish to marshal all their resources for the home front and deprived them of the ability to exercise control over their colonial empire. The residents of Spanish America were already in ferment over efforts by the Spanish king to extract higher taxes and restrict their ability to trade with Britain and the United States. Led by the nationalist "liberator" Simón Bolívar (1783–1830), Venezuela became independent almost immediately, and Colombia, Ecuador, Peru, and Bolivia soon followed suit. By 1825, Spain's three-century-old American empire was finished (except for Cuba and Puerto Rico).

In European Spain, the peasants who fought the French were motivated by a combination of religious hostility to their "atheistic" conquerors and a budding national feeling against the foreign occupier. In the field, the guerillas stymied Napoleon's army by engaging in stealthy attacks and then vanishing into the countryside. This nontraditional "asymmetric" warfare, as we would call it today, tied down a large contingent of French soldiers and prevented Napoleon from launching his entire army against Russia, now his main military objective. By invading Russia, the French emperor sought to complete his conquest of continental Europe, which he believed would force Britain to sue for peace in hopes of ending its European isolation and lifting the blockade against its manufactured goods.

In June 1812, Napoleon led six hundred thousand men and a quarter million horses into the Russian steppes. Like the Spanish, the Russians adopted their own form of nontraditional warfare. Instead of engaging Napoleon's superior forces, the tsar's army retreated eastward, drawing the French deep into the country and stretching their lines of supply. The two armies finally engaged each other on September 7, 1812, at Borodino, a village not far from Moscow, in the bloodiest single day of all the Napoleonic wars. The Battle of Borodino forms the military centerpiece of Leo Tolstoy's classic novel, *War and Peace* (1869), and it inspired one of Russia's most famous musical compositions, Pyotr Ilich Tchaikovsky's *1812 Overture* (1880).

In this epic confrontation, each side lost tens of thousands of soldiers, but the Russians, fighting at home, could replace their casualties and resupply their men, while the French could not. Rather than address these crucial problems immediately, Napoleon pressed on toward Moscow, where he planned to seize food and shelter for his troops. The Russians foiled these plans by abandoning the city and allowing its mostly wooden buildings to burn (whether they were deliberately set on fire is disputed). By the time Napoleon arrived, Moscow's food and shelter, as one top aide put it, had "vanished in air, in a whirlwind of smoke and flames."

His soldiers hungry, sick, and exhausted, Napoleon had no choice but to retreat. The problem was that he walked into the frigid Russian winter, which arrived even earlier than usual that year. Horses dropped dead from the cold, guns locked up, and food froze into inedible chunks of ice. "The unhappy men," wrote one observer, "crawled on, with trembling limbs, and chattering teeth, until the snow... made them stagger and fall." Having pushed into Russia with six hundred thousand men, Napoleon straggled out with less than a hundred thousand; he left a half million dead, mortally wounded, or in captivity.

≡ **Napoleon's Retreat from Moscow.** After suffering a great many casualties at the Battle of Borodino in September 1812, Napoleon led his depleted forces to Moscow in search of food and supplies. But the city was ablaze, and Napoleon had no choice but to retreat. Most of his soldiers—hungry, wounded, and demoralized—could not withstand the frigid, barren Russian winter.

As it turned out, Napoleon's retreat from Russia marked the beginning of the end of the French emperor's regime,

The Napoleonic Era	
November 1799	Napoleon overthrows the Directory
December 1799	Napoleon's new constitution approved
1801	Napoleon signs papal Concordat
1803	Death of Toussaint Louverture in France
January 1804	Declaration of Haitian independence
March 1804	Napoleonic Code
December 1804	Napoleon crowned emperor
May 1805	First Haitian constitution
October 1805	Britain defeats the French fleet at the Battle of Trafalgar
1806	Napoleon abolishes the Holy Roman Empire
1807	Napoleon redraws map of Europe
1808	Spanish revolt against French occupation
June 1812	Napoleon invades Russia
Fall–Winter 1812	Napoleon makes a disastrous retreat from Russia
March 1814	Russia, Prussia, Austria, Sweden, and Britain invade France
April 1814	Napoleon abdicates and is exiled to Elba; Louis XVIII restored to constitutional monarchy
February–June 1815	Napoleon escapes from Elba but is defeated at the Battle of Waterloo; Louis XVIII restored to throne for second time
1821	Napoleon dies on island of St. Helena

but he could have prevented it from collapsing around him. After two decades of warfare, Britain and the major continental powers were exhausted, their leaders willing to negotiate peace with Napoleon in exchange for the withdrawal of his troops from their remaining European strongholds. But Napoleon remained intransigent, refusing to recognize the reversal of his fortunes, and he rebuffed one peace overture after the other, either by continuing to fight or by making excessive territorial demands.

Finally, in March 1814, British, Prussian, Austrian, Russian, and Swedish armies combined in a joint invasion of France. Led by Russia's Tsar Alexander I, the anti-French coalition entered Paris on April 1, negotiating the surrender of French forces and having Napoleon's handpicked Senate strip him of his throne. Napoleon found himself exiled to the Mediterranean island of Elba, and the allies invited Louis XVIII, the brother of the slain Louis XVI, to restore the Bourbon monarchy. The apparent return of the Old Regime satisfied the allied European kings, who agreed to withdraw from France and leave the country geographically intact.

This benign settlement collapsed, however, when the deposed emperor decided, in early 1815, to return from exile, promising liberal reforms and the restoration of French glory. Napoleon's return forced Louis XVIII to flee the country, and it convinced the European powers to band together and crush the emperor for good. In June 1815, a combined European army led by Britain's Duke of Wellington and consisting mainly of British and Prussian troops—the Russian and Austrian forces had not yet arrived—amassed near France's northern border. Napoleon met them outside of Waterloo, Belgium, where his hastily assembled army suffered a decisive, if not overwhelming, defeat. This time, the victorious powers exiled the former emperor to St. Helena, an isolated island in the South Atlantic. He was kept there under guard and died a prisoner in 1821.

His legend, however, lived on. Writers compared him with Alexander the Great and Julius Caesar, and new generations of French people, hoping for a shot of glory, forgot about the 750,000 French soldiers and civilians who died in warfare during his reign. What made those negative memories recede was his extraordinary rise from obscure soldier to master of the European world. Although far from a democrat himself, Napoleon seemed to represent the unprecedented possibilities of the post-revolutionary, democratic age, a time when talent, will, and determination promised to make every man a king.

Conclusion: The Legacy of the French Revolution

The French Revolution marked a fundamentally important moment in European and world history. It produced—or confirmed—more lasting changes than any other Western historical phenomenon, save perhaps for the Protestant Reformation. If the Reformation transformed Europe's religious order, the Revolution upended its political and legal system by showing that ordinary human beings could do away with a monarchy and nobility that had existed for a millennium.

While the revolution transformed society at the highest level by abolishing monarchy and nobility, it changed social relations at the bottom by transferring vast expanses of former Church lands to French peasants and by marking the beginning of the end of serfdom elsewhere in Europe. The revolution also marked the beginning of the end of slavery, which disappeared for good in Saint-Domingue in 1793 and briefly in Martinique and Guadeloupe. Although Napoleon restored human bondage on the two small islands, the French and Haitian Revolutions had helped make opposition to slavery widespread. The institution would survive in French colonies only until 1848.

In other parts of the New World, the fledgling United States became more democratic under the influence of the French Revolution and benefited handsomely from Napoleon's defeat in Saint-Domingue. Deprived of his Caribbean jewel, Napoleon sold the gigantic province of Louisiana to the United States, doubling the size of the American republic and enabling it to become a great continental power. Meanwhile, in South America, local leaders inspired by the French Revolution responded to Napoleon's takeover of Spain in 1808 by staging rebellions against Spanish colonial rule.

Beyond these developments in society, politics, and international affairs, the French Revolution and its Napoleonic postscript transformed the way people thought. No longer did anything seem fixed forever in a "natural order of things." The revolution showed, to the delight of some and the horror of others, that little in life was permanent. Monarchies could be abolished almost overnight and ancient religious authority quickly undermined. People of humble birth could become leaders, generals, and kings, while the once mighty could fall.

In the early nineteenth century, these mental changes would coalesce into a series of new ideologies—political philosophies applied to everyday life. We will examine these ideologies—conservatism, liberalism, nationalism, democracy, and socialism—in Chapter 7. First, we must take up the other great revolution of the era, the economic transformation known as the Industrial Revolution that began in Britain and is the subject of Chapter 6.

KEY TERMS

assignats *209*

Bastille *206*

Civil Constitution of the Clergy *210*

Committee of Public Safety *215*

Concordat *228*

continental system *232*

Convention *213*

"Declaration of the Rights of Man and Citizen" *207*

émigrés *211*

Estates General *199*

Girondins *212*

human rights *223*

Jacobins *209*

Jansenists *201*

levée en masse *216*

Napoleonic Code *228*

parlements *198*

physiocrats *200*

sans-culottes *212*

Society of the Friends of Blacks *223*

tax farming *196*

Tennis Court Oath *205*

tithe *204*

Vendée rebellion *215*

For digital learning resources, please go to the Ancillary Resource Center **https://www.oup.com/he/berenson2e**. Turn to the back of the book to see the list of primary sources and writing exercises provided in the accompanying *Sources and Guided Writing Exercises for Europe in the Modern World*

The Industrial Revolution, 1750–1850

Richard Arkwright

"Arkwright was a man of great force of character, indomitable courage, much worldly shrewdness, with a business faculty almost amounting to genius. At one period, his time was engrossed by severe and continuous labor ... sometimes from four in the morning till nine at night ... After overcoming every obstacle, he had the satisfaction of reaping the reward of his enterprise. Eighteen years after he had constructed his first machine ..., George III conferred upon him the honor of knighthood."

So wrote Samuel Smiles in his immensely popular book *Self-Help* (1859). This classic of Victorian England, which became one of the best-selling books of the nineteenth century, lauded individuals said to have achieved greatness purely through their own hard work, initiative, and will. For Smiles, the greatest men of any era were those who relied on no one but themselves, and he presented Richard Arkwright (1732–1792), the creator of England's first steam-powered textile factories, as the paragon of self-help. Although Arkwright's real life was much less individualistic than Smiles portrayed it, his famous book nonetheless helped consecrate Richard Arkwright as one of the iconic figures of the Industrial Revolution.

Arkwright came from Lancashire in northwest England, the thirteenth child born to Sarah and Charles Arkwright. A tailor of extremely modest means, Charles could not afford to send his son Richard to school, which in the eighteenth century charged fees, but he had a female cousin teach him to read. Like many sons of working men, Richard became an apprentice at age twelve, and he learned barbering and wig making well enough to set up a business of his own in the early 1750s.

From his home base in the town of Bolton, Arkwright traveled the region offering to buy women's hair. He cut it for them first and then used the human hair to make wigs, which were highly fashionable at the time. He experimented with different dyes and invented a chemical process that could create the hair colors his customers wanted. His wigs became enormously popular, and he earned enough money to put some aside for future investments.

In the mid-eighteenth century, cotton manufacturing was booming, and Arkwright became interested in cotton spinning, a key step in the

manufacture of cotton yarn, or thread. Spinners took strands of raw cotton and stretched and twisted them into a tight thread of uniform thickness. Until the 1760s, spinning was done by hand with the help of a spinning wheel, usually operated by women. The process was slow, and by mid-century it could not keep up with the soaring demand for clothing and other items made of cotton cloth. Durable and easily washed, cotton was much more practical than fabrics made of wool, linen, and silk, the traditional textile products of centuries past.

The heightened demand for cotton cloth encouraged inventors to develop ways to speed up cotton spinning while employing fewer workers, whose wages were relatively high. In the 1750s and 1760s, there were experiments galore in the Lancashire region, and Arkwright realized that he could make a great deal of money by turning these experiments into a commercially viable spinning machine. Arkwright lacked the technical expertise to build such a machine himself, so in the mid-1760s, he teamed up with a clockmaker named John Kaye, who had earlier attempted, unsuccessfully, to build a spinning machine with another mechanic, Thomas Highs. Kaye brought Highs' ideas to the collaboration with Arkwright.

The key task in cotton spinning was to stretch the raw cotton as far as it could go without snapping. An experienced spinner could do this skillfully by hand, but until Arkwright, would-be inventors had failed to produce machines that could replicate the human touch. By observing their failures and integrating what Kaye and Highs had learned in their efforts, Arkwright came up with a spinning machine, the "water frame," patented in 1769, which made mechanized spinning work.

≡ **Spinning Wheel.** Until the 1760s, individuals, usually women, used this simple hand- and foot-operated device to spin raw cotton into yarn or thread. It was a slow process, which by mid-century could no longer keep up with the soaring demand for cotton cloth.

Arkwright's machine contained eight spindles for creating cotton thread, instead of the single spindle of traditional hand-operated spinning wheels. The new device thus promised to increase the amount of thread a single worker could spin by a factor of eight. How did Arkwright make his spinning machine spin? His first idea was to use horses to turn the gears that worked the machine. But horses were expensive and tired easily. His next idea, borrowed from a silk-making mill created earlier in the century, was to use flowing water to rotate a water wheel that would in turn spin the gears of his machine—hence the name "water frame."

Timeline

1750	1760	1770	1780	1790	1800	1810	1820	1830	1840	1850	1860

1764 Hargreaves' spinning jenny

1769 Arkwright's "water frame" spinning machine

1769 Watt's steam engine improves on Newcomen's

1772 Arkwright opens his first factory

1776 Adam Smith's *Wealth of Nations*

1776 Arkwright builds cotton mill at Cromford

1779 Crompton patents "mule" spinning machine

1785 Steam power used in cotton mills

1791 Trade unions outlawed in France

1793 Whitney invents cotton gin

1799 Combination Acts outlaw British trade unions

1807 Napoleon abolishes serfdom in Prussia

1811–1812 Luddite movement

1815–1848 Agricultural advances in France and Germany

1818–1883 Karl Marx

1824 Combination Acts repealed in Britain

1830–1851 Major British railway construction

1830 Belgium becomes independent, takes advantage of coal and iron ore deposits to industrialize

1833 British Parliament passes child labor laws

1834 British Poor Laws reformed

1838 Ottoman Tariff Convention prevents tariffs on British-made goods

1844 Rebellion of weavers in Silesia crushed by Prussian government

1859 Smiles publishes *Self-Help*

To test this new process, Arkwright opened a mill (factory) near a stream of falling water in 1772. This original mill turned into a four-year-long experiment that ultimately resulted in a smoothly working enterprise. It succeeded, in part, because Arkwright had also invented a carding machine that mechanically turned bunched-up raw cotton into long, thin strands suitable for spinning. In the past, carding had been done slowly and laboriously by hand.

Then, in 1776, Arkwright built a second factory that incorporated everything he had learned from the first. This new mill, established in the town of Cromford, became the prototype for all the cotton mills erected throughout Britain and, eventually, the rest of the world in the eighteenth and nineteenth centuries. By replacing handworkers with machines, Arkwright vastly reduced the cost of cotton thread and thus of finished cloth, even though weaving was still done by hand—at least for the moment. In the process, a great many hand spinners lost their jobs.

In the last decades of the eighteenth century, Arkwright dotted northern England and southern Scotland with ever-larger and more efficient cotton mills. Much of the added efficiency came from the introduction of steam engines, which had a huge advantage over waterpower. The amount and force of water depended on the weather; too little rain and too much ice reduced the flow and thus the amount of energy. Steam engines, by contrast, supplied a constant amount of power and freed mill owners from the need to build their factories near sources of water.

Arkwright did not invent the steam engine (that distinction went first to Thomas Newcomen in 1712 and then, more definitively, to James Watt in 1769 and Richard Trevithick in 1800), nor was he the first to use it in a cotton mill (that distinction went to George, John, and James Robinson in 1785). Once again, Arkwright borrowed other people's technology and learned from—and improved on—other people's experiences. He was anything but Smiles' self-made, individualistic genius working alone. But Arkwright had the ability to do what most others could not: turn decades of inconclusive experiments into immensely productive spinning machines.

Most other great eighteenth-century inventors came from prosperous families; Arkwright's life story was a rare rags-to-riches tale. His successes earned him not only a knighthood but also entry into the "respectable society" traditionally reserved for landed gentlemen. When he died at age sixty in 1792, he was one of the wealthiest men in Britain, with a fortune estimated at £500,000—the equivalent of a multibillionaire today. ≡

Origins of the Industrial Revolution: Why Britain?

Arkwright was one of the most visible architects of Britain's Industrial Revolution. That phenomenon, which unfolded between 1760 and 1850, marked a key turning point in human history and, for a time, made Britain unique. This chapter explores how and why an industrial revolution began in eighteenth-century Britain, and why it occurred there rather than someplace else.

Before the late eighteenth century, no country or region had ever developed an economic system capable of continuous growth. Certain empires or kingdoms had achieved riches and power for a time, but sooner or later all reached a ceiling of per capita wealth beyond which they could not progress. In part, growth reached a plateau because these countries devoted so many of their resources to war and to far-flung colonial empires. But mostly they ceased to expand because they lacked the know-how to increase their manufacturing and agricultural productivity rapidly enough to meet the needs of a growing population at home. Farmers were capable of increasing their production of grain and other crops only by cultivating additional lands; once all available soil had been tilled, agricultural output could grow no more. Likewise, gains in manufacturing were restricted not only because everything was made by hand, but also because the trades were organized into **guilds** dedicated to keeping prices high by holding production down.

Such was the way of the world until the late eighteenth century, when Britain emerged as the first country in history to achieve what economists have called "self-sustaining growth"—the ability to produce goods that themselves create more wealth and more productivity. A series of unprecedented changes collectively known as the **Industrial Revolution** enabled Britain to break through the age-old economic barriers to create a wholly new kind of economy.

Britain's Urban, Market-Oriented, High-Wage Economy

A key reason for Britain's industrialization after 1750 was the relative prosperity it already enjoyed. In the early eighteenth century, Britain was more prosperous on the whole than any other part of the globe save for the Dutch Republic, present-day Belgium, and perhaps Britain's colonies New York and Massachusetts. But none of these other places possessed the constellation of attributes Britain did—a market economy, high average wages, and cheap energy—which together enabled the island nation to pioneer the world's economic transformation.

Britain's seventeenth- and eighteenth-century prosperity gave its workers relatively high wages, which meant they could buy a considerable number and variety of goods on the market—food, of course, but also clothing and household items such as clocks, tables, ceramic plates, chairs, and mirrors, plus what were once purely luxury items imported from Britain's growing colonial empire: tea, sugar, spices, and chocolate. This market demand would be a key ingredient in Britain's industrial takeoff of the late eighteenth century, but it was not sufficient in itself. Crucial as well were the high price of labor and the availability of cheap, abundant energy in the form of coal. All three factors—market demand, costly labor, and inexpensive coal—ultimately gave British inventors and entrepreneurs, unlike those of other countries, the incentive to develop new processes and technologies designed to produce more goods with fewer workers. The result was a series of great inventions—spinning machines, steam engines, power looms, iron foundries, and railroads, among others—that would make Britain the first country to achieve self-sustaining economic growth.

How did Britain achieve the nearly unique prosperity that characterized it in 1700–1750? The country had not, after all, always been rich. In 1500, England and Scotland, like the rest of Europe, were poor, mostly agricultural societies. About three-quarters of their people farmed the land and did so mostly to feed themselves, exactly as in France, Germany, Poland, Russia, and the Habsburg lands (and throughout Asia as well). Almost no one lived in cities. London, destined to house a million people by 1800, numbered only fifty thousand three centuries earlier. Other British cities were little more than large villages. The same was true of Central and Eastern Europe, only more so. In 1500, the exceptions to this rule were in Italy and present-day Belgium. Venice, a center of trade and commerce in late medieval and early modern Europe, contained two hundred thousand people, as did Florence. Bruges (Belgium) had already reached that size in the fifteenth century, and nearby Ghent housed perhaps one hundred thousand (see Map 6.1).

Much of the population of these Belgian and Italian cities worked in the production and marketing of woolen cloth. Workers possessed impressive skills and labored entirely by hand. Productivity was therefore low and wages modest. Spinners and weavers in Florence and Bruges could buy their food and house themselves adequately but had little money for anything else. Still, the lightweight woolen cloth they produced was the finest in Europe, and until about 1550, these two regions dominated the market.

In the early sixteenth century, both the Belgians and Italians began to face increasingly stiff competition from an emerging English woolen industry whose raw materials—the fine fleece of long-haired English sheep—produced better-quality and even lighter fabrics. The English advantage came from their well-fed herds of sheep, which had far more land to graze on thanks to England's low population density. Good nourishment gave English sheep longer hair, which, in turn, produced superior wool.

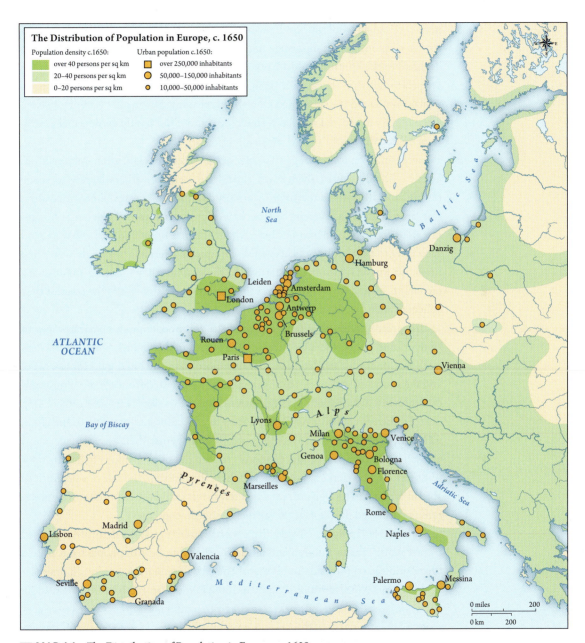

The Distribution of Population in Europe, c. 1650

Population density c.1650:   Urban population c.1650:
- over 40 persons per sq km   ▪ over 250,000 inhabitants
- 20–40 persons per sq km   ● 50,000–150,000 inhabitants
- 0–20 persons per sq km   • 10,000–50,000 inhabitants

≡ **MAP 6.1** The Distribution of Population in Europe, c. 1650

English wool, known as the "new draperies," became so popular that it put many of its continental competitors out of business. The lucrative wool trade now centered in England and especially London, where English manufacturers sent their cloth for export to a wide array of European markets. The more markets English wool captured, the more wool production stimulated the overall British economy, creating a huge number of jobs in London and attracting rural dwellers to the spinning and weaving of wool. This rural development is known as "proto-industry," because it turned farmers' cottages into mini-workshops in which women did the spinning and men the weaving. During the growing season, some of the men sowed and harvested crops, and if the family owned sheep, children tended the flock.

Increasingly, families began to specialize, since specialization increased efficiency. Some devoted themselves entirely to farming, others largely to sheep raising, and still others mainly to wool production. By the seventeenth century, this proto-industrial system had become highly organized. Merchants bought raw wool and delivered it to spinners, who made fine woolen thread and were paid according to the amount of thread they produced. Merchants then delivered the thread to weavers, also paid according to the amount they made. In many cases, merchants loaned weavers the funds to purchase their looms, and the interest they collected added to the merchants' wealth.

This proto-industrial system enriched the rural economy by paying wages to spinners and weavers and by fattening the purses of merchants, who sold finished cloth to London dealers for considerably more than they had paid for raw wool and the spun and woven cloth. Sheep raisers also profited from this system, as did the exporters in London. But the positive effects of the wool business did not stop here. Exporters needed dyers and printers to add color and patterns to the cloth, warehouses to store it, insurers to protect them against theft and damage, ships and sailors to move the product, laborers to load the ships, bankers to handle their transactions, and clerks to keep track of them. In addition, the sale of woolen cloth abroad brought in foreign currency that importers could use to purchase raw materials and finished products from various European countries.

All of these "spillover effects" from the manufacture and sale of wool created a great many jobs in London and attracted huge numbers of people from British towns and the countryside to fill them. The city's population grew at an unprecedented pace: 50,000 in 1500; 225,000 in 1600; 600,000 in 1700; 1,000,000 in 1800.

Because the demand for workers in the British capital was high, wages were generous by the standards of the time, as economic historians have shown by comparing average wages in London, Amsterdam, Vienna, Florence, Delhi (India), and Beijing. In 1500, wages (when converted to grams of silver) were about the same in all six places. They began to diverge in the late sixteenth century, with wages in London and Amsterdam topping those in Florence and double those in Vienna. By the time Adam Smith published the *Wealth of Nations* in 1776, London's average wage was 20 percent higher than Amsterdam's and three times that of Florence, Vienna, and Beijing.

London and Amsterdam were unique in that relatively high wages enabled working people to join their middle-class counterparts not only in buying a variety of British goods but also produce grown in the Caribbean, North America, and Asia. This produce, especially sugar and tea, was affordable in part because Britain's political and economic domination in the Caribbean and India had enabled it to yoke to its own economy the cheap agricultural labor of enslaved Africans and impoverished Indian peasants. The British people's ability to buy these foreign-grown products stimulated the transatlantic and Indian Ocean trade, which in turn added to the importance and size of London, as well as a few other British coastal cities, as centers of that trade. This long-distance commerce provided yet more urban jobs, and because the demand for workers remained high, so did wages.

Covent Garden, 1726. In the early eighteenth century, London was a bustling commercial city whose large outdoor markets sold a wide variety of goods. Covent Garden began life in the mid-seventeenth century as a fashionable fruit and vegetable market, but it gradually lost its aristocratic cachet. The wealthy moved out, and cafés, theaters, taverns, and other centers of popular sociability moved in. By 1726, these places had become notorious for the prostitutes who frequented them at night.

Substantial as it was, Britain's overseas trade might have been even greater and its urban population even larger had British leaders not subscribed to the economics of **mercantilism**, which dictated that countries minimize imports and maximize exports. To achieve this goal, officials imposed tariffs and other taxes on foreign goods in an effort to make them too expensive for people to buy. Doing so limited trade and the positive spillover effects trade produced.

Still, in some cases high tariffs stimulated British industry and agriculture precisely by barring foreign competition. British tariffs on French wine, imposed in 1713, shifted demand to local brewers and whisky makers and turned Britain into a nation of beer- and scotch-drinkers, unlike the French and Italians, whose preferred alcoholic beverage was wine. Mercantilism also directed colonial trade to

London instead of other European cities or colonial capitals, and for a time, these restrictions, known as Navigation Acts, may have added to London's prosperity and population.

In any case, the large number of urban workers, who lacked the time and space to grow their own food, needed to buy it from farmers. But because so many rural people had either turned to proto-industry or moved to cities, a shrinking number of farmers had to produce enough food for the growing non-agricultural population. In 1700, only about one-third of British people devoted themselves full-time to farming, as compared to at least twice that many almost everywhere else.

A small agricultural population relative to the number of urban and proto-industrial workers signaled a healthy, relatively advanced economy. It meant that agriculture had become productive enough to feed a great many people beyond those who lived on farms and that, already in 1700, Britain had a market economy in which people used their wages to buy what they needed. In England in 1500, the average farmer cultivated enough food for 1.35 people; in 1800, he produced almost enough for three, meaning that, on average, agricultural productivity more than doubled during these three centuries.

≡ **The Agricultural Revolution.** By the early eighteenth century, a revolution in agricultural techniques had made English farms far more productive than ever before. The higher productivity lowered the price of food and allowed people to spend more on manufactured goods, thus laying part of the groundwork for the Industrial Revolution. This drawing portrays a prosperous farm family returning from its fertile fields.

The Agricultural Revolution

What enabled British farmers to grow so much more than in the past? The answer begins with the urban demand for food and the declining number of farmers, as high urban wages lured people off the land and into the city, especially London. As cities grew, so did the demand for food, which gave the remaining farmers the incentive to find ways to grow more on the land they possessed and also to increase the size of their holdings.

In the mid-seventeenth century, British farmers became aware of new, more productive methods of cultivating the land known as "mixed farming." Traditionally, British farmers had had to leave one-third of their soil fallow, or uncultivated, every season, as this was the only known means of replenishing the earth with the vital nutrients consumed by plants such as wheat, barley, and rye. But thanks to new scientific knowledge and decades of experimentation in the seventeenth century, farmers now understood that they could grow new kinds of plants known as **forage crops**—field grasses, alfalfa, sainfoin, and clover—on their once-fallow lands. Not only did these new crops restore nitrogen to the soil, they also provided superior forage (food) for the livestock that until then had grazed on less nutritious pastures. By feasting on the new forage crops, cows and sheep grew fatter and healthier, richer in milk, meat, and fur. The manure they left behind fertilized a terrain already fortified by the forage crops. Farmers also grew turnips and potatoes on formerly fallow lands, adding to the supply of these basic human staples. The result of this process was better soil and better livestock, both of which enabled farmers to produce increasing amounts of food to nourish a burgeoning urban population.

Although Dutch scientists had discovered mixed farming, it was British farmers who first adopted it on a large scale. They alone had the incentive to meet a huge and growing urban demand for food. Historians once believed that the added agricultural productivity of this period resulted from the effort to eliminate Britain's traditional system of "open-field" farming. Under this system, different cultivators owned or leased a collection of small strips of land usually separated from one another by other people's strips of land. Beginning in the late seventeenth century, an "enclosure" movement gradually replaced open fields with distinct domains in which each farmer's lands were consolidated into unified farms enclosed by hedges or fences and separated from the others. In the process, cultivators with only small amounts of land often gave it up to prosperous "yeoman" farmers, who created large and supposedly more efficient agricultural domains.

It turns out, however, that enclosed farms were only marginally more productive than the remaining unenclosed open fields and that open-field farmers were just as likely to innovate as the owners or renters of large consolidated domains. The key variable was not enclosure and consolidation, but rather urban demand. Farmers innovated and became more productive not because their farms had grown in size but because of the potential to profit from the brisk demand for food.

Moreover, when farmers and agricultural wage laborers left the land, they did so not primarily as the result of enclosures but because of the lure of high urban wages. Before moving, they sold their property to prosperous landlords and upwardly mobile yeoman, who now owned larger, more efficient farms. The result was an agricultural sector with fewer farmers than in the past, but with most producing much more than their forbears had grown. This vast, unprecedented increase in productivity marked an **agricultural revolution** that had two crucial results: it expanded the size of the British market in agricultural goods, and that market, in turn, sustained ever-larger numbers of workers in commerce and manufacturing—and soon in an industrial economy about to take off.

Coal: The Revolution in Energy

All those who crowded into British cities needed to keep warm during the country's long winter months. Traditionally, the British, like others around the world, had heated their homes by burning wood. In the seventeenth century, that tradition began to change as London's burgeoning population increased the demand for wood, and therefore its price. People began to look for alternative forms of fuel, and to Britain's great fortune, the country sat atop vast seams of coal (see Map 6.2). During London's great home-construction boom of the seventeenth century, builders equipped the new dwellings with coal-burning stoves, and this produced a sky-rocketing demand for coal. In 1800 British coal production was sixty times what it had been two centuries earlier.

Most of the coal burned in London came from the rich mines of the northeasternmost part of England. Coal was expensive to move overland but relatively cheap to send by sea, which is how it made its way to London. The more the inhabitants of London demanded coal, the greater the incentive to mine it, even if that meant digging deeper than ever before.

But this posed a problem, because a water table exists underground and most coal is submerged. Shallow mines might not contain an excess of water, but deep ones almost always did. To get to the coal, the water had to be removed. Existing pumps were driven by rivers of moving water, which were rare near mines, or by the energy of people and animals, which would have been too expensive and inefficient to use in Britain's deeper shafts.

A mechanical solution seemed imperative, and in the late seventeenth century, engineers set out to create a pumping machine. They had been influenced by the natural philosophers we studied in Chapter 4, individuals who saw the world as one big machine and imagined that scientists could imitate nature and produce

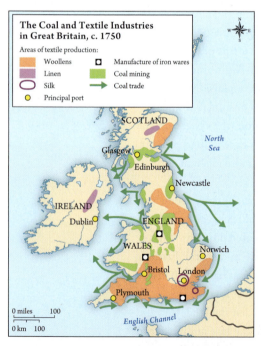

The Coal and Textile Industries in Great Britain, c. 1750

Areas of textile production:
- Woollens
- Linen
- Silk
- Principal port
- Manufacture of iron wares
- Coal mining
- Coal trade

≡ **MAP 6.2** The Coal and Textile Industries in Great Britain, c. 1750 machines of their own. In a way, the founding father of the industrial pump—and of the steam engine that powered it—was Galileo's assistant, Evangelista Torricelli, who understood that atmosphere had weight and that air could push a column of mercury up. When air was removed, creating a vacuum, the mercury dropped. The same principle could also push a lever up and then let it fall; when attached to a pump, the lever's up-and-down motion could, in theory, suck water from a mine.

But how could a lever be made to go up and down on its own? The first person to arrive at a practical solution to the problem was the Englishman Thomas Newcomen (1664–1729), who in 1712 created the world's first fully functional steam engine designed to drive a mechanical pump. By using steam to alternately create and eliminate a vacuum in an iron cylinder, Newcomen harnessed air pressure to continuously push a pump arm up and down. To make the steam, he used the

Thomas Newcomen's Steam Engine. In 1712, Newcomen introduced the world's first economically viable steam engine. It consumed huge quantities of coal and was enormously inefficient, but given its purpose—to pump water from a coal mine—its inefficiency mattered very little. The machine used unmarketable, low-quality coal readily available on the spot.

lowest-quality coal, easily harvested from a mine and good for no other purpose. Newcomen's steam engine was phenomenally inefficient, as it used a huge quantity of coal, but that mattered little because his objective was to pump water from a coal mine, and the coal he needed was right there on the spot and essentially free.

Although inventors in other countries understood the science behind Newcomen's steam engine, nowhere beside Britain would it have made economic sense to invent one. In 1700 Britain produced 80 percent of Europe's coal, and London's huge population created an enormous and ever-growing demand for the substance. To meet that demand, mine owners had the incentive to remove water from mine shafts and extract the now-accessible coal. They knew that if they could increase the supply of coal enough to lower its cost, demand would rise all the more. In no other European country was this the case. German and French demand for coal was low, giving mine owners no incentive to install steam engines and dig more of it up.

Thus for reasons of supply and demand—not any superior British inventiveness—the steam engine made its first economically viable appearance in England rather than on the continent. And only in Britain did the number of steam engines multiply rapidly. By 1800, British mine owners had installed 2,500 of them, while in

Belgium, which boasted Europe's second largest coal industry, there were just 100. France had seventy, and other countries no more than a dozen or two.

Still, the Newcomen engine was useful only in coal mines, because only there could it freely devour the huge amount of coal it needed to run. But what if steam engines, British inventors asked, could be made more efficient, requiring less energy to run? They then might be useful to power other kinds of machines. The key breakthrough came in 1769 when James Watt (1736–1819) patented a steam engine that required only half the coal of even the best Newcomen machine. At that point, Watt went into business with a financier named Matthew Boulton (1728–1809), whose money enabled him to develop his engine further by increasing its power and efficiency and thus its usability in a wide variety of machines. Beginning in the 1780s, Watt and Boulton sold hundreds of steam engines to a variety of industries, especially cotton spinning and iron smelting, whose output, as we will see, was ready to explode.

The Rise of Cotton

In the early and mid-eighteenth century, Britain manufactured a number of goods useful to consumers at home and abroad. By far the most successful product was cotton textiles. Cotton cloth was ideal for both home and overseas markets, because it could be worn comfortably in cool as well as warm climates. It was a sturdy and practical cloth that could be produced in varying levels of quality and washed with relative ease. Slave owners in the West Indies, for example, could purchase cheaper cloths for their slaves and more expensive ones for themselves. British and European consumers could buy heavier cottons for the fall and winter and lighter ones for summer and spring. Cotton fabric was useful, therefore, to master and slave alike, to colonist and colonized, European and non-European, lord and peasant, entrepreneur and worker. Its potential demand seemed almost unlimited, and as the eighteenth century progressed, English manufacturers did their best to meet it.

Between 1700 and 1750, cotton entrepreneurs responded to this increased demand by recruiting growing numbers of British families to the task of transforming raw cotton into finished cloth. There were as yet no factories and very few large workshops. For the most part, cloth was manufactured in the homes of rural laborers in a decentralized, proto-industrial system also known as "cottage industry." In this system, entrepreneurs supplied families with raw cotton and sometimes rented them spinning wheels and looms as well. Work proceeded according to the same sexual and generational division of labor as in the woolen industry described previously, which permitted men to weave for part of the week or year while performing farm labor as their primary employment. Entrepreneurs paid for the finished cloth according to its amount and quality.

This cottage system operated reasonably well, especially for the entrepreneurs, as long as demand for cotton cloth grew only gradually. But when demand, both domestic and foreign, began to accelerate in the mid-eighteenth century, entrepreneurs found themselves struggling to fill their orders. To increase output they recruited more rural families into proto-industrial pursuits. And with higher piece-rates, they encouraged men to abandon the fields to devote all of their efforts to weaving. But because it took three or four spinners to make enough yarn for one weaver, there was too little yarn to supply the growing number of weavers with work. The shortage of yarn became even worse after the 1750s when new, more efficient looms enabled weavers to cut their labor time in half. A **bottleneck** existed, therefore, at the spinning stage, and the output of finished cotton cloth could not grow fast enough to meet demand until something was done to resolve it.

It was at this point that rapidly growing demand began to call forth new technologies of production. Given the potential returns, entrepreneurs and inventors were willing to devote time and resources to an effort to break the bottleneck in spinning. The result was a series of inventions that would transform textile manufacture and launch the Industrial Revolution itself.

The Mechanization of Industry

In 1764, an inventor named James Hargreaves (1720–1778) vastly increased the speed of spinning by introducing a device called the **spinning jenny**, a simple machine operated by moving foot pedals up and down. Unlike the old spinning wheel, which could spin only one thread at a time, Hargreaves' jenny contained a row of eight spindles that could spin eight strands at once. By 1770, Hargreaves had doubled the number of spindles his machine could contain, and by the end of the century jennies were known to spin as many as 120 fibers

HARGREAVES' SPINNING-JENNY.

≡ **James Hargreaves' Spinning Jenny.** Introduced in 1764, Hargreaves' new device vastly increased productivity by enabling a single operator to spin eight strands of cotton at once, rather than the single strand of the traditional spinning wheel. The higher productivity lowered costs and thus prices and enabled growing numbers of people to clothe themselves in manufactured cotton cloth.

simultaneously. Not only did this invention enable cotton entrepreneurs to satisfy more of the demand for their product, but it actually *increased* that demand by lowering prices. Since one spinner operating a jenny could do the same work it took eight, sixteen, or more laborers to perform on a traditional spinning wheel, declining labor costs made it possible to reduce the price of cotton thread—albeit with the serious human toll of depriving hand spinners of work.

Demand continued to mount, therefore, encouraging other inventors to improve the spinning process all the more. In the 1770s, Arkwright's water frame, the spinning device that used flowing water to turn its wheels, became the first to use non-human power. It was also the first piece of equipment to take cotton spinning out of the home, because it required a source of moving water, usually a river, that was not available to each cottager. In fact, Arkwright's device required a large building, or **factory**, to house it, since moving water provided the energy to turn an enormous machine with hundreds of spindles. Given the efficiency and extraordinary output of these new devices, virtually all cotton spinning would now take place in buildings the poet William Blake would call "dark Satanic mills."

With each improvement in technology, worldwide demand seemed to increase even more, and that demand encouraged one new invention after another. In 1779 Samuel Crompton (1753–1827) patented yet another spinning machine—the "mule"—which combined the principles of the spinning jenny with those of the water frame to produce yarn of exceptionally fine quality. Thanks to Crompton, the English textile industry could now produce cotton cloth not only at lower cost than other countries, but of better quality as well.

Even so, the most significant development was yet to come. In 1785, the application of steam power freed cotton spinning from its dependence on both human strength and moving water. Steam engines

≡ **The New Spinning Mills.** In the 1770s, Arkwright's "water frame," so named because its spindles were powered by flowing water, grouped hundreds or thousands of spindles together under the same roof. These huge machines took cotton spinning out of the home and into immense buildings known as factories or mills, such as Quarry Bank Mill in Cheshire, England. By 1830, Quarry Bank was the largest textile mill in England.

provided a constant source of artificial energy dependent only upon the availability of coal, which the efficient engines of the late eighteenth and nineteenth centuries used sparingly. Since moving water was no longer essential, manufacturers were free to build their factories wherever it seemed most convenient—either close to coal mines or close to their primary supply of labor and consumers, namely the cities.

The steam-powered spinning machine thus completed the process of mechanization that had begun only two decades earlier. While spinning jennies, water frames, and mules continued to coexist alongside the new steam-powered mills for several decades, by the 1830s the latter had proved so technologically superior that older spinning methods largely ceased to exist.

A few statistics dramatically demonstrate why this was so. In the early eighteenth century, it took a hand spinner more than 50,000 hours to produce 100 pounds of cotton yarn. Crompton's mule (1779) reduced the time required to 2,000 hours, Arkwright's inventions (1780s–1790s) to 250–370 hours, and the steam-powered mule (1825) to no more than 135. These staggering reductions in labor time cut production costs to less than 3 percent of what they had been a century earlier. By the 1820s, no other cotton producing country could compete with Britain, not even India, whose highly skilled and low-paid workers had dominated the industry for centuries (see Figure 6.1).

While the new mechanized spinning technology completely eliminated the bottleneck at the spinning stage of the production process, it created several new ones before and after that point, particularly with respect to raw materials and weaving. Now that British manufacturers enjoyed the ability to produce huge amounts of yarn, they found themselves in need of vastly increased quantities of raw cotton. By the late eighteenth century, their demand for this crucial raw material became so insatiable that it transformed the economy of the American South, whose climate was ideal for growing cotton.

Spurred by this British demand, planters in the South shifted out of crops like tobacco, rice, and grain to devote their farming entirely to cotton. In the process, the southern United States became a vital annex of the British economy, allowing its supply of raw cotton to expand dramatically—although at a terrible human cost: the increased

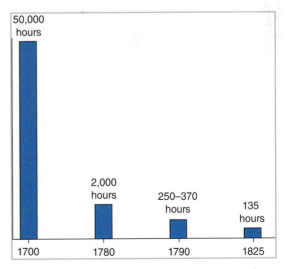

≡ **FIGURE 6.1**   Time required to produce 100 pounds of yarn.

≡ **The Cotton Plantation.** British industrialists' exploding demand for raw cotton multiplied the demand for slaves. This early-nineteenth-century drawing shows enslaved men, women, and children picking cotton in the fields.

demand for cotton multiplied the demand for slaves. Owners of large plantations purchased growing numbers of Africans from slave traders seeking to profit from the commerce in human beings. While the slave system produced untold suffering for those forced into bondage, it made certain slave traders fabulously wealthy and gave an important added boost to the British economy as a whole.

But even with the increasing amount of raw cotton and growing numbers of plantation slaves, too little cotton reached British shores to satisfy the industry's demand. Something more was required, and Eli Whitney's **cotton gin**, invented in 1793, provided the solution. His invention automated the cleaning of picked cotton, significantly expanding shipments to British mills.

At this point, the only remaining bottleneck came at the stage of weaving, for there were too few weavers to absorb the vastly increased quantities of yarn. The demand for weavers skyrocketed, and tens of thousands of men decided to abandon agriculture altogether to devote themselves full time to their looms. In 1795, Britain counted some 90,000 handloom weavers; by 1833 the number had grown to 300,000. Thanks in part to the country's rapid population growth, so many laborers were available to hand-weave machine-spun yarn that their wages remained low enough to discourage cotton entrepreneurs from investing in mechanized looms. Still, by the 1830s steam-powered looms had reduced the cost of weaving to the point that hand weaving, no matter how low the pay, became economically inefficient. Cotton manufacturers now invested heavily in the new industrial looms, and almost overnight the bulk of Britain's army of handloom weavers were put out of work. The consequences were tragic: suddenly hundreds of thousands of artisans found themselves deprived of their livelihoods, their skills now largely obsolete.

Major Inventions of the Industrial Revolution	
1712	Steam-operated water pump by Thomas Newcomen
1764	Spinning jenny by James Hargreaves
1769	Water frame by Richard Arkwright
	Improved steam engine by James Watt
1776	Steam engine–operated machinery by James Watt
1779	"Mule" by Samuel Crompton
1793	Cotton gin by Eli Whitney

The Industrial Revolution Moves Beyond Cotton

Not only did these developments in spinning and weaving transform the cotton textile industry, they helped revolutionize other aspects of the English economy as well. Cotton spinning and weaving mills required so many steam engines that entrepreneurs were motivated to seek new and more efficient methods for building those engines and for making them work. Iron and coal were crucial for doing both—iron for the engine's steam-making boiler and coal to create the steam—and the steam engine conveniently made it possible to mine more of the two minerals on which it fed. As we have seen, this was a circular process in which pumps powered by steam engines, which themselves were powered by coal, efficiently removed water from mine shafts, enabling miners to bore deeper and deeper into the earth in search of increasing quantities of coal—and iron ore as well. Meanwhile, steam-driven lifts took the minerals quickly and easily to the surface. Steam power, therefore, was crucial to mining the very materials that made steam power possible.

The creation of iron involved a process called **smelting** in which useable metal (called "pig iron") was separated from iron ore using heat. To heat the ore, iron-makers, until the mid-eighteenth century, used charcoal, which is partially burned wood. This method was not terribly efficient and had the added disadvantage of stripping Britain of its forests. Coal, when purified into **coke** by using heat, provided a much cheaper source of energy for smelting iron. And only by using coke could smelters refine pig iron into **wrought iron**, the form of the metal most useful in building and design.

The iron industry became truly mechanized when coal—and therefore coke—became cheap enough to create the steam power needed to blow a steady stream of heat into the blast furnace used to smelt the iron ore. Steam engines were thus

≡ *Coalbrookdale by Night.* In this huge iron foundry, iron ore was smelted into the pig iron used to make everything from steam engines to railroad tracks and locomotives. After textiles, iron became Britain's most important industry, and it played a major role in the country's economic advance.

crucial to all phases of the process, from pumping water out of coal mines, to refining pig iron into wrought iron, to rolling molten metal into the standard iron bars used in making everything from cooking utensils to guns, tools, nails, pipes, and bridges.

Mechanization of the iron industry reduced costs and improved the quality of the product. By 1800, English bar-iron sold for about half the price of the iron manufactured by its closest competitor, Sweden. In eighteenth-century France, efforts to smelt iron using coke failed because coal there cost more than twice as much as in Britain. Given the lack of overseas competition, British iron production rose from about 30,000 tons per year in 1760 to more than a quarter of a million tons less than fifty years later. By 1840, English iron foundries accounted for more than half the world's supply of pig iron.

Because iron was not a consumer product capable of reaching a mass market, it was less important than cotton to the early years of the industrial revolution. But once mechanized industry was fully established in the late eighteenth and early nineteenth centuries, iron quickly surpassed cotton as the key to Britain's continuing economic growth. Unlike the cotton industry, which was based on an imported raw material, every ingredient of iron production came from within Britain itself. All the proceeds of iron making accrued, therefore, to British industrialists and entrepreneurs. In addition, the more iron production increased, the greater the demand for two of Britain's most important natural resources, coal and iron ore. The iron industry thus stimulated the mining industry, creating new jobs and greater wealth in both sectors at once.

Mining was far from the only British industry enhanced by the growth in iron output. By the early decades of the nineteenth century, increasing quantities of British iron were stimulating the production of tools and hardware, military and naval equipment, telegraphic wire, gas and water pipes, building materials, and perhaps most important, industrial machinery of all kinds. Mechanized looms and spinning machines could now be made of iron instead of wood, guaranteeing that they would last longer and rely on cheaper interchangeable parts. The reduced costs that resulted enabled a wide range of English manufacturing concerns to lower their prices and thus increase their sales.

All of these developments added considerably to Britain's industrial growth, but iron's greatest contribution was to make possible a national network of rails. Railroads began in the late eighteenth century as short stretches of track, often linking a coalfield with a factory, on which wagons with grooved wheels were pulled by horses. This primitive arrangement eased the movement of coal but was hardly radical in its implications. The revolution in transportation had to await the ingenuity of inventors who, a few years later, devised a way to mount a steam engine on wheels, transforming the engine into a *locomotive*, a machine capable of moving itself. The first railroad engines, like all steam engines, were powered by coal and made of iron. Their wheels, too, were made of iron, as were the wheels of the wagons they pulled. Since the tracks themselves were also composed of iron, railroad building—begun in earnest in the 1830s—injected an enormous, even unprecedented, demand into an iron industry already straining to satisfy the mounting demand from other sectors of the economy.

Until 1830, railroad building proceeded gradually, contributing only about 200 miles of track. But at that point investors began to realize the economic and financial potential of this new mechanical means of transportation, and Britain entered the railroad age with a vengeance. By 1851, the country would possess some 7,000 miles of track with another 6,000 under construction or in the planning stages (see Map 6.3).

The railroad's effect on Britain's economy and way of life is incalculable. The ability of trains to move raw materials and finished products with unprecedented speed and efficiency dramatically lowered transport costs and therefore product prices, and this, in turn, boosted the domestic and international demand that fueled Britain's unrelenting industrial growth. Beyond this, the railroad boom of the 1830s and 1840s provided lucrative investment opportunities for those who had amassed capital in international trade and other sectors of Britain's growing economy.

The railroad also brought the country much closer together and altered people's perception of time and space. A voyage from London to Manchester (200 miles) took more than three days in pre-railroad 1750. Trains reduced travel time to one day in 1830 and to less than six hours in 1855. It takes about three and a half hours today. The reduction in time between London and Edinburgh (400 miles) was even more dramatic: ten to twelve days in 1750; fourteen hours a century later; five hours today. Suddenly, the English and Scottish capitals were only a day apart, making the 1707 union of the two countries not just a political reality but an experiential one as well.

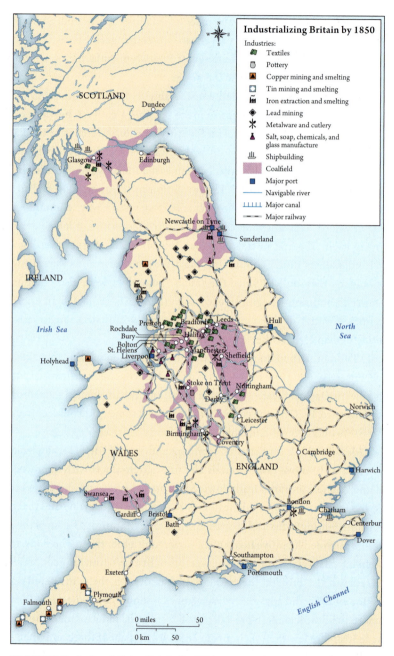

MAP 6.3 Industrializing Britain by 1850

Railroads also changed travelers' perception of the countryside, which now appeared distant and unreal to passengers who saw it as a blur through the windows of a speeding train. As trains distanced passengers from the country, they also changed travelers' relationships with one another. When people moved between cities in horse-drawn coaches, they interacted constantly with their fellow travelers, as everyone was squeezed together in close quarters for long periods and was going to the same place. Rail travel was more impersonal: people got on and off at different stops and, often spending little time together, felt minimal incentive to strike up conversations.

Beyond these experiential and perceptual changes, railroads also contributed to the economy as a major source of jobs, whose wages helped stimulate domestic demand all the more. In 1847, railroad construction employed some three hundred thousand workers, not to mention the sixty thousand engaged in running the lines already built. At the same time, railroad building absorbed more than a quarter of the nation's iron output and a major percentage of its coal. Finally, the railroad did much to complete England's transformation into an urban society, a society in which large centers of industry, employment, and consumption could keep the industrial process moving.

Taken as a whole, these developments bore witness to unprecedented change. Still, it is important to emphasize that even as late as 1850, Britain's economy was far from uniformly mechanized. At mid-century, only 27 percent of the British workforce belonged to industries directly affected by the Industrial Revolution, and certain regions of the country and sectors of the economy looked little different in 1850 from a century earlier. More manufacturers relied on human power than steam power, and some regions possessed no factories at all.

The persistence of production by hand did not mean, however, that the Industrial Revolution had left artisanal work unchanged. Although tailors, for example, continued to work with preindustrial technology long after textile production was fully mechanized, they nonetheless

≡ *The Great Western Railway.* Joseph M. W. Turner's Romantic painting of 1844 blurs the evidence of industrialism almost to the vanishing point, emphasizing light and color rather than the train itself. It is as if the artist considered the train too ugly and too disturbing to allow viewers to see it.

adopted several crucial aspects of the new factory system, especially its **division of labor**. It became increasingly rare for a tailor to work alone making whole articles of clothing from start to finish. By the mid-nineteenth century, most tailors were employed in sizable workshops in which they performed only one or two relatively narrow tasks. One tailor's sole responsibility, for example, was to cut the cloth for the backs of jackets, while another cut the sleeves. A third would sew the sleeves to the backs, and a fourth attached the front. Such specialization made manufacturing more efficient but rendered the work itself more tedious and therefore much less satisfying than in the past. The sewing machine was still decades away from widespread use, but the division of labor and other aspects of the new industrial economy had transformed the handicrafts in its image.

Even people who lived in parts of the country innocent of factories, steam engines, coal mines, and the like were indirectly affected by the Industrial Revolution, whether as consumers, travelers, readers, or citizens. They wore cotton clothes fabricated by machines, used tools and utensils mechanically produced, read books printed on mechanical presses, and were citizens of a country whose industrial prowess had made it the wealthiest and most powerful nation in the world.

Economic Development Outside of Britain

These nonindustrialized parts of Britain resembled in certain ways the other relatively advanced parts of Europe: France, the Netherlands, German-speaking Central Europe, northern Italy, the Baltic region, and sections of Scandinavia. In these places, there was little industrialization before 1850. By mid-century, however, most had developed vital market economies characterized by agricultural improvement, growing trade and commerce, and enhanced consumption—although mainly by the upper-middle and upper classes (see Map 6.4).

In France, the revolution transferred large amounts of land to peasants, and by the 1820s more French peasants were landowners than ever before. But unlike British farmers, whose holdings were growing, most French cultivators owned small and shrinking plots—thanks to French inheritance laws, which distributed lands to all children and not just firstborn sons, as in Britain. This subdivision of the land did not, however, prevent peasants from adopting the new systems of crop rotation already described and thus to expand the efficiency, and therefore the output, of their farms. By the 1820s and 1830s, a considerable number of peasants produced for the market, selling their surplus grains or shifting into wine production, silk, olives, madder (for making dye), hemp (for cloth and paper), and other cash crops, while purchasing much of their food.

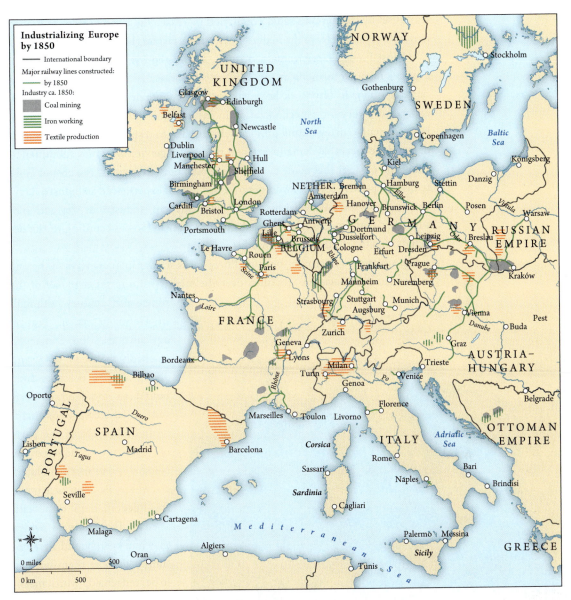

Industrializing Europe by 1850

- —— International boundary
- Major railway lines constructed:
  - —— by 1850
- Industry ca. 1850:
  - Coal mining
  - Iron working
  - Textile production

≡ **MAP 6.4**   Industrializing Europe by 1850

These developments made some peasants relatively prosperous, but most did not possess enough land to profit substantially. Since many farmers had gone into debt to expand their meager landholdings or invest in grapevines and silkworms, any drop in demand threatened to ruin them. In addition, while French agricultural production grew by 50 percent between 1815 and 1848, most of that growth was offset by the period's rapid population increase. The improvement of French agriculture did not leave the majority of France's farmers better off.

If most French farms remained small, so did the overwhelming majority of France's manufacturing firms. In 1850, most workers labored alone or with two or three others in tiny workshops where they made their goods by hand. France experienced very little mechanization in the first half of the nineteenth century, but its manufacturing output jumped substantially in response to growing market demand. To meet that demand, artisans worked longer hours, or they submitted to a division of labor that made them more productive, although at the cost of more tedious, repetitive forms of work. France had not yet experienced an industrial revolution, but it did have what historians have called an "industrious" revolution in which artisans worked more intensively than ever before—according to the demands, and the rhythms, of the market economy.

The situation in German-speaking Europe was similar in many ways to the one in France. Both societies remained overwhelmingly rural in the first half of the nineteenth century, although in Germany, as in France, agricultural life changed markedly between 1815 and 1848. German peasants, long bound to the land as serfs (unfree laborers), were emancipated abruptly in the parts of Germany conquered by Napoleon and more gradually elsewhere. Peasants welcomed this freedom, but it came with a cost. The lands to which they had been bound were not simply given to them but had to be "redeemed," which meant that the former landlord had to be compensated. In many cases, the only way peasants could do this was to return to the lord a substantial portion of the land supposedly transferred to them. Doing so left a

≡ **The French Peasantry.** In the first half of the nineteenth century, French peasants adopted the ideas and techniques of the Agricultural Revolution and significantly increased the productivity of their lands. But the added productivity did not, for the most part, turn them into prosperous farmers. Many had borrowed heavily to purchase or expand their landholdings, and even so, possessed too little land to reap significant profits. This painting of 1857, *The Gleaners* by Jean François Millet, shows peasants so poor that they were reduced to gleaning scraps of wheat from other people's harvested land.

great many peasants with too little land to make ends meet, and they had no choice but to work as agricultural laborers on their lords' domains. The serfs had been freed, only to face economic conditions that constrained them once again.

This was especially true in Eastern Prussia, where Napoleon's conquests had abruptly ended serfdom but not the political and economic power of the traditional feudal lords. In other parts of Germany, where emancipation occurred later and more gradually and lords were weaker, significant numbers of peasants accumulated enough cash to essentially buy the land to which they had formerly been bound. By the 1830s, there were thus more independent peasants in western Germany than in eastern Germany, although in both places, agricultural production came to have a great deal in common: it was now ruled by the market. Rather than farming for subsistence—that is, to feed oneself and one's family—peasants now operated in a commercial, market-oriented system, whether by working for a cash wage or by selling grain and other products to consumers.

As in France, some peasants achieved a measure of prosperity, but most led precarious lives, buffeted by the trade winds of supply and demand. Collectively, their productivity soared, but so did population growth, which meant that every peasant had to compete with an army of other peasants for employment or customers, thus keeping their incomes down.

In manufacturing, as in agriculture, the number of workers grew substantially in the first half of the nineteenth century. Most were artisans who labored by hand in tiny workshops, processing food or making clothing, shoes, and the other necessities of life. They were threatened not by industrialization, which was slow to take hold before 1850, but by the huge number of other artisans with whom they had to compete. The result was low wages and prices and a bare-bones existence for most working people.

The artisans who faced the most difficult circumstances were doubtless the hundreds of thousands of handloom weavers who worked at home in a vast cottage industry. As cheap, industrially produced British textiles flooded the German market, the price of woven cloth plummeted, and weavers' incomes declined almost to the vanishing point. In 1844, unable to make ends meet, weavers in Silesia, a large region to the east of Berlin and Prague, rose up in a rebellion of desperation, which the Prussian government mercilessly crushed.

Before long, mechanization would put virtually all remaining handloom weavers out of business, but this was a phenomenon of the post-1850 period. Until then, factory workers and miners constituted a mere 2.5 percent of the working population. As for the output of coal and iron, two key measures of industrialization, at mid-century, German-speaking Europe registered no more than 6 to 7 percent of the British level. The incentives for German mechanization were not yet in place, although they would be soon (see Chapter 8).

The Austrian Empire, like Prussia, mostly remained unmechanized and highly rural until relatively late in the nineteenth century. The great exception to this rule was Moravian capital Brno (Brünn in German), located in today's Czech Republic. Known as the "Manchester of Austria," Brno developed textile mills in the 1830s and '40s employing some 15,000 people. The mills, as the writer Jan Ohéral put it at the time, "have transplanted us from quiet, dreamy peacefulness to the uproar of the workshops [which] veil the old, many-towered town with their dark clouds of smoke."

Austria built modern port facilities along the Danube River between Vienna and Pest (the eastern section of present-day Budapest) and especially in the Adriatic coastal city Trieste (now in Italy). These ports and the railroads that gradually extended out from them advanced Austria's budding commercial economy and created new sources of wealth. The Austrian state, however, lacked the resources to stimulate this economic development further or to nudge the empire's vast agricultural regions ahead. In contrast with Austria's small, but growing, centers of commerce and industry stood the empire's Hungarian, Ruthenian (later known as Ukrainian), Polish, and South Slavic lands, where feudal social and economic relations continued to reign. Most peasants were serfs tied to a nobleman's land and forced to perform uncompensated work for him several days each week. This system was not very productive, since peasants, who worked much of the time for free, had little incentive to exert themselves. The nobles, meanwhile, were forbidden, especially in Hungary, to sell any portion of their properties by a legal tradition known as **entail**. This constraint prevented them from raising capital to improve their domains or invest in commerce and industry. In Hungary, large expanses of land remained uncultivated because nobles lacked the cash to hire peasants to farm it. As a result, a great many of Austria's people remained mired in poverty despite the notable pockets of economic advance.

Elsewhere in Europe, Belgium was already en route to industrialization when it became an independent country in 1830 and took advantage of huge deposits of coal and iron ore and proximity to markets in Britain, France, Germany, and the Netherlands. The last three countries were relatively prosperous despite their slow pace of industrialization. In addition, there were pockets of economic growth in northern Italy, Eastern Europe, the Baltic region, and western Russia and of commercial prosperity along the Ottoman Empire's Mediterranean rim. But the Ottoman Empire, in particular, suffered from the free-trade regime that Britain imposed on it.

The Ottoman Tariff Convention (1838), which the sultan signed under political and military duress, prevented the Ottoman government from imposing tariffs (import taxes) on British-made goods. It thus left Ottoman manufacturers unable to compete with Britain's cheap mass-produced goods. In addition, a series of **capitulations** gave special commercial privileges and tax reductions to Western European residents of Ottoman cities, who used their special status and ties to their home countries to elbow indigenous entrepreneurs out of the market. To make matters worse, the Ottoman state, often known as the **Porte** (the French word for a monumental gate in Istanbul), subjected its own merchants and manufacturers to punitive taxes in an effort to prevent them from gaining political power. Under these circumstances, the Ottoman Empire did not develop a modern commercial and industrial economy, which meant that its military capacity lagged behind that of its European neighbors.

The Cultural and Political Origins of the Industrial Revolution

The Ottomans were not, however, the only country to fall behind. Between 1760 and 1830, Britain alone experienced both an *industrial* and an *industrious* revolution, because its economic circumstances were unique. In 1700, Britain was the sole country in the world with the preconditions of industrialization: a high-wage, urbanized workforce; an extensive market economy; abundant, inexpensive energy in the form of coal; and the ability to ship products, easily and inexpensively, from one part of the country to the other and to the rest of the world. Only in Britain did this constellation of factors give entrepreneurs the incentive to meet the growing demand for cotton, coal, and iron with new coal-consuming, steam-operated machines.

Still, as important as the various economic factors were in sparking Britain's Industrial Revolution, other phenomena contributed as well. The British people lived in a political and cultural environment extremely favorable to industrial and agricultural investment, to inventiveness, risk-taking, and the dissemination of knowledge, all of which were crucial to the economic changes of the time.

As we saw in Chapter 4, Francis Bacon and other key protagonists of Britain's version of the scientific revolution emphasized practicality, experimentation, and inventiveness. British natural philosophers wanted their work to be useful and, if possible, to improve society. Scientific gains, they maintained, would come not so much through abstract theorizing, although this could be important, but through experimentation, through a process of trial and error designed to improve on what existed and to discover something new. In the late seventeenth and early eighteenth centuries, these ideas helped create a culture of experimentation and inventiveness that produced creative, innovative responses to economic incentives. For example, the potter Josiah Wedgwood (1730–1795), who industrialized the manufacture of pottery and ceramics, undertook five thousand experiments with clay mixtures and glazes as he developed his industrial techniques.

Even more fundamental to Britain's Industrial Revolution was the Glorious Revolution of 1688, which produced a government dedicated, among other things, to the protection and preservation of private property. England's new political system fostered confidence within the propertied elite that they could improve their land, consolidate it, add to it, and build on it without interference from the state or from anyone else. This confidence gave them the sense that such investments, so crucial to economic progress, would remain secure and that the financial benefits would accrue to themselves.

A further benefit of Britain's commitment to the unrestricted enjoyment of private property was its success in undermining the old guild system. In countries such as France, where guilds remained strong throughout the eighteenth century, master craftsmen possessed the power to determine who could enter each trade, the level and kinds of skills each craftsman had to possess, the prices of the goods they made, and the number of products they could turn out. Markets remained unfree and the incentive to innovate very weak. In dissolving such restraints, the British government encouraged the development of an unfettered marketplace in which trade and manufacture could grow quickly.

This government, moreover, was highly stable in the eighteenth century, adding to the sense of security that encouraged landlords and potential entrepreneurs to invest with the hope of future returns. The British state was also well financed, due to Parliament's willingness to levy taxes on the well-to-do at relatively high levels. Because the British political system, unlike those of most other European countries, allowed the landed elite to share power with the king, members of that elite agreed to help pay the costs of a government that ruled largely with their interests in mind. French noblemen, by contrast, refused to contribute to their king's treasury, in part because no national parliament existed to give them a say over how revenues would be spent. Finally, Britain's favorable financial situation earned it the faith of bankers and financiers who knew their loans would always be repaid and thus kept interest rates relatively low. The favorable rates encouraged not just government borrowing but also the private investment crucial to Britain's early industrial advance.

Crucial as well was Britain's commitment to **primogeniture**, a system of inheritance in which fathers bequeathed the whole of their estates to their eldest sons. This arrangement left the other children with no lands of their own, forcing them to look elsewhere for their livings. The second and third sons of aristocratic families regularly entered business and commerce, giving such endeavors a respectability they did not possess on the European continent, where a nobleman who went into business could be accused of having dishonored himself. That Britain attached no such stigma to the marketplace added to its potential for economic development by attracting members of its educated and well-connected elite to the culture of entrepreneurship.

Economic growth also gave more people than ever before the means to have their children educated, opening new opportunities to them. Literacy and numeracy enabled people to engage successfully in trade and commerce, which required written correspondence, record keeping, and the arithmetical abilities necessary to keep track of income and expense. These pivotal skills developed not only in classrooms but also in apprenticeships in which young boys learned the trade that would support them later in life. To gain an apprenticeship for their sons, parents paid a fee to the master craftsman who would train them. More and more families could afford those fees, thanks to Britain's relatively high wages, so that by the late seventeenth century, a significant number of workingmen's sons had become literate as well as skilled in a trade—Arkwright, as we have seen, fell into this category even though his family was poor.

Social Consequences of the Industrial Revolution

In general, literacy encouraged inventiveness, as would-be inventors could read scientific literature, study written accounts of relevant experiments, and correspond with people who might have essential information to share. For this reason, the rise of literacy and numeracy stood out as one of the key cultural changes underlying the Industrial Revolution and fostered by it in turn. Crucial as well was the dissemination of a "scientific" view of the world, one in which growing numbers of British people understood earthly phenomena as having natural causes rather than divine or supernatural ones. This new worldview reinforced the culture of inventiveness and gave people the sense that they could and should shape their environment and, with it, their lives.

Profoundly important changes in the nature of society accompanied these cultural developments. In 1750, most people still lived in the country and worked in agriculture and cottage industries; a century later, the majority congregated in urban centers, having left farming to just 20 percent of the population (see Map 6.5). In 1750, family members tended to work together in household units; in 1850, they were employed separately, with most working members laboring in a different

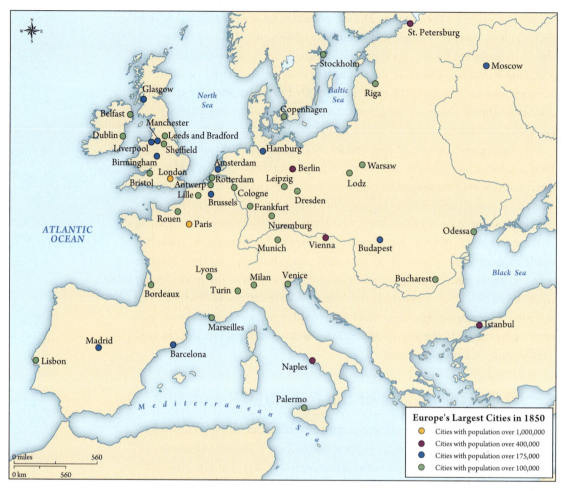

≡ **MAP 6.5**   Europe's Largest Cities in 1850

shop, firm, factory, or residence. In 1750, women and children seldom worked out-side the home, except in the case of domestic servants or apprentices who worked in someone else's home. One hundred years later, women and children were rou-tinely employed in mills, mines, and the mansions of the rich.

The Industrial Revolution enabled middle-class people to achieve levels of comfort and prosperity that until then had been reserved for a tiny elite. Members of the middle class typically enjoyed the services of cooks, maids, and nannies for their children. Their clothing was of excellent quality, their homes spacious and well furnished. Young middle-class men (though not women) ben-efited from a secondary education, and a small number gained access to universi-ties as well. More generally, the increase in overall prosperity stimulated cultural life, creating a profusion of newspapers, books, plays, and other works of art that most middle-class people possessed the means to enjoy.

As prosperous as these middle-class families became, their incomes were paltry compared to the fortunes of the entrepreneurs, financiers, and merchants who capitalized on the expanded market that mass production made possible. Some earned their money through investments, but most entrepreneurs and industrialists of the early Industrial Revolution worked extremely hard for their gains, contributing to Britain and the world through their ingenuity, foresight, and willingness to take risks.

≡ ***Swainson Birley Cotton Mill in Lancashire.*** This 1834 painting by Thomas Allom, an early example of artistic realism, depicts the inside of a factory. Here machines, not human beings, dominate the scene.

Thanks to their efforts, England's gross domestic product, averaged across the population, grew by about 50 percent between 1780 and 1850, an economic advance without precedent in any other place or time. Although the lion's share of this new wealth accrued to a minority of the population, the developments of this period set the stage for further economic advances whose benefits would eventually reach down into the working class itself.

But during the core years of the Industrial Revolution, roughly 1760–1850, working people's real incomes, their wages in relation to the cost of living, grew hardly at all, and even dropped at first, while living standards—diet, housing, education, and general consumption—probably declined. What, then, happened to the high-wage economy of the late seventeenth and early eighteenth century, the economy that helped spark the Industrial Revolution in the first place? The best statistics available indicate that average real wages for working people reached their peak around 1700 and remained steady until 1750–1760, that is, just as the Industrial Revolution was getting under way. Real wages then declined slightly for about a half-century before gradually rising above their mid-eighteenth century level.

A key reason for the fifty-year dip was Britain's unprecedented demographic growth. The population of England and Wales soared from 6.5 million in 1751 to 10 million in 1811 and 17.9 million in 1851, an increase of more than 275 percent in 100 years. (Scottish figures, unrecorded before 1831, added about four million to the total after that point.) For comparison, the population grew by somewhat less, 240 percent, between 1850 and 1950.

Rapid population growth meant more workers and thus more competition for jobs in the textile and metallurgical industries in 1850 than a century earlier. This competition came at a time when the various laborsaving devices of the Industrial Revolution—spinning machines, power looms, iron rolling mills—had replaced a great many manual workers. But the Industrial Revolution also created a wealth of new jobs, many in nonmechanized industries like tailoring, which had much more clothing to make given the explosive increase in the output of cloth. Thus the decline in job offerings relative to the size of the population in some fields was offset, though perhaps not completely, by the relative increase in offerings in others. The result was an increase in jobs that did not quite keep pace with population growth between 1760 and 1820, but exceeded the demographic advance afterwards.

That real wages remained flat at best during a time of mounting productivity and economic growth seems disappointing at first glance. But without the vast increase in agricultural and industrial output that occurred during the Industrial Revolution, the era's sharp demographic growth, according to recent economic historians, would have sent real wages per capita and living standards spiraling downward by as much as 20 percent.

The Lives of Working People

As valuable as statistics on real incomes are, they provide only a rough idea of how the Industrial Revolution affected the quality of British men and women's lives. Perhaps the most fundamental change in the structure and nature of British society between 1750 and 1850 was the shift in population away from the country and into the city. London's population tripled between 1800 and 1850 alone, and highly industrialized towns such as Manchester, Liverpool, and Glasgow experienced a fourfold increase during this time. Urbanization occurred so rapidly and so chaotically that the new industrial cities seemed to have been transformed overnight into huge teeming slums. Housing construction, sewage facilities, water supplies, street paving, and the like could not begin to keep pace with the influx of working-class immigrants. By the 1830s, laboring families found themselves increasingly condemned to cramped and unsanitary quarters and to dense urban neighborhoods devoid of light, greenery, clean water, and unpolluted air. Disease became widespread in such unhealthful and unsanitary conditions, as the periodic epidemics of cholera—then a fatal illness—tragically showed.

Working people suffered the most from blighted urban conditions, but even those families fortunate enough to escape to more pleasant middle-class neighborhoods were afflicted as well. In 1837 the average life expectancy of Manchester's most prosperous residents was thirty-eight, fully fifteen years less than that of their well-to-do counterparts in the nearby rural community of Rutland. Even more significant, the poorest agricultural laborers of Rutland could expect, on average, to live as long as the wealthiest residents of Manchester. As for the workers of that city, who earned far more on average than the laborers of Rutland, their life expectancy, with childhood mortality averaged in, was seventeen years.

Not all industrial towns were as blighted as Manchester, the place chosen by Friedrich Engels (1820–1895), the socialist writer, to illustrate the evil effects of industrial capitalism, but few were significantly better. The novelist Charles Dickens (1812–1870) referred to them all as places "reeking with lean misery and hungry wretchedness." The English civil servant and social reformer Edwin Chadwick (1800–1890) could only agree, reporting that the slums of these cities breathed an "atmosphere of filth and stink," laden as they were with "stagnant pools, ordure and heaps of refuse."

The problem was not that the workers of these cities received starvation wages. Rather, it was that the difficulties of the new urban environment surpassed the ability of individual workers, no matter how well paid, to solve them. Only an infusion of public capital could

≡ **The Ravages of Cholera.** The overcrowded, unsanitary conditions of Europe's early industrial cities made them prone to epidemics of cholera, caused by the contamination of drinking water with human waste. Working people, whose neighborhoods lacked sewage systems, suffered more than their prosperous neighbors in the elite parts of town.

alleviate these conditions, and this the new industrial magnates were not ready to endorse. The industrialists' credo was laissez-faire, the right to do what they wanted with the capital they had amassed. And the intense economic competition of the era moved them to invest in industrial expansion and improvement, not in urban renovation.

Economic Instability and Its Consequences

Another key difficulty of the new industrial economy was its instability, the regular periods of expansion and contraction known as **business cycles**. When the economy was on the upswing, employment tended to be steady and working-class families could generally make ends meet. But when the business cycle moved downward, as it tended to do every five to ten years, unemployment became widespread.

Few workers earned enough to put money aside for periods of economic distress, and even fewer could count on charity or the **Poor Laws**, England's rudimentary system of public assistance, to see them through. The Poor Laws, born under the reign of Queen Elizabeth, were designed mainly to help rural laborers; they did little for the urban poor. And after 1834, when the Poor Laws were reformed to reflect the government's new laissez-faire ideology, even rural people were reluctant to request the assistance the laws provided. Able-bodied individuals could receive help only if they agreed to enter a workhouse, a prison-like institution where husbands and wives were separated and the living conditions were spartan at best.

The paucity of support in difficult times moved increasing numbers of urban dwellers into the streets for their subsistence—to peddling, begging, crime, and prostitution. Between 1805 and 1848, the number of people tried for criminal offenses in England and Wales increased by a factor of six. This criminal activity, it should be noted, was related to the business cycle: when the economy was weak, offenses—mostly theft—increased; when it was strong, crime declined, though never to the level at which it had been before the downturn began.

Women were far less likely than men to be indicted for criminal offenses, but when economic decline left them in desperate straits, more than a few turned to prostitution. Reliable statistics are hard to come by, but it is clear that growing numbers of women resorted to prostitution as the century progressed, though not necessarily as a full-time occupation. Some used prostitution to regularly supplement inadequate industrial wages, while others sold their bodies only intermittently, especially when they faced unemployment. Because women earned lower wages than men and enjoyed fewer economic opportunities, prostitution became increasingly prevalent as the nineteenth century wore on. It was one of the few economic alternatives to industrial and commercial employment working women possessed. It was also a service that men could buy more readily than in the past, given increasing middle-class incomes and the relative anonymity of urban life.

Changes in Family Life

The prevalence of discomfort, disease, poverty, and crime made urban existence during the second half-century of the industrial revolution far from easy, and the changes in family life wrought by the new urban economy did little to alleviate these difficult conditions. In the past, it had not been uncommon for whole families to work together as a domestic unit, enabling wives and children to contribute to the family income without leaving their homes. Men, too, were often able to work in and around their places of residence. As a result, economic activity was seldom separated from child rearing, education, and other aspects of family life. Wives performed their manufacturing work while caring for children and doing the other domestic chores commonly expected of women: cooking, baking, cleaning, mending, and teaching their daughters to do all of these things as well.

Husbands generally contributed far less than their wives to child rearing and everyday household work. But beyond the discipline fathers traditionally meted out, it was their responsibility to teach their children manufacturing or agricultural skills.

Urbanization and the Industrial Revolution did much to change the relationship between the family and the economy, although the developments of the early nineteenth century did not separate the two to the extent we see today. Perhaps the most important changes in family life stemmed from the new possibilities for women to work outside the home. As technological transformation moved cotton spinning from home to factory, women followed. Partly because women had traditionally done the textile spinning and partly because entrepreneurs found it possible to pay women and children less than men, large numbers of urban women were recruited for the low-skill, repetitive tasks of the textile mills. For the most part, these women "operatives" were young and single; if married, they tended to be childless.

In taking wives and daughters out of their homes, industrial labor did much to disrupt traditional family life, especially when wives worked and their husbands were unemployed. Nevertheless, more than a few women perceived their participation in the industrial labor force as a liberation. The wages working wives earned gave them a measure of autonomy from their husbands, while daughters could achieve a certain independence from their parents. And when the economy was strong and work steady, wives and daughters could make a substantial contribution to the household income. But despite these benefits, many women found factory work far from appealing. In general, women's industrial wages remained very low—less than half the average wage of men. Perhaps even worse, the unskilled tasks to which women were typically consigned were monotonous, stressful, and exhausting. It was not uncommon for them to work twelve hours a day, six days a week.

Married women tended, therefore, to leave the factory as soon as they had children

≡ **Women Laborers in a Mill.** Because women's wages were generally seen as "supplementary" to those of men, industrialists paid them about half of what they paid their male counterparts. For that reason, large numbers of women found jobs in factories—especially textile mills—beginning in the late eighteenth century. Women were happy to earn a wage, meager as it was, but because factory work was monotonous, stressful, and exhausting, married women tended to leave the factory as soon as they had children to raise.

to raise. Mothers whose economic circumstances required them to remain in the mill did so at great cost to the health of their babies. Working mothers had either to entrust their infants to "wet nurses," women hired to breast-feed other people's babies, or to have them fed from germ-infested bottles (doctors did not yet understand the importance of sterilization). In both cases, the infant mortality rate was appallingly high.

Fortunately for mothers and their children, married women possessed other means besides factory work to enhance the income of their families. For the most part, the married women of Britain's industrial era, not unlike their forbears in pre-industrial times, worked at home and by hand—primarily in the garment industry, cutting and sewing cloth. In 1851 about the same number of British women worked at home in various nonmechanized manufacturing pursuits as in the textile mills tending machines. Each kind of manufacturing work, non-mechanized and mechanized, encompassed about a quarter of Britain's female labor force, or about 50 percent in all. The other half was employed in commerce, agriculture, and most important, domestic service, an occupation that accounted for 40 percent of the entire female labor force. Nearly twice as many English women worked as maids, cooks, and other household helpers than as factory operatives.

Thus, although many married women maintained a certain continuity with pre-industrial times by working at home, the great majority of women who worked—domestic servants plus factory hands—did so outside their own residences. The relationship between family and economy had therefore changed significantly since the beginning of the industrial era: The old model of the family as an economic unit whose members labored in or around their home no longer applied. Industrialization and urbanization gave family members a degree of autonomy that had not existed before, but it was an autonomy gained at the expense perhaps of certain psychological comforts, the comforts of working at their own rhythm and in their own space.

The Factory, Workers, and the Rise of the Labor Movement

Nowhere were such comforts more lacking than in the new factories of the industrial age. Mills were hot, smelly, dirty places in which workers—men, women, and children—were typically confined for twelve hours or more, day in and day out. Unlike the more casual work rhythms of the pre-industrial era, the factory and the machines it housed required a regular and unrelenting tempo of labor. It was expensive to fuel the machines of the textile mills and iron foundries, and for every moment they stood idle, the owner lost money. In order to prevent such losses and to maximize his returns, the employer imposed a strict discipline upon his labor force, ensuring that its members were promptly at work when their shifts began and that they worked steadily all the day through. Breaks were few and far between, as employers endeavored to extract as much labor as possible from their employees. Workers who arrived even a minute or two late, or who were caught with their attention diverted from their machines, faced a fine of a day's pay or more. Above all, employers wanted to break their workers of old pre-industrial habits, which sometimes permitted long midday recesses and often included observance of "Saint Monday," an unofficial day off when workers recovered from the overindulgences of the previous afternoon and night.

The early industrial factory, therefore, was far from a congenial place, and workers often felt as though they were imprisoned for the duration of their shifts. Not only were conditions uncomfortable, they were often unsafe as well. Intent upon producing as much as possible, industrialists paid scant attention to the hazards of their machines. Workers of both sexes regularly lost fingers and even limbs, and women faced the particular danger of having their long hair caught in the mechanisms they tended, sometimes with tragic results. Children were particularly vulnerable to industrial accidents, as was almost everyone who worked in the mines, where asphyxiation and the collapse of subterranean tunnels posed a constant threat. Beyond these dangers, the heat and fumes of the mills, along with the coal dust of the mines, created an endless number of respiratory ailments, skin problems, eye irritations, and the like. The relative poverty of most factory workers and the still-primitive state of medical care afforded little relief for those afflicted by the health and safety hazards seemingly embedded in the process of industrialization itself.

Beyond the factories that transformed the landscape of Britain's manufacturing regions, the most visible effect of the Industrial Revolution was the emergence of a new kind of worker, the factory "hand." Such individuals differed markedly from the artisans or craftsmen who had made most manufactured goods before the Industrial Revolution and who continued to populate the nonmechanized trades. For the most part, factory hands tended to possess fewer skills and to perform more repetitive tasks than did those who made products by hand, although, as we have seen, nonmechanized work was also growing more repetitive. And since the factory was a more hazardous and unhealthful environment than the handicraft workshop, industrial hands suffered infirmities largely new to the industrial era. Their skin ailments, sallow complexions, and lost and damaged limbs marked them—for some observers at least—as a race apart. Artisans often viewed factory workers as a people enslaved by the machines they tended, while middle- and upper-class writers regularly described them as so alien, so dehumanized by their bleak environments, as to constitute a threat to civilized existence itself.

After touring the manufacturing districts of Lancashire in the early 1840s, the chronicler W. Cooke Taylor described workers there as resembling bees in "crowded hives." There were "mighty energies slumbering in these masses," Taylor added, and if awakened, they could lash out at the society that had created them.

A few years later Karl Marx (1818–1883) would agree that there were "mighty energies slumbering in these masses"; unlike Taylor, however, he would embrace these factory workers not as something "portentous and fearful" but as the motive force of a new and better form of existence. In the meantime, working people, in Britain and elsewhere, set goals far more modest than the social revolution Marx would later demand. They began to search for ways to alleviate the social and economic inequality, the harsh conditions of work and life, to which the Industrial Revolution had given rise.

Those who pioneered efforts to improve the lives of working people did not, it should be noted, come from within the ranks of the factory workers themselves. They came, rather, from among the artisans whose livelihoods the new factory system seemed to put in jeopardy. Between 1790 and 1815, when textile mills began to produce cotton cloth much more cheaply than artisans could at home, certain of these craftsmen decided to attack what seemed to be the source of their woes: the machines themselves. Bands of artisans forced their way into factories and workshops to smash the machines inside. Their crusade, known as **Luddism**, took the name of General Ludd or King Ludd, a mythical folk figure who defended the workingman.

The Luddite movement reached its peak between 1811 and 1812, when well-organized bands of stocking knitters systematically smashed knitting machines belonging to entrepreneurs who had used the new technology to lower wages. Interestingly, Luddites spared the machines of employers who had not reduced

≡ **Luddites.** As machines came to replace skilled artisans, some waved the banner of General Ludd, a mythical folk figure who defended the working man. Luddites smashed the machines they blamed for taking their jobs.

workers' pay. By wielding their axe selectively, the Luddites revealed a desire to destroy not so much the machine itself as the system that used it to compromise their livelihoods. But more machines were broken than spared, and the Luddites continued their efforts until the army was called in to put them down.

Powerful and menacing as they were, the Luddites could do no more than fight a rearguard action against the machines destined to supplant them. By the 1820s and 1830s, their efforts had given way to other, more effective, means of improving workers' lives. The first was the mutual aid or "friendly society," a rudimentary insurance company whose purpose was to provide working people a measure of protection against the hazards of industrial life. As members of a friendly society, workers could come together to discuss common problems, express grievances, and share knowledge and information useful to the entire group.

Friendly societies were popular in part because trade unions were illegal, having been outlawed in Britain by the Combination Acts of 1799 (and in France by a similar law adopted in 1791). These Acts forbade employees to band together for the purpose of striking for higher wages or better working conditions. In practice, the Acts did not eliminate efforts to organize workers but rather forced those efforts underground. Although dangerous and risky for working people, strikes became relatively common, especially after workshop or factory owners attempted to reduce hourly wages. In times of high unemployment, when a large pool of idle workers existed to take the strikers' places, their work stoppages were likely to fail. But when jobs were plentiful, or when strikers possessed skills in short supply, employers met their demands.

Still, the Combination Acts imposed tough restrictions on working people and harsh penalties on individuals caught trying to organize workers or foment strikes. Working-class leaders campaigned actively to have them repealed, ultimately succeeding in 1824. Workers now enjoyed the right to organize trade unions and to use those organizations to bargain collectively for wages, hours, and better working conditions. The right to strike, however, remained sharply limited, since union members who walked off the job could be arrested for conspiracy. Still, the repeal of the Combination Acts represented a milestone for British workers that would not be equaled in France until the 1860s, and even later in Central and Eastern Europe.

The campaign against the Combination Acts highlighted the difficult conditions that workers faced, and in the 1820s and 1830s, reform-minded individuals from the British middle and upper classes joined the effort to improve them. Their first target was the exploitation of child labor, as it was not unusual for children as young as six or eight to work twelve or even fourteen hours a day. Thanks to the reformers' efforts, Parliament approved factory legislation in 1833 that prohibited all work by children below the age of nine, while limiting those between nine

Social Effects of the Industrial Revolution in Britain	
1750	Majority of people live in the country and work in agriculture and cottage industries
1799	Combination Acts forbid workers to band together to strike for better wages and working conditions
1800–1850	London's population triples to three million
1805–1848	Number of people in England and Wales tried for criminal offenses increases by a factor of six
1812	Peak of Luddite movement
1824	Combination Acts repealed
1833	Parliament approves legislation prohibiting factory work by children under nine
1834	Poor Laws reformed
1837	Average life expectancy of a well-to-do resident of Manchester was thirty-eight years; of a working-class resident, seventeen years
1850	Just 20 percent of people live in the country and work in agriculture and cottage industries
1851	Britain possesses 7,000 miles of railroad tracks

and thirteen to eight hours a day and forty-eight hours a week. "Young persons" between thirteen and eighteen could work no more than twelve hours a day and sixty-nine hours a week.

The bill did not go as far as reformers had hoped, since it applied only to textile mills, leaving out the rest of industry and excluding agriculture altogether. Nonetheless it created the important precedent of involving government in efforts to smooth away some of the harshest edges of the new economic system. Later in the nineteenth century, this precedent would serve—in Britain and elsewhere—as the basis for more substantial endeavors to improve the lives of those who performed their nation's industrial work.

Economic Liberalism

For the time being, however, most industrialists did not want these kinds of reforms to go very far. In general, entrepreneurs, bankers, merchants, and other businessmen subscribed to the doctrine of **economic liberalism**, which in their view constituted the essence of freedom. Government, economic liberals believed, should play as small a role as possible in the marketplace.

In practice, economic freedom meant that parliaments were urged to enact no laws regulating what businessmen could do in their own enterprises apart from those laws the businessmen desired. Thus, most factory owners supported the Combination Acts, maintaining that workers' organizations possessed the unnatural power to restrain the marketplace by preventing wages from achieving their natural levels. On other questions, economic liberals favored pure laissez-faire—neither laws limiting the number of hours an individual could work, nor state-imposed safety regulations of any kind. It went without saying that most economic liberals considered compensation for the sick or the unemployed to violate the basic rules of marketplace freedom.

Eventually, humanitarian sentiments would move liberals to support laws preventing very young children from working long hours in dangerous factories and limiting the number of hours women could work. Some liberals even came to support legislation to improve factory safety. But especially in the early years of industrial society, such views seldom came from businessmen themselves, who mostly believed in a marketplace free of government intervention.

Interestingly, however, a considerable number of parents and women joined economic liberals in opposing the regulation of childhood and women's labor. Parents sometimes resented the extent to which the new legislation reduced the family income, especially when they used their own children as helpers in the factory. Similarly, when British legislation of the 1840s restricted women's workday in textile mills to ten hours and banned them from mines altogether, women protested the loss of income and of opportunities to work. In the wake of this legislation, many women found themselves unemployed or forced to labor in industries that paid less than they had earned before.

The immediate impetus of this legislation, like the legislation concerning children, was the harsh working conditions reformers observed. But a number of other, underlying, beliefs also moved reformers to place women workers in a separate category from men. After all, reformers could have tried to solve the problems of factory work that affected adult workers of both sexes instead of devoting their attention to women alone. But the men who framed these laws felt not merely that women needed protection from the harsh realities of the factory, but also that they ought to spend as much time as possible at home attending to their husbands and children. Consciously or unconsciously, reformers were motivated by a set of notions, widely held in their society, concerning what was proper for men and women to do.

Conclusion: The Limits of Britain's Industrial Revolution

Viewed as a whole over the period from 1760 to 1850, the Industrial Revolution appears as an enormously complex phenomenon. On the one hand, the Industrial Revolution created the explosion of new wealth and new opportunities that made possible a high level of comfort and well-being for far more people than ever before. But on the other, it consigned working people to harsh and often dangerous factories for long days at mediocre pay, while creating industrial cities barely fit for human habitation. Ultimately, the wealth and productivity created by the Industrial Revolution would pave the way for milder working conditions and redeveloped cities, higher working-class incomes, and more prosperous lives. But most of those who toiled in the workshops, mines, and factories of the early industrial era found that the principal benefits of their labor accrued to others more than to themselves.

By 1850, the date that conventionally marks the end of the Industrial Revolution in Britain, the industrialization of other countries was only in its early stages. Not until then did the cost of operating coal-fired steam engines and blast furnaces drop to the point that it became profitable to employ them in countries in which coal was expensive and labor cheap—the case essentially everywhere but the United States. In the United States, industrialization was delayed by the prevalence and profitability of agriculture and the slow process of building a transportation network to move raw materials and finished products.

But as we will see in Chapters 8 and 9, after 1850–1860, both the United States and Germany were poised to leapfrog over Great Britain and take the industrial lead. They would do so in part because, as nearly virgin industrial lands, they could endow their entire economies with the most advanced of Britain's techniques, while Britain's own industrial landscape remained a hodgepodge of the old and the new. Factories built in 1800 or 1820 were still operating, and the expense would have been too great to replace their old machines with new ones. In Germany, there were few old machines to replace. When the newest ones were installed, German industries were instantly equipped to outcompete their British counterparts.

In effect, Britain was a victim of its early success; by the 1870s, it would lose the industrial lead it had held for a century and a half. But until then, its prosperity and relative political stability would shield it from many of the difficulties facing continental Europe, where the monarchs who had defeated Napoleon vainly struggled to keep revolutionary energies in check.

KEY TERMS

agricultural revolution *252*

bottleneck *255*

business cycles *275*

capitulations *269*

coke *259*

cotton gin *258*

division of labor *264*

economic liberalism *282*

entail *268*

factory *256*

forage crops *251*

guilds *245*

Industrial Revolution *245*

Luddism *280*

mercantilism *249*

Poor Laws *275*

Porte *269*

primogeniture *270*

smelting *259*

spinning jenny *255*

wrought iron *259*

 For digital learning resources, please go to **https://www.oup.com/he/berenson2e**. Turn to the back of the book to see the list of primary sources and writing exercises provided in the accompanying *Sources and Guided Writing Exercises for Europe in the Modern World*

Conservation, Reform, and Revolution, 1815–1852

George Sand

Aurore Dupin (1804–1876), commonly known by her pseudonym, George Sand, was France's most famous—and prolific—woman writer of the nineteenth century. She penned eighty-odd novels and plays, a five-volume autobiography, hundreds of newspaper articles, and an astonishing forty thousand letters, many to the most celebrated men and women of her time.

Part of what gave Sand her fame was the daring subject matter of her books and her willingness to violate conventions and taboos, both in her novels and in her life. She wrote about female sexuality, the suffering of unhappily married women, the attractions of incest, the cruelty of men, and the lure of love across the barriers of class. Because so much of Sand's writing was autobiographical, readers and critics never knew where—or whether—to draw a line between her fictional characters and the real people of her life, including herself. For Sand, the blurring of life and art was deliberate; she used her writing to explore alternative ways to live, and she used her life to experience relationships and human dilemmas about which she could write.

It was unusual for nineteenth-century women to write overtly about sexuality, and readers of both sexes found her work at once titillating and refreshing, while they found her life simply titillating. Sand was known to dress as a man, to smoke cigarettes and even cigars in public, and to conduct a great many love affairs, living openly with her paramours. One of her greatest loves, emotional as well as physical, may have been Marie Dorval, a beautiful actress of the Parisian stage.

In many ways, Dupin's unconventional life was given to her at birth. Her father, Maurice Dupin, hailed from aristocratic stock, while her mother, Sophie-Victoire Delaborde, came from a poor working-class family and had earned her living as a prostitute. Maurice's mother, Marie-Aurore Dupin de Francueil, the granddaughter of a Polish king, never accepted her son's wife and insisted on raising her granddaughter herself. Marie-Aurore saw to Dupin's education, organizing for her the kind of curriculum usually reserved for boys. As an adult, Sand expressed a feminist-tinged appreciation of what her grandmother had done. "Women are given a deplorable education," Sand wrote in 1837. "This is men's greatest crime against them."

Sand's education did not prevent her grandmother from insisting that she live a traditional womanly life. Marie-Aurore found Sand a suitable husband, an aristocratic military officer named Casimir Dudevant, whom Dupin married at age eighteen. Her grandmother then bequeathed to the young couple a substantial sum of money, along with a fine property in the village of Nohant in central France. By law, this inheritance fell completely under Dudevant's control, which meant that he did not need to work. Dupin gave birth to two children, Maurice and Solange, although Solange's father may not have been Dudevant.

The marriage was unhappy, as Dupin/Sand chafed against the inferiority imposed on wives by France's Civil Code, instituted by Napoleon in 1804. Within three years, she fell in love with another man and escaped into her writing, which she did clandestinely late at night. In 1830, she decided to leave for Paris. Since divorce was illegal, there was no question of ending the marriage altogether but rather of redefining it to give her the independence she craved.

In the 1830s, it was not uncommon for a young man to seek his fortune in the French capital but extraordinarily rare for a woman to do the same. Partly for that reason, Dupin/Sand found life easier when disguised as a man. A woman alone on the streets of Paris would have been noticed, even endangered; a man could be anonymous and free. Dupin's habit of cross-dressing thus began as a pragmatic choice, as did her selection of the male pseudonym, George Sand. An unknown woman writing under her own name faced obstacles to publication. When she took a draft novel, in person, to a potential publisher, his reaction showed the typical prejudice of the time. "Women," the publisher declared, "ought not to write." His advice? "Do not make books, make children." Sand had, of course, already made children, and that had not been enough.

Undaunted, she broke into print in 1831 by coauthoring a novel with her lover, Jules Sandeau, and a year later, she published her own first novel, *Indiana,* under her pseudonym. The book's central character, a melancholic woman named Indiana, stagnates in a loveless marriage much like Sand's and, like Sand, enters into an adulterous affair. Although the narrative lingers over Indiana's oppressive marriage, it does not examine marriage as an institution, as might a "realist" work. Instead *Indiana* attempts to uncover the emotions of an individual woman trapped in a relationship from which she must find an escape. Like other Romantic novels of the time, it is concerned with feelings and subjective states.

Timeline

1807 Parliament abolishes slave trade in British Empire

1814 Peace of Paris ends war against France; Congress of Vienna

1815 Germany becomes a loose confederation led by Austria and Prussia

1820 Spanish soldiers stage a coup d'état, demand constitution

1825 Decembrist revolt in Russia

1830 Polish nobles seize Warsaw, declare independence; retaken by Russia

1830 Revolution in France against Charles X and July Ordinances

1830–1848 "July Monarchy" of Louis-Philippe in France

1831 Aurore Dupin (George Sand) publishes her first solo novel, *Indiana*

1832 British Reform Bill addresses electoral system

1833 Greece becomes independent

1833–1840 Carlist Wars of succession in Spain

1834 German *Zollverein* established

1839 Aurore Dupin publishes *Spiridion*

February 1848 Rebellion in Paris; Louis-Philippe abdicates throne

March 1848 Revolution in Vienna, Berlin, Lombardy, and Venetia

April 1848 Hungarians declare independence

June 1848 Suppression of revolution in Prague and Bohemia

June 1848 Suppression of "June Days" uprising in Paris

October 1848 Suppression of revolution in Vienna

December 1848 Louis Napoléon Bonaparte elected President of the Republic

February 1849 Mazzini topples pope's government, establishes republic; later defeated

April 1849 Independent Magyar republic established

August 1849 Hungarian independence suppressed by Russia and Austria

Reviewers loved *Indiana*, and readers devoured the book, often without realizing its author was a woman. One critic thought it the work of a man stunningly alert to female sensibilities. "One would suppose this brilliant but unharmonious material to be the product of a young man [who] tightened [its] strong, vulgar tissues, and a woman [who] embroidered onto it silk and gold flowers." The novel became a sensation, and Aurore Dupin, her true identity soon revealed, a celebrity. Her next three books, each written in a matter of months, deepened *Indiana's* themes and earned Sand a hefty sum. They also focused public attention on her unconventional romantic life.

Early in her career, Sand tended to take up with other writers, but after a series of working-class rebellions in the early and mid-1830s, she found herself drawn to men who fought for—or with—the downtrodden and oppressed. One of her greatest loves was the militant republican lawyer Michel de Bourges, who introduced Sand to France's leading republican and socialist activists. Under their influence, she wrote the novel *Spiridion* (1839), which sharply criticized the Catholic Church, although without rejecting faith and spirituality. The novel highlights the importance of freedom of expression, goodness to others, and the need for moral reform.

In 1835, de Bourges became the chief defense attorney for 120 silk workers arrested during an uprising in Lyon a year earlier. At the same time, he represented Sand in her suit for a legal separation from her husband, which would allow her to regain control over her inheritance. In court, Dudevant called his estranged wife a "vile prostitute," but his greatest complaint was that "she writes novels." Writing and publishing were not, most men believed, what a good wife and mother should do.

Sand eventually won the suit, but Dudevant's accusations, all covered elaborately in the press, took a toll. Their son, Maurice, found himself mocked and bullied at school, and a great many men denounced Sand as unfeminine. She responded by sounding the notes of **feminism** to identify the politics of women's emancipation. (Scholars widely believe that the socialist writer Charles Fourier coined the term "feminism" in the 1830s; it did not, however, surface until decades later.) "I will lift women up from their abject state," Sand declared in 1837, "both in my life and my writings."

Doubts about her femininity did not prevent several of the most prominent men of the time from wanting to be involved with her romantically. Sand's most celebrated attachment was to the brilliant Polish composer and pianist Frédéric Chopin (1810–1849), who wrote several of his greatest works while living with Sand at Nohant.

Chopin showed little interest in politics, but by the early 1840s, Sand had become a committed socialist, although hers was a temperate Christian socialism that distanced itself from violent revolution. Sand advocated a "moral revolution" grounded in "the religious and philosophical conviction of equality" rather than class warfare and rebellion in the streets.

These views spilled over onto the Revolution of 1848, which began with a violent uprising in Paris. Sand launched herself into the revolutionary vortex, writing everything from circulars for the new provisional government to newspaper articles and philosophical tracts. Amid the turmoil of revolution, Sand counseled moderation and calm, fearing that a new outburst of violence would produce a backlash and undermine France's fragile new democracy. A feminist newspaper, *The Women's Voice*, asked her to run for election to the new parliament, but Sand refused. She opted to spend her time writing rather than pursuing a futile political quest—women were still forbidden to vote or hold office.

Although she disappointed Parisian feminists, Sand's moderation impressed Alexis de Tocqueville, the famous author of *Democracy in America*. Tocqueville generally "detest[ed] women who write," but to his surprise, he "liked" Sand and found in her "the natural appeal of all great minds." He shared her desire to avoid further bloodshed, a desire frustrated when a powerful Parisian uprising broke out in June 1848 and resulted in the slaughter of many thousands of working men.

After the awful violence of the June Days, Sand withdrew, disillusioned, from active engagement in politics, returning to the serenity of her country estate. She lived to age seventy-two, producing on average nearly two novels or plays every year. At Sand's funeral, Gustave Flaubert, author of *Madame Bovary* and noted cynic, "cried like an ass."

Restoration?

Sand's early career unfolded during a period misleadingly known as the **Restoration**, a time when European leaders supposedly tried to turn back the historical clock to before the French revolution. The French novelist Stendhal

(1783–1842) called this era an "age of boredom" when "the least idea with any life in it was considered grossly out of place." But Sand's remarkable career shows not only that innovative ideas were possible, but that they could be popular as well. In France, the years from 1825 to 1848 were among the most intellectually lively of any in that country's history, despite the government's often-strenuous attempts to limit what people could say. German-speaking Europe also developed a lively political culture and intellectual life—especially in philosophy—during these years, as writers defied the states' efforts to restrict public discourse and censor "subversive" texts. And although Britain showed less creativity in the cultural and intellectual realm, the Industrial Revolution, as we have seen, continued its dramatic transformation of economic life. Political repression was more successful in Russia, Eastern Europe, and the Austrian Empire than elsewhere on the continent, but governments often lacked the resources and manpower to effectively censor writings critical of their policies. Authors thus managed to produce—and circulate—impressive literary and political works, while middle-class people, sometimes together with nobles, gathered in coffeehouses and social clubs to discuss them.

Rather than restoring an earlier European order, the developments of the period from 1815 to 1848 solidified the economic and ideological foundations on which modern society would rest—and projected a newfound European power onto the rest of the world. The Industrial Revolution transformed the way the necessities of life were made and allowed Britain, in particular, to profit from a budding global marketplace that its seamen, merchants, and industrialists increasingly controlled. Meanwhile, the era's social and intellectual ferment gave rise to the ideologies that still dominate our world: conservatism, liberalism, democracy, socialism, and nationalism.

The Congress of Vienna

With these dramatic changes just beyond the horizon, the post-Napoleonic era began with the Peace of Paris on May 30, 1814, when Austria, Britain, Prussia, Sweden, and Russia formally concluded the two-decade-long war against France. The peace agreement treated France leniently, because the European allies wanted to keep nostalgia for Napoleonic glory to a minimum. This would make it easier, the allies hoped, for the French people to accept Louis XVIII, the unpopular brother of Louis XVI, as Napoleon's successor and their new king. In the Peace of Paris, the allied European forces withdrew from French territory, whose borders of 1792 were left largely intact, and they restored to France most of the Caribbean colonies it had lost—Saint-Domingue, of course, being the great exception. Still, the allies made sure to detach from France the neighboring lands in Belgium, the Netherlands, western Germany, and Italy annexed by the revolutionary and Napoleonic regimes.

In ending the lengthy, devastating war, the Peace of Paris represented a great achievement, but Europe's diplomats and statesmen still faced the daunting task of establishing a durable regime of peace. To do so, they had to create a new European order, one that acknowledged much of what the revolutionary and Napoleonic eras had wrought while creating a new framework of rules and relations among states, a framework designed to avoid the twin perils of revolution and war. The new system took shape during a gathering of top European diplomats and statesmen known as the **Congress of Vienna**, a marathon sequence of negotiations hosted by the Austrian emperor and chaired by his prime minister, Prince Klemens von Metternich (1773–1859).

The greatest challenge facing the Congress, which unfolded over nine long months from September 1814 to June 1815, was to manage the relationship between and among states of vastly unequal economic and military strength. Britain and Russia had emerged as the commanding powers of the post-Napoleonic period, each with potential to bid for domination in Europe and the world. Metternich saw as his main task the effort to prevent Britain and Russia from doing just that—that is, from threatening his own country or Prussia and France and from jeopardizing the international peace by engaging in a destabilizing conflict with each other.

Metternich planned to achieve these goals by creating a **Concert of Europe**, a group of leading European states dedicated to working in harmony to maintain peace in Europe and prevent—or suppress—revolutions, which, according to the Austrian leader, inevitably led to war. In this Concert of Europe, the different members would agree that the effort to maximize their individual powers was dangerous and destabilizing and that the best way to serve their mutual interests in the long run was to work together.

These were the Congress of Vienna's general goals; to achieve them, it had to solve two specific, though highly complex, geopolitical problems. First, Congress members had to settle the difficult "Polish question" by

≡ **Fanny von Arnstein.** During the lengthy meetings of the Congress of Vienna, several prominent women presided over salons that either became the unofficial headquarters of particular countries represented there or served as informal meeting places for diplomatic adversaries. Fanny von Arnstein, a wealthy Prusso-Austrian Jew, ranked among the most influential *salonnières* at Vienna. Her cosmopolitan heritage, together with her great wealth and cultural accomplishment, attracted the top diplomats to her home and gave her an important, albeit behind-the-scenes, role at the Congress.

punishment for France's sins, for its blasphemous Enlightenment philosophy and crimes against the monarchy and the Church. As for German conservatives, they too rejected the ultra-rationalism of the Enlightenment and French Revolution but showed a reverence for the state alien to their British and French counterparts. Outside of the state, wrote the Prussian conservative Adam Müller, "Mankind is unthinkable."

Liberalism

Conservatism was linked to a resurgent, though fearful, aristocracy, while liberalism mostly—although not uniquely—belonged to a growing, increasingly confident, middle class. **Liberalism** took different forms in different countries, focusing more on economic matters in one place and politics and culture in another. Liberals in Western Europe, men like Adam Smith in Britain and Jean-Baptiste Say (1767–1832) in France, tended to reject government intervention into economic and social life, while those in Eastern Europe advocated a substantial role for the state. Still, certain core ideas and values linked adherents of liberalism whatever their country of origin.

Most liberals saw themselves as members of a party of movement as against devotees of the status quo; they believed in progress, property, reason, and individual rights (as least for those deemed to deserve them). Liberals opposed tyranny and embraced freedom while extolling the virtues of education, self-reliance, and individual initiative; they disliked censorship, unearned privilege, and religious superstition. Liberals were optimistic, firmly believing that history was on their side.

In Western Europe, liberalism emerged in the wake of Britain and France's revolutions of the seventeenth and eighteenth centuries. It responded, all at once, to the perceived dangers of absolutism, revolutionary dictatorship (Cromwell and Bonaparte), and popular democracy (Levelers and Jacobins). Liberals thus wanted not only to guarantee individual rights—speech, assembly, and religious worship, among others—but to protect private property from potential encroachment by the state. To prevent such encroachment, liberals generally opposed democracy and favored a monarchy limited by constitutional guarantees for citizens, a group defined as adult males with enough property to give them a stake in an orderly society and a relatively weak state. Liberals dismissed the idea that women could be citizens; like children, servants, and manual workers, women were said to lack the education, maturity, and experience required for political participation.

Liberals in German-speaking Central Europe and those farther to the east agreed with their western counterparts in many basic ways but differed from them on the question of governmental authority. There had been no revolutions against absolutist monarchy in Central and Eastern Europe, and as a result few indigenous philosophies of governmental restraint emerged in those territories. This was especially true of the Austrian Empire, where in the eighteenth century, the state as embodied in Joseph II represented enlightenment, progress, and social and political reform. Joseph II had tried to limit the power and authority of the nobility, and these efforts endeared him and his successors to middle-class liberals, who wanted some of that power and authority for themselves. Thus, instead of trying, as in the west, to diminish state authority, German liberals sought to benefit from it. Liberals assumed offices in state bureaucracies and used those offices to reform and modernize government and society.

Romanticism

Romanticism, like conservatism, rejected the goals and ideals of liberalism and of the Enlightenment philosophy on which it was based. Romantics dismissed the liberal, "individualist" notion that human beings were fundamentally rational creatures and that society was a collection of separate individuals all essentially alike but largely unconnected to one another except through economic relationships or questions of power and influence. Not unlike leading figures of the Scottish Enlightenment, Romantics maintained that emotions were more fundamental human qualities than the rational intellect and that every member of society felt intimate links to all others through sympathy and compassion.

Although linked emotionally, individuals were unique, and distinct individuality was something Romantics celebrated in their writings and their art. In the classic Romantic novels of the nineteenth century, what drives the narrative is the development of the hero's own understanding of himself. Typically, the hero possesses unique qualities, ambitions, and drives that place him or her at odds with the wider society. Heroes follow the rules of their own, higher morality, even though it costs them their security and sometimes their life. In the literature of earlier periods, the outsider-rebel was a pariah, an object of scorn or

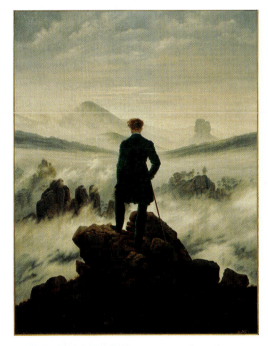

Romanticism. In this painting, *Wanderer above the Sea of Fog* (1818), the German Romantic artist Caspar David Friedrich portrays a young man, possibly himself, isolated from the world. From his lonely mountaintop, he stares—and invites us to stare—at the fog, contemplating, perhaps, his inner, spiritual life. Since the Earth is blanketed in fog, he cannot use his rational faculties to examine it, but likely stands in awe of its mystery and hidden designs.

New Lanark. Just after 1800, the British socialist Robert Owen made the textile factory at New Lanark, Scotland, into the centerpiece of an experiment in factory reform and social welfare. Owen shortened the workday, attended to the health and safety of his workers, and built comfortable housing for all those in his employ. Despite the unusual benefits Owen gave his workers, the New Lanark mill regularly earned him a healthy profit.

Remarkably, Owen regularly made a handsome profit, and he used his wealth to establish "villages of cooperation." Residents of these self-contained agricultural communities were to collaborate with one another and live harmoniously in "parallelograms"—housing built around a central square and featuring common kitchens, baths, and recreational areas. Although Owen expected to match his success at New Lanark, the agricultural villages did not catch on. Most people disliked his experiment in communal living.

Like Owen, the French socialist Charles Fourier (1772–1837) also sought to create model communities in which people lived and worked together. Fourier called these communities "phalansteries" after the ancient Greek phalanx, a fighting unit composed of soldiers tightly linked together. Work, in the phalanstery, would be a joyous exercise in creative self-fulfillment rather than a monotonous and alienating ordeal. When an individual's job became tiresome or unpleasant, he or she would simply choose a new one. Monogamous marriages would likewise give way to the natural human desire for variety. Not only would such a system make people happy, it would make the phalanstery far more productive than any other community. People work best, he wrote, when they are contented and fulfilled.

Such a message was too radical to hold widespread appeal, but it nonetheless drew groups of ardent supporters who established Fourierist communities in France, North Africa, and the United States. Most collapsed quickly, but several Fourierist leaders went on to become prominent in other, more practical, socialist movements. Many would play key roles in the Revolution of 1848.

Feminism

Although Fourier is credited, falsely, with coining the term "feminism," it was the disciples of Saint-Simon who created the most significant early feminist organization. When the French government prosecuted the Saint-Simonian leadership in the early 1830s for encouraging loose morals, prominent women members unfairly took the blame. These women Saint-Simonians, led by Suzanne Voilquin (1801–1877), then struck out on their own, establishing a newspaper devoted to applying Saint-Simonian ideas to women's needs. They considered ways to improve women's lives both at home and in the workplace and did so without the guidance or financial support of men. Voilquin and her colleagues also debated whether sexual freedom was helpful to women; this was, after all, an age without reliable means of birth control or treatment of sexually transmitted diseases. These Saint-Simonians expressed admiration for George Sand, who did not return the favor, and although unpopular in their time, they set the stage for the more successful feminist movements to come.

Perhaps the most significant woman activist of the early nineteenth century was the French-Peruvian Fourierist Flora Tristan (1801–1844). At a time when respectable middle-class women seldom went out in public alone, Tristan traveled throughout France giving powerful orations on behalf of working people of both sexes. She advocated equal pay for men and women, a radical reform that would eliminate economic competition between the sexes and, she maintained, unite all workers as a class. Despite her avant-garde views, Tristan developed a considerable following among French working people, men and women alike.

Nationalism

Throughout its history, socialism has sought to transcend national boundaries and appeal to the human race as a whole. But the more significant ideology of the first half of the nineteenth century—and perhaps the entire modern period—was **nationalism**, a body of ideas that gave supreme importance to the very national boundaries socialists hoped to erase. Nationalism sought to shape people's identities not on the basis of social class and status, as socialism did, or gender, as feminism did; for nationalists, identity grew out of membership in a bounded community shaped by language, culture, history, geography, and in some cases, religion and ethnicity. In this period, nationalists associated themselves with liberals and others who wanted to change the status quo.

Although some rudimentary forms of nationalism existed in the Middle Ages, the idea that people's primary identity resided in their membership in a nation first emerged in the late eighteenth century. Before then, most people were defined, or defined themselves, as subjects of a particular monarch, emperor or lord; as members of a guild or occupation; as adherents of a distinct religion; or as inhabitants of a particular village, town, or region. The Enlightenment did little to foster national identity, since enlightened individuals in France believed they had more in common with enlightened Poles or Germans than with their unenlightened compatriots. The same cosmopolitan connections held true among members of the aristocracy. Russian aristocrats spoke French and felt more kinship with their French counterparts than with commoners in their own land.

All that changed with the Revolution of 1789 and especially with the establishment of the republic and execution of the king three years later. Now that there was no single individual with whom French men and women could identify, revolutionaries encouraged them to transfer their allegiance to the nation, an abstract but nonetheless potent entity grounded in France's revolutionary notion of citizenship. In theory, citizens were equal members of a national community to which all adult men belonged simply by virtue of having voluntarily chosen to be French. No other status was required.

≡ **Grimms' Fairy Tales.** Jacob and Wilhelm Grimm were ardent German nationalists, who believed that the folk tales they published in the early nineteenth century revealed a deeply rooted German identity, an identity that found its origins in the myths and legends of Central Europe's ancient Germanic tribes. The brothers Grimm hoped their updated versions of these myths and legends would provide a cultural base on which a new, unified German nation could be built.

When revolutionary France began to expand beyond its pre-1789 borders on the strength of Napoleon's bayonets, its new concept of nationalism lost much of its democratic cast. The French justified their conquest of other lands by referring to the superiority of the revolutionary system, and they decided to give their European neighbors the benefits of that system, whether they wanted them or not. Napoleon's efforts to establish constitutions and other revolutionary forms in territories he controlled resembled Rousseau's belief that under certain circumstances it was necessary to "force men to be free."

Only rarely do people enjoy being forced to do anything, much less suffer the contradiction of being coerced into freedom. German intellectuals in particular resisted Napoleon's efforts, which reawakened in them a national sentiment already stirring during the Enlightenment, when German philosophers felt unfairly slighted by the French. Under Napoleon, it was not just French *ideas* that ruled, but French power as well. Not only had the experience of military conquest humiliated German leaders and intellectuals, it evoked the fear that German culture itself might cease to exist. To protect that heritage, philosophers such as Johann Gottlieb Fichte (1762–1814) and Friedrich Schleiermacher (1768–1834) began to argue that Germans needed a unified state, a solid bastion in which their culture could be preserved.

German nationalism differed from French nationalism; it arose not in the midst of a democratic and egalitarian revolution but in reaction against its excesses. The French had constructed their nation consciously and voluntarily, basing it on a constitution that possessed, at least in theory, the citizens' consent. The Germans, by contrast, grounded their nationalism in ideas of Johann Herder (1744–1803) and other philosophers who saw nationality as the product of an unconscious, even primal, attachment to an organic community grounded in language, history, culture, and custom. The French revolutionaries understood membership in the nation largely as an individual choice; for many Germans, national belonging was etched in their souls, in their blood, and in the very soil on which they lived. It also resided in the state, the entity that in the idealized terms described by the philosopher Georg Wilhelm Friedrich Hegel (1770–1831) transcended individual interests and desires to join all Germans in a community dedicated to the common good.

As French nationalism played out, many of its apparent differences from German nationalism began to recede. French writers joined their German counterparts in maintaining that national belonging could not result from a mere personal choice but rather inhered in language, culture, and ethnicity. Thus, Jews could be French only if they dropped their traditional culture and Yiddish language and began to speak and act fully French. They also needed to keep their religious observances to themselves. Later, as France colonized parts of Africa and Asia, intellectuals and statesmen argued, or implied, that colonized people, mostly non-Christian and non-white, could not be full members of a French national community.

For all these similarities with German nationalism, French nationalists, rarely joined with Hegel in idealizing the state—if only because the French took the state for granted. A French state, albeit a monarchical one, had existed for centuries, while in the early nineteenth century, a German state remained an aspiration rather than a reality, which perhaps helps explain why Hegel could idealize it. In any case, most German liberals rejected neither the state nor nationalism, whose main ideas appeared liberal, progressive, and even democratic. Liberals argued that the national ideal had fostered freedom and self-determination by liberating Germans from the French and that by encouraging national unity, nationalism promised to reduce the arbitrary power of noblemen who ruled over small princely states.

For German liberals, nationalism also implied economic development both by removing trade barriers within German-speaking Europe and erecting them between Germany and the rest of the world. The internal barriers were replaced by a customs union (**Zollverein**) that allowed raw materials, products, and labor to circulate freely within Germany, thus strengthening the economies of the different German states. To fortify external barriers in the realm of foreign trade, Friedrich

List (1789–1846) developed an economic theory devoted to serving the nation's needs rather than maximizing the wealth and productivity of individuals and their firms, as liberals sought to do. The German Confederation, List maintained, needed to surround itself with high tariffs (taxes on foreign-made goods) to serve the dual purpose of defending key German industries from more competitive British ones and German states from dependence on foreign-made goods.

If nationalism in German-speaking Central Europe was tied to liberalism and economic progress, in the Austrian Empire it meant a wide variety of things. Traditionally, it was the nobility in their capacity as members of the diets, or representative assemblies, of the empire who embodied the various "nations"—Hungarian, Bohemian, German, Croatian—that comprised the vast Habsburg domains. This definition began to change in the late eighteenth century and increasingly in the first half of the nineteenth, when "nation" came to refer to all those who spoke a particular language. Since peasants as well as nobles—or in some cases more commonly than nobles—spoke the various vernacular languages of the Austrian Empire, they claimed to belong to the nation as well. In this way, nations increasingly joined people of different social classes, and an individual's identity as, say, a Hungarian competed with—or became more important than—his identity as a peasant, a burgher (city-dweller), or even a nobleman. Still, the connection between language and nation was complicated: inhabitants of the empire not uncommonly spoke more than one language. To what nation did an individual who was bilingual in German and Czech belong? Because nations were defined geographically and not just linguistically, a "nation" such as Bohemia comprised Czech-speakers and German-speakers as well as a certain number who were bilingual. Thus, a German-speaking Bohemian could very well consider herself a member of the Czech nation—much to the displeasure of political actors who considered themselves Czech "nationalists." As the nineteenth century wore on, nationalists wanted to define nations linguistically and, in the terms we would use today, ethnically as well.

While it is true that inhabitants of the Austrian Empire increasingly saw themselves as members of a particular nation, this did not erase, or substitute for, their allegiance to the Habsburg emperor and state. In many cases, the more an individual identified with a particular nation, the more he or she also identified with the empire as a whole. Rather than contradicting each other, a given national identity and an imperial identity could be mutually reinforcing. Imperial authorities encouraged their subjects to understand the Austrian Empire as a collection of nations, each operating in cooperation with the others, so one's commitment to, say, the Croatian nation was simultaneously a commitment to the empire that granted Croatia its cultural standing.

Eventually, nationalism would help pull the Austrian Empire apart, but there was nothing inevitable about the process, frustratingly to certain nationalist organizations. Even in Italy, where nationalists agitated, after 1815, against Habsburg rule, nationalism was connected to liberalism and Romanticism and advocated the liberation of humanity as a whole. The Italian nationalist Giuseppe Mazzini (1805–1872) traversed Europe speaking in favor of Italian unity and freedom—the **Risorgimento** ("rising again"), as the Italians called it—but he saw national unity as the precondition of a united human race. Had it not been for the Balkan wars of the late nineteenth and early twentieth centuries, and especially the First World War (see Chapters 9-10), the multinational Austrian Empire, which represented a broad array of peoples, could well have survived.

Political Systems and the Quest for Reform

The Romantic movement and the ideas of democrats, socialists, and nationalists served as responses to Metternich's conservatism and vehicles for bringing it down. Already in 1820, the Austrian chancellor suspected that the revolutionary genie had escaped the bottle for good: "My most secret thought is that old Europe is at the beginning of the end."

The Autocracies: Austria and Russia

Even in the regions in which the Holy Alliance appeared to exercise its firmest control, Metternich and his colleagues faced unrest and sometimes insurrection from the beginning of their reign (see Map 7.2). Not surprisingly, the place where Metternich's system worked best was his own Austrian Empire. The Habsburg Emperor Francis I (1792–1835) maintained his absolutist rule, opposing all constitutional limits on his power. A well-staffed secret police created an elaborate system of censorship, and police spies infiltrated student meetings and maintained close scrutiny over most other organizations. Still, a considerable number of banned books were smuggled in, and censors not infrequently looked the other way—or lacked the resources and personnel to remove prohibited books, pamphlets, and newspapers. Although parliamentary liberalism was banned, individuals with liberal convictions avidly followed the movements for reform and revolution in France and Britain, and they congregated, as we have seen, in coffee houses and social clubs to discuss the events of the day and the possibility of reform. In the empire's Hungarian and Transylvanian provinces, the noble-dominated diets (representative assemblies) eventually introduced some weak but not insignificant reforms.

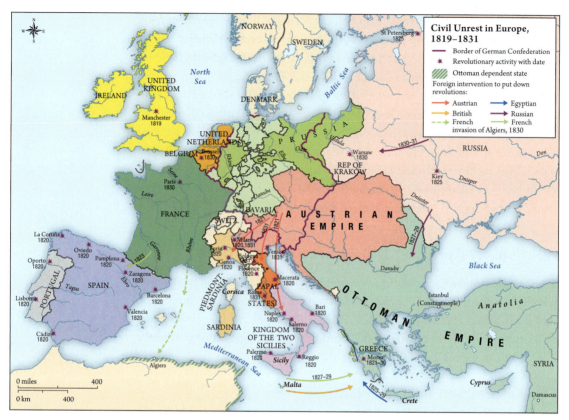

MAP 7.2   Civil Unrest in Europe, 1819–1831

While Austrian aristocratic and middle-class reformers faced severe political constraints, peasants often took action against those who oppressed them. When nobles seized fields and forests traditionally used by villagers for grazing their animals and gathering wood, peasants invaded the properties and restaked their claim to them. These peasant efforts did not as yet have revolutionary implications, but by the mid-1840s they would unsettle the regime, especially in the empire's ethnically Polish province of Galicia, where peasants staged successive rebellions. Nobles rebelled as well, although the peasants refused to coordinate with them, hostile as they were to this landowning class. Metternich's forces exploited the antagonism between the two groups to overpower the nobles and retake control, albeit temporarily.

The Russian Empire was even more autocratic than its Austrian counterpart; the tsar officially shared power with no one. No constitution existed to limit Alexander's authority, and when he wished to introduce a reform, he simply issued a decree (ukase) and the change was accomplished, at least on paper.

Because there was no prime minister, the tsar exercised direct control over his ministries, themselves staffed by autocratic and often corrupt bureaucrats. Even the highest Russian civil servants possessed little independent authority; most initiatives came from the top.

Russia reached its zenith of autocracy when Alexander's son Nicholas I (1796–1855) succeeded him in 1825. His conservatism stemmed, in part, from a serious rebellion by dissident aristocrats and soldiers on the eve of his ascension to the throne. Members of two secret societies, one composed of liberal noblemen and intellectuals, the other of impoverished army officers, emerged from their clandestine existence to challenge the new tsar. Some three thousand soldiers, known as **Decembrists** for the month in which their rebellion took place, marched to St. Petersburg's Senate Square where they demanded a constitution and the abdication of Nicholas in favor of his brother Constantine. Poorly organized and unsure of what to do next, the rebels were dispersed by troops loyal to the new tsar.

This insurrection profoundly affected Nicholas, who declared, "Revolution is at the gates of Russia, but I swear that it shall not enter as long as I have a breath of life left within me." In assuming the mantle of leadership, Nicholas reconstituted the secret police, which his father had temporarily disbanded, and gave it nearly unlimited powers of surveillance and repression. Even the mildest dissidents faced harassment and arrest. The regime kept a close watch on universities and directed Russia's educational institutions to base their instruction on three fundamental principles of the realm: autocracy, the belief in unlimited powers for the tsar; orthodoxy, obedience to the official church and its doctrines; and nationality, reverence for the traditions of "Russian national life" and opposition to foreign influence. Students and teachers accused of violating these maxims faced dismissal, arrest, and even exile.

☰ **Russia's Decembrist Revolt.** In late December 1825, some 3,000 dissident army officers and soldiers marched to Senate Square in St. Petersburg, where they demanded a constitutional government and the abdication of Tsar Nicholas I. Poorly organized, the rebellion quickly fell apart, and Nicholas severely punished the insurgents with exile or imprisonment. To stave off further rebellions, the tsar reconstituted Russia's secret police and cracked down on schools and universities, supposedly the breeding grounds of revolution.

These measures may have kept revolution from returning to Russia proper, but its Polish provinces were another matter. At the end of 1830, a group of Polish nobles opposed to the tsar seized control of the capital city, Warsaw, where they declared Poland's independence from Russia and established a provisional government. Soon, however, divisions among the insurgents weakened their movement, as did their failure to win the support of Poland's large peasant population, always suspicious of their noble overlords. Some nine months after the rebellion, Russian troops entered Warsaw and retook the city. Wishing to make an example of the Polish rebels, the tsar exacted a harsh revenge, executing hundreds of suspected rebel leaders and forcing many hundreds more into exile in the West. The country faced a brutal campaign of Russification, and for the rest of the century Poland would live under tough military rule.

Despite the repressive, reactionary nature of Russian politics, its culture took on an innovative, modern cast, especially in the work of the poets Alexander Pushkin (1799–1837) and Mikhail Lermontov (1814–1841) and the novelists Nikolai Gogol (1809–1852), Ivan Turgenev (1818–1883), and Feodor Dostoevsky (1821–1881). Still, most Russians lacked basic civil liberties and lived in bondage—and extreme poverty—as serfs. As for Russia's tiny middle class, it had nowhere to grow. The regime's aversion to Western ideas prevented the country from adopting the economic and social reforms that might have improved its dismal agricultural productivity and opened the way to industrial development. But even here in the heartland of autocracy, revolution and revolutionary ideas could not be wholly contained.

Prussia and the Non-Habsburg German States

Prussia, the third pillar of the Holy Alliance, remained an absolutist monarchy in the years after 1815, but it changed far more than either Austria or Russia. So too did the other principal states of the German Confederation: Baden, Bavaria, Hanover, the Mecklenburgs, and Saxony. By 1848, thirty-five of the thirty-nine members of the Confederation possessed at least a weak form of constitutional government in which a measure of political representation was granted, unequally, to a hierarchy of social groups (e.g., landed noblemen, city-dwellers) known as *Stände* or estates. These regimes resembled France of the Old Regime more than the new liberal France, where all wealthy landowners enjoyed equal political rights and privileged estates had ceased to exist.

Bavaria and Baden went furthest in the direction of liberal, constitutional government, having been clients of the French during the revolutionary period. In 1818 Bavaria created a two-house parliament with a degree of authority unprecedented for a German government. Württemberg, Hesse-Darmstadt, and Nassau followed Bavaria and Baden's lead. None of them developed fully liberal regimes, but their attempts to create constitutional systems, timid as they were, raised Metternich's ire. For Metternich, any constitution, no matter how weak, opened the door to revolutionary excess. As a relatively large German state, Bavaria seemed the most threatening, and the Austrian leader took advantage of a political assassination in 1819 to undermine its new political system. Metternich argued that the murder, committed by a deranged Bavarian dissident, revealed a persistent Jacobin threat. In making this exaggerated claim, Metternich successfully pressured the Bavarian king to rescind many of his country's new constitutional guarantees.

Shortly afterward, Prussian conservatives backed by Metternich convinced King Frederick William not to introduce the liberal constitution that some of his advisors desired. As elsewhere in Germany, the king ultimately granted a measure of representation, but not real political power, to the *Stände*. Suffrage was restricted to adult males of considerable social and economic standing, and censors tightly controlled what candidates and voters could say.

Still, despite censorship and narrow voting rights, post-Napoleonic Prussia departed in significant ways from the unchecked absolutism of the past. After 1815, the balance of power passed from the king to a newly professionalized civil service. Monarchical authority remained fundamental, but rulers came to exercise it through government bureaucrats who possessed expertise in particular areas of policy. Only rarely could the Prussian king and other German monarchs circumvent their ministries and govern on their own. The one exception was the Habsburg emperor, who, with Metternich's guidance, largely prevented the rise of independent bureaucratic authority, although even there, prominent people in towns and cities often took matters into their own hands in an effort to improve local conditions and gain a small measure of power.

The principal theorist and advocate of the new bureaucratic power was the philosopher Hegel, who became a professor at the University of Berlin in 1818. In an argument that resonated with the ideas of Saint-Simon, Hegel maintained that civil servants, expert in particular policy areas, were more likely than any other group to provide just and efficient government. As members of the middle class, bureaucrats, he said, avoided the prejudices of noblemen and the ignorance of working people. They stood at the center of society and thus were well placed to understand and embody the breadth of its needs. Even more important, their independence from the marketplace enabled them to transcend the particular interests of farmers or manufacturers and do what was best for everyone.

By idealizing the bureaucratic state, Hegel's philosophy did a great deal to justify the new form of absolutism emerging in early-nineteenth-century Prussia. It was an absolutism tempered by a bureaucratic apparatus with considerable authority of its own. By no means was the civil service as independent as Hegel maintained, but its growing authority and professional standing gave liberals and reformers hope that it would provide their states with the mechanisms of orderly change.

Revolution in Spain and Italy

If liberalism and constitutional government suffered setbacks in Germany, the proponents of both staged successful, although short-lived, revolutions in Spain and southern Italy. Spain, in particular, had been severely weakened by the two decades of revolutionary and Napoleonic wars. Its agriculture and industry were shattered, its navy was decimated, its trade with American colonies had been blocked, and its government had been deprived of the most forward-looking officials, many of whom had been chased from power on grounds of "collaboration" with the French.

These circumstances created opposition to Spain's absolutist king, Ferdinand VII, who unwittingly turned dissent into revolt when he attempted to recapture an American empire that was rapidly slipping away. In January 1820, a group of soldiers being readied for deployment to the Americas staged a coup d'état, seizing the government and forcing Ferdinand to grant a liberal constitution and cede power to a new parliament, the Cortes, to be elected by a wide swath of the population.

Metternich and Tsar Alexander wanted to intervene against the Spanish revolt under the banner of the Holy Alliance, but Britain opposed any joint European intervention for fear of boosting Austrian and Russian power. Given the narrow social base of Spain's liberal revolt—the country's middle class was tiny—and its apparently slim chances of success, Metternich decided not to defy Britain and kept his military forces at home. But a similar revolt in Naples (then the capital of the Kingdom of the Two Sicilies, now part of Italy) convinced him of the need to act. The Austrian prime minister sent troops into Naples and quickly quelled the rebellion, but not without triggering yet another uprising, this time in Piedmont (then part of the Kingdom of Sardinia, now in northern Italy), which the Austrians also helped to put down. These interventions prevented the spread into Italy of the liberal, constitutional governments that Metternich feared as the harbingers of a new, Europe-wide social and political upheaval. But Austria's heavy-handed tactics alienated a great many Italians and encouraged the development of a nascent nationalism on the peninsula.

Meanwhile, Spain descended into a civil war that pitted King Ferdinand's royalist supporters against the liberal leadership of the Cortes. Metternich sought to unite all the European powers against the Cortes and pressure it diplomatically, not militarily, to revoke the new liberal constitution. Britain, however, persisted in its refusal to intervene in Spain, and France decided to take matters into its own hands by sending troops across its southern border. France's conservative government sought to reestablish the country's faded hegemony in Spain and to disband a liberal regime that might, it feared, inspire imitators in France. The French intervention succeeded in restoring Ferdinand to the Spanish throne but not France's dominance over Spain, much to Metternich's relief.

The French-imposed calm in Spain did not last very long. When Ferdinand died in September 1833, the throne passed to his three-year-old daughter Isabella and effectively to her mother, Queen Maria Cristina, rather than his brother Carlos, who considered himself the rightful heir. Maria Cristina tolerated a certain liberalization of the regime, whereas Carlos was a staunch conservative, believing in God, country, and absolutist rule. Carlos also represented the northern parts of Spain, which sought autonomy from the South, considered too liberal by conservatives from the North. A violent conflict known as the **Carlist Wars** broke out between supporters of Maria Cristina and Carlos and lasted for seven bloody years, ending in the victory of the more liberal forces. This liberal/conservative conflict would resume periodically throughout the nineteenth century and, by the mid-1870s, had resulted in the deaths of more than 3 percent of the Spanish population.

France: The Rise of Constitutional Monarchy

Unlike in German-speaking Europe and countries further to the east, the idea of constitutional government had become so firmly entrenched in France by 1815 that even its revived Bourbon regime rested on a written compact called a Charter. Although the Charter was officially King Louis XVIII's "gift" to France, it was in fact a document that affirmed the most significant changes of the revolutionary and Napoleonic periods: the abolition of the old corporate hierarchy of estates and the creation of a nation of citizens. The Charter's first point reads: "Frenchmen are equal before the law, whatever may be their titles and their ranks."

In addition, the Napoleonic legal code remained in force, as did the deposed emperor's Concordat with the pope that made the French clergy servants of the state. The new regime retained Napoleon's highly centralized administrative structure and educational system, and it confirmed the ownership titles of those who had purchased land confiscated from émigré noblemen during the Revolution. The Charter called for an independent judiciary with trial by jury, and it guaranteed freedom of the press, although not without leaving open a major loophole: the government could impose restraints on journalists if it became necessary to "curb [their] abuses." Finally, Louis XVIII accepted the idea that government officials should be chosen on the basis of talent and skills rather than aristocratic birth.

If Napoleon's successors retained much of the social and legal system created during the revolutionary era, they borrowed their key political institutions from

Britain. Instead of the **unicameral** or one-house parliament established during the Revolution, the French Restoration's (1815–1830) legislature featured two houses: a Chamber of Peers modeled after Britain's House of Lords and a Chamber of Deputies that resembled the House of Commons. In theory, the Chamber of Deputies represented the nation as a whole, but in reality, its electoral base was extremely narrow. Although the French population topped thirty million, only some ninety thousand adult males possessed enough property to qualify to vote. Even fewer enjoyed the privilege to stand for election to the Chamber of Deputies.

These elevated property qualifications meant that the restoration parliament, not unlike England's unreformed House of Commons, mainly represented the wealthy landed elite. Even so, the Chamber was a genuine parliament with the right to pass legislation and enact the annual budget—or refuse to do so in case of disagreements with the king.

Although the political, administrative, and legal systems were surprisingly liberal for a regime that claimed to restore the old pre-revolutionary monarchy, many other aspects of government and society proved quite the opposite. Members of the government and leaders of the Church regularly denounced individuals who had supported the Revolution and extolled émigrés who had sided with France's enemies. Sentiments such as these helped pave the way for the "White Terror" of 1815–1816, when roving bands of ultra-royalists (extremist supporters of the king) attacked and often killed French men and women accused of being Jacobins or Bonapartists. Although the White Terror rivaled aspects of the revolutionary reign of terror in virulence, the government did nothing to stop it.

These and other developments made the new restoration regime extremely unpopular throughout much of France, as did the reparations imposed on France by the Congress of Vienna. To make these payments, the government raised taxes, which created severe economic hardship, especially after a grain shortage in 1816 tripled the price of bread.

In response, crowds of hungry people attacked markets, looted bakeries, besieged rural administrative centers and generally rioted in rage and desperation. The unrest persisted, and in 1820 a worker with Bonapartist sympathies assassinated the Duc de Berry, Louis XVIII's nephew and potential heir to the throne. Even though the assassin acted alone, conservatives saw the murder as part of a Europe-wide conspiracy to engulf the continent in revolution once again. They linked it to the 1819 killing that Metternich had used to justify his own repressive measures and placed both attacks in the context of the rebellions that had taken place in Italy and Spain.

Determined to prevent renewed unrest in France, the ultra-royalists convinced Louis XVIII to adopt a series of repressive measures, made all the more severe when his backward-looking brother, Charles X, assumed the throne in 1824. Charles tightened censorship and infuriated the middle classes by deciding to compensate nobles for the lands confiscated from them after they left France during the Revolution. His Law of Sacrilege appeared to give the Church control over the state and the hated Jesuits power over the Church.

The French Revolution of 1830

These and other similar developments outraged opponents of the regime, who took the offensive against it, winning the parliamentary elections of 1827 and then pressing the king to liberalize his regime. He ignored them for more than two years, and in the face of mounting dissent in parliament and throughout the country, dissolved the Chamber of Deputies in the spring of 1830.

To divert attention from the domestic crisis, Charles's government used a minor diplomatic affront by the Ottoman administration in Algiers to justify sending the French fleet across the Mediterranean to seize the Arab city. The ploy did nothing to subdue his opponents at home, who likened Charles X to the "oriental despots" dominant in Ottoman lands, but it had ominous implications for the future. France had mired itself—and a large Arab population—in what would be 130 years of often-brutal colonial rule in Algeria.

Meanwhile, in France, new elections resulted in an even larger majority for the opposition, now determined to tame the king. Charles struck first, however, issuing on July 26, 1830, a series of royal decrees designed to shore up his authority. With these "July Ordinances," Charles dissolved the new assembly before it could meet, censored the press, and drastically reduced the size of the electorate liable to elect his adversaries to the Chamber.

In response, three opposition newspapers, the *National, Globe*, and *Temps*, appeared on July 27 without the newly required government authorization and called for active resistance against the regime. Groups of students and working men threw up barricades in several Paris neighborhoods, and on July 28, when government soldiers refused to fire on the rebels, the protest against Charles X became revolutionary. The army's unwillingness to fight left the government defenseless and in disarray, and its ensuing collapse enabled insurgents to take control of the city in what came to be known as the **Revolution of 1830**.

The extremely swift course of events worried leaders of the Chamber's liberal opposition who preferred an orderly transfer of power to another violent revolution. As men of wealth and property, they wished to avoid at all costs a reprise of 1792. Gathering at the Paris City Hall, they agreed to remove Charles X but rejected the insurgents' demands to establish a republic. Instead, they offered the throne to Charles's cousin, Louis-Philippe, a prince known for his relative liberalism.

≡ *Liberty Leading the People.* This famous 1830 painting by Eugène Delacroix shows an allegorical figure of the Republic leading a coalition of workers and students against France's oppressive Bourbon regime. Delacroix's canvas has become one of the world's greatest symbols of revolution, recognizable to people around the globe.

Louis-Philippe agreed to be a "citizen-king" faithful to his people and to constitutional limits on his power. In the end, France's "Three Glorious Days" (July 27–29, 1830) resulted not in revolutionary change but in a new, somewhat more liberal constitutional regime.

Rebellions in the Low Countries, Switzerland, Italy, Greece, and the Ottoman Empire

Louis-Philippe's tepid—and ultimately repressive—"July Monarchy" (1830–1848) disappointed radicalized workers and their middle-class supporters, ensuring that revolutionary agitation would continue into the fall of 1830 and beyond, seconded by revolutionary movements in other European countries. In August 1830, a rebellion broke out in the Low Countries that resulted in Belgium's independence from the Netherlands a year later. In Switzerland, a radical democratic movement swept the country, ultimately producing a liberal constitution that gave all adult men the right to vote. The small duchies of central Italy experienced a short-lived insurrection in 1831, and there was considerable unrest throughout much of Germany. A Polish republic, as we have seen, achieved a brief success in 1830–1831. Greece, meanwhile, gained its independence from the Ottoman Empire after ten years of bloody struggle.

In 1827, Greek nationalists had prevailed after British, French, and Russian ships intervened to destroy the Ottoman and Egyptian forces sent to suppress their rebellion. In frustration, the Egyptian ruler, Muhammad Ali Pasha (1769–1849), officially a vassal of the Ottoman sultan, Mahmud II (ruled 1808–1839), turned on his overlords and, in late 1831, advanced toward the Ottoman capital, Constantinople. Ali's advance worried the Russians, who feared that a defeated or weakened Ottoman Empire would open the gates to an invasion of their territory, and after the Egyptian ruler won a series of battles, Russian forces moved in to stop him.

By saving the Ottomans from the upstart Ali, the tsar assumed considerable influence over a weakened Ottoman Empire and turned it into a buffer state protecting Russia's southern flank. But Russia's enhanced power over the Ottomans was balanced by Britain and France's mounting economic sway. The Ottoman sultan, Mahmud II, sought to take advantage of the standoff between Russia on the one hand and Britain and France on the other to restore a measure of independence from Russia and strengthen his government and military. In the process, however, Mahmud became heavily indebted to British and French bankers, and when he found himself unable to repay the loans, he was forced to sign treaties that gave the Western Europeans privileged access to markets in Turkey and the Middle East and substantial influence over Christian communities in Syria, Lebanon, and other places.

Meanwhile, the creation of an independent Greek nation did little to soothe the tensions that had led to the Greek rebellion in the first place. About three-quarters of those who considered themselves Greek lived outside the new state, mostly in Ottoman territories and especially Constantinople, for centuries the center of Greek culture. Efforts to annex these lands to the Greek nation kept the region in turmoil until well after the First World War.

As for Muhammad Ali, the Egyptian ruler, he returned to battle in 1839, declaring his country fully independent from Ottoman rule and sending a new military force into the heart of Mahmud's Ottoman Empire. The French regarded Ali as a liberal reformer intent on modernizing his lands; they supported his efforts, including his takeover of Syria, a province of the Ottoman Empire coveted by France. But no other European power wanted to see a French-backed strongman replace the Ottoman sultan. Such a development would give

≡ **Muhammad (Mehmet) Ali.** A commander in the Ottoman army and ruler of Egypt from 1805 to 1848, Ali led the Ottoman opposition to the effort by Greek nationalists and their European allies to win independence from the Ottoman Empire. In fighting Ali, the British and French portrayed him as a decadent "oriental despot" who had tried to wrench Greece away from its supposed destiny as the fount of Western civilization. After leaving Greece, Ali unsuccessfully tried to seize power in Constantinople and then withdrew to Egypt, where he established a government independent of the Ottoman sultan.

France a dominant position in Eastern Europe and the eastern Mediterranean, and the other great powers feared that this would upset Europe's already teetering balance of power.

Britain's powerful, perennial foreign secretary, Lord Palmerston (1784–1865), was determined to stem Ali's power, and with it, French influence in the Mediterranean region. Ali gave Palmerston a pretext for intervening against him (and indirectly, France) when public opinion in several countries reacted sharply to news that Ali's lieutenants in Syria had revived the long-discredited "blood libel" against the Jews. Dating back to the Middle Ages, this fallacious accusation maintained that Jews killed Christians to use their blood in religious rituals. The French consul in Damascus had falsely charged the city's Jewish leaders with the murder of an Italian monk and urged Ali to have them arrested. To extract confessions, Ali's agents tortured several of the Jewish leaders to death.

Even without this incident, Palmerston might well have led his country, along with allied European powers, to war against the Egyptian ruler. What made it easier for him to act were the successful efforts by Sir Moses Montefiore, one of Britain's leading Jewish citizens, to publicize Ali's failure to renounce the anti-Jewish accusations and condemn the judicial torture of Damascus's Jews. Montefiore's efforts turned influential voices in Britain against Ali and dovetailed with Palmerston's geopolitical objectives. The foreign secretary was doubly inclined to intervene in the Ottoman Middle East because he sympathized with a budding Anglican millennialism that urged Jews to return to the Holy Land, then part of the Ottoman Empire, which a British presence in the region would supposedly facilitate. According to certain biblical texts, as understood in the nineteenth century, a Jewish return to Palestine would hasten the Second Coming of Christ and the End Times when the Kingdom of God would finally reign on Earth.

In any event, Ali's refusal to absolve the Jews of ritual murder—and more important, his refusal to leave Syria and abandon his designs on Constantinople—moved the British to use military force against the Egyptian ruler. The intervention was successful, and afterward, the major European powers, France excluded, agreed to bolster the sultan's authority in Constantinople and limit French influence there for good.

The French government was enormously unhappy about this decision, but France's domestic situation left it in no position to contest the loss of standing in Damascus and Constantinople. Since the Revolution of 1830, Louis-Philippe had had to contend with three major urban insurrections in Paris and Lyon and three attempted coups d'état, two by Louis Napoléon Bonaparte (1808–1873), Napoleon's nephew and the future Emperor Napoleon III.

Britain: Social Change and Political Reform

The restoration of peace in 1815 left Britain facing considerable economic distress because it had lost markets gained during the long Napoleonic wars. The result was a harsh economic recession that caused widespread unemployment, misery, and hunger. Rather than alleviate this suffering, the government, led by the same Tory (conservative) Party that had ruled since the 1780s, made matters worse. It kept grain prices high by enacting a protective tariff, dubbed the **Corn Laws**, designed to benefit Tory landowners by barring foreign grain from the British market. The grain-producing landed aristocracy saw its fortunes rise, while those of Britain's wage earners, already suffering from high unemployment, fell even further as costlier grain raised the price of bread.

The dual dilemmas of joblessness and hunger sparked a series of peaceful, but angry, protests and a campaign for political reform. The latter was led by a group of political radicals who demanded the repeal of the Corn Laws and agitated for changes in the rules for electing members of Parliament. A more representative Parliament, they thought, would produce social and economic change.

The radicals' beliefs were perhaps naive, but their criticism of the electoral system earned them considerable support from all walks of middle- and working-class life. The rules for electing representatives to the House of Commons (the House of Lords drew its members from the titled nobility) had remained basically unchanged since the Middle Ages despite the profound demographic transformation that had taken place. By the early 1800s, after two centuries of urbanization, the largest British cities were vastly underrepresented and the countryside almost absurdly overrepresented in Parliament. London, with a population of nearly a million in 1800, had four members of parliament, while the county of Cornwall in southwestern England, with one-quarter of London's population, possessed forty-four. Manchester (population 90,000) had no MPs at all. Adding to the inequity was the fact that every British county sent two members to the House whether sparsely or heavily populated. By vastly underrepresenting commercial and industrial cities, Britain's electoral rules biased the system in favor of agricultural areas, where property qualifications limited voting rights to those who owned substantial amounts of land and disenfranchised hundreds of thousands of working- and middle-class people.

The Tories had no intention of changing an electoral system that kept them in power. Like Metternich, the Tory leadership saw even peaceful protest as the prelude to revolution, so they banned public demonstrations and subjected people to arbitrary arrest. When some 50,000 protesters gathered in Manchester in 1819 to advocate

≡ **The Peterloo Massacre.** In this bitterly ironic drawing of 1819, the anonymous artist lambasts the British soldiers who fired into a large crowd of peaceful demonstrators in Manchester. Eleven civilians were killed and hundreds wounded. The name Peterloo refers to Manchester's St. Peter's field, where the killings took place, and, ironically, to the Battle of Waterloo. There, in 1815, British soldiers fought bravely and honorably, unlike their counterparts in Manchester four years after Napoleon's defeat.

reform, heavily armed soldiers fired on the crowd, killing eleven and wounding hundreds. This event was quickly dubbed the Peterloo massacre, because it took place in St. Peter's Field and stood in bitter contrast to the Battle of Waterloo (1815), when British troops killed the French enemy rather than their own people. Afterward, the unrepentant Tories tightened the screws of repression all the more by having Parliament pass the Six Acts, the harshest repressive laws to date.

Thanks to political repression and a measure of economic improvement, protests subsided in the 1820s. By the end of the decade, the Tories felt confident enough to relax their grip somewhat, enacting a series of reforms in Britain's harsh, antiquated judicial system, its anti-union labor policies, and its treatment of religious minorities. For the first time, Catholics and Protestant Dissenters (non-Anglicans) gained something resembling full civil rights. Despite these reforms, or perhaps because of the expectations they raised, vocal members of the working and middle classes remained unsatisfied. For them, the only meaningful reform involved the country's anachronistic electoral system.

Agitation to change this system intensified in the late 1820s and came to a head in the aftermath of the French Revolution of 1830. In early 1831, the Whig Party, now in the majority, introduced a **Reform Bill** designed to reduce the number of "rotten" and "pocket" boroughs—places where a particular family or families decided who was elected to Parliament—and give more representation to London and the new industrial cities of the north. The Whigs also sought to expand voting rights by lowering property qualifications. They championed the new legislation in the hope that it would enable the country to avoid revolutionary upheaval and create a more effective and legitimate government.

Most Tories, however, expressed horror over the Reform Bill, claiming it would destroy "the natural influence of rank and property." So fierce was the opposition that it took three different votes in the House of Commons, early general elections, and intense pressure on the House of Lords to get it passed. The Commons' two initial rejections of the bill provoked rioting and mass unrest in London, Bristol, and other major towns, as well as a near revolution in Wales. When it finally passed in 1832, supporters rejoiced in an atmosphere of hope and expectation, although it would take decades for their expectations to be fulfilled.

Traditional accounts of the reform process have exaggerated the extent to which the Reform Bill enabled the middle class to share power with the aristocracy. The mythical "rise of the middle class" confuses that group's growing economic strength with its nascent political role. Although the ultimate result of Britain's political reform was to relax the aristocracy's grip on power, it would take most of the century to complete the process. In the immediate wake of the parliamentary reform, most MPs continued to hail from the landed aristocracy, and four out of five English men and all English women were still denied the right to vote.

What members of the middle classes did gain, in addition to some new representation, was a national platform for their views. They used their new foothold in Parliament to champion the cause of commerce and industry and fight for a variety of other reforms. In 1846, after a long and arduous battle, disciples of Adam Smith led by John Bright (1811–1889) and Richard Cobden (1804–1865) succeeded in creating a free trade in grain by overturning the widely despised Corn Laws, which had come to symbolize aristocratic power and the old mercantilist economy.

While placing landlords in Britain on the defensive, economic liberals moved to impose free trade on the elites of other countries as well, thus allowing British manufactured goods to penetrate markets around the world. In the 1830s, British officials pressured nominally independent Latin American governments to reduce or eliminate tariffs on British imports. And when foreign governments failed to comply, Britain sent in its navy, as it did in the Ottoman Empire in 1838 and Naples in 1840. The most spectacular case of British intervention to force free trade on recalcitrant countries was the Opium War of 1839–1842, when British gunboats forced China to accept huge shipments of Indian opium, from which British merchants made large profits. These brief British interventions in China, Italy, and Turkey point to the existence of an "informal empire" in which Britain controlled key parts of the economies of foreign countries without having to shoulder the expense of colonizing them.

≡ **The Opium War.** In 1839, the British government sent gunboats to China, where they forced that country to accept large shipments of Indian opium. Britain's victory in this naval war revealed the strength of its commercial and industrial economy and its ability to create an extensive "informal empire" over which Britain exerted powerful economic control.

As Bright and Cobden enlisted members of the British middle class in the cause of free trade, working people, eager for lower bread prices, joined them as well. Workers also formed organizations of their own, the most important of which came together in a powerful national movement known as **Chartism**, after the "People's Charter" that it sought to enact. The Charter, published in May 1838 by two of the country's most influential labor leaders, William Lovett (1800–1877) and Francis Place (1771–1854), pressed Parliament to make six fundamental reforms: annual parliamentary elections, universal manhood suffrage, electoral districts of equal size, eligibility to serve in Parliament for all adult men, pay for MPs, and the secret ballot. If enacted, the Charter would have made Britain the most democratic country in the world.

Backed by petitions with hundreds of thousands of signatures, the Charter was presented to Parliament on three occasions and rejected overwhelmingly each time. The successive refusals prompted waves of protest and often-violent social unrest, none of which succeeded in realizing Chartism's goals. It ranks nonetheless as Europe's first national working-class movement, one that gathered enormous, albeit sporadic, support. Chartism's fatal weaknesses lay in the splintered character of the British working class, divided as it was between artisans and factory workers, miners and machinists, women and men.

Ironically, Chartism's last stand took place in the spring of 1848, a moment when much of continental Europe was engulfed in revolution. On April 10, a large London demonstration proved unable to mobilize people outside the British capital, and the movement fizzled into defeat. In what was Europe's most revolutionary year (save perhaps for 1989), Chartism ended with a whimper. This once-potent movement could not muster the strength either to force radical reform or to bring down a unified, confident, and increasingly powerful British

Political Reform and Revolution in Europe, 1815–1849	
1815	Congress of Vienna
1818	Bavaria creates a two-house parliament
1819	Peterloo Massacre, Britain
1820–1821	Revolts in Spain, Naples, Portugal, Piedmont
1821–1832	Greek War of Independence
1825	Decembrist revolt, Russia
1830	Revolution in France
1830–1831	Polish republic
1831	Belgium achieves independence from Holland; revolts throughout Italy and Germany
1832	British parliament passes Reform Bill
1833–1839	Carlist Wars, Spain
1838–1848	Chartist movement, Britain
1839	Muhammad Ali declares Egypt fully independent of Ottoman Empire
1846	Corn Laws repealed in Britain
1848–1849	Revolutions throughout Europe

state. Britain was to be the only major European country west of Russia to avoid the revolutions of 1848.

1848: Europe in Revolution

The precise causes of revolution in 1848 varied from one country to the next, but everywhere the causes stemmed from one or more of the following phenomena: the development of new ideas about politics and society throughout the previous decades; the desire for political participation and an end to repressive government; the quest for economic justice, however it was defined; and the drive for national unity or for the acknowledgment by empires of the importance of their constituent national groups. New ideas were especially important, and France stood at the center of ideological innovation. Its capital city, Paris, became a magnet not only for French reformers and revolutionaries but also for those from Europe at large.

In France, the democratic and socialist ideas of the 1830s and 1840s took a somewhat more practical turn as compared with the utopian schemes of Fourier and Saint-Simon. Socialists such as Louis Blanc (1811–1882) and Pierre-Joseph Proudhon (1809–1865) challenged the prevailing economy of wage labor, which they condemned for enslaving workers to a cruel and inhumane marketplace. In his influential book, *The Organization of Labor* (1839), Blanc proposed to replace wage labor with a system of national workshops owned jointly by their workers and supported by the state. Proudhon also believed in worker-owned shops ("producers' cooperatives"), but he was suspicious of the role Blanc ascribed to the government. Elaborated in the 1840s, these ideas attracted considerable support from the skilled artisans who composed the bulk of France's manufacturing corps. These craftsmen resented the competitive pressures that reduced wages and made it increasingly difficult to keep small, independent workshops in business. They demanded the right to vote, which when combined with cooperative ownership, would set them free—or so many believed.

In German-speaking Europe, social and political ideas were not nearly so radical, but working people expressed similar demands for independence and control. Unlike their French counterparts, German workers often articulated their needs by looking not to a future of socialist cooperation but to a past of powerful guilds. In earlier times, most skilled workers had belonged to guilds or trade organizations that possessed the power to set prices and wages while limiting competition in a given field. German guilds still existed at mid-century, but only as shadows of their earlier selves. Improved transportation and communication, as well as new manufacturing techniques, increasingly subjected guild members to competitive markets. More and more, it was the market and not the guilds that determined how much an individual earned. This was especially true of the large and growing numbers of workers involved in **cottage industry**, who did not belong to guilds. These laborers—weavers, tailors, furniture-makers—worked at home (hence the name cottage industry) and were tethered to merchant capitalists who supplied them with equipment and raw materials and who bought their finished goods by the piece. By 1850, cottage industry accounted for almost 40 percent of Germany's entire manufacturing labor force, considerably more than in 1800.

The largest group of those who worked at home was handloom weavers, and by the 1840s, they found themselves in particularly dire straits. There were so many weavers that the supply of finished cloth outstripped the demand for it, and merchants continuously lowered the amount they paid until many were working long, grueling days at little better than starvation wages. In 1844, the weavers of Silesia (now part of Poland) rebelled, threatening the region's wealthiest merchants and demanding higher pay. When the protests turned violent, the government called in military force.

Protests such as these erupted regularly throughout continental Europe as severe economic difficulties created what contemporaries called the "hungry forties." The decade's economic troubles came to a head during the years 1845–1847 when bad weather throughout Europe produced a series of poor harvests, leaving much of the continent short of food. To make matters worse, a parasite attacked Europe's potato crop and turned the inexpensive and nutritious tuber into a black, inedible mush.

Because the majority of Ireland's impoverished peasants had made the potato their chief source of food and the British government refused to stop exporting food from Ireland or provide adequate relief, the ruined potato crop of the late 1840s led to mass starvation. Some two million people died of hunger in this **Irish Potato Famine** and another million perished from illnesses related to poor nutrition. A million more left the country, many emigrating to the United States. When the potato famine finally subsided, the Irish population had dropped by nearly 50 percent.

Nowhere else was the human toll so severe, but peasants and workers throughout Europe suffered the bitter effects of hunger, malnutrition, and disease. By increasing the price of food, bad harvests left people with less money to spend on manufactured goods. The reduced demand moved business owners to lay off workers, creating widespread unemployment at the very moment when the price of necessities was on the rise. The food shortage led, therefore, to an industrial depression, which in turn caused a rash of

≡ **The Irish Potato Famine.** Ireland's impoverished peasantry relied on the nutrient-rich potato for much of its nourishment. When a parasite ruined Ireland's potato crop in the late 1840s and England refused to provide relief, mass starvation ensued. As many as three million Irish people died and a million more emigrated to the United States.

bankruptcies and the failure of numerous banks. By late 1846, economic activity had slowed to a crawl.

Despite a series of violent uprisings in Prussia and Polish-speaking Austria as well as sporadic unrest elsewhere, revolution did not occur at the trough of the economic collapse. Revolutionary change is seldom the result of misery alone. It becomes possible only when significant numbers of people can express an alternative vision of what the society and economy should be, and when they possess the faith that this vision can come to pass. Only in 1847, when reformers, armed with ideas gleaned from Romantics, nationalists, democrats, and socialists, came together and agitated earnestly for change did a revolutionary situation arise.

The Revolution Begins

The narrow elites who governed almost everywhere were too distant from ordinary people to understand their plight, but by 1847 the most perceptive among them began to have premonitions of the upheavals ahead. Metternich told a visiting diplomat that the conservative order he had done so much to reconstruct had become fatally diseased. "We'll hold on as long as we can," he declared in mid-1847, "but I have doubts about the outcome." A few months later, Tocqueville voiced similar concerns, warning his colleagues in the French parliament of an impending revolution "destined not only to upset this or that law, ministry, or even form of government, but society itself."

Although an uprising in Palermo, Sicily, in January 1848 presaged the events to come, the revolution itself began in the birthplace of modern revolution, Paris. In late February, a campaign of reform-oriented meetings was to culminate in a massive banquet in Paris whose celebrants planned to demand universal manhood suffrage and a number of other changes. When the government banned the meeting, a group of radical leaders decided to hold a protest demonstration instead. A great many workers and students turned out, and the National Guard, ordered to disperse the demonstrators, refused to obey. The government then called in regular army troops, who fired on the crowd. The ensuing massacre enraged the protestors and lost the government crucial middle-class support. By the early morning of February 24, Parisian workers had erected some 1,500 barricades, and their pitched street battles with government soldiers rapidly escalated into a full-scale uprising.

Fearing the worst, King Louis-Philippe abruptly abdicated the throne. This time the radical leaders were determined to avoid an 1830s-style substitution of one monarchy for another. Almost immediately, they declared France a republic and established a provisional revolutionary government.

On February 25, the new regime enacted many of the political reforms that opponents of the deposed regime had long demanded: universal manhood suffrage; freedom of speech, press, and association; and the abolition of slavery in French colonies. Over the objections of its most moderate members, the new government then decreed that all citizens possessed the "right to work" and established National Workshops to provide state-supported jobs for the unemployed. Louis Blanc was named head of the Luxembourg Commission, a sort of workers' parliament that would study working and living conditions and propose comprehensive reforms.

The National Workshops and the socialistic right to work horrified the moderate wing of the provisional government no less than representatives of the traditional elites. Fearing that the Workshops' swelling membership could evolve into a new revolutionary army, moderates and conservatives were determined to close them down. They accomplished this goal in June 1848 after a nationwide election favorable to them. For workers, the National Workshops had come to symbolize the new Republic's commitment to economic justice; their abolition triggered an insurrection more powerful than the February revolution itself.

The **June Days**, as this uprising was called, pitted thousands of Parisian workers against a large contingent of government troops. The rebellion lasted more than three days (June 23–26) and saw some of the fiercest street fighting in modern history. In the end, more than ten thousand rebels lay dead or injured, and thousands more would die in penal colonies abroad. The generals who put down the rebellion had cut their military teeth in Algeria, where they routinely used deadly force against those who resisted French colonial rule. For the generals, Parisian insurgents and Arab rebels were one and the same.

After the June Days, the revolutionary energy unleashed in February 1848 moved into the French countryside, where it radicalized a sizable portion of the French peasantry. In December 1848, the peasantry, along with millions of their countrymen, overwhelmingly elected Louis Napoléon Bonaparte, the late Napoleon's young nephew, to the newly created office of president of the republic. Ordinary people believed that this new Napoleon, the author of *The Extinction of Pauperism* (1844), would improve their lives. But once in office, he turned away from them and sided with France's conservative elites. Revolutionary agitation continued, and a coalition of democrats and socialists threatened to take over in 1852, when Louis Napoléon, constitutionally limited to one term as president, would leave office. Rather than give up the presidency, Bonaparte staged a coup d'état, abolishing the democratic constitution of 1848 and preparing to name himself Napoleon III, emperor for life.

The Spread of Revolution

Metternich had feared that once revolution appeared it would quickly spread throughout Europe, and that is exactly what happened (see Map 7.3). It broke out in southeastern Germany just a few days after the uprising in Paris and progressed rapidly through the central German states, reaching Vienna on March 13 and Berlin less than a week later. The French experience had terrified German rulers to the point that most gave up without a fight. King Ludwig of Bavaria was the only German monarch actually to lose his throne, but ministries everywhere abruptly fell, sometimes even before rebellious crowds pushed them out. In mid-March, Metternich himself was forced to leave Austria, furtively and in disguise.

On the Italian peninsula, revolution spread from Sicily in the south to the Papal States, Tuscany, and Sardinia. With Austria itself in rebellion, the Italian revolt soon took hold in Lombardy and Venetia, the regions under direct Habsburg rule. When the Venetians declared their city an independent republic, a grand coalition of Italian states led by King Charles Albert of Sardinia joined them in a nationalistic war to rid the peninsula of Austrian influence and create a unified Italian state. But the coalition quickly unraveled after republican leaders in several Italian states refused to submit to Charles Albert's monarchical rule. With the Italians now in disarray, the Austrian army succeeded in restoring Habsburg control.

Perhaps the most dramatic events of the Italian revolution took place in Rome, where radicals toppled the pope's government in February 1849 and established a republic under Mazzini's leadership. The new republic intended to confiscate Church lands and distribute them to the peasantry, build public housing, and give Roman citizens full political rights. But Mazzini and his military commander, Giuseppe Garibaldi (1807–1882), soon faced a large French army sent by Louis Napoléon to restore the Pope's temporal power. The Romans put up a heroic fight against vastly superior forces, but the republic fell after only five months of existence. Nowhere were Italian revolutionaries successful for very long, but the events of 1848 reinforced nationalist sentiments on the peninsula and set the stage for independence from Austria and a victorious unification movement a decade hence.

In German and Habsburg Europe, liberals seemed finally to have acquired the political power they had long desired. Kings agreed to grant constitutions, establish elected parliaments, and allow individual Germans a large measure of civil rights. Perhaps most important, the revolution led to the establishment of the Frankfurt Parliament, a legislative body that brought together the more

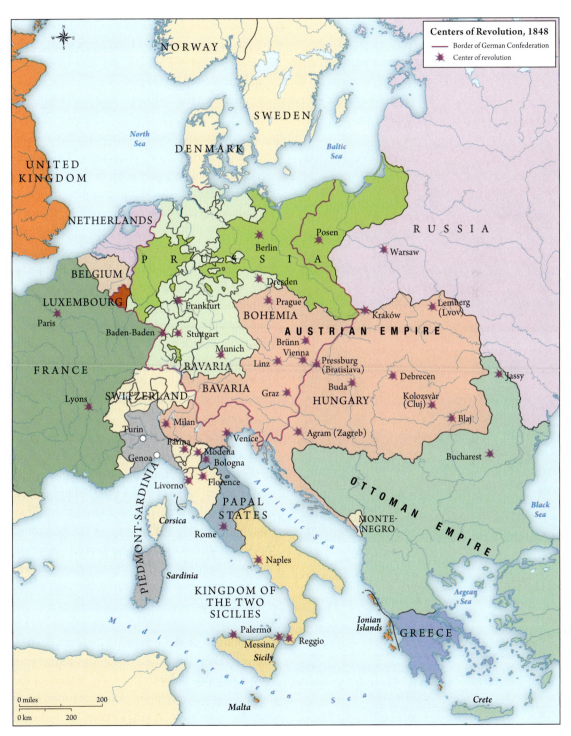

Centers of Revolution, 1848
— Border of German Confederation
✹ Center of revolution

≡ **MAP 7.3**   Centers of Revolution, 1848

than three dozen German states. Liberals and democrats hoped the new assembly would lead the way to genuine national unity. But the German monarchs and their traditional elites never supported the idea of national unification under liberal auspices. Almost immediately, they began an effort, ultimately successful, to deny the Frankfurt Parliament the legitimacy and power required to fulfill its task.

≡ **1848: Revolution in Germany.** In March 1848, revolution erupted in Berlin and Vienna, with insurgents barricading the streets and taking on government troops. New liberal regimes took shape, although most proved to be short-lived—except for parts of western Germany where "mini-republics" persisted through 1849. In Germany, as elsewhere in Europe, the revolutions took on a spiritual, even religious, hue. Radicals sought to install not just new governments here and there, but rather a universal, worldwide "democratic and social republic" in which all men (women were generally excluded) would live as brothers.

Like other new liberal governments in German-speaking Europe, the Frankfurt Parliament rejected full democracy and remained largely unsympathetic to working people's demands for radical social and economic reform. Political power for the masses, the liberals maintained, was premature, as the peasants and workers' refusal to embrace free-market economics supposedly made clear. These opposing philosophies split liberals from democrats and both groups from the bulk of peasants and working people. It would not take long for conservatives to exploit these divisions by appealing to the liberals' fear of the masses and the masses' anger over the liberals' unwillingness or inability to address their social and economic needs.

In Austria, the events of 1848 represented three different revolutions in one. The first was a revolt by noble elites in various parts of the empire who wanted to win back the power that the bureaucratic state based in Vienna had wrested from them. They would achieve this goal by gaining for the nations they claimed to embody a large measure of autonomy, or even full independence, from Austria's central government. A second revolution was led by middle-class urbanites who sought to create a constitutional government to oversee and constrain the workings of the empire's bureaucratic state. Except in Hungary and Italy, where revolutionaries sought national independence, the leaders of the noble and urban revolutions intended not to withdraw from, or break up, the empire, but rather to rebalance its power and authority in their favor. They often cheered the emperor, who they hoped would lead a reformed imperial state.

If the noble and urban revolutions were mostly concerned with the distribution of political power, the third revolution intended to change the structure of society. Its mostly peasant participants were intent on eliminating once and for all the remnants of feudalism in the empire: serfdom; compulsory, unpaid labor services for noble landlords; onerous rents and dues; the inability to buy and sell lands; and many other burdens. This revolution would free the members of Austria's largest social group and transform social and economic relations in the countryside. Its leaders were largely indifferent to nationalism, except when it threatened to harm them, as in the case of noble nationalists in Galicia and Hungary. Peasants feared that these nobles would use a newfound independence from the Austrian state to oppress them all the more. For this reason, peasants of the Austrian Empire tended to believe they were better off as subjects of the multinational empire than as subordinate inhabitants of noble-dominated autonomous or independent nations.

Although the three Austrian revolutions had different goals, they were related to one another. In many parts of the Austrian Empire, the efforts by nobles and other elites to enhance their power by gaining autonomy from, or seizing control over, the central government and its local representatives triggered the rebellions of peasants and workers, who wanted extensive social change. In Bohemia and Galicia, noble nationalists, fearful of social unrest, moved to abolish compulsory labor, but the central government outflanked the nobles by announcing the abolition first. In Galicia, Hungary, and elsewhere, peasants did not wait for official decrees: many simply stopped paying their rents and performing their compulsory labor; in some cases, peasants attacked their landlords' often opulent residences— and the Jews believed to work for them—burning the documents that listed their monetary and labor obligations. With these actions, rural-dwellers ended what remained of feudalism on their own.

These developments, like the analogous demands of urban workers, worried the leaders of the noble and urban revolutions, who, with the demise of the old regime, were left with the task of ending the violence and defending the social order. In the major cities, urban revolutionaries split into two increasingly opposed groups, liberals and democrats. The former sought to suppress the worker and peasant rebellions, while the latter tried to appease them by enacting universal male suffrage, creating public works projects to alleviate unemployment, and regulating food prices and rents. Given insufficient resources for these projects, peasants and workers generally were not appeased; they became disillusioned with the 1848 revolution when liberals, increasingly worried by the threats to social order, began to side with representatives of the pre-revolutionary regime. Under these circumstances, peasants, in particular, placed their hopes for change in the emperor and a revived empire, rather than in the noble and bourgeois revolutions that had failed them.

Throughout the period, peasants remained largely immune to the appeals for autonomy or independence of "nations" such as Bohemia, Croatia, Poland, and Hungary that came mainly from noble and aristocratic elites. This was true even of the Hungarian part of the empire, where the movement for national autonomy advanced the furthest in 1848 and 1849.

Under the able leadership of the nobleman, journalist, and lawyer Lajos Kossuth (1802–1894), Hungarians quickly took advantage of the March revolution in Vienna to declare their region independent from Austria in most fundamental respects. Kossuth demanded a separate government and parliament for Hungary and proposed to abolish the nobility's tax exemptions and end forced labor for the peasantry, although with compensation for the landlords, which most peasants could not afford. He also wanted to extend voting rights to adult men of the urban middle classes and to well-to-do peasants. In granting non-nobles the right to vote, Kossuth meant to broaden membership in the Hungarian nation beyond its traditionally narrow base in the nobility. But poorer peasants and workers plus all Jews would still be excluded from the vote, and thus from full membership in the nation.

Eager as the Hungarians were to secure their own national independence and affirm the distinctiveness of their culture, they showed little sympathy for the cultural standing and independence of the many minority groups—Croatians, Serbs, Slovenes, Italians, Ruthenians—that shared their territory. These groups, the Hungarian revolutionaries said, could be absorbed into the Hungarian nation, but only if they learned the Hungarian language and agreed to give up most of their own independent institutions. These requirements proved unacceptable to the leaders of Hungary's minority groups.

Meanwhile, in lands where Czech was spoken—Bohemia, Moravia, and Austrian Silesia, all now parts of the Czech Republic—leaders of the 1848 revolution pursued a measure of autonomy from the Austrian Empire, but their situation was doubly complicated. Not only did they seek recognition for their distinctive "national" rights, they also faced efforts by the Frankfurt Parliament to integrate them into a new, unified German state. A considerable number of German-speakers lived in these Czech-dominated territories, and certain German nationalists considered them part of Germany. But far from all German-speakers in Bohemia and Moravia wanted to join a new German nation; many identified themselves as Bohemians or Moravians rather than as Germans. This was even truer of the Czechs, who saw themselves as Slavic rather than German or considered themselves members of both groups and felt no need to choose. In any event, they resisted German rule whether it came from Vienna, Berlin, or Frankfurt.

The Austrian court looked kindly on neither the Hungarian nor the Czech aspirations for independence or autonomy; the Habsburgs resolved to keep their empire intact. In June 1848, they took advantage of a radical demonstration in Prague to send imperial troops to crush the Czech autonomy movement. Success in Prague emboldened the emperor to oust the revolutionaries from Vienna as well, which he accomplished in October 1848.

Hungary proved more difficult to subdue. The new Austrian emperor, Franz Joseph (1830–1916), encouraged Hungary's Croatian and Romanian minorities to resist Hungarian autonomy and supported their resistance with a full-scale Austrian invasion. This time military success eluded him: the Hungarians easily defeated Franz Joseph's troops, and in April 1849 made Kossuth president of a new Magyar (Hungarian) republic.

At this point, Hungarian independence would have been assured had it not been for the Russian tsar's decision to intervene. Horrified by the idea of a neighboring republic, Nicholas joined forces with the Austrians, and the combined armies soon overwhelmed the Magyar troops. With their defeat, the Austrian Empire returned to its pre-1848 state, although it did not undo the emancipation of the peasantry achieved during the revolution. Nor did it—or could it—banish the language of nationalism that had gained prominence among nobles and urban-dwellers and would become, over the next half-century, a defining political force.

In Prussia and the smaller German states, as in neighboring Austria, monarchs used military force to reassert their undiluted rule. They

≡ **Lajos Kossuth.** During the Revolution of 1848, Lajos Kossuth, a Hungarian nobleman, briefly led his people to independence from the Austrian Empire. The republic he declared in April 1849 horrified Tsar Nicholas I, who did not want a subversive republic on his western border. Nicholas sent in his army and, together with the Austrians, ended Kossuth's republican reign.

rendered the Frankfurt Parliament impotent and then reclaimed Berlin by ousting the liberal parliament established there in the spring of 1848. At this point, many liberals withdrew from active politics. Radicals, by contrast, struggled on, staging a series of violent demonstrations in which militant workers fought the rising tide of counterrevolution. They assumed power in parts of western Prussia and created minirepublics there that won the support of landowning peasants and skilled artisans.

In the end, these enclaves of democracy were no match for the increasingly confident Prussian troops. By the middle of 1849, the revolution was over. It had succumbed to military force, to the divisions between liberals and those who sought deeper political and social change, and to the revolutionaries' inability to establish the legitimacy of their rule.

Conclusion: The Meaning of 1848

Although the Revolutions of 1848 failed to realize their liberal, nationalist, or socialist aims, they managed nonetheless to achieve some important, lasting results. In France, Louis Napoléon retained the universal male suffrage instituted in February 1848. He intended his coup d'état to tame universal suffrage, not to eliminate it, as many conservatives wanted. Although George Sand was indifferent to women's suffrage, her political prominence in 1848 demonstrated just how important women's public roles could be; together with other women activists, she set the stage for feminist gains to come.

In Germany and Italy, nationalists may have failed to unify their people on the basis of liberal and democratic principles, but their experiences in 1848 did a great deal to pave the way for the successful unification movements only a decade or two away. In the Austrian Empire, nationalist ideas spread widely, although unevenly, and Hungarians would soon reassert their autonomy, this time for good. Meanwhile, the abolition of serfdom radically changed the social and economic sphere. As for the Austrian liberals, they learned a great deal from their experience, preparing themselves to move the Empire toward liberalism and constitutional government within the next twenty-five years. Finally, although Britain evaded the Revolution of 1848, it had achieved a political milestone in 1832. The Reform Bill placed the country on a gradual but steady course toward full democracy, albeit one that would not be completed until all women received the right to vote in 1928.

KEY TERMS

Carlist Wars *315*

Chartism *324*

Concert of Europe *293*

Congress of Vienna *293*

conservatism *299*

Corn Laws *321*

Cottage industry *326*

Decembrists *311*

democracy *302*

feminism *290*

Holy Alliance *299*

Irish Potato Famine *327*

June Days *329*

liberalism *300*

nationalism *305*

Reform Bill *322*

Restoration *291*

Revolution of 1830 *317*

Risorgimento *309*

Romanticism *301*

socialism *303*

socialists *303*

unicameral *316*

Zollverein *307*

 For digital learning resources, please go to **https://www.oup.com/he/berenson2e**. Turn to the back of the book to see the list of primary sources and writing exercises provided in the accompanying *Sources and Guided Writing Exercises for Europe in the Modern World*

From National Unification to Religious Revival, 1850–1880

Otto von Bismarck

At the moment of Prussia's decisive military victory over France in the summer of 1870, the German writer Gustav Rümelin exclaimed: "Before our astonished eyes, this year has become one of the great landmarks, one of the guiding lights of humanity, [and Germany], long kept standing in the wings, steps to the center of the stage." The architect of this transformation, the leader who, as Rümelin so triumphantly put it, "inscribed [Germany's ascendancy] in letters of fire upon the tablets of history," was the Prussian prime minister, Otto von Bismarck (1815–1898).

During the 1860s, Bismarck achieved what had so conspicuously eluded the revolutionaries of 1848: the unification of the various German states into a single and coherent national whole. He did so, in his words, "not by speeches and majority opinions ... but by *blood and iron.*" This ruthless approach made Bismarck the master of ***Realpolitik***, the pure pursuit of power unleavened by considerations of ethics or morality.

With his single-minded quest for power, Bismarck exemplified a post-1848 period impatient with idealistic hopes and utopian plans. His was an era known for its obsession with scientific advancement and material things and the economic development that made them possible. Its leaders were tough politicians, practical businessmen, and amoral philosophers—none of whom exceeded Bismarck's ability to get things done. But for all the prestige of science in this materialistic age, large numbers of people turned—or returned—to religion to revive a spirituality in danger of being lost.

Bismarck himself turned to religion in midlife, although his Christian beliefs did little to blunt his hardnosed Realpolitik. A Prussian Junker (landed nobleman) from the eastern reaches of the kingdom, Bismarck came from a family of distinguished government servants. Most Junkers lived and worked on their own estates, with the help, of course, of a great many peasants. When they left their farms, it was to serve Prussian kings as high public officials or military officers. Junkers tended to be highly conservative, provincial, and proud of their noble lineage. Bismarck inherited these traditionalist traits from the paternal side of his family, but from his mother, a refined woman whose father had been advisor to Frederick the Great, he developed a taste for languages and literature, a certain cosmopolitanism, and, ultimately, an

interest in public life. Those who knew him as a youth, however, could discern in him few statesmanlike qualities. What they saw was a highly emotional and rebellious young man full of undisciplined energy.

In 1832, Bismarck went to the distinguished University of Göttingen in Hanover, where he was anything but a distinguished student. Spending little time in class, he developed a reputation for drinking and dueling, fighting at least twenty-five times in three years. The 1830s and 1840s were the heyday of the *Burschenschaften,* or student fraternities, whose members devoted themselves to German nationalism and fighting duels. Bismarck enjoyed the duels, but not the politics: the members' enthusiasm for liberalism and a unified German nation were too much for a young man whose ideas remained considerably more conservative than his rebellious behavior would suggest.

Here then was the paradox that would characterize Bismarck's life. By temperament he was a rebel, by background and upbringing a conservative through and through. Later on, this paradox would help account for many of his political and diplomatic achievements. His rebelliousness allowed him to see new possibilities and to take the gamble they often required, while his conservatism enabled him to maintain the confidence and preserve the interests of his fellow aristocrats and the king.

After completing his university studies, Bismarck used his mother's connections to obtain a position in the Prussian civil service. From the start, Bismarck's rebellious spirit chafed against the rules of bureaucratic practice that required him to carry out someone else's orders whether he agreed with them or not. Early in his career, he dramatically broke those rules when he left his post, abruptly and without permission, to follow a lady friend to Switzerland. He explained his behavior by comparing a Prussian bureaucrat to an orchestra musician. "Whether he plays first violin or triangle," Bismarck declared, "he has no ability to decide what music to play and how to play it. I wish to make music that seems good to me, or none at all."

Back on his eastern Prussian lands at age twenty-four, Bismarck directed work on the estate with moderate success while conducting his life with immoderate zest. His neighbors called him "wild Bismarck," for his ability to seduce local women and his love of attention-grabbing pranks. Not until his early thirties did he begin to settle down. He fell madly in love with a woman who repeatedly told him that he was directionless and needed the discipline of religious belief. When he was ready to marry, he chose another young woman, Johanna von Puttkamer (1824–1894), who came from a devout family. To win her father's consent for the marriage, he

Timeline

1850	1855	1860	1865	1870	1875	1880	1885	1890

1852–1870 Second Empire of France

1852 Louis Napoléon Bonaparte declares himself Emperor of the French

1853–1856 Crimean War

1858 Bernadette Soubirous's vision at Lourdes

1859–1870 Unification of Italy

1859 Piedmontese and French victories against Austria at Magenta and Solferino

1859 Darwin's *On the Origin of Species by Means of Natural Selection*

1860 Garibaldi defeats Kingdom of the Two Sicilies; Victor Emmanuel proclaimed ruler of the Kingdom of Italy

1861 Czar Alexander II decrees freedom of serfs

1862 Bismarck named prime minister of Prussia

1864 Bismarck seizes Schleswig and Holstein from Denmark

1864 International Working Men's Association (First International) created

1864 Pope Pius IX releases *The Syllabus of Errors*

1865 Reestablishment of Hungarian and Croat Diets

1866 Venice seized from Austria

1866 Prussia defeats Austrians at Sadowa, extends dominance in Germany

1867 Creation of Austria-Hungary

1867 Disraeli's Reform Act in Britain

1869 Social Democratic Workers Party founded in Germany

1870 Rome, except for the Vatican, becomes part of Italy; Pope Pius IX promulgates doctrine of papal infallibility

1870 End of Second Empire; proclamation of Third Republic of France

1871 Paris Commune established; defeated

1871 Darwin's *Descent of Man*

1871 German Empire created under King Wilhelm

1871–1890 Bismarck serves as chancellor of Germany

1875 Social Democratic Party of Germany founded

1878 Romania declares independence

took a pious turn and experienced a religious conversion, which marked the rest of his life.

With his marriage and religious commitments came a new seriousness. Bismarck now embraced the public life he had earlier scorned and in 1847 was named to the Prussian Landtag (parliament). He challenged that body's rising liberal and reformist spirit by taking positions so conservative that he became more royalist than the absolutist king. The majority of his colleagues in the chamber dismissed this young, reactionary newcomer, but they would find it difficult to ignore him for long. With his sharp intellect and imposing frame—he stood well over six feet at a time when the average man reached 5'5"—he cut an impressive figure.

During and after the Revolution of 1848, Bismarck distinguished himself as one of King Frederick's most loyal and effective supporters by attacking anything that smacked of liberalism and democracy. In 1851, the monarch made him the Prussian delegate to the newly restored German Confederation, the loose governing body of German states originally established by the Congress of Vienna. In this role, which he assumed at age thirty-six, Bismarck developed crucial diplomatic experience and the conviction that Prussia should replace Austria as the dominant German state. "We each seek to breathe the same air," he wrote. "One of us must weaken or be weakened, and until then we must be enemies."

In his position toward Austria, Bismarck expressed the paradox of his rebellious temperament and conservative ideology. He was a rebel in the sense that he sought to foment an intra-German conflict that violated the traditional order of things, but conservative in seeking to do so for the glory of his absolutist king. When he finally embraced German unity, his goal was to enhance Prussian power, not to create the progressive nation of liberal dreams.

After seven years as delegate to the Confederation, Bismarck was sent to St. Petersburg and then Paris as the Prussian ambassador. He became one of King William's most trusted lieutenants, and in 1862, found himself back in Berlin as the new prime minister of Prussia. His charge was to resolve the tense standoff between the king and a newly elected parliament dominated by liberals. The parliamentary majority refused to approve the king's military budget unless he agreed to limit his powers and enhance their own. Bismarck responded by illegally collecting taxes and allocating government funds without the parliament's consent. He dared the liberals to block him, and they backed down.

Having asserted his dominance over the parliament, Bismarck proceeded to unify Germany under Prussian leadership though a series of daring, ruthless, and often brilliant moves, to be discussed in detail later in this chapter. The three wars he fought for German unity risked making enemies of all the great powers and consigning himself, if he lost, to historical oblivion. But the victory he ultimately won enabled him to create a new and distinctive German state, whose progressive economy and conservative politics combined the two poles of his being, the one forward-looking, the other anchored in the past. ≡

The New Industrialization

Beyond Bismarck's brilliance and determination and the skill of his army, what made his country so successful after the mid-nineteenth century was an unprecedented industrial boom that swept from Britain to the continent and turned Germany into Europe's dominant economic force. Germany's economic development happened so fast that few observers writing in the 1830s and 1840s would have predicted its ability to surpass France and then Great Britain before the century's end.

Prussia possessed large deposits of coal and iron ore, and by the 1850s, when the lower cost of steam engines and transportation made it economically viable to mine these crucial natural resources, the German economy began to take off—especially since other key factors were already in place. The various German states were well organized, cohesive, and stable, and the customs union (Zollverein) that had united many of them economically in 1834 gave them an integrated market free of trade-killing tariffs. German entrepreneurs were quick to learn industrial and agricultural techniques pioneered in other countries and adapt them for their own use. German citizens were better educated than their counterparts in Britain and elsewhere on the continent, and German workers equally or better skilled.

Between 1850 and 1880, German coal production grew tenfold, more than double the French increase. Even more dramatic was Germany's expansion of steam power, which during just two mid-century decades, 1850–1870, rose from less than 10 percent to 100 percent of the horsepower of British mills. The increased energy that resulted raised the Zollverein's output of iron ore and pig iron, both crucial ingredients of industrial development, by 450 and 650 percent, respectively. In Prussia, these gains led to an impressive 33 percent increase in gross domestic product over the span of just fifteen years, 1855–1870.

Germany's industrial revolution differed from the one that had begun in Britain a century earlier. In Britain, the transformation stretched over a century, as industrialization proceeded gradually from the mechanization of cotton spinning to the spread of steam engines and eventually to the rise of railways and the more generalized economic expansion they sparked. In Germany, where the factory production of textiles was visible in the 1830s but not widespread until mid-century, the revolution in textiles and the explosion of iron production and railroad building occurred almost simultaneously, thanks in part to the Germans' ability to imitate, and improve on, what the British had done (see Map 8.1).

Because Britain's industrial transformation was for several decades mainly limited to a single industry, textiles, with relatively inexpensive technology, the British could begin their economic takeoff without having to find large sources of new capital. The situation was altogether different in Germany, where entrepreneurs, spurred by the need to compete with Britain and make rapid advances, had to build spinning mills, iron-making factories, steam engines, and railroads within a short span of time. Doing so required huge amounts of capital all at once.

The fortuitous discovery of gold in California in 1848 increased the amount of currency in circulation worldwide and helped fund Germany's mid-century industrial expansion. So did profits from large-scale agriculture, especially in places like Prussia's Upper Silesia, where landowners financed mining operations—often on their own properties. After mid-century, new capital increasingly came from novel forms of banking designed to pool resources from an army of investors and loan it to industrial entrepreneurs. Crucial as well was the stock market, an institution that antedated mid-century but that assumed unprecedented importance during this period. By selling shares to a wide variety of individuals and institutions, a company could multiply its sources of capital in exchange for giving investors part ownership in the firm. German bankers excelled in raising capital and used it to underwrite potent industrial concerns.

A New Prosperity?

For Germany and elsewhere in Central and Western Europe where the industrial revolution had spread, the decades of the 1850s and 1860s were a time of prosperity such as the continent had never known. Even working people, whose lives had been so precarious just a decade earlier, enjoyed a relatively high level of employment, stable food prices, and, for many, gradually

Industrializing Germany by 1870
— International border
Major railway lines constructed:
— by 1848
— 1848–1870

Industry c. 1870:
Coal mining
Iron working
Textile production

≡ **MAP 8.1** Industrializing Germany by 1870

increasing real wages. Still, the new prosperity paid higher and more consistent returns to members of the middle and upper middle classes than to workers. Between 1849 and 1857, the income of Prussia's highest taxpayers rose by 142 percent, while that of its lowest ones advanced only 7 percent.

As much as the mid-century economic expansion did for the European bourgeoisie, it did even more for the era's leading entrepreneurs. Henry Bessemer (1813–1898), the British inventor who developed the mass production of steel, built a fortune worth several million pounds, a vast sum for the time. In France, Emile and Isaac Pereire (1800–1875; 1806–1880) controlled fifty companies with combined assets of 5 billion francs (about 1 billion mid-nineteenth-century dollars) and created an industrial and banking empire, as did the German industrialist, Werner Siemens, who declared himself "enthusiastic about founding a world-wide business . . . which would give power and reputation not only to me but also to my descendants."

Although these larger-than-life entrepreneurs dramatized the new economic possibilities of the time, most enterprises remained quite small. The typical European business in the second half of the nineteenth century was a family firm directed by a father and son or a partnership of brothers. These firms tended to employ a clerk or two and at most a handful of workers. Much of their labor was accomplished without the aid of sophisticated machines.

Thus, even though industrialization forced significant numbers of small textile and metallurgical firms out of business, it called a great many other small businesses into being. The building of locomotives, for example, required extensive engineering skills best put to use in small, specialized workshops. In addition, the growth of the middle class gave increasing numbers of

966.—Coach-making.

≡ **An English Coach-Maker.** For all its mechanization and displacement of artisans, the Industrial Revolution increased the demand for skilled craftsmen in some sectors of the economy—carriage-making, for example. As railroads accustomed people to long-distance travel and movement of goods, individuals made more local trips than ever before, whether between their homes or businesses and the new train stations or to transport and distribute goods brought in by rail. This local travel used vehicles—carriages, buggies, and wagons—powered by horses and often made by hand.

people the means to buy luxury products such as fine furniture, pianos, carriages, and other expensive items that had to be carefully crafted by hand, usually in workshops of modest size. The economic development that brought large numbers of working people to cities created the need for an army of construction workers to build everything from lavish suburban villas for the rich to low-cost housing for the poor. Expanding cities, moreover, needed new streets and bridges, sewers, lighting, sidewalks, and the like. Construction work throughout the nineteenth century was still done largely by small crews of builders working by hand.

Urbanization and the Urban World

If most firms remained small, the cities that accommodated them became numerous and large. London and Paris had long been big, but they too expanded enormously during the nineteenth century. Between 1800 and 1880, London quadrupled in population from 1 to 4 million and Paris from 500,000 to more than 2 million. The most dramatic urban growth involved places such as Manchester and Liverpool in England, Hamburg and Frankfurt in Germany, and Roubaix and Lille in France. Little more than small towns early in the century, these cities tripled and even quadrupled in population between the 1840s and 1880s. Their expansion resulted hardly at all from natural increase; urban mortality rates remained high throughout most of the century. The roots of urban growth lay in a large-scale migration away from rural areas where the poor increasingly struggled to make ends meet.

At mid-century, the movement of people from country to town was already well underway in Britain, where census-takers classified half the population as urban in 1851. Elsewhere, it was just at this point that the acceleration of industry and trade began to lure rural-dwellers to the city. Improvements in transportation lowered agricultural prices and made it increasingly difficult for those with small or inefficient farms to hold their own in an increasingly competitive marketplace. At the same time, the decline of proto-industry (manufacturing work in rural homes) deprived rural people of income from spinning or weaving, which had traditionally allowed families to remain on the land. In some regions, moreover, the consolidation of landholdings stripped farmers of their plots, as, paradoxically, did the abolition of serfdom, whose terms usually required peasants to pay compensation to their former lords. Those who could not pay, and their numbers were legion, had no choice but to give up their lands.

The result of these developments was a demographic shift in which European countries gradually, but inexorably, lost their rural character. This shift was most visible in the central and western parts of the continent, but it occurred everywhere—except for Russia, where the government discouraged peasants from migrating to the city. Interestingly enough, however, many of those who managed to remain in the country enjoyed a period of uncommon prosperity. The hemorrhage of people to the cities allowed those able to remain behind to expand their holdings and farm more efficiently. Improvements in crop rotations, fertilizers, livestock, farm implements, and machinery increased the productivity of the land. Railroads and steamships, meanwhile, gave them access to far wider markets than ever before. Thus, at precisely the moment when economic conditions forced the poorest rural dwellers from the land, those same conditions raised the more fortunate ones to a new level of affluence.

These developments led to the specialization of regions that had once hosted a mix of agricultural and industrial pursuits. Areas with good soil and access to means of transport became almost exclusively agricultural, while those with rich deposits of coal and iron ore lost most of their farms and became largely industrial and commercial. Observers at mid-century remarked on the paradox of an industrial revolution in which a number of regions became increasingly rural, even as industrial production continued to mount. Not only did the nineteenth century's revolution in industry and trade create urbanization, it produced a certain "ruralization" as well.

What mainly attracted people to the city was the promise of jobs, although for some, the lure of new ideas and experiences, plus the freedom from village and familial constraints, proved significant as well. Once people arrived in the city, what they did there depended on the kind of town it was, the skills they possessed, and, not insignificantly, their gender. In purely industrial towns, often dominated by one or two huge firms, people tended to work in large manufacturing plants. More than half the population of Le Creusot (France)—some 12,500 people—labored in the blast furnaces, rolling mills, and engineering workshops of the Schneider metallurgical company. Similarly, the iron-making firm Krupp turned Essen (Prussia) into what was essentially a company town as its workforce grew from 72 employees in 1848 to 18,000 by 1873.

In national and provincial capitals, by contrast, individuals held a wide variety of jobs in everything from heavy industry in the suburbs to small workshops close to the center of town, where skilled craftsmen catered to the growing numbers of middle-class consumers. Construction occupied a great many people during this time of urban growth; in Paris of the 1850s and 1860s, some 20 percent of the labor force belonged to the building trades. Throughout the second half of the nineteenth century, one of the largest categories of employment in major cities was domestic service, a profession that in some countries occupied as many as one-third of all urban women who worked for wages.

The other two most important female occupations involved clothing and cloth. In France, 21 percent of all women workers earned their living from garment

≡ **Paris in the Mid-Nineteenth Century.** This Charles Marville photograph was commissioned by Baron Georges-Eugène Haussmann, who oversaw the massive redevelopment of Paris between 1852 and 1870. Haussmann intended the photo to document the run-down character of mid-century Paris and the need for new housing, widened streets, and a more sanitary, healthful environment.

making and another 20 percent from textile production. The rest found employment as shopkeepers and shop assistants, office clerks, and in a variety of other, usually low-paid, jobs. Women continued to earn considerably less than men but still found themselves the object of resentment from male colleagues who believed that competition from women lowered their wages and deprived other men of jobs.

Major European cities grew so rapidly during this period that housing could not keep up. Apartments were divided and subdivided, creating living quarters of ever-shrinking size. In 1875, 40 percent of all urban households in Germany made do with a single room. Another consequence of the influx of working people was the segregation of cities by social class. Certain areas became largely and distinctively working-class, while others grew more exclusive and well-to-do. As a result, people from different levels of the social hierarchy interacted with one another less as neighbors who experienced certain similar concerns and more as members of isolated castes who increasingly viewed each other with fear, suspicion, and even contempt. Most interactions now took place within the vertical— and inherently unequal—grid of work. The urban redevelopment that transformed Paris during this period only reinforced such social and cultural shifts.

The Redevelopment of Paris

When Louis Napoléon Bonaparte declared himself Emperor of the French in 1852, Paris still looked like a medieval city. Most streets were so narrow that the sun seldom peeked in between the buildings, and people and products moved only with great difficulty. Paris was choked by its expanding population and the goods and services it created. The city's great architectural monuments—the Notre Dame cathedral, the Tuileries Palace, the Invalides memorial to Napoleon Bonaparte—were obscured behind a hodgepodge of ramshackle dwellings and shops. Worse, Parisians were drowning in an excess of sewage that had nowhere to go but into the streets.

Louis Napoléon was determined to change all that. His objectives were to open the city to the free flow of traffic, while constructing an urban environment both livable and monumental, comfortable for its inhabitants, and worthy of his illustrious imperial name. To direct the redevelopment of Paris, Napoleon III chose Georges-Eugène Haussmann (1809–1891), a gruff, dictatorial civil servant perfectly suited to operate under his authoritarian Second Empire (1852–1870), which valued order and efficiency over parliamentary procedure and democratic consultation. Louis Napoléon gave Haussmann a mandate to transform Paris, and the new Prefect intended to do just that, ignoring whatever opposition he faced (see Map 8.2).

Haussmann viewed the city as a living organism, and he sought to bring it light and air, while giving its streets and buildings an orderly uniformity characteristic of his scientific age. He planned to carve an interconnected series of broad boulevards through the capital's maze of narrow, winding streets and to punctuate the urban mass with a network of scenic parks. The boulevards, Haussmann hoped, would allow the government to launch troops into rebellious neighborhoods and nip revolutions and riots in the bud. He lined his new *grands boulevards* with sidewalks so wide as to create a kind of outdoor living area for the city. Cafes spilled out onto

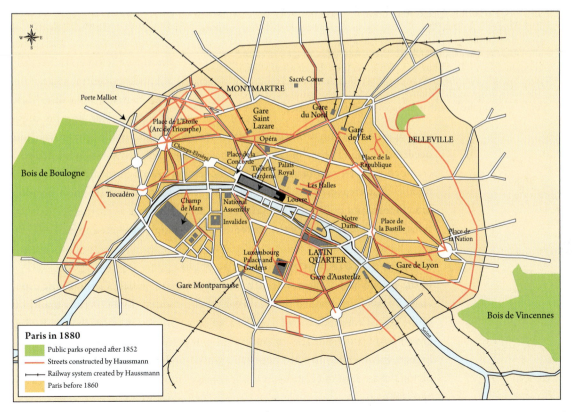

MAP 8.2 Paris in 1880

≡ **The New Paris.** This celebrated Impressionist painting by Gustave Caillebotte, *Paris Street; Rainy Day* (1877), shows the new broad boulevards and uniform apartment buildings of Haussmann's Paris. The painting also depicts the alienation a great many people felt in this new city of huge spaces and anonymous crowds. Although walking together, the man and woman in the foreground are staring into the distance rather than turned toward each other. The other people in the painting seem to be lonely figures or pairs huddled under their umbrellas and unconnected with anyone else.

these pedestrian thorough-fares, filling them with tables from which people could observe the spectacle of city life, as if seated in a theater. The boulevards and their sidewalks became so significant a feature of Parisian life that the writer Charles Baudelaire (1821–1867) immortalized them in one of his most famous essays, "The Painter of Modern Life" (1863), which celebrates the urban display and the liberating, if alienating, anonymity of the modern metropolis.

The redevelopment of Paris became a model for similar efforts in Vienna and other European cities. In virtually all of them, central areas of the city received a healthy dose of light and air, new buildings went up, and a certain urban charm was restored. But most of these improvements occurred at the expense of the poor, who often found themselves relocated to a cramped and dirty no man's land sandwiched between a beautified city and the middle-class areas beyond. Wealthier people now found urban life more pleasant than before, and political elites saw the redeveloped cities as shrines to their nations' riches and symbols of the power they increasingly projected abroad.

Europe's Worldwide Economic Role

In the second half of the nineteenth century, Belgian, French, German, and especially British firms flooded the world with their products. By 1870, fully one-third of the planet's manufactured goods came from Britain, its sales to Asia having grown by 600 percent and to Australia by a factor of thirteen since 1850. The French, meanwhile, invested heavily in Russia and the Ottoman Empire, multiplying the amount of capital sent to these places more than tenfold between 1850 and 1880.

These striking figures translated into a rapidly growing degree of British, and to a lesser extent continental European, power over Asia, Africa, and other less developed parts of the world. With economic strength came mounting military power and the ability to force open markets in China and Japan, countries that had long resisted extensive economic contacts with the West. As we have seen, China and Britain went to war in 1839 over the latter's effort to sell opium produced in its Indian colony to Chinese consumers—against the wishes of the Chinese government. The so-called **Opium War** dragged on until 1842, when the Chinese were forced to relinquish Hong Kong to the British and open Shanghai and four other Chinese ports to their merchants. The Chinese also had to make the humiliating concession of **extraterritoriality**—the right to apply British law to British subjects arrested in China. The British, together with other Europeans, won further concessions in 1858 after taking advantage of the Taiping Rebellion (1851–1864). This terrible Chinese civil war was sparked by a massive, religion-tinged uprising against the ruling Qing dynasty, itself weakened by the loss of prestige and authority occasioned by the new European ascendency.

This ascendency produced a new **globalization** in which Europe's great powers could now impose limits on indigenous elites. As much as Chinese entrepreneurs, for example, tried to develop modern industry in their country, they often found themselves thwarted by the European, American, and eventually Japanese firms implanted there. With their access to global markets and ability to import raw materials from around the world, foreign companies possessed powerful advantages over Chinese ones. Worse, China's dependence on foreign capital further sapped its economic strength and political independence. China was not completely hamstrung by foreigners, as its businessmen and workers excelled in making silk, paper, and cotton goods, among other things, but these industries tended to have low profit margins and depended on a mass of low-paid laborers too poor to inject much demand into the marketplace.

China at least remained an independent country; in the parts of the world colonized by Europeans in the late nineteenth century (see Chapter 9), the situation was even worse. British, French, and Dutch colonizers imposed tight—although not airtight—limits on the development of indigenous industry and commerce and controlled most of the trade between the mother country and the colonies. The great exception was India's textile industry, which managed to produce low-end cotton goods at competitive prices, if only because Indian workers earned rock-bottom wages. As for peasants, in India and elsewhere, Europe's economic prowess forced them to market food and industrial raw materials at the low prices beneficial to Europeans (see Map 8.3).

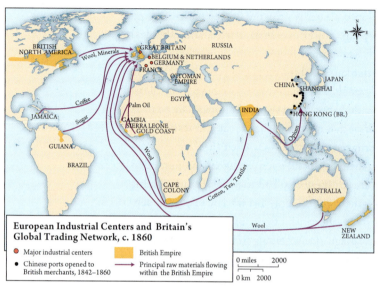

European Industrial Centers and Britain's
Global Trading Network, c. 1860

● Major industrial centers
● Chinese ports opened to
British merchants, 1842–1860

British Empire

→ Principal raw materials flowing
within the British Empire

0 miles   2000
0 km   2000

≡ **MAP 8.3**   European Industrial Centers and Britain's Global Trading Network, c. 1860

Political Change

Britain's ability to force open the vast Chinese market and to subdue this ancient empire struck a great many Britons as confirmation of their country's extraordinary influence and power. But since that power was not widely shared within Britain, the Chinese situation also highlighted the hierarchies of British society and government. Landed gentlemen continued to rule, and wealth was concentrated in the hands of a small group of elite aristocrats and industrial magnates, despite some mid-century improvement in the fortunes of working people. Rural Britain continued to be vastly overrepresented in Parliament, and 80 percent of the adult male population and all women were still denied the right to vote.

In 1865, these inequalities gave rise to a new round of agitation for electoral reform. A coalition of middle- and working-class reformers established the Reform League, which staged a series of potent demonstrations calling for universal manhood suffrage. The Liberal prime minister, William Gladstone (1809–1898), and his Conservative opponent, Benjamin Disraeli (1804–1881), sparred over which party would best respond to the call for electoral reform. Against all expectations, Disraeli's proposed reforms proved more ambitious—and more popular—than Gladstone's, and the Liberal government gave way to a Conservative one. Disraeli's Reform Act of 1867 added a million people to the electoral rolls, nearly doubling the number of eligible voters and enfranchising half of all residents of towns and cities, including a fair number of working men. The rural electorate, however, remained mostly middle- and upper-class.

Why did the Conservative politician produce the more radical bill? Part of the answer has to do with the intense political rivalry between Disraeli and Gladstone and the Conservative's desire to succeed where the Liberal had failed. Disraeli also seems to have believed that by giving working people the right to vote, the Conservative Party would earn their support and that a popular conservatism would keep a surging Liberal Party at bay.

Prosperity and Empire in France

Unlike Britain, Napoleon III's France allowed all adult men to vote. His Second Empire was not, however, a full-fledged democracy but rather a hybrid regime that brought authoritarianism and democracy together for the first time. In some ways, the political system of Napoleon III foreshadowed the populist regimes of Argentina's Juan Perón (1946–1955) and Hungary's Viktor Orbán (2010–).

On the authoritarian side, Napoleon III reduced France's parliament to a timid debating society with little more than ceremonial power. He intensified the centralized administrative system initiated by Napoleon Bonaparte and used it to harass opposition candidates and censor the press. On the economic front, his regime used its authoritarian powers to implicate itself in the country's business affairs, participating in the development of railroads, promoting certain industries, and encouraging the growth of investment banking. It went so far as to negotiate the reduction of tariffs with Britain without consulting top business leaders and over their strenuous objections.

Such were the Second Empire's authoritarian designs, but its democratic side is what made the regime so novel. When Napoleon III declared himself emperor in 1852, he preserved the universal manhood suffrage enacted by the republic he had overthrown. France remained the lone country, save for the tiny Swiss republic, which gave all adult males the right to vote. (The "democratic" United States still excluded millions of enslaved African Americans.) That Louis Napoléon was willing to allow all men to vote regardless of their economic status shows both the appeal of manhood suffrage and the extent to which he sought to attract public support. He attempted to add to that support by creating a massive program of public works designed to stimulate the economy and provide jobs for the tens of thousands of French workers who suffered from chronic unemployment and who might otherwise have been prone to rebellion.

Napoleon III's approach might have succeeded had the relative prosperity of the 1850s continued indefinitely and had French peasants and workers been as politically unsophisticated as he believed. But prosperity soon yielded to the gyrations of the business cycle, and ordinary people did not remain impressed for very long by the largely ersatz democracy the Second Empire had given them. More than a half century of revolution and counterrevolution, with the mass politicization that had accompanied them, committed many working people to the very civil liberties the Second Empire had abolished. They knew that the right to vote divorced from freedom of expression and the ability to openly oppose government candidates had only limited value. It would not be long before working people joined with middle-class liberals and republicans in advocating genuine democratic reform.

The Crimean War

In foreign policy, Louis Napoléon sought to restore some of the old Napoleonic glory to France's international standing. His first effort on the diplomatic front was to inject France into the complex relations between Russia and the crumbling Ottoman Empire. These relations necessarily involved Austria, which bordered on the two contending powers, and Prussia, which shared a frontier with Russia and had close diplomatic ties with St. Petersburg. Britain, for its part, had long been locked in a military, commercial, and diplomatic struggle to keep Russia out of Constantinople and especially out of the strategic straits connecting the Black and Mediterranean Seas. Above all, Britain wanted to prevent the Russian navy, stuck much of the year in icy harbors, from gaining warm-water ports and the ability to confront Britain's Mediterranean fleet.

France entered the fray by siding with Catholic monks in their dispute with Orthodox Christian priests over who governed the Holy Places of Ottoman-controlled Palestine. Napoleon III volunteered his aid in hopes of winning the support of ardent French Catholics suspicious of his family's revolutionary heritage. His longer-term goals were to loosen both the Ottoman and the Russian hold over parts of the Balkans and Eastern Europe and to make France the patron and protector of Catholics in these regions.

Tsar Nicholas I was incensed over Napoleon III's meddling in Ottoman-Christian affairs; for nearly a century, Russia had exercised an informal jurisdiction over the Ottoman Empire's Christian communities, many of whose members, like the majority of Russians, belonged to the Orthodox faith. In January 1853, Tsar Nicholas I sent two army divisions toward the Ottoman border to pressure the sultan to renounce the French intervention and support Russia's claims.

Backed by the British ambassador in Constantinople, the sultan rejected the tsar's demands. St. Petersburg responded by occupying the Ottoman Empire's Danubian principalities (later to become Romania). At this point, the French and British feared the Russian occupation might escalate into an effort to capture Constantinople and even an assault into Europe via the Balkans. In October 1853, the sultan declared war on Russia; six months later, the British and French entered the conflict on his side.

Dubbed the **Crimean War** (1853–1856) after the Russian territory (see Map 8.4) on which much of the fighting took place, the conflict was notable for the incompetence, suffering, and brutality displayed on all sides. The fighting was visible to noncombatants because Crimea was the world's first war covered in real time by newspaper correspondents, mainly from British papers, who could beam their dispatches to London and then Paris by telegraph. That people could read about battles less than a day after they occurred gave the war an unprecedented immediacy to people in Britain and France. At first, they cheered their soldiers with patriotic zeal, but as the conflict reached a stalemate and reports of hideous human suffering appeared on the front pages, public opinion began to sour.

It soon became clear that far more soldiers were dying from inadequate food, shelter, and medical supplies than from the fighting itself. Influential people in Britain and France began to complain about the situation, but few openly opposed the war or tried to alleviate the suffering it had caused. The one notable exception was Florence Nightingale (1820–

≡ **MAP 8.4**   The Crimean War, 1853–1856

1910), a well-to-do and well-educated English woman who embraced nursing both to address the humanitarian crisis and to escape the constraints of British society, which under ordinary circumstances, consigned middle-class women to the home.

In the extremity of war, Nightingale gained the government's permission to train a team of nurses and take them to the Crimean theater. Once there, she saw firsthand the terrible consequences of a British officer corps in which aristocratic birth, not military skill, opened the door to high military rank. Not only were a great many officers incompetent, but they also cared little for the well-being of their troops. Tens of thousands of British soldiers suffered unnecessarily from malnutrition, disease, exposure, and lamentable medical care.

Nightingale could not solve the problems created by her country's military malfeasance, but she helped save so many lives that she quickly became a national hero. Her work in the Crimean War as well as her best-selling book *Notes on Nursing* (1859) did much to raise the status of her profession and improve care for the sick. Her prestige later made her an effective advocate of military reform. In all her

≡ **Three Crimean Invalids.** This powerful 1855 photograph by Joseph Cundall and Robert Howell eschews the idealized images of warfare still common in the mid-nineteenth century. Here we see the naked reality of war, with its terrible, disabling injuries and traumatic consequences even for those who survived.

work, Nightingale became a model for women throughout Europe who wanted to take the caring, nurturing role that society reserved for them and apply it outside the confines of the family and in the realm of public life.

As significant as Nightingale's medical efforts were, she alleviated only a small fraction of the suffering in Crimea. Some 600,000 people died in that war, mostly of disease. Britain lost 22 percent of its army, France 30 percent, and the Russians half. Although the British and French prevailed after nearly two years of fighting, they did so with a notable absence of glory. The British poet laureate, Alfred, Lord Tennyson (1809–1892), captured both the selfless bravery and the murderous futility of the war in his famous narrative poem "The Charge of the Light Brigade" (1854). The allies were victorious not because their armies fought better, but largely because Western Europe now possessed a railway network that permitted Britain and France to move soldiers and supplies rapidly to the front. The Russians, backward economically and lacking a railway system, took four times as long to ship reinforcements in.

The Eclipse of Russia

After the Crimean War, Russia had to relinquish its informal control over the Danubian principalities, and this development set the stage for the independence of Romania in 1878. Russia's defeat in Crimea revealed to the Russians themselves and to their European neighbors the extent to which its power had been eclipsed. Russia's principal claim to fame had long been its military stature, but now that success in war required a potent economy, its failure to industrialize and inefficient serf-based agriculture reduced its strength relative to the Western powers.

To remedy this situation, a cadre of Russian officials examined their army and economy to pinpoint the needed reforms. The military's essential problem, beyond its outmoded transport system, was low morale, which resulted from a conscription process that relied almost exclusively on Russia's serfs. Each serf drafted into the army was condemned to serve for twenty-five years (in 1855 this was reduced to fifteen years), and although promised emancipation at the end, draftees found this dim prospect demotivating at best. How many would survive the decades of harsh barracks conditions and dangerous battles to take advantage of freedom at the end? To make matters worse, the low productivity of Russia's system of unfree labor limited the number of serfs who could be spared from the land and conscripted into the army, thus restricting its size and strength.

The solution to the problems of military ineffectiveness and low agricultural productivity seemed to be one and the same: the emancipation of the serfs. Against widespread aristocratic resistance, Tsar Alexander II decreed the freedom of serfs in April 1861, two years before Abraham Lincoln's Emancipation Proclamation. In the short term, neither military effectiveness nor agricultural productivity improved dramatically, but the freeing of serfs represented a major humanitarian advance. As in the American case, emancipation also revealed the newfound ability of the central government to impose its will on elites—nobles in Russia and plantation owners in the United States. Landowners were forced for economic and moral reasons to give up the ownership, or quasi-ownership, of human beings, although in Russia redemption payments were required from the former serfs.

Following the Crimean War, Russia reformed its judicial system along Western European lines and relaxed certain forms of censorship, but Alexander refused to align Russia's economy with the West's. He did not give the emancipated serfs farmland to cultivate as private property, but rather placed it in the hands of peasant communes, whose members farmed the land collectively. Russian officials feared that peasant landowners would sell their property and join a rootless, potentially revolutionary working class. Peasants thus remained tied to the land and largely unavailable to work in factories, which developed at a glacial pace until the late nineteenth century. As communal farmers rather than individual proprietors, the peasants felt little incentive to innovate or work harder for productivity gains. As a result, Russia continued to lag behind its European neighbors in both agricultural and industrial development.

National Unification

Despite its horrific toll, the Crimean War changed the European balance of power very little. It did, however, confirm a series of developments with the potential to alter that balance: the eclipse of Russia and the Ottoman Empire, the growing autonomy of the Ottomans' Balkan provinces, Britain's hold over the Mediterranean, France's new international ambitions, and aspirations for national unification, especially in Italy.

The Unification of Italy

The revolutions of 1848 had left Italy's territorial map essentially unchanged. The region remained a collection of kingdoms and duchies, some independent—like the Kingdom of the Two Sicilies and the Papal States—and some under the control of the Austrian Empire, including Venice and Lombardy. Nevertheless, the aspiration for national unity widely expressed in 1848 remained, and Count Camillo di Cavour (1810–1861), the prime minister of the independent kingdom of Piedmont-Sardinia, wanted to achieve the unification of Italy under Piedmont's control. He had committed his kingdom to the Crimean War on the allied side, hoping to earn the great powers' respect and enlist Napoleon III's support for the expansion of Piedmont at Austria's expense. Cavour understood that Austria, which held key territory in northern Italy, presented the primary obstacle to achieving his goal and that France was his most logical ally among the great powers. Napoleon III would be eager to weaken Austria, his country's traditional enemy, and to assert French power once again.

In the summer of 1858, Napoleon III and Cavour secretly agreed to a military alliance in which the French promised to help Piedmont oust Austria from its strongholds in northern Italy. In exchange, France would receive Piedmont's province of Savoy, where most people spoke French, and its beautiful Mediterranean city of Nice, both bordering France. When the Austrians learned of these plans in early 1859, they threatened a preemptive attack on Piedmont. This ill-advised move gave Napoleon III and Cavour an excuse to begin the hostilities they had planned. The ensuing conflict was short but horribly costly in human lives. In the two major battles of Magenta and Solferino (June–July 1859), the casualty rate exceeded that of the murderous Crimean War. European statesmen expressed horror over the devastation of the battlefield; they would soon introduce rules for the humane treatment of enemy soldiers.

The combined French and Piedmontese forces won decisively at Magenta and Solferino, but their victory alarmed Prussia, whose leaders worried that French forces might move into German parts of the Austrian Empire. To head off this possibility, German troops mobilized near the border with France and threatened to invade. At this point, French officials began to doubt the wisdom of pressing further into Italy, especially since the pope had protested vigorously against the French intervention. Napoleon decided to end the fighting before the Piedmontese victory over Austria was complete.

In the resulting peace treaty, Austria awarded the province of Lombardy to Piedmont, but little else changed, at least officially: Venice and its surrounding region remained in Austrian hands. But advocates of Italian unification throughout the small, independent kingdoms and duchies in the northern and central

Italian Unification	
1848	Revolutions throughout Europe
1853	Count Camillo di Cavour, prime minister of Piedmont-Sardinia, allies with France and Britain in the Crimean War
June–July 1859	French and Piedmontese forces defeat Austrians in battles of Magenta and Solferino
	Austria cedes control of Lombardy
Spring 1860	Garibaldi's red shirts campaign victoriously in southern Italy
	Cavour cedes Nice to France
October 1860	Armies of Garibaldi and King Victor Emmanuel II of Piedmont-Sardinia meet near Rome
February 1861	Kingdom of Italy declared with Victor Emmanuel II as its king
1866	Italy seizes Venice from Austria
1870	Italy captures Rome and makes Rome its new capital

parts of the peninsula took advantage of the unsettled conditions created by the war to oust their rulers. Wittingly or unwittingly, they then allowed Piedmontese troops to occupy their lands, which became part of a much-expanded Kingdom of Piedmont-Sardinia.

Meanwhile, Giuseppe Garibaldi (1807–1882), the nationalist leader legendary for wearing a long red shirt and for his mastery of unconventional warfare, set his sights on the island of Sicily and the bottom half of the Italian "boot." Garibaldi shared with Cavour and the Piedmontese king, Victor Emmanuel II, a common aspiration for Italian unity, despite their ideological differences: the guerilla leader preferred a republic, the Piedmontese leaders a constitutional monarchy.

In the spring of 1860, Garibaldi embarked for Sicily and then Naples, where his "red shirts" defeated the conservative monarchy that ruled the Kingdom of the Two Sicilies. When Garibaldi prepared to march north to Rome, capital of the independent Papal States, both Cavour and Napoleon III became alarmed. As always, Louis Napoléon worried about the reaction of French Catholics, who would blame him if French soldiers stationed in Rome failed to protect the pope. Cavour, for his part, feared that a red-shirt victory in Rome would shift control over Italian unification from himself to Garibaldi. To regain the initiative, Cavour had Piedmontese troops under Victor Emmanuel's command race toward Rome to prevent Garibaldi from entering the city. The two armies met on October 26, 1860, and Garibaldi, patriot that he was, agreed to defer to Victor Emmanuel and

≡ **Giuseppe Garibaldi.** An ardent nationalist and skilled guerilla fighter, Garibaldi played a major role in the Italian unification movement or Risorgimento. As a young man in the 1830s, he joined Giuseppe Mazzini's nationalist movement, and later, during the Revolution of 1848, won key victories for Milan and Rome. These victories were short-lived, and not until 1860 did Italy complete the unification process (except for Rome) begun in 1848. Garibaldi, however, was forced to take a back seat to the Piedmontese king, who became the ruler of a new Italian nation

give up his fight. In a joyous ceremony with Garibaldi at his side, Victor Emmanuel proclaimed himself the ruler of a new Kingdom of Italy.

All that remained was to bring Venice and Rome into the fold. In 1866, the new Italy allied with Bismarck and seized Venice from the Austrians. Four years later, Prussia's victory over France in the Franco-Prussian War (see below) would force Napoleon III to withdraw his troops from Rome. Defenseless, the pope saw the last bastion of his temporal power fall to invading Italian forces. Rome quickly regained its ancient status as capital of Italy, and the pope became, as he put it, "the prisoner of the Vatican," which remained officially independent of the new Italian state. Although Pius IX refused to recognize the new kingdom, the unification of Italy was complete—at least as a political-military process. The cultural unification of Italy's disparate provinces, many speaking a dialect incomprehensible to the others, would proceed gradually at best (see Map 8.5).

Throughout this Italian adventure, Cavour's diplomacy was brilliant, Garibaldi's military campaigns the stuff of legend. But none of their efforts would have succeeded without the aid of two of Europe's greatest powers: France and Prussia. Both spurred Italian unification in the pursuit of their own national interests; in the Prussian case, Bismarck's own drive for German unity helped complete the Italian task.

The Unification of Germany

The failure of revolution in 1848 may have frustrated the nationalist political aspirations of middle-class German liberals, but it did nothing to prevent the economic transformation from which many of them benefited handsomely. By the late 1850s, this transformation had given the Prussian middle class so much economic strength that it enabled liberals to vie anew for the power denied them in 1848. It also gave Prussia key advantages in its competition for domination in German-speaking Europe.

Since the late eighteenth century, Prussia's national income had increased at twice the rate of Austria's, and by the 1860s, Prussia outstripped Austria by a factor of between 5 and 10 in coal production, stream engines, railroads, and almost every other measure of industrial development. Austria sought to compensate for its relative economic backwardness by maintaining its longstanding control over a large, all-inclusive Germany, a *Grossdeutschland* (greater Germany) based on the loose federation of states established in 1815. The opponents of this greater German approach mostly consisted of liberal nationalists with Protestant beliefs, who wanted a smaller, more compact Germany, a *Kleindeutschland*, led by the largely Protestant Prussia and excluding Austria. The Austrian (or Habsburg) Empire had no place in Germany, its opponents argued, not only because the empire's population was predominantly Catholic but also because it contained more non-Germans than Germans. How, it was argued, could Austria be trusted with

≡ **MAP 8.5**   The Unification of Italy

German leadership when it had always to take account of the needs of Poles, Czechs, Italians, Hungarians, Romanians, and a variety of other nationalities?

In the early 1860s, Prussian liberals decided they now had the strength to complete part of what the Revolution of 1848 had left undone, namely the creation of a constitutional Prussian state. The first step was to limit the king's extensive powers by seizing control over Prussia's military budget. King Wilhelm wanted to skew military funding in favor of the regular army at the expense of the citizens' militia, which the liberals sought to protect. They believed the king's budget would turn an already privileged army into a state within a state and unduly benefit an officer class contemptuous of the civilian population.

The liberals repeatedly asserted their power by refusing to approve any funds for the military, and King Wilhelm repeatedly dissolved parliament and called new elections. In each successive ballot, the electorate returned an ever-larger liberal majority. By 1862, the liberal advantage had become so secure that the government became hopelessly gridlocked over the military issue. In desperation, the king appointed as his new prime minister Otto von Bismarck, a man known for bold political moves. Bismarck's charge was to overcome the parliamentary opposition by any means necessary.

The new prime minister's initial approach was simply to ignore the parliament, appropriating funds for the army without the body's approval. His actions were manifestly illegal, but for Bismarck everything was in essence a question of power, and he doubted that the parliament possessed the power to stop him. After all, it was he and not the parliament who controlled the army, and without force on their side what were the liberals to do? Bismarck understood that his policy carried some risks. The liberals might, for example, mobilize popular support against the government. To preempt them and win public opinion to his side, he sent the army to war, using its victories to stir the nationalist passions felt by a great many Prussians, whether middle-class liberals or working people.

His first triumph came against neighboring Denmark, from which Bismarck decided to wrest the tiny duchies of Schleswig, mostly Danish, and Holstein, mostly German. Traditionally, the two provinces belonged to the Danish king, but not to Denmark itself. And to further complicate the situation, Holstein resided within the boundaries of the German Confederation. The British statesman Lord Palmerston reportedly said, "Only three people have ever really understood the Schleswig-Holstein business—the Prince Consort, who is dead, a German professor, who has gone mad, and I, who have forgotten all about it." Bismarck claimed both provinces for Prussia and Austria, and in January 1864 he seized them by armed force. This military success boosted Bismarck's standing at home and built popular support for his policy of illegally funding the military over the parliament's protests.

Bismarck's next objective was to settle the competition with Austria and at the same time overpower his liberal opposition for good—once again by going to war. "With the first clash between Prussian and Austrian troops," declared a liberal leader, "the Prussian Progressive [liberal] Party will be silenced." Throughout 1865, Bismarck picked a series of diplomatic fights with Austria, all of which could have been resolved peacefully had he wanted to. But Bismarck preferred military hostilities, for they gave his superior army an excuse to occupy the independent north German states and invade Austria's allies in southern Germany, most of which supported Austria in fear of Prussian domination. After subduing these smaller states, Prussian forces moved on to the major, and ultimately decisive,

German Unification	
1815	Congress of Vienna establishes loose confederation of German states
1834	Creation of German customs union (*Zollverein*)
1848	Revolutions throughout Europe
1860s	Prussia's industrial development outstrips Austria's by a factor of between five and ten
1862	Bismarck becomes prime minister of Prussia
1864	Prussia wrests duchies of Schleswig and Holstein from Denmark
1866	Prussia crushes Austrian forces at Battle of Sadowa
1870–1871	Prussia defeats France in Franco-Prussian War
1871	King Wilhelm I proclaimed emperor of a united Germany
	Bismarck becomes chancellor

battle with the Habsburg army amassed in Bohemia. The Austrians enjoyed numerical superiority, but the Prussians were equipped with the innovative "needle gun," a weapon capable of firing three times faster than anything their opponents possessed. Prussia's industrial prowess had enabled it to build the deadly weapon and, thanks to its new railroad network, to move huge numbers of troops to the battlefield with what was then lightning speed. The Austrians found themselves overwhelmed, and Bismarck crushed them in the battle of Sadowa (Königgrätz in German) in July 1866.

Prussia's victory enabled Bismarck to oust Austria from German affairs and to collect twenty-three north German states into its own much-expanded domain. Austria's allies in southern Germany, also defeated in the war, would soon find themselves integrated into a new Prussian-led German Empire created in the wake of the Franco-Prussian War (1870–1871).

If Bismarck seems to have planned the conflict with Austria, it is less clear that he intended to go to war against France, at least immediately. Unlike the Austrian emperor, Napoleon III possessed a battle-tested army, having fought recently in Crimea and Italy, and Bismarck considered it risky to attack France with a fighting force depleted by the military campaigns of 1866. But by 1870, Napoleon III had become unpopular at home, and his military looked vulnerable. In July, Bismarck goaded the French emperor into issuing a declaration of war, and once hostilities broke out, the French army succumbed to Prussian forces in six humiliating weeks. Bismarck's forces occupied a wide swath of northern France and laid siege to Paris. The Prussian leader annexed

≡ **Prussian Military Supremacy.** Prussia's vibrant industrial economy of the second half of the nineteenth century gave it a huge technological advantage over Austrian forces in 1866 and the French army in 1870. In particular, the "needle gun," which could fire three times faster than the best Austrian weapons, was crucial to Prussia's victory over a numerically superior Austrian army. So was Prussia's railway network, which allowed Bismarck to quickly move soldiers to the front and overwhelm the Austrian forces, still thin on the ground.

the rich and strategic eastern French provinces of Alsace and Lorraine, and in early 1871, when France finally admitted defeat, Bismarck made King Wilhelm the emperor (*Kaiser* in German, from the Roman title Caesar) of a vast German Empire. Bismarck's new, unified Germany arced north and east from central France and pointed deep into Russian territory. It immediately became Europe's dominant power (see Map 8.6).

Consequences of the German Unification

The two key elements of Bismarck's new European order turned on a redesigned Austrian Empire and a new republican regime in France, both with reduced ability to shape the continent's affairs. A much-weakened Austrian Empire took new form as the "Dual Monarchy" of Austria-Hungary, and in France, Napoleon III's Second Empire gave way to what was to become a liberal, democratic regime. The Austrian emperor remained in place, but Louis Napoléon found himself a prisoner of the Prussians, who exiled him to Britain, where he died in oblivion in 1873.

The Creation of Austria-Hungary, 1867

The Habsburg monarchy had long faced the challenges of ruling a diverse empire with many languages, religions, and traditions of local autonomy. The Hungarians, as we have seen, had rebelled in 1848, creating an independent state that succumbed to the Habsburgs only after the Russians intervened militarily against it. The Austrian victory in 1849 did little to blunt the budding aspirations for recognition, even autonomy, of Hungarians, Poles, Czechs, Croats, Serbs, Slovenes, and Italians. Their elites and, to some extent, ordinary people had gradually developed a sense of themselves as belonging to distinct nations, each with its own language, history, literature, customs, and folklore. In places where no written languages existed, nationalists created them out of peasant dialects and then taught them in

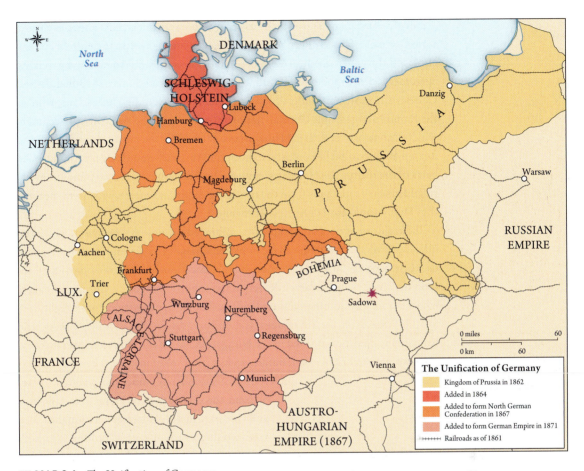

MAP 8.6   The Unification of Germany

schools. Meanwhile, scholars invented histories that supposedly traced a nation's continuous existence back into the distant mists of time. In Bohemia and some other regions, a fair number of people rejected the efforts of nationalists to assign them to one national category or the other. Still, the idea that separate "nations" existed within the Habsburg Empire had made considerable progress by the 1860s.

In the wake of Italian independence and Prussian military victories, the empire's increasingly self-aware national groups became restive. The Hungarians and Croats, in particular, demanded the reestablishment of their Diets (parliaments); in 1865, the Habsburg government granted their wishes. These concessions angered the empire's ethnic Germans, many of them liberals, who feared that national particularism would undermine the liberal, constitutional government centered in Vienna and set their own nationalist aspirations back.

But the Austrians' defeat by Prussia in 1866 and their subsequent exclusion from German affairs reduced ethnic German influence within the empire and encouraged the government in Vienna to cut its losses. It did so chiefly by making agreements with moderate nationalists in Hungary and later in Bohemia and Galicia. The most important of the agreements involved the Hungarians, who, as the Empire's largest non-German nationality, were granted their own government with full control over internal Hungarian affairs. Only the ministers of defense and foreign affairs would be common to both the Austrian- and Hungarian-controlled parts of the realm. The Habsburg emperor became king of Hungary and in theory ruled Hungary separately from the rest of the Austrian Empire, which now became the "**Dual Monarchy**" of Austria-Hungary.

The majority of the Hungarian elite embraced the new arrangement, which did little, however, for the Empire's other nationalities. The Poles obtained the right to use their language in local government and education, but received no political autonomy. The Czechs, meanwhile, remained subordinate to the German-speakers who traditionally dominated their lands, although Czech nationalists fought hard for the primacy of their language and culture. As for the Slovaks, Croats, and Romanians, they now resided in the Hungarian half of the monarchy and received no more national rights than before; in fact, their circumstances deteriorated, as they no longer enjoyed the emperor's protection from Hungarian political power or from the dominance of Hungarian language and culture. Austria-Hungary's nationality situation would remain unsettled into the twentieth century and beyond (see Map 8.7).

The New French Republic

Although some parts of France possessed their own local languages or dialects and distinctive regional cultures, the country had no organized national minorities to contend with, unlike Austria-Hungary. Still, the French military losses of summer and fall 1870 capsized its political system. On September 4, 1870, a group of republicans led by Léon Gambetta (1838–1882), a brilliant orator and spokesman for political and social change, stepped in to fill the vacuum of power left by Prussia's capture of Napoleon III. In a bloodless revolution, they established the Third Republic, a regime dedicated to the ideals

MAP 8.7 Nationalities in Austria-Hungary, c. 1880

Nationalities in Austria–Hungary, c. 1880

Croat	Magyar	Serb
Czech	Pole	Slovak
German	Romanian	Slovene
Italian	Ruthenian	Equal Croat/Serb

— Boundary of Austria–Hungary
— Boundary between Austria and Hungary

of the French Revolution. The regime was also dedicated, at least for a time, to pursuing the war against Prussia.

Determined not to surrender, even as Prussian troops laid siege to Paris, France's new leaders decided to move part of the government outside the occupied zone. In a dramatic escape from the besieged city, Gambetta boarded a hot-air balloon and floated away. Most Parisians had no choice but to remain in the city, and as the siege wore on, they lived under increasingly difficult circumstances; the Prussians refused to allow supplies into the capital. One famous cartoon from the period depicts a sizable crowd waiting to buy an allotment of meat at the "rat butcher." Not surprisingly, the people of Paris felt enormous hostility toward the Prussians. But, despite the worsening conditions, few wanted to give in. When a newly elected French parliament accepted the harsh peace agreement dictated by Bismarck in January 1871, a great many Parisians felt betrayed, especially those working- and lower-middle-class people who had suffered the most.

That sense of betrayal, along with frustration over the conservative cast of the new French legislature, revived the revolutionary passions dormant since 1851. On March 18, 1871, insurrectionaries barricaded the streets of Paris's working-class districts and quickly gained control of the city. Well-to-do Parisians fled to the countryside and pledged allegiance to the new national parliament that had already established its headquarters in Versailles, the historic home of France's Bourbon kings.

An insurrectionary Paris now confronted a conservative parliament, and rebel leaders declared the French capital independent from the rest of France. They renamed it the **Paris Commune,** as the city's government was called during the French Revolution. Elections to the Commune's governing council were historic in that they voted in a significant number of working-class people—making up perhaps 50 percent of the council. The Commune also brought several women leaders to the fore. Louise Michel (1830–1905), a schoolteacher who had come to Paris in the 1850s, wrote and spoke forcefully for women's equality, as did André Leo (1824–1900), a novelist and journalist. Both argued that women should be paid the same wages as men and that governments needed to take into account women's dual roles as mothers and workers. Along with other like-minded leaders, they established cooperative workshops in which women made uniforms and other clothing for the Commune and played a major role in supporting and defending the residents of a city under siege.

The Commune, surrounded now by French government forces based in Versailles, lived on borrowed time. On May 21, nine weeks after the declaration of Parisian independence, government troops attacked the city. For one long, bloody week, fighting raged street by street and house by house. In an effort to

≡ **Karl Marx.** One of the great revolutionary thinkers and theorists of all time, Marx began his career as a journalist. He wrote for the left-wing press and composed engaging, intellectually rich accounts of the Revolutions of 1848 in France and Germany and of the Paris Commune. In his theoretical work, Marx maintained that although human beings were shaped by a multitude of forces acting on them, the most elemental of those forces had to do with the "mode of production." By this he meant the kind of economic system—feudal, capitalist, socialist—under which a given people lived.

Although **Marxism** had only a handful of adherents in the 1860s and 1870s, a half century later it would be one of the world's most influential ideological systems. Marx's ideas would prove especially appealing to trade union movements and working-class parties whose members sought alternatives to an economic system that seemed to give them short shrift and to forms of politics that kept that system afloat. Perhaps even more important, Marxism also provided a kind of quasi-religious solace to laboring men and women, who could take great comfort in the notion that they were history's chosen people.

Trade Unions, Women's Rights, and the Rise of Socialist Parties

To enact his revolutionary vision, Marx helped create in 1864 the International Working Men's Association, commonly known as the **First International**. The new organization brought together French and British labor leaders and, inspired by Marxist ideas, held that "the emancipation of the working class must be achieved by the working classes themselves." No longer were workers to form alliances with middle-class organizations or join bourgeois parties and political movements. By fighting for electoral reform in Britain and cooperating with republicans in France, working people, Marx believed, had sacrificed their own interests to champion those of the middle class. The latter, Marx maintained, wanted only piecemeal changes; the working-class First International sought nothing less than wholesale, revolutionary social transformation.

Although the original members of the First International were mostly British and French, it was labor leaders in Germany, Marx's home country, who conformed most closely to his views. In 1869, the radical journalist Wilhelm Liebknecht (1826–1900) together with the labor leader August Bebel (1840–1913) founded the Social Democratic Workers Party of Germany (SAPD) as an explicitly Marxist organization. When the SAPD combined with another working class party to form the Social Democratic Party of Germany (SPD, founded in 1875), the new organization inherited the Marxist orientation. It was not, however, a revolutionary party. The SPD's leaders gave little more than lip service to the idea of overthrowing the capitalist state, focusing instead on achieving socialism gradually through the work of labor unions and electoral politics. Socialism itself proved elusive, but by the early twentieth century, the SPD captured more votes than any other German party. It became Europe's largest and most powerful left-wing organization and owed much of its success to the appeal in Germany of Marxist ideas.

Unfortunately for Marx and Marxism, labor leaders outside Germany possessed ideas of their own. Britain's relatively moderate trade unionists sought to extend voting rights to members of the working classes. To achieve their goals, they regularly cooperated with middle-class democrats and combined small, disparate unions into large, relatively influential organizations. Not only did these combined unions represent workers in their relationship with management, they also served as mutual aid societies to provide for working people in sickness and old age. Union leaders thus had to become responsible and efficient managers, overseeing the growing sums of money contributed by their members. This role gave them a measure of respectability in middle-class circles and helped make skillful politicians of their leaders. In 1865, British trade unions were instrumental in creating the Reform League, which set the stage for Disraeli's Reform Act of 1867.

In France, like Britain, Marxism was slow to take hold. The French section of the First International mostly supported the libertarian principles of Pierre-Joseph Proudhon (1809–1865), who opposed Marx's most fundamental beliefs, especially those that appeared to advocate a working-class seizure of the state. For Proudhon, it was not just capitalism that oppressed workers, but the state as well. As Proudhon wrote, "We want neither the government of man by man nor the exploitation of man by man." In his view, the solution to oppression was a stateless society composed of small cooperative enterprises in which the associated workers governed themselves.

Although Proudhon rejected the "exploitation of man by man," he had no quarrel with the exploitation of woman by man. He considered women inferior to men in all crucial respects and believed they should limit themselves to bearing and raising children. Nature, Proudhon wrote, "has made woman a passive being, a receptacle for the seed that man alone produces." She had no place in the world of work and no role to play in political life. Women, he added, must be carefully controlled, for their sexual enticements deprive men of the semen that Proudhon believed gave them not only their physical strength but their intellectual vitality. Proudhon's prejudices against women echoed those of the era's male politicians, academics, and writers, many of whom maintained that women were less rational and physically weaker than men. The French feminists Juliette Adam (1836–1936) and Jenny d'Héricourt (1809–1875) ridiculed Proudhon's ideas about sexuality and argued, as Adam put it, that "woman is a free being who develops to intellectual maturity exactly as man does."

To combat the widespread prejudice against women and to campaign for female suffrage, feminist leaders founded political organizations of their own. In Britain, feminists came together in London and Manchester and enlisted on their side the prominent liberal philosopher and Member of Parliament John Stuart Mill (1806–1873). Influenced by his wife Harriet Taylor Mill (1807–1858), he introduced an amendment to the Reform Act designed to extend suffrage to women. His effort failed, as critics argued that giving women the vote would destroy familial harmony and inject women into the political arena where, it was claimed, they did not belong. But Mill emerged from this effort a committed feminist. His essay *On the Subjection of Women* (1869) would inform women's rights advocates for generations to come, and not just in Britain: his book was translated into dozens of languages.

In addition to the struggle for suffrage, British activists worked to gain new educational opportunities and equal property rights for women. Cambridge University established a women's college in 1871 (although without the ability to award degrees), and the Married Women's Property Act of 1870 gave wives, rather than their husbands, control over the wages they earned. The Act left other assets in their husbands' hands.

In France, like Britain, feminists made little progress toward women's suffrage. The republicans who now governed the country feared that women would obey their priests and vote for conservative, Catholic parties, and French feminists tended to agree. Although some campaigned for women's suffrage, the majority of French feminists advocated a "familial feminism" that sought to give married women equal standing to their husbands within the family and, in the case of unhappy marriages, to legalize divorce—achieved in 1884. By the early 1900s, feminists succeeded in softening certain harsh provisions of the Civil Code—husbands' ownership of their wives' wages and assets, husbands' monopoly control over their children, and male immunity from paternity suits—but they would not gain the right to vote until 1944.

Women's rights were slower to develop in Germany, and when a national organization finally emerged in 1894, German feminists found themselves sharply divided between socialists and nonsocialists. The former supported women's rights in the workplace—higher pay and equal treatment to men—and the latter advocated the reform of Germany's Civil Code and female suffrage. The campaign for women's suffrage was stalemated until after the First World War, when German women gained the right to vote in the wake of the democratic revolution of 1919 (see Chapter 10).

In Finland and Norway, women's rights advocates won suffrage for women early in the twentieth century, 1906 and 1913 respectively, as feminists forged successful alliances with nationalists seeking independence from Russia and Sweden. In Sweden itself, both Liberals and Social Democrats supported women's suffrage after 1900 in the belief that newly enfranchised women would vote for them. Elsewhere in Europe, women's rights advanced more gradually. Women's rights organizations in Austria did not work for female suffrage until after the turn of the twentieth century. Mostly, they tried to extend public education for women, open better employment opportunities and reform marriage laws to give women more equality. Within Austria-Hungary, the quest for women's right to vote made little headway until the 1910s.

Positivism, Evolution, and the Hegemony of Science

Feminists, like liberals and Marxists, saw themselves as committed to a progressive future rather than a stultifying past. All three groups believed that history brought progress and that their ideas were consistent with the Enlightenment's empirical, scientific outlook on life. Marx, in particular, maintained that his was a scientific approach based on laws of history he had discovered. In these scientific claims, Marx resembled other prominent theorists and intellectuals of the middle decades of the nineteenth century, when science gained enormous prestige and distinguished itself from the humanities, law, and theology. In part, the prestige of science stemmed from the technological achievements of the Industrial Revolution (see Chapter 6), but it also had to do with the failure of the revolutions of 1848 and the collapse of the Romantic, utopian hopes they had inspired.

Like a great many others, Marx was influenced by the French sociologist Auguste Comte (1798–1857), whose scientific approach to human behavior was known as **positivism.** Comte rejected metaphysics, which held that people could understand the world purely through disciplined philosophical thought. Instead,

Bueberettiget Mittet & Co.

≡ **The Fight for Women's Suffrage in Norway.**
European feminists and their male allies began to campaign for suffrage in the 1860s. They were unsuccessful until the early twentieth century, when women in Finland and Norway achieved the right to vote. In Norway, the women's suffrage campaign became embroiled in the effort to separate from Sweden, which had ruled the country since Napoleonic times and showed no interest in giving women the vote. After being excluded from the successful 1905 referendum on independence, large numbers of Norwegian women signed a pro-suffrage petition. They won the right to vote in 1913.

he favored the careful empirical observation of natural phenomena and human behavior—for him, the only source of genuine knowledge. It was pointless, Comte maintained, to search for the fundamental meaning or origins of the phenomena in question, since neither could be directly observed.

Comte's philosophy made no distinctions between natural and human phenomena. Scientists, he believed, could deduce laws about the workings of individuals and society that were just as valid as laws of physics or chemistry. The science of society he called **sociology**, which for him was a largely conservative philosophy: the laws of society could be discovered but not changed. Comte's rigidly empiricist views were consonant with the materialistic industrialism of the time. Entrepreneurs, engineers, and inventors had little interest in philosophizing about what they did. They sought mainly to solve problems and get things done.

Comte maintained that Western Europe, as the world's most advanced society, had achieved its status through a three-stage evolutionary process in which human organization developed from a "theological" to a "metaphysical" to a "positive" (scientific) state. Evolutionary notions took European intellectuals by storm after 1850, and Marx in particular exemplified evolution's appeal. As we have seen, he developed a schema in which the dominant mode of production evolved from the feudal to the capitalist to the socialist stage. Both Comte and Marx had been influenced by the French zoologist, Jean-Baptiste Lamarck (1744–1829), who wrote in 1808 that plants and animals had not always been what they were in the present day—they had evolved from earlier forms. Lamarck anticipated many of the ideas later advanced by the scientist most associated with the theory of evolution, Charles Darwin (1809–1882).

Darwin had felt the influence not only of Lamarck but of the liberal notion that competition was the motor of progress and that people had to struggle to prosper or even survive. His book, *On the Origin of Species by Means of Natural Selection* (1859), melded these and other ideas to his own experimental work and proved to be one of the most important publications of the nineteenth century. In it, Darwin made four essential points. The first was that in every species, more individuals were born than could survive. The corollary to this notion, and Darwin's second point, was that life within a given species and between species involved a constant struggle for survival. The third held that differences or variations existed among members of the same species, variations that accommodated some members to the environment better than others and thus enhanced their ability to survive. Finally, the crucial implication of the first three points was that only those best suited to the environment, the "fittest" as Darwin's popularizers would put it, survived. Evolution occurred as a result of nature's selection of the most adaptive members of a given species.

In the *Origin of Species,* Darwin limited his discussion to plants and animals. Only with *The Descent of Man* (1871) would he advance the notion for which he is most famous: human beings evolved from an extinct animal species that also produced the apes. This notion aroused great controversy, for it appeared to deny the biblical account of the Creation, including the belief that God had created human life. Darwinism was controversial as well for its positivistic idea that human beings possessed no essential moral sense, that there was no such thing as a soul essentially human in character. Any species might have developed the morality generally associated with humans if the environment had enabled it to evolve far enough. Many religious thinkers found this notion disturbing, and their theological resistance to the theory of evolution has lasted until the present day.

THE LONDON SKETCH BOOK.

≡ **Charles Darwin.** When Darwin argued that people had evolved from apes, key religious figures denounced him on biblical grounds: according to Genesis, God had directly created human life. Other critics turned to satire, as in this cartoon, which places Darwin's head on an ape's body and pairs him with a simian mate.

Still, some religious thinkers saw no conflict between Darwinism and Christianity, since Darwin did not deny that God had set evolution in motion. And, more important, Darwin had documented the great bounty and diversity of what God had made. For secular intellectuals, Darwinism proved unproblematic, as a great many writers of this positivistic period wholeheartedly approved of its lack of moralism, its acceptance of what many considered the tough but nonetheless fundamental realities of competition, struggle, and the quest to survive. In many ways, these were the essential values of the reigning capitalist economic system, as of the Bismarckian era's amoral *Realpolitik.*

Although Darwin himself did not often address the political and economic implications of his work, his followers commonly did. Most prominent among them was Herbert Spencer (1820–1903), who, unlike his mentor, did not hesitate to place a positive value judgment on what he called "the survival of the fittest." In Spencer's view, the struggle to survive could only be a good thing, for it necessarily produced the fittest or best individuals. It would be a grievous mistake, he wrote, for a government to alter the outcome of this "natural" process of selection; to do so would be to allow unfit individuals artificially to survive and thereby to weaken society as a whole. For this reason, states should do nothing to aid the poor; their very poverty served as evidence that they had already failed the test of natural selection.

This outlook echoed earlier Calvinist notions concerning the elect and reinforced the prevailing liberal idea that poverty was the poor person's fault. Spencer's ideas came to be known as "social Darwinism"; they would be used to justify not only the exploitation of the poor, but imperialism, racism, and military conquest as well.

Religion in the Modern World

Although by the 1870s growing numbers of people subscribed to a scientific rather than religious worldview, organized religion retained considerable support, especially among women. As a "cult of domesticity" increasingly separated middle-class women from the materialistic world of industry and commerce, men expected them to withdraw into the private realm of the home, where they assumed the task of maintaining the family's moral and ethical standards. Since morals and ethics remained closely tied to religion, many women were open to the influence of their Christian churches, whose clergymen instilled a set of virtues consonant with their domestic role: resignation, morality, inwardness, forgiveness, patience, and charity. Moreover, as the business world became increasingly competitive and workers came to be seen as interchangeable "hands," the woman's need to preserve a caring and moral realm became all the more imperative. Thus, even when male church attendance declined, that of women increased, especially in Britain and Germany. In these countries, the Evangelical and Pietist movements that had swept through the Protestant denominations beginning in the late eighteenth century reinvigorated the faithful by encouraging a deep, personal spirituality and a recommitment to God.

While middle-class men were, for the most part, less religiously observant than their wives and daughters, only a small minority abandoned religion altogether. Some took an instrumental stance, going through the motions of religious observance to set an example for the poor, while others remained genuine believers, finding the materialism of the business world emotionally unsatisfying. In religious observance, individuals could experience feelings of solace and joy, a sense of awe and mystery difficult to find anywhere else.

Peasant men as well as women tended to keep their religious commitments throughout the nineteenth century, as did a great many women workers. Men of the laboring classes, by contrast, increasingly abandoned formal religious observance as the century progressed. Many of these workers retained deeply felt religious beliefs but rejected Europe's largely conservative clergymen and religious institutions, which seemed unsympathetic to political and social change. Heightening the detachment from organized religion was the movement of working people into large cities, where churches exercised far less influence than in close-knit rural communities.

Religious leaders found this detachment highly disturbing and took significant steps to reverse it. They engaged in a major campaign of church building, erecting more churches than at any time since the Middle Ages, in an effort to surround urban dwellers with religious edifices and bring them back into the fold. To give children a religious education, the various Christian denominations created Sunday schools and populated them with enthusiastic lay teachers eager to spread their faith. And after missionaries succeeded in converting large numbers of Africans to Christianity, religious leaders in Europe imitated these religious emissaries by establishing missions in poor urban neighborhoods with the goal of converting the irreligious at home.

Middle-class women were especially prominent in these urban missions, which enabled them to step outside the purely domestic realm. To care for the needy, women had to raise money, lobby city officials, enlist the support of business leaders, and decide who was worthy of help. These activities, partly humanitarian and partly intended to instill middle-class values and behavior in the poor, brought women back into public life. Their efforts met with mixed results among working people and the poor but not infrequently served to re-Christianize middle- and upper-class men. Bismarck, as we have seen, underwent a profound religious conversion at the behest of a woman he wanted to marry.

Beyond church building, Sunday schools, and urban missions, the different religions adopted a number of other techniques to boost attendance and revitalize the faith. They took advantage of the era's new, cheaper printing technology to produce an unprecedented number of bibles and other religious books.

The Sacré-Coeur Cathedral. In the aftermath of the deeply anticlerical Paris Commune, Catholic leaders decided to erect a massive new cathedral on Paris's highest ground. From there it would dominate the French city and remind its errant people that France remained a Christian land.

Religious organizations also began to circulate inexpensively produced newspapers, which connected growing numbers of readers to the activities of churches and synagogues—Judaism also participated in the era's religious revival—and to the worldviews and political positions of religious leaders.

In 1864, Pope Pius IX (1792–1878; papacy 1846–1878) sought to counter what he considered a dangerous secularizing trend by releasing a document entitled *The Syllabus of Errors.* This document denounced "rationalism," "indifferentism," and "secularism," the three "isms" said to separate people from God, and declared it heretical to claim that "the Roman Pontiff can and ought to reconcile himself to, and agree with, progress, liberalism, and modern civilization." The *Syllabus* horrified Catholics who sought to reconcile religion, science, and liberalism. However, in 1870, the pope went one step further by promulgating the doctrine of **papal infallibility**, the notion that any official pronouncement by the pope was necessarily true. Although secularists denounced the new doctrine, most Catholic leaders supported papal infallibility because it helped them discipline the faithful and combat Christian socialism and other nonorthodox versions of the religion. Despite the controversy surrounding it, papal infallibility may ultimately have strengthened the Church, even as it widened the rift between organized Catholicism and devotees of a scientific view of the world.

What also strengthened the Church, while alienating secularists, was the successful revival, in the late nineteenth century, of the religious pilgrimage. Catholics had long traveled to Rome, but Europe's new railroad networks made it quicker, easier, and less expensive to get there, thus enabling middle-class people to make the journey. After 1858, Lourdes, a small city in southwestern France, displaced the Italian capital as the main destination for Catholic pilgrims when Bernadette Soubirous (1844–1879), a fourteen-year-old native of Lourdes, reported eighteen visions of the Virgin Mary. In her interactions with the Virgin, she appeared to discover an underground spring to which townspeople soon attributed healing powers.

Church authorities were initially skeptical of Bernadette's claims, but after a rigorous investigation that followed scientific methods as they understood them, clerics ruled that the visions were real—as were the healing qualities of the spring waters of Lourdes. In the 1870s, priests and nuns, together with a large network of lay Catholic women, organized an annual pilgrimage to Lourdes, where the sick and disabled—soon more than a million every year—went to be healed. After being immersed in the waters, a great many claimed to have been cured. Doctors who examined those who said they could walk or see for the first time in years ruled that the waters had caused their recovery. These doctors, men of science and men of faith, showed that at the dawn of the twentieth century, educated Europeans could believe, all at once, in science and the supernatural, empiricism and the power of faith.

Popular Culture

If for these doctors there was no contradiction between religion and science, those fully committed to a scientific view of the world dismissed the claims of healing and salvation emanating from Lourdes. Foremost among them was the French writer Emile Zola (1840–1902), whose novel, *Lourdes* (1894), ridiculed the people who claimed to have been cured. Zola, like Britain's George Eliot (1819–1880) and many other writers of the late-century, presented themselves as social scientists documenting the world as it really was. Literature, they said, should be "naturalistic," reflecting nature, not fantasy.

The writing of history, too, became "scientific," as historians increasingly abandoned the great heroic narratives of the Romantic period in favor of sober works meticulously based on archival documents. Historians mined government repositories for facts the way workers excavated seams for coal. They saw themselves as little different from chemists or biologists who gathered information through empirical observation and deduced truths from what they found. History, moreover, was not just to be edifying; it was to be practical. Its purpose was to enable present-day statesmen to learn from the successes and failures of the past.

Much other writing was meant to be practical as well. Samuel Smiles' best-selling books told readers how to better themselves through hard work and the wise management of money. Although Smiles directed his books to men, women became the particular focus of the new literature of self-help. A seemingly limitless quantity of guidebooks taught women how to care for their home, create a comfortable "nest" for their husband, please their man, dress appropriately, arrange flowers, and cook elegant meals.

The large number of such works resulted, in part, from technical advancements in printing that dramatically reduced the costs of production and made printed materials cheaper and more widely accessible than ever before. Newspapers such as the *Daily Telegraph* in Britain and the *Petit journal* (Little Newspaper) in France used steam-powered rotary presses, developed in the 1860s, to increase printing speeds from a few thousand copies per day to as many as forty thousand an hour. This new technology, as well as a variety of other inventions developed between the 1860s and the turn of the century, enabled publishers with the necessary capital to expand output and lower produc-

Hawking Newspapers in Milan. In the late nineteenth century, the penny paper, accessible to almost everyone, emerged as the world's first mass medium. Throughout Europe, millions of people read one or more newspapers every day, and the penny press, published in each country's dominant language, helped stitch those countries' diverse communities into a more culturally uniform national whole. Nowhere was this unifying process more important than in Italy, which the Risorgimento had brought together politically, but not culturally.

tion costs a hundredfold. Economies of scale plus the revenue generated by the growth of advertising during this period allowed readers to buy the daily paper for the equivalent of a penny or two. The invention of a "penny press" deprived the middle and upper classes of their privileged access to information and created the very concept of "news"—information that was new every day and accessible to everyone. By the century's end, the highest-circulation papers would sell a million copies a day.

Masses of people bought these papers not only because they were cheap but because broader access to primary education gave unprecedented numbers of Europeans the ability to read. In France, illiteracy among military conscripts dropped from 40 percent in 1850 to 18 percent three decades later, and other countries registered similar improvements. In this context, the newspaper helped stitch a given country's diverse communities into a more culturally uniform, national whole. This was especially the case in countries with one dominant language. In multinational empires such as Austria-Hungary, the situation was more complex. There, newspapers extended the dominance of German language and culture while reinforcing the distinctiveness of the groups capable of publishing successful journals in their own languages. Nationalist organizations, for their part, worked hard to extend literacy among those believed to belong to the nationality in question.

As newspapers brought readers of the same language together culturally, they also gave them a common stock of information and ideas. This did not mean, of course, that every member of a given linguistic group came to share the same opinions, but there probably was more cultural uniformity than ever before. Even newspapers with widely divergent political orientations presented their readers with the same kinds of literature in serialized form. Detective novels figured prominently among these writings, as did reports of spectacular real-life crimes. Both genres boosted newspaper sales by ending each installment with a cliffhanger, which encouraged readers to buy the next day's paper.

While true crime stories enabled readers to indulge their attraction to the macabre, the works of Jules Verne (1828–1905) and other fantasy writers offered vicarious thrills and an emotional escape from the dull routines of the office and the factory. Verne's *From the Earth to the Moon* (1865) and *Around the World in Eighty Days* (1872), among many other works, sold hundreds of thousands of copies and made their author a wealthy man. His books drew on the period's fascination with new technology and inventions and helped create the genre of science fiction. But for all their forward-looking fantasies, Verne's books were anything but progressive in other ways. He routinely presented Jews and non-Europeans as devious and inferior while stereotyping women as untrustworthy and infantile. Beneath the wonder, fantasy, and drama of many of the era's new forms of popular culture lurked the messages of social Darwinism and the inherent superiority of European men.

Conclusion: A New European Balance of Power

The decades after 1850 marked a period of extraordinary change. A powerful new capitalist economy brought Europeans unparalleled wealth, some of which for the first time trickled down to the laboring classes. Significant numbers of working people began to join labor unions, and serfdom disappeared in Russia. Although most middle-class women remained cloistered at home, the "separate spheres" dividing women and men began to dissolve and new movements for women's rights emerged. Even so, working-class women continued to face low wages and discrimination not only from employers but from their male counterparts as well.

Most governments, Russia excepted, developed liberal, parliamentary institutions, and democracy gained ground in Britain and France. As for the balance of power among the different states, it shifted markedly toward Bismarck's new, economically powerful German Empire, while registering declines in the relative standing of the Ottoman Empire, Austria, Russia, and France. Italy unified itself for the first time since ancient Rome, although economically it remained relatively weak.

The leading European countries, meanwhile, positioned themselves to extend their dominance throughout the world, aided by the scientific and technological advances of the time. During the final decades of the nineteenth century, Europe would turn to conquest and expansion, endeavoring to "civilize" supposedly backward regions and subordinate them to its will.

KEY TERMS

Crimean War *354*	Marxism *370*	proletariat *369*
Dual monarchy *366*	Opium War *351*	*Realpolitik* *339*
extraterritoriality *351*	papal infallibility *377*	sociology *374*
First International *370*	Paris Commune *367*	
globalization *351*	positivism *373*	

 For digital learning resources, please go to **https://www.oup.com/he/berenson2e**. Turn to the back of the book to see the list of primary sources and writing exercises provided in the accompanying *Sources and Guided Writing Exercises for Europe in the Modern World*

European Society and the Road to War, 1880–1914

Maria Montessori

No one exemplified the New (emancipated) Woman of the late nineteenth century more than Italy's Maria Montessori (1870–1952), best known in the United States for her pioneering efforts to reform early childhood education. Born in a small Italian town, Montessori was the only child of an unusually well-educated mother and a traditionalist father. The family moved to Rome when Maria was five, and there the future educator attended the city's inadequate public schools. Classrooms seldom had enough books to go around, and the era's educational philosophy, such as it was, left little room for rigor or creativity. Worse, from Montessori's point of view, schools offered far more opportunities for boys than for girls.

Still, no laws prevented young women from pursuing an education, and Montessori was determined to do just that. Faced with a choice between traditional humanistic study and a modern technical school emphasizing mathematics and science, Montessori selected the modern curriculum. There were so few girls in Rome's technical schools that teachers did not know what to do with them at recess time. It went without saying that they could not mix with the boys, so they were forced to spend their free time shut up in a room.

Montessori performed extremely well in school, and by her late teens, her father had accepted the idea that Maria might become a teacher, although he would have preferred that she be a traditional wife and mother. When Maria announced her intention to become an engineer, her father's world turned upside down; girls did not do such things. It hardly helped when Maria dropped engineering and decided to become a doctor. No modern Italian woman had ever studied medicine, and the Medical College of Rome was not about to let her invade this exclusively male domain. Despite her almost perfect grades and strong background in math and science, her application was rejected out of hand.

Undaunted, Montessori persisted in her quest for admission, and against all the odds, she finally convinced Medical College officials to let her in. It was the right decision. At the end of her second year, she won top honors as the best in her class, despite the obstacles that confronted women in higher education. Her father had to escort her to school every day, since middle-class women were not supposed to walk about the city unaccompanied by a man.

At the Medical College, Maria was forbidden to attend the regular dissecting classes; professors deemed it unseemly for her to join the male students in looking at naked bodies, even dead ones. She had to carve her cadavers alone in a special class at night.

Maria's teachers also forbade her to enter lecture halls with her fellow students. She had to wait until all the men had taken their seats before occupying one of her own. None of these acts of petty harassment and discrimination prevented Montessori from fulfilling her dream. She graduated at the top of her class, and in the spring of 1896, became Italy's first woman doctor, specializing in pediatric medicine. She may have broken into the all-male bastion of the medical profession, but once there, she did not entirely escape her culture's conventional female roles: she turned to the care of children, as women had traditionally done.

Shortly after receiving her medical degree, Montessori found herself drawn into Europe's revived feminist movement. As one of Italy's delegates to the international women's congress held in Berlin in 1896, she won plaudits from the male journalists in attendance for exemplifying a feminism that was not unfeminine. Leaders of the women's movement regularly had to endure accusations of being more like men than women, of abandoning their femininity to compete in the world of men. Not so for Maria Montessori. Attractive and fashionably dressed, the young Dr. Montessori struck one male observer as having an "elegant and genial appearance, lady-like bearing, charm and beauty."

Montessori's acceptability to male commentators, most of them hostile to feminism, did not prevent her from impressing feminist leaders. She was invited to speak not just about professional matters, but also on the wider question of the condition of women. In an early lecture entitled "The New Woman," Montessori challenged the era's supposedly scientific proofs of female inferiority. In particular, she targeted the eminent criminologist Cesare Lombroso, who claimed that women were incomplete men, stuck, like criminals, at an earlier stage of human evolution. She also disputed the widespread belief among anthropologists that women's smaller heads made them mentally inferior to men and ridiculed doctors who maintained that the unnaturally stimulated brains of women intellectuals depleted their ovaries and made them infertile.

Beyond her political interventions, Montessori advanced the cause of women through the example of her own brilliantly successful professional life. In her medical practice,

Timeline

| 1875 | 1880 | 1885 | 1890 | 1895 | 1900 | 1905 | 1910 | 1915 | 1920 |

1878 Congress of Berlin addresses Balkan situation

1879 Zulu War

1879–1882 Triple Alliance (Germany, Austria-Hungary, Italy) established

1881 Anti-Jewish pogroms in Russia

1884 Third Reform Act in Britain

1885 Sudan becomes an independent Islamic state

1886–1905 Tory (Conservative) control of Britain

1890 Wilhelm II removes Bismarck, overturns anti-socialist law

1892 French and Russian alliance

1894–1899 Dreyfus Affair

1896 Maria Montessori becomes Italy's first woman doctor

1898 Britain recaptures the Sudan

1898–1902 Boer War

1900 Russia establishes protectorate over Manchuria

1904 British and French alliance

1905 France asserts control of Morocco

1907 Montessori establishes a school for young children in Rome

1908 Young Turks agitate in the Balkans

1911 Agadir crisis in Morocco

1912 First Balkan War

1913 Second Balkan War

1914 Archduke Ferdinand assassinated; Austria declares war on Serbia; First World War begins

she increasingly turned to the treatment of those we now label as having an intellectual disability but who were called "idiots" and "feebleminded" in her time. Authorities routinely dumped such children into asylums where they shared quarters with the criminally insane. Montessori rescued a group of these "feebleminded" kids and taught them in an environment she had devised. Within two years, her pupils, considered uneducable, were outperforming normal youths. These impressive results convinced the doctor-turned-educator that the same methods could be applied to all children, especially those whose parents were poorly educated.

In January 1907, Montessori established a school for young children in one of Rome's low-income housing projects. Known as the Children's House, this tenement school became the laboratory for an experiment in early childhood education that would ultimately become an international movement, with Montessori schools sprinkled throughout the world. In the United States, where Maria was invited to lecture in 1913, her ideas became central to the kindergarten curriculum, and in the 1960s her teaching helped inspire Head Start, the government-funded early education program.

The more she worked with children, the more Montessori realized that education was her true vocation. In 1907, she gave up medicine to devote herself full-time to pedagogy. Many of her friends wondered why she abandoned a prestigious medical career for what was considered the lowly vocation of preschool teaching. But in the years before the First World War, her Montessori schools made her one of the best-known and most admired women in the world.

After the war, Montessori developed into something of a cult figure, the increasingly authoritarian leader of what was becoming a quasi-religious sect. She had disciples but never collaborators, and she isolated herself and her movement from other educational reforms. Her ideas lost their freshness, and her once-widespread influence began to wane. Still, she remains one of the most remarkable women of the late nineteenth and early twentieth centuries, a New Woman who broke through the barriers of sex discrimination and set an example of what women could do. ≡

Life and Death and the Movement of People

Montessori came of age at a time marked by paradox. The major powers remained at peace, but there were widespread, even frenetic, preparations for war. A "Long Depression" endured for more than twenty years (c. 1873–1895), even though certain sectors of the economy grew at a rapid pace. Democratization occurred, but the newly enfranchised masses elected governments that deprived people overseas of self-rule. Women gained more rights than ever before, but almost everywhere the emancipated New Woman found herself the object of an intense critique, especially for having too few children.

Instead of the six, eight, or ten pregnancies that had been common in the past, married women in the early twentieth century typically gave birth to only two or three children. For the first time in history, Europeans possessed reliable means of birth control and voluntarily limited the size of their families. Couples did so to enjoy more of the prosperity that their growing economies promised, while women sought the freedom to work and participate in a public realm once reserved for men. Anti-feminists accused women of abandoning the home and childrearing to compete with men in factories and offices and blamed wives for the precipitous decline in the birth rate that began during this period, a decline said to weaken their countries in time of war. But men, too, wanted fewer children, and the result of these new attitudes and practices was the beginning, in Western Europe, of a lasting demographic change.

As population growth slowed in Northern and Western Europe, it exploded in the south and east, where birth control was less common. Thanks to new medical and scientific discoveries and the improved nutrition made possible by declining food prices, mortality—especially infant mortality—went down. Doctors now understood the role of bacteria in transmitting disease, and this knowledge permitted the French scientist Louis Pasteur (1822–1895) to develop a process (pasteurization) for removing the impurities from milk. Pasteurization alone significantly lowered childhood death rates, even in the poorest countries. Populations grew in Southern and Eastern Europe because people were living longer and fewer babies died.

Accompanying these changes in birth and death rates was an unprecedented movement of people, especially from the countryside to the city. By 1914, an astounding 45 percent of all English men and women lived in cities of more than a hundred thousand residents. In Germany, meanwhile, the percentage of people living in cities of that size exploded from 4.8 percent in 1871 to 21.3 percent in 1911. Southern and Eastern Europe remained overwhelmingly rural, but people from these parts of the continent poured into the industrialized countries of the north and west, while a great many left Europe altogether in search of more secure and prosperous lives. Some twenty million Italians, Russians, Greeks, and Eastern Europeans emigrated to the United States between 1880 and 1914 (see Map 9.1). Jews, who faced mounting persecution, especially in Russia, constituted more than 10 percent of all US newcomers in the early 1900s, and they migrated in unprecedented numbers to Britain and France. In part, these migrations stemmed from

≡ **The German Reichstag c. 1900.** After 1871, the new German Empire became the most powerful, economically vital, country in Europe. The massive stone façade of the Reichstag (parliament) building, opened in 1894, symbolized the strength and solidity of the German state.

it, "monarchical traditions and loyal sentiments." If that loyalty failed to hold up, Bismarck had other guarantees in reserve, the most important of which was the relative impotence of the Reichstag in the face of monarchical authority.

Still, the federal parliament was by no means powerless, for Bismarck recognized the importance of allowing the country's interest groups to express themselves at the national level. He thus gave the Reichstag and another body, the Federal Council or *Bundesrat*, the ability to set policy concerning trade and commerce, transportation and communication, the banking system, patents, and aspects of civil and criminal law. And because the Reichstag's debates were public and covered in the press, the kaiser and chancellor took them seriously and tried to ensure an ideological tone congenial to them, although they did not always succeed, as we will see.

Because all adult men could vote, the Reichstag included the gamut of political opinion (and corresponding parties) from right to left: conservatives, centrists, liberals, left-liberals, and socialists. Throughout his tenure in office, Bismarck mostly enjoyed majority support in the Reichstag, but leaders of the parliamentary parties were quick to oppose him when he violated their interests and beliefs, as he did to Catholics beginning in 1871.

A devout Protestant, Bismarck decided that Catholicism, represented in the Reichstag by the Center Party, enjoyed too much influence and power in his new German Empire, one-third of whose citizens belonged to the Catholic faith. The chancellor bristled in particular against Pius IX's anti-modern *Syllabus of Errors* and particularly the pope's 1870 declaration that he was infallible, unlike a mere political leader such as Bismarck (see Chapter 8). To limit Catholicism's reach, Bismarck unleashed a **Kulturkampf** ("struggle of civilizations") against the Catholic Church. Bismarck secularized the schools, forbade priests to express political opinions from the pulpit, banned the Jesuits, and severed diplomatic relations with the Vatican. These initiatives, warmly supported by the liberals, angered the Church and a great many Catholic voters, especially after Bismarck decreed, in

1875, that all couples had to marry in civil ceremonies conducted by government officials. Religious marriages ceased to be legal marriages, and when priests and bishops ignored the new marriage law and other of Bismarck's anti-Catholic measures, they faced stiff economic sanctions, imprisonment, and exile.

Bismarck's array of anti-Catholic initiatives mobilized the Center Party, whose leaders campaigned against him and doubled their representation in the Reichstag, where they succeeded in blocking some of his measures. By 1875, Bismarck realized that he had gone too far and abruptly retreated from his anti-Catholic positions. Most Catholics shared his political conservatism, and it now seemed pointless to alienate them. Besides, Bismarck wanted Catholic support for a new, and for him, far more important political campaign: the battle against the growing socialist party. By 1878, the Kulturkampf was over and a new struggle about to begin.

Bismarck had become so concerned over the size and strength of the socialists (Social Democratic Party of Germany) that he had them banned, forcing the SPD, as the socialist party was called, to operate outside the country or underground. Because the anti-socialist legislation failed to define precisely what constituted socialist activity, liberals feared it could be directed against them and hesitated to support it—although ultimately they did. Their hesitation, short-lived as it was, enabled Bismarck to accuse them of disloyalty and drop them from his governing coalition, thus solidifying the conservative character of the regime. He could not, however, deprive liberals of all political influence. Their importance to the German economy, prominence in the civil service, and prestige as doctors, lawyers, and professors kept them in the public eye and allowed them to shape policy from the sidelines.

Social Reform in Germany

Bismarck may have banished liberals and socialists from center stage, but his anti-socialist measures did little to stifle the public's mounting demands for social reform and even less to divert industrial workers from the SPD. In an effort to gain workers' support—and improve their lives—the chancellor dipped into uncharted waters by enacting, over liberal opposition, measures giving working people protection from sickness (1883), accidents (1884), old age (1889), and disability (1889). In an era still largely governed by the doctrine of laissez faire, Bismarck's proposal represented an unprecedented state intervention into the economic sphere.

Still, these insurance laws, innovative as they were, did not prove generous enough to satisfy most working people, especially agricultural laborers and domestic servants, who were excluded from coverage. Given the deficiencies of these laws, the SPD was anything but obsolete. Its banishment ended in 1890, when the new emperor, Wilhelm II (1859–1941, ruled 1888–1918), removed the aging

Bismarck from office and had the anti-socialist law overturned. In the first post-ban election, the SPD won a startling 20 percent of the vote.

Imperialism and Empire

In the 1880s, the SPD and other European socialists generally opposed imperialism, the conquest of people abroad. But by the early twentieth century, a great many socialists had come to accept the logic of a "civilizing mission" in which European countries supposedly hoisted "backward" societies into the modern world. If socialists supported empire, this was even truer of society at large. In the last decades of the nineteenth century, the various European powers, confident in their economic prowess, military strength, and cultural superiority, mobilized an impressive array of resources and people to bring the majority of the world's peoples under their formal or informal control. Europe's effort to colonize the globe proved to be one of the most significant—and damaging—phenomena of the modern era.

Before 1880, only Britain and France possessed colonies of any significance; the old empires of Spain and Portugal had declined almost to nothing. And even Britain and France did not devote much attention to empire, with the great exceptions of India, crucial for British trade and political prestige, and Algeria, which France claimed in 1830 and struggled for fifty years to subdue. True, Britain possessed a large **informal empire** of countries it dominated economically, but it did not seek to govern them. And although Canada, Australia, and New Zealand still belonged to Britain's "formal" empire, they had become largely independent by the late nineteenth century. As for France, it controlled some dots of territory in West Africa, Southeast Asia, and the Caribbean but encouraged settlement only in Algeria, whose European population came mostly from Spain, Italy, Greece, and Malta rather than France.

After 1880, the European powers, led by Britain and France, transformed this almost lackadaisical approach to empire into a furious and highly competitive quest to control the world. This competition featured a **Scramble for Africa**, which left much of the continent in European hands—at least nominally, because the Europeans possessed neither the resources nor the manpower to fully control the lands they claimed. They generally had to rule with the help of indigenous elites, who often exacted important concessions in return. Still, between the late 1870s and the beginning of World War I, the main European countries (plus Japan and the United States) claimed one-quarter of the globe and divided it among themselves, with Britain and France taking the lion's share—nearly 8 million square miles and more than 400 million people (see Map 9.2).

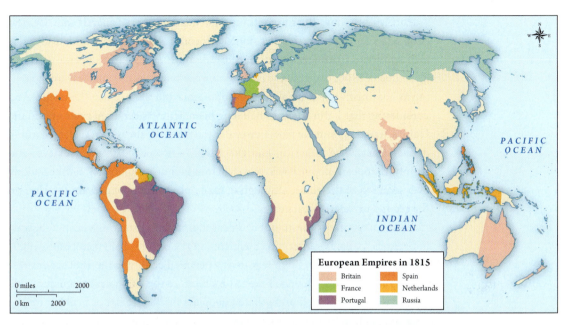

European Empires in 1815

Britain	Spain
France	Netherlands
Portugal	Russia

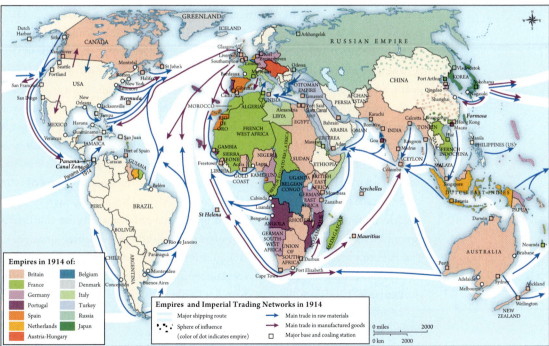

Empires in 1914 of:

Britain	Belgium
France	Denmark
Germany	Italy
Portugal	Turkey
Spain	Russia
Netherlands	Japan
Austria-Hungary	

Empires and Imperial Trading Networks in 1914

Major shipping route

Sphere of influence
(color of dot indicates empire)

Main trade in raw materials

Main trade in manufactured goods

Major base and coaling station

≡ **MAP 9.2**   European Empires in 1815/Empires and Imperial Trading Networks in 1914

During this time, Russia continued its steady imperial march into Central Asia, and China, although not colonized formally, found itself divided into foreign **spheres of influence** and then invaded during the anti-imperialist Boxer Rebellion of 1900. Even the Ottoman Empire entered the colonial fray by tightening its administrative control over Mesopotamia and the Arabian Peninsula. And considering that Latin America had long been Britain's economic colony and the United States' diplomatic pawn, virtually the whole of the non-Western World—Africa, Asia, Latin America, and the Pacific—now lived under Western, and mainly European, domination. Never before had one region claimed hegemony over so much of the globe, although in many places Europeans were too thin on the ground to exercise real power.

These colonial conquests often unleashed terrible forms of violence against indigenous peoples. After the Belgian king Leopold II (ruled 1865–1909) claimed the enormous Congo region as a personal colony in the 1880s, administrators of the so-called Congo Free State subjected the Congolese to unspeakable brutality. They murdered or mutilated people unwilling to harvest rubber for the large Belgian companies operating there. And when these tactics prompted indigenous people to escape into the jungle, colonialists captured women and children and held them hostage in appalling conditions to force their husbands and fathers to work. Between 1890 and 1910, the Belgian exploitation of the Congo produced a demographic catastrophe in which millions of Congolese died of harsh treatment, disease, overwork, and malnutrition.

France's behavior in its Congo colony resembled Belgium's, although on a smaller scale. Meanwhile, the French colonial wars in Algeria, Morocco, Indochina, and West Africa killed tens of thousands of people. The British likewise were responsible for widespread suffering and death in Jamaica, India, and southern Africa, among other colonial domains. One of the worst episodes of colonial violence took place in German South-West Africa (Namibia today). In 1904, the German army brutally suppressed an anti-colonial uprising by the lightly armed Herero people, killing some seventy thousand—nearly three-quarters of the Herero population—by machine gun fire and in the subsequent repression. In the midst of the uprising, the German commander General Lothar von Trotha announced, "I will annihilate the rebellious tribes with rivers of blood."

Why Imperialism?

Why did the various European countries undertake this unprecedented, often violent, grab for foreign lands? Part of the answer lies in the new technology, military and otherwise, of the late nineteenth century. Europe's industrial revolutions had given it the capacity to build weapons and systems of transport and communication capable of overwhelming anyone who did not possess them, no matter how culturally advanced. But important as technology was, its mere existence hardly explains why Europeans suddenly decided to use it to seize other people's lands.

How exactly to understand the race for colonies has long been the subject of heated debate. Some historians have given it mostly economic motives, others chiefly political and cultural ones. But imperialism, like most other complex historical phenomena, stemmed in reality from a combination of economic, political, and cultural roots. All countries had political motives; most had economic and cultural ones as well.

One of the key economic reasons for imperialism was

≡ **Colonial Brutality in the Congo.** The colonization of Equatorial Africa by Belgium's King Leopold II produced unspeakable forms of violence and intimidation. The Belgian companies operating in the Congo region sought to harvest rubber from vines that grew wild in the region and to do so at the lowest possible cost. Indigenous people often refused to work for the paltry wages being offered and regularly escaped labor recruiters by vanishing into the bush. To force the Congolese to work, Belgian overseers kept women and children hostage until the men contributed a set amount of raw rubber. Colonialists made an example of those who tried to abscond, or otherwise disobey them, by cutting off their hands.

the growing competition among industrialized countries for the raw materials and natural resources crucial to their new technology and inventions but largely unavailable in Europe. Bicycles and cars, for example, ran on tires made of rubber, a resource found mainly in the Congo and Amazon basins. To supply themselves with this material, the French, Germans, and Belgians looked longingly at the Congo, since the British and Americans already controlled the rubber trade in Brazil.

The automobile also required gasoline refined from crude oil, and Europeans took an avid interest in the Middle East's vast petroleum reserves. The motors that powered cars and other machines required copper, a mineral found most abundantly in the non-Western world: Chile, Peru, and central Africa. Machine tools were built with nonferrous metals, also found in what would later be called the Third (or "developing") World. So was tin, a malleable metal increasingly used in consumer products. Finally, Europeans had an insatiable demand for the diamonds and gold abundant in South Africa.

Europeans could have exploited these resources without resorting to **colonization**, as the British and Americans did in Latin America, but increasingly the different European powers, including Britain, feared that their rivals would seize overseas lands and deny them access to their raw materials. To prevent such exclusion, each European country sought to be the first to plant its flag and then claim that the region in question belonged entirely to them.

Beyond the quest for raw materials, Europeans believed that imperialism would help solve certain economic problems at home, especially overproduction—the ability to make more products than could be profitably sold. Given the limits of the home market and the tariff barriers protecting foreign ones, industrialists were eager to find new outlets for their goods, and colonized people, they hoped, would provide them. Manufacturers, therefore, figured prominently among Europe's most avid imperialists, although many suffered disappointment over what turned out to be the largely insignificant colonial demand for their products. Throughout the peak period of colonialism, 1880–1940, European countries mostly traded with one another and with the United States and spent their investment capital at home or in Russia, Eastern Europe, and the Ottoman Empire. This was less true of Britain, which traded extensively with India, Canada, and Australia while investing in Egypt and South Africa. But in general, imperialism produced meager economic returns. Its main payoff was political.

In the late nineteenth century, colonies brought prestige to the mother country and confirmed its status as a great power. Such confirmation was particularly important for France, which had suffered a humiliating military defeat by Prussia in 1870 and then a humbling relative decline of its economy from second place in 1850 to fourth in the 1880s. To compensate for these losses, French leaders turned to imperialism with a vengeance. They brought Algeria into their trading zone, and then expanded eastward into Tunisia in 1881, into the Congo the following year, and into West Africa over the next two decades. In Southeast Asia, they turned what had been little more than trading posts into actual colonies.

France claimed these territories even though most offered little economic value. Its West African lands were covered with desert or jungle; its equatorial territories, rich in natural resources as they were, proved difficult to exploit given the challenges of climate, disease, and transport. In Madagascar and Annam-Tonkin (today's Vietnam), would-be French conquerors confronted the fierce resistance of indigenous peoples and suffered extensive casualties. They also faced a domestic public opinion at first indifferent, even hostile, to these colonial ventures. It was not until France's imperial project came into direct conflict with Britain's that French opinion, galvanized by national rivalry, lent imperialism widespread support.

Nationalist Reactions to Imperialism

The Franco-British imperial rivalry began in Egypt in the 1870s and nearly ended in war two decades later. When French engineers decided to connect the Mediterranean Sea to the Indian Ocean by building a canal across Egypt's Isthmus of Suez, the British government opposed their efforts, fearing a threat to its established overland route. But between 1859 and 1869, the talented French engineer Ferdinand de Lesseps (1805–1894) completed the project, opening a sea lane via the new Suez Canal from Europe to India. The British achieved a measure of revenge for the loss of its overland Suez route by purchasing shares of stock in the Suez Canal Company from the Egyptian ruler, Khedive Ismail (1830–1895), whose excessive spending had put him in desperate need of cash.

Even after selling his Suez shares, Ismail remained in financial difficulty, and the banks to which he was indebted sent in British and French administrators to oversee Egypt's finances. When the Khedive resisted such foreign intervention, the Europeans had him deposed, outraging much of the Egyptian elite. In response, Colonel Ahmad Urabi (1841–1911) organized an incipiently nationalist rebellion, which the British, outmaneuvering the French, put down by themselves.

Having quelled the uprising in September 1882 but not the anti-European sentiments it had expressed, the British realized they could maintain their newfound control over the Suez Canal and the strategically important Nile River only by establishing a strong administrative and military presence in Egypt, something they had never intended to do. What had begun as an effort to protect British banks ended in the de facto conquest of Egypt and the establishment of informal British rule. This episode points to another crucial reason for the **new imperialism** of the late nineteenth century: the nationalist

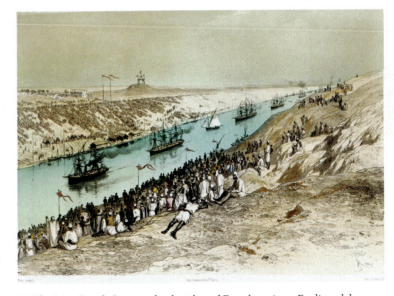

≡ **The Suez Canal.** Overseen by the talented French engineer Ferdinand de Lesseps, the Suez Canal opened to sea traffic in 1869. It allowed ships to sail from the Mediterranean Sea to the Indian Ocean, creating a shortcut of thousands of miles from Europe to India. Although the British originally opposed this French project, the canal ultimately benefited British commercial interests more than those of any other country.

responses to European interventions moved the Europeans to respond in turn with new interventions more extensive than originally planned.

Beyond Urabi's Egyptian rebellion, two other analogous anti-British reactions had a similar result: the rebellions of the Zulu people of southern Africa and of the Dutch or Boer ("farmer" in Dutch) immigrants who had settled there in the mid-seventeenth century. The British had first intervened in southern Africa to secure the sea route to India that sent ships around the tip of the continent (the Cape of Good Hope) and into the Indian Ocean. They then fanned out into the southern part of the continent but met resistance from both the Zulus and the Boers. That resistance culminated in the costly Zulu War of 1879 and ultimately, the brutal **Boer War** of 1898–1902 (see Map 9.3). The British won this war only after enduring a great many casualties and a serious loss of prestige. Most damaging was the terrible news that British soldiers had herded Boer women and children into "concentration camps" and killed a large number of civilians.

The Zulu and Boer rebellions moved the British to intervene in southern Africa more forcefully than they had intended and then to extend their original territorial claims. These additional conquests embroiled Britain in a nasty diplomatic conflict with Germany, whose kaiser strongly supported the Boers and whose businessmen hoped to wrest for themselves partial control over South Africa's lucrative gold and diamond trade. In the end, the British outflanked both the Boers and the Germans, colonizing—at considerable cost—south and south central Africa from the Cape to Rhodesia.

The sea route to India also involved the British in territories along the East African coast, territories they turned into colonies as European imperial rivalries and African rebellions intensified in the closing years of the nineteenth century. With much of East Africa secured, the British went on to tackle the Sudan, Egypt's huge quasi-colony to its south. There, an Islamic and incipiently nationalist movement was headed by Muhammad Ahmad (1844–1885), who declared himself the Mahdi or "expected deliverer" of his people and promised to drive the Egyptians and their British mentors out. In 1885, after a successful military campaign, the Mahdi delivered on his promise. The British were humiliated, and they suffered all the more from the death of

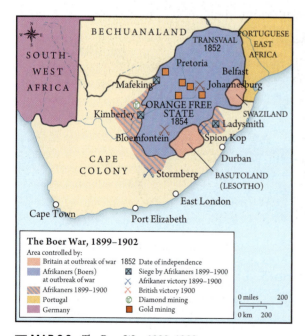

The Boer War, 1899–1902

Area controlled by:

Britain at outbreak of war	
Afrikaners (Boers) at outbreak of war	
Afrikaners 1899–1900	
Portugal	
Germany	

1852 Date of independence
⊠ Siege by Afrikaners 1899–1900
✕ Afrikaner victory 1899–1900
✕ British victory 1900
⊕ Diamond mining
◼ Gold mining

0 miles 200
0 km 200

≡ **MAP 9.3** The Boer War, 1899–1902

General Charles Gordon (1833–1885). Wildly popular at home, Gordon had gone to Khartoum, the Sudanese capital, to secure the Anglo-British position there. His death in the fighting there precipitated the fall of Gladstone's government and the redubbing of the aging prime minister from Grand Old Man (GOM) to Murderer of Gordon (MOG).

Sudan became an independent Islamic state, and British leaders feared that if left unchecked the Mahdist rebellion would spread to other parts of Africa and the Middle East and disrupt the flow of water and commerce along the Nile, the lifeblood of Egypt. To prevent this outcome—and teach the upstart Mahdists a lesson—the British government organized a powerful Anglo-Egyptian invasion of the Sudan. On September 2, 1898, the mechanized, machine-gun toting invaders confronted 50,000 Mahdist soldiers armed mainly with spears. After several hours of fighting, some 15,000 Mahdists lay dead. "It was a terrible sight," wrote a young war correspondent named Winston Churchill. The British had slaughtered their enemies, while "they had not hurt us at all."

The British had "reconquered" the Sudan, but the battle set up a potential confrontation with a French squadron encamped at Fashoda, an abandoned Egyptian military fort upriver from Khartoum. The French intended to claim Sudanese territory—and especially the upper reaches of the Nile—for themselves. Rabid imperialists in both France and Britain urged their respective governments to fight for the disputed colonial lands, and in September 1898, Britain and France reached the brink of war. The British may have been willing to fight, but the French were not. They backed down, and Britain took over the Sudan, a place that Lord Cromer, the powerful British representative in Cairo, dismissed as "worthless territory."

Britain coveted it nonetheless. Capturing the Sudan was a matter of national honor, for

The Battle of Omdurman. In 1885, Anglo-Egyptian forces suffered a humiliating defeat in the Sudan at the hands of the Mahdists, Islamic forces lead by the Mahdi or "expected deliverer." Thirteen years later, the British exacted a bloody revenge, killing some 15,000 Islamic fighters at Omdurman. On this battlefield near Khartoum, the Sudanese capital, British soldiers were armed with Europe's most advanced weaponry, the Mahdists largely with spears. This image, published in Britain's top illustrated magazine, depicts the Mahdists as wide-eyed fanatics who deserved to be killed.

the British had vowed, in 1885, to avenge the "dark stain," as Churchill put it, of their earlier defeat by the Mahdi. They also wanted to teach their French rivals a stinging lesson about military power. Once again, European national rivalries combined with an anti-imperial rebellion in Africa moved the British to extend their formal African empire far beyond what they had originally intended. The long campaign for the Sudan, as for South and East Africa, cost Britain a great deal and earned it minimal economic returns. But the political gains were significant. By the early 1900s, Britain possessed by far the world's largest overseas empire, and that distinction alone was enough to guarantee its continued status as the world's most important power.

The French followed Britain's example when they intervened militarily and then extended their territorial control in Indochina, Madagascar, and Morocco between the 1880s and the 1910s after facing proto-nationalist rebellions led by indigenous elites. The Dutch, likewise, extended their presence in what became Indonesia after facing a powerful Islamic resistance to their rule.

The Empire at Home

Not only did indigenous people and practices help determine the contours of imperial conquest and colonial policy, they also shaped key aspects of European government and society. The professional civil service is a case in point. To rule India, which Britain formally colonialized only after the anti-imperial **Indian Rebellion** of 1857, British colonial administrators created a civil service based, in part, on longstanding indigenous practices, especially concerning tax collection and judicial procedure. The British did so at a time when such a civil service did not yet exist at home. But having developed it in India, they imported it into Britain, where a new civil service devised more rational ways to administer the country. In the process, Indian methods for managing food crises were used in Ireland, where a devastating famine had occurred in the 1840s. And Anglo-Indian techniques of law enforcement such as fingerprinting were exported to Britain and Ireland, where they became staples of criminal investigation.

Similarly, the Russian effort to impose control over Asian territories conquered during the nineteenth century borrowed from local norms and swelled the size of the Russian state. Meanwhile, Europe's military leaders improved their ability to suppress insurrections at home by practicing on indigenous people in the colonies, whom they often treated with great brutality and whose military tactics—guerilla warfare and stealthy punitive raids—they adopted for themselves. The French, in particular, developed such tactics in their long war (1830–1900) to extinguish the Algerian resistance to their rule.

At mid-century, these tactics were controversial in France, but after the country's humiliating defeat at the hands of Prussia in 1871, they became less so, as a huge number of commentators decided that France had lost to Bismarck because French men lacked virility. The country needed what the writer Maurice Barrès termed "professors of energy" to teach men to be strong. The best way to train such professors, colonialists maintained, was to send young males to France's possessions in Indochina, Madagascar, Western Sudan (Mali today), and North Africa, where harsh conditions and the need to manage rebellious natives served as "schools of virility." When young, newly virile men returned to France after service in the colonies, they would, it was said, "regenerate" the homeland. They would revive France's military spirit and, as General Hubert Lyautey (1854–1934) put it, "awaken its economic activity, commerce, and the entrepreneurial spirit." Whether colonial service actually had this effect was debatable at best, but the idea became so common in the late nineteenth century that it appeared in prominent literary works. The hero of Guy de Maupassant's novel, *Bel Ami* (Handsome Friend, 1885), was a veteran of Algeria who returned to France with the energy and virility to become a powerful journalist and political leader.

From literature, imperial themes jumped to advertising, which regularly featured colonial products such as coffee, rubber, and tin and used stereotyped, often racist, images of Africans and Asians to present them. As we have seen, these products helped transform European life by allowing for the invention of the bicycle, the automobile, and the tin can, which could preserve food for an unprecedented period. Advertising helped make Europeans curious about colonial people and their ways of life. That curiosity moved a variety of entrepreneurs and officials to depict "native" ways through a cascade of newspaper articles, pictorial magazine spreads, museum displays, and especially through elaborate international exhibitions (world's fairs). These fairs, held regularly in the different European capitals, featured what were said to be replicas of "typical" African or Indochinese villages, complete with dozens of indigenous people imported,

≡ **Advertising Empire.** In the late nineteenth century, colonial imagery became common at home in Europe, especially in advertising and popular culture. This advertisement for Pears Soap, a well-known British product, suggests that the British conquest of Africa will bring civilization to "darkest Africa" by introducing them to European hygienic standards.

The Road to War	
1878	Congress of Berlin mediates border dispute in Bulgaria
1882	Triple Alliance (Germany, Austria-Hungary, Italy)
1904–1905	Japan defeats Russia in Russo-Japanese War
1905	Schlieffen Plan
1905	France and Germany nearly go to war over tensions in Morocco
1907	Triple Entente (France, Britain, Russia)
1908	Young Turk rebellion in Ottoman Empire
1911	Germany forced to back down over gunboat incident in Morocco
1912–1913	Balkan Wars
June 28, 1914	Gavrilo Princip assassinates Archduke Franz Ferdinand of Austria
July 28, 1914	Austria declares war on Serbia

like other colonial products, for the occasion. In effect, the world's fairs became human zoos, to which Europeans flocked to gawk at the "natives," who often found themselves mistreated and overworked.

These exhibitions, like advertising and colonial products, appeared to bring the empire "back home" and gave Europeans a vicarious taste of life in the colonies. So did the penny press, which elaborately covered the travels of explorers and turned several of them into heroes and celebrities. In the late 1880s and 1890s, the Anglo-Welsh explorer Henry Morton Stanley (1841–1904) became one of the most famous people in Great Britain. His return to England in 1890 after a grueling three-year-long expedition in Africa received obsessive coverage in the press, and his wedding in July of that year resembled those reserved, until then, for kings.

From Missionaries to the "Civilizing Mission"

As popular as Stanley was at home, his influence in Africa paled in comparison with the tens of thousands of missionaries sent there to save millions of souls. The first missionaries arrived before the establishment of colonies, and their objective was to convert people from their traditional religions to Christianity, not to colonize. But when the various European powers began to carve the African continent into colonial possessions, missionaries helped with the process. They did so by teaching the relevant European languages, training young Africans to be disciplined workers, and serving as de facto representatives of the colonial governments in places where officials were thin on the ground.

Despite this colonial role, the hundred thousand missionaries, who by 1900 had spread throughout Africa, maintained religious and sometimes humanitarian objectives of their own. In some places and times, they offered indigenous people a measure of protection from mistreatment by European officials, merchants, or businessmen—or by their own indigenous rulers. And by instilling the idea that all human beings were equal in the eyes of God, missionaries gave colonized people emotional and intellectual resources that would be useful in the later struggle for independence. Missionaries also gave Africans crucial leadership experience, training them as teachers, evangelists, and ultimately as pastors. After 1900, Africans led a great many of the efforts to convert indigenous people to Christianity, and ordained African ministers established their own, independent churches, creating a distinct African branch of Christianity. In some cases, African Christians would play a key role in budding anti-colonial movements.

Just as local people played a key role in the spread of European religions, so they contributed to almost everything Europeans did in the territories they conquered. The top European explorers always engaged knowledgeable Africans as their guides and interpreters and could not have completed their expeditions without them. Once explorers had staked out a territory for possible colonization, Europeans enlisted local people to fight with them and later used members of indigenous groups to help maintain order and control. Perhaps most important, Europeans could operate successfully in Africa only because non-Europeans had made crucial discoveries in the treatment of malaria, a debilitating and often deadly disease against which Europeans, unlike Africans, possess no genetic immunity.

Despite the importance of these indigenous contributions, Europeans rarely gave them the credit they deserved. British, French, German, and Belgian colonialists emphasized their own accomplishments and represented their conquests as evidence of the superiority of Western people. These conquests added luster to European governments in the eyes of their own

Missionary School in Africa. During the nineteenth century, the various European powers sent nearly 100,000 missionaries to Africa. Their objective was to save souls, but in many cases the missionaries contributed to their countries' colonial projects by socializing indigenous people to aspects of European culture and teaching them European languages. However, missionary schools also helped to give Africans the wherewithal to resist European domination. Schools taught them the Christian notion that all people were equal in the eyes of God and opened them to the nationalist ideas that would later undergird their independence movements.

people and made ordinary citizens feel important. The expansion of the British Empire convinced a working-class writer of the era that "the world was my oyster" and gave him a "proprietary view of the world." He and a great many others proudly saw the country's overseas possessions "as a symbol of the world-wide dominion of [the English] race."

Such celebrations of European superiority did not, however, leave the conquerors' consciences untroubled. They were, after all, taking other people's lands by force and exploiting indigenous people for their own material gain. Europeans needed to find moral and intellectual justifications for their deeds. The most famous of those justifications came from the English poet Rudyard Kipling (1865–1936), who portrayed the colonization of darker races as the "white man's burden." It was the Europeans' moral duty—and the Americans' too—the poet wrote, to bestow the gift of civilization on a backward non-Western world. Imperialism, according to him, was not an effort to exploit foreign people but rather a sacrifice by Euro-Americans who selflessly devoted themselves to non-Europeans, ungrateful though they often were. Europeans tended to agree with Kipling, and their leaders proclaimed a commitment to what the French called a **civilizing mission**, a sacred effort to elevate the dark-skinned people whom civilization had supposedly left behind.

Although the civilizing mission condescended to colonized people, it nonetheless brought some benefits to them—education, healthcare, political and administrative experience, and the kernel of a modern infrastructure of transportation and communication. These gains, however, affected only a small number of people, and the infrastructural projects often involved arduous, dangerous work that cost a great many African lives. Even so, European leaders routinely exaggerated the contributions of the civilizing mission while largely ignoring the extent to which the civilizations of Africa and Asia enriched European life.

Still, beginning in the late nineteenth century, a small but growing number of Europeans found solace and illumination in the apparent spirituality of the non-Western world, and some of Europe's greatest painters and musicians were deeply influenced by African, Asian, and Pacific Island forms of art. The Spaniard Pablo Picasso (1881–1973), in particular, used African methods and motifs to great effect in his painting. And the French painter, Paul Gauguin (1848–1903), found himself so moved by the people and art of the South Pacific that he spent a considerable amount of time there, adapting local artistic techniques and painting scenes of island life. The French composer Claude Debussy (1862–1918) first heard music from the island of Java (now part of Indonesia) at the 1889 International Exposition in Paris and was deeply inspired by the experience. He loved the Javanese gongs and metallophones—instruments made from rows of metal bars—and integrated their sounds into his own musical compositions. He did not, however, travel to Java or, like Gauguin, leave part of his European culture behind.

Russia, Austria, and the Balkans

Thus far we have considered imperialism mainly as overseas conquest, but it involved efforts to control neighboring territories as well. Throughout the nineteenth century, the Russian Empire expanded by pushing its boundaries deep into Central Asia and across the continent to Vladivostok, where Russians established a port and military base. Since

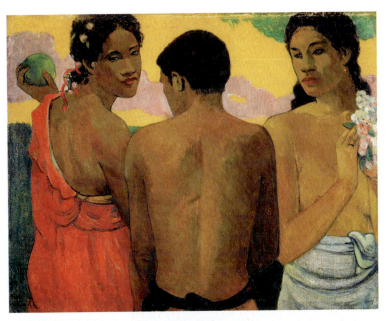

Paul Gauguin's *Three Tahitians* (1899). In this painting, as in Gauguin's many other Tahitian works, the French artist depicted the people he encountered in the South Pacific and did so using Tahitian colors and artistic forms.

Vladivostok was icebound for much of the year, the Russians decided to advance even further south into Chinese territory, where in 1897 they occupied Port Arthur (now Lüshun) on the coast of the Yellow Sea. From there they marched into Manchuria (northeastern China) in 1900, ostensibly to protect the railroad they were building there but in reality to seize control of the province, which they accomplished by 1901. The Russians also began to encroach on the nearby Korean and Liaodong peninsulas. A strong position in Korea would give them a base of operations against Japan, a regional rival, and control over the Liaodong peninsula would strengthen their hold on Port Arthur, situated on the tip of that finger of land.

While moving into China in the East, Russia also looked westward to the Balkan Peninsula, which had been slipping from the Ottoman Empire's grasp. Already in the late eighteenth century, Russia had won the right to intervene in the empire's Danubian principalities as well as to serve as "protector" of the Porte's Christian peoples. Elite Russians, like their Western European counterparts, looked down on the "Turks" as barbarians and did not trust them to oversee the Balkan Christians who lived under their rule. In the nineteenth century, Russia hoped to profit from Ottoman weakness as well as its privileged position in the Balkans to take fellow Slavs there under its wing.

As for the Balkan peoples themselves, much of the elite, whether Christian or Muslim, wanted Russia to help them break free of Ottoman rule. But the Balkan peasants, who constituted the overwhelming majority in every region, remained either content with their status as Ottoman subjects or indifferent to their political affiliation. Russia was generally willing to help with Balkan efforts to gain autonomy, although not to the point of endangering the Ottoman Empire itself. Russian leaders feared that if it fell, other Great Powers would pick up the pieces.

In 1815 Russia pressured the Ottomans to give the Serbs a measure of autonomy, and in 1829, after a Russo-Turkish war, the Principality of Serbia was granted full autonomy within the Ottoman Empire. Greece, as we have seen, gained its independence in 1830, thanks to the intervention of Russia, Britain, and France. The Danubian principalities won autonomy from the Ottomans at about the same time, thanks again to Russian military pressure. None of the Balkan mini- or semi-states was terribly strong, and they did not serve as beacons for Serb-, Greek-, or Romanian-speakers outside their borders. The appeal of nationalism in the Balkans remained narrow until late in the century, and even then, nationalists there succeeded in gaining autonomy or independence only when they enjoyed the help of one or more of the Great Powers.

≡ **The Russian Menace.** This cover drawing from a 1909 satirical Muslim magazine shows the Russian bear, a key symbol of the tsarist empire, about to assault a Muslim man caught unawares. Throughout the eighteenth and nineteenth centuries, Russia expanded into a great many Muslim-majority lands, sowing the seeds of conflicts to come.

Bulgaria is a case in point. In 1876, a small group of Bulgarians rebelled against Ottoman rule without much Great Power support; the Ottoman army crushed it easily and with great brutality, killing some 15,000 Christians. But as soon as Gladstone, the British Liberal leader, made these "Bulgarian horrors" a centerpiece of his electoral campaign, the Great Powers intervened diplomatically, demanding that the Ottomans back off. When the Sultan refused, Russia launched a full-scale invasion of the Balkans in 1877, defeating Ottoman forces and threatening to take Constantinople itself. The peace agreement dictated by the Russians in March 1878 proposed to dramatically increase their influence in the Balkans and shrink the Ottoman presence there by granting Serbia, Romania, and Montenegro full independence and creating a large independent Bulgarian state.

Meanwhile, Austria piled on against the Ottomans by taking advantage of a peasant uprising in Bosnia and Herzegovina to occupy the provinces and thus extend its empire deep into the Balkans. To sort out the new Balkan geopolitical situation created by the Russian and Austrian advances, Bismarck convened a meeting of the Great Powers in Berlin in 1878. At this **Congress of Berlin**, Britain and Germany objected to a large Bulgaria on grounds that it would give Russia too much sway in the region and their own interests too little.

In the end, Britain and Germany prevailed. The Congress of Berlin restricted Russian power by shrinking the size of Bulgaria and endorsing Austria's occupation of Bosnia and Herzegovina. Russia had hoped to place the two provinces under the control of its client, Serbia, and thus to assert indirect power there. These outcomes pointed, once again, to Russia's weakened position vis-à-vis the other Great Powers and showed that Balkan leaders did not control their countries' fate. These leaders were subject to a form of imperialism that put the interests of the Great Powers first, although they, too, had to make compromises. Austrian officials looked down on Serbia as a den of "thieves and murderers and bandits" but could not prevent that country from gaining its independence or from trying to win the allegiance of Serbs inside Austria-Hungary.

Austria-Hungary: Nationalism and the Empire

Although Austria gained territory in the Balkan conflicts of the 1870s, its successes in that region did little to strengthen or add cohesion to the empire as a whole. The "Dual Monarchy" continued to be plagued by conflicts among its different nationalities, although those conflicts, persistent as they were, did not mean, as many Austro-Hungarians believed at the time—and some historians since—that the empire was doomed to fall apart. It is true that nationalists often pushed for the autonomy and even the independence of the "nations" they defined in linguistic or ethnic terms, but people in all walks of life often refused to act as if they belonged to distinct nations understood in this way.

As we have seen, plenty of Austro-Hungarians used two or more languages in their daily lives, and even monolingual people commonly identified as much—or more—with the empire than with the ethno-linguistic nation to which nationalists said they belonged. Nationalists were political actors who claimed that their nations already existed, but in reality their efforts were designed to bring those distinct nations into being. They tried to do so by convincing people to give their allegiance to particular "nations" rather than to the Austro-Hungarian empire as a whole, and to disassociate themselves from people and institutions said to belong to an opposing nation. In some instances the nationalists succeeded in their efforts, and in others they did not. Their successes often emerged from battles over what language would be used in schools, the marketplace, and official government correspondence. These struggles regularly erupted into riots and other violent events. But in other cases, people defied the directives of nationalists and behaved as citizens of a multinational empire, cooperating with people across linguistic and cultural divides. Even so, the language of nationalism increasingly dominated the Austro-Hungarian public sphere as the nineteenth century drew to a close, and citizens of the empire had to define themselves in relation to it—even if to reject certain nationalist understandings of their world.

Not infrequently, battles over national identity and the rights and privileges to be accorded to the various national groups, as the nationalists defined them, gridlocked the Empire's parliament in Vienna, as well as its counterpart in the Hungarian capital, Budapest. In these moments, Emperor Franz Joseph (ruled 1848–1916) governed by decree, at least in the Austrian part of his lands. This situation made the regime appear more autocratic than he intended it to be, creating a vicious cycle in which apparent autocracy intensified opposition and thus the need to govern by decree.

The regime did not, in fact, possess a particularly liberal constitution. Its elitist electoral system excluded the majority of the population and gave preference to the old landed aristocracy. The emperor retained far more independent authority than did the monarchs of Western Europe. A relatively liberal ministry governed in the late 1860s and early 1870s, but it could not overcome the opposition of the conservatives and Catholics who had traditionally ruled. In the mid-1870s, the liberals left office in defeat, although they retained influential positions in business and industry, and, for a time, journalism and the arts. By the end of the century, liberal writers and artists faced challenges from traditionalists on the right and the cultural avant-garde on the left.

On the political left, a fairly powerful Austrian Social Democratic Party emerged along the lines of the German SPD. Like its sister party across the border, it found itself divided into Marxists and gradualists, but unlike the SPD, the Austrian socialists were divided by nationality as well. The socialists' cultural and linguistic rifts tended, however, to be manageable, and in managing them, their party became one of the increasingly rare organizations within Austria-Hungary that united people across the boundaries of language, region, and culture. What kept the Austrian Social Democratic Party from matching the power of its counterpart in Germany was Austria-Hungary's persistent restrictions on the right to vote. To overcome those restrictions, the Austrian Social Democrats fought hard for universal manhood suffrage, finally winning it in 1907.

"Politics in a New Key": Antisemitism and the Extreme Right

If Austria's Social Democrats spoke to ordinary people on the left, two new populist groups, the nationalist Pan-German Party and the Christian Social Party, appealed to nonelites on the right, especially the farmers, artisans, and shopkeepers squeezed by the advances of large-scale capitalism. Under the leadership of the demagogic Georg von Schönerer (1842–1921), the Pan-German Party blamed the ills of Austria-Hungary on its non-German nationalities and especially on the one group said to possess no nationality at all: the Dual Monarchy's Jewish population, which comprised 4–5 percent of the total in 1890. To reduce Jewish influence, never very significant, Schönerer sought to deprive Jews of political and civil rights, bar them from the professions, and prevent them from operating certain kinds of businesses. Later on, Adolf Hitler would gratefully acknowledge the contribution Schönerer had made to his own antisemitic views.

Throughout the 1880s and 1890s, Schönerer's antisemitism became so virulent, his rhetorical tones so feverish, that he represented a new kind of politics, a "politics," as the historian Carl Schorske called it, "in a new [sharper] key." So did another even more successful Viennese politician, Karl Luëger (1844–1910). A lawyer and self-made man, Luëger assiduously courted the landed aristocracy and sought the support of certain radical elements within the Catholic Church. But his primary constituency was a newly enfranchised lower middle class of skilled craftsmen and small shopkeepers angry over their inability to compete with factories and the era's newest commercial institution, the department store. Luëger wooed these disaffected people by blaming the Jews, falsely said to dominate the economy, for their plight; his popularity earned him several terms as mayor of Vienna.

≡ **A Russian Pogrom.** Jews were unjustly blamed for the assassination of Tsar Alexander II in 1881; in punishment, soldiers and others unleashed a wave of pogroms or violent assaults against Russia's Jewish communities. A great many Jews lost their lives, and Jewish homes and synagogues were destroyed. This photograph shows a group of men contending with the damage to their *shul*.

Antisemitism in Russia and France

While Schönerer and Luëger exploited antisemitic prejudice in Austria, longstanding anti-Jewish movements in Russia remained active. A series of **pogroms** or violent assaults against Jewish communities had taken place there after terrorists, some of them Jewish, assassinated Tsar Alexander II in 1881. The assassination may have sparked the rioting, but it was far from its only cause. A key factor was the explosive growth of the Russian-Jewish population that had begun after the absorption of Poland-Lithuania at the end of the eighteenth century. This growth evoked a widespread worry among Christians that Jews were becoming too powerful a group, even though they were legally confined to the "Pale of Settlement" along the western border of the empire. In the middle of the nineteenth century, Jews represented 3 percent of Russia's population; by the end of the century, they had ballooned to 9 percent.

The supposed problem wasn't just the mounting Jewish numbers; it was also their "alien" culture—whether the culture of traditionalist Jews, with their Yiddish language, distinctive dress, and peculiar religious habits, or the culture of Westernized Jews, said to threaten genuine Russian ways with their liberal and socialist politics, their modernist art and literature, and their commitment to competitive, atomistic capitalism. Peasants, in particular, worried that the Jews would soon dominate them economically. These fears dovetailed with longstanding religious animosities, so that when the tsar was killed, many Russians blamed the Jews and decided to make them pay.

The rioting began in urban centers to which many Jews had emigrated and where rapid economic change had disrupted the social order. Only later did peasants join in, hoping to share in the looting of Jewish property underway in the cities. The violence had not been encouraged by the Russian authorities, as many Jews thought at the time (and numerous historians since), but rather erupted semi-spontaneously from local conditions. The rioting was only semi-spontaneous because traditionalist nobles had boosted it, as had businessmen and shopkeepers, who hoped to rid themselves of Jewish competition. The result was devastating for Russia's Jews, who faced more than 250 pogroms in the southern part of the country alone. This vast wave of violence killed a large number of Jews, destroyed thousands of homes and businesses, and decimated hundreds of communities. In the wreckage of the pogroms, Jewish life in Russia persisted, although in weakened state. Even so, antisemites continued to consider Jews a mortal threat. In 1903, anonymous writers concocted a text entitled *The Protocols of the Elders of Zion*, which purported to reveal that Jews were conspiring to dominate the world. The *Protocols* first appeared in a St. Petersburg newspaper before being translated into many languages and widely disseminated as a pamphlet. It was the invention of bigoted minds, but millions of readers took it as true.

Treatment of the Jews followed the Russian pattern elsewhere in Eastern Europe, but nowhere did the so-called "Jewish question" become more politicized than in France. In that country, a particularly rabid form of antisemitism emerged in the 1880s, when the imperial encounter with Africa disseminated racist ideas and a new breed of ultra-nationalist writers and politicians directed these ideas against the Jews. Antisemites portrayed French Jews as alien to the national community and as such, a group that weakened the supposed purity of the French race. In this context, a number of French movements formed to wage political war against the Jews, turning antisemitism into a dangerous and potent form of "politics in a new key."

The Dreyfus Affair

France's antisemitic movement revealed the extent of its power and support in the notorious **Dreyfus Affair**. In September 1894, a French intelligence agent posing as a cleaning woman found a curious document in a wastebasket at the German Embassy in Paris. The document, called the *bordereau* (memorandum), listed a series of classified French military files that had come into German possession. The *bordereau* made clear that a high-ranking member of the French military command had been passing classified materials to a potential enemy.

The French army's counterintelligence service hastened to find the culprit, and without obtaining a shred of evidence, accused Captain Alfred Dreyfus (1859–1935) of having done the deed. Dreyfus happened to be the lone Jew on the army's General Staff, and given the prevailing wave of antisemitism, that fact was enough to seal his fate—although to be safe, military officials fabricated evidence against him. A military tribunal quickly found Dreyfus guilty of treason and condemned him to die on Devil's Island, a brutal penal colony off the coast of French Guiana in South America. After the verdict, a huge crowd chanted "death to the Jews" as officials publicly stripped Dreyfus of his military insignias.

The case seemed closed, except for one inconvenient detail: important classified documents continued to disappear. Clearly, the traitor was still at large, and Colonel Georges Picquart, the new chief of counterintelligence, soon identified him: Major Ferdinand Walsin Esterhazy, an officer overburdened by debt. Dreyfus was innocent, but rather than exonerate the Jewish captain, military leaders suppressed the evidence against Esterhazy and fabricated new documents incriminating Dreyfus. Top generals feared that by admitting their mistake and hence their negligence in allowing the real traitor to continue his work, they would damage the military's reputation and thus their country's defenses.

Despite the army's efforts, evidence of Esterhazy's guilt and Dreyfus's innocence began to leak out. In January 1898, the famous writer Emile Zola published a

Alfred Dreyfus Condemned. In 1894, Alfred Dreyfus, a French army captain and lone Jewish member of the military's General Staff, was hastily convicted of a treasonous act committed by another officer. France's widespread antisemitism was to blame for this injustice, but at first virtually no one challenged it. This illustration, published on the cover of a leading French magazine, shows Dreyfus being symbolically stripped of his high military rank. In the background, voices in the crowd chanted "Death to the Jews."

rhetorically brilliant polemic, "J'accuse!" ("I Accuse"), that castigated the army leadership for violating the French republic's standards of justice and decency and knowingly convicting an innocent man. Undaunted, Dreyfus's enemies only stepped up their attack, appealing to France's widespread hatred of the Jews. "International Jewry," editorialized the newspaper *La Croix*, "has decided to ruin the French people."

Dreyfus's supporters, including many of France's most prominent "intellectuals," a term widely employed for the first time, took the offensive and ultimately won Dreyfus a new trial. Although convicted again, this time with "extenuating circumstances," Dreyfus appeared innocent to France's new president, Emile Loubet, who pardoned the long-suffering army captain. Dreyfus was fully exonerated in 1906, although ultra-nationalists and antisemites never accepted the revised verdict.

If the Dreyfus Affair embodied and sustained a politics of antisemitism, it also played a role in the birth of **Zionism,** a movement to combat antisemitism by creating a national homeland for the Jews. Modern Zionism was the brainchild of Theodor Herzl (1860–1904), an Austro-Hungarian Jew who covered the Dreyfus Affair for Vienna's leading newspaper and closely observed the hatred directed against his coreligionists. French antisemitism, together with Luëger's popularity in Vienna, convinced Herzl that Jewish assimilation was impossible even in supposedly civilized countries like France and Austria. The Jews, Herzl declared, needed their own Jewish state. Herzl attracted a great many followers, and in elaborately staged performances encouraged audiences to see him as a modern-day Moses, who would lead his people to a new Promised Land.

Feminism and the New Woman

Although utterly different in objectives and ideology from the antisemitic movements of Austria and France, an energized feminism contributed to the era's politics in a new key. This was especially true of Britain, where the struggle for women's suffrage, unsuccessful using peaceful methods, descended into the streets. The Women's Social and Political Union, founded by Emmeline Pankhurst (1858–1928) and her daughters Christabel (1880–1958) and Sylvia (1882–1928), adopted highly militant tactics. They slashed valuable works of art, smashed plate-glass windows, and planted primitive bombs. They also engaged in sensational acts of civil disobedience, chaining themselves to the gates of Parliament each time the issue of women's suffrage came up.

The Pankhursts and their followers regularly found themselves in prison, where they staged hunger strikes to win sympathy for their plight. The government responded by having jailers force-feed the fasters by shoving thick rubber tubes down their throats, a procedure so painful as to be a form of torture. As a gesture of protest and martyrdom, Emily Wilding Davison (1872–1913) interrupted the Derby races by hurling herself in front of the king's horse. She was gruesomely trampled to death. Afterwards, the king expressed concern about the jockey, ignoring Davison altogether.

Such militancy and martyrdom attracted new support but also alienated those who disapproved of these tactics. Militant feminist agitation subsided, and the initiative passed to reformers and government officials who took up women's issues mainly with the goal of increasing their country's population. To achieve this goal, parliaments enacted, in the 1890s and early 1900s, legislation designed to protect women's health and conserve their strength for what was widely considered their ultimate purpose in life: to bear healthy children. Among other things, this legislation limited the number of hours women could work, forbade them to labor underground or at night, and encouraged childbearing by offering "family allowances" (payments) for each child beyond the third or fourth. Governments did not view childbirth as a purely private and familial matter but rather as connected to a public policy intended to maintain a substantial pool of potential military recruits and a large and healthy labor force.

Political leaders sought to protect women who maintained traditional female roles in part because growing numbers of women had begun to do other things. The taboos that had earlier kept most bourgeois women

≡ **Emmeline Pankhurst under Arrest.** As the leader of Britain's women's suffrage movement in the early twentieth century, Pankhurst engaged in militant tactics and regularly found herself arrested and condemned to prison. While behind bars, Pankhurst and her two daughters went on hunger strikes to protest their treatment, only to find themselves force-fed through rubber tubes painfully jammed down their throats.

≡ **The Bicycle.** In the 1890s, the bicycle came into widespread use, and women took to it with great enthusiasm. The new contraption gave women the unprecedented ability to move around independently of men. Artists were fascinated by the spectacle of women whizzing past them on two wheels and drew them obsessively.

out of the workforce and public life had begun to dissolve, and a **New Woman**, as commentators called her, emerged. The New Woman went to school, and even the university; she held her own in conversations with men; and she chose her marriage partner, rather than having her parents decide.

She also enjoyed considerably more freedom of movement than had her mother and grandmother. Although it was still considered improper for an unmarried woman to walk about the city unchaperoned—Montessori's father, as we have seen, accompanied her to class—some were daring enough to venture into the street alone. They wore less constraining clothing than in the past and took, with great elan, to the bicycle, which came into widespread use in the late 1890s. The new invention offered an exhilarating ease of movement and general sense of freedom in keeping with the times.

The changes in women's lives registered during the pre-1914 years convinced a great many men that the "weaker" sex was fast becoming a threat. Because the New Woman was said to be more interested in intellectual pursuits than motherhood, feminism took the blame for declining birthrates and ultimately for a nation's potential vulnerability in war.

Origins of the First World War

Already in the late nineteenth century, people and nations throughout Europe were preparing for the eventuality of war. Some avant-garde intellectuals went so far as to declare that European society had become so corrupt and materialistic that its only salvation lay in a violent upheaval, in a purifying war that would wash the old civilization away. The leading German philosopher Friedrich Nietzsche (1844–1900) hoped for a war that would "say yes to the barbarian, even to the wild animal within us." When adopted by people more hotheaded than he, such ideas helped create an intellectual climate in which war could be embraced. A violent conflagration, it was said, would awaken Europe from its materialistic slumber, from the boredom and alienation of industrial, bureaucratic society and its divorce from nature, community, spirit, and religion.

The Road to War

These ideas may have helped create an intellectual climate open to war, but they could hardly have made it occur. The phenomenon that did the most to pave the way for war was a system of alliances that, in time, created two rigid blocs poised in a cold war against each other and increasingly on hair-trigger alert. Bismarck originated this system with his **Triple Alliance** (Germany, Austria-Hungary, and Italy) established between 1879 and 1882. The German chancellor brought the three countries together in an effort to shore up the Austrian Empire, which Bismarck saw as a crucial buffer against Russia.

Once the existence of this supposedly secret Triple Alliance became known and Germany refused to renew its nonaggression pact with Russia in 1890, the French and Russians realized that they possessed common enemies and that they stood to benefit strategically from forging an alliance of their own, which they did in 1892. The one nation that remained outside this alliance system was Great Britain, which had long sought a balance of power on the continent without definitively joining one side or the other. But British leaders changed their position after the turn of the century in response to the German government's decision to build a navy to rival the powerful British fleet, which since the eighteenth century had constituted their country's principal means of defense. A world-class navy, the Germans declared, would give them the dominant position in Europe and the world that they now deserved.

In response, the British added to the size and strength of their fleet and looked for new allies as well. The logical choices were the two powers already allied against Germany. In 1904, Great Britain entered into an Entente Cordiale (friendly alliance) with France, which meant that given the latter's existing agreement with Russia, it would eventually join with the tsarist regime as well, although Britain and Russia came together in fits and starts. The German government, which had counted, overoptimistically, on British neutrality, was shocked to find its Triple Alliance balanced by a **Triple Entente** (see Map 9.4). It now felt "encircled" by hostile powers and choked by "the ring [that] tightens around us."

Count Alfred von Schlieffen (1833–1913), Chief of the German army's General Staff, realized that in the event of war his country would have to fight on two fronts—against France in the west and Russia in the east. It would be folly to divide his forces in half and fight on the two fronts simultaneously, so he devised a scheme to tackle one front after the other. His **Schlieffen Plan** (1905) envisaged sending the bulk of German troops through neutral Belgium and into France with the intention of overwhelming French forces in a matter of weeks, as in 1870. Germany would then turn virtually the whole of its army against Russia.

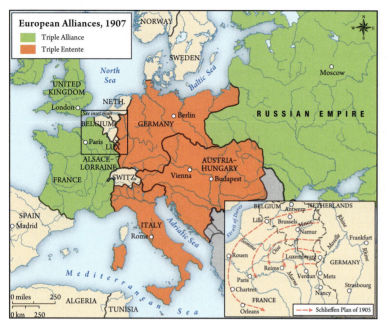

≡ **MAP 9.4** European Alliances, 1907

As the Germans planned for war, the French, British, Austrians, and Russians undertook preparations of their own. They did so not only by devising a new military strategy, but also by joining an arms race whose potential destructiveness was unprecedented in human history. European industry now had the ability to manufacture guns, planes, mortars, bombs, and chemical weapons capable of destroying millions of lives. Some voices warned that the arms race was dangerous, but they went unheeded. All the major countries relentlessly pursued their military buildups, each convinced that to do otherwise would not only give the enemy the upper hand in war but also encourage him to attack.

Given these preparations and the fears surrounding them, the arms race became a self-perpetuating phenomenon that helped propel Europe toward war. So did a series of domestic crises in which members of some political groups attempted to discredit their opponents by accusing them of weakness toward—or even sympathy for—the country's supposed enemies. The resulting war talk reinforced the idea that enemies were waiting to strike and prepared Europeans emotionally for a fight.

France had been divided over the Dreyfus Affair, and in the early years of the twentieth century, its citizens clashed fiercely over relations between Church and state, over a wave of militant strikes, and over whether every young man should serve in the army for two years or three. Those who supported secularists, strikers, and a shorter term of service found themselves accused of weakening France in the face of the German enemy.

Germany, for its part, was increasingly divided by social class, especially after the socialists emerged as the country's largest political party. Interestingly, the left-wing SPD was more hawkish toward autocratic Russia than a great many German conservatives, who tended to sympathize with the tsarist regime. Conservatives also resisted the higher taxes that war preparation required, and they disliked the idea of drafting large numbers of socialist workers into the aristocrat-dominated military. The resistance to taxes moved army leaders to push for an early **preventive war** that could be fought before budgetary problems cost Germany its lead in the European armaments race.

In Britain, an analogous conflict between aristocratic landowners and middle-class liberals moved leaders of the ruling Liberal Party to castigate conservative elites for refusing to support the taxes required to build **dreadnoughts**, the heavily armed battleships that were key, Liberals believed, to the race for naval supremacy. Landed elites, the Liberals charged, had, in effect, sided with the enemy. So, they added, had suffragists who tried to paralyze the state through civil disobedience and terror, and labor leaders who staged a record number of strikes.

The domestic situation was even more polarized in Russia. In 1905, the tsar suffered a double humiliation, first in a military defeat at the hands of the Japanese, supposedly an inferior non-European race, and then in a successful, albeit short-lived, revolution against his autocratic regime (see Chapter 11). With much of Russia's middle class in open rebellion and revolutionaries threatening to turn society upside down, a European war seemed to some traditionalists the only way to redeem the authority of the tsar.

As for Austria-Hungary, domestic conflicts were linked even more than elsewhere to international ones. Serbs outside Austria-Hungary sought to rally to their side the Serbs and other Slavic groups who lived inside its borders. In doing so, Serb leaders threatened the integrity of the Dual Monarchy and raised the temperature of war fever in the region. Meanwhile, the aristocratic elites who had traditionally governed Austria-Hungary and enjoyed its greatest privileges found themselves menaced by the mounting power of socialist

≡ **The Dreadnought.** In the early 1900s, Britain responded to the rapid expansion of the German navy by building a series of enormous, heavily armed warships designed to restore British dominance of the seas. During the First World War, these dreadnoughts proved highly effective, although they were so expensive to build that they nearly bankrupted the country.

workers and nationalist members of the middle and lower-middle classes. For a fair number of aristocrats, the prospect of war seemed appealing, since it might enable them to squelch popular democracy and reimpose top-down, quasi-authoritarian rule.

Morocco and the Balkans

In 1905, the French and Germans nearly came to blows over the question of who had rights to Morocco. The British had conceded the country to France in compensation for its own takeover in Egypt, an arrangement that left the Germans out of the picture. In protest, Kaiser Wilhelm II traveled to Tangier, the diplomatic headquarters of Morocco, to stake out a claim of his own. Some German military leaders were prepared to go to war over Morocco, but when Britain and Russia unequivocally supported the French, the kaiser withdrew. His ill-conceived effort had driven Germany and France even further apart while anchoring Britain, and soon Russia, to the entente with France.

Franco-German antagonism reached a fever pitch in 1911, when the kaiser sent the gunboat *Panther* into the Moroccan port of Agadir. The German ruler threatened to seize the city if France persisted in its attempts to monopolize Morocco's affairs. Since the beginning of the century, France had seized control of Morocco's finances, deposed its sultan, and launched a series of bloody wars against its fiercely independent tribes. In the wake of Agadir, skillful French diplomacy, backed by strong British support, forced the Germans once again to retreat. This second humiliation over Morocco inflamed German nationalists, who openly called for war. The kaiser rejected these demands but privately affirmed that war was "inevitable" and "the sooner the better."

If anything, the Balkans produced even more tension than the situation in North Africa. In 1908, a rebellion by reformers called **Young Turks** against the Ottoman sultan Abdul Hamid II (ruled 1876 –1909) weakened his already faltering empire and encouraged Austria to annex the Ottoman provinces of Bosnia and Herzegovina. This action infuriated Serbia, which wanted these territories, and Serb leaders called on their Russian patrons to take military action against Austria. Russia backed off, however, after Germany threatened to intervene on Austria's side. "Russia is not yet ready with her army," the Russian foreign minister told his Serbian counterpart, "and cannot now make war." This assessment would change, with disastrous results, in July 1914.

In 1908, these conflicts did not explode into a wider European war—at least not yet. But the situation in the Balkans remained highly unstable, and that instability moved Serbian, Romanian, and Bulgarian leaders to attempt to expand their countries' boundaries beyond those created in 1878 by the Great Powers. Such expansion could only come at the expense of Austria-Hungary and the Ottoman Empire, for they contained people who identified as Serbs, Romanians, and Bulgarians. Greek leaders, meanwhile, set their sights on Ottoman Macedonia, although it housed only a minority of Greeks.

Beyond the nationalist agitation in Serbia, Romania, Bulgaria, and Greece, nationalist rebels in the Ottoman province of Albania demanded that Albania become an independent state. In response, Italy, excluded until now from the imperial contest, staked a claim to Albania and seized Libya, still officially part of the Ottoman Empire. Under these circumstances, Austria joined with Italy in claiming Balkan lands from which the Ottomans were being dislodged. In doing so, both countries entered into direct competition with the various small Balkan states.

In 1912, Russia encouraged Serbia, Bulgaria, Greece, and Montenegro to come together in a defensive alliance, the Balkan League, designed to check any Italian or Austrian advance. But instead of standing firm against Austria, the four countries attacked Turkey, whose dwindling position in the Balkans Russia wanted to preserve—in part to prevent the Ottomans from seeking a protective alliance with Germany. Having for decades encouraged Balkan nationalism at Turkey's expense, Russia now found that Balkan nationalists had gone too far.

In the First Balkan War (1912), the Balkan League's campaign against Turkey reduced the Ottomans' European possessions to a tiny ring around Constantinople, a city now exposed to attack, and Serbia and Greece expanded into the territories vacated by the Turks. Bulgaria, meanwhile, was unhappy with its share of the spoils, and in the Second Balkan War (1913) opened hostilities against its former allies in the Balkan League, which defeated Bulgaria easily. To prevent Serbia and Greece from expanding further and threatening Austria, the Great Powers recognized the independence of Albania (see Map 9.5).

The two Balkan wars left Turkey humiliated and vulnerable and drove it into the arms of Germany, exactly as Russia had feared. In early 1914, a leading Turkish newspaper declared that the Ottoman Empire could be preserved "only by war" and with Germany as its ally. Meanwhile, the Serbian gains at Turkey's expense emboldened Serbian nationalists to demand that their country now expand into the Slav-inhabited regions of Austria and create a large Serbian state. It was amid such nationalist demands that a Serbian student, Gavrilo Princip (1894–1918), assassinated Austria's Archduke Franz Ferdinand, heir to the Habsburg throne, as he toured the Bosnian capital Sarajevo on June 28, 1914.

proportions. Between the 1870s and 1914, Europe's balance of power had changed dramatically, and the new rebalanced Europe was unstable. Bismarck's German Empire had become an economic and political powerhouse threatening to France and, by the turn of the century, to Britain as well. The weakened Austrian and Ottoman Empires allowed for a series of wars in Southeastern Europe, and imperial rivalries between Britain and France and between them and Germany extended continental tensions to Africa and beyond.

Underlying these geopolitical developments was a series of technological innovations that reshaped the way people lived and created new, extraordinarily destructive weapons of war. Meanwhile, social and cultural changes added domestic tensions to the growing international ones. Working people joined political parties and labor unions dedicated to overhauling the existing order, whether through reform or revolution, and their efforts evoked both repression and accommodation. Bismarck banned the German Social Democratic Party, and he and other leaders sent soldiers and police to put down strikes. But governments also extended voting rights to most working men, and, in Germany, created fledgling social insurance programs intended to improve workers' lives.

While socialists blamed the captains of industry for unemployment, poor working conditions, and inadequate wages, new antisemitic parties emerged in Austria and France to lay the blame on Jews. In Russia, antisemitism led to murderous attacks on Jewish communities and moved a great many Jews to migrate to Western Europe and especially to the United States. Alongside these and other conflicts, women's movements emerged to advocate female suffrage and a general equality between women and men. Maria Montessori was emblematic of the era's emancipated New Woman, who began to populate schools and universities and enter professions once reserved for men.

Intellectuals and politicians criticized the New Woman for supposedly abandoning her sex's traditional domestic and maternal roles. In some countries, they blamed her for a decline in the birth rate and thus for manpower shortages that would weaken their armies and encourage potential enemies to attack. These criticisms were blatantly unfair, for the main causes of war lay elsewhere, as we have seen. When armed conflict broke out in August 1914, the Great European Powers launched their people—and eventually those of the United States, Asia, Africa, and the Middle East—into the abyss.

KEY TERMS

Boer War *406*

civilizing mission *412*

colonization *404*

Congress of Berlin *415*

dreadnoughts *425*

Dreyfus Affair *419*

economic nationalism *393*

finance capitalism *390*

home rule *395*

incandescent filament
  lamp *392*

Indian Rebellion *408*

informal empire *400*

internal combustion
  engine *391*

Kulturkampf *398*

Long Depression *388*

new imperialism *405*

New Woman *422*

pogroms *418*

preventive war *425*

Schlieffen Plan *423*

Scramble for Africa *400*

spheres of influence *402*

tariffs *392*

Triple Alliance *423*

Triple Entente *423*

Young Turks *426*

Zionism *420*

For digital learning resources, please go to **https://www.oup.com/he/berenson2e**.
Turn to the back of the book to see the list of primary sources and writing exercises
provided in the accompanying *Sources and Guided Writing Exercises for Europe in the
Modern World*

The First World War, 1914–1919

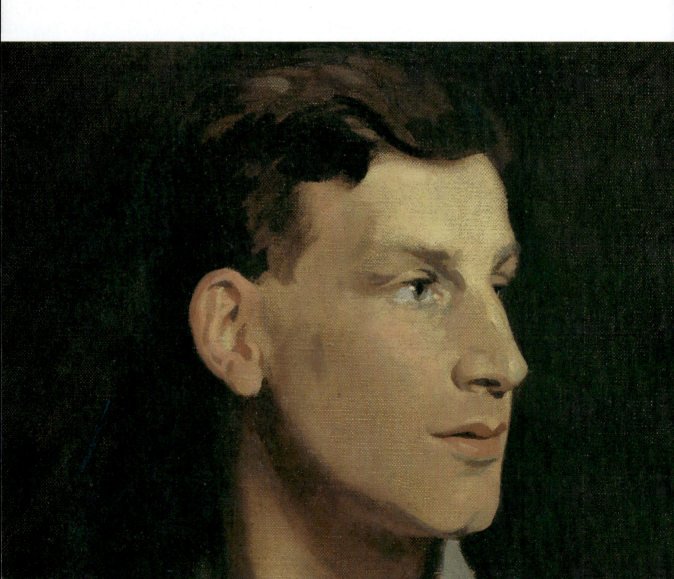

Siegfried Sassoon

The First World War drew an entire generation of young men into its vortex of death and destruction and transformed the lives of those who survived it. After the war ended in 1918, people from all walks of life struggled to make sense of what had happened. Once optimistic, middle-class people no longer looked to the future with the confidence typical of the nineteenth century, nor could they take for granted the benevolence of science and the inevitability of progress. The twentieth century seemed a darker and far more troubled time.

No one reveals this transformation of perception better than the British poet Siegfried Sassoon (1886–1967), whose autobiographical writings give a powerful sense of the disillusionment that war could produce and of what it meant and felt to be a soldier at the front. Sassoon was born in Kent in 1886, where he lived a peaceful and apparently happy country life. His well-to-do mother had artistic inclinations, and she encouraged the young Siegfried's interest in drawing and poetry. She sent him to a good boarding school and then to Cambridge, where he studied law and history. But scholarship was not for him, and he left school without earning a degree. Sassoon much preferred his comfortable rural life at home, where an inheritance allowed him the full-time pleasures of cricket, fox hunting, book collecting, and writing romantic verse. After the war, a sadder but wiser adult Sassoon, his memories laced with irony, described his prewar self as overly "impressed by the urgency of tremendous trifles."

When the war suddenly intervened in August 1914, the twenty-eight-year-old Sassoon rushed to enlist, as did a great many others of his generation. He joined the cavalry, expecting his excellent horsemanship to be valuable to the war effort. But this war was to be different from those of the previous century. On the Western Front (southern Belgium and northern France), cavalry gave way to infantry (foot soldiers), and horses ultimately to tanks. Ironically, a riding accident prevented him from being sent to France right away, and he did not take his place at the front until late 1915.

It was clear by then that the war would not be short, as most believed—or hoped—in August 1914, and Sassoon was aware of the conflict's horrible toll. His brother had just been killed in Britain's ill-fated campaign to capture the straits leading to Constantinople. But knowing and experiencing

were two vastly different things. As he later wrote in his *Memoirs of an Infantry Officer* (1930), the reality of the war did not fully hit him until he saw "an English soldier lying by the road with a horribly smashed head."

Sassoon himself was wounded twice—once by a German sniper and once by friendly fire. Expecting to die, Sassoon took such excessive, foolhardy risks that his comrades called him Mad Jack. One night he set out alone, for no good reason, to destroy a German machine gun. Returning to the trench at dawn, he was mistaken for an enemy soldier and shot in the head. His wound was superficial and the outing fruitless, but his superiors awarded him the Military Cross for bravery. He nonetheless concluded that British leaders were needlessly sacrificing hundreds of thousands to a war that should not have been fought. In protest, he threw his award away.

Despite his mounting opposition to the war, Sassoon remained wedded to the comradely struggle going on in the trenches of France. The war may have been wrong, but he owed it to his fellow soldiers to continue the fight. Another famous memorialist of the time, Robert Graves (1895–1985), described Sassoon as a man who "varied between happy warrior and bitter pacifist."

By 1917, the pacifist in Sassoon seemed to have won out. He wrote a series of poems that chronicled both the horrors of the Western Front and the cynical ineptitude of his military superiors. Published as *Counter-Attack and Other Poems* (1918), these works made him one of the best known of Britain's "war poets." He portrayed his fellow soldiers as "citizens of death's grey land" and denounced his country's military leaders as unfeeling old men who "speed glum heroes up the line to death"— while they are safely "guzzling and gulping in the best hotel."

Sassoon's bitter words aroused considerable controversy at home—one conservative commentator later called them "feeble and depressing rubbish"—but his greatest notoriety came with the publication of his open letter "Finished With the War: A Soldier's Declaration" (1917). This tract was so critical of Britain's military establishment that he expected to face a court-martial. "I am making this statement as an act of willful defiance of military authority," he wrote, "because I believe that the war is being deliberately prolonged by those who have the power to end it." This was no mere pacifist denunciation of the evils of war, but a starkly political condemnation of the premises on which it was being fought: "I believe that this war, upon which I entered as a war of defense and liberation, has now become a war of aggression and conquest."

Timeline

August 1914–November 1918 World War I

August 1914 German advance into Belgium and France under Schlieffen Plan

August 1914 Russians defeated by Germany at Tannenberg

August 1914 Siegfried Sassoon enlists in the British cavalry

September 1914 Russian victory against Austrians at Lemberg

September 1914 Britain and France halt German advance at Battle of Marne

October–November 1914 Stalemate at the Battle of Ypres

December 1914 Serbs repel Austrians from Belgrade

April 1915–February 1916 Allied Gallipoli campaign against Ottoman Empire

May 1915 Italy joins Allies; German U-boat sinks *Lusitania*

October 1915 German and Austrian armies cross Danube River, occupy Belgrade

February–December 1916 Battle of Verdun

June 1916 Russian Brusilov Offensive against Austria

July–November 1916 Battle of the Somme

April 1917 The United States joins the Allies

July 1917 Sassoon writes his open letter "Finished with the War: A Soldier's Declaration"

July 1917 German Reichstag passes a "peace resolution"

October 1917 Unsuccessful Allied offensive at Passchendaele

November 1917 Balfour Declaration

March 1918 Germans launch Spring Offensive

May 1918–April 1919 The influenza pandemic

July 1918 Allies launch counterattack

September 1918 Austria requests a separate peace

October 1918 Ottoman Empire surrenders; Britain captures Palestine and Mesopotamia

November 1918 "November Revolution" leads to German Republic; Germany surrenders

June 1919 Treaty of Versailles signed

January 1920 League of Nations created

Thanks to Graves's intervention, Sassoon avoided a court-martial; a medical board deemed him "shell-shocked" (an ancestor term for "post-traumatic stress disorder") rather than treasonous. To recover, Sassoon was sent to a comfortable hospital in Scotland, where he met Wilfred Owen (1893–1918), a younger war poet, who had as yet published only a handful of verses. Owen idolized Sassoon and said of his work, "Nothing like his trench life sketches has ever been written or ever will be written."

After the war, Sassoon's best poetry was behind him, but he wrote obsessively, publishing five volumes of poems in the 1920s before turning to prose. He failed to produce a great novel, but his three-part fictionalized memoir, based as it was on careful, real-time diary entries, not only provided a gripping account of the war but also helped shape the way future generations would perceive it. Sassoon found it a futile, meaningless, and tragic waste, which is how it would mostly be remembered after the 1920s. But as we will see, it was not uncommon for soldiers and civilians to see the war in more positive terms while it was taking place. For many in the various belligerent countries, the Great War was a necessary patriotic struggle and a battle for values that people held most dear.

But already in 1917, Sassoon no longer found idealism or silver linings in the wartime experience. He became bitter and cynical, much like the young soldier in his platoon who rejoiced when his foot was blown off during a raid. "Thank God Almighty for this," the young man said. "I've been waiting eighteen months for it, and now I can go home." When Sassoon himself returned to England after being wounded, he reflected sardonically on the difference between the way those at home imagined the war and the reality of being at the front. He saw a father who had not been to the war attending to his son who had lost a leg. "I heard [the father] telling one of the nurses how splendidly the boy had done in the Gommecourt attack [part of the disastrous Battle of the Somme, 1916] . . . I wondered whether he had ever allowed himself to find out that the Gommecourt show had been nothing but a massacre of good troops, [that] it had been a bloody nightmare."

The Outbreak of War

How different this postwar Sassoon was from the young men in every European country who had been eager in August 1914 to march off to war. From London to St. Petersburg, men rejoiced on being mobilized for battle. There were festive parades, featuring all the pomp and circumstance associated with great events. One new German recruit proclaimed, "the war had made everything beautiful, [and] I was giddy with … human love." Amid the festivities, the ordinary man "could become a hero," as a Viennese observer put it. "The clerk, the cobbler had suddenly achieved a romantic possibility in life [and] everyone who wore a uniform was already being cheered by the women."

≡ **Enthusiasm for War.** In European cities, much of the population seemed exhilarated over the prospect of war, and this photograph shows Parisian women giving soldiers a warm send-off to the front. The countryside was different; the harvest season was approaching, and peasants were apprehensive about being away from their farms.

These mostly urban scenes were rarely repeated in the countryside, where peasants left their lands reluctantly at best, fearing that their crops would remain unharvested and their livelihoods would be destroyed. Whether eager or reluctant, few of these recruits knew that their leaders could have avoided going to war. But the Austrian government, backed by their German allies, had decided to initiate a war, and the other powers quickly joined the fray.

In the early days of August, Russian troops raced westward toward Habsburg lands, and French troops headed east and north to face the German invasion. On August 3, two German armies poured into Belgium, violating that country's neutrality. Their intention was to sweep down into France, circle to the west and south of the French forces and push them eastward, up against a third German army lying in wait. Surrounded by German soldiers, the French army would have no choice but to surrender—or so the kaiser's commanders believed.

Fortunately for the French, the Schlieffen Plan worked better on paper than in practice. The Germans expected that Britain would send an expeditionary force to France, but they underestimated the significance of its role in the early fighting. The invaders thus faced a stronger opposing force than they had bargained for. The Germans had also neglected to account for the spirited Belgian resistance that slowed their army's advance. These two developments and several others—a

German failure to follow through on its offensive successes, inadequate German supplies and reinforcements, and some skillful maneuvering by French generals— made the Schlieffen Plan fall apart. Instead of sweeping the French army from west to east, capturing Paris along the way, the Germans missed the French capital altogether and became bogged down along the Marne River, just east of the city.

The Battles of the Marne and Ypres

There on the Marne, Britain and France, representing two of the three Allied Powers (the third ally, Russia, fought entirely in the east), opposed Germany in what was to be the most decisive battle of the month-old war. On September 4, French forces under General Joseph Joffre (1852–1931) counterattacked, opening a gap between the two German armies operating in northern France. Together, French and British soldiers moved into this gap and began to push the German armies back—thanks, in part, to the morale-building efforts of Parisian taxicab drivers, who transported six thousand French soldiers to the front. The Germans, meanwhile, exhausted from more than a month of ceaseless advance, their leadership now in disarray, decided to retreat. Their withdrawal was orderly and well organized, and the reinforcements that were rushed in enabled them to take up a strong defensive position well within French territory. But they could not regain the initiative; the German commander-in-chief, Helmut von Moltke (1848–1916), had to divert troops to the east, where the Russians were doing better and the Austrians worse than expected.

With the conclusion of the Battle of the Marne, the two opposing forces tried to maintain a war of movement by attempting to outflank each other to the north and west. Instead, they simply extended the front throughout northern France and all the way to the Belgian

≡ **The Destruction of Ypres.** In September and October 1914, the Germans tried to blast open a hole in the Franco-British line near the Belgian town of Ypres. In a month of bloody fighting, no significant territory was gained or lost, but 150,000 soldiers were killed or wounded. The town itself was reduced to rubble.

coast. Before this front was solidified, however, the Germans tried to open a hole in the Franco-British line near the southern Belgian town of Ypres. The fighting there lasted more than a month without either side gaining any significant new territory, but at the cost of 50,000 casualties for the British, who represented the Allied side, and 100,000 for the Germans. The Flanders countryside became a wasteland, the town of Ypres a ruin. This battle provided a gruesome taste of what the war on the Western Front was to become: fighting of unprecedented brutality with hundreds of thousands of casualties and no vital territory gained or lost.

The Western Front

After Ypres, the nature of the conflict on the Western Front changed entirely. The freewheeling war of movement that had characterized its first months now bogged down into a stalemate war of attrition in which the two sides dug themselves into 12,000 miles of parallel, opposing trenches. Soldiers on both sides spent most of their time crouched in these trenches, which extended from coastal Belgium to the Swiss frontier and formed two, mostly immobile, lines.

Each line consisted not of one trench, but three: a front or firing trench constructed between fifty yards and a mile from the opposing front line, a support trench a few hundred yards to the rear, and a reserve trench well beyond the range of enemy artillery. Between the two opposing front lines stood the forbidding **no man's land**, the terrain on which offensives took place and which, for defense, was studded with barbed wire, observation and listening posts, grenade-throwing positions, and machine gun nests. Soldiers had to traverse this no man's land in order to attack the enemy, their movement hindered not only by these defensive devices but also by the residues of earlier fighting: water-logged shell craters, burned-out tree stumps, mud, and rotting corpses.

On the Franco-British side, a typical front-line trench was six to eight feet deep, affording soldiers inside a measure of protection from opposing gunfire. There could be no protection, of course, from the artillery shells that regularly landed in or near a trench, killing most of those trapped inside. Soldiers fired at the enemy from behind parapets of sandbags but otherwise ate, slept, and fought in the dank and muddy trenches to which they were assigned. They were always wet and cold, thanks to the

The Trenches. For most of the war, French and British soldiers crouched in hastily dug trenches perpetually filled with rainwater, thanks to the damp climate of northern France. Front-line soldiers were always cold, wet, and deprived of sleep.

dreadful climate of northern France, and the filth and stench were so bad that those entering the trenches for the first time immediately felt sick. Lice infested most soldiers' bodies, and rats thrived on the dead. No one could endure such misery for very long, especially given the constant risk of injury and death. After a week, front-line soldiers were released first to the support trenches, and then a week later to the reserve line where conditions were a bit better and they were relatively safe. After a period of rest, they returned to the front line (see Map 10.1).

Because the Germans were concerned as much with defending their captured territories as with returning to the offensive, they built considerably more elaborate trenches. It was not uncommon for a German dugout to be thirty feet deep and to feature bunk beds, water tanks with taps, and wood planks on the walls and floors to protect soldiers from the mud. The writer Ernst Jünger (1895–1998) described himself, not without exaggeration, as "master of an underground dwelling" so deep that even the heaviest shells "made no more than a pleasant rumble when we sat there over an interminable game of cards."

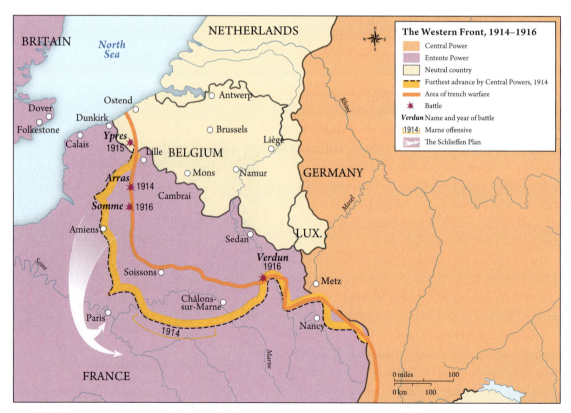

≡ **MAP 10.1** The Western Front, 1914–1916

Trench Warfare

From the end of the battle of Ypres in November 1914 to the German offensives of spring and summer 1918, the war on the Western Front took place mostly in and around the trenches. These dugouts formed a de facto line of fortresses that made it extremely difficult to penetrate the opposing side, thus giving the defending army an enormous advantage over the attacking one. To attempt to dislodge an entrenched enemy, attackers had to leap out of their own trenches onto no man's land, where they soon appeared within the sights of the other side's machine gunners. Artillery shelling had so denuded the strip of land separating the opposing trenches that there were few places to take cover, allowing machine gunners to mow attackers down. Those who managed to survive the first machine gun blasts inevitably ran into a wall of barbed wire, which they had to cut laboriously by hand. While attempting to do so they were sitting ducks. Offensive troops rarely made it past the barbed wire; those who did remained vulnerable not only to machine gun fire but also to artillery, grenades, and rifles. If against all odds the attackers succeeded in overwhelming the firing trench, they then had to confront those encamped in the support and reserve trenches. Not until the final months of the war did the two sides develop the weapons and tactics to break through all three.

Despite the enormous advantages of the defenders, leaders of both the Allies and the **Central Powers**— Germany, Austria-Hungary, and the Ottoman Empire—clung steadfastly to their belief in offensive operations. Both sides feared they lacked the resources and perhaps the morale to win a lengthy war and repeatedly tried to end it by achieving a breakthrough in the enemy lines. In theory, once a breakthrough occurred, it would be relatively easy to surround the enemy force and then annihilate it. That the German invasion of August 1914 came close to surrounding French forces convinced German generals—and their French counterparts—that an offensive strategy could succeed.

Generals on both sides drew confidence from the unprecedented destructiveness of the new military technology. In 1815, a musket had a maximum range of 150 yards and could fire two rounds a minute. A century later, the rifle's range had increased to a mile and frequency to ten

≡ **The Battlefield's Open Graves.** Both sides' powerful artillery killed so many men so quickly that their surviving comrades could not keep up with the toll. Corpses lay unburied for days, and soldiers often had to do battle amid the dying and the dead.

bullets a minute. Machine guns could sweep a wide area and fire 400–600 rounds a minute, and heavy field guns could hit targets as far as five miles away while launching up to twenty rounds a minute. What the generals mostly failed to accept—perhaps because they did not want to—was the huge inherent advantage the new technology gave defenders over attackers.

This advantage held true until attackers developed the technology to advance behind a nearly impermeable wall of artillery fire complemented by tanks and planes. Although the various armies did not develop this technology until late in the war, military leaders knew all along that such an attack was theoretically possible and regularly came to the premature conclusion that they were ready to mount one and thus that their next offensive would succeed. This belief transformed the Western Front into a theater of futile slaughter (see Map 10.2). By the end of 1914, after five months of war, French and German casualties exceeded eight hundred thousand each. The following year was particularly bloody, with the French losing one and a half million men and the British another three hundred thousand in the West. During the battles that claimed these hundreds of thousands of lives, no significant territory changed hands. Political leaders and journalists pointed out that the offensive strategy was not working. But generals on both sides replied that even if a breakthrough had not taken place, the enemy was being ground down by a war of attrition that promised to weaken its morale, manpower, and resources to the point that an offensive would ultimately achieve its goals. In this context, 1916 was destined to be the most murderous year of the war. Each side decided that the time was ripe for the breakthrough they had been seeking since the stalemate war had begun.

The Battles of Verdun and the Somme

The Germans opened their operations in 1916 with a massive attack on the French fortress at Verdun, 140 miles east of Paris. Both sides viewed Verdun as a crucial symbol, and the Germans believed a triumph at Verdun would be decisive. In an attempt to overwhelm the French, they assembled a gigantic army, transferring in troops from the Eastern Front and fielding an unprecedented array of artillery and other materiel.

The kaiser's forces struck on February 21, 1916, showering the French with the most intensive bombardment of the war—"an avalanche of steel and iron, of shrapnel and poisonous gas shells," wrote the French general in charge of the defense, Philippe Pétain (1856–1951). The Germans had introduced poisonous

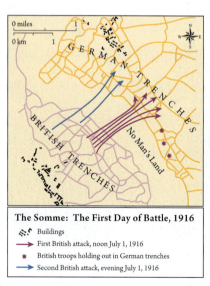

The Somme: The First Day of Battle, 1916

🏛 Buildings
→ First British attack, noon July 1, 1916
✳ British troops holding out in German trenches
→ Second British attack, evening July 1, 1916

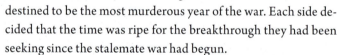

≡ **MAP 10.2** The Somme: The First Day of the Battle, 1916

gases (chlorine, phosgene, and diphosgene) as offensive weapons the year before, and the Allies quickly followed suit. These chemical armaments raised the Great War to yet new levels of barbarity, especially with the addition of **mustard gas**, which seared bodily tissue, destroyed the lungs, and made men blind.

Under the hail of artillery and poison gas, Pétain's French forces fought back effectively, holding the Germans to only minor gains. The German offensive stalled altogether when their commander, Erich von Falkenhayn (1861–1922), had to divert troops away from Verdun to counter a massive Russian offensive on the Eastern Front. Meanwhile, the British launched an attack along the Somme River, intending to draw more German troops away from Verdun and give the Allies the breakthrough they sought. The Battle of the Somme (July–November 1916) raged for 141 days and ended with the Allies gaining a tiny piece of territory, thirty miles long and six miles wide, without the slightest strategic value. The almost unfathomable cost was 600,000 casualties on the Allied side and 680,000 for the Germans.

As the British and Germans fought at the Somme, the French staged a counteroffensive at Verdun, erasing the German gains registered earlier that year. When the Battle of Verdun finally came to a close on December 18, 1916, it stood as the longest battle in history—almost ten months. The French sacrificed more than a half million men killed and wounded, while the Germans lost nearly as many. The kaiser's forces had succeeded in their plan to bleed the French white, but they could not do so without hemorrhaging themselves. The strategic result, once again, was nil. The war had now been in progress for nearly three years; the Western Front remained virtually unchanged.

These battles damaged the soldiers' morale on both sides, as Sassoon's writings—and those of his German

≡ **Poison Gas.** In 1915, the Germans introduced poison gas as a weapon of war, and the Allies followed suit the following year. Mustard gas proved particularly damaging, as it seared bodily tissue, destroyed the lungs, and made men blind. To protect themselves, soldiers donned gas masks to prevent the toxic chemicals from seeping into their lungs.

counterparts—made clear. In the past, a soldier's skill, intelligence, and courage had counted for a great deal; the best warriors were often the likeliest to survive. But the terrible new weapons introduced during the First World War made soldierly talent beside the point. When the enemy unleashed a barrage of artillery and machine gun fire, survival or death seemed a pure matter of chance. The infantrymen's inability to defend themselves under these circumstances created feelings of hopelessness and led many to complain bitterly about the callousness and stupidity of the generals who sent them to slaughter.

The Eastern Front

Ever since the German failure on the Marne, their generals had faced what they most wanted to avoid: a two-front war. Because a major part of the German army remained entrenched on the Western Front, only a relatively small force could be dispatched to the east, where it had to face a numerically superior Russian army. Fortunately for the Germans, manpower was less decisive in this war than in earlier ones. Although well equipped with men, Russia's army, hampered by the country's relatively backward economy, proved inferior to its German counterpart, which benefited from weapons and equipment far more advanced than those of the Russians and a superior officer corps. In early campaigns against the Reich (German regime), Tsar Nicholas's forces suffered a series of defeats, the worst taking place at Tannenberg (August 26–30, 1914) in East Prussia, where 100,000 Russians were killed or taken prisoner. The two victorious German generals, Paul von Hindenburg (1847–1934) and Erich Ludendorff (1865–1937), assumed the aura of heroes and by 1916 would come to dominate the government in Berlin.

The tsar's forces fared significantly better against the Austrians, whom they defeated at Lemberg (now Lviv in Ukraine) in September 1914 but at the cost of nearly 400,000 Russian casualties—the Austrians suffered 350,000 killed and wounded. The Austro-Hungarian army lost at Lemberg in part because it, too, was fighting on dual fronts—against the Serbs in the south and the Russians in the north. By dividing their already inadequate army in two, Austrian generals found themselves outmanned and outgunned on both fronts.

They had invaded Serbia in the early days of the war, but the Serbs fought back effectively, and the Austrian campaign stalled almost immediately. Rather than shift all their troops to the north for the vastly more consequential battle against Russia, the Austrians persisted in their effort to occupy Serbia, which they wanted to punish for the assassination of their future emperor the previous June. In the process, Austrian troops committed a great many atrocities against Serbian civilians, some 4,000 of whom were summarily killed. The Austrians finally took Belgrade, the Serbian capital, in early December, but Serb forces quickly regrouped and ejected the invaders within a week. Much of the Austrian army was shattered, and as a result, largely ineffective in its campaigns against Russia. By mid-December the Austrians had suffered 957,000 casualties, leading their German allies to conclude that they were "shackled to a corpse."

In these battles and those that followed, a great deal of territory changed hands, making the campaign in the east, unlike its stalemated western counterpart, a war of movement. In the east, troops advanced or retreated from one military engagement to the next (see Map 10.3). This kind of war relied on cavalry as much as infantry and neutralized some of Germany's technological advantage. With the German army bogged down in France and unable in combination with the Austrians to rout the Russians, the odds now turned against the kaiser's troops. He had to confront three nations with combined resources far surpassing his own, aided only by Austria and the Ottomans, a pair of empires crumbling under the weight of the war. Still, the German army demonstrated impressive strengths, and the nation's leaders proved adept in mobilizing their potent industrial economy in single-minded support of the war. The Germans may have been at a disadvantage, but during four long years they overcame it with convincing force.

Having defeated the Russians at Tannenberg in August 1914, the Germans began a drive in early 1915 that ultimately pushed the Russian forces out of their strongholds in the westernmost regions of their empire: Galicia, Poland, Lithuania, and parts of Latvia and Belorussia. The effect of these victories was to keep the Habsburg army, close to collapse in 1914, in the field and demonstrate the weakness of the Russian army, which suffered not only from outmoded weapons but also lackluster leadership in the field.

Part of the German-Austrian campaign against Russia involved a new detour through Serbia, which

Nur über meine Leiche geht Dein Weg „Koloß"

≡ **Paul von Hindenburg.** Together with Erich Ludendorff, Hindenburg led several highly successful campaigns against Russian forces in the fall of 1914. The two generals, and Hindenburg in particular, quickly assumed the aura of heroes, as this worshipful 1915 painting of Hindenburg makes clear. Although these and other images of the time portray Hindenburg as a man of great vitality, he was nearly seventy years old and beginning to slow down.

The Eastern Front, 1914–1917

- Central Powers
- 1915 Neutral state that joined Central Powers, with date of joining
- Entente Powers
- 1914 Neutral state that joined Allied Powers, with date of joining
- Country that remained neutral
- Furthest advance by Central Powers on date marked
- Furthest advance by Allied Powers on date marked
- Brusilov Offensive, June–Sept 1916
- Borders in 1914

0 miles 200
0 km 200

≡ **MAP 10.3** The Eastern Front, 1914–1917

stood in the way of direct communications between Germany and the Ottoman Empire and gave Russia an important foothold in the Balkans. In early October 1915, the combined Austrian and German armies crossed the Danube River and quickly occupied the Serbian capital. They were aided by Bulgaria, which had recently joined the war on Germany's side and now sent troops north to prevent the Serbian army from escaping into Greece. With this southern route blocked, the Serbs were forced to retreat through snow and bitter cold toward the Albanian coast, where British ships rescued the survivors—only about a third of the original 420,000 men. As a proportion of its population, Serbia lost more soldiers than any other participant in the war.

The defeat of Serbia made Russia all the more intent on achieving some victories against its Austrian and German foes. In June 1916, the Russian general Aleksei Brusilov (1853–1926) launched a massive offensive against Austria in what is now western Ukraine. In his initial thrusts, Brusilov routed the depleted Austrian army, taking more than 200,000 prisoners and forcing the Germans to divert troops away from their offensive at Verdun to prop up their flailing ally once again. After two months of intense fighting, the Germans succeeded in halting the Russian advance but not in preventing the further breakdown of the Austrian army, which suffered more than 600,000 killed, missing, and wounded. Although the Russians were judged to have won this engagement, they registered nearly a million casualties, making the **Brusilov Offensive** one of the costliest in the history of warfare. Its horrible toll moved a great many Russian soldiers to desert and may have led to the collapse of the Russian army in 1917. It likely played a role in creating the revolutionary situation of that year (see Chapter 11).

The War Outside Europe and at Sea

Although most of the dramatic fighting took place on the Western and Eastern Fronts, the belligerent powers fought a crucial ancillary war in other parts of Europe and around the world. The "world war" they were fighting was aptly named: because Europeans claimed so much of the globe—and virtually all of Africa—the fighting could not fail to spill over into their colonies, where each of the two European alliances sought to weaken the other (see Map 10.4).

Given Britain's naval strength, the Germans recognized their inability to launch a successful attack against the British Isles. They hoped instead to knock Britain out of the war by threatening its empire. The kaiser's plan was to launch military attacks in British Africa and to support nationalist opponents of British rule, especially in India and Ireland. The Germans also sought to unsettle the tsarist empire

SOTTOSCRIVETE AL PRESTITO

Wartime Propaganda. In the heat of the war, each side enlisted a small army of artists and writers for the propaganda effort to demonize the enemy, to portray him as barbaric and subhuman. This Italian poster alludes to the "barbarian" invasion of the "civilized" Roman Empire in the fourth and fifth centuries, depicting the German as a savage, club-wielding Hun. Italy is represented by a Classically garbed woman both to refer to the goddesses of ancient Rome and to emphasize the feminine innocence of Italy, a nation victimized by German atrocities.

The governments of the belligerent powers seemed almost surprised by the level of support their people gave the war, but officials never quite trusted that this consent would persist. To bolster and deepen it, governments enlisted leading intellectuals and writers to create propaganda to extol their cause and condemn that of the enemy. In every country, their efforts began with the attempt to assign all blame for the war to the other side. People would be more willing to fight and to keep fighting, most governments believed, if they could be convinced that the war was purely the result of enemy aggression.

The Home Front

Another key way to maintain the soldiers' willingness to fight, and the civilian population's willingness to support them, was to give soldiers periodic "leaves" from the battlefield to return home, despite the hardships their absence created. One overriding irony of the First World War, at least on the Western Front, was that home was so close to the fighting. Just fifty or a hundred miles from "this stinking world of sticky trickling earth," as one soldier called the trenches, was the gaiety of a Parisian cafe, the plush tranquility of a London theater, the comforting sights and sounds of the family hearth. It was not uncommon, observed the writer Arnold Bennett, for a British officer to have "breakfasted in the trenches and dined in his club in London."

As much as soldiers relished their leaves, the proximity of home and its normal life profoundly disoriented them, as they moved so quickly between two wholly different worlds. Back in London, Paris, Berlin, or another city or town, soldiers on leave from the trenches glimpsed enough of the home front to resent those who permanently enjoyed its pleasures. The comforts soldiers experienced at home, moreover, only sharpened their perceptions of the cold, damp, filth, lice, and rats they suffered at the front, not to mention the unrelieved danger of pain and death. With each leave, their resentment mounted, as did their reluctance to absent themselves from loved ones yet again. The policy of granting leaves from the battlefield often did not have the desired effect.

Women's Contributions to the War

Also evoking resentment in soldiers was the wartime employment of women in traditionally male jobs. With so many young men dead and wounded and the rest fighting at the front, all the belligerent countries faced a shortage of labor, only a small portion of which could be supplied by captive enemy civilians or imported colonial men. Increasingly, the European powers solved their manpower problem with women. A quarter of those employed in French defense industries were women; in Germany and Britain, the percentages in these industries rose even higher—40 and 60 percent, respectively. France's supreme commander, General Joffre, exaggerated only slightly when he declared, "If the women in our war factories stopped for twenty minutes, we would lose the war." In Germany, the number of women workers increased by 52 percent over prewar levels and in the big factories by 700 percent. In the United States, the ranks of women workers grew 250 percent between 1917 and 1918.

Most women took these jobs because they needed the money, not as a feminist statement, although many saw their work as a patriotic contribution to the war. This view was reinforced by government slogans such as "Shells Made by a Wife May Save a Husband's Life," although a great many male workers remained unconvinced by such propaganda. Some complained that for each woman employed, another man became cannon fodder at the front. Others worried that with women now accustomed to traditionally male jobs, especially the ones that paid the best, men would be deprived of work at good wages after the war. Still others feared that women's newfound economic independence would strip men of their traditional power and respect.

By working in munitions plants and other war industries, women became indispensable to their country's war effort and to its economy as a whole. Even more directly involved were the women who

≡ **Woman Working in a Wartime Factory.** With so many men at the front, the belligerent powers recruited large numbers of women for the kinds of jobs that, until 1914, had been reserved for men. This photograph shows a woman making an airplane propeller.

served as nurses, many of whom became so horrified by the carnage they witnessed firsthand that they turned against the war. Former nurses figured prominently among the disproportionately large number of women who fueled the pacifist and antiwar movements that emerged in 1917.

Wartime Propaganda

Partly because of these stirrings of antiwar sentiment, governments feared it would no longer be enough simply to maintain that the enemy was evil and one's own cause just. Propagandists had to convince their compatriots that their country was winning the war—that their generals were firmly in charge and the enemy would soon collapse. These messages were powerfully and widely conveyed through the new mass media, especially the penny press, cinema newsreels, and gramophone records. To ensure that only uplifting and optimistic messages got through, officials subjected the media to extensive government censorship and pressured journalists to sanitize the news. Newspapers ignored or played down enemy gains, while they cast disastrous military campaigns in the best possible light. Above all, the extraordinarily high casualty figures could never be revealed. Germany's censorship was so strict that when their forces surrendered in November 1918, the public was shocked to hear the news. They had no idea the German army had been in danger, let alone on the verge of defeat.

In many cases, journalists willingly complied with the demands of propaganda; they did not need the threat of censorship. One prominent British newspaperman extolled "the open-air life [of the trenches], the regular and plenteous feeding, the exercise, and the freedom from care and responsibility, [which] keep the soldiers extraordinarily fit and contented." The reality was so far from such descriptions that they increasingly undermined themselves. According to the French historian Marc Bloch (1886–1944), who fought in the war, "The prevailing opinion in the trenches was that anything might be true, except what was printed."

Despite such cynicism, most soldiers continued to fight, and most civilians maintained the belief that their countries were battling for a just cause. Love of country had become a powerful emotion during the nineteenth century, when, for many, it replaced or reinforced religious belief. Such deeply rooted and widespread patriotism, fortified as it was by pro-war propaganda, limited the appeal of antiwar movements and enabled the respective countries to remain militarily engaged despite the horrendous losses they incurred. Still, some Europeans did speak out against the war, especially in 1917, when the work of Sassoon and other soldier-writers began to appear, and a certain war-weariness took hold.

The First World War, 1914–1916	
June 28, 1914	Archduke Ferdinand of Austria-Hungary assassinated by a Serb nationalist in Sarajevo
July 28, 1914	Austria declares war on Serbia
August 3, 1914	Germany invades Belgium
August 23–September 11, 1914	Battle of Lemberg; Russia defeats Austria-Hungary
August 26–30, 1914	Russia invades Germany and is defeated at Tannenberg
September 4–10, 1914	German advance on Paris halted at Battle of the Marne
December 15, 1914	Serbia recaptures Belgrade from Austrian forces
February 19, 1915	Allied forces land in Gallipoli
April 22, 1915	Germans use poison gas in Second Battle of Ypres
April 24, 1915	Start of Armenian genocide
May 7, 1915	Germany sinks the *Lusitania*
May 23, 1915	Italy enters war, joining the Allies
October 14, 1915	Bulgaria enters war on side of Central Powers
December 1915	Over 2.5 million British men enlisted since start of war
January 9, 1916	Last Allied forces evacuated from Gallipoli
February 21, 1916	Battle of Verdun begins; lasts until December 18
June 4, 1916	Brusilov Offensive begins; Russian forces against Austria suffer 1 million casualties
June 6, 1916	Arab revolt begins
July 1, 1916	Battle of the Somme begins; lasts until November 18
August 27, 1916	Romania enters the war on the side of the Allies

From Protest to Mutiny

Already in 1915, an antiwar meeting had taken place in Zimmerwald, Switzerland, which attracted feminists and leftists from all over Europe. Follow-up gatherings took place in 1916 and 1917, but attendance was slim. Governments did their best to prosecute those who attended these meetings, but the more immediate problem for European officials was the mounting unrest among industrial workers.

Wartime inflation everywhere reduced the real wages of workers at a time when the profits of industrialists had reached unprecedented levels. This growing disparity produced a burgeoning number of strikes, which threatened to disrupt the manufacture of crucial war materials. When workers won higher wages, their rebelliousness declined; when their demands remained unmet, they threatened to turn against the war.

Challenging as the workers' disaffection could be, wartime governments worried most about angry, disheartened soldiers. When they became upset, the country risked defeat. Given the hideous conditions of battle, it is a wonder that more troops did not rebel. But in the spring of 1917, after the murderous failure of yet another Allied offensive, the French army faced a mutiny of serious proportions.

During the Battle of Verdun, French forces had counterattacked successfully by saturating the German lines with a massive artillery barrage and then moving up the infantry behind it. These tactics pushed the Germans back and convinced their main architect, General Robert Nivelle (1856–1924), now France's commander-in-chief, to use them in a large-scale offensive. In April 1917, Nivelle launched a ferocious attack against the German line east of Reims in the battle of the Chemin des Dames. He fielded a new, much-heralded weapon, the tank, whose armor plate and caterpillar tracks would supposedly allow it to penetrate enemy lines. But after just a single day of fighting, only 11 of Nivelle's 132 tanks had survived; their effect was next to nil. The French captured a mere four miles of territory and suffered more than 100,000 casualties—ten times as many as Nivelle had predicted. After three weeks of fighting, 20 percent of his troops had been killed or wounded.

When Nivelle refused to halt the offensive despite its evident lack of success, French soldiers rebelled. The commander had claimed the Chemin des Dames offensive would overcome demoralization and antiwar agitation by achieving a decisive military victory. Instead, it intensified the unrest. Amid the battle itself, 35,000 French soldiers declared themselves on strike, attacking their officers and refusing to fight. Most of these soldiers did not demand that France unilaterally abandon the war, whose essential objectives—the preservation of nation and civilization—they continued to support. What the rebellious soldiers wanted, as one fighter put it, "was to call the government's attention to us, make it see that we are men, and not beasts for the slaughterhouse."

These mutinies represented France's worst wartime crisis since the battle of the Marne. To solve it, the government removed Nivelle and replaced him with Pétain, who treated most mutineers leniently—although he executed forty-five putative ringleaders—and soothed the army's morale. The new commander had long advocated a military strategy oriented toward defense, and he now maintained that any new offensives should await the American intervention and the production of planes, guns, and artillery powerful enough to overwhelm enemy defenses.

The British did not take Pétain's advice. In October 1917, they launched an offensive of their own near the Belgian town of Passchendaele. Like the French offensive of the previous spring, it ended in disaster. Allied forces suffered some 300,000 casualties (as did the Germans) but did not push the enemy back—much less achieve a breakthrough against them. At about the same time, the Italians, who had joined the Allies in 1915, lost 700,000 soldiers in the Battle of Caporetto (October–November 1917). Although officially one of Germany's allies in 1914, Italy had declined to enter into the war. In 1915, it switched sides in hopes the Allies would eventually compensate it with territory seized from Austria. But given the paucity of the Italian contributions, Britain and France would be disinclined to give them any rewards.

As if the Allies' situation was not bleak enough in the fall of 1917, it deteriorated still further in November when the Bolshevik Revolution swept away Russia's Provisional Government, a coalition dominated by socialists who had overthrown the tsar the previous March (see Chapter 11). The revolution's communist leaders pulled Russia out of the war and in doing so enabled Germany to concentrate most of its military force on the Western Front. The Russian peasants and workers who had helped the Bolsheviks seize power wanted peace, and peace is what their new leader, Lenin, gave them in the Treaty of Brest-Litovsk (March 3, 1918). The price, however, exacted by Germany was steep: a million square miles of Russian territory, 90 percent of its coal, 50 percent of its heavy industry, and 30 percent of its population (see Map 10.6). If the end of hostilities pleased a great many Russians, it horrified Britain and France, which now had to confront the full, undiluted force of the German army.

The American Intervention

What gave the Allies hope amid the litany of terrible news was the intervention of the United States in April 1917. Until 1916, the majority of Americans, including President Woodrow Wilson (1856–1924, president 1913–1921), were loath to join what seemed to them a European folly unworthy of American troops. But after the sinking of the *Lusitania*, two events finally tipped the US government and public opinion to the Allied side: Germany's resumption of unrestricted U-boat warfare in early 1917, and the publication in February of an intercepted German cable, the so-called **Zimmermann telegram**. The cable, sent by Arthur Zimmermann, chief of the German Foreign Office, directed his ambassador in Mexico to propose a

MAP 10.6 The Treaty of Brest-Litovsk

German-Mexican alliance against the United States whose goal would be to seize Texas, Arizona, and New Mexico. This disclosure moved Congress to declare war on Germany.

The United States was not, however, well prepared to fight. In April 1917, it possessed an army of only 100,000 men—less than the typical number of casualties in a single European battle. Naval strength was somewhat more impressive, but the country possessed only fifty-five reliable military airplanes. What is remarkable about the American intervention is the speed and efficiency with which the country mobilized for war. In a matter of months, the United States drafted and equipped four million men and sent nearly half of them to Europe.

In doing so, the American government transformed an antiquated militia into a modern fighting force, spending more on war preparations in 1917 and 1918 than the cumulative total of federal expenditures since the ratification of the Constitution in 1788. By November 1918, American industry had turned out 3,200 fighter planes, millions of artillery shells, and 367 modern naval ships. Many of these vessels were organized into convoys, which successfully protected American merchant ships from the U-boat threat. Now US products could reach Europe, where they replenished soldiers and civilians with armaments and food. The American ability to mobilize and equip its army so quickly while fulfilling European needs revealed the extraordinary might of a US economy that now led the world.

Both Sides Prepare for All-Out Victory

With the US mobilization under way, German leaders knew they had to do everything in their power to win the war before large numbers of American soldiers arrived, which would not occur until the spring of 1918. Until then, the Germans appeared to hold the upper hand, especially after the Russian withdrawal had enabled them to focus virtually all of their resources on the Western Front. But appearances were deceptive; thanks to the Allied blockade, the German people were on the brink of starvation, and their army, underfed and undersupplied, was exhausted. Throughout the country, shortages of food, coal, and other necessities led to strikes and other forms of unrest. Even the Reichstag, until then firmly in support of the war, had become weary and demoralized. In July 1917, it passed an ambiguous "peace resolution" that could be interpreted as offering a German withdrawal from foreign territory in exchange for an end to the fighting.

For the Allies, the resolution was too ambiguous to take seriously; for the German military, it amounted to treason. The army leaders, Hindenburg and Ludendorff, convinced the kaiser to replace the sitting chancellor with one committed to stripping the peace resolution of whatever force it might have contained. To ensure that it would remain a dead letter, the army High Command launched a new Fatherland Party to campaign for an annexationist "German peace"—that is, the seizure of other countries' lands—and against the Reichstag, whose majority now advocated democratizing reforms and civilian control over the military. The new party was financed by leading industrialists and within a year had recruited 500,000 members, showing not only that a great many Germans still supported the war but did so ardently.

Thanks in part to the Fatherland Party, Hindenburg and Ludendorff succeeded in marginalizing the Reichstag—and even the kaiser—while maintaining effective control over the government. They reiterated the maximalist war aims that military leaders and their nationalist allies had wanted all along: annexation of strategic parts of France and Belgium, including their richest industrial areas; seizure of the French and Belgian colonies in the Congo; and the establishment of German hegemony over Poland, the Baltic countries, and Ukraine, plus huge reparation payments from the Allies. Some extremist organizations went even further than this, and a chorus of voices throughout the political spectrum argued that the promise of annexations would boost the patriotism of restive German workers and focus their sights on national glory rather than social change. But given the deteriorating conditions of the home front and the mounting desire for reform, it was too late to win over working people in this way.

In contrast to Germany, the French and British had, by 1917, asserted civilian control over the military, but, like Hindenburg and Ludendorff, Allied leaders possessed unshakable war aims of their own—Alsace and Lorraine returned to France, Belgian sovereignty, the security of their respective empires, constraints on German "militarism," and significant changes to the Austrian and Ottoman Empires. Although these aims paled in comparison with what the Germans hoped to gain, they were nonnegotiable both with respect to the German government and to citizens of Britain, France, and Germany who sought a compromise peace. The Allies were just as eager as the Germans for a total victory, and like the Germans, they cracked down even harder than before on those who sought solutions short of that end.

In 1917, France's new premier, Georges Clemenceau (1841–1929), jailed a prewar prime minister, Joseph Caillaux (1863–1944), for seeking a negotiated settlement and issued an uncompromising hard line. "You ask me for my policy," Clemenceau declared before the Chamber of Deputies. "It is to wage war. Home policy? I wage war. Foreign policy? I wage war. All the time, in every sphere, I wage war." Germany's leaders might have said exactly the same thing, and at the beginning of 1918, it was their turn to try another offensive, hoping to break the Allies before the American intervention definitively changed the balance of military force.

The Allied Victory

≡ **France's Bréguet BR 14.** Airplanes, which had previously been used for reconnaissance, were introduced for fighting in the summer of 1917. Their bombs were inaccurate but served to scar all the more an already devastated French countryside.

Ludendorff poured everything he had left into this effort, fielding 199 divisions, each with about 12,000 men, against a total of 158 divisions for the British and French. Almost immediately, the Germans ended the war's long stalemate, ejecting Allied forces from their trenches and forcing them to retreat. They did so by employing massive artillery barrages—half a million shells an hour—that prepared the way for an assault by "storm troops," or mobile infantrymen, carrying portable machine guns and other light but deadly weapons. By late April, the Allies had lost about 300,000 men and were reeling backward throughout northern and northeastern France. But along with the Germans' territorial gains came huge, unsustainable sacrifices of troops—some 350,000 by late April and 800,000 two months later—and this at a time when 300,000 American soldiers were pouring in every month. In early July, Ludendorff's last-ditch offensive stalled, his lines of supply and communications overextended, his forces exhausted, depleted, and demoralized.

Without the American intervention, the Germans might have been able to hold out, but the seemingly bottomless reservoir of US troops definitively turned the tide against them. In mid-July, the Allies, who now included a million American soldiers, regrouped for an all-out counterattack, which for the first time used tanks to excellent effect. Aircraft also came into their own, as the Allies employed planes for surveillance and bombing in combination with infantry attacks. On the first day of the July offensive, Allied forces penetrated seven miles into German-held territory and took tens of thousands of prisoners, handing the kaiser's army its first outright defeat in four years of fighting. By the end of September, after a series of Allied victories, Ludendorff told the kaiser that there was no chance of winning the war.

Meanwhile, Germany's allies collapsed in defeat. Having suffered several military reverses in the summer of 1918, non-German members of the Habsburg army deserted en masse, and their political leaders announced the intention to separate from the Dual Monarchy. In September, the government in Vienna requested a separate peace. Allied troops now moved into the Balkans, retaking Serbia and forcing the Bulgarians out of the war. The Ottoman Empire was the next to go, surrendering on October 30, as the British completed their capture of Palestine and Mesopotamia.

On the Western Front, the end of the war was only a matter of time. In early October, Germany's new political figurehead, the liberal nobleman Max von Baden, appealed to President Wilson to negotiate a ceasefire agreement on behalf of the Allies. The American leader, having earlier announced a willingness to compromise, now took a much tougher line. Tens of thousands of American soldiers had died, and the American people seemed in no mood for concessions. Wilson responded that he would negotiate only if Germany unconditionally laid down its arms, ended its de facto military dictatorship, and established a constitutional state.

Ludendorff, the all-powerful generalissimo, refused these preconditions; he sought only a temporary halt to the fighting so that if he disliked the outcome of the talks, he could continue the war. But the Allies, increasingly confident of military victory, endorsed Wilson's demand for an unconditional German surrender. Bowing to the inevitable, the kaiser forced von Baden to agree, thus saddling the civilian government with the stigma of having "given in." Later, Ludendorff and many others on the German right would claim that their country had not been defeated; treasonous civilians had "stabbed it in the back."

Meanwhile, the German commander, dismissed from his post in late October, maintained that he could somehow mobilize the German nation to repel an Allied invasion. But the already reeling German army had been weakened all the more by a microscopic enemy that had infiltrated its troops. That enemy came to be known as the "Spanish flu," a deadly strain of the influenza virus that would ultimately kill tens of millions of people around the world—more even than the war itself.

The Influenza Pandemic of 1918–1919

In May 1918 Spanish journalists reported that "a strange form of disease of epidemic character has appeared in Madrid." Because Spain was neutral during the war, its press suffered less censorship than that of the belligerent powers, and reporters there, unlike elsewhere in Europe, were free to publicize the disease. Although the flu virus had almost certainly infected people in other countries, the early Spanish reports about its ravages made it appear to have originated in Spain, hence the name it was given, "Spanish flu."

Some historians now think that the disease did not first surface anywhere in Europe, but rather in China. In late 1917, a large corps of Chinese laborers traveled across Canada in sealed railroad cars en route to France where they were to help rebuild the country's damaged infrastructure. While on the trains, several thousand became sick, but the Canadian doctors who examined them did not take their symptoms seriously and sent them on to France. When they arrived in early 1918, hundreds were dying, but not before they transmitted their illness to other Chinese workers and soon to French men and women.

It seems likely that this first European outbreak was relatively mild, but that the virus worsened in the early summer, leveled off briefly, and became much more deadly in September. It then mushroomed quickly in part because people's immune systems had been weakened by malnutrition and other deprivations of the nearly four-year-long war. Soldiers on the Western Front were particularly vulnerable because they were traumatized, deprived of sleep, and undernourished while being crammed together in dank, dirty trenches where germs could easily spread. When soldiers went home on leave, which they regularly did, the virus jumped to family members and friends. Some people recovered rapidly, but others became seriously ill, especially twenty- to thirty-year-olds, exactly the age group that did most of the fighting. Normally, older people are more susceptible to viruses than younger ones, but for reasons still unclear, the Spanish flu was topsy-turvy, devastating the young at least as much as the old.

Symptoms of the 1918 flu included headaches, exhaustion, a dry cough, and gastro-intestinal distress. In people severely affected, the illness sank into the lungs and caused pneumonia, which may have been the main cause of death. Deaths mounted rapidly as the disease spread around Europe and hopped to Britain during the summer of 1918. By August and September it had reached— or perhaps returned to—North America, where there may have been an earlier outbreak. The flu then appeared in Africa, New Zealand, and India, among many other countries. It was now a **pandemic**, an epidemic of global proportions.

Doctors and public health officials had no means to battle the flu except to take measures to slow its reach. They told people to stop shaking hands, avoid large groups, and wear protective masks. Schools and theaters were closed, but the virus could not be stopped. Before burning itself out, it infected as many as 500 million people worldwide and perhaps a quarter of the European and American population. The global death toll has been estimated at between 20 and 50 million.

It is unclear to what extent the Spanish flu affected the final months of the First World War. Soldiers with the disease doubtless continued to fight, but the German troops—exhausted, malnourished, and increasingly sick—could not withstand the influx of fresh American "doughboys," despite Ludendorff's desire to keep them in the fight. The German general's efforts were especially futile in the face of the militant strikes, massive antiwar demonstrations, and military desertions that in October 1918 increasingly said "no" to continuing the war. Any effort to keep it going threatened to tip Germany into revolution, as in Russia the previous year, or to trigger an Allied intervention that would have crushed Germany altogether.

As if to prove Ludendorff wrong, sailors stationed at the Kiel naval base in northern Germany mutinied after receiving orders, in late October, to attack the British navy. Their action sparked a revolution in Germany that sealed its exit from the war. On November 11, 1918, a German delegation headed by Matthias Erzberger (1875–1921), leader of the Catholic Center Party, met Allied representatives in a railroad dining car parked in France's forest of Compiègne. They signed an armistice that formalized Germany's unconditional surrender and foreshadowed the peace agreement soon to be imposed on it at Versailles. At long last, the world war was over.

Germany's Aborted Revolution

Even before the armistice was signed, Germany's "November Revolution" extended from Kiel, where rebels created a sailors' soviet (governing council modeled on those of Bolshevik Russia), to Germany's largest naval base at Wilhelmshaven. Columns of sailors and workers then invaded the city halls of Hamburg and other north German towns. By November 9, the insurrections had reached all the way to Berlin. Meanwhile, in the Bavarian capital of Munich, a rebellious crowd of soldiers and peasants led by the left-wing socialist Kurt Eisner (1867–1919) seized the city and proclaimed Bavaria a "democratic and social republic."

These events convinced the liberal and Majority (moderate) Socialist leaders of Germany's parliament that only dramatic political change would stem the revolt: the kaiser had to go. On November 9, as mass demonstrations gripped Berlin, the

Social Democratic Party (SPD) leadership announced: "The Hohenzollerns have abdicated. Long live the great German Republic." With the German army in defeat and the country in rebellion, the German socialists seemed the only political organization capable of forming a viable government. Friedrich Ebert (1871–1925), the leader of their moderate majority, became chancellor of the German state.

During the war, the SPD majority had sided with the government and largely abandoned their party's original revolutionary goals. This "reformist" turn moved the SPD's more radical members to split off and form their own Independent Socialist Party still dedicated to the abolition of capitalism. For some on the German left, even the Independents were too moderate; a group of socialists influenced by the Russian Revolution established an even more radical group, the Spartacus League, soon to be renamed the German Communist Party.

For the Spartacists, Ebert was as much the enemy as Ludendorff, and they sought to overthrow his fledgling regime. For Ebert, revolution was to be avoided at all costs. He wanted to establish a secure democracy and then move gradually to reform the economy and society. The new chancellor and soon president of the German republic feared that it would be impossible to achieve either goal if Germany's revolutionary disorder were to persist.

The country was certainly chaotic in the aftermath of its wrenching military defeat, but Ebert and his colleagues among the Majority Socialists exaggerated the threat of a Bolshevik-style revolution. The Spartacists enjoyed only minimal support, and with patience, Ebert might have used the relatively moderate workers' and soldiers' councils established in November to build popular enthusiasm for the new regime. He might also have succeeded in creating a police force at once loyal to the fledgling republic and capable of maintaining order. But Ebert's fear of unrest moved him instead to turn to the German army, whose leaders were only too happy to restore order—but at great cost to the nascent regime.

Rather than use regular military forces, most of whose members had no interest in fighting their countrymen, army leaders encouraged the establishment of volunteer militias, or Freikorps ("Free Corps"), composed of demobilized soldiers unable to adjust to civilian life. Most of these volunteers held conservative and nationalist views, sympathizing little with the new German republic and even less with the idea of socialist revolution. They were eager to do battle with left-wing demonstrators.

When the Communists staged an uprising in January 1919, the Free Corps brutally put it down. The Spartacist leaders, Rosa Luxemburg (1871–1919) and Karl Liebknecht (1871–1919), were murdered in captivity, their bodies unceremoniously dumped in a Berlin canal. Their martyrdom attracted more working people to the Communists than would otherwise have been the case. And because the socialist Ebert was complicit in sending the Free Corps into battle, the two murders helped consummate a lasting split within the German left. The mutual hostility of socialists and communists became so venomous that they would be unable to unite even to block Adolf Hitler. In the early 1930s, the Nazi leader would ride to power on a wave of economic grievance, nationalist passion, and resentment against the war-ending Treaty of Versailles.

The Treaty of Versailles

In January 1919, the world's leaders and diplomats converged on Versailles, once the home of Louis XIV, to put a formal end to the war and establish a lasting peace.

In some ways, the Versailles Peace Conference was reminiscent of the Congress of Vienna a century earlier. Both sought to refound and rebuild a European order devastated by revolution and war.

At the peace conference, the leaders of the Big Four—Wilson, Clemenceau, Britain's David Lloyd George (1863–1945), and Italy's Vittorio Orlando (1860–1952)—had to come to grips with two key problems: the collapse of three huge empires—Austria-Hungary, the Ottomans, and tsarist Russia—and the future of Germany. They also sought, at Wilson's urging, to create an international organization, a League of Nations, designed to preserve the peace.

The Big Four's approach to the fall of empires differed from one former empire to the next. In the case of the old Austria-Hungary, the negotiators, operating under Wilson's principle of the right to national "self-determination," mostly ratified the new or enlarged nation-states—Poland, Czechoslovakia, and the Kingdom of Serbs, Croats and Slovenes (renamed Yugoslavia in 1929)—that nationalist leaders had already established. The negotiators then divided the Dual Monarchy's two principal parts into a pair of separate countries, Austria and Hungary, vastly reduced in size, and expanded the borders of Romania, Greece, and Italy. Finally, they punished Bulgaria, a former German ally, with the loss of part of its land.

In theory, the principle of national self-determination, one of Wilson's famous **Fourteen Points** or list of postwar goals, sounded good to a great many ears;

≡ **Versailles—The French Desire for Revenge.** This postwar propaganda poster exhorts the French public to remember Germany's wartime aggression, represented here by a burning gothic (that is, French) cathedral. A sword-wielding French goddess of liberty demands that nothing be given to the Germans at the Versailles Peace Conference and, by implication, that France should receive reparations from them.

in reality, it worked imperfectly at best. Croats, Serbs, Slovenes, and Bosnian Muslims found themselves uncomfortably squeezed together in the same south Slav state, while significant ethnic minorities remained, often against their will, in nearly every newly created country. Hungarians ended up in Romania, Russians in the Baltic states, and Germans in Italy and Czechoslovakia. All told, the Versailles settlement left the new and existing nations of Central and Eastern Europe with thirty million members of minority groups.

If self-determination worked unevenly in Central and Eastern Europe, it played a minimal role in the former Ottoman Empire, where Britain and France divided the region between them instead of allowing Arabs the independence they sought. In what the treaty called **mandates**, Britain gained effective control over Palestine, Transjordan (renamed Jordan in 1949), and Iraq (arbitrarily created out of the Ottoman provinces of Mosul, Baghdad, and Basra), while France assumed jurisdiction over Syria. According to the official language of Versailles, countries under mandates "were inhabited by peoples not yet able to stand by themselves under the strenuous conditions of the modern world" and would remain under the tutelage of "advanced nations." Mandates, in other words, were updated versions of nineteenth-century colonialism in which self-determination was promised, but only at an unspecified future date (see Map 10.7).

The Arabs felt betrayed by these developments, and especially by special provisions for European Jews in Palestine. In 1917, the British Foreign Minister, Arthur Balfour, issued his famous **Balfour Declaration** promising "the establishment in Palestine of a national home for the Jewish people." Britain made this declaration without consulting Arab leaders in the region and in apparent conflict with its earlier promise to turn this land over to them after the war. Essentially, the British government pledged the same piece of territory to two different peoples, each making a historical claim to Palestine and believing they possessed the right to live there. The resulting conflict between Jews and Arabs was destined to endure.

After detaching Arab lands from the former Ottoman Empire, the Allies imposed a draconian settlement on the Turkish heartland. They awarded Greece substantial territory on the Anatolian mainland and placed the Straits and the former Ottoman capital, Constantinople, under international supervision. France and Italy asserted control over large parts of Turkey proper, while Kurdistan gained autonomy and Armenia independence.

The Ottoman sultan, confined to occupied Constantinople, signed the Treaty of Sèvres under protest, and nationalists under the leadership of the war hero Mustafa Kemal took up arms against it. The Allies authorized the Greek army to put down the rebellion, but after two years of fighting, the Turks emerged victorious. In 1923, a new treaty, the Treaty of Lausanne, overturned the original punitive one and

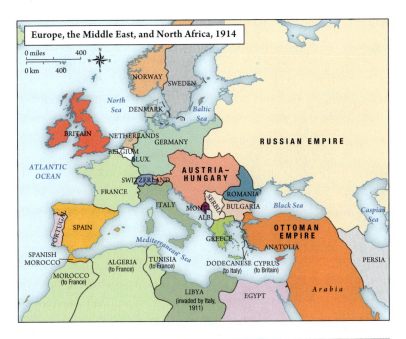

Europe, the Middle East, and North Africa, 1914

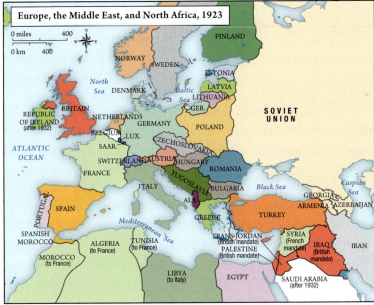

Europe, the Middle East, and North Africa, 1923

≡ **MAP 10.7**   Europe, The Middle East, and North Africa, 1914/Europe, the Middle East, and North Africa, 1923

≡ **Atatürk.** Europe's postwar peace agreements awarded Greece large amounts of territory at Ottoman Turkey's expense. Turkish nationalists vehemently opposed what they considered the usurpation of their land, and under the leadership of the war hero Mustafa Kemal, later dubbed Atatürk or "father of the Turks," took up arms against the Greeks. In 1923, after two years of fighting, the Turks emerged victorious, retaking the whole of Anatolia (the Asian part of Turkey today), Constantinople (Istanbul), and a small strip of European land.

enabled the Turks to regain control over the whole of Anatolia as well as Constantinople and the strip of European territory they had possessed before the war. A new Turkish Republic was born, although at great cost to over a million "ethnic Greeks" ejected from their ancient homes in Anatolia and a smaller number of "Turks" forced out of Greece. These ethnic designations were arbitrary, with Greeks defined as individuals of the Orthodox faith—even if they did not speak Greek—and Turks as Muslims. Their expulsions would later be called "ethnic cleansing."

The Turkish victory had extraordinary significance for Europe's relationship to the non-Western world. The Allies had tried to partition Turkish territory, and Kemal prevented them from doing so by the force of arms. This was, in many ways, the first successful anticolonial effort by a non-European people since the Haitian Revolution; it foreshadowed the anticolonial movements of the next half-century and revealed the extent to which the war had weakened the Europeans' hold over the rest of the world.

That weakness could be seen as well in Europe's inability to preserve its interests in China or protect that country from Japan's imperial designs. China had contributed to the Allied effort and expected Western support after the war, but Europeans lacked the resources and Americans the will to thwart Japan's superior power in the region. When the Big Four transferred the strategic Shandong Peninsula from Germany to Japan rather than restoring Chinese sovereignty there, the Chinese representative stalked out of the peace conference and refused to sign the treaty. Shortly afterward, China erupted in anti-Western demonstrations.

Turning to Russia, the third old empire to fall, Western leaders at Versailles did their best to contain the fledgling Bolshevik regime by shaping the new states of Eastern Europe into bulwarks of anticommunism. This region was to become a buffer zone, a quarantine belt, as it was called, insulating Europe from Soviet Russia. A series of Allied interventions against Russia at the end of the war helped make these political and territorial solutions possible; to ensure that the Bolsheviks could do nothing to reverse them, they were not invited to join the League of Nations. The Soviet Union was to remain a pariah state, one whose authoritarian government and efforts to abolish capitalism earned it the lasting enmity of the West.

Germany was the other major power forbidden to join the League and represented the second major problem to be resolved at Versailles: what was to become of it after the war? The Allies, and especially the French, sought to dictate a punitive peace, one that would seriously weaken Germany and prevent the return of militarism and authoritarian government. To justify such a settlement, the treaty featured a "war guilt" clause, which assigned Germany sole responsibility for the conflict. The actual responsibility, as we have seen, was more widely shared.

To weaken Germany economically, the Allies required it to make large reparations payments to the countries it had attacked; return the lands it had occupied in France, Belgium, and Poland; and cede to its neighbors other economically important territories. Altogether, Germany was stripped of 13 percent of its prewar surface area, 15 percent of its prewar productive capacity, and 10 percent of its population. In addition, Germany had to give the Allies most of its merchant marine plus 200,000 tons of ships to be built, a large part of its railroad stock, and substantial amounts of coal.

In political terms, the treaty was intended to reduce Germany to a second-rate power through the effective abolition of its navy and air force and by limiting its army to 100,000 men. Germany had to give up its overseas colonies, which the British, French, and Japanese divided among themselves. In addition, the treaty forbade Germany to station troops in the part of the country bordering on France (the Rhineland). As if to rub salt in these wounds, Allied leaders refused to allow the German delegation to participate in the peace negotiations, keeping its members imprisoned behind barbed wire. Six weeks after the Germans received the completed treaty, they were ordered to sign it essentially as is, or fighting would resume.

The German representatives at Versailles bitterly opposed most provisions of the treaty. They argued that such punitive measures would frustrate efforts to rebuild their country as a stable democratic state and that the economic weakness the treaty imposed on it would shackle the rest of the European economy, which depended on trade with an economically viable Germany. The economist John Maynard Keynes (1883–1946), who participated in the British delegation at Versailles, echoed these points in an extraordinarily influential book of 1919, *The Economic Consequences of the Peace.*

In fact, the treaty did not hamstring the German economy or turn it into a second-rate power, although it would play a major role in the German hyperinflation of 1923 (see Chapter 12). Because the inflation proved so devastating, the British and American governments ultimately adopted Keynes' argument as their own. After 1923, they only lightly enforced Germany's reparation payments, which ultimately amounted to just 16 percent of the sum originally imposed, and offered it lenient terms for repaying wartime debts. Meanwhile, German industrialists rebuilt much of their country's economic infrastructure and did much to restore its prewar stature. Although the treaty placed severe restraints on the German military and its armaments industries, leaders there managed to resurrect both during the 1920s and 1930s. Even so, the Versailles Treaty created the widespread perception among Germans that the victorious powers had deliberately humiliated their country, meting out forms of retribution it did not deserve. Reactions against the treaty created a powerful desire for political and military revenge, a set of emotions that Hitler would brilliantly exploit.

Beyond the collapse of empires and the future of Germany, the final key issue for the leaders and diplomats gathered at Versailles was the creation of an international organization, a **League of Nations** designed to resolve problems between countries before they came to blows. Most European nations agreed to join the League, but in the United States, Wilson's Republican opponents raised two objections to the organization as the Democratic president had conceived it. It would, they said, unconstitutionally commit the United States to go to war in Europe without due congressional deliberation, while failing to provide for France's defense in the event of a renewed German threat. Republicans wanted to amend the treaty accordingly, and Wilson refused. When the treaty came before the Senate, it failed to receive the two-thirds majority required for ratification, which meant that the United States could not join the League of Nations. With the world's leading power uninvolved and Germany and Russia excluded, the League would have minimal effect. The legacy of the treaty as a whole would, however, cast a long shadow over the twentieth century, setting up potential conflicts in Palestine, Iraq, the Balkans, Central and Eastern Europe, and between China and Japan.

Conclusion: Results of the First World War

We have seen the extent to which the Great War altered the face of Europe and decimated its population. During the four years and three months of fighting, more than ten million soldiers died, with perhaps another thirty million wounded. Broken down by country, these figures are even more startling. Of the 8.5 million soldiers mobilized in France, 60 percent were either killed or wounded. In Germany, Austria-Hungary, and Britain the percentages were 41, 38, and 37, respectively. Fully 10 percent of France's active male population died during the war, including 18 percent of those sent to the front. On average, nine hundred Frenchmen and thirteen hundred Germans died each and every day of the war. Those who survived had all too often been disfigured or disabled and left in emotional ruin. No one knows the extent of the civilian losses, but it is likely that Europe as a whole suffered about fifty million casualties between August 1914 and November 1918. These staggering numbers set this conflict apart as

The First World War and Its Immediate Aftermath, 1917–1923	
February 1, 1917	German U-Boats begin unrestricted attacks
	Zimmerman telegram published
March 11, 1917	British forces capture Baghdad
March 15, 1917	Russian tsar is overthrown and forced to abdicate (the "February Revolution"); Provisional Government is established in Petrograd
April 6, 1917	United States enters war on Allied side
April 16–May 9, 1917	French offensive of the Battle of the Chemin des Dames; 35,000 soldiers mutiny
July 31, 1917	Start of the Battle of Passchendaele; lasts until November 10
October 24– November 12, 1917	Italian forces defeated by Austrians at Battle of Caporetto
November 2, 1917	Balfour Declaration expresses British support for a Jewish homeland in Palestine
November 16, 1917	Vladimir Lenin and Bolsheviks come to power in Moscow (the "October Revolution")
December 9, 1917	British forces capture Jerusalem
January 8, 1918	Woodrow Wilson issues his "Fourteen Points"
March 3, 1918	Treaty of Brest-Litovsk
	Russia withdraws from the war
June 1918	German army advances to within 60 miles of Paris
August 1918	British victory at Amiens
August–September 1918	Allied counteroffensive succeeds
October 29, 1918	"November Revolution" begins in Germany
October 30, 1918	Ottoman Empire and Austria-Hungary surrender
November 11, 1918	Austria and Germany sign armistice agreements with allies
	War ends with more than fifty million casualties
January 4–15, 1919	Spartacist uprising in Germany
January 12, 1919	Paris Peace Conference begins; lasts until January 21, 1920
1920	League of Nations founded
1923	Treaty of Lausanne defines borders of Turkish Republic

the world's first **total war**, a kind of warfare that mobilized entire societies and victimized millions of soldiers and civilians alike.

Although nothing compared in horror with the war's loss of life, the economic havoc it caused added enormously to Europe's self-inflicted misery. The fighting laid waste to farmlands from northern France to the Russian heartland, producing famine and malnutrition in virtually all the belligerent countries. Russia was barely able to feed its population before the war; it fell into the grip of starvation during the period of civil strife that followed the long years of fighting and revolutionary upheaval. In addition to these agricultural setbacks, Europe's industrial machine sputtered as well, as the inability to keep it properly maintained under wartime conditions took a lasting toll. The result was frequent postwar mechanical breakdowns and reduced productivity, which was the last thing Europeans needed; they had to pay off enormous wartime debts, mostly to the United States. The effort to do so transferred massive amounts of capital from Europe to America and confirmed the United States' new status as the world's leading economic and financial power.

The huge amount of resources the war required, combined with the need to mobilize societies and economies from top to bottom, vastly strengthened the role and power of the state. Governments could not entrust private enterprise with the responsibility to organize war production on its own. A central authority was required to allocate scarce resources, direct investment capital to the most appropriate firms, and decide who would go to the front and who would continue working at home. Other key new roles for government included food rationing, mass propaganda, medical services, and the organization of transport and communications.

Even as the state grew in power and responsibility, democracy and democratic expectations advanced as well. By making women pivotal to military production, the war bolstered their claims to equal rights; after 1918, they won the right to vote in Great Britain, Germany, Finland, and the United States, having gained the suffrage during the war in Russia, Norway, and Denmark. Among the major powers, only France delayed, withholding voting rights from women until 1944.

The war also bolstered the standing of labor unions and democratic and socialist political parties, which had played crucial roles between 1914 and 1918. Contributing as well to the advance of democratic expectations was Allied wartime propaganda, which tried to convince soldiers that they were making the world "safe for democracy." If the war's goal was to make Germany and the other Central Powers democratic, most soldiers felt that the least their countries could do was to enhance their own democratic rights at home. Ordinary people tended to define democracy not just in terms of political rights but of economic opportunity as well. When workers returned from the front to find widespread unemployment—a problem caused by the war's depletion of raw materials and natural resources, the destruction of factories, and the reduced demand for manufactured goods—they felt betrayed. Working people had made great sacrifices for their governments and believed they were owed something in return. Unemployment seemed hardly a just reward.

Intellectuals also felt betrayed and disillusioned by the war. Like Siegfried Sassoon, most young authors had entered the conflict with high spirits and the belief that they were fighting for a noble cause. By 1917 and 1918, a significant number joined Sassoon in bitterness toward the societies and political systems that had sent so many young men to die. Writers and intellectuals returned from the fronts questioning not only the war itself but the culture that had made it possible. The optimism of the nineteenth century, already under attack before the war, subsided in its wake. People now questioned the value of scientific knowledge, for the weapons it had created—the tanks, guns, bombs, and poison gas—had enabled human beings to kill one another on a previously unimaginable scale.

Some rejected the realm of science and rationality altogether, turning instead to the irrational, to the landscape of feelings and emotions that came to seem more authentically human. Others turned to the romance of radicalism, either of the right or the left. In Italy, the ultra-nationalist poet Gabriele D'Annunzio (1863–1938) denounced the Versailles Treaty as anti-Italian and developed emotive political techniques (rows of black-shirted followers, special salutes, rousing balcony harangues, and other forms of political stagecraft) that strongly influenced the fascist leader Benito Mussolini (1883–1945) and perhaps Hitler as well.

If D'Annunzio veered to the right, others embraced the radical left. In every European country, new left-wing organizations sought to turn postwar discontent into revolutionary movements. Increasingly, European radicals found inspiration in Bolshevik Russia, a country that appeared to demonstrate the possibility of thorough-going socialist transformation. The Bolshevik Revolution, itself a product of the First World War, intended to build an entirely new egalitarian society. How and why the revolution occurred and what it accomplished is the subject of Chapter 11.

KEY TERMS

Balfour Declaration *472*	League of Nations *476*	pandemic *468*
Brusilov Offensive *447*	mandates *472*	total war *478*
Central Powers *441*	mustard gas *443*	Zimmermann telegram *463*
Fourteen Points *471*	no man's land *439*	

 For digital learning resources, please go to **https://www.oup.com/he/berenson2e.** Turn to the back of the book to see the list of primary sources and writing exercises provided in the accompanying *Sources and Guided Writing Exercises for Europe in the Modern World*

The Russian Revolution and the Rise of the Soviet Union, 1905–1940

Aleksandra Kollontai

In March 1938, at the peak of the Soviet Union's Great Terror, Aleksandra Kollontai, the first woman to serve in Russia's revolutionary government of 1917, described her horror and bafflement over the reign of terror taking place. "I cannot accept," Kollontai wrote, "that even [the most dedicated revolutionaries] have fallen under the 'wheel of history.'" Kollontai worried that she, too, would be crushed by that wheel, that implacable instrument of progress, which according to Joseph Stalin, the Communist Party chief, required the taking of so many lives. The great Soviet Revolution, the millennial event for which Kollontai had risked so much, was systematically—and inexplicably—slaughtering its most devoted servants. Thanks in part to the recent opening of Soviet archives long off-limits to historians, we can begin to comprehend what remained obscure to Kollontai herself.

Kollontai (1872–1952) turned out to be one of the rare Old Bolsheviks (original members of the Bolshevik Party) who did not fall under the "wheel of history." And perhaps even more miraculously, her private diaries also managed to survive. It was extremely risky under Stalin's reign (1928–1953) to write down, even in private, the kind of doubts she expressed; agents of the political police routinely searched people's homes and confiscated their papers. Individuals could be executed not just for acts of disobedience, which were rare during the Stalinist period, but also, as Kollontai put it, for "thought crimes," for "the mental state of the offender, not his objective behavior." It is likely that Stalin spared her because she had flattered him in a flirtatiously feminine way and as a woman seemed unthreatening. A gruff plebian, Stalin was perhaps attracted not just to Kollontai's beauty and charm, but also to her cultivated, aristocratic manner.

Born in 1872 to a prosperous family of minor nobles, Aleksandra Mikhailovna Domontvich (Kollontai was her married name) received an excellent liberal education from tutors at home. Her parents refused to send her to university, fearing the revolutionary ideas circulating there. Besides, marriage, not education, was her family's goal for her. When she turned sixteen, her parents tried to arrange a union with a much older man; instead, she eloped with an impoverished army officer and soon gave birth to a son.

In her autobiography, Kollontai said she raised her son "with great care," but that "motherhood was never the kernel of my existence" and marriage "became for me a cage." She soon left her husband and son to join Russia's revolutionary movement. It was the early 1890s, and Marxism had just come to Russia, where its ideas about class struggle seemed to explain the conflicts taking place in the huge new factories of St. Petersburg and other large cities. Kollontai "read voraciously" in the newly translated Marxist literature and became a member of the radical intelligentsia, the Russian term for the educated—and often highly alienated—elite.

In 1899, Kollontai joined the Russian Social-Democratic Workers' Party, the party of Lenin and Leon Trotsky. Although she resumed caring for her son, she found "love, marriage, family" only "secondary, transient matters." More important was the struggle for workers' rights, which exploded into the Russian Revolution of 1905 and a brief liberalization of the autocratic regime. But the persecution of political dissidents quickly resumed, and Kollontai was forced to flee the country after publishing a book calling for a Finnish uprising against Russian rule.

She lived mostly in Germany, where she associated with many of the country's leading Marxist intellectuals and lectured widely on the condition of working women. She took European socialists to task for having "little understanding, and even less interest" in the "cause of women's liberation." These Marxists, in turn, dismissed Kollontai as a "bourgeois feminist," who falsely imagined that all women belonged to the same social category rather than being divided by class. The condition of women, they maintained, would improve only when the class struggle overturned bourgeois society and allowed the working class to rule.

Although equally opposed to "bourgeois" feminism, which mostly focused on the right to vote, Kollontai argued that socialists needed to pay special attention to working-class women because they were doubly exploited—as factory workers and as wives and mothers. Socialists, Kollontai said, needed to think not just about overthrowing bourgeois society but also about altering the kind of family structure it had created.

Kollontai's own complex situation as a single mother and emancipated woman could not but shape her political and intellectual work. As a tireless speaker and organizer, she traveled to a dozen European countries, often leaving her son behind, while in her romantic relationships with men, mostly fellow revolutionaries, she longed to be treated as an intellectual and political equal and not just an object of

Timeline

1905	1910	1915	1920	1925	1930	1935	1940	1945	1950

January 1905 "Bloody Sunday" massacre by St. Petersburg police

1905 Peasant revolts throughout Russia

October 1905 General strike in St. Petersburg; Nicholas issues October Manifesto, establishes a Duma

1907 Nicholas changes electoral laws to reassert control of Duma

1914 General strike in St. Petersburg

1916 Rasputin assassinated

March 1917 Petrograd strike, "February" Revolution; Nicholas abdicates; Provisional Government established

April 1917 Lenin returns to Russia

May 1917 Kerensky and moderates take over Provisional Government

July 1917 Unsuccessful Petrograd uprising

August 1917 Failed coup attempt by Kornilov

November 1917 Bolshevik forces depose Provisional Government in "October Revolution," establish Petrograd Soviet; Aleksandra Kollontai becomes People's Commissar for Social Welfare

1917–1921 Russian Civil War

1918 Russians and Germans sign the Treaty of Brest-Litovsk

1921 Kronstadt naval base rebellion suppressed

1921–1929 New Economic Policy (NEP)

1922 Union of Soviet Socialist Republics (USSR) established

1923 Bolshevik government bans all other political parties

1923 Kollontai becomes Soviet Ambassador to Norway

1924 Lenin dies

1928–1932 First Five-Year Plan

1929 NEP ends; collectivization begins

1933–1937 Second Five-Year Plan

1936–1939 Stalin's Great Purge

desire. In this quest, Kollontai found only frustration: time and again, she had to "shake off the chains" of love.

Kollontai's life changed dramatically after the overthrow of the tsar in March 1917, which lifted her exile and allowed her to re-enter Russia's political fray. In April, she joined Lenin in opposition to the moderate post-tsarist Provisional Government and struggled to radicalize the new regime. Bourgeois opponents called her a "mad female Bolshevik," as she helped lead a six-week-long strike of women laundry workers and organized a women's bureau of the Party, whose ruling Central Committee she joined in the fall of 1917. After the Bolsheviks' October Revolution, she became the People's Commissar of Social Welfare, making her the lone woman in the new Soviet government.

At first exhilarated and optimistic, she was quickly overwhelmed by the tasks of providing social welfare to an immense population shattered by revolution and war. She did not retain her government position for long. Like many others before and after her, Kollontai succumbed to the Bolshevik demand for ideological uniformity and to the Party's efforts to monopolize Russia's political arena. Her support of the "workers' opposition," an effort to create an independent trade union movement, nearly led to her ouster from the Party and effectively ended her career as a Soviet leader. Rather than ban her altogether, officials sent her to Norway, where she lived in de facto exile as a Russian diplomat.

After three years in this position, Kollontai returned home and rejoined the debate over the future of women under the new communist system. Just as communists foresaw the "withering away of the state" in a harmonious socialist utopia, Kollontai looked forward to the "withering away of the family." In the communist future, she said, private property would cease to exist and everyone would live and work in collective settings. Members of each collective would eat together in communal dining halls, their food prepared in large, institutional kitchens. Children would be raised not in individual families but rather in communal nurseries and schools, and they would belong at once to their parents and to the collective, whose members would feel responsible for everyone's children, not just their own.

These arrangements, Kollontai maintained, would liberate women from the day-to-day drudgery of child care and housework and enable them to fulfill themselves in work for the common good, which she saw as humankind's highest calling. Such views attracted interest in the 1920s, when younger Russians were thinking about new socialist ways to live. But by the 1930s, most Bolshevik leaders wanted women to maintain their traditional roles and, if anything, sought to strengthen rather than dilute the nuclear family. Their main goal was to develop Russian industry; there was no time or energy for experiments in new forms of family life.

Besides, a great many Bolshevik leaders expressed shock over Kollontai's apparently radical, if contradictory, views about marriage and sexuality. Although she seemed at times to promote "free love," she mostly favored communal living situations in which all members of the collective would be bound together by platonic, familial affection, which in some cases would include a sexual dimension as well. In this way, sex would always be paired with love and never promiscuously free, although it would not necessarily be limited to monogamous couples.

Such views earned her a new period of exile, first to a diplomatic post in Mexico and later to Sweden, where she served as modern Europe's first woman ambassador. Her diplomatic service distanced her from Russia's deadly political storms and gave her the confidence to continue committing her "thought crimes" to paper. When she learned of Stalin's confiscation of peasant lands in 1930 and the deportation of tens of thousands of uprooted families to Siberia, she expressed horror over this violation of "communist humanity." How, she asked in her diary, could Bolshevik officials, in the dead of the Siberian winter, herd "children, parents, the elderly and the sick into [railroad] cars like sheep," throwing dead babies into the snow? ≡

Origins of the Russian Revolution

How did revolution in Russia come to this? It was, after all, a revolution whose leaders professed a belief in human equality and an end to the exploitation of the powerless by the powerful. To some extent, the barbarity of the 1930s, a decade of expropriations, deportations, state-induced famine, and political murder, followed from the extreme brutality of the First World War and the ensuing Russian Civil War. Together, the two episodes, which stretched from 1914 to 1921, produced millions of deaths and human suffering that dwarfed the already unimaginable suffering that had gripped the rest of Europe. But for a fuller explanation of the tragic trajectory of the Russian Revolution, we must begin with its antecedents in the late nineteenth century, when the incomplete emancipation of peasants and extremely rapid industrialization led to social conflict on a massive scale.

The Travails of Agricultural and Industrial Life

The "Great Reforms" of the 1860s did not, as Russian leaders had promised, emancipate the peasantry—about 80 percent of the country's population. Farmers found themselves free from the bondage of serfdom only to be indentured to their villages and the state. The government assessed an annual tax on villages in compensation for the noble land transferred to the villages and then to individual peasants during the Reforms. Each peasant was responsible for a part of the village's tax assessment and became indebted to it for the amount owed. This obligation bound peasants to their villages much as they had been bound to their lords under serfdom.

In allocating former noble lands first to villages and then to peasants, the Russian government created forms of communal control that inhibited agricultural improvement and kept most peasants miserably poor. Communes distributed land according to family size, not industriousness and productivity, and peasants usually received a number of separate strips of terrain rather than one consolidated farm. Both policies led to low agricultural output, which meant that, at best, the majority of peasants produced only enough for their own consumption and had little to sell. The resulting rural poverty retarded industrial growth, since entrepreneurs had little incentive to develop mass production for a peasant population that could not afford to buy manufactured goods.

The industrial situation began to change in the last two decades of the nineteenth century, when nobles put some of the government's compensation payments to productive use. Their capital made possible the financing of roads, railroads, and the kind of industry that did not rely on consumer demand (e.g., iron and steel). Foreign capital helped as well; European investment in Russian infrastructure and industry multiplied by a factor of ten between 1880 and 1900. Suddenly, Russia's industrial economy began to grow at a rapid pace (see Map 11.1). Because this process had occurred so late, Russia was able to borrow the West's most advanced technology, making Russia's industrial enterprises more modern and efficient than many of their counterparts in Britain, France, and Germany.

Russia's industrial technology was so advanced that it required mostly unskilled labor; its workforce came chiefly from the ranks of the peasantry, whose men left their villages for several months of the year to work in the new factories and mines. Women and children stayed behind to till the land. Even the small number who labored in factories year-round often left their families in the village—or commuted daily or weekly from village to factory—and continued to identify as much with a rural, agricultural life as with an urban, industrial one. In turn-of-the-century Russia, there was no clear-cut distinction between peasants and workers, a situation confusing to the country's budding Marxist revolutionaries for whom

≡ **MAP 11.1** The Economic Development of European Russia, 1860–1914

industrial workers, not "backward" peasants, were supposed to be the agents of
revolution.

Much to the Marxists' surprise, these worker-peasants were extraordinarily
militant, even revolutionary, thanks in part to Russia's haste to industrialize. There
was no time or money to build adequate housing or social services for workers, and
to finance continued industrial expansion, factory owners kept wages extremely
low. In an effort to improve these conditions, workers resorted often to strikes,
which many were unafraid to do, since they had village homes to return to in case
of a lengthy work stoppage.

Unwilling to tolerate such "indiscipline," the tsar's autocratic government did
not hesitate to call in troops against strikers, and these confrontations sowed the

seeds of militancy all the more. That many of these workers retained a peasant mentality only added to their radicalism, since Russian peasants had a long tradition of violent rebellion, which the inadequate emancipation from serfdom had not overcome.

The Radical Intelligentsia

Although workers struck of their own accord and peasants had periodically rebelled on their own initiative, middle- and upper-class Russians saw themselves as the people's saviors and guides. The best-educated members of these groups, known by the mid-nineteenth century as the **intelligentsia**, often adopted radical politics and sought the wholesale transformation of their country by trying to mobilize the peasant mass.

The intelligentsia's radicalism stemmed in part from the lack of opportunity to participate in Russia's political life. Most positions in government were reserved for members of the high nobility, and there were no parliaments, either local or national, to which educated people could seek election. Even the zemstvos, the local government councils created in 1864, gave most seats to high nobles and then lost much of their power in 1890, when Tsar Alexander III decided to rein them in. In addition, there were few professional organizations from which the intelligentsia could exert influence, and Russia lacked the clubs, advocacy groups, and other voluntary associations common in Britain, Germany, and the United States.

Unable to participate in or influence politics and policymaking, educated Russians could see no way to reform their society. For many, revolution seemed the only option, and in the second half of the nineteenth century, members of the intelligentsia formed a variety of radical groups, most of them conspiratorial and clandestine by definition, since they were illegal and persecuted by the police. Members of these groups drew up utopian designs for a reordered society and did so mostly with Western European experiences and ideologies in mind. Some wanted to avoid what they considered the devastating Western experience of industrialization, said to have stripped people of their healthy rural roots and made them slaves of the machine. Known as **populists**, individuals with these views believed in a form of socialism grounded in Russia's supposedly egalitarian agricultural commune (*mir*). Populists romanticized the peasantry and flocked to Russia's villages in the 1870s, determined to help peasants realize their revolutionary potential.

But the populist students and urban intellectuals who went "to the people" seemed utterly alien to Russia's peasants, who saw them as likely exploiters and not infrequently denounced them to the police. The populists' frustration over this situation turned some to terrorism in hopes that a spectacular attack would spark a general uprising and bring the entire tsarist system down. In 1881, a group called the "People's Will" assassinated Tsar Alexander II, but instead of triggering a revolution, their dramatic act sparked a series of violent pogroms—massacres against Jewish communities, falsely blamed for the death of the tsar. The government cracked down not on the architects of the anti-Jewish attacks but on populists and other opponents of the regime, many of whom found themselves deported to prison camps in Siberia.

From the rubble of populism emerged a new group of Russian revolutionaries, the **Marxists**, who also belonged to the intelligentsia but, unlike the populists, admired the West. This new group became especially wedded to the Marxist notion that history moved forward in predictable stages thanks to the class struggle and that socialism was scientifically programmed to result. The problem for Russia was that by the late nineteenth century, the class struggle had created at best a glimmer of capitalism, which meant, according to Marxist theory, that the country would have to undergo a bourgeois, capitalist revolution before a socialist one could ensue.

Most Russian Marxists were willing to wait, reassured as they were by the inevitability of socialism and the successes of capitalism in the West, whose modern, efficient factories and mechanized agriculture they admired. Such views paradoxically made Russian Marxists into advocates of capitalism, although only as a necessary way station along the road to socialism. Some Marxists—Petr Struve (1870–1944), for example— became so enamored of capitalist modernity that they dropped the long-term goal of socialism and embraced liberalism, itself a new ideology in Russia. Still, most Russian

≡ **Russian Peasant Commune (*mir*).** After the tsar emancipated the serfs in 1861, he did not give them farmland as private property but rather assigned it collectively to agricultural communities known as *mir*. Since individual peasants did not own the land they farmed, they had little incentive to improve it, and Russian agriculture stagnated. This photograph, staged by a British photographer in 1900, shows a meeting of the male heads of household in a *mir*.

Marxists clung to their socialist faith, although some favored tactical alliances with liberals and some did not. Lenin, in particular, denounced such alliances, arguing that the Marxists' role was to build a compact, militant party focused solely on organizing workers to hasten the socialist revolution to come. His insistence on that principle at the Second Congress of the Russian Social-Democratic Labor Party held in 1903 created a split between his hardline centralist faction, which became known as the Bolsheviks ("majoritarians," because they had gotten their way in a key political debate), and the group favoring a loosely organized, more democratic party, which became known as the Mensheviks ("minoritarians").

The Revolution of 1905

Thanks to the Russo-Japanese War of 1904–1905, revolution arrived much sooner than anyone expected. Russia's expansion into the Far East brought it into conflict with Japan, which harbored competing ambitions in the region. After war broke out in January 1904, the Russian army and navy suffered one disastrous defeat after the other. These setbacks seemed especially humiliating because they came at the hands of a supposedly inferior Asian race. Russia's military failures tarnished Tsar Nicholas II's already blemished reputation and emboldened his growing number of opponents: nobles in the zemstvos who felt excluded from power; liberals who wanted a national parliament and limits on the tsar's authority; teachers, doctors, and lawyers who felt stymied in their professional lives; socialists who sought revolutionary change; and workers and peasants already in ferment and ready to revolt.

On January 22, 1905 (**Bloody Sunday**), unrest turned into rebellion when the St. Petersburg police fired on a huge demonstration of workers demanding better pay and working conditions and hoping the tsar would hear their pleas. The police massacred 130 of the protestors, dashing their hopes and galvanizing Russia's amorphous oppositionist groups. Liberals came together in the Constitutional Democratic Party (also known as Cadets), and the moderate wing of the Social Democrats, the Mensheviks, supported their efforts to create a constitutional government. Lenin's

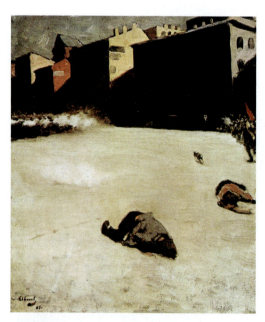

≡ **Bloody Sunday.** On January 22, 1905, the St. Petersburg police fired on a large group of peaceful demonstrators, killing 130 people. This massacre galvanized Russia's disparate opposition groups and laid the groundwork for revolutionary upheaval. The painting reproduced here, *Shooting* by S. V. Ivanov, evoked widespread sympathy for the demonstrators and their efforts to achieve better pay and working conditions.

Bolshevik faction, along with the peasant-oriented Socialist Revolutionaries (SR), encouraged militant strikes, demonstrations, and peasant unrest.

In the summer of 1905, peasants throughout Russia rebelled against the nobility in what was to be the most extensive rural uprising since the Pugachev revolt of the late eighteenth century. Peasants sacked and burned nobles' residences and attacked landowners and government officials. The rebellion raged until the end of the Russo-Japanese War in September 1905, when troops finally became available to quell it. The revolt flared up again the following year (see Map 11.2).

Meanwhile, leaders of Russia's many national minorities (e.g., Poles, Georgians, Tatars) began to demand autonomy or independence, and radicalized soldiers rebelled. By August 1905, opposition had swelled to the point that the tsar felt he had no alternative but to allow the creation of an elected **Duma** or parliament with the ability to advise the ruler but no right to frame legislation or shape policy. By this point, however, the demands for change had become so widespread and impassioned that the tsar's opponents rejected a purely advisory Duma.

Agitation intensified, and at the end of October, the months' long crescendo of labor unrest coalesced into a massive general strike in St. Petersburg, which paralyzed the Russian capital for nearly two weeks. To direct this strike, workers formed a leadership council—*soviet* in Russian—whose members made the work stoppage one of the most successful in history. On October 30, the tsar gave in, issuing the October Manifesto, which granted Russians civil liberties and established a Duma with real legislative powers.

With these reforms, the tsar appeared to transform his autocracy into a constitutional monarchy. In doing so, he calmed the unrest and prevented the further erosion of his power by dividing his opposition. Liberals and moderates expressed satisfaction with what he had done; socialists wanted considerably more. When police arrested the members of the St. Petersburg Soviet, workers alone rebelled. Middle-class liberals largely withdrew from the revolutionary struggle, focusing their energies on the coming elections to the Duma. Meanwhile, groups of ultra-rightists known as the "Black Hundreds" joined with policemen in beating and sometimes killing workers, intellectuals, and Jews accused of opposing the regime.

The split between moderates and radicals enabled the tsar to rescind many of the reforms he had originally proposed. Then, in 1907, Nicholas abruptly and illegally changed the electoral laws to ensure his government a permanent majority in the Duma. With a compliant Duma in place, the Russian government returned to business as usual: repression. Opponents of the regime faced prison, exile, and execution. Newspapers were closed down, editors jailed, and labor unions kept in check. These actions sent opponents underground and revived

War and Revolution in Russia, 1904–1907

- Peasant revolt in 50–75% of area, 1905–1907
- Peasant revolt in over 75% of area, 1905–1907
- ● Strike in urban area, 1905/1906/1907
- ○ Soviet of Workers' Deputies established in urban area, 1905
- □ Armed uprising in urban area, December 1905
- ◇ Military mutiny, 1905/1906/1907
- ☠ Pogroms, 1905–1906

The Russo-Japanese War of 1904–1905

- ⚔ Naval Battle
- Russian sphere of influence

≡ **MAP 11.2** War and Revolution in Russia, 1904–1907

the terrorism largely dormant since the 1880s.

On the positive side, industrial development resumed at a rapid pace, providing more jobs for workers and opportunities for peasants unable to support their families on the land. The plight of workers and peasants improved enough to make them realize that change was possible but not enough to satisfy them. Frustrated expectations added to the political discontent. Liberals, too, pushed for further changes, heartened by the existence of a parliament, however power-

Early Oil Wells in Baku. In the late nineteenth century, Russia's new oil wells in Baku, the capital of Azerbaijan today, produced about half of the world's petroleum. Russian oil helped fuel its burgeoning industrial plants and became one of the country's most valuable export commodities.

less it was. Only the revolutionaries remained disillusioned and depressed, most festering impotently in exile, unable to prepare the working class for a revolution that seemed to shrink into the distant future. But workers did not need the Bolsheviks' help. Strikes became commonplace during the run-up to the First World War, especially in St. Petersburg, where a powerful general strike in the summer of 1914 made some officials fear that Russian workers would defy orders to mobilize for war. In the end, most workers readily went to the front, as a wave of patriotism washed over the country. But before long, the rigors of war would open the way for a new revolution and ultimately a new era in Russian history.

The Russian Revolution

As we have seen, the war effort did not go well for the Russians. Although the tsar's forces fought with some success against Austria, the Germans subjected them to one loss after another. Defeat in war, especially in a troubled, unstable country like Russia, saps morale and makes soldiers and civilians unwilling to put up with the deprivations and sacrifices that war entails. Thus, after a brief burst of patriotism in 1914, the Russian people increasingly turned against the war. Their detached, unappealing tsar proved incapable of reviving the national sentiment of those early days, and when

MAP 11.3   The Russian Civil War, 1917–1922

empire. To do so, the Bolsheviks offered a measure of autonomy to several of the dominant ethnic groups.

In most cases, autonomy meant that each of the regions in question became a quasi-independent "Soviet Socialist Republic" under the umbrella of a nascent Union of Soviet Socialist Republics (USSR), formally established in 1922. Thus, when the smoke cleared, the former tsarist empire was divided into eight repub- lics (ultimately, there would be fifteen) dominated by the huge Russian Soviet Federal Socialist Republic (RSFSR). Each had the trappings of its own govern- ment, but in reality the republics were controlled by, and subordinated to, the Central Committee of the Bolshevik Party (soon renamed the Communist Party) in Moscow (see Map 11.4). To soothe local sensibilities, Lenin and his colleagues encouraged the expression of ethnic and regional culture, with local languages taught in schools alongside Russian and ethnic traditions celebrated in public events. The Bolsheviks did not want to see themselves as imperialists, so the cul- tural and linguistic celebrations were designed to soothe their sensibilities as well.

Religious minorities in these republics received favorable treatment—especially Muslims, whom the atheistic Bolsheviks encouraged to practice their faith. This toleration was partly sincere and partly designed to prevent Muslims from allying with their coreligionists in nearby Turkey. Religious freedom did not extend to Muslims within the Russian Republic, nor did the many non-Russian peoples within the RSFSR receive the same consideration as those outside it, setting up future ethnic and religious conflicts. Since each republic was to have a dominant ethnic group, the Russians felt free to dominate their own.

MAP 11.4   The Soviet Union in 1924

Outcome of the Russian Civil War

Although few observers expected the Bolsheviks to prevail, they ultimately emerged from the civil war bloodied but victorious. The Red Army had outmaneuvered the Whites, and the majority of peasants, although enamored of neither side, ultimately saw the Reds as the lesser evil. The Bolsheviks, after all, had endorsed the peasants' seizure of land, while the Whites had taken it back—or promised to when they could.

The transformation of the countryside and several other developments made the Civil War more revolutionary than the revolution itself. It created a powerful security police, the Cheka, which did not hesitate to terrorize villages and regions suspected of sympathy with the Whites, who resorted to terror as well, and set a precedent for further political terror to come. The Civil War also created a potent Red Army, which served both to socialize young men to the new regime and give the Bolsheviks a fighting force with which they could secure their monopoly of political power. In many ways, the Red Army militarized the Party, as the new communist fighting force grew to five million men and became the Bolsheviks' largest and most important institution, the only institution that functioned tolerably well. Reliance on the Red Army accustomed Party leaders, even more than before the Civil War, to getting things done by force.

In a sense, the Civil War re-created the Party by bringing in a half-million new recruits and transforming it from a small, conspiratorial group into a mass political organization. The war also set a precedent for the party's oversight of all areas

the country after Bukharin and Stalin joined forces against him. (Trotsky was assassinated in 1940, almost certainly on Stalin's orders.) In supporting Trotsky's excommunication, Bukharin and his followers unwittingly set the stage for a similar move against themselves.

Bukharin may have been the party's most prestigious policy maker and editor of its official newspaper, *Pravda* (Truth), but the real, everyday political muscle increasingly belonged to Stalin. On his deathbed, Lenin had warned his potential successors to beware of Stalin's machinations, but the latter's command of the party apparatus enabled him to brush his mentor's admonition aside. As general secretary of the party, Stalin controlled the local bureaucratic appointments that gave people jobs, power, and the prospect of social mobility. Rank-and-file party members coveted these posts, and Stalin's ability to decide who received them gave him the ability to appoint and promote people loyal to him and remove those who were not.

Stalin's rank-and-file support was to prove crucial in the party's internal debates over who would control policy and what that policy would be. In 1927, Stalin declared himself disillusioned with NEP for its failure to industrialize the country rapidly enough. The underlying problem, as Bukharin had to admit, was the peasants' low productivity and unwillingness or inability to market a sufficient quantity of grain, either for domestic consumption or export.

Stalin decided to remedy this situation by sending agents into the countryside to forcibly requisition agricultural produce. His firm grip on the party apparatus enabled him to undertake this effort even in the face of substantial opposition within the Politburo. In particular, Stalin's agents targeted the richest peasants, known as **kulaks**, arguing that they had prospered too much from NEP and that they should be compelled to contribute to society as a whole.

Stalin's forced grain collections caused rioting and resistance in the countryside, as some peasants destroyed their produce rather than give it to government officials. Food shortages began to appear, and the relative social harmony of the NEP period threatened to dissolve. By 1929, Bukharin and his allies on the right realized that Stalin had to be stopped but found themselves stymied by their opponent's control over the party's bureaucracy.

It is likely that Communist Party officials supported Stalin's policies not only because they owed their jobs to him, but also because they agreed more with him than with Bukharin. Stalin's drive for rapid industrialization and support of "class struggle" against the kulaks was consistent with the Bolsheviks' longstanding ideological objectives and seemed much bolder and more revolutionary than Bukharin's relatively cautious, evolutionary designs. What is more, Bukharin's gradualist approach likely appeared weak in the face of a widely feared, although nonexistent, military threat from the capitalist powers and of the widespread belief that kulaks, as "class enemies," were plotting against the regime. Bukharin might have tried to calm these fears and taken his criticism of Stalin beyond the party's inner sanctum, but his belief in a monolithic, authoritarian party prevented him from acting decisively in this way. Bukharin thus acquiesced in his own defeat, opening the way for Stalin to transform his control over the party apparatus into a personal dictatorship.

Stalin's Revolution

Stalin, the political alias of Ioseb (Joseph) Dzhugashvili, was one of the few Bolshevik leaders who came from the working class. A native of Georgia, a once-independent nation in the Caucasus, Stalin was the son of a shoemaker. After a brief stint as a theology student, he joined Lenin's Social Democratic party in 1903 and quickly became an effective revolutionary conspirator. He played a prominent role in the revolutions of 1917 and the ensuing civil war. In 1922, he was appointed general secretary of the Communist Party, the position that, as we have seen, allowed him to concentrate power in his hands. By mid-1929, there was no one to stop him from introducing his plan to abruptly transform Russia's still-backward peasant society into a modern industrial economy.

His first step was to order the collectivization of the Russian peasantry, which would place all agricultural property in government hands and, in theory, allow it to extract from that property whatever resources it wanted. Those resources, destined to finance industrial investment, would come at the expense of peasant consumption, which would be kept at subsistence levels or below.

For obvious reasons, Russia's peasants had no desire to bear the brunt of industrialization in this way, and they resisted, often strenuously, the collectivization effort. In response, the government announced the

≡ **The Annihilation of Kulaks and Priests.**
During Stalin's brutal effort to collectivize Soviet agriculture, a great many peasants, especially the relatively prosperous kulaks, resisted the effort to seize their lands. They hid grain, slaughtered livestock, and attacked government agents. In response, the regime dubbed kulaks "class enemies" and undertook a violent campaign against them and their supposed allies in the Orthodox Church. This poster belonged to the propaganda side of that campaign.

"liquidation of the kulaks as a class," sending into the countryside brigades of party activists to "dekulakize" the villages. Terrified, millions of peasants fled to nearby cities, while many of those who remained were rounded up and sent in sealed boxcars to the new industrial plants under construction, often to toil as captive laborers. Some of those who refused to vacate their lands were shot or deported to harsh labor camps administered by a new government agency, the **Gulag**.

Before fleeing or being deported, a great many peasants rebelled by burning crops and killing livestock to prevent them from being turned over to the new collective farms. Peasants slaughtered four million horses and fourteen million cows, leaving too few horses to plow the fields at a time when the government had not yet built enough tractors to take their place. The government had no choice but to halt the collectivization drive, but did so only long enough to bring in what harvest was left. In 1931, a new effort began.

This time, peasants reacted even more strongly than before, cutting the number of livestock in half and burning wide expanses of crops. Officials now deported larger numbers of kulaks to the Gulag. The destruction of crops and animals, along with the chaotic transformation of individual farms into state-run collectives, vastly reduced the size of the harvests in 1932–1933. The result was a terrible shortage of food, made infinitely worse by the government's decision to seize the amount of grain and other crops it wanted, regardless of the cost in peasant lives. The result, as officials understood in advance, was a deadly year-long "terror famine" that cost between three and four million human lives.

The survivors learned their lesson: never again would Russian peasants massively resist the Soviet state, which quickly pushed the collectivization effort to its conclusion. By 1936, the government had transformed 25,000,000 peasant domains into 240,000 collective farms. Stalin considered large state-owned farms inherently better than small peasant ones and expected this transformation to improve Russia's agricultural productivity. Just the opposite occurred, however, as the peasants who survived found themselves malnourished and unmotivated to work at full strength. Productivity proved so weak that the government had no choice but to allow collectivized peasants to till small, private plots and sell their produce in what resembled a free market. Although in 1937 these plots represented just 5 percent of Russia's cultivated land, they produced 25 percent of the country's food. Clearly, collectivization had made little sense in terms of productivity, but it enabled the government to subdue a long-restive peasantry and obtain the food it wanted at the low prices it was now able to set.

Even though the grain harvest in 1933 was five million tons below that of 1928, the state doubled the amount of grain it procured during this period. It then sold this enlarged portion to food processing plants and urban consumers at substantially higher prices than it had paid the peasant collectives. The difference between the state's buying and selling prices for grain remained in government coffers as a kind of "profit" used to finance a series of massive investments in heavy industry. That this profit left the peasantry malnourished and in many cases starving to death was a matter of indifference to Stalin; he had found a way to fund the economic development he desperately wanted.

The Five-Year Plans

Stalin's economic development focused on the construction of several gigantic factories modeled on the largest ones of the United States. His goal was to catch up with, and eventually overtake, the world's leading manufacturing power. The general secretary considered this effort a matter of life or death for Soviet Russia, for, as he put it, "the pace of Soviet industrialization would determine whether the socialist fatherland survived or crumbled before its enemies." Rapid industrialization also became synonymous during the 1930s with the effort to "build socialism," now defined in purely economic terms (see Map 11.5). Stalin's version of socialism thus stood in contrast to classical Marxist theory, which understood capitalism as the engine of economic development and socialism as the prosperous, classless, egalitarian society that economic development made possible.

The Soviet leader established goals for the development of his country in a series of **Five-Year Plans** that outlined what the economy was to look like a half decade hence. The first Five-Year Plan, soon squeezed into four (1928–1932), focused on iron and steel. It assigned each industry and industrial plant quotas specifying the quantities to be produced, creating what looked like an organized, rational set of goals. But government officials immediately undermined the plan by rewarding managers and workers for exceeding their quotas, thus encouraging them to throw the entire project off kilter. When a given plant, say a steel mill, produced more than the planned amount, it forced the firms supplying it with parts and raw materials to ignore their own quotas as they hastened to keep up. When they succeeded in meeting the steel plant's elevated demands, the mill inevitably produced more metal than the rest of the economy, operating under its own quotas, could absorb. Its haste, moreover, led to the production of brittle, low-quality steel.

The first Five-Year Plan's most ambitious project was the mammoth metallurgical plant at Magnitogorsk, a brand new industrial city created to house the plant and its workers. When the first laborers arrived at what was to be Magnitogorsk, they found themselves in the middle of nowhere, some 900 miles southeast of Moscow. There were no roads or buildings—not even housing. Workers lived in tents, barely protected from the bitter cold of the Russian steppe. Eventually, there would be crude wooden barracks, and finally grey apartment blocks. As for the factory itself, the new Soviet plant would resemble the huge United States Steel factory opened in Gary, Indiana, in 1908. To design it, the Russians even hired the same Chicago engineering firm, Henry Freyn and Co., that had produced the steel mill in Gary.

The Five-Year Plan had supposedly laid out the Magnitogorsk factory and related industrial concerns according to a rational design fully thought out in advance; in reality, a chaos of improvisations reigned. The Magnitogorsk region was extremely well endowed with iron ore but possessed none of the coking coal required to fire the plant's huge blast furnaces. Officials had to import coal from Western Siberian mines some 1,200 miles away. But since the Plan had given mining and railroad building lower priority than metallurgy, the factory took shape well before officials could adequately supply it with the materials it needed to run. Worse, Magnitogorsk constantly suffered from a shortage of technicians and engineers, to say nothing of ordinary workers, who were in demand throughout the country.

Still, despite the frequent bottlenecks, delays, engineering gaffes, and often terrible working conditions, by the end of the Second Five-Year Plan (1933–1937), Magnitogorsk had come on line, as had several other huge enterprises: Gorky Auto, Stalingrad and Kharkov Tractor, and Dnieper Steel, among others. And although Soviet statistics are unreliable, it is clear that the two completed five-year plans proved successful in purely economic terms—successful in the sense that they gave Russia a new industrial base and prepared it to build the military machinery it would need in the Second World War.

At the time, Russia's apparent economic progress seemed to compare favorably to the depressed economies of the West, and observers in Europe and the United States expressed admiration over the factories and cities that seemed to spring up overnight. What they did not say, or did not know, was that much of what the new factories produced was shoddy or unusable and that the economy as a whole did not supply the Russians' most basic needs.

The Social Consequences of Stalin's Revolution

We have already discussed what the peasantry had to endure to make industrialization possible, and virtually every other social group suffered as well. Real wages dropped by 50 percent, while the legions of new workers who crowded into Russia's industrial cities confronted an acute shortage of housing. The economic historian Alec Nove called the Soviet period from 1928 to 1933 "the culmination of the

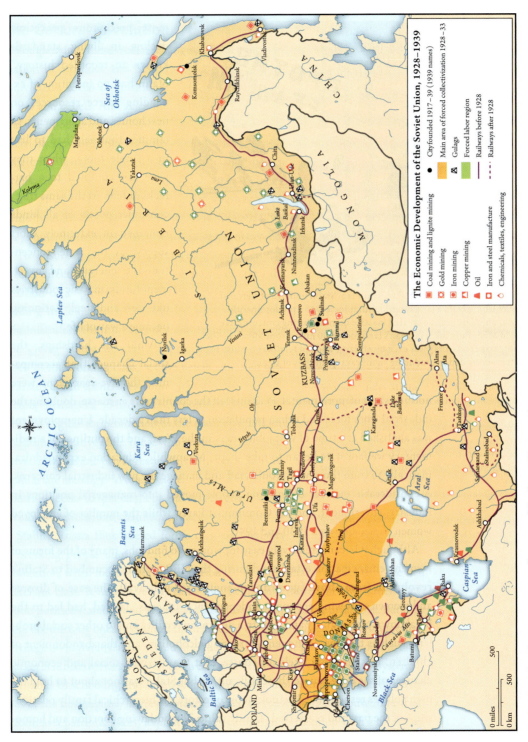

The Economic Development of the Soviet Union, 1928–1939

Coal mining and lignite mining
Gold mining
Iron mining
Copper mining
Oil
Iron and steel manufacture
Chemicals, textiles, engineering

City founded 1917–39 (1939 names)
Main area of forced collectivization 1928–33
Gulags
Forced labor region
Railways before 1928
Railways after 1928

≡ **MAP 11.5**   The Economic Development of the Soviet Union, 1928–1939

were mobilized for war. Special Communist Party agitators traveled from factory to factory, encouraging "socialist competition," meting out rewards, and emphasizing the importance of high productivity in the face of "capitalist encirclement" and, later, "international fascism."

It is difficult to know the extent to which workers internalized such exhortations, but a productivity movement known as **Stakhanovism** suggests that more than a few took them seriously. Stakhanovism emerged from the herculean efforts of a coal miner named Aleksey

☰ **Alexei Stakhanov.** In 1935, Stakhanov set a record for extracting the most coal from a seam in a single day. Stalin's propagandists made Stakhanov into a national hero, and other workers felt compelled to follow his example. Stakhanovism became a movement embraced by some, but opposed, subtly and silently, by those who considered it a new form of exploitation.

Stakhanov, who in August 1935 set a record for extracting the most coal from a seam on a single day. After his achievement became widely known, workers in other industries found themselves moved, either by their own ambitions or by external pressure (or both), to set records in their fields. They came to work early and stayed late, while making doubly certain that machines were well maintained. Their ability to increase production and break records became a matter of personal pride. Others showed less commitment, working harder when exhorted to do so and cutting back when the pressure was relaxed.

Still, a growing number of workers took the Stakhanovite challenge seriously, turning it into a kind of sport in which competing workshops kept scorecards of who produced what and going to great lengths to come in first. In the process, the most productive workers received prizes such as motorcycles and cash bonuses; several became celebrities touted in the press. One older Stakhanovite from Magnitogorsk made speeches contrasting the work he had done for "exploiters" under the tsarist regime with what he now accomplished "only for the people." Statements such as this should perhaps not be taken at face value, given their usefulness as propaganda for the regime, but they were common enough to suggest that significant numbers of workers considered their labor more meaningful now than it had been in tsarist times.

Workers who did not believe as much learned that it could be suicidal under the repressive Soviet regime to publicly air skeptical or dissenting views. When one Magnitogorsk steel smelter complained that Stakhanovism amounted to the enslavement of workers, he found himself sentenced to forced labor in the Gulag. Such treatment taught workers what *not* to say, but they also learned what they *should* say in order to conform to the expectations of the regime and keep themselves out of trouble; they learned, as one historian has put it, to "speak Soviet." That new form of public discourse often included boasts of a decades-long working-class pedigree and assurances that their jobs gave them satisfaction and that they eagerly toiled to fulfill the Plan. Workers commonly spoke of visiting the factory on days off, and nonworking wives endorsed their husbands' claims. Wives also joined with other women to shame husbands who drank too much and worked too little.

In learning to "speak Soviet," workers did not have to believe what they said and may, in reality, have thought the opposite. But the more they said what was expected of them, the more it made psychological sense to believe—or half-believe—the official discourse. It can be painful and confusing to constantly say one thing and believe another, and it is often soothing therefore to bring private beliefs and public statements into harmony. For these reasons, a great many Soviet workers came to feel a certain allegiance to the regime, despite the often severe hardships it imposed on them.

There were other, larger, reasons for allegiance to Stalin's system—in particular, ignorance of the outside world. In the 1930s, foreign publications were banned, travel impossible for all but a tiny elite, and information tightly controlled. What Soviet citizens learned about capitalist countries, mired as they were in severe economic depression, made Russia seem happy and prosperous by comparison. And even though a great many people experienced their lives in hardly these terms, they often comforted themselves with the belief that an idyllic socialist future was on the horizon and, as Marxism-Leninism had taught them, scientifically certain to arrive.

These ideas took on religious overtones, as the official discourse presented the socialist future as a heaven on earth and Lenin and Stalin as saviors and saints. Lenin's body was embalmed and kept on view in a special Kremlin crypt, where secular worshippers could pay their respects. Stalin became a kind of transcendent father figure whom people were encouraged to love and worship, often by mounting pictures of

≡ **Lenin's Tomb.** After Lenin died in January 1924, Soviet officials had his body embalmed and placed in a quasi-religious shrine, where the public could view it. Although the USSR was officially an atheistic country, Soviet leaders recognized that the people's religious and spiritual feelings had not disappeared. To satisfy them, they canonized Lenin as a secular saint. This painting of 1939 shows thousands of people on the pilgrimage to Lenin's tomb.

the great leader on their walls. For some, this was doubtless a display of fearful loyalty, but for others, it marked a genuine reverence for the man. For perhaps the majority, such signs and symbols bore witness to both feelings at once: fear and reverence, the imperative to bow to a coercive reality, and the desire to be part of something larger than oneself. It may be that a majority of Soviet citizens found themselves suspended between disbelief and belief, between a palpable awareness of the bleak reality of Stalin's regime and a quasi-religious faith that they would one day find salvation in a socialist Promised Land.

The Great Terror

Despite a widespread belief in—or hope for—the socialist millennium, there was no way to completely deny the inadequacies of the present day, no matter how hard the regime worked to paper them over. Most Russians lived less well in the late 1930s than they had ten years earlier. Housing was grossly inadequate, agriculture unproductive, food supplies meager, working conditions difficult, and decent consumer goods largely unavailable. Since the Soviet system was fundamentally sound, or so political leaders and the captive media constantly said, the problems people were experiencing must be the work of enemies and saboteurs. Counterrevolutionary "wreckers" were disrupting Soviet agriculture and industry, while foreign and domestic enemies, it was said, were plotting to overthrow the regime. In reality, the regime's opponents had long since been exiled, deported, and killed, or silenced by fear. No matter: Stalin purged several hundred thousand members from the Communist Party rolls.

Still, as late as 1932–1933, Stalin faced opposition—not to the regime, but to his excesses—within the upper reaches of the Communist Party. After the fiasco of collectivization and the murderous famine of 1932–1933, several party leaders criticized Stalin in private. A group of "Rightists" even tried to slow the pace of collectivization and industrialization and push the General Secretary aside. Stalin wanted to have these critics executed, but his colleagues allowed him only to expel them from the party.

Stalin thus felt his power and authority under threat. In late 1934, he took advantage of the assassination of Sergei Kirov, the popular Leningrad leader, to crack down on his opponents. Stalin blamed Kirov's murder on Grigory Zinoviev and Lev Kamenev, two of his former opponents among the original Bolshevik leaders. There is no evidence that either had anything to do with Kirov's death, but Stalin had them executed after a sham trial in 1936. The following year, Stalin incriminated another pair of key party leaders for this crime, and then in 1938 staged an elaborate "show trial" for Bukharin and two others—all of them long-standing, prominent Bolshevik leaders—in which they were forced to confess to efforts to sabotage the regime. As "enemies of the people," they were summarily shot.

Stalin had begun his campaign against the party elite in the face of a real, if publicly invisible, opposition to him in 1933–1934. That opposition apparently convinced him that he had enemies everywhere in the Party and that it was imperative to eliminate them. After the arrests of Zinoviev and Kamenev in 1936, Stalin undertook a massive purge of the Communist Party as a whole. In 1937, some five hundred thousand members found themselves excommunicated, and many were subsequently shot or sent to the Gulag. The higher an individual's position in the party, the more likely he was to die: 110 of the 139 members of the Central Committee elected in 1934 were killed or driven to suicide. By 1940, Stalin was the only member of Lenin's Politburo who remained alive.

After these mass purges of the Communist Party, the secret police and the army suffered a similar fate. In 1938, Stalin ordered the arrest and later the execution of Nikolai Yezhov, the secret police chief who had carried out much of the **Great Purge**. The general secretary then had several of Russia's most important generals shot or deported. All told, Stalin's regime sent more than a half million new political convicts to the Gulag, where they joined the 800,000 already there. More than 680,000 purge victims were shot before reaching the labor camps, and perhaps another 500,000 died in the Gulag or shortly after being released. To these 1,200,000 deaths must be added the three to four million who perished in the famine of 1932–1933 and the tens of thousands shot resisting the collectivization drive. Altogether, perhaps five million Soviet citizens died of political causes during the terrible initial decade of Stalin's rule.

The execution and deportation of more than a million party members and leaders gave the general secretary a huge number of positions to fill. In them, he placed a new cadre of people entirely loyal to him. In a sense, Stalin's Great Purge of 1936–1939 constituted a coup d'état against the original Bolshevik regime, one that gave powerful positions to young men such as Nikita Khrushchev, Leonid Brezhnev, and Aleksei Kosygin—future Soviet leaders all—educated and shaped politically during Stalin's "revolution from above."

≡ **The Party after Stalin's Purge.** The Great Terror of 1936–1939 constituted a coup d'état against the Soviet Communist Party, which Stalin transformed into an organization led by people entirely loyal—and beholden—to him. This photograph shows those people, many destined to rise to the summit of the party. The young Nikita Khrushchev, the future head of the Soviet Communist Party, appears in the lower left-hand corner of the frame. Khrushchev remained utterly loyal to Stalin until the dictator was safely in his grave.

The new industrial capacity this revolution produced helped prepare Russia for the Nazi onslaught to come, but it also weakened a population that would soon have to face even more severe hardships than it had already endured. After the Jews, the Soviet Union was the enemy Hitler most wanted to crush.

Conclusion: The Rise of a Powerful Communist State

In the late nineteenth century, Russia was a backward country with only a tiny industrial base and a mass of mostly impoverished peasants. Its autocratic tsar was all-powerful at home but weak in the international sphere. In 1905, Russia suffered a humiliating defeat at the hands of Japan and during the First World War endured a series of crushing military blows.

Failure in war did much to trigger the revolutions of 1917, which overturned the tsar and allowed the country's most radical force, the Bolshevik Party, to take charge. But revolution led to civil war and to another three years of suffering on top of what the Russian people had already endured between 1914 and 1917. Ultimately, the Bolsheviks prevailed, but at the cost of millions dead, a devastated countryside, a ruined economy, and a decimated industrial and managerial elite.

Under these circumstances, the Bolsheviks, now calling themselves the Communist Party, had no choice but to put Marxist ideological prescriptions on hold in favor of a New Economic Policy designed to restart an economy that had essentially ground to a halt. Lenin's NEP succeeded in a great many ways, producing a revived agricultural system and allowing for unprecedented social mobility and women's emancipation. Kollontai became the public face of a New Soviet Woman, granted the ability to earn a living and a certain independence from men.

But a great many Soviet leaders, Stalin foremost among them, were dissatisfied with the gains of NEP. Stalin wanted a full-fledged collectivist system with consolidated state-owned farms and vast factories capable of competing with those of the West. The general secretary created this system on the backs of the peasantry, expropriated and starved in the service of industrial growth. Millions of peasants died in government-engineered famines and in gruesome labor camps. By the end of the 1930s, millions more had succumbed to the Great Purges.

Stalin's murderous policies dismantled the party and military elite but enabled the Soviet dictator to replace former officials with new men utterly loyal to him. In the economic sphere, agricultural collectivization took an appalling human toll and made Soviet farming less efficient than under NEP. But by transferring vast resources to heavy industry, Stalin's policies laid the groundwork for a powerful industrial regime, one capable of fielding an army potent enough to stymie Hitler's advanced military machine.

The Soviet Union, 1922–1939	
December 1922– January 1923	Lenin dictates his "testament" advising the party leadership to beware of Stalin
January 1924	Death of Lenin sparks succession struggle; Stalin expounds on idea of "socialism in One Country"; Bukharin tells peasants to "enrich themselves"
December 1927	Stalin and Bukharin defeat "Left Opposition"; Trotsky expelled from Communist Party
Late 1928	First Five-Year Plan launched; beginning of cultural revolution; Stalin defeats the "Right Opposition" and starts "revolution from above"
January 1929	Trotsky expelled from Soviet Union
November– December 1929	Beginning of mass collectivization and dekulakization; Stalin calls for the liquidation of the kulaks as a class; the cult of Stalin begins
December 1932	Kremlin declares the First Five-Year Plan a success after four years
1932–1933	Several million peasants die in a famine caused by collectivization
December 1934	Sergei Kirov assassinated in Leningrad
August 1935	Beginning of Stakhanovism
1936–1939	The Great Terror; five million citizens killed in collectivization, state-induced famines, and purges

KEY TERMS

For digital learning resources, please go to **https://www.oup.com/he/berenson2e**. Turn to the back of the book to see the list of primary sources and writing exercises provided in the accompanying *Sources and Guided Writing Exercises for Europe in the Modern World*

12

Fascism and Nazism: Mass Politics and Mass Culture, 1919–1939

Leni Riefenstahl

"Finally, quite late, Hitler appeared . . . the people jumped up from their seats, screaming dementedly: Heil, Heil, Heil . . . I had in the same moment an almost apocalyptic vision that I could never forget. It seemed to me as though the earth's surface . . . suddenly split in the middle and a monstrous jet of water came spurting out, so strongly that it touched the sky and shook the earth. I felt paralyzed."

This is how the thirty-year-old Leni Riefenstahl (1902–2003) described her first impression of Adolf Hitler as he spoke at a Nazi rally in 1932. A talented dancer, actress, and filmmaker, Riefenstahl is best known for her lyrical propaganda film *Triumph of the Will* (1934), which glorified Hitler and his Nazi movement. Although Riefenstahl made excellent films that had nothing to do with **Nazism**, *Triumph of the Will* identified her for all time as a "Nazi filmmaker" and implicated Riefenstahl in Hitler's crimes against humanity. Her Nazi connections do not, however, negate the artistry of her work. The quality of her photography and editing made *Triumph of the Will* a masterpiece of visual propaganda.

Born into a prosperous middle-class family, Riefenstahl spent a comfortable and highly protected childhood in a well-to-do suburb of Berlin. In her autobiography she called herself "a dreamer and an athlete," and unlike most middle-class girls her age, she pursued sports with a vengeance. She loved swimming, gymnastics, and skating—especially the latter two, for they appealed to her artistic side as well. Against her father's wishes, she enrolled in ballet classes and soon began to perform in public. When a knee injury seemed to jeopardize her dancing career, she discovered the relatively new art of the cinema and was drawn in particular to the director Arnold Fanck's visually powerful "mountain films" set in the Alps. Impressed by Riefenstahl's fresh looks and athletic grace, Fanck launched her career in the cinema by writing *The Holy Mountain* (1926) especially for her.

After making a series of films with Fanck, Riefenstahl created her own film company and directed its first production, *The Blue Light* (1931). For this feature, she used a new, highly sensitive film stock for the first time in the history of motion pictures. It produced a mesmerizing, eerily romantic effect that made her scenes look as though they had been shot in another world.

The Blue Light quickly became a critical and commercial success, so much so that it drew the attention of Hitler himself. An avid filmgoer, the Nazi leader admired the tone and texture of the movie and enlisted Riefenstahl in the Nazi cause.

Thus began the extraordinarily controversial period of her life when she lent her considerable talents to the National Socialist regime. Although Riefenstahl always enjoyed Hitler's support, other members of the Nazi hierarchy did their best to sabotage her efforts. "The Nazis were by tradition antifeminist," Hitler's chief architect, Albert Speer, explained, "and could hardly brook this self-assured woman, the more so since she knew how to bend this man's world to her purposes."

In the summer of 1934, Hitler asked Riefenstahl to create a documentary of the Nazi party's annual gathering, scheduled for early September in Nuremberg. Although Riefenstahl always claimed to be nonpolitical, she must have been aware that Hitler was not interested in a critical, or even a neutral, portrayal of the movement he led.

In his book, *Mein Kampf* (My Struggle), which Riefenstahl read in 1932, Hitler maintained that there was nothing more important to the kind of emotional politics he embodied than visual effects. As Hitler understood, no medium was better suited than film for creating those effects and thus for manipulating the emotions of the masses. Under Hitler's guidance, Riefenstahl set out to produce a propaganda film as effectively and artistically as she could. The result stood out as perhaps the best piece of documentary filmmaking to date. Riefenstahl's *Triumph of the Will* created a powerful vision of a reawakened and revitalized Germany whose happy, untroubled, and hard-working people stood united in support of the new Nazi regime.

Such a portrait of Nazi Germany was illusory at best. By September 1934, when the party convention chronicled in *Triumph of the Will* took place, Hitler's regime had already destroyed what was left of German democracy. It had killed or jailed thousands of dissidents, infiltrated or abolished most of the country's formerly independent institutions, enacted policies that discriminated against Jews and women, and, most recently, conducted a bloody purge of the Nazi Party itself.

Riefenstahl's film ignored all of this, concentrating instead on the crowds of rapturous Germans cheering Hitler as his motorcade glided through the city of Nuremberg, resplendent with its medieval German charm. Her camera lingered over the faces of clean-cut young Germans ecstatic in the presence of their

Timeline

| 1915 | 1920 | 1925 | 1930 | 1935 | 1940 | 1945 | 1950 | | | |

1919–1933 Weimar Republic governs Germany

March 1919 Mussolini founds *Fasci Italiani di Combattimento* ("Italian combat league")

1921 Hitler assumes leadership of National Socialist German Workers' Party (Nazi Party)

1921 Polish republic created

1922 Fascist Blackshirts march on Rome; Mussolini becomes prime minister

1923 Great inflation and economic crisis in Germany; France occupies Ruhr Valley

November 1923 Hitler's failed "beer hall putsch" in Munich

1925–1926 Hitler publishes *Mein Kampf*

1926 Pilsudski stages a coup in Poland

1929 Great Depression begins

1931 Germany, Britain, and Austria leave the gold standard

1931 Leni Riefenstahl releases her first film, *The Blue Light*

1933–1945 The Third Reich

January 1933 Hitler named Chancellor of the German Reich

February 1933 Nazis take control of Prussian state police; deputize SA and SS; Reichstag fire

March 1933 Nazis gain control in parliament; pass Enabling Act

1934 Riefenstahl releases her propaganda film *Triumph of the Will*

June 1934 Night of the Long Knives

August 1934 President Hindenburg dies; Hitler becomes head of state and government

1935 German Jews lose citizenship, are forbidden to marry other Germans

1936 Olympic Games held in Berlin

1938 Riefenstahl's *Olympia: Festival of Nations and Festival of Beauty*

1938 Jewish property confiscated; Jews forbidden to run most businesses; *Kristallnacht* (Night of Broken Glass)

1939 Nazis gas to death 70,000 mentally ill and disabled people

Führer (Leader). It presented loving close-ups of a smiling Hitler as he shook hands with his followers and admired their children. And it showed hundreds of thousands of uniformed German men, most of them young, fit, and blond, marching in formation, symbolizing Hitler's promise to overcome the divisions of class, region, and religion. Through Riefenstahl's lens, we see a united Germany voluntarily falling in behind the firm but benign leadership of a great man.

Riefenstahl's film presents itself as an actual record of an important event in the life of Nazi Germany. But no documentary can be an exact replica of the events it depicts; the filmmaker selects what scenes to use, how to edit them, what music to put in the background, what to show in close-up or from a distance. Riefenstahl's film altered the chronological sequence of the Nuremberg rally and used creative lighting, camera angles, and above all, editing to produce rhythmic pulses of excitement and repose. Riefenstahl had an army of 120 technicians at her disposal and used thirty cameras plus an array of the most modern equipment, including telephoto lenses and sophisticated microphones mounted on trucks. In filming Hitler, whose "will" she placed at the center of her work, she had her crew dig trenches in front of the speakers' platform so she could point her cameras upward at the Führer to make him appear to loom high and mighty above his loyal flock.

Riefenstahl's film allowed viewers to participate vicariously in the great Nazi rally, making the film seem to be a window onto the reality of the event. That Riefenstahl succeeded in producing such an illusion, especially within the confines of a propaganda film, testifies to her artistic and directorial skills and earned her several international awards, including the Grand Prize at the Paris Film Festival of 1937. But since her success served

≡ *Triumph of the Will.* This still from Riefenstahl's classic Nazi propaganda film gives the impression that Germany had liberated itself from the Treaty of Versailles and built a vast military and paramilitary force. Three huge swastika banners, symbolizing the Nazi ascendency, loom over the seemingly endless rows of assembled men.

the interests of what was perhaps the most brutal political regime of all time, she bears some responsibility for what it did.

Riefenstahl's responsibility is less clear in her next film, *Olympia: Festival of Nations and Festival of Beauty* (1938). Commissioned by the International Olympics Committee and not by the Nazi Party, *Olympia* depicted the 1936 Olympic Games held in Berlin. The games themselves were extraordinarily controversial; they seemed to lend international recognition to a Nazi regime already seen as routinely violating human rights. Hitler very much wanted the Olympics to take place in his country precisely to win a measure of legitimacy abroad and as a means of advertising the achievements of his regime. Thus, to the extent that the Olympics itself obscured the terror and racism so central to Nazi policy, Riefenstahl's film did as well. But beyond this admittedly important effect, *Olympia* had little overt propaganda value. The film itself beautifully depicted the grace, strength, and elegance of the human form.

If the film had a star, it was the brilliant African American runner Jesse Owens (1913–1980), the man Hitler had wanted to exclude from the games on racial grounds. Ignoring Nazi doctrines, Riefenstahl revealed the drama of a black athlete whose talent and determination enabled him to prevail against all the odds. For Owens, the gold medals he won represented something of his own triumph of the will. ≡

The Failure of Liberalism and Democracy after World War I

Although the Nazi regime was the most extreme to emerge in Europe (outside the Soviet Union) during the interwar period (1919–1939), it was far from alone in its authoritarian rejection of liberalism and democracy. Woodrow Wilson may have proclaimed that the United States, in entering the First World War, would make the world "safe for democracy," but as things turned out, the war and the treaties that ended it pushed most European governments toward dictatorship instead.

By 1939, the vast majority of European countries, including most of the new ones created at Versailles, were governed by dictators, military elites, or other agents of authoritarian rule. The victors—Britain, France, and the United States—retained their existing democratic governments, as did the Scandinavian countries, but a small fascist party emerged in Britain, and anti-democratic movements threatened the French republic throughout the 1930s. Czechoslovakia, created in 1918 from the rubble of Austria-Hungary, featured Central and Eastern Europe's lone democratic regime, but the sharp ethnic rivalries among its Czech, Slovak, German, and Ruthenian (Ukrainian) peoples threatened its stability and ultimately allowed Hitler to destroy its democratic government.

The Fragility of Postwar Parliamentary Regimes

Throughout much of the rest of Central and Eastern Europe, ethnic rivalries also helped undermine liberal, parliamentary regimes, but they did so much sooner than in Czechoslovakia and without outside help. As we saw in Chapter 10, the different ethnic groups long under Ottoman and Austro-Hungarian imperial rule moved to create independent nation-states even before the war was over. The postwar treaties endorsed the nations invented, or reinvented, by the largest ethnic groups—Poles, Czechs, Serbs, Greeks, Romanians—but in doing so inevitably created new multiethnic states; there were too many peoples, too dispersed geographically, for each to have its own country (see Map 12.1).

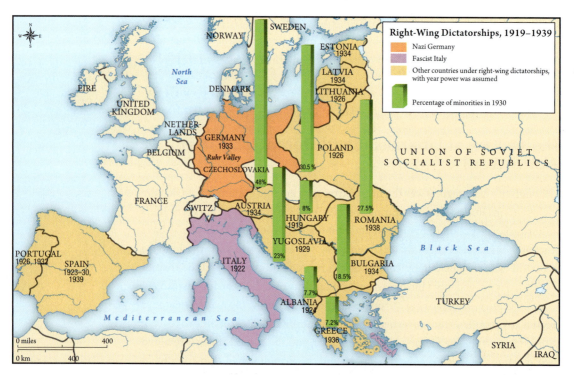

≡ **MAP 12.1**   Right-Wing Dictatorships, 1919–1939

The result was countries like Poland, with a dominant ethnic group, the Poles, but several significant "national minorities": Ukrainians, Germans, Belarusians, Czechs, Lithuanians, and Jews. The creation in 1921 of a Polish republic with a parliament and democratic elections encouraged members of minority groups to form their own political parties, or coalitions of ethnic-based parties, designed to foster the perceived interests of their group. When the parliament convened, it became a forum for the expression of the various parties' particularistic inclinations and seemed to invite conflict rather than effective policymaking. These conflicts were exacerbated by a growing left-right polarization and a mounting hostility to Poland's three million Jews. To impose order, the country's military hero, Jozef Pilsudski (1867–1935), staged a coup d'état in 1926 that gave him near dictatorial control, albeit with a minimum of violence and repression. In Poland, ethnonationalism had undermined the country's new parliamentary institutions and opened the way to authoritarian rule.

This was also true of Yugoslavia, where political parties were also organized along ethnic lines. Members of parliament were known to throw chairs and punches at one another and sometimes to wave pistols as well. In 1928, a Serb legislator shot and killed the Croatian opposition leader Stjepan Radić inside the parliamentary chamber itself. Afterward, King Alexander dissolved the legislature and revoked the constitution, vesting most political power in himself.

To make matters worse, in Yugoslavia and elsewhere in Europe, seats in postwar legislatures tended to be allocated according to proportional representation, which meant that each party's share of seats corresponded to its proportion of the popular vote—20 percent of the vote resulted in 20 percent of the seats. On the surface, this system seemed fair and democratic, but it led to political instability because in most countries, six, eight, ten, or more parties competed in elections, making it nearly impossible for a single party to capture a majority of the vote. Politicians had to piece together coalitions of two or more parties to achieve a majority, and because different political parties, by definition, represent different interests and ideas, conflicts between and among coalition partners inevitably—and regularly—made governments fall apart. In the early 1920s, the average French and German government lasted eight months, the average Italian government five.

Intellectuals' Disillusionment with Liberalism and Democracy

The constant rise and fall of governments added to the disillusionment with parliamentary democracy and left people in the various European countries, including a longstanding democracy like France, clamoring for alternatives. Already in 1918,

Thomas Mann (1875–1955), the great German novelist, wrote, "I don't want the trafficking of Parliament and parties that leads to the infection of the whole body of the nation with the virus of politics . . . I don't want politics. I want impartiality, order, and propriety." (Mann later repented these views.) Although Mann's model was Bismarck's tempered authoritarianism, the English novelist D. H. Lawrence (1885–1930) wanted an outright dictatorship. Society, he wrote, "must culminate in one real head, as every organic thing must." Spain's influential philosopher José Ortega y Gasset (1883–1955) maintained that democracy undermined the traditional values of the West, and Oswald Spengler's (1880–1936) widely read *Decline of the West* (1918) saw democracy as the end product of a decadent civilization.

Left-wing intellectuals joined conservatives such as Ortega y Gasset and Spengler in the era's antidemocratic chorus, as did communist parties, contemptuous of "bourgeois" democracy. When the Great Depression hit in 1929, desperate citizens of all political stripes wanted their governments to turn the situation around but witnessed parliamentary paralysis instead. By the 1930s, outside of Britain, France, and Scandinavia, political parties fully committed to parliamentary democracy had become difficult to find.

The Dangers of Mass Politics

One of the terrible ironies of the period was that the opponents of democracy often used its institutions and procedures with considerable skill. In many ways, democracy made **fascism** possible, as we will see in detail in the sections that follow. Fascist regimes came to power in Italy and Germany not through coups or revolutions, but by mobilizing masses of people and winning support in elections in which all adult citizens now possessed the right to vote. In Hungary, by contrast, where a fascist-style movement surfaced immediately after the war, the country's lack of democratic institutions prevented it from taking control. Without elections and electoral campaigns, the fascists enjoyed no means to harness the people's discontent and had to cede the country's leadership to its traditional landed elites.

To achieve success, fascist politicians and movements needed not only to exploit democratic institutions but to use violence, or the threat of violence, to intimidate their opponents. Thus, one of the key obstacles to the establishment, after 1918, of durable parliamentary governments was the legacy of violence from the First World War. Although the majority of those who had survived the trenches were happy to leave murderous fighting behind, a significant minority came to see it as a defining feature of masculinity and sought after the war to achieve their aims through fistfights, beatings, intimidation, and gunfire. For these men, parliaments were gatherings of the weak, places where feminized males debated with one another and got nothing done. Some of those too young to have fought in the trenches also embraced violence after the war to prove they were just as manly as their elders. Such men expressed nothing but contempt for liberalism and democracy, preferring the supposed hardness and strength of authoritarian rule, whether of the right or the left.

The Rise of Fascism in Italy

In many ways, Benito Mussolini (1883–1945), the future leader of Italy's fascist regime, was typical of those who had been schooled in the violence of war and who carried its hatreds into the postwar period. Like so many other European countries, Italy proved unable, in the postwar years, to establish a vital parliamentary, democratic regime. Its problems did not, however, stem entirely from the war but rather had been brewing since Italy's unification a half-century earlier, when it inaugurated a series of feeble, unstable parliamentary governments and suffered from a weak, underdeveloped economy.

Italy finally began to industrialize in the 1880s and 1890s, although its overall economy remained fragile. In the early 1900s, Giovanni Giolitti (1842–1928), destined to dominate Italian politics until after the First World War, encouraged further industrial expansion. But this effort made him liable to charges of excessive "materialism," of promoting a mundane bourgeois existence as life's highest goal while failing to "engender faith" in Italy as a "great nation." Such views became increasingly common among a group of young writers who called themselves Nationalists. If liberals promoted the individual above all, nationalists thought individuals should be subordinated to the nation, which would unify and strengthen them and give them a set of ideals. The best way to promote allegiance to the nation, the nationalists said, was to send Italians to war.

Giolitti did just that by invading Libya in September 1911. But the operation was too expensive for Italy's cash-poor treasury, and Italian forces proved incapable of fully controlling the would-be colony. The Libyan debacle made

≡ **Benito Mussolini.** A leftist schoolteacher-turned-journalist, Mussolini lurched sharply to the right after the First World War. Mussolini's ultra-nationalist Fascist Party gained seats in parliament, but Italians mostly felt its presence in the streets and the countryside, where black-shirted paramilitary toughs intimidated, beat, and killed their leftwing opponents. Violence and the threat of further violence ultimately catapulted Mussolini into the highest political office in the land.

Giolitti reluctant to enter the First World War, but after being badgered by the Nationalists—and promised large territorial gains by the Allies—Italy finally joined their side. Although the socialists generally opposed the war, other elements on the left supported it, especially anarcho-syndicalists (radical labor unionists), who thought the extremities of the conflict might spark a revolution at home. One of the leftists who took this view was a hot-blooded schoolteacher-turned-journalist named Benito Mussolini, soon to veer to the extreme nationalist right.

As we have seen, Italy's war effort did not go very well, but it nonetheless landed the country on the winning side. This outcome should have given the liberal government a much-needed boost, but the lands Italy actually received in the post-war peace agreements did not measure up to the Allies' promises. The Nationalists blamed Italy's liberals for what they called "the mutilated victory" imposed at Versailles, and it was they rather than government leaders who profited politically from the outcome of the war.

In September 1919, the nationalist writer Gabriele D'Annunzio (see Chapter 10) sought to improve his country's share of the postwar spoils by leading a squadron of demobilized soldiers into the Adriatic port of Fiume (now Rijeka in Croatia), claimed by both Italy and the new Kingdom of Serbs, Croats, and Slovenes (later Yugoslavia). D'Annunzio made himself Fiume's ruler and invented an aesthetic, stage-managed form of politics that would become a hallmark of fascist movements. Italy's liberal government discredited itself all the more by allowing D'Annunzio's illegal takeover to stand for fifteen months.

The government's passivity toward D'Annunzio went hand in hand with its in-action on the economic front. Inflation had reduced the Italian currency to a fifth of its prewar value, creating widespread misery for middle-class people on fixed incomes and sharply reducing the real wages of workers and landless peasants. When liberal officials proved unable to alleviate the situation, Italians increasingly turned toward the right or the left, especially after the dramatic electoral reform of 1919, which in compensation for the suffering and sacrifices of the war gave all adult men the right to vote.

Suddenly, Italy became a mass democracy, but its liberal leaders, accustomed to a small electorate and to campaigning through networks of local elites, had no idea how to navigate this brave new world. The Socialists, by contrast, could mobilize masses of people through their unions, Chambers of Labor, and political leagues, while the new Catholic party, the Italian People's Party (PPI), could use parish priests to galvanize the peasants.

The Socialists triumphed in Italy's first postwar elections, and their new status as the country's largest political party encouraged peasants and workers to rebel.

Impoverished farmers occupied their landlords' fields, and industrial workers went massively on strike, in some cases seizing factories with the intention of operating them on their own. This rural and urban unrest terrified powerful landowners and industrialists, who feared the Bolshevization of their country.

Many of these property owners had already been attracted to the nationalists' anti-leftist propaganda, and when they found their economic interests in jeopardy, they turned to them for protection and support. Before the war, nationalism had been a largely intellectual affair, but the long conflict transformed it into a hardened, violence-prone phenomenon whose militant leaders were eager to intervene muscularly in Italian political life. D'Annunzio had staged one kind of intervention; Mussolini was preparing another.

In March 1919, he founded a new political movement called the *Fasci Italiani di Combattimento,* or Fascists for short. While some Fascists ran for election to parliament, most preferred physical combat to electoral combat and grouped themselves into small bands (*squadre*) of young, paramilitary fighters known as *squadristi* or squad members. They wore distinctive black shirts and dedicated themselves to attacking strikers, socialists, and labor union members.

≡ **Fasces.** A collection of wooden rods bound together, fasces symbolized political authority in Ancient Rome. In modern Italy, fasces (Italian *fasci*) gave the Fascist Party its name. The term *fasci* for tight-knit groups was first used by radical Sicilian workers in the 1880s; for Italy's extreme nationalists, fasces represented the Italian people bound together in reverence for the nation. The fasces shown here were carved onto the façade of Milan's main railroad station.

In November 1920, a Fascist squad attacked Bologna's socialist-controlled city hall, killing six people and threatening to take over the city. Other squads then fanned out into the fertile Po River delta in northern Italy, where they destroyed socialist and labor union offices and newspapers while beating and torturing socialist officials. During the first three months of 1921, 102 people died in the fighting. Although socialists struck back, they were no match for the Fascist toughs, who often enjoyed the support of local policemen and soldiers. In less than a year, the once-solid socialist control of the region had collapsed. Similar developments took place almost everywhere socialists were entrenched.

The Fascist successes attracted mounting numbers of young men to the squads, and by mid-1921, fascism had become a mass movement. Its members made the exaggerated claim that they were saving the Italian nation from the clutches of Bolshevism, but it did appear to take the kind of decisive action foreign to the weak liberal government. Leading members of that government, recognizing the Fascists' growing strength, invited Mussolini to bring his organization into an alliance with the mainstream political parties. Giolitti reasoned that by linking the radical right-wingers to the governing coalition, he would benefit from their mass appeal while moderating their excesses. Instead, Mussolini and his lieutenants used Giolitti for their own purposes. The Fascists took advantage of their new connections to the government to gain a sizable foothold in parliament, and at the same time, stepped up, rather than moderated, their violent attacks in the countryside.

Mussolini sought to use the squads, which now counted 300,000 members, to demonstrate his political muscle but not to attempt a revolutionary coup d'état. The Fascist leader feared that such an effort might not succeed and that, if it did, he would be overly beholden to the squads, whose violence-prone members he might be unable to control. He wanted to be invited into the government through regular procedures and then to extend his power through a combination of legal and illegal means. He thus played a double game, telling the squads he intended to seize power thanks to them, while assuring liberal leaders he would keep his rank and file under control and respect the rules of the parliamentary game.

The squads feared that Mussolini would betray them, and they decided on a show of paramilitary strength by having their members march on Rome. On October 28, 1922, about 29,000 young black-shirted men headed toward the Italian capital. The police stopped about two-thirds of them before they could reach the city, and the 10,000 who did were poorly armed, drenched from rain, and in disarray. Mussolini hung back in Milan, ready to flee to Switzerland if the army intervened.

The March on Rome. On October 28, 1922, some 30,000 young black-shirted men marched toward Rome in an effort to demonstrate the strength of their fascist, paramilitary movement. The march nearly fizzled out before the bulk of the *squadristi* reached the Italian capital, and Mussolini allowed himself to be photographed only at the beginning of the march. He hung back in Milan, ready to flee to Switzerland if the army intervened.

The military was ready, having been placed on alert the day before, but for reasons never made clear, King Victor Emmanuel III refused to allow it to neutralize the Fascist stragglers—he may simply have lacked the stomach for violence in his capital. Before the **march on Rome**, the government had begun negotiations with Mussolini, and now, in its wake, the king made him prime minister, following regular constitutional procedures. The Fascist march on Rome, later mythologized as a great popular uprising, was in reality little more than a bluff that the king refused to call. It formed the context in which Mussolini came to power but did not catapult him into office. In reality, the liberal government had opened the door to Mussolini, and the king invited him in.

Italy's Fascist Regime

Mussolini began his reign by appearing to accept the norms of parliamentary government, although with the help of Fascist squads, whose members terrorized rebellious workers and intimidated his political opposition. Most of Italy's middle-class politicians, whether Catholic, liberal, or conservative, tolerated such tactics, driven as they were by misguided fears of a communist revolution. It soon became clear that these same mainstream politicians would do little to prevent a Mussolini dictatorship, which he convinced them to accept in 1924.

With his Fascist Party firmly in control of the government, Mussolini and his henchmen set out to eliminate the still-significant left-wing opposition. They began with Giacomo Matteotti, the moderate socialist leader, who had presented parliament with solid evidence of Fascist corruption and electoral fraud. Not long after Matteotti's speech, Blackshirts kidnapped him on a Roman street and later dumped his battered corpse outside the capital. It is unlikely that Mussolini had ordered the political murder, but the Fascist leader knew that assassinations were being discussed and did nothing to prevent them.

The crime was so brazen that even Mussolini's closest non-Fascist allies were outraged, as was the king. They might have been able to remove the prime minister at that point but proved too fearful and uncertain to act. Meanwhile, Fascist militants urged Mussolini to crush all remaining opposition and threatened to take matters into their own hands if he did not. After some hesitation, Mussolini, in early 1925, defiantly took responsibility for Matteotti's murder and other acts of violence. He then closed Italy's remaining channels of dissent by dissolving all political parties but his own, outlawing labor unions, and banning most independent newspapers. Now, anyone who openly criticized the regime became subject to physical attack, imprisonment, and even assassination.

By the mid-1920s, *Il Duce*, or "the leader," as Mussolini liked to be called, had created an absolutist dictatorship built on political terror and mass propaganda. These two pillars of his regime worked hand in hand: terror intimidated and

≡ **Il Duce.** Italian for "the leader," Il Duce was the exalted title Mussolini gave himself. The leader was said to embody the collective spirit, virtues, and values of the Italian nation. Pope Pius XI deemed Mussolini "a man sent by Providence," and this haut-relief (carving on a building or monument), sculpted for the 1942 world's fair, depicts the Italian dictator as just such a man. He is the leader who has rallied the entire nation—workers, soldiers, women, and children—to his banner.

punished dissenters while the propaganda value of parades, public spectacles, posters, and slogans built mass support. Fascist propaganda conveyed a few simple, but potent, ideas. Above all, it denounced parliamentary government for supposedly dividing people into mutually hostile groups and creating a chaos of competing interests. Mussolini's movement promised to bring people back together, uniting them into a collective, organic whole under the guidance of a single charismatic leader, namely himself.

As "a man sent by Providence," according to Pope Pius XI, Mussolini was said to embody the collective strength, spirit, and virtues of the nation. And nationalism, the ideology that glorified the nation, lay at the core of fascist belief. Nationalists extolled the superiority of Italy and Italian culture and claimed the right to dominate those deemed inferior to them. Nationalists in Italy, as elsewhere, preached that individuals must submit—and freely want to submit—to the national will as expressed by the leaders of the state. "The maximum of liberty," wrote the Fascist intellectual Giovanni Gentile, "coincides with the maximum power of the state."

The nationalism at the heart of fascist ideology implied overseas conquest, not just as a means of demonstrating Italy's superiority but as a vehicle for the action and "will" that fascism claimed to represent. Mussolini appeared to embody that will, which together with his vivid personality gave him a charisma that reached beyond his own country to many parts of the world. Famous foreign intellectuals such as Ezra Pound and T. S. Eliot expressed admiration for Mussolini, as did no less a figure than Winston Churchill. The Portuguese strongman Antonio Salazar (1889–1970; dictator, 1932–1968) learned from Mussolini, as did General Francisco Franco (1892–1975), who became Spain's dictator in 1939 and ruled until his death in 1975. Mussolini's most significant foreign disciple was Adolf

The Rise of Fascism in Italy	
1915	Italy enters the First World War on the side of the Allies
1918	All male citizens aged twenty-one and older or who had served in the army given the right to vote
June 1919	Italy signs Treaty of Versailles; Nationalists denounce "mutilated victory"
March 1919	Benito Mussolini founds the *Fasci Italiani di Combattimento*
September 1919	Gabriele D'Annunzio seizes Fiume with a squadron of demobilized soldiers and holds the port for fifteen months
November 1920	Fascist squad attacks Bologna's socialist-controlled city hall, killing six people
January–March 1921	*Squadristi* kill more than one hundred people across northern Italy
Summer 1921	Fascist squads count 300,000 members
October 28, 1922	March on Rome; King Vittorio Emmanuel III appoints Mussolini as prime minister
1924	Socialist leader Giacomo Matteotti murdered by Fascists
1925	Mussolini assumes dictatorial control over Italian government

Hitler, who built on Il Duce's fascist experience and later made him Germany's junior partner in the Second World War.

Hitler and the Origins of the Nazi Movement

Adolf Hitler, like Mussolini, had been hardened by his service in the First World War and schooled on the nationalist passions it had unleashed. Born in Linz, Austria, in 1889, Hitler migrated to Vienna in search of fame and fortune as an artist, but he lacked both the discipline and the talent to do more than ordinary work. Rejected from prestigious art schools and unable to make a regular living, he floated around the city penniless and increasingly resentful of those more successful than he. The city's many populist and antisemitic politicians appealed to that resentment, and Hitler found himself drawn to them. Above all, Hitler was attracted to Georg von Schönerer, the German nationalist demagogue, and Karl Luëger (see Chapter 9), the longtime mayor of Vienna and master antisemite, whose views would shape his own.

Hitler remained in Vienna off and on until 1913, when he left for Munich, Germany, disgusted with the "rotten" Habsburg empire, which in his view favored inferior Slavs over superior Germans. He probably would have drifted anonymously in Munich and elsewhere for the rest of his life had it not been for the First

World War. This conflict, so terrible for so many people, proved a great boon to Hitler, for it rescued him from his impoverished existence and gave him, through military service, the purpose and discipline he had lacked.

Passing as a German in the country with which he now identified, Hitler volunteered for a Bavarian regiment of the German army and spent four long years at the front, fighting bravely and winning two important decorations. In October 1918, he was temporarily blinded in a poison-gas attack, and while confined to a hospital bed, learned of Germany's defeat: "Everything went black before my eyes," he later wrote, as he reacted in disbelief to the "catastrophe" of the German surrender.

Still a soldier in early 1919, Hitler attended a political indoctrination course developed by army leaders to instill right-wing, nationalist ideas in its rank and file. Hitler excelled in the course, and his teachers sent him to scout out one of the ultra-right-wing, antisemitic groups that flourished in postwar Munich. That group was the German Workers' Party, a fledgling organization that saw itself as at once nationalist and socialist, ethnocentric and anti-capitalist, although it defined capitalism as an economic system dominated by the Jews. Hitler's superiors in the army ordered him to join the party, and while still an undercover agent, he became its star speaker.

In his speeches, Hitler claimed that Jews and left-wing politicians had "stabbed the army in the back" and caused Germany's defeat. He denounced the "shameful" Treaty of Versailles and called for revenge against Britain and France. Above all, Hitler denounced Bolshevism, which, for him, was a Jewish doctrine bent on subverting German society and taking over the world. In Hitler's view, Jews were not a religious group but a distinct "race," a people inherently menacing to a superior, but nonetheless vulnerable, German race. Thus even those who had converted from Judaism to Christianity remained Jews in Hitler's view; an individual could no more shed his race than his skin. Because the impure, corrupt "Jewish race" lived amid the once-pristine German *Volk* ("racial" Germans), "the poisoning of the people will not end," Hitler declared, "as long as the causal agent, the Jew, is not removed from our midst."

Although in his milieu there was nothing distinctive about Hitler's racist and nationalist ideas, what set him apart from

≡ **The Young Adolf Hitler.** The future German dictator (*seated on the right*) poses with members of his regiment during the First World War. The military life rescued Hitler from the failures of his youth and gave him the purpose, resolve, and discipline he had lacked.

his peers was his exceptional oratorical skill. During the war, Hitler's military superiors had singled him out as a "born popular speaker who through his fanaticism and populist style positively compelled his audience to take note and share his views." On the strength of these abilities, he left the army and quickly rose to the top of the ultra-nationalist pack. In 1921, at age thirty-two, Hitler assumed leadership of the National Socialist German Workers' Party, later abbreviated as "Nazi," which was an expanded version of the group he had infiltrated in 1919. The National Socialists' membership was small, but its adherents were determined. Hitler's rhetorical gifts were such that he even attracted the interest of the region's more traditional conservatives, well-to-do individuals who shared many of the Nazis' nationalistic and antisemitic views. Some of them were so taken with Hitler that they introduced him to "respectable" society and enabled him to make converts—or at least sympathizers—of certain prosperous and influential members of Bavaria's elite.

Weimar Politics and the Rejection of Democracy

If Bavarian politics simmered on the right, Germany's new central government, housed in the town of Weimar and known as the **Weimar Republic**, began life on the democratic left. The first elections, held in January 1919, returned a left-of-center coalition headed by the moderate wing of the Social Democratic Party (SPD) and included two other democratic parties: the German Democratic Party (DDP) and the Catholic Center Party (Zentrum). Together, the three parties of the "Weimar coalition" received 76 percent of the vote, and the SPD leader, Friedrich Ebert, became the first president of the Republic.

But Weimar's left-of-center politics was not destined to last. Within eighteen months, the Weimar coalition would foreshadow Europe's general anti-democratic trajectory by losing its majority for good. Even members of the coalition itself would distance themselves from Weimar's democracy, as the Democratic and Center parties moved steadily to the right and President Ebert regularly circumvented the Reichstag and ruled by decree. The SPD, too, was ambivalent about the Weimar Republic, supporting it in practice but not in theory. Its official Marxist ideology led it to prefer a socialist regime to the existing capitalist, democratic one. As for Weimar's other major parties, they all opposed Weimar democracy, although they did not hesitate to use it to build support, wield power, and undermine the regime. The German Communist Party (KPD), which had split off from the SPD, was openly hostile to Weimar, as were Germany's two explicitly conservative parties, the German People's Party (DVP) and the German National People's Party (DNVP), or Nationalists.

By 1924, the DNVP, which represented much of the business and aristocratic elite, had garnered 20 percent of the vote and stood as the country's second largest party after the SPD (25 percent). The DNVP called for the restoration of the kaiser and the repudiation of the Versailles Treaty, and was "emphatically opposed to the prevalence of Jewdom in the government and in public life." (Jews represented less than 1 percent of the German population.) In the mid-1920s, Germany's political configuration meant that the majority of German people stood closer ideologically to the Nationalists than to the SPD. That majority wanted a restoration of the now-idealized prewar regime, with its potent authority, military values, and stable, hereditary rule. What it got instead under Weimar was a typical parliamentary regime characterized by political maneuvering, unsatisfactory compromises, and divided authority.

Weimar's Undemocratic Institutions

With most of Weimar's political parties unenthusiastic at best about their democratic republic, the regime did little to democratize Germany's bedrock institutions—the army, judiciary, government bureaucracy, and educational system. Led by conservative, aristocratic officers, the army remained wedded to the defunct kaiser's regime. And like the army, Germany's judicial system clung to its traditional imperial ways. It regularly meted out harsh penalties to left-wing opponents of the regime, while treating their right-wing, anti-democratic counterparts leniently.

If most military leaders and judicial officials had been trained under the kaiser's regime and continued afterward to share its anti-democratic values, so too did most of Weimar Germany's civil servants (government employees) and educators. The former often used their considerable authority to undermine or dilute progressive legislation, and the latter did little to instill respect for, or even understanding of, democracy.

It did not take long before some of the republic's opponents attempted to do away with the regime. In March 1920, an East Prussian politician, Wolfgang Kapp, led a band of Free Corps (irregular troops) into Berlin, intending to seize control of the German government and create a right-wing, authoritarian alternative. A few weeks later, a communist "Red Army," bent on overthrowing the government, marched into industrial centers in western Germany. To President Ebert's horror, the army did nothing to stand in Kapp's way, although it put down the communist rebellion quickly and brutally.

Given the anti-republican orientation of the judiciary, civil service, and educational system, the army's unwillingness to defend the regime when attacked by nationalist opponents did not bode well for the future. This did not, of course, make the Weimar Republic's collapse inevitable, much less ensure Hitler's rise to power; without Weimar's two severe economic crises, the great inflation of 1923 and the Great Depression of the early 1930s, it might have limped along, even matured into a conservative republican regime. But after the majority of German voters, including growing numbers of Communists, abandoned the Weimar coalition for good and middle-class parties, terrified of Bolshevism, began moving to the anti-democratic right, the republic found itself highly vulnerable to political and economic shocks.

The Economic Crisis of 1923

The first of those shocks came with the hyperinflation of 1923, which resulted directly and indirectly from the First World War. Like its enemies, Germany had borrowed vast sums during the war, expecting to repay them afterward by seizing prosperous industrial regions in neighboring countries and forcing defeated nations to transfer gold and other resources to its coffers. Germany's military defeat ruled out these solutions, and in the aftermath of the war, its leaders found their country massively in debt and lacking the funds to pay it off. As a result, international lenders lost confidence in Germany, and the value of its currency relative to the dollar declined sharply. In 1913 one German mark was worth about twenty-five cents, in late 1919 about two cents.

Germany might have been able to quickly regain its economic footing and restore international confidence had the Allies not imposed large reparations payments. But, as we saw in Chapter 10, the French had suffered cruelly from Germany's wartime occupation of their country and wanted compensation. The Allies argued long and hard over the size of the reparations bill and finally agreed on an amount: 50 billion gold marks pegged to the prewar gold value of the German currency, or about 12 billion dollars—payable in annual installments of 4 billion gold marks. The price for failure to pay would be an Allied occupation of Germany.

Der Goetze

≡ **Contempt for the Weimar Republic.** In the 1920s, a great many Germans, longing for the supposed order and discipline of their prewar regime, rejected the democratic, parliamentary republic that replaced it in 1919. This cartoon depicts that rejection, figuring Weimar's political party system as an idol—a false god. The country's corrupt politicians bow and scrape before this idol, while the German people, represented by the woman in the foreground, look on with anger and contempt.

Americans were no longer in a position to loan much money to Europe, nor were they able to buy as many European products as before the crash. European currency continued to flow to the United States in loan repayments and stepped-up investments, which now earned relatively high rates of return, but the United States could no longer send that money back. A severe balance of payments problem resulted for the major European powers, which to stay on the gold standard now had to either restrict the movement of their currencies toward the United States or spend down their precious gold reserves.

Germany found itself in a particularly difficult situation, because it possessed neither huge reserves of gold nor strong foreign currencies like the dollar that could stand in for gold. It could not afford to lose gold to the United States or other countries, which meant that the Weimar regime had no alternative but to stanch the outflow of German marks. It did so by raising interest rates and cutting government spending. The higher interest rates retained capital at home, but they also discouraged business investment and consumer purchases on credit. The lower government spending reduced the money available to buy both foreign and German products. The result was to further contract a German economy already plunging into recession.

In an ideal world, German officials would have tried to stimulate their economy by taking the opposite policy steps. But like all the other countries on the gold standard, Germany had above all to prevent the outflow of gold. To retain the precious metal, it had no choice but to respond to economic contraction by contracting its economy all the more. Doing so sharply cut demand and thus production and jobs, sending the German economy spiraling downward, powerless to pull itself up by the bootstraps, let alone help its European neighbors, whose economies suffered a similar fate.

Under these circumstances, US banks feared that the German banks to which they had loaned money would no longer be able to service their debts; the American banks refused to roll over their loans. German banks now had to repay the principal, which they did by dangerously depleting their reserves of cash. Depositors were horrified, and they ran to withdraw their money before the reserves disappeared altogether. These "runs" forced hundreds of German banks to close, causing the country's financial system to collapse. The same developments unfolded in Britain, France, Austria, and around the world.

With banks in collapse, millions of individuals and businesses lost their money and credit froze up. The short-term loans that grease the wheels of any economic system disappeared, and with them a great deal of economic activity. Production plummeted and unemployment soared (see Map 12.2). Deflation set in, often reducing prices below the cost of production and discouraging people from purchasing goods and services on the grounds that prices would be lower in the future.

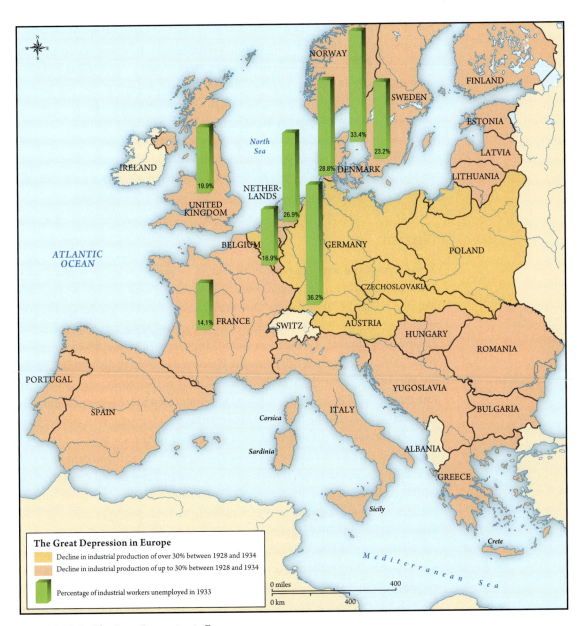

The legend reads:

The Great Depression in Europe

- Decline in industrial production of over 30% between 1928 and 1934
- Decline in industrial production of up to 30% between 1928 and 1934
- Percentage of industrial workers unemployed in 1933

0 miles   400
0 km   400

≡ **MAP 12.2** The Great Depression in Europe

Economies everywhere were falling apart, mired now in what would be called the
Great Depression.

The only answer, as one government after the other belatedly realized, was to
leave the gold standard behind, which Britain, Austria, and Germany did in 1931
and the United States two years later. They had remained on it as long as they did

out of fear that the absence of fixed exchange rates and gold values would reproduce the runaway inflation of the early 1920s, when the gold standard had not yet been restored. But in the 1930s, the problem was deflation, not inflation, and most governments eventually understood that the perils of remaining on the gold standard outweighed the risks of abandoning it. Once untethered to gold, the economies of most countries improved—in some cases dramatically. They were now free to devalue their currencies, thus increasing exports, and to stimulate their economies through deficit spending and reduced interest rates. The demise of the gold standard did not, by itself, end the Great Depression, but it allowed the different countries to set out on a road to recovery.

Nazism

It was a long and winding road, especially in Germany, where fear of inflation had reached pathological proportions. In June 1931, Reich Chancellor Heinrich Brüning (1885–1970) declared, "One must either go along with deflation or devalue the currency. For us only the first could be considered, since, six years after experiencing unparalleled inflation, new inflation, even in careful doses, is not possible." With views such as this, even the German exit from the gold standard did not alleviate its catastrophic economic crisis. And as the country spiraled deeper into the depths of depression, a great many people lost what remaining confidence they had in the established order of things. Millions of Germans were now open to radical solutions and to the demagogues who advanced them.

Communists on the extreme left as well as Nazis on the extreme right proposed such solutions, and although the German Communist Party gained strength in the terrible economic climate, the nature of Weimar politics predisposed most Germans to the right. After Ebert died in 1925, a majority had voted to replace him with the monarchist First World War general Paul von Hindenburg, who served as a substitute kaiser and embodied the conservative, nationalist values Germans commonly held. Again, Germany's rightist center of gravity did not make the Nazi rise to power inevitable. If Brüning, who held the chancellorship during the crucial years from 1930 to 1932, had responded more vigorously and creatively to the economic crisis, the economy might have improved just enough to avoid Hitler's extremes. Or if the Social Democrats and Communists had been able to join forces in a common anti-Nazi front, or had the conservatives not underestimated and misunderstood the nature and designs of the Nazi Party, Germany might have followed a different path.

The Nazis, after all, were still a tiny fringe party as late as 1928, when they won just 2.6 percent of the vote. Hitler's organization began to pick up support in the fall of 1929, when the entire German right campaigned against the Young Plan, a new American proposal to reduce and reschedule reparations payments, which conservatives and nationalists wanted to abolish altogether. This campaign also lent the Nazi leaders some much-needed respectability, as they appeared on the same platform as leading nationalists, many of them wealthy aristocrats and industrialists. In these meetings, brown-shirted, jackbooted Nazis, marching in disciplined formations, seemed to many Germans more dynamic and energetic than the often dull, somberly dressed mainstream politicians. Young men, in particular, many of them restless and contemptuous of their elders, were attracted to the uniformed Nazis, especially as Germany began to slip into the Great Depression.

The Nazi Takeover

Germany's unemployment figures, already high in 1928–1929, tell much of the story of the country's economic and social devastation during this time. At the beginning of 1930, joblessness stood at 3 million. By December of that year it had jumped to 4,380,000, and twelve months later to almost 6 million. By 1932, nearly 40 percent of German workers were out of a job.

While Weimar's inept centrist government continued to worry about inflation—even with prices dropping, production falling, joblessness mounting, and the banks in crisis—the Nazis promised a new and dramatic approach to the country's problems. They did so not through any formal program for economic recovery, but through a series of simple and powerful ideas and images designed to blame Germany's plight on others and appeal to popular prejudices.

The economic recovery would come, the Nazis said, when the German people bonded themselves into a cohesive "racial community" under Hitler's leadership. Only then would they throw off the economic and political shackles of Versailles and seize the "living space" in Eastern Europe necessary to realize their economic potential. In the process, they would suppress the Jews, said to exploit and weaken the German *Volk*.

Because the National Socialists kept their message deliberately vague but backed it with skillful propaganda and moving atmospherics—torchlight processions, swastika banners, emotional speeches—they became the sole party of the Weimar Republic capable of drawing significant support from a broad array of social groups. Still, Hitler won his greatest number of converts from the middle ranks of German society, from the shopkeepers, clerks, small businessmen, farmers, and modest government officials who had suffered severe hardship in the German inflation and again after 1929. As the economic crisis deepened, the Nazis gained working-class recruits, although unemployed laborers were more likely to vote for the Communists.

The National Socialist success can be measured by its stunning electoral ascent between 1930 and 1933. With the country mired in depression in 1930, the Nazi vote tally skyrocketed from 2.6 to 18.3 percent, making it the nation's second largest party after the SPD (24.5 percent). Between a quarter and a third of those who had voted for the Nationalists, Democrats, and People's Party in 1928 now judged them inept and backed the Nazis. Hitler's party was increasingly seen as the lone political organization strong enough to protect the middle and upper classes from the communists. One-tenth of Social Democratic voters defected to the Nazis as well. Large numbers of women, many of whom had never voted before, now supported Hitler's party.

Two years later, during the presidential election of March–April 1932, Hitler audaciously challenged the eighty-four-year-old Hindenburg. The sitting president was endorsed by every major party except the Nazis and Nationalists, who backed Hitler, and the Communists, who championed their own leader, Ernst Thälmann. Hitler and Thälmann forced Hindenburg into a second-round runoff by denying him an absolute majority, and in the second round Hitler received 37 percent of the vote, by far the highest Nazi total to date. The election showed that Hitler had national appeal, although not enough to dislodge the incumbent president.

≡ **Nazis on the March.** Two years before the Nazis began their electoral ascent in 1929, they dramatized their movement by goose-stepping through German cities and towns. In this photograph, storm troopers give their leader, Adolf Hitler, the Nazi salute.

In poor health, Hindenburg had agreed to run for re-election only to deny the presidency to Hitler. As his new chancellor, Hindenburg chose Franz von Papen, a conservative aristocrat with close ties to the most traditionalist forces in the country. Like other conservatives, Papen believed he could bring Hitler and the Nazis into a grand right-wing coalition without giving them the upper hand. He clung to this belief despite his own scant popular support and the Nazis' standing as the largest and most dynamic political organization in the country.

New parliamentary elections in July 1932 confirmed the Nazis' status as by far the largest party, with 37.4 percent of the vote.

They achieved this result, in part, by launching their paramilitary Brownshirts (*Sturmabteilung* or SA) against their political opponents in what amounted to an unprecedented campaign of violence. The Communists fought back, but Social Democratic leaders ordered their forces to stand down in a misguided—and unilateral—commitment to legality. Still, the Social Democrats managed to hold onto most of their seats with 21.6 percent of the vote, while the Communists (14.3 percent) and Center Party (12.4 percent) actually increased their parliamentary numbers. Most of the other, now discredited, Weimar parties all but vanished from the electoral map.

As powerful as the Nazis had become, they represented considerably less than a majority of the German electorate. The problem was that there existed no viable parliamentary majority that excluded them. Hoping somehow to clarify the political situation, Papen called for yet another legislative election in November 1932. This time, the Nazis registered their first electoral decline, dropping from 37.4 to just over 33 percent and losing two million votes, as former supporters protested the party's escalating violence. The SPD and KPD together received considerably more votes and seats than the Nazis, although the SPD vote dropped, while the KPD's increased. The Communist advance from 14.3 to nearly 17 percent terrified property owners and the middle class all the more and enabled the Nazis to present themselves, despite their loss of support, as the lone bulwark against German Bolshevism, which in reality did not pose much of a threat.

More problematic was the government's lack of legitimacy. Papen had little party backing and less public support, and the faltering Hindenburg was in no position to exercise energetic leadership. The government found itself stalemated, even as the economy continued to decline. The president rejected the idea of replacing the republic with a frankly authoritarian regime. He feared that doing so would infuriate the Nazis and Communists, which both thrived on Weimar's democratic elections, and plunge the country into civil war.

Under these circumstances, Hindenburg overcame his hesitations about Hitler's character and background and named him Chancellor of the German Reich on January 30, 1933. An enthusiastic Papen proclaimed, "We've hired him," showing that he had learned nothing of the realities of the new mass politics. Hitler may not have believed in democracy, but he planned to use his large, if not majoritarian, electorate to do away not only with the Weimar Republic but with old-school aristocrats like Papen as well.

The Nazi Regime

Once in office, Hitler showed how little he intended to be the traditionalists' hired hand. In mid-February, the Nazis took control of the state police of Prussia, the German province that contained about two-thirds of the Reich's population. They then effectively deputized members of the Nazi's two paramilitary forces, the SA and SS (*Schutzstaffel*, Hitler's elite police force), and directed them to terrorize potential Nazi opponents. The uniformed toughs beat up centrist and leftist politicians, closed down newspapers, disrupted public meetings, and harassed anyone who dared to oppose these actions. Goebbels then turned the German state radio network into an arm of Nazi persuasion, broadcasting Hitler's major speeches and giving his party an enormous advantage over any potential opposition group.

Army leaders worried about competition from the armed, uniformed SA, which had grown to two million members—twenty times the size of the regular military. But Hitler secured the generals' acquiescence to SA violence and intimidation by promising to restore conscription, destroy communism and social democracy, and overturn the Treaty of Versailles. With the army's tacit blessing, SA members murdered, in public, the Social Democratic mayor of Stassfurt and nearly beat to death a former Center Party cabinet minister. Papen's confident prediction that power would tame the Nazis looked increasingly absurd, as did the Communists' belief that Hitler's actions represented the last gasp of a capitalist system about to collapse.

≡ *The Reichstag Fire.* In February 1933, an unstable Dutch anarchist named Marinus van der Lubbe set the German parliament building (Reichstag) ablaze. Hitler and his lieutenants used van der Lubbe's act to justify a brutal crackdown on communists and others who dissented from their rule.

The Communist view became even less plausible after an arsonist burned down the German parliament building (Reichstag), giving Hitler a pretext for even harsher repression. On February 27, an unemployed Dutch anarchist named Marinus van der Lubbe set fire to the Reichstag, imagining that his spectacular act would spark a rebellion of German workers. It is still unclear whether van der Lubbe acted alone or at someone else's behest, but Hitler declared unequivocally that the Reichstag fire was the opening act of an attempted communist coup d'état. He ordered police officials to arrest as many communists as they could find and then to shoot them all. Some 4,000 communists were rounded up, although police officials ignored the directive to kill them. Many were eventually sent to **concentration camps**, harsh detention centers where inmates were routinely abused, starved, tortured, and killed.

In this atmosphere of terror and repression, with SA and SS members patrolling the streets, Hitler called new parliamentary elections for March 5, 1933. The deck was clearly stacked against all non-Nazi candidates, but even so, Hitler's party failed to win the absolute majority it coveted, attracting just 43.9 percent of the vote. The Social Democrats and Center Party maintained most of their support, while the Communists, their leaders in jail or in hiding, still managed 12.32 percent. The Nazis achieved a majority in parliament—-not that majorities mattered any more—only by allying with the Nationalists, who received 7.97 percent of the vote.

The Consolidation of Nazi Power

In the wake of these elections, the SA and Nazi-controlled police felt free to round up tens of thousands of people and dump them in the growing network of concentration camps. Hundreds, perhaps thousands, were shot outright. When even Hitler's Nationalist partners protested against these actions, the Führer decided to give them a veneer of legality through a proposed "Enabling Act" that would rewrite the Weimar constitution and award the new chancellor something close to dictatorial powers. Hitler threatened to punish any Reichstag member who resisted the Enabling Act, and over the Social Democrats' objections, it was approved by a resounding majority. The Führer now enjoyed the power to do essentially what he pleased.

Almost immediately, Hitler purged the civil service, dissolved the governments and parliaments of Germany's individual states, and abolished Germany's venerable trade union movement. In addition, the new government placed under direct or indirect Nazi control virtually every other institution and organization in the country. Hitler even purged his own Nazi organization. During the infamous Night of the Long Knives (June 30, 1934), the SS joined with elements of the regular army to stage an assault against the leadership of the SA, whose mounting power worried both Hitler and the army's high command. Just before dawn, SS gunmen shot dozens of men in cold blood, including the SA leader, Ernst Röhm. As soon as the deeds were done, Germany's top generals solemnly swore eternal loyalty to the Führer; when President Hindenburg died five weeks later, they embraced Hitler's decision to consolidate all executive power in his hands. Although the high command did not realize it, they had set the stage for their own submission to Hitler four years later.

The Nazi Dictatorship

In the absence of any genuinely independent institutions, it became extremely difficult to organize opposition to the Nazi regime or even to voice dissenting ideas. Once in power, the Nazis moved quickly to establish control over Germany's major channels of communication—radio, film, theater, publishing, and print journalism. Nazi officials forced Jews and known leftists out of these industries and sharply limited foreign films and other media from abroad. With these measures in place, Germans found themselves largely isolated from ideas and information that did not conform to Nazi views.

But even this was not enough for Hitler and his lieutenants. They wanted not just to block opposing ideas but to instill the Nazi outlook in the German people and evoke from them a thunderous approval of the new regime. Under Goebbels' direction, Nazi leaders pursued these goals through public symbolism, mass meetings, and elaborate rituals such as the gigantic Nuremberg Party Rally filmed by Riefenstahl in 1934. Goebbels also ensured that even the most basic human interactions would express allegiance to Hitler and belonging to his new national community. Germans now greeted one another with the cry "Heil Hitler" (Hail Hitler) while extending their arms in the Nazi salute. Although people who failed to use this greeting could run afoul of the political police, it seemed genuinely popular, as did Hitler himself. The American journalist William L. Shirer reported that a great many Germans "looked up at him [Hitler] as if he were a Messiah."

The New Regime: Dissent and Consent

These rituals and other forms of Nazi propaganda convinced skeptics and dissenters that it would be dangerous to buck the apparent Nazi tide, while also producing the positive effects Goebbels intended. Still, support for the regime was far from unanimous, especially early on. Given the pervasive threat of arrest, most people did not act on any reservations they felt, but some brave souls did try to resist the regime. By mid-1933, small, clandestine groups of Social Democrats and Communists had begun to produce crudely printed anti-Nazi newspapers, which they distributed in secret. Their members maintained contact with exiled party leaders and on occasion managed a brief public demonstration. But these groups lacked leadership and coordination, and the **Gestapo**, the Nazis' political police, was constantly on their heels, picking off members one by one and torturing them for information about their colleagues. By the end of 1935, both the Social Democratic and Communist undergrounds had been destroyed. Even so, personal beliefs and commitments were not so easily undone; millions of Social Democrats and Communists maintained their political views throughout Hitler's **Third Reich** (1933–1945), while keeping those views to themselves.

Not just left-wingers, but conservatives, too, registered opposition to the regime, albeit in private. Friedrich Reck-Malleczewen, a wealthy physician with highly traditionalist views, kept a carefully hidden diary into which he poured his venomous hatred of the Nazis. He called Hitler "a piece of filth" and ridiculed his fellow Germans for idolizing this "unclean . . . monstrosity," this "power-drunk schizophrenic."

The physician's opinions were startling and uncommon within his social group. There is reason to believe that the middle class generally approved— or did not disapprove—of the Nazi regime. Elisabeth Braunschweig, a bureaucrat's

Germans Rally to Hitler's Regime. Although the Nazis never enjoyed an electoral majority under the Weimar Republic, they became increasingly popular after seizing absolute power in 1933. By photographing huge rallies such as the one pictured here, Nazi propagandists demonstrated—and exaggerated—the extent of their support.

wife whose voluminous correspondence has survived, was perhaps typical of bourgeois Germans in the evolution of her views. Braunschweig rejoiced when Hitler was named chancellor and accepted the need for what she called "ruthless, decisive action by the national government," by which she meant the purges, beatings, and roundups of those deemed to represent the discredited Weimar Republic. Initially, Braunschweig criticized Goebbels and Göring's antisemitic speeches and disliked the regime's attacks against Jewish artists and intellectuals. But she soon justified those attacks by claiming, as Hitler did, that Bolsheviks and Jews were conducting a "smear campaign against Germany" and had to be stopped.

Nazi propaganda clearly had its effect, and by 1935, the twin pillars of propaganda-inspired consent and implied coercion served to maintain not just acquiescence to the regime but also widespread allegiance to it, even enthusiasm, especially in the middle class. The Nazis were now able to tighten their apparatus of terror, which they unleashed mainly against those considered on the margins of society: Jews, Roma (Gypsies), homosexuals, beggars, and the disabled and mentally ill. For these people, no outward acquiescence to the regime would do; they became targets purely for who they were.

≡ **Strength through Joy.** This Nazi program created government-subsidized leisure activities for working people. The most popular of these activities was weekend excursions to lake or seaside resorts. Wealthy people often resented the "invasion" of their vacation spots by the lower class, but Strength Through Joy helped solidify working-class support for the National Socialist regime.

Nazi officials ordered the central bank to print five billion Reichsmarks to stimulate the economy. In this effort, Hitler did nothing to undermine German capitalism; he used government funds not to create state-run enterprises, although some war-related ones were eventually built, but to subsidize the private businesses contracted to manufacture armaments and fortify the country's infrastructure.

Between 1933 and 1939, the government devoted the equivalent of 20 billion dollars to a massive rearmament campaign designed to restore Germany's status as a great military power. On the domestic front, Hitler's centerpiece was the creation of a national highway system (the *Reichsautobahnen*) more advanced than any in the world. The unprecedented government spending involved in these military and domestic projects reduced Germany's official unemployment from the six million inherited by the Nazis to less than one million by 1937. By the eve of the war, labor shortages set in, and the government began to conscript people into the less desirable jobs. But even the relatively desirable ones did not pay very well and subjected workers to long days and harsh factory conditions. Hitler wanted to devote as many resources as possible to his ambitious rearmament plan and gave priority to investment in plant and equipment, not wages. Still, the overall economic situation was immeasurably better than it had been in 1933.

Leisure for the Masses

Partly because Nazi authorities had kept wages low, they took a variety of steps to prop up the workers' morale. Their most successful venture, an organization called the National Socialist Community Strength Through Joy (STJ), provided government-subsidized leisure activities for working people and their families. Strength Through Joy's most notable project was the creation of vacation packages at prices affordable to factory workers. These packages ran the gamut from weekend excursions to weeklong cruises and attracted hundreds of thousands of people in what became an unprecedented democratization of tourism.

It goes without saying that Jews and other "undesirables" were barred from STJ activities, and even the good "Aryans" who participated in them had to endure the presence of Gestapo and SS spies. Still, working-class travelers for the most part enjoyed themselves and appreciated the Nazis' efforts, clumsy as they often were, to offer them travel and leisure activities that, until then, had been beyond their means. These opportunities, and especially the millions of newly created jobs, earned Hitler the acquiescence, if not the loyalty, of the bulk of the German working class, including a great many women, who also found employment despite the official Nazi objective of keeping wives and mothers in the home.

Hitler and the Rise of Nazism in Germany	
1913	Adolf Hitler leaves Austria for Munich, Germany
1914	Germany enters the First World War
November 11, 1918	Germany surrenders to Allies
January 1919	First general elections under new Weimar Republic
June 1919	Germany signs Treaty of Versailles and is forced to accept harsh terms
September 1919	Hitler joins the ultra-rightwing, antisemitic German Workers' Party
December 1919	German mark is worth about 2 cents
Spring 1920	Political violence from both left and right weakens support for Weimar government
May 1921	Allied powers and Germany settle on reparations bill of 50 billion gold marks, pegged to the prewar gold value of the German currency
July 1921	Hitler assumes leadership of National Socialist Workers' Party (Nazis)
August 1922	One German mark is worth about one-tenth of a penny
January 1923	French forces occupy Ruhr Valley in response to Germany's failure to make reparation payments
Spring–Summer 1923	Rampant hyperinflation; German currency collapses
September 1923	Germany negotiates withdrawal of French troops from Ruhr Valley in exchange for reparation payments in the form of coal; French troops leave in 1925
November 8, 1923	"Beer hall putsch"; Hitler wounded and jailed
1924–1928	Most major countries return to the gold standard
Spring 1924	Inflation disappears; German economy recovers
1925	Paul von Hindenburg elected president of Germany
1925–1926	Hitler publishes *Mein Kampf*
May 1928	Nazi party gains just 2.6 percent of the vote in German federal elections

Hitler and the Rise of Nazism in Germany	
Summer–Fall 1928	US Federal Reserve Bank raises interest rates; American banks turned inward, rather than making loans abroad; European economy contracts
October 1929	New York stock market crashes; Great Depression begins
1930	Nazis gain 18.3 percent of the vote in national elections
1931	Britain, Austria, and Germany abandon gold standard
1932	Nearly 40 percent of German workers are unemployed
January 30, 1933	Hindenburg appoints Hitler as chancellor; beginning of Third Reich and massive German rearmament
February 27, 1933	Reichstag fire; four thousand communists rounded up by Hitler
March 5, 1933	Nazis fail to win absolute majority in parliamentary elections
June 30, 1934	Night of the Long Knives; Hitler purges Nazi party
1934	*Triumph of the Will* filmed by Leni Riefenstahl
1935	German Jews lose their citizenship; Social Democrat and Communist parties destroyed; persecution of Jews, gypsies, homosexuals, the disabled, and mentally ill intensifies
1937	Number of unemployed German workers falls to less than 1 million
November 8, 1939	*Kristallnacht* (Night of the Broken Glass)
1939	Population of German Jews drops to 202,000 from 523,000 in 1933

Conclusion: The Fascist "Revolution"?

The murders of disabled people, Jews, and dissidents, the violent purge of the SA, the sadistic treatment of inmates of concentration camps—all these shocking Nazi acts, awful as they were, did not constitute a social revolution like the one engineered by Stalin in Russia. Nor did Mussolini's less extreme, though still brutal, Fascist state. Hitler was no less ruthless than his Russian counterpart, but the German leader's goals for Germany differed markedly from Stalin's goals for the Soviet Union.

Hitler had no intention of transforming German society. He inherited an industrial, capitalist country, and he left its basic socioeconomic structure intact. Hitler's goal, like Mussolini's, was a cultural revolution rather than a socioeconomic one, a revolution designed to create an obedient, culturally uniform, and ostensibly unified people. To accomplish this objective, the fascist leaders did not need to upend society and eliminate millions of people, as Stalin did in transforming Russia from a semi-capitalist, peasant-dominated society into an industrialized, collectivist one in the space of a dozen years. Under Stalin, the machinery of terror continued until the Soviet leader had erased the traditional peasantry and bourgeoisie and created a new, largely proletarian ruling group completely loyal to him. Hitler, by contrast, required only an initial burst of terror, after which the mere threat of further terror generally sufficed—except, of course, for the Jews and other "inferior" people.

The great Nazi violence would come after Hitler's war of aggression had begun. Between 1939 and 1945, his effort to make Europe into a haven for the German "master race" and a hell for everyone else would lead to a staggering, unprecedented number of deaths.

KEY TERMS

concentration camps *565*	gold standard *556*	Nazism *529*
consumerism *555*	Great Depression *559*	newsreel *552*
fascism *536*	*Kristallnacht* *568*	Third Reich *566*
Gestapo *566*	march on Rome *541*	Weimar Republic *545*

 For digital learning resources, please go to **https://www.oup.com/he/berenson2e**. Turn to the back of the book to see the list of primary sources and writing exercises provided in the accompanying *Sources and Guided Writing Exercises for Europe in the Modern World*

13

The Second World War, 1939–1945

Primo Levi

> The need to tell our story to "the rest," to make "the rest" participate in it, had taken on for us, before our liberation and after, the character of an immediate and violent impulse, to the point of competing with our other elementary needs.

The Italian writer Primo Levi (1919–1987) penned these lines in his memoir, *Survival in Auschwitz* (1947), to explain why he felt compelled to relive the agony of his year in the most notorious Nazi concentration camp. Although he never overcame his guilt for having survived when so many others did not, he wanted "to tell the story, to bear witness" to the incomprehensible horrors the Nazis had devised. Hoping that in the future others might be spared his fate, Levi used his gift of prose "not to live *and* to tell, but to live *in order* to tell."

Primo Levi was one of some 6,400 Italian Jews deported by his country's German occupiers to the Nazi death camp at Auschwitz (Poland). Italian Jews were relatively lucky, since the Nazis did not begin sending them away until late in the war. Jews from Poland, Russia, and elsewhere in Eastern Europe found themselves the objects of Hitler's "final solution" beginning in 1941. In camps specifically designed as murder factories, the Nazis killed nearly three million Jews—about half the number they slaughtered altogether. The rare survivors stayed alive, in Levi's words, by sheer luck.

Born in 1919, Primo Levi grew up in the northern Italian city Turin, where he passed a comfortable and undramatic childhood. He went to one of the best secondary schools in the region, and in 1937 entered the University of Turin where he studied chemistry. Levi was able to complete his studies because he had matriculated before the enactment of Fascist Italy's "racial" laws barring Jews from public schools and universities. His pleasure in graduating summa cum laude was marred, however, by a notation on his diploma—"of the Jewish race"—intended to deny him employment opportunities and subject him to a variety of other indignities.

Until this point, Levi had suffered little anti-Jewish discrimination. Italian Jews had long been integrated into civic and economic life, and it was not until Mussolini's alliance with Nazi Germany in the late 1930s that Italian officials began to enact antisemitic laws. And even then, the discrimination was mild enough that Levi did not feel himself to be the victim of excessive persecution.

That perception changed abruptly in September 1943, when the Nazis, threatened by the Allied invasion of southern Italy, occupied the central and northern parts of the peninsula and turned Mussolini into a puppet. Rebel bands formed to resist both the local Fascists and their Nazi overlords, and early one morning Levi found himself under arrest for membership in one of these resistance groups. Rather than admitting such political involvement, which Levi believed would bring him certain torture and death, he identified himself as a Jew. At this late stage of the war, Levi was still so unaccustomed to the poisonous effects of antisemitism that he believed it safer to reveal himself a Jew than an anti-Fascist partisan.

But as much as the Nazis hated those who opposed them, their highest priority was to annihilate the Jews. In February 1944, a squad of German SS men loaded Levi and 649 other Italian Jews onto freight cars bound for Auschwitz. Of those 650 people, only twenty-three returned home alive. During the four-day-long trip, SS officers struck people with their guns for no reason and denied their victims, freezing in unheated cars, food and water.

When Levi and his fellow deportees arrived at Auschwitz, SS men sorted them into two groups, the fit and the unfit. In the first group the Germans placed most of the young men and a sprinkling of women. Into the other they herded the ill, elderly, women, and children—three-quarters of the Italian deportees. Within two days, all the "unfit" were dead, murdered in gas chambers built to asphyxiate thousands of people a day.

As a member of the group deemed fit enough to work, Levi entered the world of the camp. Over its entrance stood a sign that read *Arbeit macht frei* ("Work makes you free"), its message purposefully and grotesquely ironic, for the Nazis meant to work or torment Levi's group to death. The Auschwitz motto caricatured the famous dictum of the German Enlightenment, "Knowledge makes you free," and recalled the emblem that adorned the entrance to hell in Dante's *Inferno*, "Abandon all hope, you who enter."

The torment of the camps began with the effort to deprive new inmates of their identity. After a quick, boiling shower to "disinfect" them and a forced sprint, naked, their heads shaved bald, to an unheated hut, Levi and his compatriots were given identical prison uniforms and somebody else's ill-fitting shoes. They now resembled one another, generic inmates of the camps. Like cattle, prisoners had their wrists branded with a number, and camp officials referred to them not as people but as "pieces," distinguished only by the marks seared into their skin.

Timeline

1936	1937	1938	1939	1940	1941	1942	1943	1944	1945	1946

1936 Hitler sends German troops into the Rhineland

1936–1939 Spanish Civil War

March 1938 Hitler annexes Austria (*Anschluss*); seizes Czechoslovakia

September 1938 Munich Pact grants Germany the Sudetenland

March 1939 Germany seizes Czechoslovakia

August 1939 Nazi-Soviet pact agrees to nonaggression between Germany and Russia and divides Poland between them

September 1939–May 1945 World War II in Europe

September 1939 Germany invades Poland; Britain and France declare war on Germany

April 1940 Germany attacks Denmark and Norway

May 1940 Germany launches attack against Western Europe

June 1940 Germans occupy Paris; Pétain rules a rump France headquartered in Vichy

August–November 1940 Battle of Britain

March 1941 United States passes Lend-Lease Act

May 1941 Greece and Yugoslavia in Germany's hands

June 1941 Germany's Operation Barbarossa begins against Soviet Union

December 1941 Japan attacks Pearl Harbor; United States enters war

January 1942 Wannsee Conference formalizes "final solution"

October 1942 Allies launch attack against German forces in Egypt

August 1942–February 1943 Battle of Stalingrad

August 1943 British and American forces take Sicily, advance into Italian mainland

February 1944 Primo Levi sent to Auschwitz

June 6, 1944 D-Day—Allied forces storm Normandy coast

December 1944 Battle of the Bulge

April 1945 Soviet army takes Berlin; Hitler commits suicide

August 1945 Bombing of Hiroshima and Nagasaki

As Levi looked at his fellow prisoners, shorn of their clothes and hair, starved and humiliated, he understood that it was not enough for the Nazis merely to kill. They meant to humiliate and dehumanize, to delight in turning human beings into objects without names, too hungry to think, too weak to resist. *Survival in Auschwitz* was not, therefore, purely a record of Levi's existence in the camp. It was an effort to explore to what extent the human spirit can remain alive under conditions of abject brutality.

What Levi observed acknowledged the Nazis' diabolical success. Exhausted and harassed, laboring on five hundred calories a day, prisoners took advantage of others weaker than themselves. They lied and stole, debased and humiliated themselves, and readily took the lives of others if it allowed them to extend their own. This was the reality of the camp, a place whose motto became, "Eat your bread, and, if you can, that of your neighbor too."

But there was another side to the life of the camp, one in which inmates opposed brutality with kindness, degradation with dignity. Upon discovering a source of water, Levi, though desperately thirsty, shared it with a friend. A non-Jewish Italian laborer working under contract at the camp put his life at risk by bringing Levi extra bits of bread at a time when he was literally starving to death. Another relatively privileged Auschwitz resident regularly intervened on behalf of the Jewish prisoners and encouraged Levi to think beyond the hellish reality of the camp by remembering the great literature he had read.

Most significant for Levi was an act of human solidarity he witnessed on the eve of Auschwitz's liberation by Russian soldiers. A prisoner accused of attempting to incite rebellion against the Germans was to be hanged in front of the assembled inmates to show them what happens to those who dare to resist. A moment before the trap door of the

≡ **The Gates of Auschwitz.** All those doomed to die in Auschwitz, the most notorious of the Nazi death camps, were greeted with the words *Arbeit macht frei*—"Work makes you free." These words were cruelly, grotesquely ironic and signaled not the possibility of freedom but the torments of hell.

gallows opened, the doomed man cried out, "Comrades, I am the last one," taunting his executioners, who, with the Russians at their gates, would soon have to abandon the camp.

Levi was at once awed by the courage of this man, who "had found in [himself] the strength to act," and shamed by his own inability to emulate him. In this and other parts of his memoir, Levi was too hard on himself, for although he did not openly rebel, he proved himself a man in a great many ways: his countless acts of kindness, his risky efforts to keep a record of life in the camp, his refusal to debase himself before the Nazis. As the Germans evacuated the camp, Levi, overcome by illness and fatigue, summoned all his strength to care for those sicker than himself. He emerged from the Nazi hell with his humanity intact. ≡

The Enormity of the Second World War

Most of Europe's Jews did not, of course, emerge at all. Nor did millions of other Nazi victims, not to mention the tens of millions of soldiers and civilians who perished in the Second World War. In Europe, this terrible conflict lasted from September 1939, when the Germans invaded Poland, to May 1945, when the Nazis finally gave in. (Overall, the war extended from July 1937, when the Japanese invaded China, until August 1945, when the atomic bombings of Hiroshima and Nagasaki forced the surrender of Japan.) It destroyed more people, land, and resources than any prior conflict in human history (see Map 13.1).

What made this war especially dangerous for European civilians was the fact that the Germans decided, as an integral part of the conflict, to destroy or displace entire populations to make room for German colonists. The Jews were to be annihilated, the Poles killed or enslaved, the Russians killed or removed to the eastern reaches of their lands. Communists, homosexuals, Roma, the physically and mentally disabled—all were to perish in a systematic campaign of murder conducted under the cover of the war. Atrocities always accompany the violence of war, but never before had the systematic murder of civilians been such an integral part of a conflict.

How did so terrible a war come so closely on the heels of an earlier world war, itself the most destructive conflict to date? Why were men and women who had survived the earlier trauma unable to prevent the new one? And how are we to explain the barbarism that the Second World War unleashed? To answer these questions, we must first return to the conclusion of the First World War.

≡ **The Munich Pact.** Returning from Munich at the end of September 1938, British Prime Minister Neville Chamberlain displays to reporters the "document of peace" he has just signed with Hitler. While Chamberlain believed he had secured "peace in our time," Hitler used the Munich Pact purely as a tactic of delay, as a strategic pause in his campaign of aggression and war.

give up these highly strategic lands, only to find that this too was not enough. The dictator now insisted that German troops be permitted to occupy the entire western third of Czechoslovakia immediately and that its other neighbors be allowed to claim pieces of Czech territory as well. Here, the British and French finally drew the line, refusing to endorse Hitler's latest demands.

At this point, Hitler's only choices were to back off temporarily or go to war. With his military leaders opposed to an immediate conflict and public opinion lukewarm at best, Hitler decided to negotiate. At the end of September, he met with Mussolini, Chamberlain, and the French Prime Minister Edouard Daladier in Munich, where the French and British leaders agreed, in the **Munich Pact**, to allow Germany to occupy the Sudetenland in exchange for the Führer's promise to leave the rest of Czechoslovakia intact.

In the short run, the Munich Pact prevented the outbreak of war, and for this reprieve, ecstatic crowds greeted Chamberlain and Daladier on their return from the German city. Chamberlain announced that he had secured "peace in our time" and boasted that the "friendship agreements" with Germany he and Daladier had secured meant that Hitler could be trusted to uphold the Munich accords.

In this belief, the Western leaders were naïve at best, for Hitler understood the Munich Pact as yet another sign of weakness from Britain and France. Had Chamberlain and Daladier refused to appease Hitler, the German High Command might have blocked any further moves against Czechoslovakia, even endorsed a planned coup against the Führer, but after Munich, neither eventuality was possible. So much did that agreement enhance Hitler's prestige that he now seemed infallible. German military leaders bowed to his apparently superior diplomatic and strategic ability, freeing him to do as he pleased. In March 1939, just six months after the Munich Pact, Hitler violated it by sending the German army into Prague, seizing Czechoslovakia and showing his contempt for the West, whose leaders, he rightly believed, would do nothing to thwart him (see Map 13.2).

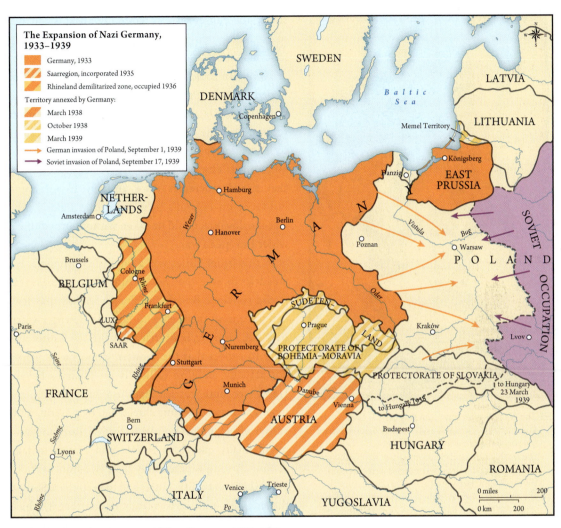

The Expansion of Nazi Germany, 1933–1939

- Germany, 1933
- Saarregion, incorporated 1935
- Rhineland demilitarized zone, occupied 1936

Territory annexed by Germany:
- March 1938
- October 1938
- March 1939
- → German invasion of Poland, September 1, 1939
- → Soviet invasion of Poland, September 17, 1939

≡ **MAP 13.2** The Expansion of Nazi Germany, 1933–1939

Prelude to the Second World War

Under these favorable circumstances, Hitler planned his next move: the conquest of Poland. One of the provisions of the Treaty of Versailles most hated in Germany had awarded Poland a corridor of land dividing Germany proper from its province of East Prussia and made Danzig, formerly a German city, an independent city-state under the protection of the League of Nations. Hitler and other German nationalists had long sought to reclaim these territories and to punish Poland for taking them away. But this was not all Hitler wanted. "It is not Danzig that is at

تقدم التعاون الألماني الروسي

≡ **The Nazi-Soviet Pact.** On August 23, 1939, Nazi Germany and Soviet Russia, widely believed to be ideological opposites and mortal enemies, shocked the world with a public promise not to attack each other. Their pact included a secret agreement to divide Poland between them. This caricature shows the twin, mustachioed dictators joined at the knee, if not the hip, and dancing, revolvers in hand, to the same menacing tune.

stake," the Führer secretly wrote. "For us it is a matter of expanding our living space in the east and making food supplies secure."

To obtain that **living space** (*Lebensraum*), Hitler hoped to take Poland piece by piece, as he had Czechoslovakia, but when the Polish government refused to cede Danzig and parts of the corridor to Germany, the Führer plotted to conquer Poland all at once. The West's timidity had convinced him that the democracies were unlikely to intervene militarily on Poland's behalf and that Poland, like Czechoslovakia, could be taken without provoking a wider European war.

In this belief Hitler was a little too optimistic. He failed to foresee that his seizure of Czechoslovakia would convince British and French leaders that they had to commit themselves to Poland's defense, which they did, formally, in March 1939. But the Führer was right to expect that the Western democracies would not actually mobilize militarily on Poland's behalf. He was far more worried that the Soviet Union might intervene instead, feeling threatened by a German invasion of neighboring Poland. Such a Russian move might finally embolden Britain and France to take action, creating a potentially fatal two-front war. To avoid this eventuality, Hitler had to keep the USSR on the sidelines until he was ready to confront it, which would not occur until after his armies had neutralized Poland, France, and Britain one by one.

To allow this strategy to unfold, Hitler had his diplomats approach Stalin with an offer of a mutual nonaggression pact, an agreement in which each country pledged not to attack the other or ally with an enemy of the other party. Although Stalin had been negotiating with the West since April, the talks with Germany proved far more serious. On the surface, it seemed inconceivable that these two implacable ideological foes could forge an alliance, but the two dictators decided that, under the circumstances, it made strategic sense. Both wanted to buy time—Hitler to avoid a two-front war, and Stalin to rebuild an officer corps decimated by the purges of the late 1930s. Stalin also feared that Britain and France might join with Germany in an alliance of "capitalist powers" against the Soviet Union or that he might have to fight a two-front war against Germany in the west and an increasingly aggressive Japan in the east. On August 23, 1939, Hitler and Stalin stunned the world with their announcement of the **Nazi-Soviet Pact**. In secret, they had agreed to divide Poland between them, and both readied their forces to attack.

The War—Phase I: Hitler's Quest for Domination

On September 1, 1939, two German Army Groups struck Poland with an impressive array of modern weapons and techniques: Stuka dive-bombers, swiftly moving mechanized columns, extremely efficient infantry assault teams, and excellent air-to-ground coordination. Britain and France declared war against Germany two days later, but even though the combined French and British armies outnumbered their German counterpart by seventy-six divisions to thirty-two, the Western forces remained in place, their governments and peoples still hoping to avoid the reality of war.

Had the French and British attacked Germany from the west, the course of the war would have been dramatically different, for despite Germany's impressive show of strength in Poland, the German army (Wehrmacht) was not without its flaws. During the brief Polish campaign, there were frequent problems with supply and communications, as well as a great many mechanical breakdowns. The German economy, powerful as it had become, was not quite ready to support a mechanized war effort of major proportions.

But instead of intervening to defend Poland, as they had promised, Britain and France ceded the initiative to Hitler, whose forces quickly seized control of the western two-thirds of the country. And as the remnants of the Polish army retreated into eastern Poland, the Soviet army moved in to wipe them out. The surviving Polish officers were systematically murdered by Stalin's secret police, which also killed thousands of other members of the Polish elite, dumping them in mass graves in Russia's Katyn forest. The German military and SS had already slaughtered nearly 60,000 Poles, including 7,000 Polish Jews. By the beginning of October, Poland had ceased to exist, its territory now divided between Germany and the Soviet Union.

Hitler's Attack on the West

When it became clear that the British and French were not going to attack Germany, Hitler began to plan his campaign against them, taking advantage of the West's inaction during the "phony war" (September 1939–May 1940) to refine his strategy and strengthen his armaments and military forces. To prevent Britain from blocking German trade routes to Sweden, which supplied it with crucial iron ore, Hitler's forces seized Denmark and Norway in April and May 1940.

Germany's Invasion of the Low Countries and the Fall of France, May–June 1940

- ▬ ▬ German offensives
- ➤ Movement of Allied forces
- ▬ ▬ Maginot line

≡ **MAP 13.3** Germany's Invasion of the Low Countries and the Fall of France, May–June 1940

These ominous developments triggered the fall of Chamberlain's weak, passive government and the establishment of a British war cabinet led by the far more resolute Winston Churchill (1874–1965). The change took place none too soon, as the Germans immediately threatened Britain by launching a ***Blitzkrieg*** or lightning attack against France and the Low Countries. Hitler's objective was to entrap French and British forces in northern France and destroy so much of their armies that both countries would have to sue for peace. In case Britain did not immediately withdraw from the war, the Germans aimed to capture coastal bases in northern France and the Low Countries from which they would launch an assault against the British Isles (see Map 13.3).

As the Germans advanced from the north and east toward the English Channel coast, Churchill decided to evacuate as many troops as possible. Some uncharacteristic German hesitation enabled Allied forces to converge on the port city of Dunkirk, where they were rescued in an extraordinary operation. Virtually every vessel that could float crossed the Channel to Dunkirk, and from there ferried some 220,000 British and 120,000 French soldiers to safety in England. With those troops was a young, as yet unknown, French general named Charles de Gaulle (1890–1970), the man destined to lead France's wartime resistance against the Germans.

With many of France's best military units now ensconced in England, the Germans quickly battled the rest of the French army into submission. The

Wehrmacht occupied Paris on June 14, 1940, and although a few French leaders wanted to relocate the government to North Africa and continue the fighting from there, a demoralized majority decided to surrender instead. On June 16, France's republican government resigned, and the parliament vested near-absolute political authority in the First World War hero, Philippe Pétain.

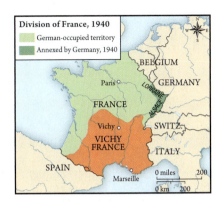

MAP 13.4   Division of France, 1940

Named prime minister at age eighty, Pétain promised to give his country "the gift of my person," supposedly to spare his compatriots the rigors of occupation and defeat. This was a dubious gift, for Pétain hoped to shield his people by collaborating actively with the Germans in an effort to help them win the war. From London, de Gaulle denounced Pétain's plans, going on the radio to urge French men and women to continue the fight, which many would later do under his leadership. In the meantime, Hitler imposed harsh and humiliating terms on the defeated French, annexing Alsace and Lorraine, the two provinces that had seesawed between France and Germany since 1871, and dividing France in two. The Germans occupied the prosperous and strategic parts of the country and consigned Pétain and his government to the town of Vichy, a faded resort in central France that gave the collaborationist government its name, **Vichy France** (see Map 13.4).

Despite these harsh conditions, most French men and women felt relieved by the settlement. They had not wanted to fight in the first place, and now no more blood would be spilled—or so they believed. In addition, many French people, especially those of conservative temper, applauded the armistice for abolishing the tired Third Republic and looked forward to what they believed would be a purer, stronger, and more tradition-bound regime.

From the Battle of Britain to the Early Campaigns in Greece, North Africa, and the Middle East

With Germany's occupation of France and the Low Countries, Hitler hoped the British government would sue for peace, thus allowing him to pursue his primary objective, the conquest of the Soviet Union. But Churchill vowed to resist the Nazi onslaught, bellowing in the House of Commons, "You ask, What is our aim? I can answer in one word: Victory—victory at all costs, victory in spite of all terror; victory however long and hard the road may be." Churchill made it clear that the road ahead was mined with sacrifice and death, but he assured his people that at the cost of "blood, sweat, toil, and tears," they would prevail.

Enraged by Britain's refusal to concede defeat, Hitler directed his powerful air force to attack. In the **Battle of Britain** (August–November 1940), German

≡ **The Battle of Britain.** British Prime Minister Winston Churchill, his trademark cigar tucked in his mouth, inspects the damage to London inflicted by a hail of German bombs. In the summer of 1940, Hitler had ordered the destruction of London, and although some 30,000 were killed and entire neighborhoods reduced to rubble, Britain did not give in.

planes first tried to knock out Britain's air defenses, but when British gunners and pilots held out against difficult odds, the Führer ordered the terror bombing of London, which he wanted destroyed. Although London suffered enormous destruction and perhaps 30,000 deaths, Britain did not succumb. It resisted the German Blitz thanks in part to the Polish gift of a cloned Enigma machine, Germany's encryption device, which enabled British intelligence to decipher the enemy's military communications. In November, Hitler canceled his plans to invade the British Isles, thus allowing Britain to remain in the war.

The British had won a major defensive battle, but given the German occupation of much of the European continent, their offensive options were limited. In November 1940, they tried to help Greece fend off a bungled invasion by Italy, but the British contribution did not amount to very much. When Germany came to Italy's rescue the following spring, the British army proved far too weak to withstand the German assault. By May 1941, both Greece and Yugoslavia, which Hitler had conquered en route to Greece, were in German—and later, Italian—hands.

In its futile effort to defend Greece, Britain diverted troops away from Libya, where, for a time, its forces had fought successfully against the Italian and German armies stationed there. British leaders had hoped to build on those victories to stage an invasion of Italy and knock it out of the war. However, by transferring soldiers from North Africa to Greece, the British sacrificed a winning campaign for a losing one. As a result, the invasion of Italy would be delayed by two years.

Still, the British managed to achieve some notable successes in 1941. Relying on Indian, Australian, and African soldiers, they defeated Italian forces in East Africa (British Somalia, Eritrea, and Ethiopia) in the winter of 1941, thus undoing Italy's conquest of Ethiopia and denting Mussolini's already faltering prestige. These operations foreshadowed the much wider use of African troops in the latter stages of the war, when nearly a million black and Arab men would be involved— at the cost of 50,000 lives. For the time being, the British victories kept the crucial Suez Canal under their control. They also prevented East Africa from becoming a staging ground for German and Italian assaults on Allied positions in North Africa and the Middle East, where the British won another important battle. Together with a new **Free French** army organized by de Gaulle, British forces seized Syria from the Vichy administration and turned it over to de Gaulle.

These victories, however, were the exceptions that proved the rule of German supremacy. By mid-1941, Hitler's forces dominated the European continent and controlled the lion's share of its resources: iron ore from Sweden, oil from Romania, food and raw materials from Eastern Europe, and a huge amount of supplies looted from Greece. These resources proved crucial to the German war effort and made ineffective any British effort to blockade the continent as it had in the First World War.

Thus, independent as it was, Great Britain could not, on its own, reverse these vast German gains. Churchill needed help, and this only the Americans and Russians could provide. For the moment, however, American isolationism prevented President Franklin D. Roosevelt (1882–1945) from intervening militarily. But Roosevelt did convince Congress to supply food and military equipment to Britain and its allies through the Lend-Lease Act of March 1941. Stalin, meanwhile, appeared pleased with his German alliance, which had allowed the Red Army to occupy eastern Poland and the Baltic states.

But to Hitler, it mattered little that Stalin had sided with Germany since the beginning of the war. With the rest of the continent in his grip, the Führer now turned his attention toward the Soviet Union, whose lands Hitler wanted for the same reasons he had conquered those of Czechoslovakia and Poland: to enrich his country and give his people vastly expanded "living space" in the East. He also sought to destroy "Jewish Bolshevism" and to enslave the supposedly inferior Slavs.

Operation Barbarossa: The Invasion of Russia

On June 22, 1941, three German Army Groups poured into the Soviet Union. The first headed north through the Baltic states toward Leningrad, the second northeast through Minsk and Smolensk toward Moscow, and the third south through Ukraine. Because significant numbers of German troops had to remain in western, northern, and southeastern Europe as occupying forces, Hitler could send no more troops into Russia than he had a year earlier into France and the Low Countries. And thanks to the Battle of Britain, the Germans had fewer aircraft to devote to the Russian invasion than to the earlier one in the West. But Hitler had grown so overconfident and so dismissive of the Russians' military abilities that he considered these resources more than sufficient for what he called **Operation Barbarossa**, named after a crusading twelfth-century German emperor (see Map 13.5).

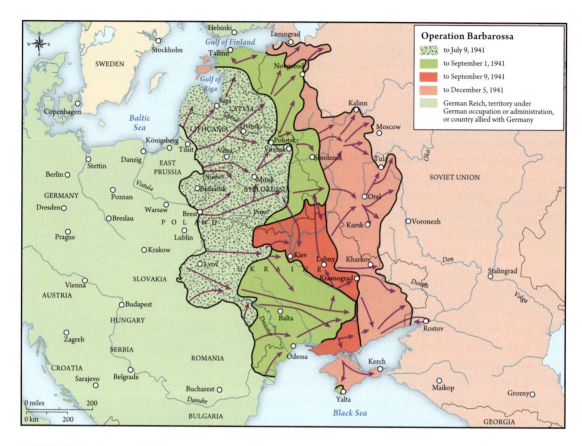

≡ **MAP 13.5**   Operation Barbarossa

The early weeks of the German campaign went exceedingly well. Taken by surprise, the Red Army had to retreat hastily, leaving the Germans in control of much of its equipment and supplies and more than a million square miles of Soviet territory. In the process, the Germans killed some four million people and took nearly four million prisoners—many of whom would be murdered or left to die.

As the Russians retreated, they drew the Germans further and further into Soviet territory, stretching the Wehrmacht's lines of communication and supply and exposing its Achilles heel: the lack of planning for a long-drawn-out war. Hitler's generals had made no provisions to replace soldiers and equipment lost in the fighting, which meant that German manpower and effectiveness declined just as the Russians were beginning to activate large numbers of new troops.

This they did quickly, for once over the shock of the surprise attack, Stalin used the levers of his centralized communist state to draft young men by the hundreds of thousands into the army; send women, already accustomed to factory work, to labor in munitions plants; and divert resources to military use. Stalin had entire factories moved from the western to the eastern part of the country to prevent the Germans from capturing them and then built new enterprises far from the Wehrmacht's reach.

By December 1941, the Red Army had halted the German advance outside Moscow and begun a counteroffensive against a German army unprepared to fight through the long, bitterly cold Russian winter. Hitler ordered his soldiers not to retreat, and they suffered massive losses. This military reversal lifted Soviet spirits and motivated them to continue the fight; it also cheered the British, now allied with the Russians in a battle to the death against Nazi Germany. When the United States entered the war after the Japanese attack on Pearl Harbor on December 7, the prospect of a victorious British-American-Russian coalition came into view.

The War in Asia and the Pacific

Before their assault on the US navy in the Hawaiian port of Pearl Harbor, the Japanese had been fighting a brutal war in China that included the killing and rape of large numbers of civilians. To resupply their forces in China, the Japanese coveted the oil and other resources of the British, French, Dutch, and American possessions in Asia and the Pacific, especially British-controlled Burma (Myanmar today) and Malaya (Malaysia and Singapore today), French Indochina (Vietnam, Cambodia, and Laos today), the Dutch East Indies (Indonesia today), and the Philippines, which the United States had claimed in 1898. Once Hitler had France and the Netherlands under his control, and Britain under bombardment—all this by the summer of 1940—the European powers could no longer defend their Asian colonies, which were now vulnerable to a Japanese takeover.

What gave the Japanese pause was the fear that the United States would intervene to prevent such a move and especially to defend its bases in the Philippines. To encourage the Japanese to act, Hitler promised their leaders that he would join a war against the United States as soon as Japan attacked it. The promise convinced the Japanese to seize strategic European and American possessions in Asia and the Pacific, but first they had to neutralize the US navy to prevent it from interfering with their imperial plans. On December 7, 1941, Japan undertook a surprise peacetime assault on the US vessels parked in Pearl Harbor.

This unprovoked attack shocked the bulk of the American people and US Congress and ended whatever isolationist sentiments remained. The United States would now embark on an all-out war against Japan, which also meant a war against Japan's de facto ally, Germany. Although the struggle did not begin very well for the Americans, it would soon unfold better than Japan expected. The

Japanese pilots conducting the raid thought they had sunk the US ships docked at Pearl Harbor, but most of them had simply taken on water and settled into the mud of the shallow port. They could be repaired and returned to service. As for the thousands of seamen assigned to the ships, most survived the assault and would return to the fighting, although over 2,000 sailors and hundreds of soldiers and airmen were killed.

In the short run, though, the Japanese succeeded in many of their aims. They seized Malaya and Singapore, where they murdered and raped thousands of

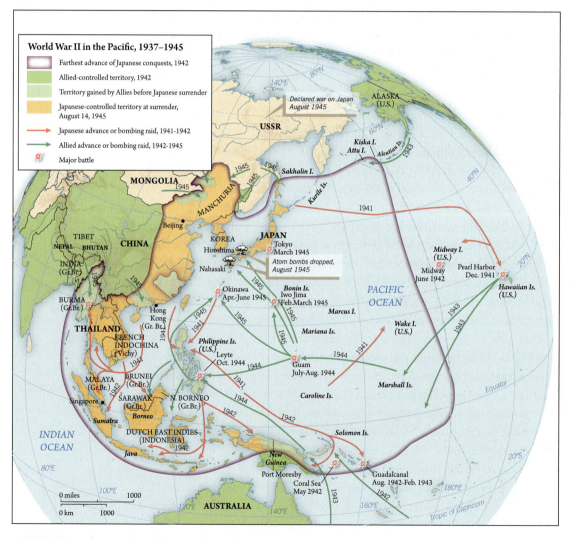

≡ **MAP 13.6**   The Second World War in the Pacific

people, and took Hong Kong as well as the US possessions Wake Island and Guam. They ultimately won the Philippines, too, although only after encountering considerable resistance from US forces, which fully surrendered only after six months of fighting. Thousands of the American servicemen captured on the Philippines' Bataan peninsula were murdered by Japanese soldiers. The survivors were herded, after a long death march, into miserable camps in which many more succumbed to forced labor, malnutrition, disease, and gratuitous attacks (see Map 13.6).

After finally taking the Philippines in June 1942, Japanese forces seized Burma and the Dutch East Indies, while occupying parts of Indochina. In the aftermath of these victories, and with the Germans in control of Europe, Japan and Germany confidently proposed to divide the world between them. Japan would receive most of Siberia and India plus the whole of Indochina and China, Australia, New Zealand, several Pacific islands, Alaska, western Canada, Washington State, Central America, the Caribbean, and South America save for Brazil. Germany would retain Europe, including the Soviet Union, North Africa, the Middle East, and the European colonies not claimed by the Japanese.

Such a division of the world assumed, of course, the defeat of the United States, Great Britain, and the Soviet Union, which even at the war's nadir in late 1941 was far from assured. After the Red Army stopped the Germans in early 1942, a few months later US and Australian forces blocked a Japanese effort to threaten Australia by seizing the neighboring New Guinea and the Solomon Islands. In June, the United States won an even more consequential engagement, the most important victory so far, in the **Battle of Midway**, which took place near a pair of tiny islands in the Pacific Ocean (midway, as their name suggests, between Asia and the Americas). With this crucial victory, the United States halted Japan's advance into the Pacific and destroyed enough of the Japanese navy as to make further offensive operations extremely difficult.

Hitler's Europe

Although the United States had stemmed the Japanese advance in June 1942, the American need to devote huge numbers of soldiers and resources to the Pacific theater of the war prevented it from intervening decisively in Europe until 1943. The Americans could thus do nothing to reinforce the successes the Soviets were beginning to achieve at the end of 1941. In the meantime, Hitler and the Nazis enjoyed nearly free rein to impose an unbearably harsh occupation on virtually the whole of Europe.

The Nazi Plans

Even though the Germans had encountered unexpected difficulties in the Soviet Union, at the end of 1941 they still controlled essentially all of Europe from the Atlantic coast of France to the gates of Moscow and from the North Sea to North Africa. Within this vast territory, the Nazi leadership had ambitious ideas for the new order they intended to establish. They would incorporate into Germany the genetically acceptable people of northern Europe—Norwegians, Dutch, Belgians, and Luxembourgers—but only as second-class citizens of the Reich. The Nazis would allow France to survive, but only as a truncated and totally dependent protectorate of Germany, which would annex France's choicest regions. Denmark alone, with its superior "Nordic" people, would persist as an independent country (see Map 13.7).

In the east and southeast, Poland, Czechoslovakia, and Yugoslavia would cease to exist, and the borders of Germany would extend all the way to the Ural Mountains, which separated the European and Asian parts of Russia. In this huge eastern space, the Germans planned a "war of annihilation" in which the native populations would either be killed or removed to make way for ethnic German settlers who would claim the land for themselves. City dwellers would simply be starved to death, as would most prisoners of war. Disabled and seriously ill people would also be killed, along with anyone who seemed likely to cause trouble. Other Slavs would either be deported to regions east of the Urals or forced to become servants or slaves of the German colonists. As a supposedly subhuman species, Slavs would live on subsistence rations and be deprived of an education. They were to "know just enough," Hitler declared, "to understand road signs, so as not to get themselves run over by our vehicles."

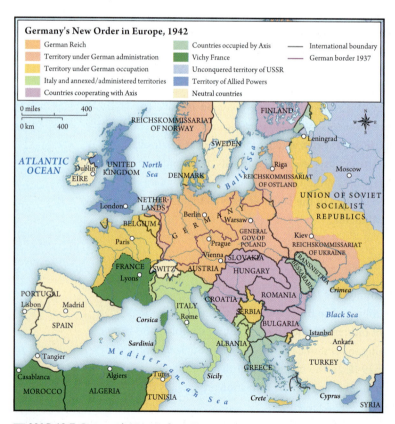

Germany's New Order in Europe, 1942

German Reich	Countries occupied by Axis	—— International boundary
Territory under German administration	Vichy France	—— German border 1937
Territory under German occupation	Unconquered territory of USSR	
Italy and annexed/administered territories	Territory of Allied Powers	
Countries cooperating with Axis	Neutral countries	

≡ **MAP 13.7** Germany's New Order in Europe, 1942

The large number of Jews who lived in this region would be removed altogether. Hitler's original idea was to deport Europe's entire Jewish population to the island of Madagascar in the Indian Ocean, where they would live in a vast concentration camp administered by the SS. The persistence of British naval power, however, made that scheme impossible, and in 1941, Hitler and his lieutenants began to devise a far more radical alternative: **genocide**.

Fortunately, Germany's military difficulties in Russia and a growing resistance movement against Nazi forces in the East prevented them from carrying out many of their plans. But Hitler's highest priority, the genocide of the Jews, proceeded to its awful conclusion—even when it conflicted with his other war aims—and the Poles suffered mightily as well.

The Terrible Results

Of the 35 million Poles, more than 5.5 million died under the German occupation, only 664,000 having perished as a result of military operations. Of those who died, 2.6 million were Polish Jews. The Russians killed another 400,000 Poles, and because both the Germans and Russians targeted the Polish elite, there the death toll was particularly horrific: 30 percent of its academics, 57 percent of its lawyers, and 39 percent of its doctors. Hans Frank, the Nazi who administered the General Government of Poland, boasted about his cruelty to the Poles: "If I wanted to have a poster put up [announcing each of the] Poles who were shot, the forests of Poland would not suffice for producing the paper for such posters."

Beyond Jews and Poles, those who suffered most horrendously from the German invasion were the 3.9 million Soviet prisoners of war. By February 1942, just eight months after the beginning of Operation Barbarossa, only 1.1 million, or 28 percent, of the Soviet POWs remained alive, and most were too sick and emaciated to work. While refusing to feed Russian POWs, the Germans looted Poland, the Ukraine, and Belorussia of virtually everything that could move. And although mid-level Nazi officials tried to harness local economies to the German war effort, the racism of the top Nazi leaders often got in the way; they

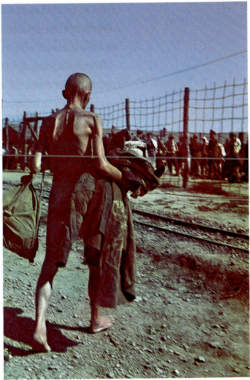

≡ **German Atrocities against Soviet Prisoners of War.** The German invasion of Russia in 1941 turned nearly four million Soviet soldiers into prisoners of war. Violating the fundamentals of international law, German military leaders resolved to starve them to death. Nearly three million perished, and survivors like the one shown here became walking skeletons. They remained alive, at least for a time, by escaping from the Germans' makeshift camps and joining bands of resisters known as "partisans."

☰ **Hiroshima.** On August 6, 1945, an American plane dropped an atomic bomb
on the Japanese city Hiroshima, employing this fearsome new weapon in an
effort to force the surrender of Japan. Heat from the atomic blast seared human
beings to the bone and melted cars and trucks into barely recognizable, twisted
heaps. Some eighty thousand people died instantly, and tens of thousands more
later succumbed to injuries from the blast and radiation poisoning.

office when Roosevelt died in April 1945, knew from deciphered Japanese cables
that some members of the Imperial government favored surrender and decided
that an atomic bomb might convince the rest of Japan's rulers to end the war.

On August 6, an American plane, the *Enola Gay*, dropped the world's first atomic
bomb on the city of Hiroshima. The device incinerated much of the urban region,
instantly causing as many as 80,000 deaths and wounding perhaps 100,000, not
including the countless others who later died from radiation poisoning. With the
bombing of Hiroshima, a single plane and a single bomb unleashed the destructive
power that until then had required hundreds of planes and thousands of bombs.
The A-bomb was truly a horrific weapon, one capable of flattening a major city and
literally burning the skin off human beings.

The effect of the nuclear device was so devastating that it has been the object
of great controversy since 1945. Some have argued that the United States actually saved lives by dropping the bomb, thereby avoiding a bloody invasion of
Japan. Others have condemned its use as immoral and unjustified under any circumstances, and still others have maintained that rather than targeting civilians,
the United States should have dropped a "demonstration" bomb on an uninhab-
ited island.

We will, of course, never know whether an invasion would have taken more or fewer lives than the Hiroshima bomb, but the nuclear explosion did not, in any case, move the Japanese to surrender. It took a second atomic bomb, this one dropped on the city of Nagasaki, plus Soviet attacks on Japanese positions in Manchuria, China, to force the Japanese to give in. They did so only after the Emperor, believed to be semidivine, made an unprecedented personal intervention by going on the radio to announce his country's unconditional surrender.

Conclusion: The Consequences of the War

With the Japanese capitulation, the long and unbearably cruel war had finally come to an end. Its costs in human and material terms almost defy belief; in all, about 60 million people lost their lives. The Soviet Union suffered the most, registering some 27 million dead and countless millions physically maimed and emotionally scarred. That only one-third of the Russian dead belonged to the military dramatizes the martyrdom of its civilian population. The Chinese took second place on the rolls of death and devastation, with some 15 million killed. About 7.6 million Germans lost their lives, as did nearly 6 million Poles. Japan suffered 2 million deaths, Yugoslavia between 1.5 and 2 million, and Great Britain some 400,000. The United States, touched directly by the war only at Pearl Harbor (and in Alaska's remote Aleutian Islands), also endured about 400,000 deaths.

Those who survived the European war found themselves living amid rubble and ruin. Bombing had rendered whole sections of cities unrecognizable, while the loss of factories and the devastation of the land brought economies to a halt. The war made millions homeless and millions more stateless as well. Hitler had preached the unity of all ethnic Germans, and after the war, his words came back to haunt those of German descent. Some thirteen million ethnic Germans found themselves expelled from their homes in Eastern Europe and forced to migrate to Germany, often under horrendous circumstances. Meanwhile, many of the Jews who had survived the camps were unwilling or unable to return to their own countries, thanks to the persistence of antisemitism. Large numbers emigrated to the United States or sought refuge in Palestine, which Britain, still the colonial power there, tried to prevent.

Such death, dislocation, and destruction could not fail to have major political consequences, and nowhere were those consequences more profound than in Germany. Occupied by the British, French, Americans, and Russians, Germany was ultimately divided into two separate countries, one allied with the West, the other with the Soviet Union. Internally, Germany experienced profound change as well, as the war and the subsequent war crimes trials discredited the military and Germany's traditional ruling elite.

The Second World War, 1944–1945	
June 4, 1944	Allied forces capture Rome
June 6, 1944	D-Day: Allied invasion of Normandy
July 1944	German officers attempt to assassinate Hitler
December 1944–January 1945	Battle of the Bulge
January 1945	Auschwitz liberated by Soviet forces
February 1945	Allied air forces firebomb Dresden
April 30, 1945	Hitler commits suicide
May 2, 1945	Soviet forces capture Berlin
August 1945	United States drops atomic bombs on Hiroshima and Nagasaki; Japan surrenders

In 1945, much of Eastern Europe found itself occupied by Stalin's Red Army, which would help impose unwanted communist governments there over the next three years. As for Britain, it was scarred by bombing but had not suffered occupation or fighting on its soil. It emerged from the conflict with its political system intact, although with voters' attitudes toward laissez-faire government transformed. The postwar reaction in France was similar, although there, the collaborationist regime gave way to a revived democratic republic. In both Britain and France, the most dramatic effect of the war may have been the terminal damage it did to their world empires. Japan's wartime success in overturning European colonial regimes in Asia convinced nationalist leaders from India to Algeria that they too could rid themselves of their British and French masters. India and Pakistan's independence in 1947 marked the beginning of the end of European colonial rule.

The Soviet Union experienced almost unprecedented devastation but nonetheless emerged from the conflict as a major world power. Its army had played a dominant role in Germany's defeat, and not only did the USSR gain political hegemony over Eastern Europe, but its own territory also grew significantly. As for the people of the USSR, already traumatized in 1939 by the forced collectivization, hothouse industrialization, and Great Terror of the previous years, the searing ordeal of the "Great Patriotic War" (as the Russians call the Second World War) unified them as nothing else could have done.

Like the Soviet Union, the United States emerged from the war as a major world power, but without any of the destruction the Russians had endured. Indeed, the

United States ended the war with its economy vastly stronger than it had been in 1940. During the conflict, American factories, operating with considerable government assistance, had supplied not only the US army, but the armies of Britain and the Soviet Union as well. The sheer numbers of planes, tanks, jeeps, artillery, and bombs that the United States turned out testified to the extraordinary depth of its resources and the productive power of its economy. Although the Soviet Union could compete politically and ideologically with the United States, in economic terms the Americans enjoyed overwhelming superiority.

Beyond the realms of politics and economics, the war left a legacy of brutality and inhumanity that raised questions about the nature of human existence itself. During this conflict people did things to one another that violated the most basic standards of civilized life. The effort to destroy entire peoples by systematically murdering millions represents the most egregious example of such inhumanity, but there were countless other horrors as well: the routine torture and murder of prisoners; the killing of hostages in retaliation for acts of resistance; and the use of firebombs and ultimately atomic bombs on cities, incinerating hundreds of thousands of civilians.

Since the Second World War, these evils—or the threat of them—have emerged again and again. But the two that have left the most ominous legacy are genocide and the use of atomic weapons. Auschwitz represented the destruction of entire categories of people; Hiroshima made conceivable the elimination of life itself.

KEY TERMS

Axis Powers *615*

Battle of Britain *593*

Battle of Midway *599*

Battle of the Bulge *620*

Blitzkrieg *592*

British Commonwealth of Nations *582*

D-Day *618*

Final Solution *614*

Free French *595*

genocide *601*

living space *590*

Maginot Line *585*

Munich Pact *588*

national self-determination *581*

Nazi-Soviet Pact *591*

Operation Barbarossa *595*

Popular Front *584*

Vichy France *593*

Wannsee Conference *611*

 For digital learning resources, please go to **https://www.oup.com/he/berenson2e**. Turn to the back of the book to see the list of primary sources and writing exercises provided in the accompanying *Sources and Guided Writing Exercises for Europe in the Modern World*

14

The Postwar, 1945–1970

Ho Chi Minh

Visitors to Hanoi, the capital of Vietnam, commonly make a pilgrimage to the gray-granite mausoleum housing the embalmed body of Ho Chi Minh (1890–1969). Ho (the surname comes first in Vietnamese) was a nationalist and communist revolutionary who led his country to independence after the Second World War. The architects of Ho's mausoleum designed a Vietnamese version of the Lenin mausoleum, which holds the pride of place in Moscow's Red Square. Not only did Vietnam ape Russia's design, but it imported expert Soviet embalmers to preserve Ho's body. These embalmers had kept Lenin's corpse looking fresh, if with a waxy sheen, for nearly a half-century, and they would do the same for Ho. In both cases, specialists substituted flesh-colored plastics for patches of skin that had deteriorated, and every eighteen months they performed a major overhaul of the bodies, adding fluids and other substances to keep them from breaking down. Every day in Moscow and Hanoi, long lines of people wait patiently for a glimpse of the apparently unspoiled remains of the two icons of twentieth-century communism, both transformed after death into secular saints.

Ho Chi Minh, born Nguyen Sinh Cung, came from a small village in north central Vietnam sandwiched between the Gulf of Tonkin and the Laotian border. Today, the region is peppered with monuments to Vietnam's founding father, familiarly known as Uncle Ho, although he did not adopt the name Ho Chi Minh ("He Who Has Been Enlightened") until 1942. In the late nineteenth century, Ho's birthplace was an impoverished area plagued by cycles of drought and flooding and the food shortages they caused. It was further devastated by the French conquest of the country between the 1860s and 1890s.

Ho's father taught him the rudiments of the Chinese language and the traditional Confucian morality—the belief in human dignity, loyalty, good conduct, wisdom, and faithfulness—that would guide much of his life. (Vietnam, ruled by China for a thousand years, has been deeply influenced by Chinese culture.) Ho then attended an elite school, where he was introduced to the French language, showed a gift for writing in his native tongue, and became fascinated by the French Revolution. He resolved to travel to France, and in 1911 took a job as a chef's assistant on a ship bound for Marseilles. He liked many things about the land of his colonizers but was put off by the

immorality and indiscipline he observed. "Why don't the French civilize their own people," he asked, "instead of trying to civilize us?"

After a brief stay in France, Ho spent the next two years at sea and a fair amount of time in London and the United States. He disliked Britain's mistreatment of the Irish and America's oppression of the blacks. Weary of the English-speaking world, Ho moved to Paris, where he joined a small, active community of Vietnamese intellectuals and political activists. The highlight of their efforts was a petition demanding freedom and equal rights for Vietnam addressed to the Allied leaders involved in crafting the Treaty of Versailles. The Allies ignored the substance of the petition, but the ideas behind it attracted the interest of France's security services, which assigned three agents to surveil the now thirty-year-old Ho. Much of what we know about his six-year stay in Paris (1917–1923), and we know quite a bit, comes from these agents' reports.

In 1920, Ho joined France's newly created communist party and dedicated himself to the study of the party's ideology, Marxism-Leninism. He was passionate about the liberation of colonized peoples, and several French communists took an interest in him. One described Ho as "very appealing—reserved but not shy, intense but not fanatical, and extremely intelligent." Another praised him for having "a spirit of tolerance and respect for freedom that was rare among Marxist-Leninists." That tolerance and respect would be crucial to his success in the years to come.

Ho's budding Marxism attracted the interest of key Soviet figures, who in June 1923 invited him to Moscow to be further schooled in Marxism-Leninism. Ho took up residence in Moscow but found the Soviets insufficiently interested in colonial liberation. The USSR's leaders told him that national independence would be achieved only after revolutionaries overthrew Europe's "bourgeois" regimes in favor of communist ones. Ho did not want to wait.

He believed that revolutions could succeed in places such as China and Vietnam, thanks to their huge, exploited peasant class. Eventually, authorities in Moscow gave him permission to travel to China, where he observed the revolutionary movement getting underway. While in China, he married a woman fifteen years younger than he ("I need a woman," he said, "to teach

Timeline

1945	1950	1955	1960	1965	1970	1975

1945 Yalta Conference; Potsdam Conference; United Nations established

1945 Indonesia, Vietnam, Syria, and Lebanon declare independence; France crushes Algerian revolt

1946–1954 First Indochina War

1946 Jordan gains independence

1947 Cominform created; India and Pakistan gain independence

1948 Israel created; Communist coup in Czechoslovakia; Soviet blockade of Berlin

1948–1952 Marshall Plan (European Recovery Program)

1949 NATO established; West Germany and East Germany created; first Soviet atomic bomb test

1950–1953 Korean War

1952 Elizabeth II ascends to British throne

1952–1956 Mau Mau Revolt in Kenya

1953 Stalin dies replaced by Khrushchev

1954–1962 Algerian War of Independence

1955–1975 Vietnam War

1955 Warsaw Pact signed

1956 Tunisia and Morocco gain independence; Suez Crisis; Hungarian rebellion

1957 Malaysia and Ghana gain independence

1957 Treaty of Rome creates European Economic Community (EEC)

1960–1975 Most of Africa achieves independence

1961 Berlin Wall constructed

1962 Cuban Missile Crisis; Vatican II

1964 Brezhnev becomes Communist Party leader

1968 Student rebellions in France, Italy, and Germany; Prague Spring suppressed

1969 Death of Ho Chi Minh

me the [Chinese] language and to keep house"). The marriage was short-lived; he had to flee China alone after that country's nationalist leader, Chiang Kai-shek, began to arrest communists like him.

Ho returned to Moscow in 1927 but set out a year later for Siam (Thailand), the only independent country in Indochina. From there, he began to organize Vietnamese revolutionaries and helped found the Indochinese Communist Party, an organization dedicated to throwing off French rule and creating an egalitarian society through revolutionary change. The fusion of these two goals—independence and social revolution—created complications, since some members of the new party were more interested in the former than the latter and vice versa. This conflict resided in Ho himself, as he swung back and forth throughout much of his career between privileging national independence or social revolution.

On a trip to Hong Kong, then a British possession, Ho was ambushed by British agents, who threatened to extradite him to France where he faced a death sentence for his "subversive" activities. An English lawyer kept him from French clutches, but to remain safe, Ho faked his death and escaped, in disguise, to China, where he spent the years 1937–1941. There, he helped the Chinese communist forces in their dual struggle against the nationalists and the Japanese, whose armies had conquered a great deal of Chinese territory. The Japanese had also landed in Vietnam, gaining an important foothold there after France's humiliating surrender to Germany in June 1940 weakened its colonial empire. Like the Japanese, Ho took advantage of Vichy's feeble authority in Vietnam, only in his case, it was to return to his native country. He had been away for thirty years.

In Vietnam, he lived in a cave and subsisted on a thin soup of corn and bamboo shoots. His goal was to overthrow the French regime and evict the Japanese. To achieve these ambitions, Ho combined the energies of nationalism and communism into a broad anticolonial organization called the Viet Minh (short for "League for the Independence of Vietnam"). In this phase of his life, Ho seemed to prefer nationalism to communism. As he told a Chinese friend, "I am a communist, but what is important to me now is the independence and the freedom of my country, not communism."

Between 1942 and early 1945, the Viet Minh gradually seized control over much of northern Vietnam, forcing French and Japanese authorities and troops to retreat to the south. Ho now travelled to Hanoi, where in September 1945, he wrote a declaration of independence for a new Democratic Republic of Vietnam. The declaration expressed an aspiration more than a reality, since Ho faced opposition on several fronts: from Vietnamese and Chinese nationalists opposed to communist rule; from a variety of ethnic groups hostile to Ho's efforts to centralize authority in Hanoi; from Catholics concerned about communism's anti-religious stance; and especially from the French, who wanted to reestablish their colonial control—albeit under the guise of a new French Union.

Having been humiliated during the Second World War, the French were intent on restoring their standing as a great power by holding on to their empire, by force if necessary. The French readied their Far East Expeditionary Corps (FFEE), and armed hostilities began in December 1946 with a preemptive Vietnamese attack against them. The two sides fought to a stalemate over the next two years, but the Viet Minh gained a great advantage in 1949, when Chinese communist forces under Mao Zedong defeated Chiang Kai-shek. Now, Ho had two communist allies, China and the USSR, to support his efforts against the French, and he could get supplies from just across the border. But this communist front horrified the Americans, who now saw the world through the lens of the Cold War, which pitted the capitalist world against the communist world. The Americans, having opposed the continuation of French colonialism in 1945, now leapt to France's support, supplying weapons and other material aid.

In Vietnam, the battle between France and the Viet Minh dragged on and on, with vast casualties and suffering among the Vietnamese. But it was the French public, whose sons were fighting and dying in a distant land, that wanted out of this war. So did members of the FFEE. In May 1954, the French suffered a devastating defeat at Dien Bien Phu in northwestern Vietnam. Afterwards, the French forces were in tatters, and France's new prime minister, Pierre Mendès France, called for a truce. A peace conference in Geneva would decide Vietnam's fate.

Ho Chi Minh and his top general, Vo Nguyen Giap (1911–2013), had achieved a decisive military victory, but their small, impoverished country was too weak to fully win the peace. At Geneva, the great powers—the United States, Britain, the USSR, and France—brokered an end to the fighting, which Ho desperately wanted, but in exchange he was forced to cede the southern half of Vietnam (south of the seventeenth parallel) to forces friendly to the United States. The division of the country, it was promised, would end in 1956 with nationwide elections intended to unify the north and the south. But Ngo Dinh Diem, who ruled the territory south of the seventeenth parallel, refused to participate in these elections, and two halves of Vietnam hardened into separate countries—the communist Democratic Republic of Vietnam (North Vietnam) and the anti-communist Republic of Vietnam (South Vietnam).

Having landed on opposite sides in the Cold War, the two Vietnams now seemed worlds apart. Under these circumstances, Ho found himself under pressure from the USSR to adopt a Soviet-style economic and social system. His land reform, having initially distributed some two million acres of farmland to impoverished peasants, quickly morphed into a forced collectivization that transferred these lands to the state. At the same time, all businesses were collectivized, and individuals who refused to relinquish their properties found themselves accused of being "counterrevolutionaries." Many were imprisoned, while others had to endure Chinese-style "self-criticism" sessions in which they admitted to a variety of "crimes against the people." In more than a few cases, "self-criticism" turned into denunciation by others, and denunciation into violence. At least 15,000 people—and perhaps many more—lost their lives in the murderous conflicts unleashed by the land reform and collectivization. Eventually, Ho realized that things had gotten out of hand, and he put a stop to the violence, although not to the collectivization that had triggered it.

In the meantime, Ho did not forget that Ngo Dinh Diem had sabotaged the Geneva agreement and thus the unity of Vietnam. The North Vietnamese leader considered the South Vietnamese government, now a virtual dictatorship, illegitimate, and he resolved to overthrow it. In 1960, communist guerilla forces in the South (known to their enemies as Viet Cong, "Vietnamese Communists") allied with the Army of North Vietnam and attacked Ngo's regime. By 1965, the communist forces were winning this new Vietnamese war; the United States, which had been advising the South and giving it a measure of military support, decided to intervene massively on the South's behalf.

Now North Vietnam faced the greatest military power on the planet, and the odds seemed stacked against it. But the United States was ill-equipped for guerilla warfare, and it largely lost the battle of public opinion both internationally and at home. In part, this loss was due to the mythology that had grown up around Ho Chi Minh. He was "Uncle Ho," the kindly, if frail, underdog, the David who stood up to the American Goliath. In his own country, an aura of heroism surrounded Ho, an aura that pictured him as a providential figure anointed to save his people from the "imperialists." Ho had played a major role in creating this aura, which was designed to motivate and mobilize the Vietnamese to persist in their difficult fight.

North Vietnam would eventually win, but Ho died six years before the victory was complete. By then, he had become a quasi-religious figure, a nationalist and communist icon immortalized in a mausoleum and preserved forever. ≡

The Toll of the War

The Vietnam wars extended for decades the already unprecedented toll of death and destruction caused by the Second World War. And beyond Vietnam, millions more would die in Asia and Africa in a host of other anticolonial wars of independence. In Europe, the killing and dying stretched beyond the formal end of the war in May 1945. Civil wars between communists and anticommunists in Greece and Yugoslavia took tens of thousands of additional lives. And during the capture and postwar occupation of Berlin and Vienna, Russian soldiers systemically assaulted and raped some 200,000 German women, killing a considerable number and leaving many of their 150,000 "Russian babies" to die.

Reports of the Red Army's atrocities sent millions of ethnic Germans fleeing Eastern Europe for their lives. And once the war formally ended, the remaining Germans outside Germany proper—3 million in Czechoslovakia; 3.3 million in Hungary, Romania, and Yugoslavia; 7 million in Poland—found themselves abruptly expelled from the Eastern European towns and villages in which their families had, in many cases, lived for centuries. "We must expel all the Germans," declared the Polish communist leader, Władysław Gomułka (1905–1982), "because countries are built on national lines and not on multinational ones." Germans, that is, had no place in the new, ethnically pure postwar Poland; they were pushed—in some cases literally—into a postwar Germany greatly reduced in size. Several hundred thousand of the thirteen million German refugees—the largest population movement in European history—died during their trek toward the former Reich (see Map 14.1).

As Germans fled or were expelled from their homes, several other countries added to the human flood. Bulgaria sent 160,000 Turks to Turkey, while Hungary and Czechoslovakia traded their Slovak and Hungarian minorities, leaving both countries more ethnically "pure." Meanwhile, many of the Jews who had managed to survive the "Holocaust by bullets," the ghettos, the extermination camps, and

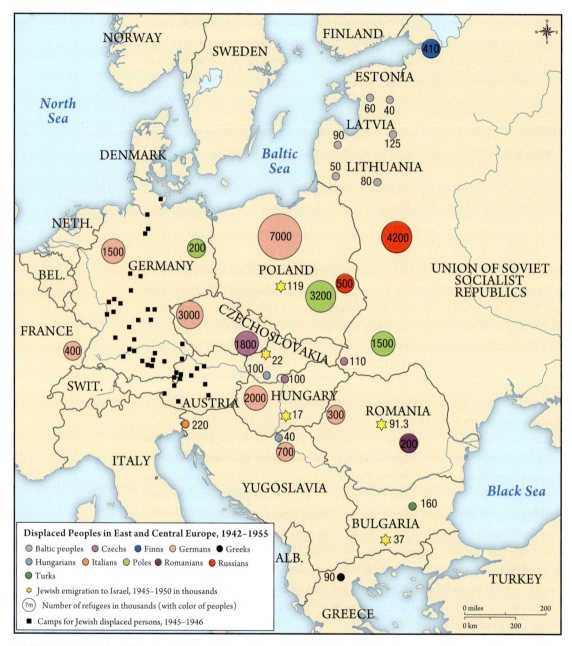

≡ **MAP 14.1**   Displaced Peoples in East and Central Europe, 1942–1955

the death marches were greeted with death threats, murder, and a wave of pogroms when they tried to return home to Poland. And with the refusal of Western
European countries to admit Jewish survivors—or in the case of Britain, to allow
them to emigrate to Palestine—hundreds of thousands of Jews had no choice but

to take refuge in "displaced persons" (DP) camps, established, ironically enough, in Germany. Most remained in these facilities until 1948, when the United States and Canada agreed to admit several hundred thousand, and the creation of Israel gave Jews a country of their own.

The result of the wartime genocide and the massive postwar movement of people was the creation of countries nearly devoid of minority groups. The German population of western Czechoslovakia dropped from 29 percent in 1930 to under 2 percent in 1950. In Poland, after the murder of nearly three million Polish Jews and the postwar expulsion of Germans, Ukrainians, and Belarusians, the country's non–Polish Catholics declined from one-third of the population almost to zero. Germany, which had included a large number of Poles before the war, was almost exclusively German after 1945 (except for the foreign refugees temporarily encamped there).

Since Western and Northern European countries were already quite homogenous ethnically and culturally before the war, postwar Europe became a collection of states largely uniform in ethnocultural terms. As this situation became ingrained as the "new normal," it exacerbated simmering conflicts in Romania, Hungary, and Yugoslavia, the rare countries in which significant minorities remained.

Assessing Responsibility for the War

Adding to the suffering and death caused by the forced population movements was the retribution taken in virtually every country against those suspected of wartime collaboration with the enemy. In France, some 10,000 were killed before de Gaulle disarmed the resistance movements and created an official, extremely forgiving, state-run process for assessing responsibility for wartime collaboration. De Gaulle established the convenient fiction that most French men and women had resisted the Germans and that only a handful of collaborators, exemplified by Pétain and Laval, had pushed France into an unholy alliance with the occupier.

Although members of the Italian resistance killed collaborators in the closing months of the war, the official postwar reckoning was even less severe in Italy than in France. In Greece, communists had led the anti-Axis resistance, and much of the country's elite had supported the Italian and German occupiers. But when communists seemed likely to seize power, the British sided with the compromised elites in hopes of keeping Greece in the Western camp, to which Stalin had tacitly agreed. The result was a topsy-turvy situation in which the wartime collaborators prosecuted the resisters and thus not only went unpunished for having aided Greece's occupiers but succeeded in dominating Greek politics for decades to come.

In Eastern Europe, where communist governments took power, wartime collaborators who resisted the communist takeovers faced punishment, even death, while collaborators who supported or joined the communists tended to be spared. As for the Germans themselves, they were the lone national group deemed to include individuals guilty of "crimes against humanity," although such crimes had been common enough among the notorious Croatian fascists, the many Austrian members of the SS, and among soldiers of the Red Army. But the Germans had, of course, been responsible for the war, and their crimes against civilians and opposing soldiers were so many and so horrible that the victorious powers decided that Nazi leaders should be publicly tried and made to answer for their heinous acts.

The most important of the trials took place between November 1945 and October 1946 in the German city of Nuremberg, the birthplace of the Nazi movement. The **Nuremberg Trials** prosecuted several of those considered the most serious war criminals, although not the top Nazi leaders—Hitler, Himmler, and Goebbels—who had committed suicide at the end of the war. Of the twenty-four men tried, twelve received death sentences, three were acquitted, and the rest were sent to prison for terms varying from ten years to life.

In a series of other trials, 5,000 were found guilty of war crimes or crimes against humanity, leading to 486 executions over a five-year period. Beyond those convicted, the Allies considered a great many other Germans complicit in the Nazi crimes, but since they were too numerous to put on trial, the victorious powers had them undergo a re-education and "denazification" campaign. But if anything, the effort to dissolve Nazi ideology and instill Western, democratic values intensified the nationalistic attitudes it was

≡ **Hermann Göring at Nuremberg.** After the Second World War, the victorious Allied powers prosecuted Nazi leaders for the "crimes against humanity" they committed during the conflict. The trials took place in Nuremberg, Germany, birthplace of the Nazi movement. Göring, who had founded the Gestapo and headed the German air force, was the most notorious of those put on trial; the other top Nazi leaders committed suicide at the end of the war. Göring was convicted and sentenced to death.

designed to root out. At the prodding of German leaders, the Americans quietly dropped the effort.

The "German Question"

The Western powers and the Soviets had cooperated to some extent in the prosecution of Nazi war criminals, and immediately after the war, they set out to cooperate over the future shape of Germany. At the Potsdam Conference of July 1945, the Big Three—the United States, Britain, and the Soviet Union—agreed to temporarily divide Germany into US, British, and Soviet zones of occupation. Eventually, the French would receive a zone carved from the American one, and the city of Berlin, deep inside the Soviet sphere, would itself be split into four sectors, one for each of the occupying powers. Austria was severed from Germany and also divided among the United States, Britain, France, and the Soviet Union, as was the city of Vienna. Poland received a large portion of eastern Germany, and France regained Alsace and Lorraine. Altogether, Germany lost nearly a third of its prewar territory (see Map 14.2).

Because "the Germans [had been] able to fight all the rest of the world," as Dean Acheson, the future US secretary of state, put it in 1945, the Big Three decided to establish an international organization, the **United Nations**, designed to foster peace, security, and economic prosperity. The UN's most important body, the Security Council, excluded the defeated powers, Germany and Japan, and gave permanent representation to China, France, Great Britain, the Soviet Union, and the United States, each of which—at Stalin's insistence—would have veto power over any resolution of the council.

The United Nations would play a major role in the care of millions of European refugees

The Division of Germany at the End of the Second World War

Future Soviet bloc countries	Areas controlled by Soviet Union
Western Allies and countries liberated by Allies	Meeting of Soviet and Western forces in April 1945
Neutral countries	International borders, 1945
Germany	German boundary in March 1939
Areas controlled by Western allies	City divided into four occupation zones

≡ **MAP 14.2**   The Division of Germany at the End of the Second World War

and displaced persons, but it would have little to do with the resolution of the German question, which quickly stalemated the big four. The United States, after initially seeking to weaken the German economy, changed course and sided with the British, who had come more quickly to the belief that only a revitalized Germany would allow Europe to recover economically. American leaders also feared that an impoverished Germany would be an embittered Germany and that under such conditions the country would be vulnerable to a new Hitler or a communist takeover.

The French objected strenuously to this view, declaring that Germany would remain a permanent threat—it had, after all, invaded France three times in the past seventy-five years—unless it was dismantled into weak, separate states and rendered economically and militarily impotent. In addition, France demanded substantial reparations in cash and in kind along with complete access to the coal and other natural resources of the highly industrialized parts of western Germany.

Although French leaders could not convince the British and Americans to endorse the harsh settlement they wanted to impose, Paris succeeded in blocking any solution to the German question that involved the reunification of the country, which the British and Americans—and, in theory, the Soviets, too—had hoped to achieve. When the French reluctantly came around to the Anglo-American point of view, the Western allies and the Soviet Union had become so distant from each other that agreement over Germany was no longer possible.

The Cold War and the Division of Europe

Although allied during the war, the Soviets and the Anglo-Americans had never gotten along. But their alliance had held, and they tried to extend a measure of cooperation into the postwar world. At Yalta, where Roosevelt, Churchill, and Stalin met in February 1945 to discuss the shape of postwar Europe, the three leaders agreed to "the right of all people to choose the form of government under which they will live" and to organize in their respective spheres of influence "free elections of Governments responsive to the will of the people." But Churchill and Roosevelt recognized that given the disposition of military forces, "the Russians had the power in Eastern Europe" and that for reasons of national security, Stalin was likely to impose Soviet hegemony on the neighboring countries of Poland, Romania, and Bulgaria and likely others as well.

Churchill and Roosevelt acquiesced to this hegemony not only because Stalin had armies there but also because they needed the Soviet leader's cooperation to complete the victory over Germany and Japan and especially for all decisions about postwar Germany. "Realist" American policy makers such as George F. Kennan (1904–2005) saw no alternative to the permanent division of Europe into opposing Western and Soviet spheres and considered that division a way of stabilizing the continent after the war.

American and British leaders did not publicly give up on free elections in Eastern Europe, and they planned to offer economic aid to the region, but the Soviets considered both elections and aid as efforts to ensure American political and economic dominance in their sphere of influence. Experience had shown that free elections would not install communist governments sympathetic to the Soviet Union, and by infusing Europe with dollars, American economic aid would subordinate the continent to the US economy and turn it—and the Soviet Union—into a set of vassal states—or so the Soviets believed.

Stalin had good reason to worry about US economic domination. His country emerged from the war with much of its industry and agriculture shattered, its lines of transportation pummeled, its population decimated. The United States, by contrast, doubled its gross domestic product during the war and in 1945 produced about half of the world's manufactured goods. There was no way the Soviet Union could compete economically, at least in the short run, and Stalin's solution to the imbalance was to withdraw his country and the surrounding states of Central-Eastern Europe from the US-dominated economic system and preside over a separate system of his own.

≡ **The Yalta Conference.** Shortly before Hitler's demise, the leaders of the soon-to-be victorious powers, Winston Churchill (*left*), Franklin D. Roosevelt (*center*), and Joseph Stalin (*right*) met at Yalta, a Soviet resort, to discuss the shape of postwar Europe. The negotiations were tough, but the conference was not without its light moments.

For all these reasons, neither country is exactly to blame for initiating the **Cold War**. Each had opposing political and economic interests, and each contributed, often unwittingly, to the mutual suspicion and mistrust that had framed their wartime alliance and postwar relations. It is difficult to see how a postwar conflict could have been avoided.

Economic Recovery

Intimately related to the developing Cold War between West and East was Europe's extraordinarily difficult postwar economic situation. At the war's end, industrial production stood at less than 40 percent of its prewar level in Belgium, France, and the Netherlands and at less than 20 percent in Germany and Italy. Things were even worse in Eastern and Southeastern Europe. Circumstances were so dire that, throughout Western Europe, governments, industrialists, and labor union leaders came together in an unprecedented collaborative effort to restart economic growth.

The European commitment to rebuilding their economies produced much faster growth than anyone had expected, but postwar conditions imposed sharp limits on how far that growth could proceed. Traditionally, most European countries had depended on Germany to sell them industrial machinery, coal, and other natural resources in exchange for food and consumer items. But given Germany's devastated state and the initial unwillingness of the occupying powers to allow the revival of German production, its neighbors could not obtain the equipment and products their economies required.

The other key obstacle to European economic growth was the controls on wages and prices governments had imposed during the war and were loath to lift afterwards

≡ **Queuing for Coal.** Conditions were bleak in immediate postwar Europe, and there were shortages of almost everything. This photo shows a long line of people waiting for the meager ration of coal they received to heat their homes.

for fear of igniting runaway inflation. The problem with this arrangement was that, with prices artificially low, farmers had little incentive to sell their goods and hoarded them instead. Employed people, meanwhile, felt little motivation to go to work because their pay was kept artificially low, and given hoarding and the scarcity of consumer goods, there was little to buy. Instead of working, people spent their time trying to barter their possessions for food.

With wages low and absenteeism high, tax revenues remained inadequate, and governments ran deficits to pay for imported food, which for Britain and France included the cost of feeding the Germans in their occupation zones. To finance their deficits, officials required banks to buy government bonds, which meant that they constantly printed money. This was a terrible catch-22: governments risked inflation by printing money, and to contain inflation they had to maintain the very wage and price controls that made deficits, and therefore money-printing and inflation, such a risk.

The only solution to this impossible situation was to end wage and price controls. But how to do so without sparking a devastating inflation? The answer was for governments to eliminate their budget deficits and thus the need to print money, but they could do so only with the United States' help. The Truman Administration rose to the occasion by enacting the **Marshall Plan**, an initiative that injected $13 billion (over $100 billion in today's dollars) into the European economy between 1948 and 1952.

The Marshall Plan

On June 5, 1947, Secretary of State George C. Marshall (1880–1959) announced that the United States would undertake a multiyear European Recovery Program (ERP) designed to boost the flagging European economies. No longer would the United States limit its aid largely to loans for disaster relief; it would now offer significant grants of cash and American goods, which could be consumed or sold. The American government was motivated by humanitarianism, on the one hand, and, on the other, by the desire for Europe to develop healthy capitalist economies compatible with that of the United States.

Marshall and his colleagues also hoped to ensure the existence throughout Europe of governments friendly to the United States. The Marshall Plan was conceived before the Cold War was fully under way, so it should not be understood entirely in that context. But since it aimed to foster market economies opposed to the state-driven, non-market-oriented Soviet system, Stalin saw it as a threat and prevented Poland, Czechoslovakia, Hungary, Bulgaria, and Albania from participating in the ERP.

To administer the Marshall Plan, the United States and its European partners created an eighteen-member **Organization for European Economic Cooperation (OEEC)**, although most of the US money went to just three countries, Britain, France, and West Germany. All three—and others as well—took advantage of their Marshall Plan funds to lift price controls without sparking inflation. They did so by using the American money to offset the negative effects of price increases on working people not through wage increases, which would have been inflationary, but by giving them improved social benefits (e.g., health care and pensions) and higher take-home pay through reduced taxes. The latter could now drop as Marshall Plan funds helped pay off budget deficits. With higher take-home pay, working people could help stimulate their economies by purchasing more and better food and new products.

Throughout Western Europe, the ability to allow most prices to rise to market levels ended hoarding almost overnight and quickly increased industrial output now that higher prices made production profitable. Workers' absenteeism dropped, since they now had things to buy, and with more people regularly on the job, productivity increased. This expanding economic activity boosted tax revenues, which in turn lowered government deficits all the more, while essentially eliminating the need to print money and thus risk inflation. As the threat of inflation receded, businessmen felt more confident to invest, and banks more confident to issue loans.

What helped the Western European economies all the more was the use of Marshall Plan money to facilitate and stimulate intra-European trade. The new opportunities to trade heightened demand and allowed the different economies to expand, in some cases rapidly. Between 1950 and 1952, Austrian exports to OEEC countries increased by 89 percent and German exports by 87 percent.

≡ **Marshall Plan Aid.** Greece had suffered especially cruelly during the war, and the Marshall Plan provided funds to help their recovery effort. This photo shows Greek children waiting for a morsel of bread.

The "Economic Miracle"

By the mid-1950s, Western and Northern Europe had not only recovered from their postwar disastrous state, they had launched themselves into an extraordinary twenty-five-year period of growth unmatched either before or since. Between 1950 and 1973, the economies of Western Europe grew on average 4.5 percent per year, more than four times the prewar rate and more than double the rate between 1973 and 2000.

The postwar period, therefore, was an anomaly, a time when European economies grew at several times their normal pace and considerably faster than the United States. How to explain this shotgun growth? Part of the answer is that after the war, the European economies made up for the decline of economic activity between 1939 and 1945 and for the destruction caused by the relentless wartime bombing campaigns. But this "catch-up" growth does not explain very much, since the wartime destruction of infrastructure (roads, railroads, bridges, electricity) and industry was less extensive than observers thought in 1945 and rebuilding relatively quick. Housing suffered more, but it, too, was relatively quickly restored. As for industrial production, already in 1947 European output exceeded its 1938 level.

What explains Europe's **economic miracle** is rather its unprecedented level of investment in factories, machinery, mining, and other key economic areas. French investment was 40 percent higher in the 1960s than in the 1920s and 1930s, German investment 63 percent higher, and UK investment 133 percent higher. The increased investment was sparked by the explosion of intra-European trade discussed earlier. Each country's export markets expanded to such an extent that it now made sense for entrepreneurs to invest in the techniques of mass production (assembly lines, automation, interchangeable parts, and the extreme division of labor) that US firms had adopted decades earlier. The new techniques significantly reduced costs of production, which in turn expanded markets and resulted in additional economic growth.

Only a small amount of the funds for this investment came from the Marshall Plan, which as we have seen mostly served to reduce budget and trade deficits, improve benefits for workers, and facilitate intra-European trade. Some of the investment funds came from tax revenues, which government planners directed to particular, favored industries, but most were generated by the profits the different companies earned. Profits were relatively high because wages were relatively low, and they remained low for many years because huge numbers of people were looking for work.

This was especially true in Germany, which had absorbed nearly thirteen million ethnic Germans ejected from Eastern Europe. In addition, as farming

high but later skidded to a halt, and where people had to endure Soviet-style authoritarian political systems that few citizens would have chosen on their own.

The Communist Takeover in Eastern Europe

Once the Red Army completed its occupation of Eastern Europe, Stalin moved to turn the countries there into a ring of buffer states closely tied to the Soviet Union and poised to slow any future German- or US-led invasion of Soviet territory. There was no question of conquering these lands and incorporating them into the Soviet Union, as Stalin feared that such a blatant act of aggression against sovereign states would have mobilized the West against him. His shattered country, moreover, did not possess the resources to govern them directly.

The only practical way for Stalin to establish control over the governments in Central and Eastern Europe was to put friendly politicians, namely communist ones, in charge and to do so under the guise of democratic elections, which he had pledged at Yalta to allow. But outside of Czechoslovakia, the postwar communist parties in the region were weak and incapable of winning elections on their own. Stalin thus encouraged the formation in each country of broad "anti-fascist" coalitions in which the communists participated as one party among many. This seemed reasonable—or at least unchallengeable—to the other coalition partners, whose leaders had to face the reality of the Soviet military occupation. But once given a foothold within the various governments, the communists, under Moscow's direction, claimed the main levers of command, especially the ministries of the interior and justice, which placed the police, security forces, and judicial systems under communist control.

Increasingly, communist parties used their influential government positions to manipulate the electoral process and their police and judicial powers to intimidate, physically attack, arrest, and even kill their opponents. These tactics progressively narrowed the political field and by 1948 enabled communists to emerge victorious from rigged elections almost everywhere. Any potential resistance bowed to the overpowering presence of the Red Army, which remained in the region into the late 1940s and beyond, depending on the country.

The two exceptional cases were Yugoslavia and Czechoslovakia. In the first, Marshall Tito had liberated the country without the Red Army's aid, and in the second, Soviet forces voluntarily withdrew. With no Soviet soldiers to contend with, Tito showed little inclination to take orders from Stalin, who soon came to see him as an enemy. In Czechoslovakia, by contrast, the withdrawal of Soviet forces left in its wake a left-leaning, although not communist-dominated, government committed to friendly relations with the Soviet Union. Having been abandoned by Britain and France at Munich in 1938, Czechoslovakia now looked to the Soviet Union for protection and support. Its pro-Soviet leaders dutifully complied with Stalin's order to decline Marshall Plan support, but even this sacrificial show of cooperation did not satisfy the Soviet dictator. In February 1948, Stalin engineered a communist coup d'état against the popular government of Edvard Beneš.

Beneš's replacement by a communist puppet government intensified the East-West

≡ **The Soviets Say Nyet to the Marshall Plan.** To keep Eastern European countries in the Soviet Union's orbit, Stalin required them to decline Marshall Plan support. Stalin feared that Marshall Plan largesse would connect Eastern Europe to the US economy and give his satellite countries a measure of independence from him.

Cold War already underway. It convinced a great many influential people in the West that Stalin would be content with nothing less than total domination and that he would now threaten Western Europe by using communist parties there, as he had in the East. If this strategy failed, many Cold Warriors feared that Stalin would try to conquer Western Europe by force. In hindsight, it is clear that Stalin intended to take neither step, but at the time, Western leaders and policy makers assumed the worst.

The Hardening of the Cold War

Fear of Stalin and ideological hostility to communism had already moved the postwar coalition governments of Italy and France to expel their communist cabinet ministers in mid-1947. In response, Stalin ordered Italian and French communists to suspend their political and economic cooperation with the efforts to recover from the war. Communists now organized a wave of strikes and, especially in France, did their best to unsettle the society, which still suffered the aftershocks of the war and left a great many people impatient for reform. The communists now promised to bring about that reform through confrontation rather than cooperation.

To limit the communists' influence, US agents intervened covertly in elections in Italy, France, and elsewhere in an effort to assure the victory of moderate, pro-American and anti-Soviet political parties. The Americans need not have bothered. Centrists had developed large followings on their own after the war, while socialists and social democrats, disturbed by the Stalinist coup in Czechoslovakia, mostly sided with the West.

In Germany, meanwhile, the British, French, and US governments definitively rejected the idea of lifting the occupation to create a united neutral Germany, which the Soviets wanted. Instead, the Western powers decided to turn their occupation zones into a new West German political entity firmly in the American camp. The Soviets were outraged, and in April 1948 responded by blockading Berlin, which lay deep within the Soviet zone. In preventing all access by ground to the Western-occupied parts of the city, the Russians sought to use West Berlin as a bargaining chip to prevent the creation of an independent West German state, or failing that, to integrate the whole of Berlin into East Germany.

Britain and the United States resolved to foil the Soviet blockade by airlifting food and supplies into the besieged city. The airlift proved successful, and after more than thirteen months, Stalin gave in, unable to starve West Berlin into submission. He reopened the city in May 1949. In the aftermath, the United States, Britain, and France proceeded with their plan to create a new West German state, which came into existence in May 1949 as the Federal Republic of Germany. The Soviets answered a few months later by making their occupation zone into a (nominally) independent state known as the German Democratic Republic (commonly called East Germany). Berlin was then divided into western and eastern halves and later (1961) bisected by the **Berlin Wall**, which was built by East Germany to prevent its citizens from escaping to the West.

The communist coup in Czechoslovakia and the Berlin blockade firmly established in the minds of Western leaders and policy makers that the Soviet Union had aggressive designs against them and that they needed to formally band together in an alliance for mutual defense. They thus established in April 1949 the **North Atlantic Treaty Organization (NATO)**, which brought together twelve countries on both sides

≡ **The Berlin Airlift.** In 1948, the Western powers decided to merge their zones of occupation in western Germany into what would become an independent German state. To disrupt this effort, the Soviets blockaded the city of Berlin, which lay deep within their German occupation zone. To overcome the blockade and reconnect Berlin to the outside world, the United States led an effort to airlift food and supplies into the western, Allied-controlled sectors of Berlin.

of the Atlantic. The United States, whose leaders had hoped to substantially withdraw from Europe, now decided to lead this alliance and commit itself to stationing troops in Germany—and elsewhere in Europe—for the foreseeable future.

Although mainly designed to deter the Soviet Union, the positioning of US troops in Germany allowed the West to keep a close eye on that country as well. For this reason, NATO was especially reassuring to the French, who now felt

The Cold War, 1945–1968	
February 1945	Yalta Conference
May 1945	End of Second World War in Europe; Germany and Austria divided into occupation zones
July 1945	Potsdam Conference
October 1945	United Nations founded
1947	Cominform set up by Soviet Union; United States pressures France and Italy to expel communist cabinet ministers
1948–1952	United States injects $13 billion into European economy through the Marshall Plan
February 1948	Communist coup d'état in Czechoslovakia
April 1948	Soviets blockade West Berlin, and US and Britain airlift food and supplies
April 1949	NATO founded
May 1949	Soviet blockade lifted
	Federal Republic of Germany (West Germany) founded
September 1949	German Democratic Republic (East Germany) founded
1950–1953	Korean War
1953	Stalin dies
1955	Warsaw Pact created by Soviet Union
1956	Suez Crisis
	Hungarian "counterrevolution" violently put down by Soviet forces
1961	Berlin Wall erected
1962	Cuban Missile Crisis
1968	Prague Spring

protected from any future German invasion and who were pleased that the main line of defense against the Soviet Union would stretch not along their eastern border but in the middle of a weakened Germany now divided in two. Expressing a general West European approval of the new arrangements, Lord Hastings Ismay, NATO's first secretary general, quipped that the organization was designed "to keep the Russians out, the Americans in, and the Germans down."

The Beginnings of European Cooperation

The belief in the necessity of NATO grew even stronger after the Soviet Union tested its first nuclear bomb in late 1949 and then supported communist North Korea's invasion of anticommunist South Korea in what became the Korean War (June 1950–July 1953). The United States entered the war as head of a United Nations military force, and the tensions that resulted from the conflict, which both sides feared would spill over into Europe, led to a massive military build-up in Western Europe. This build-up, the British and Americans believed, required the rearmament of Germany.

The French, deeply worried about any German resurgence, acquiesced to a German rearmament and role in NATO only after German leaders agreed to subordinate key elements of their economy to the French. Operating under a joint Franco-German High Authority, Germany would be required to sell French steelmakers the coal they needed, and Germany's steel industry would agree not to undercut the prices of French steel.

German leaders embraced these ideas in the hope that by cooperating with France and joining NATO, their country would shed its pariah status and be able to integrate its economy into a larger European whole. The Franco-German steelmaking arrangement appealed to Italy and the Benelux countries (Belgium, the Netherlands, and Luxembourg), and in 1951, the six nations came together in the **European Coal and Steel Community** (ECSC), Europe's first common economic project.

The British declined to join in, fearing that the ECSC's High Authority, however weak its actual powers, would compromise the United Kingdom's national sovereignty and weaken its economic links to the Commonwealth, the successor to its colonial empire. Much of the British elite and people did not identify themselves primarily as Europeans but rather as the head of a world empire centered in London. This view found elaborate expression in the coronation of Queen Elizabeth II in June 1953, a highly choreographed event awash in the symbols of empire. But this British view of itself represented wishful thinking rather than political and economic reality. The United Kingdom would suffer from its self-imposed exclusion from Europe.

With Britain aloof from the ECSC and Germany still stigmatized by the war, France led the new European project, which turned out to be more important as a political phenomenon than an economic one. European economies recovered not because of the ECSC or even the Marshall Plan, but for the more complex reasons of investment, wage restraint, and export growth already discussed. Politically, however, the ECSC was crucial, because it represented the first step toward a process of European unity that promised to make war between Germany and the rest of Europe a thing of the past.

Stalinist Politics and the Command Economy in Eastern Europe

While Western Europe came together as a political and economic bloc, the Soviet Union organized its satellite countries as a separate bloc of its own. In 1947, it created the **Cominform**, an organization of European communist parties, and in answer to NATO, the **Warsaw Pact** in 1955. During these years, the Eastern economies and political systems were reshaped in the Soviet image and their states became quasi-colonies of the USSR (see Map 14.3).

Although Stalin had established friendly communist governments throughout Eastern Europe, he decided that those communists were not friendly enough. In the wake of a perceived threat from Tito and from Cold War with the West, the Soviet leader wanted pure obedience. To ensure it, he organized a great purge of Eastern Europe's communist officials, a political bloodletting that closely resembled the purges

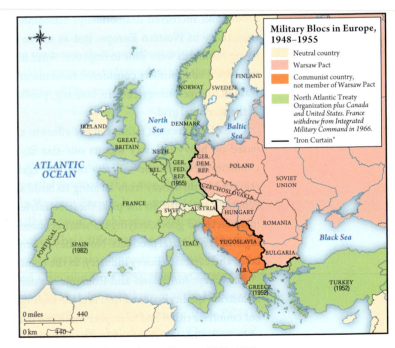

≡ **MAP 14.3** Military Blocs in Europe, 1948–1955

Of all the Eastern European satellites, Hungary traveled furthest down the path of reform, much to its peril. In 1955, after a series of demonstrations, student leaders boldly established an independent, noncommunist organization and advocated economic reforms, democratic elections, and free speech. Revolution was in the air, as the student demonstrations grew larger and more militant and workers joined the fray. In an effort to calm the situation, the Hungarian Communist Party, with reluctant Soviet backing, decided to resurrect the highly popular Imre Nagy (1896–1958), ousted two years earlier, as Hungary's leader. Once in office, Nagy publicly acknowledged the legitimacy of the people's grievances and declared Hungary "free, democratic, and independent."

This declaration, in the Soviet view, turned the Hungarian rebellion into an impermissible "counterrevolution," and the Kremlin sent in an army to put it down. The Hungarians fought valiantly, if futilely, and nearly 3,000 died in the effort to assert their independence. The victorious Russians replaced Nagy with the compliant János Kádár (1912–1989), who immediately nullified his predecessor's reforms and jailed more than 35,000 people. Some 200,000 fled the country, many to the United States and Canada. As for Nagy, the Soviets executed him in 1958.

Given the simultaneous Suez crisis, there was little the West could do. The British and French could hardly criticize the Soviets for invading a foreign country, and the United States had long since conceded Eastern Europe and its people to the Soviet Union. But the Hungarian repression was not without consequences for the Soviet Union, which more than ever showed itself to be an imperial power unhesitant to suppress independence movements. After the Hungarian revolt, it became increasingly difficult to see communism and the USSR as representing equality and workers' rights: tens of thousands abandoned the Italian, French, British, and Spanish communist parties. Throughout Eastern Europe, communism lost much of the legitimacy it had managed to retain until 1956.

As for Khrushchev, the architect of the Hungarian repression, he never succeeded in modulating his efforts to reform the Soviet Union and its satellite states. His attempt to "thaw" Soviet and Eastern European societies and moderate the "excesses" of Stalinism evoked demands for change much more radical than Khrushchev and his colleagues were willing to allow. The result was an oscillation between reform and repression that ultimately worried conservative Kremlin leaders and brought on Khrushchev's demise.

The pretext for ousting him came from the Cuban Missile Crisis of October 1962, when Khrushchev was widely believed to have "blinked" in a tense, nuclear-tinged standoff with President John F. Kennedy (1917–1963). The American leader had demanded the removal of Soviet nuclear missiles deployed in

Cuba, and Khrushchev gave in, although not without gaining some reciprocal concessions from the United States. But it seemed as though Kennedy had won, and Khrushchev's standing never recovered at home.

The Consumer Society

To compensate for Khrushchev's failure to deliver on political reform, governments in Eastern Europe made consumer items more available and affordable than before and improved overall living standards to some extent. Their progress did not, however, begin to compare with the explo-

≡ **The Hungarian Rebellion of 1956.** After Hungary's popular leader Imre Nagy declared his country "free, democratic, and independent," the Soviet Union sent a fleet of tanks to Budapest to crush him and his people. Some 3,000 people died in the futile effort to resist the Soviet intervention.

sion of prosperity evident in the West, where economic growth rates, already high after 1955, rose even further in the 1960s, reaching 5–6 percent a year. Even more than in the 1950s, this growth was fueled by exports and international trade, which advanced at a rapid pace.

The mounting prosperity sparked an unprecedented population increase, making the postwar "baby boom" generation the largest the West had ever seen. Between 1950 and 1970, the West German and French populations expanded by 28 percent—four times the interwar rate—and the Dutch by an extraordinary 35 percent. Prosperity made people optimistic about the future, and that optimism encouraged them to have children. So did the ability to feed relatively large families, as real wages went up—by 300 percent in Germany and Benelux between 1953 and 1973—and the cost of nutrition declined.

Because people now devoted less of their incomes to food than ever before, they had more left over to spend on the array of consumer goods rolling off Europe's new assembly lines. Car ownership, still reserved for the wealthy in 1950, became common among members of the middle class two decades later. Europeans also bought refrigerators, washing machines, and especially televisions at an increasingly rapid pace. In 1953, France counted only 60,000 TV sets (one for every 720 people), and no other

France, Maurice Papon, a former Vichy official responsible for the deportation of 1,600 Jews, became prefect of the Paris Police in 1958. In that capacity, he ordered a brutal police attack on a peaceful 1961 demonstration that left two hundred people dead, many of them Algerians who supported the nationalist FLN.

Although lethal attacks against North African immigrants were rare, discrimination, harassment, and arbitrary arrest were not. In France, as elsewhere in Western Europe, the mistreatment of immigrants from North and sub-Saharan Africa, the Caribbean, India, Pakistan, and Turkey revealed the limits of postwar democracy. So, in many cases, did attitudes toward women. Under the Italian Penal Code, a marriage that took place after a rape nullified the rapist's crime, and women who had suffered a sexual assault were regularly pressured to marry the perpetrator. In 1965, a seventeen-year-old Italian woman, Franca Viola, caused a sensation when she refused to wed the man who raped her after she had declined his marriage proposal. With no marriage to nullify the rape, the man was tried and sent to jail. This incident dramatized the mistreatment of women and ultimately led to the revision of laws that discriminated against them.

Elsewhere, women campaigned against double standards that allowed men alone to commit adultery with impunity and against the common practice of paying women less than men for the same work. In Switzerland, women had to fight hard for the right to vote, which they did not obtain until 1971. Throughout Europe, women writers influenced by Simone de Beauvoir's (1908–1986) seminal feminist book *The Second Sex* (1949) decried "the Madame Bovary syndrome," which imposed most child-rearing responsibilities and household tasks on women and left all too many frustrated and depressed. More generally, women, like immigrants, protested against the gap between what their democratic constitutions promised them and what they actually enjoyed.

≡ **Simone de Beauvoir.** The philosopher and feminist writer and activist Simone de Beauvoir (*center*) prepares to testify at a 1972 trial in defense of women arrested for having abortions. Beauvoir, author of *The Second Sex,* was one of the world's most influential feminist thinkers.

The Student Revolt

Students, too, pointed to this gap, with many calling democracy a "myth" because Western political systems seemed all too compatible with brutal colonial or neocolonial wars. Although the Vietnam War, in particular, galvanized large numbers of European students, many were also moved by issues more mundane and closer to home. They protested against distant, authoritarian teachers and professors, against overcrowded universities, poor educational facilities, and the often indifferent education they received.

These complaints were prompted by an increase in the number of university students so rapid that it overwhelmed systems of higher education built centuries earlier for a tiny elite. Prosperity gave many more families than in the past the means to keep their children in school rather than have them go to work at age twelve or fourteen. Equally important, the growing complexity of the European economies required ever-larger numbers of educated people.

The building of new campuses and university buildings could not keep up with the demand, and suddenly, large numbers of relatively privileged young people found themselves faced with scarcity—not the food and housing scarcity of their parents' generation, but the scarcity of classrooms, courses, dormitories, libraries, and cafeterias. Something was bound to give, and in 1966, rebellions broke out in Italian universities, where overcrowding was especially severe and the quality of instruction poor.

The best-known episode of student rebellion began at the University of Paris. On March 22, 1968, about 150 students plus members of small ultra-leftwing groups occupied an administration building at the university's suburban campus, Nanterre. In strident Marxist rhetoric, they demanded more university funding and condemned capitalism, US imperialism, and the "authoritarianism" of French officials. The police surrounded the campus and threatened to arrest anyone who refused to leave the occupied building. The radicals eventually complied but kept the school in ferment over the following weeks.

Finally, on May 2, the Rector of the University of Paris closed the campus. At that point, the demonstrations moved to the Sorbonne, the grand medieval university building in the heart of Paris. Police forces sealed off the structure, and more than 20,000 students, teachers, and their sympathizers gathered to confront them. Wielding heavy truncheons and hard vinyl shields, the police charged into the crowd, cracking dozens of heads. The demonstrators withdrew behind hastily constructed barricades and hurled paving stones at the officers, who responded with tear gas and hundreds of arrests.

In clashes the following week, the police force's rough treatment of demonstrators, displayed on TV and the front pages, evoked widespread sympathy for the students. The French Communist Party, initially hostile to demonstrators it did not understand and could not control, now felt compelled to make a show of support. Together

≡ **Paris, May 1968.** An immense throng crowds the streets of Paris to show support for the student protestors attacked by battalions of riot police armed with tear gas, truncheons, and shields. The events of May '68 alternated between street-fighting and speech-making, with the bullhorn the students' weapon of choice.

with their own labor union and several independent ones, communist leaders called a one-day general strike on May 13; with Paris shut down, hundreds of thousands of people poured into the streets. In the following days, young workers throughout France joined the rebellion by occupying factories and going on strike, often in defiance of union leaders. The strikes snowballed throughout the month, ultimately involving millions of workers and making it France's largest protest movement since the French Revolution.

With much of France paralyzed, the unions took advantage of the situation by negotiating a 35 percent increase of the minimum wage and average pay hikes of 10 percent. But even this did not end the strikes, for the movement had spiraled into uncharted territory. Workers, now in de facto alliance with radical students and vastly overshadowing them, demanded fundamental—utopian, critics said—changes to society and government. What was perhaps most evident in the demands of young workers and students was a hostility to all established authority, whether of the government, labor unions, or traditional left-wing parties. It was as if the "generation gap" had spilled over into the political arena, making it impossible for the young, in age or spirit, to come to any understanding with the old.

As the strikes wore on, French people became weary of the lack of services, the absence of paychecks, and the breakdown of government. De Gaulle made a secret visit to the French army's headquarters in West Germany, where he won assurances of the military's support against any effort to overthrow the regime. He then dissolved the parliament and called for new elections at the end of June. On Election Day, the Gaullists routed their socialist and communist opponents and won a huge majority in the National Assembly.

With the Gaullist landslide, the French "Events of May '68" were over. Still, ephemeral as it was, **May '68** would live on as a set of positive memories capable of shaping future events. To many younger people, May 1968 was a time when the powerless had nearly succeeded in overturning the powerful and when activists had made a valiant effort to replace a listless consumer society with something authentic and alive.

For all the intense rhetoric, mass demonstrations, and occupied factories, the French rebellion was relatively peaceful. Property was destroyed and students and policemen injured, but no students were killed. The situation was more violent in Italy, where student radicals quickly allied with dissident workers. Strikes began at the Pirelli rubber factory in Milan in September 1968 and continued there and elsewhere for more than a year, making it the largest strike wave in Italian history. A great many younger strikers rejected the Italian Communist Party (PCI), supposedly the embodiment of the working class, as too moderate and too wedded to the establishment. Some found the PCI's version of Marxism overly tame and turned instead to more radical forms of the doctrine, especially Maoism, which Italian radicals—like some in France—admired for the "Cultural Revolution" then taking place in China. But European radicals viewed the Chinese events through rose-colored lenses, mostly unaware of the awful violence Mao's new revolution had unleashed. While most European radicals simply romanticized these events, in Italy, a small minority tried to imitate their violence by staging a series of terrorist attacks.

The German student movement, like its Italian counterpart, turned to violence in the late 1960s. Many of the protests began with complaints against overcrowded and underfunded universities and against distant, uncaring professors. But they soon fed on revelations of Chancellor Kiesinger's Nazi past and on his supposed complicity with the war in Vietnam, which radicals insensitively likened to the Holocaust. During the German demonstrations of spring 1968, three people were killed and four hundred wounded in violent clashes with the police.

The 1960s in the East

Political ferment and violence also erupted in Eastern Europe in the late 1960s, although their causes and consequences differed markedly from those of the West. Khrushchev's successor, Leonid Brezhnev (1906–1982), ended the cultural thaw and cracked down on dissidents in his own country while keeping a close eye on Eastern Europe, where intellectuals, students, and even some political leaders were showing new signs of independence.

Brezhnev tolerated a set of economic reforms in Hungary, whose party leaders enacted them in exchange for political calm. Factory managers now enjoyed the leeway to decide what and how much to produce and to price about half of

denounced capitalism for exploiting the working class. Even in Scandinavia, the Netherlands, Germany, and Austria, countries in which the collaboration between government, business, and labor had become institutionalized, workers now demanded and received significant increases in wages. Prices rose as well, while profits and productivity declined.

By the early 1970s, the unique conditions of wage restraint and high productivity that had fueled the extraordinary economic growth of the 1950s and 1960s had come to an end. So too had the vitality of the "Fordist" economy of assembly lines and mass production of industrial goods; diminishing returns had set in. The European future would belong to information technology, the fuller automation of industrial plants, and the export of jobs to cheaper labor markets overseas. At home, well-paid factory jobs gave way to lower-paid positions in the service sector: government, schools, healthcare, sales, and tourism.

What the Germans called the "economic miracle" and the French the "thirty glorious years" had run its course. A new era of economic difficulty, of high unemployment and high inflation, was about to begin—and nowhere more so than in Great Britain. There, the postwar centrist moderation would succumb to militant strikes and then to a new radical conservatism that widened inequality and deepened poverty even as it boosted the prosperity of the well-to-do.

Conclusion: A European Continent Reshaped

The European states and societies of the 1970s had come a long way from the devastation of 1945. The physical destruction of the war had vanished for the most part, and Western Europe had achieved extraordinary economic growth—thanks in part to the creation of the European Economic Community. The communist East had industrialized as well, and even though economies there were not nearly as successful as those of the West, most Eastern Europeans lived considerably better in 1970 than they had in 1945. The Cold War division of Europe had saddled Eastern Europeans with unpopular communist governments, while Western Europeans, especially younger ones, often felt that their democratic regimes were not democratic enough. In the East, major uprisings occurred in Hungary and Czechoslovakia, while in the West, students and workers rebelled in the late sixties against regimes deemed hierarchic and unfair.

Already before the Second World War, Western and Northern European societies had revealed a great deal of ethnic homogeneity; in Central and Eastern Europe a new ethnic homogeneity reflected the terrible toll of the war. The genocide of the Jews and other mass killings, the forced migrations of ethnic Germans after 1945, and the shifting of national boundaries turned once multiethnic countries like Poland and Germany into ethnically uniform states. The Soviet Union, by contrast, remained a multinational empire and Romania and Hungary retained significant minorities, although fewer than before the war. Yugoslavia was still composed of a potentially explosive mix of Muslims and Christians, Serbs, Croats, and other groups.

Perhaps the most important development of the Postwar was the collapse of Europe's overseas empires. By the early 1960s, the peoples of Africa and Asia had, for the most part, wrested independence from their colonial rulers, reducing Britain, France, Germany, and the Netherlands to nations rather than empires, and giving dozens of newly sovereign states room to maneuver between the US and Soviet Cold War blocs. The Cold War was not, however, destined to last, and the abrupt downfall of Europe's communist regimes between 1989 and 1991 would reshape Europe and the world in dramatic ways.

KEY TERMS

apartheid *659*

Berlin Wall *648*

Christian Democrats *653*

Cold War *640*

Cominform *651*

economic miracle *643*

European Coal and Steel Community *650*

European Economic Community (EEC) *653*

Marshall Plan *641*

May '68 *672*

North Atlantic Treaty Organization (NATO) *648*

Nuremberg Trials *636*

Organization for European Economic Cooperation *642*

Prague Spring *674*

United Nations *637*

Vatican II *668*

Warsaw Pact *651*

 For digital learning resources, please go to **https://www.oup.com/he/berenson2e**. Turn to the back of the book to see the list of primary sources and writing exercises provided in the accompanying *Sources and Guided Writing Exercises for Europe in the Modern World*

15

Economic Dilemmas, European Unity, and the Collapse of Communism, 1970–2010

Mikhail Gorbachev

Born to a peasant family in 1931, Mikhail Gorbachev experienced the Soviet Union's greatest upheavals as a young boy. One grandfather was briefly deported to Siberia during the forced collectivization of the 1930s, the other grandfather arrested during the Great Terror. His father was seriously wounded during the Second World War. The family was lucky, however, as all three returned home. In another time, the very provincial young Gorbachev would have become a farmer, like his father and grandfather. But the prewar purges and massive wartime deaths opened opportunities for those who had survived. Mikhail set his sights on a university education, and not a merely local one. He had done brilliantly in his secondary school and impressed local authorities with his tireless work during the harvest of 1948. With their help, Gorbachev gained admission to Moscow State University's prestigious school of law.

At the university, he encountered several of the USSR's leading academics and gained introductions to members of Moscow's cultural elite. He met his future wife at a ballroom dancing class and joined the Communist Party, an essential step for any ambitious young Soviet citizen. But Gorbachev was no opportunist; he became a dedicated communist and remained so throughout his career. He took pleasure in reading Marx and Lenin, and his senior thesis claimed to demonstrate the superiority of socialism over capitalism.

After graduating in 1955, Gorbachev took a job as a junior prosecutor in the small capital city of his home province, Stavropol. He was put off by the petty corruption he found there and by the primitive conditions of life in a small city with no running water and entire families crammed into a single room. He jumped at a position in the Communist Youth League, which entailed traveling to remote towns and villages and teaching young people there about the wider world to which he, as a college student, had escaped.

Gorbachev himself learned more about the wider world—or at least the real world—when shown a copy of Khrushchev's "secret speech" of 1956 detailing the crimes of Stalinism. Despite the repression in Hungary, Khrushchev's speech seemed to mark for communists of Gorbachev's generation a new beginning. The Soviet Union would relax its internal restraints, reform its economy and society, and assert its standing as a great power.

Gorbachev found himself thrilled and inspired by the launch in October 1957 of Sputnik, the first artificial satellite to orbit the earth. And he took pride in the pro-Soviet revolution in Cuba and Khrushchev's dramatic intervention at the United Nations, where he claimed that socialism was destined to outlive capitalism. Still only thirty years old, Gorbachev felt honored to attend the Twenty-Second Party Congress (1961) at which communist leaders proclaimed that by 1980 the Soviet Union would make the transition from socialism to communism and thus reach what, according to Marx, was history's highest stage.

These developments left Gorbachev optimistic not only about the future of his country but also about the future of humankind, for which the Soviet Union would set a shining example. His career also gave him grounds for optimism. At age thirty-one, he moved from the relative backwater of the Communist Youth League to a position in the central administration of the Communist Party. From there, Gorbachev quickly ascended the party's bureaucratic ranks, becoming the party leader for his entire province in 1970 at the still-tender age of thirty-nine.

This new position made him a member of the communist elite and entitled him to privileges denied everyone else, especially the ability to travel to Western Europe. Driving with his wife through France and Italy in the early 1970s, Gorbachev was amazed by the Westerners' high standard of living and personal liberties. The trip convinced him that Khrushchev's boasts at the United Nations had been overly optimistic and that the Soviet Union had a great deal of catching up to do. He also learned, on a trip to Czechoslovakia, that the Red Army had not been welcomed with open arms in 1968, as Soviet propaganda maintained.

Eager to remain a member of the party elite, Gorbachev was in no position to act on these revelations; first, he had to continue to climb the party hierarchy. When Yuri Andropov, head of the Soviet Union's ruthless security agency, the KGB, convalesced in Gorbachev's home province, the older party dignitary befriended his charming younger host. Andropov became Gorbachev's patron and, in 1978, saw to his appointment to the Communist Party's Central Committee or ruling group.

At age forty-seven, Gorbachev was by far the youngest member of the Central Committee, where he faced a powerful gerontocracy (elderly rulers). Its leaders were the ailing Leonid Brezhnev (seventy-four in 1980), a man so disabled by arteriosclerosis and tranquilizer overdoses that he could barely work two hours a day. Brezhnev's main lieutenants ranged from age sixty-six to seventy-eight, and few

Timeline

| 1970 | 1975 | 1980 | 1985 | 1990 | 1995 | 2000 | 2005 | 2010 | | |

1971 Collapse of Bretton Woods exchange rate system

1974–1975 Greece transitions to a democratic republic

1975 Franco dies, ushering in democratic era in Spain

1975 Helsinki Accords establish détente, elaborate broad human rights

1978 Gorbachev appointed to Communist Party's Central Committee

1978 First Pole elected pope, as John Paul II

1978–1979 Iranian Revolution

1979–1989 Russian intervention in Afghanistan

1979 Margaret Thatcher becomes British Prime Minister

1980 Solidarity created in Poland; Yugoslavia's Tito dies

1981 Greece joins EEC; AIDS epidemic begins in the United States

1985 Gorbachev becomes Communist Party leader

1986 Explosion of nuclear reactor at Chernobyl; Spain and Portugal join EEC

1988 Gorbachev introduces glasnost and perestroika

1989–1995 Dissolution of Yugoslavia

May 1989 Slobodan Milošević elected president of Serbian province

1989–1991 Collapse of the Soviet Union

June 1989 Poland names a noncommunist prime minister

November 1989 Berlin Wall falls

December 1989 Communist party leadership resigns in Czechoslovakia; Ceaușescu executed in Romania

1990 German reunification; free elections in Hungary, Bulgaria, and East Germany; Lithuania, Russian Republic, Ukraine, Belorussia, and Moldova declare sovereignty from the Soviet Union

June 1991 Yeltsin becomes president of the Russian republic; Slovenia and Croatia secede from Yugoslavia

December 1991 Soviet Union dissolved

1992 Maastricht Treaty

1995 Austria, Finland, and Sweden join EU; Dayton Accords

2000 France adopts "parity" for women in elections

social inequality; the East would not. Rigid, state-controlled economies, poor living standards, the lack of civil liberties, and aged, inflexible leaders mired the various Eastern European countries in economic malaise and threatened the existence of their communist regimes once Gorbachev opened the floodgates of change.

Stagflation

Classically, economic contraction and the unemployment that resulted produced a decline in the prices of goods and services as joblessness reduced the ability to pay for them. But in the 1970s, world economies came down with a new economic disease, namely "**stagflation**," the unholy combination of stagnation and inflation, of economic contraction, unemployment, and skyrocketing prices.

This unprecedented constellation of problems had taken root in the late 1960s, when the productivity of workers began to decline and wages to rise. The resulting squeeze on profits lowered investment and set the stage for at least a modest economic contraction. What combined contraction with inflation to produce stagflation were two huge shocks to the international economic system: the collapse in 1971 of the **Bretton Woods** system of exchange rates set in 1944 and a dramatic increase in oil prices beginning in 1973.

Meeting at Bretton Woods, New Hampshire, forty-four of the world's major countries replaced the prewar gold standard with a new arrangement in which they all agreed to peg their currencies to the dollar at fixed, but adjustable, rates of exchange. The dollar alone would be pegged to gold, now valued at $35 an ounce, and the US Treasury guaranteed the new currency structure by promising to redeem with gold all paper dollars submitted to it.

The great virtue of the Bretton Woods system was that it allowed for both stability and flexibility—stability in that importers and exporters would know in advance the value of their own country's currency in relation to any other, and flexibility in that if a country experienced a significant balance of payments deficit or surplus, it could adjust its exchange rate accordingly.

The Bretton Woods arrangements worked well into the 1960s, when speculators accumulated the capital to disrupt the system and the United States amassed huge budget and trade deficits to pay for the Vietnam War. Suddenly, people and institutions overseas demanded gold for the piles of dollars they possessed, and in August 1971, US President Richard Nixon (1913–1994) moved to preserve the country's gold reserves by announcing that the Treasury Department would no longer redeem dollars for gold. Doing so ended the fixed relation between the dollar and gold and allowed the value of the dollar to fall, thus making American products less expensive for foreigners.

In order to compete in the international marketplace, other countries devalued their currencies as well. But devalued currency increased the relative prices of raw materials and other imports bought from countries that had not devalued, or devalued as much. As a result, prices went up: nonfuel commodities by 70 percent and food by 100 percent. To offset the domestic price increases, workers bid wages up, which in turn caused prices to rise all the more.

These inflationary pressures formed the backdrop to a dramatic increase in the price of oil. In the wake of a new war between Israel and Egypt in October 1973, the Middle East's major oil-exporting countries announced an abrupt, unprecedented hike in oil prices, which nearly tripled from $15 to $44 a barrel (in 2010 dollars). The price per barrel climbed to $72 during the Iranian Revolution of 1978–1979.

By the 1970s, oil had become so fundamental to the world's industrial economies that it accounted for 60 percent of Europe's energy consumption, up from 8.5 percent just twenty years earlier. Europe and the United States could not do without oil, but the relationship of the price hikes to inflation was indirect. Because higher-priced oil greatly increased manufacturing costs, industries cut other expenditures, especially labor, by laying off workers. The layoffs caused economies to contract and moved governments to pump in resources through government spending and interest-rate cuts, both to support the unemployed and to encourage enterprises to hire people back. But in the poor economic climate, businesses did not rehire at an adequate pace, and the increased money supply that resulted from higher government spending and interest-rate cuts added to the inflation already caused by the devaluation of the world's major currencies in 1971. Inflation soared from a European average of 4 percent in 1968 to 14 percent in 1975— and 24 percent in Britain.

≡ **The Oil Shock, 1973.** When the Organization of Petroleum Exporting Countries (OPEC) dramatically reduced production and therefore supply, prices skyrocketed. Shortages became common, especially of heating oil and gasoline. People everywhere shivered in frigid homes and buildings, and motorists waited in long lines to buy a partial tank of gas. The owners of the Volkswagen bus shown here had apparently given up on the internal combustion engine.

and overtaxed by a government overly generous to it. Haider, like Le Pen, was highly nationalist, condemning the European Union (the successor to the EEC) for sacrificing Austria's national interests and the United States for subjecting his country to the storms of globalization.

In 1999, Haider's Freedom Party attracted 27 percent of the vote, outdistancing Austria's main conservative organization and drawing nearly even with the Social Democrats. Workers, like rural-dwellers, had become susceptible to the anti-immigrant message. Similar parties appeared in the Netherlands, Germany, Denmark, and Norway, and even when their vote counts declined, their influence persisted. Earlier electoral successes had convinced mainstream parties of the right and the left to take a tough stance against immigrants, especially the Muslims among them.

Fixing Stagflation

Wherever unemployment remained high, immigrants shouldered much of the blame, but the solution to unemployment was not, as Le Pen claimed, to deport immigrant workers. It was to address the root causes of the problem, which experts identified as the inflationary spiral of the time.

By the late 1970s, Germany, Denmark, and the Benelux countries had succeeded in limiting inflation by negotiating wage restraint and maintaining a tight monetary policy (high interest rates). The latter was extended to the rest of the EEC, but at the cost of even higher unemployment: 9–11 percent in France, 10 percent in the United Kingdom, and 14 percent in Ireland.

In the early 1980s, France's newly elected socialist government, the first since 1936, abruptly shifted from contraction to reflation (government spending and low interest rates), hoping to stimulate the economy and reduce unemployment. But international speculators attacked the French franc as inflation heated up, and in the face of a plummeting currency, François Mitterrand (1915–1996), the new French president, faced a difficult choice: he could either stay the course and risk a break from the EEC, which required exchange rates to stay within a narrow range, or contract the economy and maintain the franc's value in relation to the mark. Mitterrand adopted the latter course, satisfying his European partners but not the leftist electorate that had voted him into office. Working people in particular suffered the consequences of the new economic austerity.

In Britain, a country also plagued by high inflation and poor productivity, Margaret Thatcher (1925–2013), a Conservative leader with radical intentions, became prime minister in 1979. She sought to conquer inflation, tame the country's traditionally powerful labor unions, and dramatically reduce the size and scope of the state.

Shortly after taking office, Thatcher moved to choke off inflation by having the Bank of England dramatically increase interest rates. The economy contracted and shed millions of jobs, doubling the unemployment rate between 1979 and 1981 and shrinking the country's GDP by a full 5 percent. Between 1981 and 1985, Britain was judged to have the fourth highest "misery index" in Europe—after Ireland, Italy, and Spain.

Thatcher's drastic economic contraction did little, however, to lower the inflation rate, which remained stubbornly high at 11 percent. Unions continued to demand—and receive—wage increases, and the huge number of unemployed people sharply increased government spending on unemployment insurance, which added to the inflationary pressures.

Although Thatcher's policies created a great deal of unemployment, they weeded out a considerable number of inefficient, uncompetitive firms in steelmaking, shipbuilding, coal mining, and textiles, many of which had remained in business only because previous governments had subsidized them. Britain's labor productivity went up as a result, but millions of people who had devoted their careers to these industries would never find work again.

Given the large number of jobless people, Britain's labor unions began to lose their clout. This development found dramatic confirmation in 1984–1985 when government forces crushed a violent, emotional miners' strike intended to prevent the closure of inefficient, unprofitable mines. A chastened, emasculated labor movement could no longer obtain significant wage increases, and widespread layoffs brought down general labor costs. This reality, combined with new interest-rate hikes, finally broke the inflationary spiral, returning Britain by the mid-1980s to low, 1960s-level inflation, although seemingly freezing unemployment at high 1970s rates.

Having successfully conquered inflation, Thatcher

≡ **The British Miners' Strike.** In the early 1980s, Prime Minister Margaret Thatcher's efforts to conquer inflation produced a huge spike in unemployment, especially in the less efficient rust-belt industries. Coal mining was hit particularly hard. With high unemployment, the miners' union lost its clout—as the bitter, but futile, coal miners' strike of 1984–1985 starkly revealed.

moved to privatize what, since the war, had been a large state-owned sector of the economy. She sold off the telecommunications network, utilities, the state-owned airlines, and a large portion of the country's public housing stock. In many cases, Thatcher's privatizations made overly bureaucratic enterprises far more efficient, and the private capital that poured into them modernized their operations, created more consumer choice, and gave individual citizens more investment opportunities. But critics accused her government of sacrificing public services for private profits, the comforts of community for the unequal fruits of individual gain.

The Politics of Terror

The economic troubles of the 1970s had produced a great deal of labor militancy, but the decade also saw a far more violent, confrontational form of politics that expressed itself through murder, kidnapping, and other terrorist acts. Perhaps the most powerful terrorist movement took shape in the six counties of Northern Ireland, which although contiguous with the Republic of Ireland, belong to the United Kingdom. The population there is divided between Catholics and Protestants, the latter strongly, emotionally tied to Great Britain and eager not to be integrated into the overwhelmingly Catholic Irish Republic. Protestants formed the majority in Northern Ireland, also known as Ulster, and they excluded Catholics from positions in government and from the most desirable jobs (see Map 15.1).

Catholics fought back through the Irish Republican Army (IRA), which as a nationalist organization aimed to detach Northern Ireland from Britain and unite it with the Irish Republic. In the late 1960s, the rebellious temper of the time spilled over into the IRA, whose new youthful leadership turned to violence to pursue their cause.

After a series of bloody incidents in 1969, British troops arrived to maintain order, but their presence only increased the mayhem. In 1972, 146 soldiers and 321 civilians were killed in Northern Ireland and some 5,000 wounded. Protestant organizations contributed significantly to the carnage, killing hundreds of Catholics, but the IRA alone brought the struggle to England by murdering politicians, bombing civilian targets, and even attempting to assassinate Margaret Thatcher. By the 1990s, when the two sides began to negotiate, 1,800 people had been killed in the futile conflict, which did not reach a resolution until the end of the decade.

Beyond Northern Ireland, Germany and Italy also saw the political ferment of the late 1960s fester into **terrorism**. In Germany, two young radicals, Andreas Baader and Ulrike Meinhof, created the Red Army Faction (RAF), dedicated to the

Ireland and Northern Ireland

🟩 Population in Northern Ireland that is predominantly Catholic

🟧 Population in Northern Ireland that is predominantly Protestant

0 miles   50

0 km   50

≡ **MAP 15.1** Ireland and Northern Ireland

violent destruction of the West German state, condemned as imperialist and neo-Nazi, and its replacement by a communist alternative. In 1977, the RAF kidnapped and killed the chairman of the automobile company Daimler-Benz, assassinated the president of one of the nation's largest banks, and murdered the attorney general. All told, the RAF was deemed responsible for more than thirty deaths. In Italy, the ultra-left-wing Red Brigades killed nearly four hundred people, including three politicians and nine judges. The organization's most notorious

☰ **"The Troubles" in Northern Ireland.** In the late 1960s and throughout the 1970s, conflict between the Catholic Irish Republican Army and its Protestant counterpart resulted in a series of bombings and other attacks. The aftermath of one of them is graphically shown in this picture.

act was the kidnapping in March 1978 of Aldo Moro, a former Italian prime minister, whom the group murdered two months later.

Italian groups on the extreme right heightened the violence by killing eighty-five in the bombing of the main Bologna railroad station in 1980, and the Mafia added to the violence by murdering judges, policemen, local politicians, and journalists. Although intended to destabilize a fragile Italian state, this constellation of terrorist acts ultimately had the opposite effect. Terrorism forced politicians, judges, police leaders, and civil servants to put aside their differences in a common effort to withstand the assault. By the mid-1980s, the Red Brigades and their right-wing counterparts had been reduced to impotence, as had Germany's RAF. But as we will see in the Epilogue, Europe would soon face a new kind of terrorist threat, one stemming from the injustices that certain radicalized Muslims believed they faced from the West.

The New Democracy in Greece, Portugal, and Spain

Although the 1970s was generally a bleak decade, Greece, Portugal, and Spain shared the happy experience of making successful transitions from dictatorship to democracy. The first to do so was Greece, which in the 1950s and 1960s was ruled by a traditionalist king and undemocratic politicians and, after a coup in 1967, by a military dictatorship. The junta's leader, Colonel George Papadopoulos, censored the press, banned strikes, and outlawed the study of several ancient Greek philosophers. Papadopoulos deemed these two-thousand-year-old works subversive. The military regime also forbade long hair and miniskirts, and generally deadened Greek society. The economy suffered, and in 1969, the EEC rejected Greece's bid to join the EEC.

Although Greeks quietly endured the military regime, it was unpopular. To bolster its standing, the government plotted in 1973 to annex Cyprus, an independent island nation whose population was 82 percent Greek and 18 percent Turkish. But Turkey got wind of Greece's plans and dispatched soldiers to Cyprus, foiling Papadopoulos's plan. Humiliated, the Greek military relinquished power in July 1974 to a new civilian regime, which adopted a democratic constitution and abolished the monarchy. By mid-1975, Greece's transition from military dictatorship to democratic republic was complete.

Unlike Greece, which had allowed elections up until the military coup, Portugal had been governed autocratically since 1932. Its ruler, António Salazar, kept his country in a backward, impoverished state, and its largely illiterate peasant population mostly accepted the status quo. What disrupted Portugal's stable authoritarianism was a 1961 rebellion in its African colonies—Angola, Mozambique, and two other small territories. Portugal's untested army, which had sat out both world wars, could not contain the rebellion, and by 1970, when Salazar died, the government was spending fully half of its defense budget in Africa.

Thousands of young Portuguese men were dying there every year, and by the mid-1970s, young conscripts were increasingly unwilling to fight in the futile African wars, especially for a government that had deprived them, like their African counterparts, of basic liberties and human rights. Finally, in April 1974, army officers calling themselves the Armed Forces Movement (MFA) ousted Salazar's successor, Marcelo Caetano, and created a provisional government dedicated to democratization, decolonization, and economic change.

Uncharacteristically for army officers, the MFA supported Portugal's now-legalized communist party, which sought to nationalize banks and major industries and redistribute land from large proprietors to peasants. This program proved unpopular in most of the country, and in the inaugural elections of 1975, the largest vote getter was Mário Soares's moderate socialist party. In 1976, Portugal's parliament approved a new democratic constitution, and Soares formed the country's first democratically elected government in a half-century.

Although Spain's economy in the 1960s was more advanced than Portugal's, Francisco Franco maintained the repressive rule he had inaugurated in 1939. Political parties were banned and speech, assembly, and protest constrained. What opposition there was existed, albeit quietly, within Franco's own administration. When Franco died in November 1975 at age eighty-two, government officials, eager to bring Spain up to general European standards, managed a quick transition to democracy. Juan Carlos, the grandson of Spain's last king, was crowned the country's new constitutional monarch, and his democratic inclinations did much to smooth the country's political transition.

With the king's support, the existing Francoist parliament, until then without real power, approved a host of democratic reforms, and in 1977, an elected assembly wrote a new democratic constitution. Among

≡ **Prince Juan Carlos and General Francisco Franco of Spain.** In 1969, Franco (*right*), the longtime Spanish dictator, named Juan Carlos (*left*), the grandson of Spain's last reigning king, as his heir apparent. Juan Carlos pledged to maintain Franco's authoritarian form of rule, but after Franco died in 1975, the young monarch abandoned authoritarianism in favor of democracy.

other things, the new charter decentralized the country and gave the different regions considerable autonomy from Madrid. This autonomy failed, however, to satisfy separatists in the Basque country and Catalonia, who threatened to tear the country apart. Juan Carlos rallied the country against them, while facing the trauma of hyperinflation.

Not until October 1982, when Felipe Gonzáles's Socialist Party won an absolute majority in parliament, did the economy begin to improve. Gonzáles served as prime minister for fourteen consecutive years and acted more like a Thatcherite than a socialist, imposing budgetary austerity and privatizing much of the public sector. The policies were painful and made unemployment soar, but inflation eventually receded and the modernization of the economy began. Gonzáles brought Spain into NATO, against the wishes of many in his party, and in 1986 ushered his country into the European Economic Community.

New Political Movements: Feminism, Gay Rights, and Environmentalism

As the countries of Southern Europe moved toward democracy, the nature of the existing democracies in Western and Northern Europe had begun to change. People's allegiance to the reigning political parties, whether Christian democrat, socialist, or communist, loosened considerably. Younger people in particular developed new political concerns, often expressed through "movements" rather than political parties.

The most important of these movements was **feminism**, which had been dormant for decades and came back to life in the wake of the student and worker protests of the late 1960s. To some extent, this revival stemmed from a reaction by women against the traditionalism of the student radicals, whose leaders were mostly male and seemed more concerned about the oppression of Vietnamese peasants than about the plight of women at home, their own movements included. But the new feminism also resulted from the era's dramatic changes in women's lives.

Between 1950 and 1970, the proportion of married women who worked outside the home more than doubled in many European countries. By the 1990s, women constituted between 40 and 50 percent of the workforce everywhere except Italy and Portugal. Middle-class, married women were thus much more likely to work for wages or salary than ever before, but they typically earned considerably less than men.

This differential did not go unnoticed, and new feminist organizations addressed it by demanding equal pay for equal work. They also petitioned governments and employers for reasonably priced child-care facilities and paid leave to care for newborn children. But even when women began to benefit from new day-care centers and expanded nursery schools, they still found themselves bearing the lion's share of responsibility for their children.

Gender roles changed gradually at best, and many women now worked what amounted to a "double shift" every day, sandwiching child-care and household responsibilities around full-time jobs. One common response to this situation was to want fewer children, and women's organizations demanded access to contraception and, increasingly, to legal abortion. These developments, along with the inflated cost of living, later marriage, the growing divorce rate, and couples' desire to cohabit rather than marry, resulted in a sharp decline in the birth rate—from nearly three children per woman to less than two. By the 1980s and 1990s, not a single Western European country produced enough children to replace the previous generation.

Smaller families threatened to reduce Europe's vitality in the near future and made their welfare states, already under strain, increasingly unaffordable. Retirement pensions are based on the ability of working people to support, through taxation, the retirement of their elders. As people lived longer and the working population shrank, European leaders began to worry about the future of their countries' generous pension systems.

Women's movements did not, of course, intend to jeopardize the welfare state, but they did seek to give women a larger role in politics, government, and society. In Scandinavia, the number of women in parliament increased dramatically between 1975 and 1990—to as high as 39 percent in Finland. But in the United Kingdom and France, and throughout southern Europe, the major political parties tended not to run women for office, and their representation in legislatures remained low—8 percent in Italy, 7 percent in Britain, and just 6 percent in France.

In 2000, the French parliament moved to remedy this

≡ **Italian Women Demonstrate for the Right to Divorce.** In 1971, the Italian government made divorce legal for the first time in the country's history. Italy's powerful Catholic Church had long opposed the legalization of divorce, which Catholic doctrine does not permit. In 1974, Italy's ruling Christian Democrats held a referendum designed to overturn the law of 1971, but the proponents of divorce won by a 60/40 majority.

situation by enacting a law requiring political parties to run equal numbers of male and female candidates in local elections and imposing financial penalties on parties that failed to do so in elections to the National Assembly. This "parity" law was successful at the local level: female representation on municipal and regional councils reached 48 percent by 2010. But in parliamentary elections, parties paid the fines rather than run equal numbers of women and men. Even so, female representation in the National Assembly rose from just 10.9 percent in 1997 to 27 percent in 2012.

Related in certain ways to the revival of feminism was the emergence in the 1970s of movements for the rights of lesbians and gay men. Among other things, these movements called for the decriminalization of same-sex relations, an end to discrimination against homosexuals, and for the abolition of laws that classified homosexuality as an illness. In the mid-1970s, lesbian feminists broke away from the various gay liberation movements in protest of their domination by men.

In the 1980s, the AIDS epidemic both intensified anti-gay hostility and evoked sympathy for the plight of homosexual men, especially as well-known, respected figures in public life and the arts began to perish from the disease. Because hospitals often refused to release information to the partners of AIDS patients, some gay rights organizations began to call for the legalization of same-sex marriage so that homosexual partners would enjoy the same rights as heterosexual husbands and wives. But not all gays and lesbians supported same-sex marriage, as some saw wedlock as a repressive "bourgeois" institution that homosexuals ought not to support.

Another key movement that took shape in the 1970s was environmentalism, the effort to reduce air and water pollution and to curb the growth of nuclear-generated power. In some cases, environmentalists created new political parties, usually known as "greens," and in others they tried to achieve their goals through demonstrations and other forms of direct action or by reshaping the policies of existing parties or both.

Environmentalism represented a disillusionment with the postwar focus on unbridled economic growth, a sense that Europeans had sacrificed the natural world on the altar of economic progress. In a way, the environmentalists' timing was ironic, since economic growth had slowed considerably in the 1970s, and pollution-prone "smokestack" industries were on the decline. Still, the environment had suffered during the "economic miracle" years, and new challenges had arisen with the creation of nuclear power plants, which had the potential not just to harm the environment but make it uninhabitable.

Although small green parties surfaced in various European countries, only in Germany did they become a major political force. In 1983, they won more than two million votes in parliamentary elections, and two years later, they entered the ruling coalition in the state of Hesse. By the late 1990s, they were influential enough to join the Social Democrats in governing the country and remained in the ruling coalition from 1998

≡ **The Amoco Cadiz Oil Spill.** In March 1978, a huge oil tanker named *Amoco Cadiz* ran into a rock formation three miles off the coast of Brittany, France. The tanker split into three pieces, releasing 4,000 tons of oil into the sea. It was the largest oil spill in history to that date. The oil killed countless fish and birds and covered the shoreline in a thick black muck. The cleanup occupied a small army of workers for many months.

to 2005. Green parties and movements succeeded in cleaning up polluted lakes and rivers and in improving the quality of the air, although the growing number of cars continued to lace the atmosphere with greenhouse gases and leave urban areas clouded in smog. Still, environmentalism had a profound effect on public views and corporate and government policies, and increasingly the EEC and its successor, the European Union, regulated the emission of toxins into the water and the air.

Dissent and Decline in Eastern Europe

The situation was completely different in Eastern Europe and the Soviet Union, where authorities outlawed all organizations, including environmentalist ones, independent of the communist party. Although budding environmentalists in the West expressed concern about environmental degradation in Eastern Europe and developed contacts with dissidents there, Western European governments paid little attention to pollution in the East. In general, the 1970s was an age of **détente** between Western and Eastern Europe, a time when leaders on both sides committed themselves to reducing the tensions of the Cold War by improving political relations, increasing trade, and facilitating loans by Western banks to needy Eastern European countries.

The Helsinki Accords

This "Ostpolitik" (new Eastern policy), as the Germans called it, sought to normalize relationships between the two halves of the divided continent and did much to legitimize the Eastern regimes, at least in the West. The new relationships received formal recognition in the **Helsinki Accords** (1975), which bound the thirty-five Western and Eastern signers to a policy of détente and recognized the territorial integrity of the Eastern countries. But buried within the accords was a set of principles outlining not just the rights of states but also requiring respect for "the human rights and fundamental freedoms" of individuals. The accords did not merely affirm these principles but obliged all thirty-five signatories to "promote and encourage the effective exercise of civil, political, economic, social, cultural and other rights and freedoms."

These clauses, which diplomats intended as cosmetic boilerplate, ultimately proved to be political dynamite. Suddenly, a variety of groups sprang up in the Soviet Union and Eastern Europe demanding that their countries live up to the accords they had signed. The communist governments took these groups very seriously, but from the dissidents' point of view, they had one key shortcoming: they seemed to concern intellectuals far more than the bulk of working people, who were primarily interested in improving their wages and living conditions.

What ultimately brought the Soviet system down was not a rebellion of ordinary people, but the machinations of its leaders. When Gorbachev and his colleagues tried to restructure the Soviet Union, the political and economic supports that had held the ungainly structure in place crumbled with breathtaking speed.

Gorbachev's Dramatic Reforms

As we have seen, the nuclear catastrophe at Chernobyl deeply shocked the new Soviet leader and convinced him that the effort to reform the Soviet system required that it first be opened up. Gorbachev hoped to do so carefully and progressively, with the goal of erasing the all-too-evident gap between the ideals of socialism and its often-dismal realities. He went on television to appeal directly to the people and over the heads of crusty, secretive bureaucrats. He freed the prominent dissident Andrei Sakharov from house arrest, allowed Jews to emigrate to Israel, and loosened censorship. Gorbachev took several well-publicized foreign trips designed to advertise his open, energetic leadership and strike up relationships with his counterparts abroad and especially President Reagan, with whom he formed a strong working partnership.

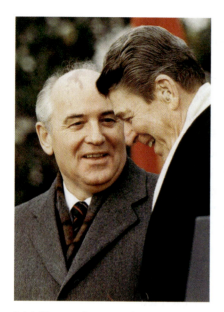

≡ A "Summit" Meeting between Gorbachev and President Ronald Reagan. The Soviet and American leaders were said to enjoy a close personal relationship, and in 1988 they made a dramatic agreement limiting their countries' respective stocks of nuclear weapons. In the spirit of this accord, and for internal Soviet reasons as well, Gorbachev also ended his country's long, costly war in Afghanistan.

Beyond the openness of glasnost, Gorbachev now initiated an ambitious new campaign to restructure the economy, which he labeled **perestroika**. He gave industrial firms a measure of autonomy, had managers elected rather than appointed, and released enterprises from some requirements of centralized planning by allowing them to deal directly with one another. To free up resources for consumer-oriented industries, he reduced military spending, which had reached an extraordinary 20–30 percent of GNP.

Gorbachev then tried to cut military costs even further by proposing to Reagan a large mutual reduction of the two superpowers' nuclear arsenals. Initially wary, Reagan came to believe in Gorbachev's sincerity, and the two leaders reached a dramatic agreement in 1988. Perhaps most important in terms of military spending, the Soviet leader began a phased withdrawal from Afghanistan, which finally cut the Soviet Union's losses there and brought all Russian troops home by 1989.

The measures of perestroika seemed to hold great promise when Gorbachev first initiated them in 1986, but he quickly ran into serious obstacles. The party and government bureaucracies, on which the Soviet leader relied to implement his plans, did their best to block them, fearing that decentralization and firm autonomy would deprive them of their authority, their jobs, or both. Beyond these problems, Gorbachev's economic advisors had him invest large sums in obsolete factories in the vain hope of reviving them, while doing too little to encourage the manufacture of consumer goods, always in high demand. To make matters worse, a steep drop in world oil prices in 1986 reduced the value of the Soviet Union's main export commodity and gave it much less foreign currency with which to buy consumer goods from abroad. The Soviet people's standard of living sank as a result, and their new hardships moved them to raise questions about the value of perestroika.

These economic issues were debated in the Soviet media, which had been given unprecedented freedom of expression under the policy of glasnost. Economic concerns quickly spilled over into virtually all areas of Soviet life, allowing festering problems—alcoholism, drug addiction, poverty, marital breakdown—to be openly discussed. Long-banned books and films became accessible, even Aleksandr Solzhenitsyn's *Gulag Archipelago* (published in the West in 1973), a powerful indictment not just of Stalinism but of the entire Soviet project. A variety of writers now published devastating critiques of the war in Afghanistan, the treatment of ethnic minorities, and the Chernobyl disaster. Glasnost gave the Soviet Union its first genuine public sphere.

With these publications, the exhilaration of the early glasnost period, when people felt almost intoxicated by the ability to speak freely, gave way to public expressions of disillusionment. Journalistic revelations about the evils of the Soviet past and the long-hidden problems of the present made a great many people feel as though their government had fed them nothing but lies. This feeling made people impatient with Gorbachev's gradual reforms and unsympathetic to his effort to make socialism live up to its ideals. Increasingly, members of the intelligentsia and ordinary citizens came to believe that socialism was the problem, not the ideal, and that their country needed not piecemeal reform but radical change.

These beliefs quickly spread into the various Soviet republics, where dissident voices now called for autonomy and even independence from the Soviet Union. Some demanded the dethroning of the communist party and the establishment of a multiparty pluralistic democracy, while others called for the end of state ownership and an economy based on private property. Such demands represented nothing less than the negation of the entire Soviet system, something that Gorbachev, who wanted only to improve that system, could barely understand, let alone allow. But he had set these demands in motion by calling for glasnost and perestroika,

in the communist party led by Ion Iliescu. After rebaptizing his party as the National Salvation Front, Iliescu was elected president of a largely unreformed Romanian state.

Neighboring Bulgaria experienced a similar transition, as party reformers capitalized on the events of 1989 to oust the country's seventy-eight-year-old leader and install themselves in his place. Elections were held, and former communists, now calling themselves socialists, easily won a majority. Their main opposition came from Bulgaria's Muslim and Turkish minorities, who gained equal rights with the dominant Orthodox population and won representation in parliament.

The dizzying succession of events in Eastern Europe meant that, by the beginning of 1990, the **Iron Curtain** separating East from West, as Winston Churchill had named it, was everywhere in tatters. Communist regimes that had seemed secure only a year earlier had all but disappeared (see Map 15.2). Although Gorbachev had not been the architect of communism's fall in Poland, Hungary, Czechoslovakia, East Germany, Romania, and Bulgaria, he was in many ways responsible for it. Between July and December 1989, the Soviet leader declared on three different occasions that his country would not block reform in Eastern Europe, and he assured President George H. W. Bush (1924–2018; in office 1989–1993) that the USSR would not intervene militarily to keep the teetering communist regimes in place.

Without the threat of Soviet tanks, Eastern Europe's communist regimes proved fragile at best. But even given Gorbachev's benign neglect, why did the fall of communism happen so fast? Part of the answer has to do with television, the now-pervasive medium that beamed the revolutionary events into almost every household and moved huge numbers of people to become involved. Those numbers deterred the repressive apparatus in every regime, for leaders knew that any and all police violence would unfold "with the whole world watching." Important as well was the commitment of Eastern European dissidents to nonviolence. Their pacifism convinced stalwarts of the old regime that they could give up power without risking their lives—Ceaușescu's Romania being the exception—and allowed former leaders the hope that, under democracy, they might be able to govern again.

One final reason for the speed of communism's fall was the lure of the European Economic Community, soon to be reborn as the European Union in 1993. The EEC/EU was an increasingly powerful organization of European states that the different countries of Eastern Europe could aspire to join once they had shed the albatross of communism. Above all, the promise of a united Europe meant that "Eastern Europe," with its implications of backwardness and otherness, could cease to exist.

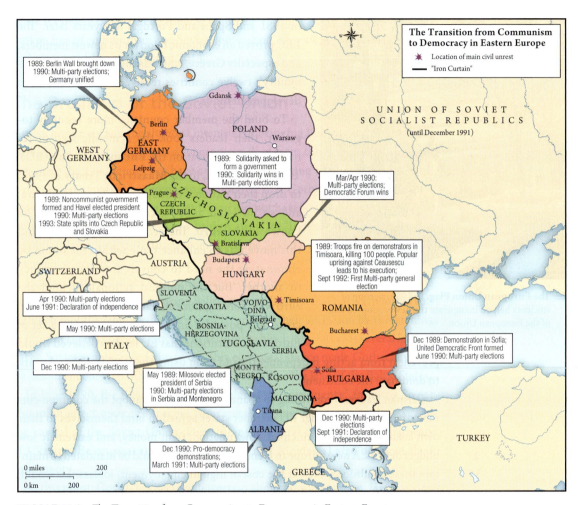

The Transition from Communism to Democracy in Eastern Europe

- ✶ Location of main civil unrest
- —— "Iron Curtain"

1989: Berlin Wall brought down
1990: Multi-party elections; Germany unified

UNION OF SOVIET SOCIALIST REPUBLICS
(until December 1991)

Gdansk ✶

POLAND

Berlin ✶

EAST GERMANY

WEST GERMANY

Warsaw ○

Leipzig ✶

1989: Solidarity asked to form a government
1990: Solidarity wins in Multi-party elections

Mar/Apr 1990: Multi-party elections; Democratic Forum wins

C Z E C H O S L O V A K I A

Prague ✶

CZECH REPUBLIC

1989: Noncommunist government formed and Havel elected president
1990: Multi-party elections
1993: State splits into Czech Republic and Slovakia

SLOVAKIA

Bratislava ✶

AUSTRIA

Budapest ✶

1989: Troops fire on demonstrators in Timisoara, killing 100 people. Popular uprising against Ceausescu leads to his execution;
Sept 1992: First Multi-party general election

SWITZERLAND

HUNGARY

SLOVENIA

Apr 1990: Multi-party elections
June 1991: Declaration of independence

CROATIA

VOJVO-DINA

Timisoara ✶

ROMANIA

Belgrade ○

May 1990: Multi-party elections

BOSNIA-HERZEGOVINA

YUGOSLAVIA

Bucharest ✶

ITALY

SERBIA

Dec 1989: Demonstration in Sofia; United Democratic Front formed
June 1990: Multi-party elections

Dec 1990: Multi-party elections

MONTE-NEGRO

KOSOVO

Sofia ✶

May 1989: Milosovic elected president of Serbia
1990: Multi-party elections in Serbia and Montenegro

BULGARIA

MACEDONIA

○ Tirana

Dec 1990: Multi-party elections
Sept 1991: Declaration of independence

ALBANIA

TURKEY

Dec 1990: Pro-democracy demonstrations;
March 1991: Multi-party elections

GREECE

0 miles   200
0 km   200

≡ **MAP 15.2** The Transition from Communism to Democracy in Eastern Europe

European Unification and Its Discontents

In 1970, the six original members of the European Economic Community agreed to expand membership to Britain, Ireland, and Denmark. Their entry was uncontroversial, since except for Ireland, the new countries were prosperous and thus guaranteed to expand the EEC's budget without incurring many additional costs. It was the next group of applicants, the newly democratic Greece, Spain, and Portugal, that raised a variety of concerns. All three were poor and in need of financial assistance. However, the core countries were committed to expansion and to rewarding the democratic transitions in these countries; Greece was admitted

☰ **Boris Yeltsin Acclaimed by the Moscow Crowd.** In mid-1991, Gorbachev and Yeltsin, president of the Russian Republic, signed an agreement that all but dissolved the Union of Soviet Socialist Republics, formed in 1922. To prevent the implementation of this agreement, conservatives in the Soviet government staged a coup d'état, placing Gorbachev under house arrest and sending tanks to Moscow. But Yeltsin took refuge in his Moscow office and foiled the coup. As this photograph suggests, the people of Moscow supported Yeltsin en masse.

But the newly declared Soviet leader, Vice-President Gennady Yanaev, stumbled through his opening remarks and appeared to be drunk. Three members of the State Committee, including the head of the KGB, did not bother to participate. The five sober putschists sat there wooden-faced and looked anything but leaders. The press conference was a disaster, and the coup collapsed within a matter of days.

Gorbachev arrested these "cowardly geezers," as one KGB official called them, and in a joint press conference with Yeltsin stood by while the Russian president dissolved the Communist Party of the Soviet Union and then the Soviet Union itself. Although Gorbachev had equivocated toward the end and tried, if half-heartedly, to stop the process of democratization and dissolution that he had set in motion, he nonetheless allowed it to proceed. As late as 1990, he could have mobilized the Soviet Union's gigantic military and KGB apparatus against the secessionist republics, against Yeltsin, and against all those who wanted to go beyond the reformed version of communism he had in mind, however vague and romantic it was. But it was precisely that idealized version of communism that ruled out repressive violence and allowed the Soviet Union to fall.

The Soviet Union was replaced by a loose, powerless organization called the **Commonwealth of Independent States**, which left Gorbachev without a job. On December 25, 1991, he stepped down as leader of what turned out to be Europe's last great empire.

The Violent Collapse of Yugoslavia

Not only did the Soviet Union's outer and inner empires dissolve with astonishing speed but it happened with relatively little bloodshed. The former Soviet republics peacefully went their separate ways, with the tragic exception of Armenia and

European Unification	
1952	European Coal and Steel Community formed
1957	Treaty of Rome creates the European Economic Community (EEC)
1973–1974	Britain, Ireland, Denmark, and Norway join the EEC
1973	Oil shocks threaten European prosperity
1992	Treaty of Maastricht creates European Union (EU)
1995	Austria, Sweden, and Finland join the EU
1998	European Central Bank founded
1999	Euro instituted as a common currency but without Britain and Denmark
2004	First wave of former communist states admitted to EU; Cyprus and Malta join
2007–2013	Romania, Bulgaria, and Croatia join the EU

Azerbaijan, which fought a bloody war between 1992 and 1994 over disputed territory. Some 20,000 died and perhaps a million people were displaced. In Eastern Europe, Czechoslovakia broke into two ethnically distinct halves—the Czech and Slovak Republics—with no violence to speak of. Only a single Eastern European country, Yugoslavia, marred the otherwise peaceful transition to post-communism in that part of the world, and marred it in a terrible way.

The Yugoslav crisis began with the death in 1980 of its longtime ruler Josip Broz Tito, who had done a great deal to bring his fractious country together and soothe ethnic tensions. He gave the different regions—Slovenia, Croatia, Bosnia-Herzegovina (BH), Serbia, Montenegro, and Macedonia—a measure of autonomy and protected their ethnic minorities—Croats in Serbia, Serbs in BH, Albanians in Kosovo.

With Tito gone, ethnic tensions revived, especially after the Serbian election of May 1989, when Slobodan Milošević (1941–2006), a former communist party boss, won the province's presidency after running a stridently nationalist campaign. Milošević stigmatized Croats and Muslims and especially Serbia's Albanian minority, most of whom were clustered in the officially autonomous, although Serb-controlled, region of Kosovo. Even though Serbs constituted less than 20 percent of Kosovo's people, they gave the region great significance as the place where their ancestors had made a heroic, if futile, last stand against the invading Turks in 1389. Kosovo was thus a Serbian shrine and its Albanians, mostly Muslims who had adopted their religion under the Ottomans, were deeply resented and badly treated.

Despite the revival of ethnic tensions and mistreatment of Albanians, the most explosive problems in Yugoslavia were economic. As president of Serbia, Milošević manipulated Yugoslavia's carefully balanced federal system to award his province the lion's share of Yugoslavia's tax receipts. The leaders of the other provinces saw no reason to contribute disproportionately to Serbia's coffers, and in June 1991, Slovenia and Croatia followed the example of the Soviet Union's breakaway republics by seceding from Yugoslavia and declaring themselves independent states.

In response, Milošević sent the Yugoslavian army, now consisting entirely of Serbs and Montenegrins, into Slovenia, setting off a potentially explosive conflict based on the ethnic passions the Serbian ruler had aroused. Fortunately, the stakes in Slovenia were low, since only a tiny number of Serbs lived there, and after eleven days of inconclusive fighting, the Yugoslavian forces withdrew.

The situation was far more serious in Croatia, where more than a half-million Serbs lived in ethnic enclaves. When the Serbs of Croatia, their ethnic fears stirred by Milošević, rebelled against the province's secession from Yugoslavia, the Serbian dictator invaded to "protect" them. The two sides fought fiercely for several months until the United Nations imposed a ceasefire in January 1992 and sent in a peacekeeping force. Since Croatia did not have a formal army at the beginning of the conflict, it lost a substantial amount of territory to the Serbs, who wanted to annex the Serb-dominated parts of Croatia to a "Greater Serbia." The UN presence blocked the annexation but did nothing to stop the expulsion of non-Serbs from their homes in the parts of Croatia occupied by the Yugoslavian (read Serbian) army.

While an uneasy calm settled over a truncated Croatia, the Croats and Muslims of Bosnia voted overwhelmingly for BH's independence from the Serb-dominated Yugoslavia. Immediately, Bosnian Serbs declared war on the new independent republic of BH, and as in Croatia, the Serbian army intervened to support them. In early fighting, the Bosnian Serbs succeeded in creating their own mini-state within BH, where they undertook a bloody effort to "cleanse" the area of non-Serbs.

This **ethnic cleansing**, a terrible term that would define the Yugoslavian wars, mostly affected BH's Muslims, who in January 1993 also found themselves at war with the Croats of their fledgling state. As the death toll of Muslim civilians mounted, the UN's "peacekeeping" forces did little to stop it, and NATO remained aloof, despite urgent demands by leading public figures for a "humanitarian intervention."

Emboldened by Western inaction, Serbian soldiers entrenched in the mountains surrounding Sarajevo, the capital of BH, launched an artillery shell into the city's central marketplace in February 1994, killing sixty-eight people. Under these circumstances, NATO finally reacted, promising to answer further shelling of the city with air strikes. The Serbs backed down, and the danger to Sarajevo subsided for a time.

But the Yugoslavian wars were far from over. In May 1995, a now battle-worthy Croatian army ejected Serbian forces from their country, and in response, the Bosnian Serbs resumed their attacks on Sarajevo. NATO bombers returned fire, but only briefly, as the Serbs took 350 UN soldiers hostage and threatened to kill them if the air strikes continued. The international forces stood down, and Serbian soldiers, led by a fanatic named Ratko Mladić, burst into Srebrenica, a Muslim town deemed a "safe area" by the UN and manned by 400 Dutch peacekeepers. With the Dutch passively looking on, the Serbs rounded up Srebrenica's men and boys and marched them to the outskirts of town, where Mladić's men killed all 7,400 of them in cold blood. It was the largest European mass murder since the Second World War. But once again, NATO sat on its hands. Only when the Serbs resumed the shelling of Sarajevo, killing another thirty-eight people, did NATO finally act—and then only because President Bill Clinton finally overruled the European opposition to stepping in.

A NATO bombing campaign rousted the Serbs from their perches in Bosnia and forced them to lay down their arms. Peace talks held in Dayton, Ohio, gave each of Bosnia's peoples, Serb, Croat, and Muslim, a measure of autonomy within a unitary Bosnian state and stationed a large contingent of NATO forces there to maintain the peace. But nothing could undo the ethnic cleansing that had taken place. Most of those uprooted from their homes would never return, and three million former Yugoslavs looked for asylum abroad. Some 300,000 had lost their lives.

After the Dayton agreements of 1995, there was a violent coda to the Yugoslavian wars. A weakened, humiliated Serbia took out its frustrations on the oppressed Albanian majority of Kosovo, whose leaders now demanded independence from Milošević's rule and undertook an intense resistance campaign. The Serbian dictator sent in special police forces to kill the "terrorists," and it soon became clear that he intended to cleanse the region of its Albanian population.

☰ **Mass Killings in Srebrenica, 1995.** At the height of the Bosnian War, Serbian soldiers led by Ratko Mladić stormed into the Bosnian village of Srebrenica and killed 7,400 Muslim men and boys in cold blood. Most were hastily buried in mass graves, recalling the Nazi massacres of 1941.

≡ **MAP 15.4**   War in the Former Yugoslavia, 1991–1999

Having learned the lesson of Bosnia, NATO wanted to intervene but preferred to do so under a mandate from the UN. But China and Russia, which supported the Serbs and opposed NATO, blocked any action by the international organization, and NATO hesitated until Serbs massacred forty-five Albanians in a tiny Kosovo town. At that point, NATO launched a major air attack on Serbia that battered its army and forced Milošević to withdraw all Serbian personnel from Kosovo. The region was given autonomy under NATO protection, but not before half of its Albanian population had fled (see Map 15.4).

This latest humiliation finally put an end to Milošević's reign. He lost the presidential election of September 2000, and when he refused to step down, demonstrators filled the streets of Belgrade and forced him from office. His successors agreed, on Western insistence, to turn him over to the War Crimes Tribunal in The

Hague, where the international court charged him with genocide, among other crimes. He died of a heart attack during the course of his trial.

The Challenges of Post-Communism

In Yugoslavia, the transition away from communism proved particularly cruel; elsewhere, the advent of post-communist regimes occurred peacefully but not without difficulty. Even in the former GDR (East Germany), which disappeared in October 1990 with the reunification of Germany, the transition was far from smooth.

German Reunification

At first, political leaders everywhere thought that changes in East Germany would occur gradually and that the GDR might join in a federation with West Germany rather than vanish altogether. French and British officials were wary, as always, of a huge united Germany in the heart of Europe, and Gorbachev, not to mention members of his military establishment, feared the revival of German might.

Whatever the world's political leaders said, East Germans voted with their feet. Thousands moved to West Germany every day in search of jobs and a better life, and Helmut Kohl (1930–2017), the West German chancellor, feared that his country would become overcrowded as East Germany emptied out. The only way to have East Germans stay put was to erase the border between the FRG (West Germany) and the GDR and merge the two Germanys into one. With US backing, Kohl quickly put the prospect of German reunification to a vote, and in March 1990, the citizens of East Germany overwhelmingly said yes.

Despite the popularity of reunification in Germany, it still had to receive the endorsement of Britain, France, the United States, and the Soviet Union, which each occupied a part of Berlin and had troops on German soil. Once Kohl made clear that a united Germany would remain in NATO and bound to the European Economic Community, Britain and France agreed to reunification. But Gorbachev came around only after Kohl agreed to make Germany's eastern border with Poland permanent—it had been left unfixed after the war—and offered multibillion-dollar payments to the Soviet Union.

Germany's political reunification was thus relatively easy; its economic reunification proved far more difficult. The former GDR's infrastructure of roads, railroads, telephone lines, plumbing, electricity, and the like was antiquated, and it cost the German government vast sums to bring it up to date. Even more problematic was the state of East German industry, which featured old-fashioned technology and low productivity; it could not, for the most part, produce internationally competitive products.

Compounding the problem of productivity and competitiveness was the successful effort on the part of West German labor unions to quickly raise wages in the former GDR to West German levels. But with output per Eastern worker less than half that of Western ones, the real cost of labor in the East was double that of the West. Since few capitalist businessmen wanted to manage antiquated industries with high labor costs, a great many former GDR enterprises collapsed.

To shield the many workers who lost their jobs, the German government provided high unemployment benefits—about 70 percent of their lost wages—and generous social services. These benefits helped working people weather the transition from communism to capitalism, but they cost the German government a fortune, as did the effort to rebuild the East German infrastructure. During the early years of the transition, the former FRG transferred to the former GDR some $200 billion a year, for a total of $2 trillion by the early 2010s. Even so, joblessness in the former GDR remained high, reaching 18 percent in 1998, double the rate in the former West Germany.

Although the East continued to lag well behind the West into the twenty-first century, the former East Germans did not, at least, have to invent a stable, functioning democratic government or systems of civil and administrative law relevant to a modern capitalist economy. Nor did they have to create a modern banking system and the know-how to manage capitalist firms. These key elements of Western capitalist societies automatically enveloped them as they were integrated into West Germany. The inhabitants of Russia and Eastern Europe were not so fortunate. As they navigated the transition from state-run to private-enterprise economies, they had to create, essentially from scratch, the new political, administrative, and legal structures that liberal capitalism requires.

The Transformation in Eastern Europe and Russia

No country had ever made the transition from communism to capitalism before, and without precedents to follow, it proved much more difficult to accomplish than anyone, including a great many Western experts, had thought. One commanding idea, championed by certain Western economists and adopted in Poland and the Czech Republic, was that the transformation from communism to capitalism should take place through a "shock therapy" in which the supports of the state-run economy would be removed overnight. Deprived of the crutches of government subsidies and controlled prices, institutions and individuals would quickly and automatically adjust—or so the experts claimed.

But this idea proved naïve at best. The personnel and institutions of liberal capitalism do not emerge instantly and on their own; they had, after all, taken centuries to evolve in the West. The former communist countries needed to train managers of private companies and develop modern banking systems capable of raising capital and acting as intermediaries between firms seeking to do business with one another. They had to build legal systems with the personnel and institutions to enforce contracts, resolve economic disputes, impose penalties on fraudulent operators, and adjudicate conflicting claims. And they had to develop political institutions supple enough to oversee and regulate the workings of a private enterprise economy while managing the inequality it inevitably creates.

Despite these challenges, Poland and Czechoslovakia decided to dive headlong into the cold waters of economic liberalism. At the beginning of 1990, Poland ended all price controls, canceled subsidies to money-losing enterprises—thus allowing them to fail—and tried to attract hard (Western) currency by raising interest rates. Predictably, unemployment in both countries rose sharply as inefficient companies went out of business, and real wages fell as working people had to contend with a much higher cost of living.

To cushion these blows, both governments provided unemployment benefits and welfare for the elderly and indigent, but these policies produced growing budget deficits and rampant inflation—46 percent in Czechoslovakia and 1,000 percent in Poland. Fortunately, Czechoslovakia had developed a successful private enterprise economy before the Second World War and retained some of its earlier, if outdated, expertise. Poland and Hungary had some experience with small private farms and businesses during the communist period, and once communism fell, they tended to privatize small, competitive enterprises rather than large uncompetitive ones, allowing the private sector to expand productively and even attract some foreign investment.

Gradually, these and other former communist countries and Soviet republics developed a body of laws and institutions to govern the private economy and protect those who invested in it. The European Union offered incentives to deepen this process by promising admission to the organization once the legal and administrative systems of the eastern countries, as well as their political institutions and economic standing, met the EU's standards.

By the mid- and late 1990s, capitalism in Poland, the Czech Republic, Hungary, and the Baltic states had begun to work. Much of the rubble of the old communist enterprises had been cleared away, and new firms that made things people wanted to buy rose in their place. Some of these products were

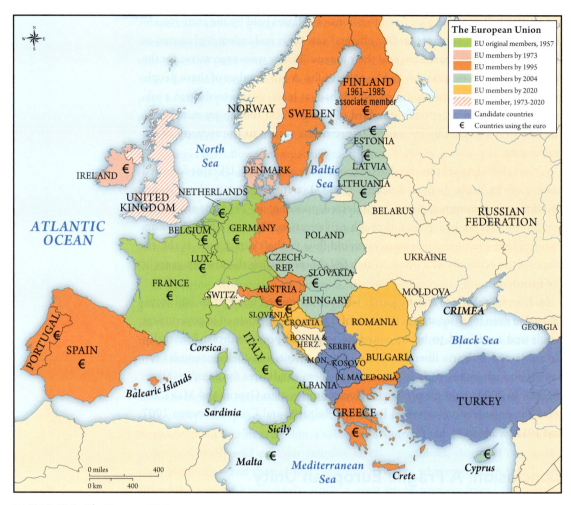

The European Union
- EU original members, 1957
- EU members by 1973
- EU members by 1995
- EU members by 2004
- EU members by 2020
- EU member, 1973-2020
- Candidate countries
- € Countries using the euro

≡ **MAP 15.5**   The European Union

Europe had become mired in debt and stuck in an economic recession triggered by the United States' financial collapse of 2008. While the United States began to recover, Europe's economic problems became deeper and more pervasive, as the EU and European Central Bank imposed austere monetary and fiscal policies at Germany's behest. The economic situation became so dire in the EU's poorest countries—Greece, Portugal, Ireland, and Spain—that politicians and policy makers began to wonder whether the Eurozone, and even the European Union itself, would persist.

KEY TERMS

Bretton Woods *684*

Charter 77 *698*

Commonwealth of
 Independent States *714*

détente *697*

ethnic cleansing *716*

euro *710*

European Union *710*

feminism *694*

Gastarbeiter *686*

glasnost *682*

Helsinki Accords *697*

Iron Curtain *708*

Maastricht Treaty *710*

oligarchs *722*

perestroika *702*

Solidarity *700*

stagflation *684*

terrorism *690*

velvet revolution *707*

For digital learning resources, please go to **https://www.oup.com/he/berenson2e**.
Turn to the back of the book to see the list of primary sources and writing exercises
provided in the accompanying *Sources and Guided Writing Exercises for Europe in the
Modern World*

EPILOGUE

Europe in the Twenty-First Century

Ayaan Hirsi Ali

Born in Mogadishu, the capital of Somalia, Ayaan Hirsi Ali (1969–) grew up in East Africa and Saudi Arabia and emigrated as a young adult to the Netherlands. Intelligent and resourceful, she escaped the poverty to which most African immigrants were consigned and became an outspoken, controversial critic of Islam, which she condemned for its treatment of women.

When Hirsi Ali turned five, her traditionalist grandmother decided she should undergo female circumcision, even though her Western-educated father, a jailed Somali dissident, opposed the custom. A great many Somali girls have their genitals cut in a procedure intended to prevent them from being possessed by devils and to make them pure. The practice existed before the advent of Islam, but in Somalia the religious authorities (Imams) supported it in the name of the Muslim faith. Hirsi Ali's description of how it was done is unbearable to read, and she makes clear that its physical and emotional scars helped shape her later life.

A year after this traumatic childhood event, a civil war in Somalia drove Hirsi Ali's family out of their country. Her father then escaped from prison and joined them in their new homeland, Saudi Arabia, which Hirsi Ali found strange and depressing. In Somalia, women wore colorful, flowing robes; in Arabia, they wore black burqas, their bodies covered except for their eyes.

When it was no longer safe for Hirsi Ali's father, now a leader of Somalia's rebel movement, to remain in Saudi Arabia, he moved the family several times until it finally landed in 1980 in Nairobi, Kenya. Her parents enrolled her in an elite Muslim girls' school, where instruction was entirely in English, a language she learned to speak fluently. While at the school, Hirsi Ali mastered a variety of other languages and developed academic knowledge and skills rare for a Somali girl. Still, an arranged marriage was always on the horizon, and when Ayaan turned twenty-two, her father promised her to a cousin in Canada, whom she had met just once.

For the wedding and her new life, Hirsi Ali was to fly to Frankfurt, Germany, and then to Canada. But after completing the first leg of the journey, she decided to escape, unwilling to turn her body, as she later put it, into "a factory of sons." She boarded a train bound for the Netherlands, where she received

the country (the various shades of green on Map E.2), by contrast, were settled by Slavs in the seventeenth and eighteenth centuries and have since then attracted a large number of Russians, many of whom reject the West and support Russia.

Ukraine seemed safely in Russia's orbit until the early 2000s, when the central parts of the country joined its western-most regions in seeking to link their country with the European Union and its capitalist, welfare-state economies and democratic politics. Things came to a head in 2004, when Ukraine's pro-Russian prime minister, Viktor Yanukovych (1950–), tried to catapult himself into the presidency by rigging the elections of that year. Widespread protests broke out, and in what became known as the **Orange Revolution**, the mostly young pro-Western demonstrators succeeded in having the election annulled. A new contest, supervised by international observers who declared it "free and fair," gave the pro-Western candidate, Viktor Yushchenko (1954–), a clear victory. This result seemed, for a time, to launch Ukraine onto a more democratic path.

But Yushchenko did not succeed in diminishing the power of Ukraine's oligarchs, many of whom remained sympathetic to Russia, or in improving Ukraine's economy. Nor did he make progress in narrowing the country's ethnic, ideological, and linguistic divisions. The election of 2010, which resulted in a narrow victory for the pro-Russian Yanukovych, starkly revealed just how wide those divisions were—and how closely they conformed to Ukraine's ethnic and linguistic map.

Yanukovych thus won the presidency with only marginal support in the western two-thirds of the country. And heeding, perhaps, the latter's pro-Western views, he tentatively accepted a proposal to connect the country's economy to that of the European Union. But in November 2013, under Russian pressure, he changed his mind, rejecting the path toward the EU. Infuriated by this about-face, legions of young Ukrainians descended once again into the streets of

☰ **The Orange Revolution, 2004**. Waving orange flags, a throng of young people in Kiev, the capital of Ukraine, celebrate the defeat of their country's pro-Russian prime minister and the victory of his pro-Western opponent, Viktor Yushchenko.

Kiev and occupied the city's Independence Square, hoping to pressure Yanukovych to sign the accord with the EU. The protestors also condemned the corruption of the regime, ranked among the worst in the world, as well as its economic stagnation.

Rather than relent, Yanukovych sent troops to break up the demonstrations; in the confrontations that ensued, nearly 150 people lost their lives—many shot by police snipers firing from rooftops into the crowd. The deadly repression caused widespread outrage, and a great many Ukrainians now demanded the president's resignation. Finally, in late February 2014, after two months of extreme unrest, the Ukrainian parliament voted to remove Yanukovych from office. He then fled to his home base in eastern Ukraine and ultimately to Russia, where he has remained.

Clearly, events in Ukraine did not work out the way Putin had wanted, and he retaliated in March 2014 by slipping Russian soldiers wearing unmarked uniforms into the Crimean Peninsula. Crimea had historically belonged to Russia, but in 1954, the Soviet leadership transferred it to the Ukrainian Soviet Socialist Republic. When Ukraine gained its independence in 1992, Crimea remained with it, although as a semi-autonomous region with a majority of Russian speakers and Russian military bases on its soil.

The unmarked Russian soldiers quickly took over the peninsula in a patently illegal violation of Ukraine's sovereignty. Putin followed up with a referendum asking Crimea's inhabitants to confirm their allegiance to Russia. According to the Russian government, some 97 percent said yes, a result that independent observers viewed skeptically. Still, the announced outcome gave Putin's aggression a fig leaf of legitimacy, and in any case, no Western country was willing to risk a military confrontation over a dot of territory long considered in Russia's sphere of influence.

In the wake of Russia's annexation of Crimea, a rebellion against the ouster of the pro-Russian Yanukovych erupted in eastern Ukraine.

≡ **Russia's Annexation of Crimea, 2014.** Putin announces the incorporation of Crimea, formerly a province of Ukraine, into the Russian Federation. The Russian president justified the move on the grounds that until 1954 Crimea had been part of Russia.

Ostensibly, this was a local insurrection carried out by Ukrainians hostile to their new pro-Western government, but one of the key rebel leaders was a Russian citizen and former member of Russia's security services. Putin's government backed the rebellion with arms, money, and tactical support—including soldiers in unmarked uniforms. What is more, thousands of Russian troops lined the border between Russia and Ukraine within hailing distance of the rebellion.

When the Ukrainian army moved to put it down, Russia armed the rebels with ever more sophisticated weapons, including advanced surface-to-air missiles. According to Western officials, Ukrainian separatists used those missiles to blow up, likely inadvertently, a civilian airliner carrying 298 people. Although Russia pinned responsibility on the Ukrainian air force, the evidence pointed to the Russian-backed rebels. The Ukrainian government now stepped up its offensive against them, and in response, Putin sent Russian troops, tanks, and artillery across the border to push the Ukrainians back. The Russian intervention moved Europe and the United States to impose sanctions on Putin's regime, and although its economy suffered, the Russians have defiantly held firm in eastern Ukraine, claiming to protect the Russian-speakers there from pro-Western "fascists" in Kiev.

The Crisis of the Eurozone

The standoff in Ukraine took place against the backdrop of a **Great Recession**, whose severity and persistence resulted, in part, from the earlier decision to create a common European currency and especially from the perils of **globalization**. The modern world saw its first globalization in the late nineteenth century, when Europe's largely completed Industrial Revolution brought the world closer together through faster transportation (railroads and steamships) and quicker communications (telegraph, mass-circulation newspapers, telephones). The second globalization of the late twentieth century also brought the planet closer together, although at light speed compared to a century earlier. Electronic communications connected people instantaneously and enabled individuals and business to buy and sell stocks, bonds, currencies, and a vast number of goods and services with a few clicks of a keyboard—and later, taps on a phone. At the same time, the EU, which had already eliminated tariffs and other trade restrictions within its borders, now began to reduce them with other parts of the world. These developments often resulted in lower prices for consumers, but they also led to increased competition with foreign producers, which could now sell steel, cars, industrial machinery, and many other things at prices so low as to threaten, in some cases, the very existence of European manufacturers.

Beginning in the 1970s and increasingly over the next three decades, many European firms either closed their doors or moved their manufacturing operations abroad. Reduced transport costs, minimal tariffs, and global supply chains in which parts of a product were made in several different places made it increasingly easy for European firms to relocate their manufacturing operations to countries where labor costs were much lower than in Western Europe and expensive environmental regulations weak or nonexistent. The lower costs of making products abroad enabled European companies to cut prices still more, benefiting consumers yet again, but often at great cost to the workers at home whose jobs had been eliminated. Some never found new employment and others were forced to take positions in the growing service sector—healthcare, tourism, food preparation, administration—where pay tended to be considerably lower and jobs less permanent than in the old manufacturing concerns. By the early 2000s, two-thirds to three-quarters of Europeans were employed in the service sector. Some of these service workers faced competition from immigrants whose often-precarious situations enabled employers to pay them even less than natives of the countries to which they had moved.

Although service workers could buy domestic- and foreign-made products at reasonable prices, low wages could put these products out of reach. Other Europeans, however, were more fortunate. Some 10 to 20 percent of the populations of the different EU countries benefited handsomely from globalization. These were people with the education, "cultural capital" (educated, well-connected families), and know-how to qualify for jobs in the burgeoning high-tech sector, the various knowledge industries (consulting, legal services, applied sciences), banking and finance, management, real estate development, and a few others. These people saw their incomes soar high above those confined to service sector jobs. Inequality thus widened as a consequence of globalization. In many countries, those in the top 1 percent of the income distribution earned more than the bottom 20 percent combined, while the incomes of the top 10 percent equaled those of the bottom 50 percent. In 1998, elite business executives in the United Kingdom earned forty-seven times as much as their average employee did. By 2014, executives made 143 times as much. If the average employee took in $40,000 a year, top bosses took in almost six million.

Inequality widened not only within countries but also between countries, as the richest nations (Germany, the Netherlands, Britain, France) became even wealthier in relation to the poorest ones—mostly former communist states (Bulgaria, Romania, Ukraine). The average GDP of the countries admitted to the EU in 2004—Estonia, Latvia, Slovenia, Poland, and Slovakia—was less than half that of members admitted before then. The GDP gap was even worse in 2007, when Romania and Bulgaria joined the union with GDPs less than a third of the EU average. Wages in the new member countries hovered at a quarter or less of the average in the wealthier states. Businesses throughout the EU showed inequality as well. The largest concerns tended to benefit from globalization, as their huge sales volumes enabled them to cut prices to meet their global competition and thus to increase their sales all the more. Smaller businesses did not have that luxury, and a great many went under.

If globalization reordered manufacturing, it transformed banking and finance even more. New electronic technologies allowed transactions to hop over borders and across oceans instantaneously, and the ability to move capital anywhere, anytime, encouraged individual countries to relax, or eliminate, their regulations on the flow of money. Deregulation enabled traders to buy and sell a plethora of financial instruments—currency, stocks, bonds, futures, debt, insurance contracts— free of the constraints that governments have placed on such transactions in the past. It did not matter which countries had issued the currency or financial instruments. This development increased wealth but distributed it unevenly. It also encouraged banks and other financiers to devote themselves to making money from manipulating money rather than to making money from producing things. As a result, Western economies focused increasingly on finance rather than manufacturing. Doing so created high-paying employment for some but eliminated a considerable number of manufacturing jobs. The availability of finance capital also encouraged governments to borrow money rather than raise taxes; taxes were politically unpopular, while borrowing saddled future generations—and shielded the current one—from the bills. Beyond the postponement of financial obligations, the mounting pile of debts rendered sovereign governments dependent on international bankers and vulnerable to a financial system over which they exercised little control.

Globalization and Neoliberalism

With globalization already in full swing, the European Union added to the speed and strength of phenomenon when in the Maastricht Treaty of 1992 its twelve members agreed to retire their national currencies and adopt a common currency known as the euro (see Map E.3). For the first several years after 1999, when the euro was introduced, the **Eurozone** seemed to operate smoothly, facilitating trade and reducing the costs of doing business among member states. By the early 2000s, many of Europe's leaders were convinced that the good times were here to stay. Even leftish politicians such as Tony Blair, who led the British Labour Party, and Gerhard Schröder of the German Social Democrats, whose parties had traditionally favored strong states, progressive taxes, and government intervention in the economy, embraced globalization and the "neoliberal" policies that had facilitated it: lower taxes (especially on corporations), reduced government expenditures, deregulation, unrestrained global finance, and relaxed trade restrictions. Blair, Schröder, and social democrats in other countries tried to combine neo-liberalism with social welfare, gambling that continued economic expansion would foster prosperity and reduce the need—and cost—of the social welfare benefits that their parties had long endorsed.

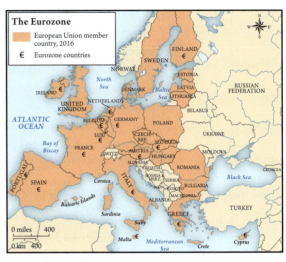

≡ **MAP E.3** The Eurozone

They also banked on the prospect of ampler revenues coming not from high rates of taxation but from the proceeds of economic expansion.

These hopes were largely fulfilled between the late 1990s and the mid-2000s, but dangers were built into the EU's neoliberal turn from the start. As we have seen, the creation of the European Central Bank (ECB) took monetary policy out of the hands of individual countries and deprived them of the ability to stimulate their economies by lowering interest rates during recessions. In addition, the EU required all countries adopting the euro to sign a Growth and Stability Pact that imposed stringent limits on budget deficits, inflation, and national debt. Countries that largely respected these limits found themselves unable to deploy deficit spending to boost their economies when unemployment spiked upward and recession loomed. Countries that ignored these limits tended to run up large public and private debts, as governments and businesses borrowed ever larger sums to keep their economies afloat.

Many commentators argued at the time that a common European monetary policy and EU-wide limits on deficits and inflation would work equitably only if EU countries were more integrated politically. Such integration would allow a European government to give economic aid to less advantaged member states without burdening them with unsustainable debt or forcing them to suffer the consequences of high interest rates decreed by the ECB. A strong economy such as Germany's might benefit from a tight monetary policy, but weaker ones inevitably suffered from the slower growth that high interest rates tended to produce.

The problem, as a series of referenda showed, was that the citizens of EU countries registered only minimal support for greater political integration. Without such integration, the weaker EU countries could not hope to receive significant financial aid from the stronger ones. Instead, the weaker states continued to borrow and to violate the limits on deficit spending. The resulting indebtedness, public as well as private, did not seem to matter in the early and mid-2000s, when credit was readily available. German banks were particularly eager to lend, since their country's excess of exports over imports placed a great deal of cash in their coffers.

The Financial Collapse of 2008 and the Great Recession

This ill-conceived system broke down, however, when the collapse of the United States' banking sector in 2008 spilled over into Europe. Banks and other financial institutions in EU countries had made extremely risky loans or invested in the same "toxic" assets—subprime mortgages, mortgage-backed securities, credit default swaps—that had poisoned their US counterparts. These banks, faced with worthless investments and insolvent borrowers, suddenly lost the ability to make loans to the governments and businesses that needed them to pay interest on debts, buy raw materials, and compensate their workers. The banking collapse thus rippled outward, paralyzing governments and businesses now deprived of the liquidity (money) that was their lifeblood. National economies, especially in the weakest countries—Greece, Portugal, Italy, and Spain—went into free fall. They could no longer pay the interest on their debts, and this, in turn, sent the big European lenders—particularly banks in Iceland, Britain, and Ireland—even further down the road to bankruptcy. By late 2008, credit had evaporated, and a great many governments, financial institutions,

≡ **Crisis of the Eurozone**. Referring ironically to the John Lennon song, Greek demonstrators protest the severe austerity measures imposed by the European Union.

and individual borrowers were left high and dry. Millions lost their homes and businesses, and unemployment began to soar. With household incomes down, tax receipts plummeted, leaving most EU countries, especially Greece, Portugal, Italy, and Spain, in difficult, even dire, economic straits.

In the relatively wealthy countries, governments stepped in to save the flailing banks. They legislated huge bailout packages, and in several cases, essentially nationalized (took over) the banks. These actions prevented a collapse of the European financial system, but at great cost to taxpayers, who paid for the bailouts, usually without being consulted. In effect, ordinary people, many of them already suffering from the 2008 crash, were now required to subsidize Europe's largest banks—and their highly compensated CEOs. The political fallout from this massive transfer of resources from the bottom to the top would be severe. People throughout Europe lost faith in their national leaders, who faced accusations that they had ranked the needs of banks and bankers above those of ordinary citizens. Most governments in office in 2008, whether of the right, left, or center, were ejected from power in the first elections following the crash of 2008.

Although the bailouts largely stabilized Europe's—and the world's—financial system, the powerful aftershocks of the 2008 crash left the major banks unable or unwilling to extend credit to the countries accustomed before 2008 to rolling over their loans (that is, paying off old loans with new ones). With no new loans coming in, the debt-ridden countries of southern Europe, in particular, faced the prospect of defaulting on their loans, which would have heaped new financial pressures on Europe's already ailing banks.

Under these dangerous circumstances, three international institutions—the ECB, European Commission, and International Monetary Fund (IMF)—stepped in to support the countries mired in debt. But in doing so, these institutions exacted a heavy price: "austerity." They required Portugal, Ireland, Italy, Greece, and Spain to drastically cut their budget deficits by reducing pension and welfare benefits, laying off government workers, slashing the minimum wage, and reducing subsidies to businesses and individuals.

These measures dramatically contracted the economies in question, producing the worst joblessness since the Great Depression of the 1930s. In Spain, overall unemployment reached 20 and youth joblessness 40 percent. Things were even direr in Greece, where the economy shrank to three-quarters of its pre-2008 size while overall unemployment topped 25 percent. By 2012, one-third of Greeks officially lived in poverty and tens of thousands resided on the streets. The situation was almost as bad in Italy, where economic output plummeted by 25 percent, and in the Baltic states, whose collective GDP dropped by 18 percent.

Critics of the EU-imposed austerity plans argued, with considerable justice, that they were counterproductive. Although the IMF and other agencies justified austerity as a way to reduce budget deficits and national debt, in several countries, austerity had the opposite effect. Economies contracted so much that tax revenues continued to plummet, and large budget deficits persisted—despite the sharp cuts to government-financed social services. Worse, the shrunken economies made it even more difficult for the Greek, Spanish, and Italian governments to repay their debts, which instead kept increasing.

Greece faced the direst situation, since even under the best circumstances, the inefficiency of its government and widespread tax evasion among its citizens kept the country in debt. By mid-2015, it became clear that the IMF, ECB, and European Commission would either have to forgive a substantial portion of Greece's debt or face a Greek default. The latter would probably force Greece to leave the Eurozone, setting a precedent that could encourage—or compel—other countries to leave as well, thus calling the Eurozone into question.

What made the situation in Greece, Italy, Spain, and Portugal seem even worse to its inhabitants was that several of the traditionally wealthy member nations recovered relatively quickly from the crash. By 2010, Germany was once again growing at the enviable rate of 4 percent per year, and the Scandinavian economies were expanding handsomely as well. In Poland, one of the newer members of the EU, a tiny banking system meant that it had been little effected by the financial collapse of 2008. And because Poland had retained its national currency rather than adopting the euro, its leaders enjoyed the freedom to devalue and indulge in deficit spending. Both projects succeeded in stimulating the economy, the former by making Poland's exports less expensive and the latter by putting more money in the hands of businesses and consumers. Poland never fell into recession and registered healthy growth in the early 2010s.

Much of the rest of the Eurozone began to recover in 2012, when the ECB lowered interest rates to near zero and printed money to prevent **deflation**, the devastating drop in prices that paralyzes an economy. When deflation sets in, consumers delay their purchases, knowing that prices will be lower next month or even next week. These delays, continually repeated, prevent businesses from selling their products, especially since when prices drop, wages drop as well. With less money coming in, many consumers cannot buy anything beyond basic necessities. Mario Draghi, president of the ECB, succeeded in preventing deflation, but his policies managed to create only modest growth in France, the United Kingdom, and several other key EU countries. Still, compared to Greece and Spain, France and the UK were doing well.

Changing Attitudes Toward the European Union

Even so, the EU was increasingly seen in virtually all member states as a distant, faceless bureaucracy. In 2004, about 50 percent of EU citizens expressed "trust in the European Union." By 2016, that number had dropped to only 35 percent, although since then, "trust" has trended slightly upward as most economies have improved. If the trend lines are similar in the various EU countries, some show less trust than others. In the UK, trust had dropped to 35 percent already in 2004, and it sank to just 19 percent in 2013 before recovering to 35 percent in 2017. In the Netherlands, by contrast, trust reached 64 percent in 2007 and dropped only to 42 percent in 2017.

Despite the relatively low numbers for trust, when European citizens are asked whether they support their countries' membership in the EU, the figures are much more positive. Across the EU as a whole, support held steady at an average of between 50 and 55 percent between 1993 and 2017. In mid-2018, the number endorsing their country's membership reached above 60 percent, on average, for the first time since 1991, when the then twelve members voted for free movement around the European Community. In general, since 2016, support for the basic ideas of the EU—a common currency, free movement of European citizens, and the establishment of a common defense, security, and foreign policy—has reached levels not seen in decades. (It should be added that support for these ideas drops when people are asked if they would agree to pay higher taxes to finance them.) Sixty percent back the common currency and 80 percent the free movement of EU citizens. Beyond the general economic gains registered since 2015, these improved numbers may represent a reaction against the turmoil surrounding Britain's efforts to leave the EU (see below) and the perceived threats to Europe from Putin and US President Donald Trump, who has expressed hostility to NATO and to the EU's policies on trade.

It is important to keep in mind that the better-than-50-percent support for membership in the EU represents averages, and averages can mask substantial variation within a given country. In fact, the citizens of most EU member states are divided between those who generally back the international organization and those who generally oppose it. This divide mirrors to some extent the split between those who have benefited from globalization and those harmed by the deindustrialization that globalization has produced. Critics of the EU—commentators, political organizations, and ordinary citizens skeptical of the European Union's benefits—have been dubbed "euro-skeptics."

Euro-skepticism has fueled the rise of "populist" parties, mostly on the right, but in Spain and Greece on the left as well. Populist parties claim to speak for "the people" as opposed to supposedly uncaring, incompetent, and self-interested experts and "elites." Each group, "people" and "elites," are depicted as if there were no significant differences within them. In addition, populists tend to champion the interests of small towns and rural regions, promote demagogic leaders, denounce immigration, and use anger as a political tool. Populists wrap themselves in the mantle of the nation, accusing their opponents of a "globalism" that favors foreigners over their own compatriots. In the 2010s, rightwing populists won national elections in Hungary and Poland and became the junior partners in Austria's right-of-center coalition government. Populism made significant gains in the United Kingdom, France, Germany, the Netherlands, and Italy, where in June 2018 they joined a shaky coalition government with the Five Star Movement, an anti-establishment organization. Originally opposed to both the euro and membership in the EU, Italy's populists, once in office, revised their views to say that they would work to change the Eurozone and the EU from within. With this change, they have heeded Italian public opinion, which, however hostile to the EU's traditional policies, favors continued membership in the organization. The same is true of most of Europe's other populist parties, whether of the right or the left: they have dropped earlier plans to lead their countries out of the Eurozone or the EU.

Although populists, for the most part, have not succeeded in winning national elections—Italy and Greece are the exceptions—they have played a key role in the decline of traditional parties of the right and the left. In the French presidential elections of 2017, both the socialist and the conservative candidates, whose parties had taken turns ruling France since 1981, were eliminated in

The Yellow Vest Movement. The "Yellow Vest" movement began in 2018 and was a working- and middle-class protest in France against high fuel prices, housing costs, and inequities in the nation's tax structure and the growing sense of a severe wealth imbalance in society. One national poll showed that as much as 83 percent of the population supported the protestors. The French demonstrations inspired similar movements from Portugal to Pakistan. By January 2019, ten French protestors had been killed and more than 1,800 injured. More than 1,000 police were wounded as well.

the first round of France's two-round presidential contest. In the second round, the National Front, a right-wing populist party led by Marine Le Pen, faced off against a new centrist party (France on the Move) assembled expressly for the election by Emmanuel Macron. Le Pen had never held any national office, and Macron's lone political experience was a short stint as minister of the economy under the previous socialist government. Although Macron won the election by a landslide, he has faced powerful protests from the **Yellow Vest** movement, so named for the emergency outerwear that all French drivers must keep in their cars. The Yellow Vests mainly represented disaffected voters from small towns and rural areas hit hard by globalization and unhappy with Macron's neoliberal policies.

In other EU countries—Germany, Austria, Britain, and Italy, among others—populist parties have siphoned votes away from traditional parties, especially social democrats (center-left) and Christian democrats (center-right). In the May 2019 elections to the European Parliament—Europe-wide elections typically exaggerate the political developments occurring within individual countries—the traditional parties lost considerable support. Those parties were widely seen as representing an EU status quo disliked on the left and the right. The big winners in these elections were intensely pro-European parties that nonetheless advocated major reforms within the union, especially stronger environmental policies, a clearer stance on immigration, and more democratic governance. The populist parties also did well in these elections, although not as well as expected. These nationalist organizations paradoxically promised to work together on a common European program, mainly to severely limit immigration and give individual countries more independence within the EU. They promised not to withdraw their countries from the union, but rather to transform it from within.

Brexit

The great exception to the general acceptance of the EU, however grudging in some quarters, is the United Kingdom, which in the 2010s became the ground zero of euro-skepticism. Because Britain had left its borders completely open to immigration from within the EU, people from the former communist countries flocked there in search of higher wages and more opportunities as soon as their countries were admitted to the union. The numbers were so large that British working people began to fear that the migrants would take their jobs or allow employers to reduce their pay. There is some evidence that the wage reductions, in particular, had taken place. Many Britons also worried that the demographic makeup of their country was changing too rapidly, and some said they no longer felt at home in their own homeland. Populist politicians intensified these fears by claiming, falsely, that immigrants would bring terrorism with them—terrorists turned out to be overwhelmingly British-born citizens—and that newcomers would monopolize the resources of the country's underfunded public services (welfare, national health, public housing, transportation).

In the 2014 elections to the European Parliament, Britain's anti-EU party, the United Kingdom Independence Party (UKIP), won a higher percentage of the vote than any other political organization. The UKIP's success put pressure on the two mainstream parties, Labor and Conservatives, to take a stand on continued membership in the EU. In the national elections of 2015, David Cameron, the Conservative leader and candidate for prime minister, promised that, if he won a majority, he would hold a referendum on membership in the EU. He personally favored remaining in the union and probably calculated that his prospective coalition partner, the pro-EU Liberal Democrats, would block the referendum. Unexpectedly, the Conservatives won an absolute majority and did not need to govern jointly with the Liberals. Cameron had miscalculated and now had no choice but to go ahead with the referendum, a vote either to Leave the EU or to Remain within it.

The campaign, quickly dubbed **Brexit** (for "British exit"), was fierce and marked by demagogy on both sides, although the Leavers' scare tactics proved more intense. The Conservatives split into pro-Leave and pro-Remain factions, with Cameron leading the forces to Remain. Labor, for its part, was divided as well, only here the split was between the party's members of Parliament, who overwhelmingly wanted to Remain, and the rank-and-file, who in their majority, sought to Leave. Labor's leader, Jeremy Corbyn, long identified with the most euro-skeptic faction of his party, seemed tacitly to back the campaign to Leave.

The referendum took place on June 23, 2016, and it resulted in a narrow victory for the Leavers, 51.9 to 48.1 percent. The big cities had voted strongly to Remain, while small towns and rural areas had voted to Leave. Younger, well-educated people wanted to Remain, while their older, less-educated counterparts wanted to Leave. These divisions roughly conformed to the split between the beneficiaries and victims of globalization. Ominously for national unity, the referendum had also separated England and Wales on the one hand from Scotland and Northern Ireland on the other (see Map E.4). The first two parts of the United Kingdom had voted to Leave, the latter pair to Remain. England and Wales possessed large "rust belts," where deindustrialization had left people unemployed or with low-paid work, while Scotland had long sought protection from English domination through membership in the EU. As for Northern Ireland, its Catholic population,

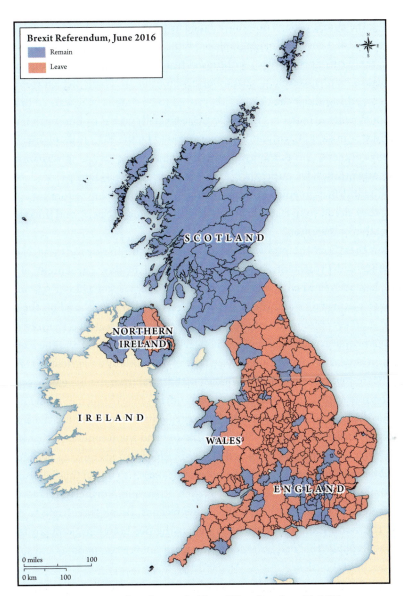

Brexit Referendum, June 2016
- Remain
- Leave

SCOTLAND

NORTHERN
IRELAND

IRELAND

WALES

ENGLAND

0 miles   100
0 km   100

≡ **MAP E.4**   Brexit referendum in the United Kingdom, June 23, 2016
(*NY Times*, May 24, 2019)

slightly less than half of the total, sided with the overwhelmingly Catholic population of the Republic of Ireland, a staunch member of the EU. The younger, well-educated Protestants of Northern Ireland also elected to Remain, giving the province a pro-Remain majority.

After the Brexit vote, Cameron resigned as prime minister, and Teresa May, a convert to the Leave campaign, replaced him. May and the EU leadership negotiated the terms of the British withdrawal from the union, agreeing to complete the British exit by March 29, 2019. But beyond this timetable, which would not be met, nothing about the negotiation proved to be simple. May wanted to retain certain benefits of membership in the EU, especially access to European markets and European capital, without being constrained by the EU's rules on migration, the environment, the economy, financial contributions to EU governance, and many other things. Unsurprisingly, this was unacceptable to Europe's leaders, who feared that if Britain enjoyed the benefits of EU membership without its obligations, they would soon face a Frexit, Italexit, Grexit, and Spexit and thus the disintegration of the union.

Then there was the problem of Northern Ireland. The peace there between Catholics and Protestants, achieved in the **Good Friday Agreement** of April 1998, had been hard-won, and its success turned in part on a closer relationship between the province and the Republic of Ireland next door—and on the possibility of an eventual union of the two. The relationship featured the free movement of people across the boundary between Northern Ireland and the Republic and a great deal of cooperation between the two, especially on agricultural policy, healthcare, and transportation. A British withdrawal from the EU would separate Northern Ireland from the Republic of Ireland, because the former would now be outside the EU and the latter inside. Such a separation would require the erection of a hard border between the Northern Ireland and the Republic so that import and export taxes could be collected on EU-produced goods moving between the Republic and Northern Ireland. The two political entities would thus be distanced economically and psychologically from each other, and Northern Ireland would be yoked more tightly to the UK. For these reasons, Brexit threatened to undermine the Good Friday Agreement as well as the ties between Northern Ireland and the Republic that had boosted the prosperity of the two peoples and soothed tensions between them.

Prime Minister May sought to paper over Brexit's Northern Ireland problem by proposing that the UK, including Northern Ireland, remain for an unspecified period inside a customs union with the EU and subject to its rules. This attempted compromise infuriated hardcore Brexiteers, who wanted a complete break with Europe, while it alienated advocates of remaining within the EU, for whom May's compromise did not go far enough. The result was a complete deadlock within the British Parliament, which could not muster a majority for any of the successive deals that May would propose. Finally, in May 2019, with no agreement on Brexit in sight, May announced her resignation as prime minister.

May's successor was the hardline Brexiteer Boris Johnson, a former mayor of London and foreign secretary. Johnson resolved to leave the EU, with or without a deal. When he too faced a deadlock in Parliament, he called for a new general election, which took place in December 2019. The balloting gave Johnson and the Conservatives a massive victory and a large majority in Parliament. The opposition Labour Party suffered its worst defeat since the 1980s. With Johnson and pro-Brexit Conservatives firmly in power, the United Kingdom formally withdrew from the European Union, although without fully resolving the issue of Northern Ireland and several other matters to be negotiated in the years to come. Brexit also clouded Scotland's relationship to the United Kingdom, since a large majority of Scots wanted to remain within the EU. In the wake of Johnson's election as prime minister, key leaders in Edinburgh called for Scottish independence from the UK.

Mass Immigration and the Refugee Crisis

A key reason for the effort to take Britain out of the European Union was, as we have seen, the absence of restrictions on immigration from other EU countries. Most of the UK's counterparts blocked migration from new EU countries for seven years after they joined the union. Britain was doubly attractive to immigrants, because globalization had made English the world's most common second language and young Poles and Hungarians already had some facility with it before crossing the English Channel. The result was an explosion of immigration from Eastern Europe, especially Poland. In 2001, about 58,000 people of Polish origins lived in Britain. Ten years later, the number had soared to 678,000, more than a tenfold increase. The British economy was booming in the early and mid-2000s, and not only did it seem capable of absorbing these immigrants; it needed them to fill jobs in healthcare and other areas where labor was scarce. Still, in the least prosperous parts of the country, immigrants were said to take jobs from British citizens and to push their wages down.

After the limits on intra-EU immigration expired in the other wealthy European countries, they saw similar developments: EU citizens flocked from east to west and south to north in search of jobs. Meanwhile, business owners in several of the wealthier EU countries moved factories and other enterprises to Eastern Europe, where labor costs were considerably lower than at home. The resulting loss of jobs in Western Europe turned many working people there against their governments and especially against the EU.

At first, crowds of people from Germany and Austria, which also promised to admit large numbers, enthusiastically greeted the refugees at train stations in Munich and Vienna and offered them food and clothing. Germans and Austrians had been moved by media reports of the migrants' harrowing escape from their war-ravaged countries, often with young children in tow. Leaders of the two countries doubtless also wanted to show that no vestiges of Nazi-era inhumanity remained. Germany, in particular, moved quickly to integrate the newcomers, giving them food and shelter and teaching them German.

But it was unrealistic to think that a single country, even one as wealthy as Germany, could quickly integrate a million newcomers, virtually none of whom spoke German or had any familiarity with German culture or with its dominant religions, Lutheranism and Catholicism. It is true that Germany had admitted a fair number of Turkish "guest workers" between the early 1960s and early 1970s, but only a total of about 375,000, or less than 30,000 a year, remained in the country. And Germany had actively recruited these workers, deemed essential to the country's booming economy, rather than accommodating them as a humanitarian gesture.

The more significant immigrant experience for Germany was the influx of German citizens and ethnic Germans expelled from Eastern Europe and the Soviet Union in 1945–1946. But this phenomenon was utterly different from the migration of 2015. The Western and Soviet forces that occupied Germany after the war required the defeated country to admit the 12–14 million expellees. And in any event, it was mainly the British and American occupying authorities who provided for them. By the time the Federal Republic of Germany and the German Democratic Republic were created in 1949, most of these forced immigrants had already established themselves in one of these countries. This was a huge number to accommodate in a country recovering from nearly five years of war, but it helped enormously that a large percentage spoke German, understood German culture, and had been raised as Christians. The mostly Muslim immigration of 2015 and beyond posed a completely different set of challenges.

It did not take long for German citizens to express hostility to the newcomers, increasingly seen as alien and dangerous. After a group of immigrant men molested and sexually attacked German women in Cologne on New Year's Eve 2015, opposition to the Muslim newcomers exploded on social media and in the German press. The Cologne police had mishandled the situation, but even so, it was troubling. Anti-immigrant organizations, and especially the Alternative for Germany, a far-right political party, denounced Merkel for having allowed so many refugees to settle in their country.

Merkel got the message and tried to convince other EU countries to accept some of the migrants. Hungary, Poland, Slovakia, and the Czech Republic flatly refused, while these and other EU nations declined even to contribute funds to provide for the displaced people. Finally, Merkel essentially bribed Turkey to admit many of the refugees who had initially settled in Germany, Austria, and elsewhere, but who were no longer welcome there.

By 2016, the flow of refugees from the Middle East, Afghanistan, and North Africa had subsided to some extent, but given the ongoing conflicts in these places, the EU will continue to attract large numbers of people fleeing for their lives. Others will come in search of jobs and other opportunities denied them at home. Clearly, no country can accommodate an unlimited number of immigrants, but Europe has had to face the fact that, like the United States, it exerts a powerful pull on people from Asia, Africa, and Latin America seeking a better life. Whether the EU can find a humane way to manage this situation, as Angela Merkel said in 2018, stands as one of the West's most "vital questions." It will shape the future of Europe's experiment in multinational, democratic cooperation.

The COVID-19 Pandemic

Between 2012 and 2018, several European leaders tried to block the entry of migrant people by closing borders and preventing them from landing on Greek and Italian shores. To some, the refugees seemed to threaten Europe's way of life. But beginning in the winter of 2020, a new presence on the continent—as elsewhere in the world—threatened life itself. A novel, microscopic strand of genetic material, a deadly pathogen called a "coronavirus," settled into the European environment and made a great many people sick. The virus takes its name from the corona, or crown-like shape it reveals under a microscope. Its official medical name is COVID-19 (CO for corona, VI for virus, D for disease, and 19 for the year in which it emerged). Coronaviruses are zoonotic diseases, which means they take root in animal populations but can jump to human beings. This is what happened with COVID-19, as with two earlier coronaviruses. The first was Severe Acute Respiratory Syndrome (SARS), which infected humans in 2002, having been transmitted by civet cats. The second was Middle East Respiratory Syndrome (MERS), which may have developed in camels and spread to humans in 2012.

COVID-19 emerged in Wuhan, China, a large city in the center of the country, in December 2019. Over the next three months, it spread to every continent except Antarctica and to more than 200 countries. In March 2020, the World Health

Organization (WHO) officially labeled COVID-19 a pandemic, an epidemic disease that has spread across an exceptionally large geographical area. The WHO's announcement was late, since the virus had already circled the globe weeks earlier. When the pandemic reached Europe in the late winter of 2020, Italy quickly became the continent's most severely affected country, with about 225,000 cases as of mid-May, compared to China's (reported) 83,000 and 1.5 million in the United States. On March 19, Italy surpassed China in the number of deaths (3,405) from the disease. Other European countries with large numbers of cases included Germany with 177,000 and France with 180,000. These numbers likely understate the incidence of the disease, because test kits had were in limited supply.

Since there was no known cure for the disease or vaccine against it, the main way to prevent its spread involved **"social distancing,"** discouraging people from congregating in groups in which this extremely contagious disease could spread. The consequences of social distancing quickly became dire: bars and restaurants shuttered, sporting events canceled, schools and universities closed, and people forbidden to travel—or even to leave their homes. These measures dramatically disrupted national economies by cutting the production of goods and the delivery of services and by throwing people out of work. Adding to the misery, the disruption of fragile supply chains unequipped, in some cases, to produce goods for consumers as opposed to businesses, or stretching uncertainly to China, led to hoarding and shortages of food and essential supplies.

Europe's welfare states helped alleviate the economic distress, although even before the coronavirus crisis they lacked the resources to cover all their citizens' basic needs. In the wake of the coronavirus, the greatest social welfare problem became the overtaxing of hospitals and medical systems, which had too few beds for patients sick with the disease and a scarcity of test kits to determine who had contracted it. Most ominously, hospitals had inadequate numbers of the ventilators needed to treat Acute Respiratory Distress Syndrome (ARDS), a lung failure that the coronavirus can cause and from which patients can die. As this book goes to press, the number of new COVID-19 infections has subsided in many countries, although the overall number of cases and deaths continues to rise. Public health officials hope that social distancing will continue to slow the increase and moderate future waves of the disease while buying time for researchers to devise effective treatments and eventually a vaccine. In their efforts to contend with the disease, governments assumed a wartime stance; their actions, however justified, constrained the personal liberties to which Europeans have long been accustomed and raised questions about the free movement of people and goods that has been the hallmark of both the EU and the globalized world.

KEY TERMS

Brexit *748*

Chechnya *732*

deflation *744*

Eurozone *740*

globalization *738*

Good Friday Agreement
(1998) *750*

Great Recession (2008) *738*

Orange Revolution *736*

social distancing *756*

Yellow Vest *747*

For digital learning resources, please go to **https://www.oup.com/he/berenson2e**.
Turn to the back of the book to see the list of primary sources and writing exercises
provided in the accompanying *Sources and Guided Writing Exercises for Europe in the
Modern World*

Glossary

Note: The number at the end of each definition indicates the chapter in which the term is discussed.

95 Theses Martin Luther's ninety-five statements of faith questioning the doctrine of the Church, including the sale of indulgences, presented in 1517. (1)

Absolutism Political theory that rulers possess complete and total authority over their realms and subjects. (3)

agricultural revolution Innovations in farming techniques that resulted in increased productivity in the seventeenth and eighteenth centuries, beginning in the Netherlands. These innovations included the planting of forage crops on fields formerly left fallow and, in places, the consolidation of smaller farms into larger, more efficient farms. (6)

Anglicanism England's official version of Protestantism, established by Queen Elizabeth and embodied by the Church of England. (1–3)

animistic Relating to Aristotle's description of natural phenomena as resembling living things in having goals and aspirations and in being motivated to reach a particular state. (4)

apartheid Racial segregation and discrimination enforced through legislation, as practiced by South Africa against its black population. (14)

assignats Paper money created by the French parliament in 1789 to pay off France's debts. Lacking backing, the value of the assignats plummeted, becoming essentially zero by 1796. (5)

astrolabe Astronomical instrument introduced to European seafarers via Muslim Spain during the Middle Ages. The astrolabe can be used to measure the altitude above the horizon of a celestial body, to identify stars or planets, and to determine latitude. (2)

Axis Powers The coalition founded by Germany, Italy, and Japan (and later including Bulgaria, Romania, and Hungary) in the Second World War. (13)

balance of power Political theory embodied by the Treaty of Westphalia in 1648 that the object of statecraft in Europe should be to assure that no single country, kingdom, or empire should be allowed to dominate the continent. (1)

Balfour Declaration The 1917 declaration by British Foreign Minister Arthur Balfour promising a national home for the Jewish people in Palestine. (10)

barometer A device invented by Evangelista Torricelli that measures the pressure of air. (4)

Bartolomé de las Casas Sixteenth-century Dominican friar whose account of the atrocities committed by Spanish colonists in the New World—*A Short Account of the Destruction of the Indies*—helped to improve Spain's treatment of indigenous peoples. (2)

Bastille A once-notorious prison for political prisoners in Paris, stormed by insurgents on July 14, 1789. (5)

Battle of Britain A series of air attacks by Nazi Germany on Britain, which occurred between August and November 1940. The Battle of Britain was supposed to knock out Britain's air defenses and hurt civilian morale, but failed at both. (13)

Battle of the Bulge The battle in 1944–1945 in which the Allies stopped the last-ditch advance of the German army in the Ardennes region of Europe. (13)

Berlin Wall The wall built by East Germany in 1961 to divide the city of Berlin and prevent East German citizens from escaping to the West; it was torn down in 1989. (14)

bishoprics Religious jurisdictions of the Catholic Church under the supervision of a bishop. (Introduction)

Blitzkrieg A "lightning attack" by the Germans at the beginning of the Second World War. Hitler's Blitzkrieg against France was designed to entrap French and British soldiers and bring a quick end to the war. (13)

Bloody Sunday A demonstration of workers demanding better pay and working conditions before the tsar's palace in St. Petersburg in January 1905. It turned bloody when police fired on the march. (11)

Boer War The war fought from 1898 to 1902 in South Africa between the Boer settlers and the British Empire that extended British control in the region. (9)

bottleneck A point of congestion in a production sequence in which one stage of the sequence is incapable of processing the work of the prior stage in a timely fashion, or in which one stage of the sequence is incapable of supplying the next stage in a timely fashion. (6)

Bretton Woods A meeting of the major nations of the world in 1944 that replaced the gold standard with a new arrangement that pegged all currencies to the dollar at initially fixed rates of exchange, although these rates could be modified. The system began to fail in the mid-1960s as the US economy weakened thanks to trade deficits and the high costs of the Vietnam War. (15)

British Commonwealth of Nations An organization of the predominately white colonies of Great Britain, formed after the end of the First World War. (13)

Brusilov offensive A massive offensive against Austrian forces launched by Russia in June 1916. Germany was compelled to reinforce the Austrian army, and Russia is considered to have won the engagement, but at the cost of a million casualties. (10)

business cycles Regular periods of expansion and contraction in an industrial economy. These cycles raised and lowered employment as well as the overall economic fortunes of a large number of people. (6)

capitulations Agreements to a set of special conditions. The Ottoman Empire agreed to capitulations that gave special commercial privileges and reduced taxation to Western European residents of Ottoman cities. (6)

Carlist Wars A series of civil wars in Spain from 1833 to 1876 that began with a conflict over succession to the Spanish throne between the supporters of Carlos, the royalist brother of the late Ferdinand VII, and the supporters of the infant heir Isabella and her mother Queen Maria Cristina. Carlists were traditionalists and their opponents liberals and republicans. (7)

Central Powers The coalition of Germany, Austria-Hungary, and the Ottoman Empire in the First World War. (10)

centrifugal force The outward force on a body moving around a rotating center. Newton explored the relationship between centrifugal force and gravity. (4)

Charter 77 Published criticism of the Czech government, written by Václav Havel and a group of Czech intellectuals. They criticized the government for not living up to the human rights provisions of the Helsinki Accords. (15)

Chartism A workers' movement in Britain that sought, in the 1830s and 1840s, to enact the "People's Charter" designed to achieve electoral reform and make Britain the most democratic country in the world. (7)

Chechnya A small landlocked region in southwestern Russia between the Black and Caspian Seas; Chechnyan separatists advocate for an independent state. (Epilogue)

Cheka The secret political police established by the Soviet government during the Russian Civil War to kill, imprison, or exile its foes; it was rebranded as the GPU in 1922. (11)

Christian Democrats Center or center-right political parties initially with explicit ties to the Catholic Church. Christian Democratic parties held power consistently in Italy, West Germany, and Austria, and were popular in Belgium and the Netherlands beginning in the mid-twentieth century. (14)

Civil Constitution of the Clergy French Decree of 1790 that subordinated the Catholic Church to the

that conducted trade (mostly in textiles and spices) in South and Southeast Asia. It was disbanded in 1799. The VOC was one of the world's first publicly traded companies. (2)

East India Company (EIC) Joint-stock company, founded in England in 1600, that conducted trade in the Indian Ocean region. At the height of its power, the EIC controlled large parts of India. It was disbanded in 1874. (2)

economic liberalism Doctrine holding that the government should play as little role as possible in the economic sphere. (6)

economic miracle Term used to describe the extraordinarily rapid economic growth, especially in Germany, following the Second World War. (14)

economic nationalism Encouraging the purchase of a nation's own products, especially via tariffs. Economic nationalism became popular in the late nineteenth century with the growth of industrial competition among the various European nations. (9)

Edict of Nantes A decree establishing religious toleration for Protestants issued by King Henry IV of France in 1598. The Edict made France one of the few European countries to allow both Protestants and Catholics to worship legally. When Louis XIV revoked the Edict in 1685, a great many Huguenots left the country. (1, 3)

Edict of Worms A decree issued by Holy Roman Emperor Charles of Hapsburg in 1521 after Martin Luther's speech at the Diet of Worms, which sentenced Luther to death as a heretic and banned his writings. (1)

El Niño A weather pattern that affects the equatorial Pacific region and beyond every few years, characterized by the appearance of unusually warm water off northern Peru and Ecuador, typically in late December. (3)

ellipse An oval shape; the term was used by Tycho Brahe to describe the shape of planetary orbits. (4)

émigrés Individuals who have left one country for another. This term surfaced during the French Revolution to refer to opponents of the revolution who had left the country. (5)

Enlightenment The body of philosophical writings of the eighteenth century which denied that God had established the parameters of social, political, and religious life and asserted that human beings could shape society, government, and religion for themselves. (4)

Epidemic A disease that is actively spreading and is out of control.

Estates General France's kingdom-wide representative body. It consisted of three chambers—one each for the clergy, the nobility, and the commoners. Louis XVI agreed to convene the long-dormant Estates General in 1789 to address the kingdom's serious financial and political problems. (5)

ethnic cleansing The effort to remove an ethnic minority from a region through intimidation, violence, and murder. (15)

euro The common currency of the European Union adopted as a result of the Maastricht Treaty of 1992; it replaced national currencies such as the franc, mark, and lira. (15)

European Coal and Steel Community Europe's first attempt at an integrated economy, founded in 1951. It united six European nations in an attempt to aid their common recovery from the Second World War. (14)

European Economic Community (EEC) The European common market, created in 1957, that envisaged the gradual reduction of tariff barriers and the ultimate establishment of a free trade zone; it brought greater political and economic unity to Europe. (14)

European Union The successor of the European Economic Community, the EU was officially founded in 1992 with the Treaty of Maastricht, when member states adopted a common currency and governmental structure. The euro was designed to promote trade and economic growth, and some EU members hoped it would prevent a reunified Germany from dominating the continent politically or economically. (15)

Eurozone The group of the European Union member states that share a common currency (the euro) and abide by the monetary policies of the European Central Bank and agree to fiscal restraint. (Epilogue)

evangelicalism A term meaning "bringing good news" used to describe the religious movement sparked by Martin Luther, which would later be called Lutheranism. (1)

extraterritoriality Sometimes shortened to "extrality." In diplomacy, the practice of exempting resident citizens or subjects of a country from the laws of that country; diplomatic immunity is a form of extraterritoriality. In Japan until 1899 and China until 1943, the practice was a centerpiece of the "unequal treaties" and the "treaty ports" that benefited the Western powers. In China the exemptions were extended to include territorial concessions and ultimately the Chinese converts of Christian missionaries. (8)

factories Establishments for traders conducting business in a foreign country. (2)

factory A building in which manufactured goods are mass-produced. Arkwright's mill established in Cromford in 1776 is an example of a factory, as are the many mills that proliferated afterward. (6)

fascism An authoritarian and nationalistic form of right-wing government that uses intimidation and violence to win electoral contests and suppress opposition. (12)

feminism An ideology and movement that promotes the social, political, and economic rights of women and their equality to men. (7)

Final Solution The attempt to eliminate through murder the entire Jewish population of Europe. The Nazis committed genocide by shooting more than a million people and dumping their bodies in mass graves, by herding millions more into lethal ghettoes, and by confining them in death camps, where more than three million were asphyxiated with poison gas. (13)

finance capitalism An economic arrangement pioneered in Germany in the late nineteenth century in which large banks entered into de facto partnerships with key industrial concerns. The banks loaned large sums to these concerns and in exchange were given seats on their boards of directors. (9)

First International The International Working Men's Association, founded by Karl Marx and numerous other European radicals in London in 1864; it held that the working classes must emancipate themselves through their own independent efforts rather than through alliances with middle-class reformers. (8)

Five-Year Plans A series of plans outlined by Stalin for the development of the Soviet Union. The first Five-Year Plan (1928–1932) focused on iron and steel production. (11)

forage crops Crops such as grasses, alfalfa, sainfoin, and clover that are planted on a field that otherwise would have been left fallow. Livestock then graze on these crops and fertilize the fields with their manure. (6)

Fourteen Points A series of postwar goals issued by US President Woodrow Wilson in 1918. (10)

Free French The fighting force created in 1940 by General Charles de Gaulle, who had exiled himself to London. Initially, the Free French forces worked to liberate France's colonies from the pro-German government of Vichy France. Beginning in 1943, the Free French participated in the liberation of Europe from its Nazi occupiers. African soldiers comprised a large percentage of the Free French forces. (13)

Fronde Uprising in France beginning in 1648 in which top noblemen turned against Mazarin, the young Louis XIV, and his mother Anne to protest high taxation and arbitrary rule. (3)

Gastarbeiter Guest workers in Germany, many of whom were Turkish. They were allowed to live and work in Germany but could not gain German citizenship. (Epilogue)

gender The socially constructed roles, behaviors, and characteristics attributed to women and men and commonly seen as given by nature to each of the two biological sexes. (4)

genocide The purposeful attempt to exterminate an entire racial or ethnic group. The term was invented in 1944 to describe the Holocaust, the Nazi attempt to wipe out the Jews of Europe. (13)

Gestapo The secret political police of the Nazi Party, created by Hermann Göring in 1933. (12)

ghettos Parts of a city in which members of a disfavored group (originally Jews) take up residence, either by custom, economic necessity, or force. (Introduction)

Girondins A faction of the Jacobin Club that seceded to form its own group under the leadership of

Jacques Brissot. The faction supported Louis XVI's call for war against Austria and opposed the execution of the king. (5)

glasnost A policy of openness to discussion of political and economic matters initiated in the Soviet Union by Gorbachev. (15)

globalization The international, planet-wide process of economic, political, and cultural integration and interdependence. (8, Epilogue)

Glorious Revolution of 1688–1689 Political transformation engineered by Parliament's Whig leaders that deposed James II and anointed William and Mary as joint rulers of England, Scotland, and Ireland. It barred Catholics from the throne, strengthened the powers of Parliament, and limited the powers of the monarch. (3)

gold standard The system of using a set price for gold as the standard for valuing currency. Holders of paper currency had the right to convert paper currency into gold at the set price, and all international currencies had a fixed relationship to one another based on their respective fixed values in gold. (12)

Great Depression (1929–1936) The global economic crisis that followed the crash of the New York Stock Exchange on October 29, 1929, and resulted in massive unemployment and economic misery worldwide. (12)

Great Recession The result of the collapse of the US banking system in 2008. European banks failed as well, and governments went into debt bailing them out and paying welfare and unemployment benefits to the victims of the crisis. The EU and other institutions were forced to support newly shaky governments but required austerity measures in return. (Epilogue)

Great Terror Brutal efforts, beginning with show trials in 1936, by Joseph Stalin to eliminate anyone he considered an enemy of the Soviet Union. (11)

Great Trouble Also known as the "Time of Troubles," it was a time of social and political unrest between the death of Tsar Fedor I in 1598 and the accession of Michael I in 1613, which established the Romanov dynasty. (3)

guilds Professional associations dedicated to protecting the interests of a particular trade or monopolizing a production process. (Introduction)

Gulag The governmental agency created in 1930 in the Soviet Union to manage the forced labor camps where rebellious peasants and political dissidents were sent. (11)

Helsinki Accords A formal recognition of detente, the Accords made permanent the borders of Europe established after the Second World War. They also bound all signatories to respect human rights; the failure to do so fueled dissident movements in various Soviet-bloc countries. (14)

Holy Alliance Coalition of Austria, Prussia, and Russia established by Metternich in 1815 to intervene in the affairs of sovereign states deemed vulnerable to revolution and likely to spread social and political upheaval beyond their borders. (7)

home rule The advocacy of a large measure of administrative autonomy for Ireland within the British Empire between the 1880s and 1914. (9)

Huguenot A term for French Calvinists, engaged in bloody conflict with Catholics in sixteenth-century France. (1)

Humanism An educational movement of the Renaissance that cultivated young men for careers in business and public engagement by giving them broad training in literature, history, mathematics, and the arts, the sources of which were the great writers and statesmen of ancient Greece and Rome. (Introduction)

human rights The notion that a set of fundamental rights—especially the freedom from servitude—applies to all human beings without exception. (5)

incandescent filament lamp The electric light bulb, invented at the same time by Thomas Edison and Joseph Swan in 1879. (9)

Indian Rebellion An 1857 rebellion in India against the rule of the East India Company that resulted in Britain's formal colonization of India. (9)

indulgences A pardon of sins by the Catholic Church that shortened a person's time in purgatory; these were merited by a spontaneous act of charity or by payments to the Church. The practice was criticized by Martin Luther in his 95 Theses. (1)

Industrial Revolution The advent of mechanized mass production that began in Britain in the mid-eighteenth century. Beginning with cotton textiles, the Industrial Revolution vastly increased productivity and made Britain the "workshop of the world."(6)

informal empire An empire "ruled" by means of economic domination rather than outright colonization. The term particularly refers to the British Empire until the late nineteenth century. (9)

intelligentsia The Russian term for the educated—and often highly alienated and radical—elite. (11)

intendants Royal representatives first sent by Cardinal Mazarin into the French provinces to attempt to enhance the king's power and win the support of local elites for his policies. (2)

internal combustion engine A device that mixes a fuel, often gasoline, with air to create power. (9)

Irish Potato Famine The mass starvation caused by a parasite that attacked Europe's potato crop, 1845–1849. The effect of the parasite was particularly vicious in Ireland because Irish peasants made the potato their chief source of food. At least one million Irish people died, and a million more emigrated. (7)

Iron Curtain The imaginary line separating communist Eastern Europe from the rest of the continent. The term refers to the fact that, especially at the beginning of the Cold War, there was little commerce or communication between the two halves of Europe. (15)

Jacobins A political club formed in Paris in 1790 that supported a democratic republic, dominated the Convention, and called for the execution of the king. (5)

Jansenists A group of reform-minded French Catholics who criticized the luxury and worldliness of official Catholicism. (5)

Jesuits Members of the Society of Jesus religious order founded in 1540. Jesuits sought to provide a high-quality Catholic education and combat Protestantism. The order was dedicated to the strength and glory of the Church and became central to the Catholic reformation and Counter-Reformation. (1)

joint-stock company A company jointly owned by its shareholders and managed by a board of directors, such as the Dutch East India Company. (2)

June Days A Parisian uprising of workers in June 1848 triggered by the closing of the National Workshops; the fierce fighting left thousands dead or injured. (7)

"justification by faith alone" Religious doctrine advanced by Martin Luther, which held that in order to achieve salvation, all individuals had to do was have faith in God's goodness and mercy, while recognizing their inherent sinfulness. (1)

Kristallnacht The "Night of Broken Glass," November 9, 1938. On that night, the Nazi government unleashed widespread attacks on Jewish businesses, synagogues, and homes. These attacks left 100 dead and 30,000 condemned to concentration camps. Many of Germany's remaining Jews left the country, just as Hitler had wanted them to do. (12)

kulaks Russia's best-off peasants, they were deemed by Stalin to represent a threat to his regime. A great many alleged kulaks became the victims of the forced agricultural collectivization of the early 1930s. (11)

Kulturkampf Otto von Bismarck's "cultural war" of the 1870s against Catholicism in Germany. (9)

League of Nations The international organization created after the First World War to peacefully resolve conflicts between countries. (10)

levée en masse The French revolutionary conscription (August 1793) of all males into the army and the use of women and children in the interests of national defense. (5)

Levellers Radical political group during the English Civil War that demanded civil rights and religious toleration. (3)

liberalism An ideology that promotes the ideas of political, social, and economic liberty; liberalism opposes tyranny and embraces the virtues of education, self-reliance, and individual initiative. (7)

Little Ice Age The period between the late sixteenth and early eighteenth centuries when global temperatures cooled. The effects of the Little Ice Age exacerbated the political, religious, and social conflicts of the seventeenth century. (3)

living space (German *Lebensraum*), The territory in Eastern Europe into which Hitler wanted Germany to expand, both to provide more living space for the German people and to bolster its food supply. In that way, the supposedly superior Germans would displace the supposedly inferior Eastern Europeans. (13)

Long Depression Worldwide economic depression lasting from about 1873 to 1893, when declining prices, interest rates, and profits hurt small farms and small businesses in Europe. The Long Depression resulted from a relative decline in the supply of money and an oversupply, relative to demand, of food products and other goods, thanks to sharply reduced transport costs and mass production on a global scale. (9)

Luddism A movement in the early nineteenth century in which artisans protested against and attacked machines and the factory system, which they saw as a threat to their livelihoods. (6)

Maastricht Treaty The 1992 treaty in which twelve members of the European Union agreed, among other things, to retire their national currencies and adopt the euro. (15)

Maginot Line A string of border fortifications built to protect France from Germany in the aftermath of the First World War. It failed to prevent France from falling to the German army in 1940. (13)

magnates Wealthy and influential individuals, either in business or in landed estates. (3)

mandates Quasi-colonies created by the League of Nations, which mandated key territories of the defunct Ottoman Empire to Britain and France. (10)

march on Rome An attempted Fascist show of strength led by Benito Mussolini's Blackshirt squads, March 22–29, 1922. King Victor Emmanuel III refused to use the army to defuse the march, and instead made Mussolini prime minster, confirming his rise to power in Italy. (12)

Marshall Plan A US initiative, formally known as the European Recovery Program, to boost war-torn European economies by offering European countries significant grants of cash and American goods, which could be consumed or sold. (14)

Marxism The economic, political, and social theory advanced by Karl Marx, which defined history as a struggle between two opposing social classes and the end of history as the victory of the working class over the bourgeoisie. That victory would place the means of production in the workers' hands and ultimately lead to a classless society. (8)

Marxism-Leninism Lenin's theory of Marxism, tailored to the Russian situation. It denied the orthodox Marxist idea that Russia needed to pass through a bourgeois capitalist phase before a socialist revolution could be successful and insisted on the essential role of a centrally controlled vanguard party of professional revolutionaries. (11)

Marxists Individuals who subscribe to the politics and ideas of Karl Marx. (11)

mass A standard church service of the Catholic Church. (1)

May '68 A month of unrest that began with a student rebellion at the University of Paris and spread throughout French society. The student rebels and their counterparts among young workers turned against all forms of authority, including that of the traditional left-wing parties and unions, which supported the rebellion tepidly at best. After a month of often violent protests, and even more violence from the police, much of the French public wearied of the chaos and endorsed President de Gaulle in a landslide vote. (14)

mechanistic Relating to a view advanced by seventeenth-century philosophers that the natural world worked by purely mechanical processes which scientists could discover and understand, and that inanimate objects possessed no will, intention, or desire, as Aristotelians had long believed. (4)

mercantilism An economic theory prominent in the seventeenth and eighteenth centuries that held that international trade was a zero-sum game in which the wealth gained by one state necessarily came at the expense of the others. Under mercantilism, individual states tried to gain monopolies over trade in certain commodities and certain regions; they forbade their colonies to trade with other countries, prevented foreign ships from transporting their goods, and subsidized exports. (2)

monarchies Forms of government in which one person holds all executive power and usually gains his or her position by inheriting it. Monarchs often govern in collaboration with parliaments and in harmony with established laws. (4)

Munich Pact The agreement in 1938 between Germany, Britain, and France that allowed Germany to occupy the western regions of Czechoslovakia (the Sudetenland) in exchange for Hitler's promise, later violated, to leave the rest of Czechoslovakia intact. (13)

mustard gas A poisonous gas that seared bodily tissue, destroyed the lungs, and made people blind. (10)

Napoleonic Code The body of civil law established by Napoleon in 1804. This form of law was grounded in statute rather than precedent and applied to a great many realms of life. In family law, the Napoleonic Code subordinated women to men and treated married women as minors. (5)

national self-determination One of the major principles enshrined in the peace treaties that ended the First World War. It gave people who claimed the same national identity the right to have nation-states of their own. Under this principle, the defunct Austrian and Ottoman Empires dissolved into a variety of often weak nation-states. (10)

nationalism An ideology that gives supreme importance to membership in the nation, that is, in a bounded community shaped by language, culture, history, geography, and, in some cases, religion and ethnicity. (7)

natural law The set of rules that derive from qualities inherent to human beings, because either God or nature had made them that way. Natural law is often contrasted with human-made or "positive" law, the laws developed by communities, societies, or states. (4)

Nazism A set of political beliefs associated with Hitler and the Nazi Party in Germany, including antisemitism, authoritarian rule, and extreme nationalism. (12)

Nazi-Soviet Pact The 1939 nonaggression agreement between Germany and the Soviet Union, also called the Molotov–Ribbentrop Pact, which also secretly set the terms for the division of Poland, the Baltic states, and Finland between the two countries. (13)

New Economic Policy (NEP) An economic policy established by Lenin in 1921 that encouraged peasants to produce food by allowing them to sell it on the market and earn profits from those sales. NEP denationalized the country's small-scale industry and trade, ended grain requisitions, and restored key features of capitalism. (11)

new imperialism The extensive colonial conquests by the major European states in the late nineteenth and early twentieth centuries. (9)

New Model Army Fighting force created by England's Parliament to counter the royalist army raised by King Charles I in the English Civil War. (3)

New Woman Term coined for the emancipated women who entered the workforce, the public sphere, or both. The New Woman sought equal standing with men. (9)

newsreel A film selection of news and current events presented as part of a program in movie theaters; it was a precursor of televised news programs. (12)

no-man's-land The space between the two opposing front lines in World War I and the terrain on which offensives took place; it was studded with barbed wire, observation and listening posts, grenade-throwing positions, and machine-gun nests. (10)

nobles of the robe Nobles in France who gained their titles mainly by purchasing them from the king. Robe nobles served as magistrates and in high government positions. Many robe nobles earned the right to pass their titles to their heirs, thus enabling them to resemble, in certain ways, nobles of the sword. (2)

nobles of the sword France's traditional hereditary nobility, individuals who derived their wealth from the land and their prestige from their role as defenders of the realm. Just as robe nobles came to resemble sword nobles, so the opposite was also true, as sword nobles accepted offices and became courtiers to the king. (2)

North Atlantic Treaty Organization (NATO) The organization created in 1949 by Western leaders as an alliance for mutual defense against the Soviet Union. (14)

Nuremberg Trials A series of trials that prosecuted Nazis accused of what would later be called crimes against humanity; they took place 1945–1946 in the German city of Nuremberg. (14)

oligarchs A small group of men who became multibillionaires when they acquired Russia's valuable commodities industries such as oil and gas after the downfall of the Soviet Union. Most of them were close confidants of Russian president Boris Yeltsin, and their resources helped keep him in power. (15)

Oliver Cromwell English general who led the parliamentary army during the English Civil War. Cromwell made himself England's dictator after the execution of Charles I. (3)

Operation Barbarossa The Germany military campaign of 1941 to invade the Soviet Union and acquire territory for an expanded Germany. (13)

Opium Wars Two wars resulting from a trade dispute between China and Great Britain over China's efforts to curtail the sale of opium by Great Britain. The first Opium War took place 1839–1842 and the second 1856–1860. (8)

Orange Revolution Widespread protests by young pro-Western demonstrators in Ukraine in 2004 against the rigged election of Viktor Yanukovych; the election was annulled and a new election held. (Epilogue)

Organization for European Economic Cooperation Created to administer the Marshall Plan, the US-led effort to rebuild Europe after the Second World War. Marshall Plan money was primarily used to reduce taxes and increase social benefits, improving the economies of European nations, especially Great Britain, France, and West Germany. (14)

Pandemic An epidemic that spreads far beyond its geographical source and affects an entire country and even the world. It sickens an exceptionally large number of people. (Epilogue)

papal infallibility The doctrine established by Pope Pius IX in 1870 that any official pronouncement by the pope was necessarily true. (8)

Paris Commune The short-lived rebellious government that declared Paris independent from the rest of France in March 1871. The Commune sought to create an egalitarian "democratic and social republic."(8)

parlements The thirteen regional judicial institutions in France that had the power to review royal decrees and reject those they considered flawed. The parlements' decisions could be overruled by the king. After the death of Louis XIV, the parlements asserted greater authority than they had under his reign. (5)

Parliament England's legislative assembly, consisting of two chambers, Lords and Commons. (2)

parliamentary Pertaining to a parliament. The term also refers to those loyal to Parliament during the English Civil War. (2, 3)

Peace of Augsburg Agreement in 1555 in which the princes of the Holy Roman Empire gained the right to determine the official religion of the territories they ruled but that effectively prohibited any form of Protestantism other than the Lutheran faith. (1)

perestroika The restructuring of the Soviet economy initiated by Gorbachev; it gave industrial firms a measure of autonomy, had managers elected rather than appointed, released enterprises from some requirements of centralized planning, and reduced military spending. (15)

philosophes French for "philosophers"; public intellectuals of the Enlightenment, applied to all regardless of their homeland. (4)

physiocrats A group of French economists who convinced Louis XVI to remove price controls on grain. They believed that allowing grain prices to rise naturally with demand would encourage French farmers to produce more and that the larger supply would bring prices down. (5)

pogroms A series of assaults on a particular ethnic group, such as the Jewish communities of Russia after the assassination of Tsar Nicholas II; the Russian word *pogrom*, literally 'destruction, devastation,' became specialized to an organized brutal assault, especially on Jews. (9)

Politburo The small leadership committee of the Soviet Communist Party, ranging in number from five to a dozen or more. (11)

Poor Laws A rudimentary system of public assistance established by Queen Elizabeth I and designed to help rural laborers; it did little for the urban poor. (6)

Popular Front A center-left coalition in France that came to power in 1936. It sought to enact extensive social reforms and prevent right-wing extremists from gaining power. There was also a popular front government in Spain. (13)

populists Russian political revolutionaries who believed in a form of socialism grounded in agricultural communities. They romanticized the Russian peasantry and attempted to recruit them to revolution in the 1870s. (11)

Porte The name (derived from French) for a monumental gate in Istanbul; also Sublime Porte. The term is also used as a synonym for the Ottoman sultan or the Ottoman state. (6)

positivism A philosophy advocated by Auguste Comte that favors the careful empirical observation of natural phenomena and human behavior over metaphysics. (8)

Prague Spring An uprising against Communist control in Czechoslovakia, it was sparked by the appointment of Alexander Dubček, a reformer, as head of the Communist Party. Dubček's attempt to liberalize Czech society and government was eventually put down by the Soviet Army. (14)

predestination Religious belief advanced by John Calvin that God decided in advance who would be saved and who would not, and that salvation was reserved for a small "elect."(1)

preventive war A war that is initiated to prevent an opposing military force from taking action first. (9)

primogeniture A system of inheritance practiced in Britain in which fathers bequeathed their entire estates to their eldest sons. This arrangement left the other children with no lands of their own. (6)

Prince Henry the Navigator. Fourth child (1394–1460) of Portuguese king John I who was a pivotal figure for the early development of Portuguese exploration and maritime trade through the systematic exploration of the coast of West Africa and the islands of the Atlantic Ocean. (2)

probabilistic A form of knowledge which holds that science provides explanations whose truths are probable rather than certain or absolute. (4)

proletariat The Marxist term for the class of people employed in industry, who work as either skilled or unskilled laborers. Proletarians were said to produce more value for their employers than they earned in wages. (8)

public sphere The formal and informal institutions outside of the home in which Enlightened ideas were developed and disseminated. (4)

Realpolitik The pure pursuit of power unleavened by considerations of ethics or morality. (8)

Reform Bill Passed by the British Parliament in 1832, the Reform Bill extended the right to vote to about 10 percent of the adult male population. In addition, it eliminated two problematic aspects of the British electoral landscape: "rotten boroughs," grossly overrepresented in Parliament as the result of population declines in the wake of industrialization, and "pocket boroughs," in which a small number of influential people controlled elections to Parliament. (7)

Renaissance The fifteenth-century rebirth of classical art, architecture, and literature in Europe. (Introduction)

republic A form of government not headed by a monarch. The classic early republics existed in Ancient Rome and in the Italian city-states of Renaissance and Early Modern Europe. (4)

revolution from above Government-engineered revolution of Russian society. Stalin's revolution from above was designed to promote extremely rapid industrialization and economic growth. (11)

Revolution of 1830 The "Three Glorious Days" in Paris (July 27–29, 1830) that overturned the monarchy of Charles X in the wake of his autocratic "July Ordinances"; the revolution resulted not in a republic, as many had hoped it would, but in a new, somewhat more liberal monarchical regime. (7)

Rikstag The national legislature of Sweden (2)

Risorgimento "Resurgence," literally; the name given to the nineteenth-century movement for Italian national reunification. (7)

Romanticism An ideology and movement that dismissed the liberal, "individualist" notion that human beings were fundamentally rational creatures and that society was a collection of separate individuals all essentially alike but largely unconnected to one another except through economic relationships or questions of power and influence. Romantics maintained that emotions were more fundamental human qualities than the rational intellect and that every member of society feels intimate links to all others through sympathy and compassion. (7)

royalist One who has loyalty to the king or queen. During the English Civil War, the term signified those loyal to King Charles I. (3)

salons Gatherings in which hostesses invited people to their homes for the reading and discussion of plays, poems, and other writings. In the eighteenth century, salons encompassed an intellectual and social elite, becoming part of the public sphere that disseminated Enlightened ideas. (4)

sans-culottes A phrase meaning "without knee breeches" and used by the Parisian working people during the French Revolution to distinguish themselves from aristocrats. (5)

Schlieffen Plan The plan developed by army chief Alfred von Schlieffen in 1905 to send German forces first to France and then to Russia to avoid conducting a two-front war. (9)

Sejm The national legislature of Poland. (2)

serfs Unfree laborers forbidden to leave the landed estate where they worked and whose income and resources were kept artificially low by their inability to bargain with any landowner. (2)

smelting A process by which usable iron (pig iron) is separated from iron ore using heat. (6)

Social Democratic Party (SDP) Political party founded in Germany in 1875 that sought to achieve socialism through electoral politics and the labor movement. (9)

socialism An egalitarian political and economic ideology promoting the idea that the means of production should either be shared cooperatively by the people, or by the state in the people's name. (7)

Social distancing The practice of preventing people from congregating in schools, stadiums, workplaces, restaurants, and the like in an effort to slow the spread of a highly contagious disease. (Epilogue)

Society of the Friends of Blacks An organization founded in 1788 in France in response to the mistreatment of slaves in the colonies; it advocated the abolition of slavery and the slave trade. (5)

sociology Term brought into use by Auguste Comte that refers to the scientific study of human society. (8)

Solidarity The national trade union created in Poland in 1980 by Lech Wałęsa and other activists. It was banned in 1981 and then legalized in 1989, winning the democratic election of that year and seating Poland's first noncommunist prime minister. (15)

soviet A leadership council of workers and soldiers formed in Russia during the revolutions of 1905 and 1917. (11)

spheres of influence Regions, cities, or territories over which powerful foreign nations exercise influence and control. (9)

spinning jenny A device created by James Hargreaves in 1764 that mechanized the spinning of cotton, greatly increasing the number of threads that could be spun at once. (6)

stadtholder Chief magistrate of the United Provinces of the Netherlands. (2)

stagflation The combination of stagnation and inflation characteristic of the 1970s. During this decade, Western economies experienced, all at once, economic contraction, unemployment, and soaring prices. (15)

Stakhanovism A movement in the Soviet Union in which workers sought to set productivity records in their fields as a matter of personal and ideological pride. (11)

tariffs Taxes imposed on foreign goods to discourage the consumption of foreign-made products. (9)

tax farmers Private individuals or companies that collected taxes for a government, usually an Early Modern monarchy. Tax farmers advanced a fixed sum to the monarchy; all receipts in excess of that amount constituted their profit, often substantial. **Tax farming** refers to the practice of allowing private individuals or companies to purchase the right to collect taxes on behalf of the government. (2, 5)

technology The application of scientific knowledge to accomplish practical ends through new inventions and procedures. (4)

Tennis Court Oath Assertion by the Third Estate in 1789 that their newly created National Assembly, not the Estates General, was the official parliament of the French nation. The oath took place at an abandoned indoor tennis court and marked the beginning of the French Revolution. (5)

terrorism The use of violence, often against civilians, to sow fear in an effort to achieve a political, social, or economic goal. (15)

theodicy An attempt to answer the "problem of evil," which asks why God allows terrible things to take place. For Leibniz, the answer to this problem was that certain phenomena may look evil from the limited perspective of human beings, but if they could understand the world from God's point of view, which by definition they cannot, they would see that everything God does is for the best. (4)

Third Reich, 1933–1945 The German regime ruled by Adolf Hitler and the Nazi Party. *Reich* is German for "empire" or "kingdom"; the First Reich was the Holy Roman Empire (962–1806) and the Second Reich was Otto von Bismarck's German Empire (1871–1918). (12)

Thirty Years' War A series of wars in Europe from 1618 to 1648 that were grounded both in religious conflict between Protestants and Catholics and in territorial and political disputes between the Holy Roman Empire and other European powers. The war was concluded by the Treaty of Westphalia in 1648. (1–3)

tithe A tax, typically of 10 percent (*tithe* is another form of the word *tenth*), levied by the Church. During the French Revolution, it was protested in the "lists of grievances" submitted to the Estates General in 1789. (5)

total war A conflict whose scope mobilizes not only armies but entire societies. The First World War is often considered the first total war. (10)

Treaty of Brest-Litovsk Treaty signed in 1918 between Germany and Russia ending hostilities between the countries; Russia renounced all claims to Ukraine, Finland, Lithuania, Estonia, and Livonia (now split between Latvia and Estonia), which would be controlled by Germany. (11)

Treaty of Westphalia Agreement signed in 1648 to end the Thirty Years' War. The Treaty established the principle of "balance of power" in Europe, froze Europe's religious divisions for centuries to come, and opened rulers to the compromise solutions of diplomacy. (1)

Triple Alliance The alliance between Germany, Austria-Hungary, and Italy forged by Otto von Bismarck between 1879 and 1882 to shore up the ailing Austrian Empire and serve as a buffer against Russia. (9)

Triple Entente The alliance between Britain, France, and Russia sealed between 1904 and 1907 that served as a counter to the Triple Alliance. (9)

Twelve Articles of Memmingen Anabaptist document of 1525, during the Peasants' War, that linked the Word of God with the requirements of economic and social righteousness. The articles called for the abolition of serfdom, the restoration of hunting and fishing rights, tax reductions, and an end to obligatory unpaid labor. (1)

unicameral Pertaining to a parliament consisting of one chamber or legislative body. (7)

United Nations The international organization established after the Second World War to foster peace, security, and economic prosperity. (14)

Vatican II A Vatican Council convened in 1962, whose purpose was to reform Catholicism and make the Church more attuned to the modern world. Vatican II replaced the Latin mass with masses in vernacular languages, advocated better relations with Protestant churches, and condemned antisemitism and authoritarianism. (14)

velvet revolution The largely peaceful overthrow in 1989 of Czechoslovakia's communist regime. (15)

venal Susceptible to being purchased, referring in the early modern period to an office or title. (2)

Vendée rebellion An anti-revolutionary civil war that took place in western France in 1793. The rebellion began as a reaction against military conscription and the perceived persecution of priests. (5)

Viceroyalty of New Spain Territories of the Spanish Empire in North America, the Pacific Ocean, and Asia. Mexico City was the capital of the Viceroyalty. (2)

Viceroyalty of Peru Spanish imperial administrative district, created in 1542, that encompassed modern-day Peru and most of Spanish-ruled South America. Its capital was Lima. (2)

Vichy France The regime established in 1940 in the unoccupied zone of France; it took its name from the spa town of Vichy, which became the capital of a truncated France. Led by Philippe Pétain, the Vichy regime collaborated with the Germans. (13)

Wannsee conference A meeting, held near Berlin in January 1942, where plans for the "final solution" of the "Jewish Question" were discussed with top Nazi leaders. This meeting resulted in the expansion of the death camps and an infrastructure dedicated to genocide. (13)

War Communism The authoritarian, statist economic policy adopted by the Bolsheviks during the Russian Civil War. Under war communism, banks, heavy industry, railroads, and grain fell under government control. (11)

War of Spanish Succession The twelve-year conflict (1702–1714) over whether Philip of Anjou or Archduke Charles of Austria should be crowned king of Spain; it pitted France against the Habsburg family, which forged anti-French alliances with England, the Dutch Republic, and parts of the Holy Roman Empire. The treaties of Utrecht and Rastatt granted Spain to Philip and Spanish territories in Italy and the Netherlands to Charles. (3)

Warsaw Pact The Treaty of Friendship signed in 1955 by the Soviet Union and seven Soviet satellite states in Central and Eastern Europe. The Warsaw Pact was the Soviet counterpart to NATO during the Cold War. (14)

Weimar Republic The German democratic republic established in 1919 following the abdication of the kaiser and Germany's defeat in the First World War. It was replaced by the Third Reich in 1933. (12)

wrought iron A highly malleable form of iron created by a special smelting process. (6)

Young Turks A group of reformers who rebelled against the Ottoman Empire in 1908. (9)

Zimmermann telegram Intercepted cable message sent by Germany in 1917 to its ambassador in Mexico proposing a German-Mexican alliance against the United States. (10)

Zionism A movement, begun in the 1890s, to combat antisemitism by creating an independent Jewish state. (9)

Zollverein A customs union created in 1834 that allowed raw materials, products, and labor to circulate freely within a coalition of German states. Prussia was the Zollverein's leading state, and Austria was excluded from the union. (7)

Table of Contents for *Sources for Europe in the Modern World with Guided Writing Exercises*

Part V. Tools for Refining Meaning and Correcting Stylistic Mistakes

12. Creating the complex "noun phrases" of academic writing

Learn to write more efficiently by using noun phrases to reduce the number of words in a sentence.

13. Using passive voice, *it*-shifts, and *what*-shifts to tell your reader what matters most

Learn techniques for adding emphasis.

14. Using parallelism to simplify complex ideas

Use techniques to revise mediocre paragraphs into stylish and coherent texts.

15. Using coordination and subordination to find and fix common-punctuation mistakes

Identify and correct classic coordination mistakes, such as run-on sentences and comma splices, and subordination mistakes, such as sentence fragments and dangling modifiers.

Epilogue. Double Focus

Use the technique of "double focus" to emphasize the most important ideas in a sentence.

Suggested Readings

Introduction

Cameron, Euan. *Early Modern Europe: An Oxford History*. New York: Oxford University Press, 2001.

Man, John. *The Gutenberg Revolution: How Printing Changed the Course of History*. London: Bantam Books, 2009.

Chapter 1

Collinson, Patrick. *The Reformation*. London: Weidenfeld & Nicolson, 2003.

Davis, Natalie Zemon. *The Return of Martin Guerre*. Cambridge, MA: Harvard University Press, 1984.

Duffy, Eamon. *The Stripping of the Altars: Traditional Religion in England, 1400–1580*. 2nd ed. New Haven, CT: Yale University Press, 2005.

Ginzburg, Carlo. *The Cheese and the Worms: The Cosmos of a Sixteenth-Century Miller*. Translated by John and Anne Tedeschi. Baltimore, MD: Johns Hopkins University Press, 1976.

Hsia, R. Po-Chia. *The World of Catholic Renewal, 1540–1770*. New York: Cambridge University Press, 2005.

Kittelson, James M. *Luther the Reformer: The Story of the Man and His Career*. Minneapolis, MN: Fortress Press, 2003.

MacCulloch, Diarmaid. *The Reformation*. New York: Penguin Books, 2005.

O'Malley, John. *The Jesuits: A History from Ignatius to the Present*. London: Rowman & Littlefield, 2014.

Chapter 2

Burbank, Jane, and Frederick Cooper. *Empires in World History: Power and the Politics of Difference*. Princeton, NJ: Princeton University Press, 2010.

Elliott, J.H. *Empires of the Atlantic World: Britain and Spain in America, 1492–1830*. New Haven, CT: Yale University Press, 2006.

Ertman, Thomas. *Birth of the Leviathan: Building States and Regimes in Medieval and Early Modern Europe*. Cambridge, UK: Cambridge University Press, 1997.

Fernández-Armesto, Felipe. *Pathfinders: A Global History of Exploration*. New York: W.W. Norton, 2006.

Mann, Charles C. *1493: Uncovering the New World Columbus Created*. New York: Vintage Books, Random House, 2012.

Pierce, Leslie. *Empress of the East: How a European Slave Girl Became Queen of the Ottoman Empire*. New York: Basic Books, 2017.

Snyder, Timothy. *The Reconstruction of Nations: Poland, Ukraine, Lithuania, Belarus, 1569–1999*. New Haven, CT: Yale University Press, 2003.

Chapter 3

Appleby, Andrew B., "Epidemics and Famine in the Little Ice Age," *Journal of Interdisciplinary History*, X (1980), 643–63.

Beik, William. *A Social and Cultural History of Early Modern France*. New York: Cambridge University Press, 2009.

Kishlansky, Mark. *A Monarchy Transformed: Britain 1603–1714*. London: Penguin Books, 1996.

Le Roy Ladurie, Emmanuel. *Times of Feast, Times of Famine: A History of Climate Since the Year 1000*. New York: Doubleday, 1971.

Lockhart, Paul Douglas. *Sweden in the Seventeenth Century*. New York: Palgrave McMillan, 2004.

Parker, Geoffrey. *Global Crisis: War, Climate Change and Catastrophe in the Seventeenth Century*. New Haven: Yale University Press, 2013

Chapter 4

Broadie, Alexander. *The Scottish Enlightenment*. Edinburgh, UK: Birlinn, 2007.

Dear, Peter. *Revolutionizing the Sciences: European Knowledge and Its Ambitions, 1500–1700*. 2nd ed. Princeton, NJ: Princeton University Press, 2009.

O'Brien, Karen. *Women and the Enlightenment in Eighteenth-Century Britain*. New York: Cambridge University Press, 2009.

Outram, Dorinda. *The Enlightenment: New Approaches to European History*. 3rd ed. New York: Cambridge University Press, 2013.

Pagden, Anthony. *The Enlightenment: And Why It Still Matters*. Oxford, UK: Oxford University Press, 2013.

Seigel, Jerrold. *The Idea of the Self: Thought and Experience in Western Europe Since the Seventeenth Century*. New York: Cambridge University Press, 2005.

Shapin, Steven. *The Scientific Revolution*. Chicago: The University of Chicago Press, 1996.

Wolff, Larry. *Inventing Eastern Europe: The Map of Civilization on the Mind of the Enlightenment*. Stanford, CA: Stanford University Press, 1994.

Chapter 5

Chartier, Roger. *The Cultural Origins of the French Revolution*. Translated by Lydia G. Cochrane. Durham, NC: Duke University Press, 1991.

Desan, Suzanne, Lynn Hunt, and William Max Nelson, eds. *The French Revolution in Global Perspective*. Ithaca, NY: Cornell University Press, 2013.

Englund, Steven. *Napoleon: A Political Life*. New York: Scribner, Simon & Schuster, 2004.

Kaiser, Thomas E., and Dale K. Van Kley, eds. *From Deficit to Deluge: The Origins of the French Revolution*. Stanford, CA: Stanford University Press, 2011.

Popkin, Jeremy D. *A Concise History of the Haitian Revolution*. Malden, MA: Wiley-Blackwell, 2012.

Spang, Rebecca L. *Stuff and Money in the Time of the French Revolution*. Cambridge, MA: Harvard University Press, 2015.

de Tocqueville, Alexis. *The Old Regime and the French Revolution*. New York: Harper & Brothers, 1856.

Chapter 6

Allen, Robert C. *The British Industrial Revolution in Global Perspective*. New York: Cambridge University Press, 2009.

Davidoff, Leonore, and Catherine Hall. *Family Fortunes: Men and Women of the English Middle Class, 1780–1850*. London: Routledge, 2002.

Mokyr, Joel, ed. *The British Industrial Revolution: An Economic Perspective*. 2nd ed. Boulder, CO: Westview Press, 1999.

Mokyr, Joel. *The Enlightened Economy: An Economic History of Britain, 1700–1850*. New Haven, CT: Yale University Press, 2010.

Pomeranz, Kenneth. *The Great Divergence: China, Europe, and the Making of the Modern World Economy*. Princeton, NJ: Princeton University Press, 2000.

de Vries, Jan. *The Industrious Revolution: Consumer Behavior and the Household Economy, 1650 to the Present*. New York: Cambridge University Press, 2008.

Chapter 7

Bayly, Christopher. *The Birth of the Modern World, 1780–1914*. Malden, MA: Wiley-Blackwell, 2004.

Jack, Belinda. *George Sand: A Woman's Life Writ Large*. New York: Knopf, 2000.

Jarrett, Mark. *The Congress of Vienna and Its Legacy: War and Great Power Diplomacy after Napoleon*. London: I.B. Tauris & Co., 2014.

Schroeder, Paul W. *The Transformation of European Politics, 1763–1848*. New York: Oxford University Press, 1994.

Sperber, Jonathan. *The European Revolutions, 1848–1851*. Cambridge, UK: Cambridge University Press, 2005.

Vick, Brian E. *The Congress of Vienna: Power and Politics after Napoleon*. Cambridge, MA: Harvard University Press, 2014.

Chapter 8

Blackbourn, David. *History of Germany, 1780–1918: The Long Nineteenth Century*. 2nd ed. Malden, MA: Wiley-Blackwell, 2002.

Broadberry, Stephen, and Kevin H. O'Rourke, eds. *The Cambridge Economic History of Modern Europe*, Vol. 1. New York: Cambridge University Press, 2010.

Judson, Pieter M.. *Exclusive Revolutionaries: Liberal Politics, Social Experience, and National Identity in the Austrian Empire, 1848–1914*. Ann Arbor, MI: University of Michigan Press, 1997.

Judson, Pieter M. *The Habsburg Empire: A New History*. Cambridge, MA: Harvard University Press, 2016

Schivelbusch, Wolfgang. *The Culture of Defeat: On National Trauma, Mourning, and Recovery*. New York: Picador, St. Martin's Press, 2004.

Seigel, Jerrold. *Modernity and Bourgeois Life: Society, Politics, and Culture in England, France, and Germany since 1750*. New York: Cambridge University Press, 2012.

Steinberg, Jonathan. *Bismarck: A Life*. New York: Oxford University Press, 2013.

Chapter 9

Berenson, Edward. *Heroes of Empire: Five Charismatic Men and the Conquest of Africa*. Berkeley and Los Angeles, CA: University of California Press, 2010.

Cain, Peter J., and Anthony G. Hopkins. *British Imperialism: 1688–2000*. 3rd ed. London: Routledge, 2013.

Hall, Catherine, and Sonya O. Rose, eds. *At Home with the Empire: Metropolitan Culture and the Imperial World*. New York: Cambridge University Press, 2007.

Hochschild, Adam. *King Leopold's Ghost: A Story of Greed, Terror, and Heroism in Colonial Africa*. New York: Houghton Mifflin, 1998.

Mazower, Mark. *The Balkans: A Short History*. New York: Modern Library, Random House, 2002.

Montessori, Maria. *Dr. Montessori's Own Handbook*. New York: Frederick A. Stokes Company, 1914.

Todorova, Maria. *Imagining the Balkans*. New York: Oxford University Press, 1997.

Chapter 10

Audoin-Rouzeau, Stephane, and Annette Becker. *14–18: Understanding the Great War*. New York: Hill and Wang; Farrar, Straus and Giroux, 2014.

Barry, John M. *The Great Influenza: The Story of the Deadliest Pandemic in History*. New York: Penguin, 2005.

Clark, Christopher. *The Sleepwalkers: How Europe Went to War in 1914*. New York: HarperCollins, 2014.

Fussell, Paul. *The Great War and Modern Memory*. 2nd ed. New York: Oxford University Press, 2013.

Keegan, John. *The First World War*. London: Hutchinson, Random House, 1998.

Credits

Introduction

Erich Lessing/Art Resource, NY, p. xxxiv;
(a) FEDERICO GAMBARINI/EPA/Newscom,
(b) Boris Roessler/dpa/picture-alliance/Newscom,
p. xxxvii

Chapter 1

© DHM/Bridgeman Images, p. 2; © DHM/
Bridgeman, p. 8; (a) © Clynt Garnham Architecture,
(b) © Werner Otto/Alamy p. 12; AKG Images, p. 19;
Sueddeutsche Zeitung Photo/Alamy Stock Photo,
p. 23; Private Collection/The Stapleton Collection/
Bridgeman Images, p. 28; Château de Versailles,
France/Bridgeman Images, p. 32; De Agostini
Picture Library/G. Dagli Orti/Bridgeman Images,
p. 35; Musee des Beaux-Arts, Orleans, France/
Bridgeman Images, p. 39; Manuel Cohen/The Art
Archive at Art Resource, NY, p. 43

Chapter 2

Heritage Image Partnership Ltd/Alamy Stock
Photo, p. 48; Nation of Islam Research Group,
p. 55; Bridgeman Images, p. 61; Hispanic Society
of America Museum and Library, New York, p. 62;
Bridgeman Images, p. 63; Vincenzo Negro, p. 67;
Bridgeman Images, p. 71; Granger Collection
0007542, p. 77; Bridgeman Images, p. 84;
Bogomyako/Alamy Stock Photo, p. 87; Bridgeman
Images, p. 90

Chapter 3

© RMN-Grand Palais/Art Resource, NY, p. 98;
Bridgeman Images, p. 105; Bridgeman Images, p. 109
(a and b); Bridgeman Images, p. 114; Peter Eastland/
Alamy Stock Photo, p. 120; Bridgeman Images,
p. 125; Bridgeman Images, 127; Bridgeman Images,
132; akg-images, p. 135; Bridgeman Images, p. 137

Chapter 4

Nicolo Orsi Battaglini/Art Resource, NY, p. 142;
Mihai Simonia/Shutterstock/stock photo ID:
162613688, p. 153; CCI Archives/Science Source,
p. 154; Bridgeman Images, p. 156; Courtesy of the
Library of Congress, p. 158; Erich Lessing/Art
Resource, NY, p. 161; akg-images, p. 162; Courtesy
of the Library of Congress, p. 165; Courtesy of the
Library of Congress, p. 166; © RMN-Grand Palais/
Art Resource, NY, p. 176; Bridgeman Images, p. 179;
Bridgeman Images, p. 182; Bridgeman Images, p. 187

Chapter 5

Musee de la Ville de Paris, Musee Carnavalet, Paris,
France/© Leemage/Bridgeman Images, p. 200;
© RMN-Grand Palais/Art Resource, NY, p. 203;
© RMN-Grand Palais/Art Resource, NY, p. 205;
© DeA Picture Library/Art Resource, NY, p. 206;
Musee de la Ville de Paris, Musee Carnavalet, Paris,
France/Bridgeman Images, p. 207; © RMN-Grand
Palais/Art Resource, NY, p. 208; akg-images/De
Agostini Picture Lib./G. Dagli Orti, p. 211; Musee
Carnavalet, Paris, France/Archives Charmet/
Bridgeman, p. 212; Erich Lessing/Art Resource,
NY, p. 215; © BnF, Dist. RMN-Grand Palais/Art
Resource, p. 218; Erich Lessing/Art Resource, NY,
p. 223; (a) Erich Lessing/Art Resource, NY, (b) ©
Musée de l'Armée/Dist. RMN-Grand Palais/Art
Resource, NY, p. 229; © Musée de l'Armée/Dist.
RMN-Grand Palais/Art Resource, NY, p. 235

Chapter 6

Photo © Philip Mould Ltd, London/Bridgeman
Images, p. 240; ©SSPL/The Image Works, p. 242;
Yale Center for British Art, Paul Mellon Collection,
USA/Bridgeman Images, p. 249; © Look and Learn/
Bridgeman Images, p. 250; Private Collection/

Bridgeman Images, p. 253; Private Collection/© Look and Learn/Bridgeman Images, p. 255; PRISMA ARCHIVO/Alamy Stock Photo, p. 258; Science Museum, London, UK/Bridgeman Image, p. 260; Science Museum, London, UK/Bridgeman Image, p. 263; Erich Lessing/Art Resource, NY, p. 266; Science & Society Picture Library /Getty, p. 273; Private Collection/Ken Welsh/Bridgeman Images, p. 277; Chronicle/Alamy Stock Photo, p. 280

Chapter 7
© RMN-Grand Palais/Art Resource, NY, p. 286; HIP/Art Resource, NY, p. 293; Bridgeman Images, p. 295; © Wilberforce House, Hull City Museums and Art Galleries, UK/Bridgeman Images, p. 298; Hamburg Art Collections/Elke Walford/Art Resource, NY, p. 301; New Lanark Trust, p. 304; akg-images/Interfoto, p. 306; Moscow, Puschkin-Literaturmuseum/AKG Images, p. 311; Erich Lessing/Art Resource, NY, p. 318; Private Collection/Bridgeman Images, p. 319; incamerastock/Alamy Stock Photo, p. 322; ©Pictures From History/The Image Works, p. 324; Watts Gallery, Compton, Surrey, UK/© Trustees of Watts Gallery/Bridgeman Images, p. 327; bpk Bildagentur/Art Resource, NY, p. 335

Chapter 8
Bridgeman Images, 338; Private Collection/© Look and Learn/Bridgeman Images, p. 345; © Musée Carnavalet/Roger-Viollet/The Image Works, p. 348; The Art Institute of Chicago/Art Resource, NY, p. 350; Royal Collection Trust/© Her Majesty Queen Elizabeth II 2016, p. 356; PVDE/Bridgeman Images, p. 360; Photo 12 /Universal Images Group/ Getty, p. 368; akg-images, p. 370; photographer: unknown, published by: Mittet & Co., owner: National Library of Norway., p. 373; HIP/Art Resource, NY, p. 375; © LL/Roger-Viollet/The Image Works, p. 377; Copyright DEA/A. DAGLI ORTI/Granger, NYC— All rights reserved., p. 379

Chapter 9
Granger, p. 382; HIP/Art Resource, NY, p. 391; ullstein bild/GRANGER, p. 403; ©Mary Evans Picture Library/The Image Works, p. 405; Private

Collection/© Look and Learn/Illustrated Papers Collection/Bridgeman, p. 407; Time Life Pictures/ The LIFE Picture Collection/Getty, p. 409; Chronicle/Alamy Stock Photo, p. 411; National Galleries of Scotland, Dist. RMN-Grand Palais/ Art Resource, NY, p. 413; Courtesy of the Library of Congress, p. 414; HIP/Art Resource, NY, p. 417; HIP/Art Resource, NY, p. 420; Fotosearch/ Getty Images, p. 421; DEA/G DAGLI ORTI/AGE Fotostock, p. 422; SeM/Universal Images Group/ Bridgeman Images, p. 425; Private Collection/ Peter Newark Military Pictures/Bridgeman Images, p. 429

Chapter 10
Fitzwilliam Museum, University of Cambridge, UK/Bridgeman Images, p. 432; Archives Larousse, Paris, France/Bridgeman Images, p. 437; Photo by © Hulton-Deutsch Collection/CORBIS/Corbis via Getty Images, p. 438; © Hulton-Deutsch Collection/ CORBIS, p. 441; AKG Images, p. 443; AKG Images, p. 445; © Albert Harlingue/Roger-Viollet/The Image Works, p. 449; ©Mirrorpix/The Image Works, p. 454; De Agostini Picture Library/Bridgeman, p. 456; Universal History Archive/UIG/Bridgeman Images, p. 458; © Classic Image/Alamy Stock Photo, p. 466; Private Collection/The Stapleton Collection/ Bridgeman Images, p. 471; Atatürk Research Center Library, p. 474

Chapter 11
Photo by Alfred Eisenstaedt/The LIFE Picture Collection/Getty Images, p. 480; V&A Images, London/Art Resource, NY, p. 489; Photo by Fine Art Images/Heritage Images/Getty Images, p. 493; © Heritage Image Partnership Ltd/Alamy Stock Photo, p. 495; HIP/Art Resource, NY, p. 497; bpk, Berlin/ Art Resource, NY, p. 499; Private Collection/ Peter Newark Pictures/Bridgeman Image, p. 501; © Sovfoto ID: SOV-B-5569, p. 506; © ITAR-TASS Photo Agency/Alamy Stock Photo, p. 510; © ITAR-TASS Photo Agency/Alamy Stock Photo, p. 515; © Sovfoto ID: SOV-C-001, p. 520; IAM/akg-images, p. 522; IAM/akg-images, p. 523; © ITAR-TASS/ Sovfoto, p. 525